In Quest of Justice

In Quest of Justice

*Protest and Dissent
in the Soviet Union Today*

EDITED BY

Abraham Brumberg

PRAEGER PUBLISHERS

New York · Washington · London

PRAEGER PUBLISHERS
111 Fourth Avenue, New York, N.Y. 10003, U.S.A.
5, Cromwell Place, London S.W.7, England

Published in the United States of America in 1970
by Praeger Publishers, Inc.

© 1970 by Praeger Publishers, Inc.

Library of Congress Catalog Card Number: 69–12700

Printed in the United States of America

Contents

Part Three: Literature of the Underground

Editor's Note

Most of the essays and documents in this volume appeared originally in the July–August and September–October, 1968, issues of *Problems of Communism* (Washington, D.C.). Because of space limitations, I was faced with the disagreeable task of discarding some of the material included in *Problems of Communism*, and with the even more disagreeable—and somewhat perilous—necessity of appearing to assign relative priorities to the various categories of dissent in the U.S.S.R. The selection of material was further complicated by what would probably be called in academic jargon the "dynamics of dissent"—that is, by the fact that politics generates new issues, that these issues tend to provide dissidents with new causes, and that these causes, in turn, generate more material, which an editor cannot, in good conscience, disregard. The results, then —arrived at after considerable soul-searching—are as follows:

Sections I and II of Part 2 ("The Moscow Trials of 1967" and "The Ginzburg-Galanskov Trial"), pertaining to the two events that, together, provided the catalyst for the emergence of open dissent in the U.S.S.R., are reproduced in full from *Problems of Communism*. Furthermore, Section II has been amplified by the inclusion of documents that reached the United States in recent months. Therefore these two sections represent, to my knowledge, the most comprehensive compendium available of Soviet writings on the violation of constitutional and legal rights of Soviet citizens.

The body of documents dealing with the Ukraine and the Crimean Tatars (Section III) has been drastically cut, chiefly because some of the relevant material has already appeared elsewhere.[1] The same applies to Section IV, "Religious Dissent."[2]

Again to the best of my knowledge, no comprehensive collection of documents relating to the "Solzhenitsyn affair" has hitherto appeared in the English language. For this reason, Section V, like the first two, is reproduced in its entirety from *Problems of Communism*, with the addition of one document (Document 56) that was unavailable earlier.

Section VII, "Stalinism Redivivus?" contains all the material that appeared in *Problems of Communism*, albeit in a slightly abridged form, while Sections VI, "In Defense of Czechoslovakia," and VIII, "Reprisals," include much material that has not appeared elsewhere in print.

[1] See references in the article by George Luckyj.
[2] See references in the article by Peter Reddaway.

The "Literature of the Underground" (Part 3) was represented far more extensively in *Problems of Communism*, and the interested reader is urged to look up the relevant pages (September–October, 1968, pp. 66–114). The section was cut purely for reasons of space. Regrettably, Professor Maurice Friedberg's analysis of the Soviet literary underground also had to be deleted.[3]

The persons responsible for rendering the immense Russian material into English deserve special mention and praise. The names of the translators of Part 3 appear at the end of the literary selections. The following persons translated the documents in Part 2: Rev. Michael Bourdeaux, Richard T. Davies, Maurice Friedberg, Theodore Guerchon, Zoreslava Kushner, Elizavetta Lomonosova, Sidney Monas, Penny Poppof, Peter Reddaway, Elisavietta Ritchie, Arlo Schultz, and Gloria Sosin. At the risk of sounding platitudinous, let me also say that this volume would certainly not have seen the light of day were it not for the invaluable advice of Mr. Alexander Barmine, of the U.S. Information Agency, and the painstaking labor of my colleagues on the staff of *Problems of Communism*: Marie House, Clarke Kawakami, Gordon Sterner, and Rosalind Avnet, the last of whom also assisted in the translations. I acknowledge my debt to them with gratitude and pleasure.

[3] "What Price Censorship?" *Problems of Communism*, September–October, 1968.

Sources and Credits

Novoe russkoe slovo (New York): Document 1 (April 6, 1968); Documents 5, 6 (April 7, 1968); Documents 8, 17 (March 11, 1968); Documents 9, 22 (February 29, 1968); Document 10 (June 6, 1968); Documents 14, 25, 32 (March 2, 1968); Document 15 (March 1, 1968); Document 18 (February 27, 1968 and March 7, 1968); Document 20 (February 5, 1968); Document 23 (June 9, 1968); Document 24 (June 7, 1968); Document 26 (March 14, 1968); Document 27 (February 25, 1968); Document 30 (March 10, 1968); Document 31 (March 31, 1968); Document 35 (March 24, 1968); Document 63 (September 3, 1968); Document 64 (September 18, 1968); Document 65 (September 18, 1968); Document 21 (November 23, 1968); Document 39 (October 12, 1968); Documents 67, 68 (November 3, 1968); Documents 79, 80 (November 24, 1968); Document 81 (December 21, 1968); Document 72 (March 19, 1969).

Atlas (New York): Document 62 (March, 1968).

Grani (Frankfurt-am-Main): Document 4 (No. 62, 1966); Documents 66, 75 (No. 67, 1968).

Le Monde (Paris): Document 58 (June 5, 1967); Document 61 (April 28–29, 1968).

Literaturnaia gazeta (Moscow): Document 29 (No. 17, April 24, 1968).

The New York Times: Documents 2, 3 (December 27, 1967); Document 7 (January 13, 1968); Document 16 (March 8, 1968); Document 76 (July 22, 1968); Document 49 (June 5, 1967); Document 67 (August 29, 1968).

Nouvel observateur (Paris): Document 13 (March 7, 1968).

Novyi zhurnal (New York): Documents 51, 52, 60 (1968, No. 93).

Possev (Frankfurt-am-Main): Documents 35, 36, 52, 73 (1968, No. 8); Document 57 (1968, No. 7); Documents 56, 77 (1968, No. 10); Document 82 (1969).

Radio Moscow: Document 34 (March 26, 1968).

Survey (London): Documents 50, 53, 54, 55 (April, 1968).

Tagebuch (Vienna): Document 74 (January–February 1968).

Thought (New Delhi): Documents 2, 3 (January 27, 1968).

Tra. Autoritismo Sfruttamento (Milan: Jaca 1968), Documents 51, 59, 60.

The Washington Post (Washington, D.C.): Document 69 (September 29, 1968); Document 70 (October 15, 1968); Document 71 (September 29, 1968).

Voices of Human Courage: Appeals from Two Soviet Ukrainian Intellectuals to Soviet Authorities (New York: Association for Free Ukraine, Inc., 1968): Document 37.

V. Chornovil (ed.), *Lykho z rozumu* (Paris: First Ukrainian Printing House, November, 1967): Document 38.

Sources for documents pertaining to religion are indicated in the article by Peter Reddaway.

With the exception of the aforementioned works, all the poetry, stories, and literary essays in this volume have been translated from the following issues of *Grani*: No. 52, 1962; No. 58, 1965; No. 63, 1967; No. 64, 1967; No. 65, 1967; No. 66, 1967. The remaining documents have not been previously published in the West.

PART ONE

Commentaries

The Rise of Dissent
in the U.S.S.R.

ABRAHAM BRUMBERG

If terror and despotism are—as has been alleged—endemic to the "Russian soul," then so, surely, are hatred of despotism and a passion for justice, as well as a penchant for idealism often carried to the point of self-immolation. It has long been fashionable to explain the success of Communism in Russia in terms of innate national characteristics, such as authoritarianism, the need for a "father figure," lack of democratic traditions, and so on. Yet the history of Russia is also replete with struggles against tyranny—from the peasant revolts of the seventeenth and eighteenth centuries to the revolutionary outbreaks of the nineteenth and twentieth centuries—with countless instances of men and women risking imprisonment or death for some principle higher than life, be it political liberty or the right to pursue their own religious practices.

Equally fashionable is the image of Russian "extremism," a lack of moderation with regard to ends as well as means. This assumption is not altogether off the mark: denial of elementary human rights, if long continued, is bound to evoke a violent response. In the absence of legal methods of effecting political change, illegal methods will prevail. The young revolutionaries who threw bombs at Tsarist officials and, in many cases, perished together with their victims were driven to these acts by despair. The incidence of such acts declined perceptibly after 1905, when Nicholas II granted his subjects a constitution and a quasi-representative parliament. When the Tsar's most determined opponents again took to assassinations and "revolutionary mass action," it was because the promises of 1905 soon turned out to be largely sham.

These parallels come to mind as one considers the current manifestations of dissent and protest in the U.S.S.R. Under Stalin, political opposition was first driven underground and then effectively decimated. The powerful apparatus of terror not only removed both actual and potential opponents from the political arena but made it impossible for anyone to express even the mildest misgivings about the wisdom of the regime. Stalin's ultimate weapon was the feeling of helplessness that gripped all Soviet citizens, from the lowliest *kolkhoz*-peasant to the members of the Politburo.

3

With his death in March, 1953, mass terror came to an end. Yet the ubiquitous inertia that Stalinism had engendered could not vanish overnight, notwithstanding the new regime's halfhearted economic and administrative reforms, the amnesties of certain categories of political and criminal offenders, and the vague promises of better days to come. It was precisely this state of affairs that led former First Secretary Khrushchev, in his "secret" speech to the Twentieth Party Congress in February, 1956, to brand Stalin a mass murderer whose ideology was riddled with lies.

In restrospect, it is clear that Khrushchev's aim was to restore a sense of confidence to the Party as well as to the population at large and to replace fear and blind obedience by at least a semblance of popular consensus as the basis of Party rule. It is equally clear that he failed in this endeavor. Much like the Tsar's Constitution of 1905, Khrushchev's speech aroused vast popular expectations that subsequent policies did little to fulfill. Yet, again like the Tsar's Constitution, Khrushchev's dethronement of Stalin marked an epochal break with the past. However specious and inconclusive it was, it created a psychological climate that permitted, even encouraged, some measure of criticism and dissent. With the foremost leader of the Party repudiating the misdeeds and crimes of nearly thirty years of Party rule, Stalinism—or, rather, the "cult of personality," as it came to be called—was fair game. All that remained to be seen was what the authorities would consider to be the "legitimately" negative features of the "cult," and how they would view its causes and its effects on Soviet society.

The answers to these questions were not slow in coming. In a series of pronouncements, the Party made it clear that Stalinism was to be regarded as an ephemeral stage in an otherwise successful and undeviating march toward a bountiful Communist future. While no doubt unfortunate from the viewpoint of its "thousands of illegally repressed" victims, the "cult," it was claimed, was not an outgrowth of "the Soviet social system," nor had it vitiated the fundamental achievements of the Soviet order—a thesis with which, incidentally, many foreign Communists, including the late Palmiro Togliatti, strongly disagreed. This formulation, first adumbrated in June, 1956, has remained essentially in force to this day.[1] Yet it was sufficiently flexible to allow for various interpretations, which Soviet intellectuals were quick to exploit. First to benefit from the new spirit of permissiveness were drama and literature. Instead of being inundated by dreary "construction novels," Soviet readers were offered works that dealt—some more honestly, some less so—with the traumatic experiences of the Stalin era. Literary journals published debates on matters of aesthetics and on the role of the artist in a socialist society; some writers even went as far as to question, albeit only indirectly, certain aspects of Party control over the arts.

In a country where the question of whether the hero of a novel should make love to a milkmaid or to a tractor is apt to be the subject of an official Party decree, no sector of public life is devoid of political significance. By and large, however, criticism and dissent under Khrushchev were directed, not at political issues *senso strictu*, but, rather, at what might be termed "dogmatic" restrictions on the pursuit of truth and artistic or intellectual freedom. True, such controversial works of the early and middle 1950's as Ehrenburg's novel *The Thaw*, Dudintsev's novel *Not by Bread Alone*, or the remarkable essay by the young literary critic Vladimir Pomerantsev, "On Sincerity in Literature"— these were hardly exercises in *l'art pour l'art*; but the debates to which they gave rise were of an essentially *literary* character. The questions that were voiced were: How much experimentation should Soviet writers be allowed? Would preoccupation with "innovation" lead to the sin of "formalism" or, on the contrary, to the genuine emancipation of literature and, hence, of intellectual life in general? Should Soviet artists be prevented from depicting the seamy side of Soviet life without (in the words of the venerable writer Konstantin Paustovsky) "first making an exculpatory 'bow' by mentioning our achievements"?[2] Should there be a place in Soviet art for the expression of private emotions such as love, sadness, and introspection? Should the works of formerly "repressed" writers be resurrected or be left in limbo?

There is no need to recount the subsequent developments in Soviet cultural life, the principal features of which are more than adequately dealt with by Mr. Monas. Suffice it to say that, under Khrushchev, the Party proved willing neither to suppress the growing ferment by Stalinist methods nor to relax its controls sufficiently to allow for the growth of an autonomous, *non-Party* art. The result of this ambivalent attitude was, on the one hand, a more combative *esprit* and a sharpening of restiveness and dissent among the Soviet intelligentsia and, on the other, a reluctance on their part to invest the continuing struggle against "Stalinism" with an overtly political mantle. As late as 1964, therefore, it was still accurate to describe the situation in the words of the American poet and historian Peter Viereck: "An intellectual revolt, a revolt of the heart? Yes. Political freedom? Hardly."[3]

This situation was abruptly changed by a single event in February, 1966—the trial of writers Andrei Siniavsky and Yuli Daniel, whose works, under their respective pen names of Abram Tertz and Nikolai Arzhak, had for several years been smuggled out to and published in the West. In legal terms, the trial symbolized, at one and the same time, the progress of Soviet jurisprudence since Stalin's days, its setbacks in the past few years, and—most important—the feebleness of legal guarantees when political issues are at stake. The regime was obviously interested in trying the two writers—whose identities had long been a *cause mystérieuse* both in Russia and abroad—as an object lesson to all nonconformist intellectuals. The days of Stalin were gone; a prearranged spectacle, in which Daniel and Siniavsky would confess to "placing broken glass in workers' butter" and then plead for mercy, was therefore out of the question. On the other hand, since the publication of manuscripts abroad, pseudonymously or not, does not constitute a violation of Soviet law, their "crime" had to be defined in different terms. Accordingly, the two writers were charged with having engaged in "anti-Soviet propaganda and agitation," which is punishable, under Article 70 of the Criminal Code of the Russian Republic, by up to seven years of forced labor or exile. As proof, the prosecution offered the literary works of Siniavsky and Daniel, ascribing the views of some of their characters to the writers themselves.

The trial, then, was a judicial farce, compounded as it was by the inordinate length of the pretrial detention; by the attacks in newspapers and on radio virtually condemning the defendants in advance as "traitors"; by the packing of the courtroom; and by the browbeating of witnesses—all of which, incidentally, had been long ago condemned by Soviet legal spokesmen. To the dismay of the authorities, however, the defendants behaved throughout the trial in a courageous and dignified manner (which an outraged *Izvestia* denounced as a manifestation of "extreme cynicism"). Nor was the intended lesson driven home; on the contrary, the trial, with its throwbacks to the discredited methods of the past, served as a warning that Stalinism was still a viable weapon in the hands of an unscrupulous regime.

Deeply disturbed by these implications, the liberals rallied to the defense of their colleagues. In a series of unpublicized petitions to the highest organs of Party and government, writers, artists, scientists, and scholars vigorously condemned the judicial proceedings as playing into the hands of "bourgeois propaganda" and "impeding the progress of Soviet culture."[4] Characteristically, most of the protests still addressed the problem of intellectual freedom; others, however, went beyond such "traditional" demands, comparing the trial to the travesties of the 1930's and pointing out that not even "in the history of Tsarist Russia . . . has a writer been arrested and tried on a charge of antistate crimes which consisted in his writing antistate works of literature and publishing them at home and abroad." Perhaps the most eloquent statement came from the pen of Lidia Chukovskaia, daughter of the noted writer and scholar Kornei Chukovsky, addressed to Mikhail Sholokhov, author of *And Quiet Flows the Don*. Sholokhov had not only welcomed the persecution of Siniavsky and Daniel but demanded that they be treated with the same "rough justice" meted out to "counterrevolutionaries" in the early 1920's. Miss Chukovskaia's letter bluntly branded the Nobel Prize winner a traitor to the traditions of Russian literature, denounced the trial as "illegal," and warned that the Soviet people were in danger of being "robbed" of "the most precious achievements" of the past decade—the "persistent attempts to return to the rule of law."[5]

And so the die was cast. Intellectual freedom without political freedom was unthinkable. From then on, political freedom became a major battle cry of Russia's dissenters.

The first to bring this cry into the open were the young—students and aspiring poets and writers—whose "underground" literary activities had frequently involved them in difficulties with the police. In January, 1967, two demonstrations were held in Moscow to demand the release of Siniavsky and Daniel and the overhaul of the notorious Article 70. They were followed by arrests and subsequently by the trial of Viktor Khaustov in February and of Vladimir Bukovsky, Vadim Delone, and Yevgeni Kushev seven months later. Having (in the words of Bukovsky) "demonstrated in defense of legality" (Document 2), the young writers now learned that demonstrations, too, were a serious "breach of legality." They were charged with participating "in group activities that grossly violate public order" (Article 190-3 of the R.S.F.S.R. Criminal Code). Khaustov received a three-year prison sentence, and Bukovsky was sent to a forced-labor camp for three years. The others were released on probation, having been "encouraged" to "express remorse" (Document 1). In December, Pavel Litvinov, grandson of the late Commissar for Foreign Affairs, performed an unprecedented act of defiance: he publicly distributed the text of Bukovsky's final trial statement (Document 2) and a transcript of a KGB interrogation in which Litvinov himself had been threatened with "criminal responsibility" if he went through with his plan to disseminate Bukovsky's statement (Document 3). To Litvinov, the attempt at intimidation "clearly revealed tendencies that should be made public and that cannot but alarm our progressive society and the world in general."

Then, in January, 1968, came the trial of Aleksandr Ginzburg, Yuri Galanskov, Aleksei Dobrovolsky, and Vera Lashkova. The first two had long been active in various "underground" literary activities. Galanskov, a remarkable prototype of the Russian idealist, had also drafted a program for universal disarmament and had earlier staged a one-man demonstration in front of the American Embassy to protest U.S. intervention in the Dominican Republic. Dobrovolsky, as it turned out, had been "persuaded" to turn state's evidence against his erstwhile friends, and the young student Lashkova was accused of nothing more than having typed the various "incriminatory" manuscripts (including Ginzburg's compilation of documents on the Daniel-Siniavsky trial, the so-called *White Book*). Since these writings could by no stretch of the imagination be labeled "slanderous fabrications which defame the Soviet state and social system" (Article 70), the young writers were fancifully accused of collaborating with the anti-Soviet émigré organization NTS. Not a single piece of creditable evidence was offered in support of this charge. Again, the trial was ostensibly "open," but in fact only a handful of KGB agents and "indignant citizens" were admitted to the courtroom. The defendants were interrupted and jeered; numerous individuals wishing to testify in their behalf were prevented from appearing in court; and the presiding judge, Lev M. Mironov, provided the final touch of hypocrisy by openly cooperating with the prosecution.

The storm produced by this trial, as may be seen in the letters, appeals, petitions, and protests comprising Section II of the documents, was extraordinary. In the words of one observer, "the single voice raised by Pavel Litvinov . . . in 1967" now "turned into a roar."[6] The "generation gap" vanished overnight. The young dissenters suddenly found that they were no longer alone; they were joined by literally hundreds of Soviet citizens, some famous, some less well known, some with notable records of nonconformism, and some who had never before taken part in public life. Not only writers and artists but also teachers, mathematicians, engineers, librarians, doctors, physicists, and even factory workers, high-school students, and at least one collective-farm chairman (see Document 16) were galvanized into action. In the past, intellectual ferment had been restricted to Moscow and Leningrad; now it spread to Magadan, Kharkov, Dubna, and other cities throughout the country. Nor did the signatories court discretion; they addressed their letters and petitions to Soviet state and judicial authorities, to Party leaders, to the newspapers, to foreign Communists, and even (in the case of Litvinov and Larisa Bogoraz-Daniel, wife of the imprisoned writer) to "World Public Opinion" (Document 7), making sure that copies got into the hands of Western newspapermen and tourists for dissemination abroad.

As one leafs through the voluminous "literature of protest," one is struck again and again not only by its content but by its tone. Courage, passion, a sense of martyrdom—these are qualities we have surely come to expect from Russian rebels against authority. *Viz.*, Bukovsky: "I absolutely do not repent having organized this demonstration. . . . When I am free again, I shall again organize demonstrations" (Document 2) and Ginzburg: "I know that you will convict me because not one person charged under Article 70 has ever been acquitted. I will go off to camp calmly to serve my time. You can put me in a prison or send me to a camp, but I am sure that no single honest person will condemn me" (Document 10). Or consider some of the terms employed by the protesters: "base," "treacherous," "disgusting," "dishonorable," "cruel," "bestial." But whence, one wonders, come the composure, the *sang-froid*, the intellectual sophistication, the familiarity with Soviet law, and the occasional flashes of caustic humor displayed by the dissenters?

In a country racked first by "revolutionary justice" (so nostalgically recalled by Mr. Sholokhov) and then by years of arbitrary terror, it comes with the force of revelation to see political prisoners challenging and confounding their accusers by drawing them into intricate discussions of Soviet law (Documents 2 and 10) and defense attorneys deftly demolishing the cases against their clients (Documents 2 and 3). The Soviet Union has never—even during the comparatively liberal 1920's—enjoyed a free press. Yet letter after letter exposes the prevarications, inconsistencies, and distortions of both the prosecution and the information media. Consider, for example, the letter by poet and translator Anatoli Yakobson (Document 23), which, in a few contemptuous sentences, exposes an alleged NTS agent by the name of Brocks-Sokolov, the "major trump card of the prosecution," as nothing but a creature of the police—and an inept one at that. "It used to be said," observes Yakobson, "that a windbag is a boon to a spy. Such a spy as Brocks-Sokolov is a boon to the KGB." (Brocks-Sokolov "confessed" to having arrived in the Soviet Union in December, 1967, in order to establish contact with Galanskov and Ginzburg, not having been briefed, apparently, that his fellow agents had been arrested nearly a year earlier.)

Cynicism and blundering were characteristic features of the Moscow trials of the 1930's, when various old Bolsheviks confessed to having met either Trotsky or his emissaries in a nonexistent hotel in Copenhagen or at an airport near Oslo at which, it turned out, no foreign plane had landed for months before or after the alleged encounter, much less during. Soviet citizens who could see through such inane deceptions communicated their feelings in "Aesopian language"—the only means of expressing any criticism in the U.S.S.R., save that which was officially sanctioned and encouraged. Surely the abandonment of this language in favor of direct refutation and criticism is of no mean therapeutic value.

Whence, then, come the audacity, the erudition, the self-confidence displayed by such people as Yakobson? Two answers suggest themselves, one rooted in history, the other in ideology. The reader will find a perceptive discussion of the similarities between the dissenters of today and of the past in Mr. Monas's essay. Let me merely stress the references to radical democrats of the late nineteenth century, who welcomed the judicial reforms of Alexander II, seeing in them an ideal means of effecting more profound changes in the political and social order. It is surely not without significance that an "underground" journal chose to reprint, from a "legitimate" Soviet publication, an essay on the Russian revolutionary Serno-Solovevich that emphasizes his view of legality as a weapon to be used against the Tsarist regime (pp. 405-10).

The second reason for the preoccupation—and familiarity—with legal issues is directly related to the profound contrast between ideology and reality in the U.S.S.R. It is the Soviet Constitution itself, after all, that guarantees to the Soviet citizen freedom of speech, of the press, and of assembly (including meetings and demonstrations) and, as was pointed out by the indomitable Major-General Piotr Grigorenko,[7] "the greatest weapon of the working class: the right to strike" (Document 1). The promises embodied in this solemn document have not been lost upon Soviet citizens, nor has the fact that they have been patently vitiated by the regime. As Mr. Weiner points out, the dissenters' emphasis on "the rule of law" takes many forms: criticism of specific abuses of procedural norms; criticism of the subordination of law to politics; criticism of the absence of legal safeguards; but, above all, criticism of the violation of the Soviet citizen's constitutional guarantees, of the "trampling on the rights of man" (Document 32) in a country that—to quote another statement—"proclaimed the slogans of freedom and justice to the whole world" (Document 15).

Having examined the origins and some of the characteristics of current dissent in the Soviet Union, we must now ask ourselves: What are the over-all aims and demands of this movement? Is it, indeed, a movement in any recognizable sense of the term, with clearly defined goals and a consistent program of action?

For an answer to these questions, let us turn to the specific issues that have agitated Soviet dissenters over the past two years or so, indicated by the titles of the various documentary sections. There is, first of all, the overwhelming concern with legality—that is to say, the question of whether Soviet society is to be ruled by arbitrariness and police repressions or by due process of law (Sections I and II). Closely linked to that is the demand for intellectual freedom (Section V), a demand that has undergone profound radicalization ever since Aleksandr Solzhenitsyn openly appealed to his fellow writers, in May, 1967, to join him in a struggle for the abolition of any form of censorship whatsoever (Document 49). Despite the abusive press campaign against him, despite the fact that his printed works have been withdrawn from circulation and two of his novels, *The First Circle* and *Cancer Ward* (both now published in the West), have been suppressed in Russia, despite all the demands that he revise his "slanderous" works and cease engaging in "anti-Soviet activities"—despite all this, Solzhenitsyn has continued to adhere to his demand, which has now been taken up by numerous other intellectuals, including even so eminent an "Establishment" figure as the physicist Andrei Sakharov (Document 76).

Discontent among Russia's ethnic minorities and the often brutal suppression of their national and cultural rights have given rise to yet another category of protest and dissent, "the nationalities problem" (Section III). Official and quasi-official anti-Semitism, of course, has long been a target of the liberal intelligentsia. With the growing realization of the fundamental similarities of all totalitarian ideologies, whether Stalinist or fascist (a point stressed by Sakharov), criticism of this noxious phenomenon has acquired both greater depth and greater urgency over the years. But it is in the Ukraine that nationalist ferment has been most intense, and it is the Ukrainian intellectuals—most of them in their thirties and forties—who have provided us with the most eloquent pleas for national freedom and ethnic harmony (including pleas for understanding between Ukrainians and Jews, both traditional victims of Moscow's discriminatory practices—*e.g.*, Document 38). In the past few years, there have been more arrests and trials of nonconformist intellectuals and "bourgeois nationalists" in the Ukraine than anywhere else in the U.S.S.R., and it is in the painstaking accounts of such people as Vyacheslav Chornovil (Document 37)—a young Ukrainian journalist whose efforts in behalf of political prisoners landed him in a forced-labor camp in 1967—that we find the most sophisticated analysis of the suppression of both civil and national rights and the struggle against it.

Also in this category are numerous protests against the persecution of the Crimean Tatars, who, together with six other national minorities, were forcibly expelled from their native republics during World War II on grounds of collaborating with the Germans and were deported to Central Asia (Documents 39 and 40). Though rehabilitated in September, 1967, they were allowed neither to return to the Crimea to reconstitute their republic nor even to refer to themselves as Crimean Tatars. It is fascinating to note among the signatories of the relevant documents not only "representatives of the Crimean-Tatar people" but also numerous individuals who played an active part in the broader revolt against judicial iniquities, such as Grigorenko and Aleksei Kosterin.[8]

The tendency of many dissenters to embrace any cause involving the suppression of human rights, whether national or international, is borne out most dramatically in the protests against Soviet action in Czechoslovakia, the first of which were issued weeks before the invasion. On August 25, a number of young people mounted a demonstration in Moscow's Red Square calling for the immediate withdrawal of Soviet troops from Czechoslovakia. The demonstration was broken up by the police (shouting, according to one of the demonstrators, Natalia Gorbanevskaia, "These are all dirty Jews—beat the anti-Soviets!"), and some of the participants were put on trial in October. The two principal figures were Pavel Litvinov, who was sentenced to five years of exile in a remote region of the country, and Daniel's wife, who followed her husband into exile for a term of four years. The forty-year-old linguist Konstantin Babitsky was exiled for three years, and two other defendants were sentenced to terms of three and two and one-half years in jail. "Those who do not approve of the verdict," said Larisa Daniel in her final statement in court, "if they should express their disapproval, will also find their way here" (Document 69). She was right. More protests followed—and more arrests. As these words are written, the American press has just reported on a trial of six young dissidents in Leningrad, convicted under Article 70 for decrying the Soviet invasion. Three of them received prison sentences, and three others were subjected to that most repulsive form of political repression in the U.S.S.R. —confinement to mental institutions.

Finally, a few words about one of the most extraordinary chapters in the "literature of protest"—documents pertaining to the suppression of religious worship in the U.S.S.R. (Section IV). In his essay, Mr. Reddaway notes that over 300,000 words have already been published in the West, representing "only a small part of the whole." The fact, as Mr. Reddaway observes, that, for the most part, these materials were written by ordinary citizens rather than by members of the intelligentsia makes their familiarity with the Soviet laws governing religion (whose violations they document and denounce) all the more astonishing. Also noteworthy is the fact that religious freedom has become a cause of the nonreligious dissenters as well (*e.g.*, Document 48).

The current dissent in the Soviet Union thus covers a wide gamut of issues, ranging from literary censorship to anti-Semitism, from freedom of conscience to freedom for Czechoslovakia. But does it amount to an organized political opposition with a systematic political program and platform? Hardly. To be sure, there have been several trials in Leningrad within the past year or so—all held behind closed doors, and all unreported in the Soviet press—involving small groups accused of concerted political action aimed at the overthrow of the Soviet regime. One group in particular, the "All-Russian Social-Christian Union for the Liberation of the People" (see Mr. Reddaway's article), had formulated a set of political goals and organizational principles, all of them painfully naive and clearly derived from the at-once utopian and ultra-conspiratorial notions of such nineteenth-century figures as Bakunin and Nechaev. There is no evidence, however, that the majority of Soviet dissenters have ever attempted to organize themselves or to work out any concrete guides to political action (or, for that matter, that the official charges against the Leningrad group—"treason" and "dangerous crimes against the state"—had any substance whatsoever).

Yet, in a larger sense, dissent in the Soviet Union today *does* represent a very genuine movement—and a political one at that. It lacks an organizational framework and, indeed, does not seek one. It is heterogeneous, embracing people who wish to reform the system from within, people concerned with the correction of certain specific abuses, as well as individuals thoroughly alienated from the official ideology, even in its "purest" and most "Leninist" form. Still relatively small, it confronts not only a hostile regime but also a largely indifferent population, vast segments of which are imbued with a traditional suspicion of "smart-alecky" intellectuals and "Jews." It would therefore be wrong to ascribe more importance to the dissent than it actually has or to see it as a serious political challenge to the regime.

Yet it is a movement, and a very Russian movement, in that it is inspired by one central idea—an overriding concern for justice and liberty. Whatever the differences among its adherents, they are bound together—as Mr. Monas points out—in a spiritual and moral kinship. It is this kinship that makes it so natural for them to turn from one specific issue to another without resort to the "organizational weapon" or to a set of ideological and strategic principles. And it is without the benefit of such typically twentieth-century political tools that this small and diverse group of people has succeeded in presenting, in effect, a comprehensive indictment of some of the fundamental features of the Soviet system. The dissenters, then, do not pose any real threat to the power of the regime. But to the extent that they have—for the first time in history—laid bare the regime's ideological and historical pretensions, to the extent that they have effectively exposed the myths that provide the only moral justification for Communist rule in Russia and for Moscow's leadership of the international Communist movement, they have confronted the regime with its most serious moral and ideological challenge to date.

The Soviet leaders are aware of this challenge and, above all, of the fact that its strength rests upon palpable truth. It is this awareness that explains the stridency of the official reaction (Section VIII, "Reprisals"). The first serious manifestations of dissent erupted in 1967, during the celebrations of the fiftieth anniversary of the "Great October Socialist Revolution." Embarrassed, the regime's initial response was silence— silent arrests and confidential appeals for *some* decorum, at least, on this of all occasions (wasn't the disgraceful defection of Stalin's daughter enough?). When these measures proved unsuccessful, the time came for overt "action": trials, confinement to mental institutions, expulsions from jobs, police interrogations, and threats. The press was filled with ominous allusions to such unsavory elements of the past as "Russian capitalists" and "Trotskyites," with calls for more severe censorship and other measures aimed at increasing Party control over the arts, and with appeals for "vigilance" against Western intelligence agencies bent on the ideological subversion of "morally unstable" and "politically immature" segments of the Russian intelligentsia. Finally, the campaign— somewhat erratic until then—to cleanse Stalin's image of some of the "slander" that had been heaped upon it in recent years became considerably more vocal. Nothing, of course, was more likely to evoke a sense of outrage among the dissenters, for whom "the exculpation of Stalin" is "tantamount to the defamation of socialism" (Document 74).[9]

Perhaps at no other moment in history has Soviet society been so rife with contradictions as it is today. The Brezhnev-Kosygin leadership— an uninspired conglomeration of mediocre *apparatchiki*, suspicious of innovation and wedded to the preservation of the *status quo*—has nullified most of its predecessor's reforms and created an atmosphere of intimidation and repression more pervasive than at any other period since 1953. Yet, thirteen years after the dethronement of Stalin, the present leadership finds it impossible to restore his heritage in full. At no time since 1953, perhaps, have Soviet citizens been so fearful of contacts with Westerners as they are today, or has the popular mood been permeated with so much weariness and hopelessness. Yet never before, too, has there been such pronounced defiance or such extensive and incisive criticism of the social and political system. Despite all the measures taken against them, as a scandalized proregime writer acknowledged in *Literaturnaia gazeta* (April 8, 1968), "There are those who to this day remain stubborn and fail to draw the appropriate conclusions for themselves." And so, most likely, they will continue to do. For it is the regime that is unwilling to "draw the appropriate conclusions": that discontent breeds restiveness; that restrictiveness (in the words of the same writer) creates "alarm"; and that alarm leads to reprisals—and thus to more restiveness, defiance, and dissent—a story as old as Russia itself.

Notes

1. "Resolution of the Central Committee of the Communist Party of the Soviet Union, June 30, 1956," *Pravda* (Moscow), July 2, 1956. English text in *The Anti-Stalin Campaign and International Communism*, ed. Russian Institute of Columbia University (New York: Columbia University Press, 1956).

2. Konstantin Paustovsky, "Indisputable Thoughts and Controversial Ones," *Literaturnaia gazeta*, May 20, 1959.

3. Peter Viereck, "The Mob Within the Heart: A New Russian Revolution," *Tri-Quarterly*, Spring, 1965.

4. See Max Hayward (ed. and trans.), *On Trial: The Soviet State Versus "Abram Tertz" and "Nikolai Arzhak"* (New York: Harper & Row, 1967), pp. 287–302.

5. For a subsequent letter by Chukovskaia, see Document 73.

6. Paul A. Smith, Jr., "Protest in Moscow," *Foreign Affairs*, October, 1968, p. 156.

7. One of the most indefatigable of the protesters, Grigorenko was deprived of his rank and sent to an insane asylum in 1964. "When I asked precisely when my husband lost his sanity since I had never noticed it," his wife wrote subsequently in an open letter to Brezhnev, "I was told by the investigators . . . that my husband's political views and his dissemination of them rendered him socially dangerous" (Document 36).

8. Aleksei Kosterin (born 1896), a writer and journalist who spent seventeen years in Stalin's labor camps, was, to many Russians, the very embodiment of ascetic selflessness and courage. He died on November 12, 1968, and, at his funeral two days later, his friend and admirer Piotr Grigorenko delivered an unprecedented oration denouncing the "totalitarianism that hides behind the mark of so-called Soviet democracy" and the "soulless" Party bureaucracy. Unfortunately, no full text of this address—reported in the Western press—has reached us as of the time this volume goes to press.

9. See also G. S. Pomerantz, "Address to the Institute of Philosophy in Moscow": "to restore respect for Stalin would be to establish something new—to establish respect for denunciation, torture, execution" (Document 75).

Engineers or Martyrs:
Dissent and the Intelligentsia

SIDNEY MONAS

It is surely unusual for literature to become the occasion for a constitutional crisis. Yet this is, in essence, what has happened in the Soviet
Union as an outgrowth of the February, 1966, trial of Andrei Siniavsky
and Yuli Daniel. At their trial, the two writers defended themselves on
literary grounds against the charge of having carried on "anti-Soviet
propaganda." The judge even accused them of attempting to turn the
court proceedings into an elementary course in literary criticism; yet he
himself called in a panel of literary experts whose presence at the trial
was difficult to explain *except* on literary grounds. Everything seemed
confused, contradictory, paradoxical, and against expectations.

The sentences handed down by the court turned out to be extremely
harsh, and the amnesty that many expected has so far not been granted.
On the other hand, literary dissent has not been silenced either. On the
contrary, the trial stirred up a wave of protest that has since spread to
the very fringes of the intelligentsia, if not beyond, and that has, at the
same time, become much broader than a demand for mere literary and
artistic freedom. Indeed, because it has had the effect of polarizing the
articulate Soviet public into opposing authoritarian and libertarian
camps, the trial has been likened in its divisive impact to the Dreyfus
case in France of the 1890's.[1]

Yet, too, how Russian! One is immediately reminded of the historic
role of nineteenth-century Russian literature, of the special relationship
between Nicholas I and Pushkin, of the secretly circulated manuscripts
of Griboedov, Pushkin, and Lermontov, of Belinsky's letter to Gogol,
and of the publications of Hertzen's *Free Russian Press* in London.

Because literature was an island of relative freedom in a censor-ridden
country, hopes for the expression of grievances and the authentication of
private experiences and predicaments—hopes that elsewhere might have
found other outlets—in Russia became centered in literature. It should
be added that Russian literature embodied a Christian sensibility in
secularized form and thereby served to orient intellectuals who had lost
their religion, but not their religiosity. It tended to glorify compassion,
the notion of "beautiful suffering" and the acceptance of suffering as
one's lot, and the subordination of self to some larger cause.

15

Before the occurrence of the Revolution that aimed at changing the
conditions that produced beautiful sufferers and superfluous men, there
was a literary revolution that anticipated the type of the revolutionary.
This was the project of the "new man," the "positive hero," which was
inaugurated by Belinsky, Chernyshevsky, and Gorky and much admired
by Lenin.[2]

Now there is once again in Russia something like an intelligentsia—
not merely, as Stalin defined the term, a "social segment" of professionals and "white collars" recruited from among the workers and peasants but a "spiritual brotherhood" bearing a *special burden of conscience*
and equipped with a special sensibility. In a recent article ostensibly
about America, the Soviet sociologist Igor Kon prefaces a discussion of
the particular problems of the American intelligentsia with an analysis
of the problems involved in the general concept "intelligentsia," presenting some especially interesting ideas regarding the importance of a
psychological approach. On the role of a literary avant-garde, he quotes
Lewis Coser, the American sociologist, as follows:

> It would be absurd to attribute the alienation of many avant-garde authors
> solely to the battle with the censors; yet one may well maintain that those
> battles contributed in no mean measure to such alienation. To these
> authors the censor came to be the very symbol of the philistinism, hy-
> pocrisy, and meanness of bourgeois society.
>   Many an author who was initially apolitical was drawn to the political
> left in the United States because the left was in the forefront of the battle
> against censorship. The close alliance of avant-garde art with avant-garde
> social and political radicalism can be accounted for, at least in part, by
> the fact that they came to be merged in the minds of many as a single
> battle for freedom against all repression.[3]

The relevance of this passage to the current situation in the Soviet
Union is attested to by its requotation, this time deliberately and overtly
in a Soviet context, by the extraordinary physicist-academician A. D.
Sakharov in his "underground" essay, which recently found its way
abroad and appeared in the *New York Times*.[4]
   The Revolution ravaged but did not destroy the old Russian intelligentsia, with its distinctive public-mindedness and literary education.
What was left was joined—perhaps "swamped" would be a better word
—by a large, new, crudely trained group, newly empowered and newly
privileged, ambitious, dynamic, and perhaps more than a little frightened
underneath its new perquisites and accomplishments. This new amalgam
was further devastated by the purges, the war, and the Stalinist terror,
giving place only slowly and reluctantly to the better-educated, more
finely honed, and intellectually more secure generation that came of age
in the postwar world.

It is *their* situation that recapitulates at least some aspects of the situation of the nineteenth-century intelligentsia—a ravished public life,

something of which may, perhaps, still be redeemed, and a heavy burden of guilt toward "the people."[5] With the collapse of Stalinist authority, the claims of which were as absolute as those made on behalf of any divinity, the very authority of the Communist Party itself seemed to tremble and waver, and, with it, the very sense of a purpose to life. Questions were asked and not answered. The call for *glasnost* (publicity) was stifled by the same Party organs that had issued it. Significantly enough, it was in the wake of the Twentieth Party Congress that Andrei Siniavsky wrote his essay "On Socialist Realism," and only two years later that he sent it abroad under the pseudonym of Abram Tertz.

This was the period of the "thaw" that somehow never quite passed on to spring. Publication became much freer, yet not altogether free. The formulas of socialist realism were torn to shreds; yet the basic idea of an *organized* literature remained. It was not merely that the journals and the publishing houses were controlled by the Party through the Writers' Union. The Party refused to relinquish its control over the life of literature as such and over the lives of writers; it continued to decide who should have access to a typewriter and a *dacha*, who could give a public recital, and who could go abroad. And precisely to the degree that the Party felt this control slipping, the need to preserve it was frantically invoked. From 1956 on, spontaneous literary gatherings that easily spilled over into politics became commonplace. The mimeographed journals began to appear in 1958. There were poetry readings in Maiakovsky Square. "Underground literature" assumed a certain bulk.

In genre, this literature varied greatly, and, in quality, it ran the gamut from brilliant to unmitigatedly awful. Something of that range is represented in the examples provided in this volume. Among the discursive writings, all remain more or less within the revolutionary if not necessarily the strictly Bolshevik tradition. None are antisocialist, and none are antipatriotic. There are no "witches' covens" represented—perhaps, among the intelligentsia at least, none exists. Similarly, the more personal and lyric works, while reflecting an assiduous effort to affirm the value of private experience and personal desire, reveal no real opening of the sluice gates of personal repression. While the political rhetoric is sometimes fairly strong, the rhetoric of sex seems remarkably restrained and old fashioned.

With the arrest and trial of Siniavsky and his disciple Daniel, the repressive mechanism—from the *Glavlit* censorship to the KGB—clamped down hard. Curiously enough, however, intimidation proved ineffective. Protest mounted. An increasingly wide range of people became involved. In April, 1968, a plenary session of the CPSU Central Committee declared the "consequences of the personality cult" officially liquidated and called for strengthened ideological discipline in the face of what was termed a renewed bourgeois ideological offensive. Six weeks later, writing in *Literaturnaia gazeta*, a Party ideologue attempted to belittle the entire protest movement as the work of a few "politically immature" writers.

Misconceptions of the place of the intelligentsia, false conclusions concerning the writer's role in the ranks of the whole intelligentsia, and finally, overestimation of their own relative weight in the writers' community—these are what have nurtured the childish arrogance of some of our comrades.[6]

Yet this rings most unconvincingly, and no one really believes that either protest or *samizdat* (underground writing) has been terminated. Within the ranks of the intelligentsia, the regime has unleashed a small-scale and highly selective, yet at the same time vicious, terror.[7] This, however, only seems to have deepened the divisions within Soviet society rather than to have silenced dissent effectively.

The real preface to the current intellectual turmoil was written by Nikita Khrushchev back in February, 1956. However carefully planned and "engineered" the secret speech may have been, it also seems unquestionably to have contained a personal Khrushchevian element of great significance. Into the planned unmasking of Stalin there crept—or, rather, welled up—a sense of personal outrage, a sense of humiliation lived through and resented, a genuine need for self-assertion and self-authentication. It took place within a strictly Party context, of course, and it was entirely on behalf of the corporate personality of the Party, standing as a surrogate for the Soviet Union as a whole—indeed, for all mankind—that the Stalin icon was smashed. Khrushchev "bore witness" on behalf of the upper leadership of the Party. But there were millions who had suffered far more, yet were allowed no such luxury.

Within a few months, foreign Communist newspapers and leaders began to ask questions that the speech had obviously raised. The asking was reluctant, painful, enmeshed in a sticky, murky, half-apologetic vocabulary, and surrounded by exhortative reminders of the "objective" achievements of the Soviet Union—as though the whole Stalinist notion of "objectivity" were not precisely what was hanging in the air. Why did the Stalin exposure come so late? What was the complicity of the current leadership in Stalin's misdeeds? How could Marxists, of all people, rest content with the attribution of the personality cult merely to one personality—or, if Beria were thrown in, two personalities? What were its historical-institutional bases, and what was being done to alter them? Why was the exposure made through a "secret" speech that first came to the attention of many sincere Communists through publication in a bourgeois newspaper?

Ten years after these questions were first raised, they were still neither satisfactorily answered nor withdrawn. They floated in the air, out of reach and for short periods almost out of sight, then reappearing in all their perplexity. To answer them fully may well be impossible. Even to make a real effort might put the authority of the Party leadership in grave danger; yet failure to make such an effort produces the same results.

Communist party leaders outside the Soviet Union have their own constituencies, and their power in many instances depends more on pleasing those constituencies (which include intellectuals) than on acting as "transmission belts" for the will of Moscow. Notwithstanding the current military occupation of Czechoslovakia, the possibilities for the Soviet Union to exert naked force have substantially diminished since 1956, and the political losses that result from such action have increased. At home, terror and naked force come more readily to hand; yet there, too, limitations have closed in. Prestige abroad is one factor limiting the use of force. A changed and changing social and economic structure is another and more important one.

In a society that presumes to compete technologically with the United States, the intelligentsia is not merely a crucial element but one that, even if it could simply be kicked and pummeled into submission, would then be incapable of performing the socio-economic task demanded of it. For youth especially, between the ages of sixteen and thirty-six, be they *intelligenty* themselves, children of the intelligentsia, or merely intelligent, sensitive, and aspiring young people, the questions asked or implied by Khrushchev's speech are questions of orientation to the world of their parents, and they pose the most crucial problem of integrity of personality.

For many of their parents, in turn, they are questions of the authentication of experience. Was what they went through meaningful, did it have a purpose, was it real? Have the ends of socialism been irretrievably corrupted by the means used to achieve them? Should they believe experience or what is printed? Can what is printed be validated by experience? If the parents refuse to face these problems—as many do—the children must do it for them. A world in which what is known, what is felt, and what is desired—though disharmonious factors among themselves—are all three so assiduously sealed off from what is publicly proclaimed and officially permitted cannot but create a sense of confinement and unreality in the people who live in it.

The Soviet Union is now a predominantly urban society, and the sophistry of the city has replaced what Marx called "the idiocy of rural life." The intelligentsia possesses professional skills that are of unprecedented importance to such a society; yet its position has not ceased to be extremely vulnerable. For all its modernization, the Soviet Union still contains a very massive "dark" population, aspiring to bourgeois amenities, on the one hand, yet immersed in socialist rhetoric, on the other. And, within this population, there is a strong element of "grudge"— crude, primitive, often all too well founded, a kind of legendary force in its own right—which views all privilege as corruption, and which is directed equally against the political and managerial elite of the Party and against the intelligentsia. Here, however, the intelligentsia is at a disadvantage, for it still carries the traditional burden of guilt toward the people, and the lines of manipulation are in the hands of the Party. It is wrong, of course, to speak of the Party and the intelligentsia as separate entities: they interpenetrate each other, both sociologically and psychologically speaking. Nevertheless, the Party's standards are political, organizational, and institutional. As an organization, it is all-embracing —its founding mission, after all, was world revolution and the total transformation of man. Like all organizations, however, it directs much of its energies toward maintaining, justifying, and reproducing itself. The intelligentsia, on the other hand, is not an organization. Not all "professionals" belong to it, but only those who have a more general concern with ideas and experience than can be satisfied within the bounds of their professions. Yet there is a certain "community of professionals." The highly trained physicist appreciates the pyrotechnics and playful technical proficiency of Voznesensky's poetry, just as Voznesensky has a feeling in his poems for the modernity of physics. Professional skill becomes a pride and nourishes a secret elitism *vis-à-vis* the "mere administrators" and still more so in relation to those whose career has been built not on skill and accomplishment but on proclaiming the correct ideological view at the right time.

Not only is the Party an organization, it is a revolutionary organization dedicated to the triumph of world socialism in its own special version. Militancy has always been its watchword. In its early days of power, the need for militancy often served as an excuse for crudeness. To justify the terror, Stalin advanced the theory that the class struggle, instead of diminishing as it moves toward victory, grows sharper. With the exposure of Stalin and the rejection of his theory, it became apparent that crudeness had served as an excuse for militancy. The cultural thaw at home and the officially proclaimed policy of coexistence abroad encouraged the intelligentsia to hope for a new era. Khrushchev, however, very quickly proclaimed "no coexistence in the realm of ideology." Literature, unlike the study of language as such, was said to belong to the realm of ideology.

It was, of course, not the intelligentsia alone that reacted against the Party's tendency to insist on total militancy. Every working girl who read a novel or went to a play was tired of the heroine whose main distinction was her overfulfillment of the production norm, tired of the hero who made love only to tractors. The demand for some acknowledgement of the literary legitimacy of such things as personality, personal distinctiveness, and the poignance of private feelings, apart from their relation to the Party or to socialist construction, went far beyond the intelligentsia. The intelligentsia's demands were, of course, still more comprehensive, embracing the whole realm of private experience— thought, doubt, speculation, and dreams.

The Party relaxed the standards of socialist realism—which, under Stalin, had tended to become increasingly rigid except for the brief interlude of the war years—with regard to both style and subject matter. Control of publication, however, remained entirely in the Party's hands as part of its ideological monopoly. How much freedom of expression would be allowed came to depend on literary politics—on who controlled what journal; on whether the "liberals" controlled or merely had a slight foothold in, say, the editorial board of *Novyi mir*; on the degree to which the party favored *Oktiabr*; on how the "waverers" (those, like K. Simonov, V. Kataev, and many others, who were neither "liberal" nor "conservative" but wavered within themselves and between the camps) resolved or failed to resolve their doubts. Above all, it depended on who could decisively influence the ideological commission of the Party Central Committee, where the final say resided. The resultant policy was far from consistent. There were many *little* thaws and freezes, and at present the situation is about as "frozen" as it has been at any time since 1956.

A rigidification of literary policy might signal, therefore, not only a deprivation of felt personal needs—the need for a certain playfulness, if not necessarily for bourgeois "entertainment"; the need for imaginative exploration of personal possibilities, for public recognition of deeply felt experiences, for a sense of life not circumscribed by political expediency or couched in an outworn and discredited rhetoric; and, above all, the need to "bear witness" and "receive testimony" to the importance of this larger sense of life, in which the conscious and the unconscious, the self and the other, the mind and the heart, the language and the reality, are not so irreparably riven apart as they have generally come to be in the current officially commended literature. It might signal as well a return to militancy and crudeness in all walks of life. The Chinese stand as a frightening example of the present possibilities of Stalinism.[8]

Against the threat of renascent Stalinism in the U.S.S.R., the Soviet intelligentsia invokes the civil-rights provisions of the Stalin Constitution, the International Declaration of Human Rights (of which the Soviet Union is a signatory), the concept of socialist legality, and the possibility (terribly remote!) of countervailing forces such as the Writers' Union, which, by acting in the writers' interests and defending them *as* writers, might modify the monolithic nature of the Party and at the same time induce a greater sense of responsibility and caution in the *apparatchiki*. The battle for literary freedom and independence—of which both *samizdat* and publication abroad are important aspects—is thus central to the entire struggle for civil and constitutional rights.

Against the intelligentsia and against the struggle for civil rights, the Central Committee of the Party has invoked the supposed menace of a "bourgeois ideological offensive" in which the foreign publication of works critical of the Soviet regime, all publicized dissent, the broadcasts of Radio Free Europe, the operations of the NTS and CIA, and the "political immaturity" of a few famous writers are all seen as linked and related factors.[9] It will be recalled that the same kind of threat was invoked in an attempt to bring fraternal Communist parties, most recently the Czechs, under closer Soviet discipline and control. Since the April meeting of the Central Committee, this "new threat" has been referred to many times, and repeated efforts have been made to build a logical case for repression—not, of course, *as* repression but, rather, as a strengthening of social discipline—precisely on the basis of this alleged offensive.

No doubt there are members of the Central Committee who now cast a nostalgic eye on the Stalinist theory of "the sharpening of the class struggle as victory nears," which they themselves had a hand in discrediting. But, unfortunately for them, the case for the existence of a genuine bourgeois offensive is difficult to maintain before a well-informed public. In the Czech crisis, for instance, whatever fanciful Soviet claims were made regarding American involvement, it is clear that the United States did not intervene in any way. Moreover, while the United States remains no less committed than the Soviet Union to the defense and propagation of its own values, it is absurd to picture the U.S. as chiefly responsible for encouraging and sponsoring the dissidence among Soviet intellectuals. Indeed, the Soviet underground writers' most effective channel of protest and appeal has been not the official organs of Western governments but, rather, those of the diffuse "New"—and even the Communist —Left, both of which remain, on many issues, sympathetic to the Soviet Union.

Nevertheless, the charge that "the enemy is using your work!" has a certain cogency for the Soviet intelligentsia. There are, of course, segments of the intelligentsia—to say nothing of the broader public—that simply are not very well informed. Hostility to the Soviet Union is not a rarity in the Western press and is often handily cited, too often with a disregard for the context or the finer shades of difference. Even among those who *are* well informed, however, the spell of the Party and of Party discipline in the face of a potentially hostile world has not entirely worn off. Their quarrel, after all, is not with the concept and the dream of "socialism" but with those who have sullied and vitiated the dream. To the extent, therefore, that the Soviet leaders can conjure up a creditable image of war-mongering, "imperialist" powers bent on annihilating the very *goal* of Communism, they can count on a certain amount of loyalty even from some of their fiercest domestic critics.

In writing the history of the Peasant War in Germany, Engels expressed an extraordinary sympathy for, and, indeed, a certain identification with, the religious rebel Thomas Muenzer. And Mikhail Pokrovsky, the dean of Soviet historians in the early postrevolutionary years, attempted to write a Marxist history of Russia in which the relationship to the modes of production could be seen as the decisive factor in all historical stages. Thus, Engels emphasized the singular pathos of a revolutionary "ahead of his time," and Pokrovsky, the pathos of Russian backwardness in relation to the West. Stalin, on the other hand, placed the triumph of his own system at the center of the world-historical process. Whatever contributed to it was progressive; everything else was reactionary.

"Objectively speaking," that is, for sentiments and intentions make no difference. Ivan the Terrible, for instance, may have lopped off heads, but, since he strengthened the power of the military monarchy over and against the divisive aristocratic factions and thus prepared the way for the Petrine Empire, which in turn became the locale for the great Revolution, he was a progressive ruler. Since centralized power, a massive army, strong borders, and the terrorization of potential opponents at home were still "necessary" elements of policy, Ivan emerges as not only progressive but prophetic as well. On the other hand, Shamil, leader of the nineteenth-century resistance to Russian occupation of the Caucasus, though once much admired by Russian revolutionaries as a fellow fighter against Tsarist oppression, was now branded a reactionary, because, if he had succeeded in what he attempted, the Trans-Caucasus would have been absorbed by either the Persian or the Turkish Empire, and the "emancipation" of its people through the Great October Revolution would have been immeasurably delayed.[10]

World science and world literature of the past, since they contributed to the consciousness of revolutionaries, were progressive, but contemporary scientists and (foreign) writers were judged, "objectively speaking," by their usefulness to the cause. Among the Russian classical authors, all who were safely dead were progressive—though some were more progressive than others. Dostoevsky, in his religiosity and morbid psychologizing, was dangerous; Gorky, in the years of his Stalinist enthusiasm, basked in a glory second only to Stalin's.

Religion was intrinsically reactionary, and no good could be said of it, although, insofar as it served Russian patriotic ends, it could be tolerated. For the strength of the Russian state was one of the factors that made the strong Soviet state possible, and, insofar as priests, generals, and Tsars contributed to that power, they were progressive, no matter how many peasants they oppressed. In general, the farther back in time, the more progressive they were: Ivan the Terrible was more progressive than Alexander II, Peter the Great was a hero, and Alexander III a slob. Patriotism was progressive. The Russian people were intrinsically progressive and invented almost everything from the steamboat to the radio, but the reactionary social system prevented such inventions from finding useful application.

Not only were the Russians great inventors, but as revolutionaries they were by no means behind their counterparts in the industrially more advanced West. Indeed, in many important respects, they were more advanced. Radishchev, the Decembrists, Hertzen, Belinsky, and Chernyshevsky—though not Marxists—all pointed to the eventual socialist revolution. Their works help validate the Revolution, and the Revolution in turn validates them. Of course, as the Revolution actually approached, reactionary revolutionaries began to make their appearance—*i.e.*, Social Revolutionaries, Mensheviks, Trotskyites.

Russian nationalism was on the whole a progressive force, especially since it embraced Russian literature and science and the Russian revolutionary movement. But the nationalism of the minor nationalities of the empire was somewhat more problematic. On the one hand, their national self-consciousness could be viewed as having played a vital role in cementing their "alliance" with the Russian people, since it was the latter who "liberated" them and in some instances actually created their national consciousness, with the result that they received the blessings of socialism far sooner than they might have on their own. On the other hand, nationalism that looks away from Russia is reactionary and "bourgeois."

Stalin's rewriting of Party history and his debonair way with facts are sufficiently well known. Indeed, Khrushchev himself lingered with some vehemence on this aspect of the cult of personality. The old Bolsheviks who were called in to criticize the third volume of the new *History of the CPSU* were indignant that some of the most prominent names in Party history had not yet been restored. I wish to emphasize here, however, not so much the falsification or omission of facts as the view of history that treats all past life as merely a prelude to the current organization and policy of the Party.

Of course, there is a hunger for sheer fact that was whetted by the Twentieth and Twenty-second Congresses and that still remains unsatisfied despite a considerable growth in the richness and complexity of Soviet historiography. In connection with the history of the Revolution, the Civil War, and World War II, V. Kardin has stressed the need for "the black bread of facts, . . . the unremitting desire, characteristic of our times, to drink from 'the river of fact'," and has attempted to demythologize a number of incidents and anecdotes.[11] He was immediately attacked, however, by no less than Field Marshal Rokossovsky, with Admiral Baikov and General Khlebnikov joining in. "The people's grateful memory," these dignitaries wrote, "has made poetry of outstanding events in the history of the Soviet state."[12] Defending such poetry on the ground of its patriotic exaltation, they argued that it contributes to the ultimate victory of Party policy and is therefore "objectively" true! (This is, of course, my own interpolation; and I would not deny a legendary kind of truth to legends.)

More ominously, there has been a recent attempt to "objectivize" Stalin himself. In spite of the abuses of the cult of personality, the authors of this attempt contend, much that was worthwhile was accomplished during the Stalin period. Against this line, however, Kopelev, Galanskov, and others cry out in protest—Kopelev with particular brilliance since he uses with great effect the logic and language of the "objectivity" argument itself (see Document 74). Addressing himself to the Austrian Communists (who could be counted on to know very well the range and degree of fascist terror), Kopelev reminds them that "more Communists were confined in Stalin's prisons and camps than in all the capitalist and fascist countries taken together." As for the "good" side of Stalin, he says:

> We ascribed to him all the virtues we saw in our best people. We believed the myth of the great, the all-knowing leader, because we wanted to have such a leader; we ourselves had created this myth—some consciously, others unconsciously—and we were convinced of its reality or quasi reality. Beyond that, we were convinced that it was an absolute historical necessity, for we believed that victory was impossible without an unlimited authority and unlimited faith.

Kopelev goes on to call Stalin a repulsive "naked emperor," referring
to a witty satirical play by Yevgeni Shvarts, *The Naked King,* based on
the Hans Christian Andersen story. Against the myth of Stalin, he cites
disaster in agriculture, the purges, the near-genocide of more than a
half-dozen peoples, the mistrust deliberately inculcated in the population for all "returnees" after the war, and finally the Yugoslav fiasco.
Above all, he insists, Stalin must be condemned for the effects of Stalinism on "the intellectual and moral consciousness of youth," for the
alienation of an entire generation from Communism.

Kopelev sees the efforts to rehabilitate Stalin as leading to "hypocrisy,
civil apathy, and a contemptuous disbelief in those very ideas to which
the restorers of the cult pay lip service." "Quite independently of the
subjective intentions of the authors," he warns, these efforts "objectively
damage our country and our Party, strengthen our opponents, and disarm or repel our friends." He concludes, however, that "the experience
of history" shows that censorship is always harmful—and therefore he
does not recommend its use against Stalin's defenders!

In November, 1962, aided by the personal intervention of Khrushchev, Aleksandr Solzhenitsyn appeared in print for the first time. His
One Day in the Life of Ivan Denisovich was hailed as a masterpiece
by almost almost everyone who read it, and Solzhenitsyn won instant
recognition as one of the very best living Russian prose writers. Yet the
book's impact can hardly be explained solely in terms of its literary
merits.

It was the first, as the Russians would say, "unlacquered" account of
the Stalinist concentration camps to appear legally in print in the Soviet Union. There were many known convicts' songs, many of them
actual products of the camps, and some poems, stories, and accounts
in underground circulation; but this was the first legally published
novel. Its very appearance was a deliberate political gesture against a
recrudescence of Stalinism. The public greeted it with wonder and re-
lief; it was as though a great lid had been taken off. Hundreds of poems,
stories, novels, and reminiscences about the concentration camps began to pour into Soviet journals and publishing houses. Then the lid
quickly came down again, and the manuscripts were returned. Solzhenitsyn himself succeeded in publishing only three or four more short
stories, although it became known that he was the author of a much
larger body of work. A number of official and semiofficial attempts were
made to isolate and discredit him. Meanwhile, despite his own efforts
to discourage it, he became a kind of Archpoet of the literary underground, and concentration-camp writings were indiscriminately attributed to him, much as liberal odes had once been ascribed to Pushkin
and pornography to Barkov.[13]

A long underground essay by D. Blagov[14] insists on viewing the appearance in print of *Ivan Denisovich* not as a literary but as a cosmic
event—a crucial incident in the religious destiny of the world, a kind
of second coming. Not many literary men, whatever their talent, are

hailed as redeemers. It should be added that Blagov, though wild and far-out and not a critic, is, nevertheless, neither ignorant nor foolish. What makes Solzhenitsyn seem, to this eccentric Russian, a figure in theology rather than in literature?

Like many Russians, Blagov attributes theological values to literature as a whole. Even so, the place he accords to Solzhenitsyn is an extraordinary one. To account for this, we must go beyond the touch of madness and obvious personal eccentricity in the article to examine the attitude it expresses.

For other dissident Soviet intellectuals, Solzhenitsyn may not be a redeemer in exactly the same sense that Blagov sees him as one, but he *has* redeemed a vast and weighty area of experience. For millions of Soviet citizens, the concrete meaning of Stalinism is expressed in the concentration camps—not merely in their physical horror, but in the distrust, suspicion, cynicism, and hypocrisy they engendered, and in the whole power mechanism of the permanent purge that kept filling them with their living dead. There is scarcely a Soviet family that has not been touched by this horror in the person of some member. Yet, so vast and pervasive has been the network of propaganda and repression that public discussion has been virtually impossible. Confined to private or family conversation, and with the air of public disgrace still clinging, the most shattering experience of many men's lives seemed, after so many years of public silence, to waver and tremble on the edge of unreality. How could one be a socialist, a Russian, and a human being in the presence of this unspoken horror? And yet, the dynamism of the regime, its genuinely ameliorative and productive aspects, and the impact of its populist and patriotic propaganda made it difficult for the intelligentsia—even for those who had suffered arbitrary imprisonment—to set themselves in polar opposition. It is in the context of this inner conflict, or something like it, that the impact of *One Day in the Life of Ivan Denisovich* needs to be understood.[15]

In addition, Solzhenitsyn struck chords that have deep resonance in Russian culture. In both *Ivan Denisovich* and the remarkable short story "Matriona's House," he seemed to draw on themes and images that had not been successfully organized into the purposive mechanism of socialist realism and "objective" history.[16] He created characters who seemed to combine the lost qualities of the secret Christian with those of the hidden socialist and who appeared convincingly life-affirming, healing, and restorative, even in the most miserable circumstances. The miserable circumstances, realistically and unflinchingly portrayed, merely tend to emphasize the power and the pathos of an ongoing humanity. And this is done in a language that recovers some of the range and flavor and expressiveness of spontaneous human speech—in stark contrast to the rhetorical, abstract, rallying-cry sort of prose that pervades Soviet print.[17]

Finally, like Dostoevsky, he himself has suffered; he has been there. And his courage and his power to resist did not fail him. However solitary, however eccentric a figure, he never confessed, never recanted, never modified his inner voice in order that the words might more easily slide into print. He demanded rights—the independent rights of a writer—and forsook privilege. Living austerely as a schoolteacher in Riazan to this day, he recalls some of the more stalwart characters of the Soviet past who are now being granted some grudging scrap of official recognition—Mikhail Bulgakov, the novelist and playwright who, when he couldn't publish, worked on as an obscure assistant-director in the theater until his death in 1940; or the painter Pavel Filonov (who died in 1941), whose magnificent expressionist canvases are still stored invisibly underground, and who supported himself as an ordinary factory worker. It was Solzhenitsyn who appealed to the Writers' Union to cease being an instrument of repression and control and to assume the function of a real union—to protect the interests of the writer (see Document 49). Not against Communism, Solzhenitsyn insists, but against the possibility of an arbitrary interpretation of Communism imposed at any given moment by men who happen to control the levers of power.

Andrei Siniavsky, who published abroad under the name of Abram Tertz, seemed to express the sense and drift of the young writers and the young generation of the intelligentsia more brilliantly, imaginatively, and boldly than anyone else. At the same time, he was critical of them, mocking and ironical. He seemed to be more masterfully in control of what the great writers of the 1920's had attempted to do, and he seemed to have absorbed an over-all literary education more thoroughly. If Solzhenitsyn echoed Dostoevsky's *Notes from the House of the Dead,* Siniavsky drew inspiration from that supremely subversive book, *Notes from Underground.*

For all his brilliance, he is not always sure of himself. He repeats; he does not exactly shout, but there is in his repetitions some of the insecurity of shouting. Curiously enough, his tone seems more secure and his style less repetitive and more even in the works he published abroad as Tertz, as if he knew better what to expect from his foreign audience. Yet he has an extraordinary sense for the vital issues and how they impinge on men ten or twenty years his junior.

For five years he published abroad, and his identify remained a mystery. Was he an old *intelligent,* or one of the new wave? Christian or Jew? Soviet citizen or *émigré?* For a time, it was rumored that he was an expatriate, possibly a Pole—perhaps because his work first appeared in *Kultura,* the Polish *émigré* journal in Paris, or perhaps simply in order to discredit him. He did not seem to be, like Pasternak, an "inner Christian," though he drew freely on religious motifs. He seemed more like a "secret Communist" or a Goliard mocking the official monastic culture.

The narrators and characters of Siniavsky's stories are alienated, isolated, exiled, underground men, always on the edge of halucination, yet driven to communicate—to stuff the message in the bottle, even if only to drop it into some blind ocean. He writes about madness and inspiration and about demonic possession. He stretches hard for the sense of another world impinging on the familiar, conventional world of worn clichés and used-up attitudes, a sense that might yet renew the world with some as yet undiscovered purposefulness. He writes about exile, about repression (which is exile from one's own emotions), and the resultant dissociation or fragmentation of reality in which, nevertheless, inspiration, breakthrough, and a renewed wholeness are possible—in which some inspired graphomaniac, too long under the delusion that *he* writes, suddenly discovers that he *is being* written.[18]

Siniavsky's choice of the pseudonym Abram Tertz is in itself thematic. It is: (1) a Jewish name, suggesting a stiff-necked people with a stubborn capacity for survival, abnormal, exiled, "individualistic," living by values they consider higher than mere good citizenship; (2) the name of the first martyr, Abraham; (3) a reference to a ribald song about an unsavory black-marketeer, which apparently originated in Odessa in the 1920's, and which is also rather funny; the "return of the repressed"; libido asking its own back; Pugachev proclaiming himself the true Tsar.

Tertz's most memorable work to date is still his essay "On Socialist Realism." The articles he published as Siniavsky, the stories, the aphorisms, the novella, and his book on the poetry of the 1920's are all remarkable efforts, but the essay is still the core of Tertz, just as the first philosophical letter was the core of Chaadaev. The essay resembles Chaadaev's letter in its power of generalization and its superbly sustained rhetoric. It presents the notion of Communism as a theology, a logically elaborated vision of the Godhead, now breached by the disclosures about Stalin (the essay was written almost immediately after the Khrushchev speech). It advocates "a phantasmagoric art, with hypotheses instead of a Purpose," precisely in order to rediscover a larger sense of purpose. Irony, which Tertz ironically calls "that unworthy device," becomes a way of avoiding head-on collision with the old shibboleths; they cannot be saved, but perhaps something of what they were *for* can still be saved. Tertz also introduces the theme of the relationship between means and ends, which he illustrates and elaborates further in *The Trial Begins*.

"In Defense of Pyramids" (see p. 411) was written by Siniavsky and accepted for publication before his arrest and arraignment made its appearance impossible. The essay is a critique of Yevtushenko, poet of the thaw and acknowledged spokesman for the young generation of Soviet citizens. Siniavsky appreciates and sympathizes with Yevtushenko's basic project—the restoration of the lyric "I" to Russian poetry, making autobiography the subject of poetry. But he is subtly aware of Yevtushenko's deficiencies and the difficulties posed by his particular environment for the fulfillment of this attempt.

Fighting against the rhetorical grain of Soviet poetry in the spirit of Maiakovsky and Tsvetaeva, Yevtushenko asserts himself loudly and engagingly. He brings back some of the rhetorical splendor of voice and gesture that Maiakovsky brought to public readings—indeed, along with Voznesensky, he has created the somewhat erroneous impression abroad that poetry readings in the Soviet Union have always been typically as massive and popular as sporting events are in the West. His charm, good looks, outgoing nature, friendliness, and adaptability have endeared him greatly to the young people for whom he speaks. Indeed, he has made spokesmanship part of his role. His self-assertions and travails are implied to be of general significance. And yet, in Siniavsky's view, he "lacks the stamp of an exclusive personality:" He is too eager to please; his demands are too easy and too mild, too readily responded to. In poets like Yesenin or Maiakovsky, "the hypertrophy of the ego is paid for . . . by a cross, a burden, a destiny; it has been motivated by the scale of the legend that has been formed and the tragedy lived through. When the situation is not motivated, it becomes ordinary self-love."

In the situation of the thaw, somewhere between freedom and repression, with the enormous felt need for the authentication of private experience and for a fresh set of references (modern art, the glamour of foreign places, the importance of personal feelings, high-mindedness, and idealism expressed in other than a Party way, etc.), talent is too easily tempted. Yevtushenko is too hasty, unstable, diffuse; he has "too much education" and is prone to display more of it than he has fully absorbed. "The desire to 'seem' overmasters the thirst to 'be'; the agitation over 'What am I like?' is interrupted by concern over 'How do I look?' " The illusion of significance passes too rapidly for the real thing. "Perhaps," Siniavsky reflects, "a writer had better not touch at all those aspects of life about which, for whatever reasons, he cannot say more than others have said."

And yet Siniavsky is excruciatingly aware of the need for artistic ego, for precisely the sense of a personal destiny and of the writer's mission, in order to cross the depersonalized wastes of socialist realism. One imagines him as indulgent toward SMOG, that club of self-styled geniuses to which his friend Aleksandr Ginzburg belonged. (The initials may be deciphered in two ways: [1] *smelost, mysl, obraz, glubina*— boldness, thought, metaphor, depth; or [2] *samoe molodoe obedinenie geniev*—"the youngest association of geniuses.") Siniavsky, after all, is the author of that great story "Graphomaniacs"—an expression that even the Party has now taken over, although without Tertzian irony. He suggests also a motto for graphomaniacs and SMOGists, whatever their petty vanities and self-delusions: "One of us will get through."[19]

If the Siniavsky-Daniel trial seems reminiscent of the Dreyfus case, its Colonel Picquard was undoubtedly Aleksandr Ginzburg, whose indefatigable and undaunted publicity and inspired propaganda kept alive an affair that the instigators of the trial would have preferred to see buried.

Probably, if Siniavsky and Daniel had confessed or pleaded for mercy, they would have received very light punishment, or none, and the case would indeed have faded away. But, as one of the documents contained

in Ginzburg's *White Book* on the Siniavsky-Daniel trial (Document 4)
points out, Siniavsky and Daniel behaved more like the right SR's in
the trial of the early 1920's than like the accused Bolsheviks in the
purge trials of the 1930's: "They accepted their sentences like men."
Whatever slight concession they made to their accusers during the trial—
namely, that perhaps without their intending it, their works had lent
themselves to abuse by "enemies" abroad—was later withdrawn by
Daniel in his (unpublished) letter to *Izvestia*. But the credit for keeping the case alive belongs to Ginzburg, along with Mrs. Daniel, Galanskov, and a small band of intrepid graphomaniacs, who attempted—
obviously with a considerable degree of success—to carry their protests
to the very fringes of the intelligentsia and beyond.

"A Letter to an Old Friend," the identity of whose author Ginzburg
denied knowing at his own trial in January, 1968, recalls, at least by
title, Hertzen's "Letters to an Old Comrade" and in general evokes
something of the atmosphere of nineteenth-century revolutionism, the
underground *élan* of those who struggled against Tsarist oppression.
The experience of the Stalinist camps, writes the unknown author, cries
out the need to bare more fully "the bloody corruption of those in
power," and he cites the Twentieth and Twenty-second Party Congresses as evidence of the self-acknowledged bad conscience of the *apparatchiki*. Where, he asks, are the obelisks promised by Khrushchev,
which were to have the names of the rehabilitated victims of Stalin's
terror engraved on them? And not even a beginning had been made
toward dispelling the mystery surrounding the murder of Kirov. The
letter concludes with a quotation from Piotr Dolgorukov, Hertzen's
friend and collaborator on the *Free Russian Press* and his fellow exile
in London of the late 1850's:

> Many of our compatriots say: "There's no need to tell the truth about
> Russia to a foreigner. . . ." These words, in our opinion, are completely
> opposed to logic, to personal dignity, to love of country, to true enlighten-
> ment. . . . People who want to hide and conceal their sores are like the
> critically ill who prefer to suffer and die rather than ask the help of a skilled
> doctor who could cure them and give them back their strength, refreshed
> and renewed. For Russia, this doctor is publicity.

The world is not an easy place for graphomaniacs. Discredited as Stalinism and "the cult" may be, the Party of Lenin is a powerful and ubiquitous force—not only in its control of the levers of power, the publishing houses and journals, the courts and the newspapers, the *druzhinniki*
and the KGB, but in its control over the prestige machinery, the distribution of public accolades and material rewards, as well. Every schoolbook,
every park of culture and rest, every recreation club—indeed, almost
every word in the dictionary—is impregnated with the influence of the
Party; every monument on every public boulevard, even the Tolstoy
home at Yasnaia Poliana, is inscribed with a quotation from Lenin.

But it is not, in any case, against Lenin and Lenin's Party that the
graphomaniacs set themselves. For the most part, they are not (like

Pasternak) secret Christians able to resist a powerful world view with an equally powerful and more ancient one. For most of them, the question is: How can one recover from the grip of bureaucracy and inhumanity the cause of the revolution one still believes in? It is no easy task. They are weak, young, isolated, inexperienced. The Christians among them have an easier time; yet those, like Levitin, who try to reconcile Christian with socialist idealism have no bed of roses either, dealing as they are with a corrupted church as well as a corrupted Party. It takes a certain craziness (graphomania and egomania have always gone hand in hand), a certain eccentricity, a kind of youthful sans-culottism grounded in energy, exuberance, and naiveté.

We have some rather extraordinary people here. Take, for example, Yuri Galanskov (still in his twenties) writing to Nobel Prize winner Sholokhov (Document 62) that the protests in the Writers' Union, which Sholokhov had so crudely denounced, were, after all, "still the protests of slaves" still bound by the general predicament:

> The writer is hypnotized by general Communist ideals, on the one hand, while, on the other hand, he cannot accept the disgusting aspects of a Communist reality that includes Stalinist concentration camps. The Communist concentration camps prevent him from praising Communist ideals, and the same ideals prevent him from criticizing the concentration camps.

He calls literature "the most specific, concrete, and available way of learning about the world . . . , developing feelings, and shaping points of view," and he regrets "the stupefaction and atrophy of feelings" in contemporary Soviet literature. Finally, for the mental and emotional improvement of the old Cossack writer, he recommends that Sholokhov look into Dostoevsky's *Notes from Underground*!

This is the same Galanskov who carried out a personal protest demonstration (in a land where such happenings are commonly organized and conducted "by the numbers") before the United States Embassy at the time of the Dominican intervention and who represented a plan for world government, disarmament, and world citizenship not unlike that of the American Garry Davis. His poetry, while not remarkably talented, is suffused with this same passionate and somewhat aristocratic idealism.

And there is Galanskov's friend Vladimir Bukovsky, the organizer of poetry readings and student-protest demonstrations. And the extremely gifted poet Batshev, sentenced by a Moscow court—like Brodsky in Leningrad—for parasitism. It is quite natural that these young rebels should form a club—for graphomania *is* a club—and that the club, fortified by a spirit of common exaltation and dedication, a feeling of living dangerously and at the same time supremely virtuously, should move in the direction of a secret society and even a conspiracy. It is not by chance that the editors of *The Russian Word* call themselves "The Ryleev Club." Ryleev was not only a patriotic poet and one of the very first professional journalists in Russia; he was also the key figure in the Northern Society of the Decembrists. I do not mean to suggest that there *is* a conspiracy and that the mysterious Leningrad case of 1967, which involved the

"Berdiaev circle" and many others connected with Leningrad University and the Academy of Sciences, was in some sense justified. I do not know; I suspect not. But, given the present policy of half-hearted repression, the shape of ninetenth-century Russian protest seems inevitably to recur.

All the graphomaniacs are interested both in literature and in politics; that is intrinsic to their situation. Yet one can discern differences of emphasis among them in this respect. The very titles of the *samizdat* publications that have been appearing irregularly since about 1959 indicate differences of emphasis: *The Russian Word* (taken from the name of the paper with which Pisarev was identified in the 1860's, and which, thereafter, became radical-populist); *The Notebook of Social Democracy*; and, on the other hand, literary titles such as *Phoenix* and *Sintaksis*.

In all these journals, the level of competence is "amateur"—very uneven and, on the whole, rather low. A few writers quite clearly come up to professional standards in almost everything they write; some have also appeared in the "ordinary" journals and might never have published underground at all but for the vagaries of the Party line. This is clearly true of Brodsky, Akhmadulina, Okhudzhava, Stefanov, Batshev, and a few others. Some, such as the Bukovsky who produced the rather appalling anecdote-allegories, write no worse than many who are published "normally," but their views are such that no *likely* swing in the Party line, at least in the foreseeable future, could conceivably accommodate them. Some of the overtly political, discursive writing has bounce and feeling, but, on the whole, it shows little mastery. But these *are*, after all, amateur journals; so their amateurishness is hardly to be wondered at. Moreover, professional skill in itself involves a certain repression, and amateurishness may be a way of impressing on public consciousness aspects of experience that conventional standards of skill might not be capable of conveying.

Leo Strauss tells us that it is in the nature of all "persecuted" writing to rely not merely on a coded, Aesopian language but even more on a between-the-lines kind of reading.[20] It relies on a "secret" audience *within* the audience that normally reads such things—a "secret" audience that can be relied upon to have the right associations for words and allusions and trusted to read *implicitly*. While this is true of some of the writing we are dealing with—and it may be attributable as much to *modernism* as to persecution—a good deal of it seems, on the contrary, to suffer from a heavy, Russian overexplicitness. This, it seems to me, signifies not only a lack of skill but an insecurity *vis-à-vis* the audience that is being addressed.

What we might call the range of "experiment" is not very great. Contributors to these underground journals are for the most part very young people for whom, in general, experimentation consists of trying out the manners and mannerisms, the subjects and attitudes, of the "forbidden" writers of a previous generation. There was, of course, no Russian avant-garde of their fathers' generation. So the young writers must go back to the 1920's, to the emigration, to foreign writers like

Berthold Brecht or T. S. Eliot, to Khlebnikov and his "transintellectual" language, to Mandelshtam, Akhmatova, Pasternak, and Zabolotsky. And yet, as Siniavsky points out in comparing Maiakovsky with Yevtushenko, the mannerisms of the past are not always appropriate; experiences differ. The weight of the intervening period lies most heavily upon the new generation of writers. To some degree every poet has become his own KGB, and it is not easy to move in the wished-for direction. The level of repression from which many of these poets write is very deep indeed. Some can find no better model for their verses than Ryleev or—worse still—the sentimental-romantic poets of the 1880's, Nadson and Apukhtin.

I find it tempting to divide the underground writers into two categories more or less analogous to the "engineers" and "martyrs" of my title. Instead of "engineers," let us call one group the "politicals," and, instead of "martyrs," let us call the other group the "metaphysicals." The "politicals" strike a political attitude that the reader is asked to share. It may not be a stance of out-and-out rebellion, but it is one that says: "Cross over here with us—on the outside." But, on the outside, they tend to use the same language, the same modes of apprehending reality, the same "engineering" stance as on the inside. They do not primarily seek a new understanding of the world they wish to change, or a more appropriate or more subtle accommodation of experience and understanding, or a new language. While opposed to Stalinism, they tend to use all the rhetorical gestures, if not of Stalinism itself, of the head-on, revolutionist-confrontation politics that formed the historical background of Stalinism. The "metaphysicals," on the other hand, are not directly interested in politics. Their aim is to confirm and affirm the reality of their experience.

The "politicals" express a protest that is still, in the terms of Galanskov's letter to Sholokhov, "a protest of slaves." They are within the tradition of Communism, which is a revolutionary tradition. To oppose the dominant official "church" of Communism, they are forced back to its earlier traditions—to Lenin and Leninism. But the "church" already occupies that ground, having at its command formidable means of publicity and propaganda enveloping not merely the public at large but the young underground writers themselves. After all, they went to school in it.

They seek a sanction for their grievances, some "justification" bigger than they are. They push back further into the revolutionary tradition, into pre-Bolshevik times—and there they find it. They find it in the populist tradition, in the idea of "going to the people" and, more specifically, of "sacrificing oneself for the people."

This tradition is by no means limited to the 1870's, the heyday of populism. It takes in the Decembrists, and even Radishchev and—with some juggling—Griboedov and Pushkin. It embraces Hertzen, Ogarev, Bakunin, Chernyshevsky, and Pisarev, as well as the Serno brothers. One of the troubles with it is that it by no means requires a concrete knowledge of "the people" or of long-range politics. On the contrary, it helps *not* to have these. The young idealists who sacrifice themselves for the people become a kind of elect, a club, an aristocracy. Sacrificial populism, mingled with Jacobinism, is part of the tragedy of Russian history.

It is interesting to note that the revolutionaries who seem to have the most appeal to the young writers are those who were also aristocrats in a more literal sense—that is, aristocrats by birth and, even more, by virtue of a certain elegant style, wit, and bearing: *e.g.*, Pisarev, Hertzen, the Serno brothers. Even Chaadaev and Montesquieu, who were aristocrats but not revolutionaries, are given revolutionary laurels, for they associate the struggle for freedom with a certain aloofness from the common herd.

Revolutions create their own elites, which provoke the revolutions of the future. The "good of the people"—which Chernyshevsky thought was the same as "enlightened self-interest"—demanded for its fruition an extreme of discipline that was at the same time an extreme of exclusiveness. The price of such discipline was the suppression of all immediate feeling and sense of affect. For the loneliness of prison and exile, Chernyshevsky substituted an obsession with counting and measuring. Carried to an extreme, this kind of discipline produces a dissociation of sensibility—a separation of emotion from reason in the apprehension of experience—which it is the goal of the metaphysicals to overcome.

The ability to see things freshly is not something that "comes natural"; it has to be learned. In an environment so thoroughly infested with Stalinist stereotypes, clichés, and conventions, the learning does not come easily. The first attempt of the metaphysicals is to deal with the everyday world, with common experience—to demythologize it and divest it of its associations with an abstract and worn-out vocabulary.

I use the word "metaphysical" not because I think these Russian writers are conscious philosophers, but because I see a fruitful analogy with the work of John Donne and the English metaphysicals and their revival in modernist English and American poetry. It will be recalled that Donne wrote in what was, politically, an immediately prerevolutionary period. Intellectually, the stability of the world order had already begun to waver ("New philosophy calls all in doubt . . ."), and Cromwell was waiting in the wings. Modernism in poetry has its origins in the generation preceding World War I and the Russian Revolution. At first, and for a long time, modernist poetry, like that of Donne, was viewed as disintegrative and disruptive. Now, I think, both can be seen in quite the opposite light—as attempts at integration. What the poets attemped to hold together, however, was not the political world or the *status quo* but a way of apprehending reality that might survive the impending chaos.

One of the great innovations of John Donne and the English metaphysicals was to introduce into their poems the theme of sexual love *as* sexual love—as an experience of very great seriousness in its own right, with its own psychology, divested of its Petrarchan trappings—a very touchy subject, for a long time deeply swathed in protective ritual. The Petrarchan love poem invoking divinity in high-flown language is really talking about sex. Donne reversed the process: talking about sex, he invoked divinity.[21] Yet, in spite of his daring imagery and bold psychology and his linking of the exalted with the vernacular, Donne was only doing in an especially vigorous and robust way what all poetry does. For poetry can proceed only by analogies. It is a discovery of the relatedness of things, a sewing together of the seeming separateness of the things of this world. The Russian metaphysicals, not much on sex and lacking Donne's poetic power and his Christian faith, nevertheless share his interest in fusing the fragments of their splintered world.

The most interesting of the modern Russian metaphysicals is Yosif Brodsky. Having begun as an underground poet, he was subjected to an absurd trial and exile at hard labor for "parasitism," but he has now returned home and has even been accepted to some degree as a "legitimate" poet. A favorite of Akhmatova's, and himself an admirer both of T. S. Eliot's poetry and critical prose and, through Eliot, of Donne and the English metaphysical tradition, he is nevertheless his own poet, sure in his taste, detached from politics and the temptations of spokesmanship. Although some of his poems are less sure-footed than others (the symbolic significance he attaches to the syllables of words in his long poem "*Isaak i Avraam*," for instance, does not quite come off), almost everything he writes is of the greatest interest. And he has not yet turned thirty.

For Brodsky as for Pasternak, art is inherent in the world, not a matter of form but, in Pasternak's words, "a secret, hidden part of content." Words are hiding in things:

> I am surrounded by silent verbs.
> They are like strange heads—
> verbs
> hungry verbs, naked verbs,
> major verbs, mute verbs . . .[22]

The verbs are grasped first as nouns, as things that are there, possible, latent, surrounding him. He must release their movement so that

> poems about fish,
> like fish,
> stick in the throat.[23]

It is in the world of sensuous objects that reality inheres; it is that world, and that world alone, that one experiences. It is also that world that contains eternity.

In "A Long Elegy for John Donne," the theme is wholeness, integrity, the binding-up of wounds, the bridging of gaps. Slowly, laboriously, the poem creates objects out of words, then a world, then a perspective. It is full of the imagery of "bridge" and "junction": sleep as a meeting of life and death; birds, needles, snow, tears; dialogue between a man and his "lost" soul. The perspective opens out from earth to eternity. The verbs

"to sleep" and "to weep" oddly link the most banal everyday objects—
bread, a breadknife, china, pots and pans, houses, roads—with an entirely
different order of objects—the saints, the Devil, God, their wicked servants, their children, John Donne's distant soul. By the time the concluding passage has been reached,

> Man's cloak does gape with holes. It can be torn
> by him who will, at this edge or that.
> It falls to shreds, *and* is made whole again . . .[24]

The abstraction has been eloquently prepared and concretely anchored
not only by the description of Donne's torn cloak but by the image of
sleep, snow, tears, as kinds of sewing-up.

Peace, persistence, reconciliation, the coming together again of shorn
members, the mending of what has been torn apart, integrity, authenticity, wholeness—such is Brodsky's theme. In his poem about the Jewish
cemetery located "four miles from the last trolley stop," out of the main
swing of travel, he plays ironically on what is said about the Jews and
what he knows to be there behind "the rotting plywood fence":

> They didn't sow grain.
> They never sowed grain.

He echoes the anti-Semitic canard, only to dispose of it:

> They just planted *themselves*
> in the cold earth, like seeds.
> And fell asleep forever.
> Then they were strewn with earth;
> they had burned candles,
> and on the Day of Atonement
> the hungry old men with high voices,
> panting with cold, shouted of reconciliation.
> And they achieved it.
> As dissolution of matter.[25]

(The Russian word *"zasypali"* is repeated as a pun—another bridge—
meaning in the first instance "fell asleep" and in the second "were
strewn," but in both instances both meanings might apply.) Brodsky
ends the poem by stating once more the actual location of the cemetery.

There is almost a kind of providence in Brodsky's very name, for its
root, *brod-*, implies wandering, and one of his major themes has been
"inspired wandering"—the procession, the pilgrimage. "Past Hippodromes" and all that, but—to where?

> You keep spinning through your best years
> like a little boy along his life, like a youngster,
> with a beat-up, life-affirming face,
> snot-rag in your hand, the inscription—"nowhere."[26]

A "beat-up, life-affirming face" and going "nowhere." There is nowhere to go—but it is the "going" that counts.

The metaphysical poems are not necessarily without political thrust. When Akhmadulina's simple-minded bar-girl confuses her seducer with God, political analogies immediately present themselves. Whatever politics may be implied, however, the vocabulary of these poems is not overtly political; it shuns argument and purposive discourse and spokesmanship. The poems propound no theory or theories. On the contrary, by the skillful use of paradox and irony, they tend to call existing theory into question. They appeal to what Eliot praised in the English metaphysicals—the unified sensibility in which thought and feeling are one, a sensibility that sensuously apprehends thought.

In the long run, I believe it is the metaphysicals who will be discovered to be not only the true poets but also the true revolutionaries, for their secret knowledge is that in order to change the world you have to make it new from within yourself. Meanwhile, poetry has become a rallying cry and a constitutional cause, less divisive and more inclusive than nationalism or religion—a breathing-in, a welling-up, a battening of energies. And, at the same time, poetry is a slowing-down and a release, a detachment from the bonds of belief and the modes of perception of a world that has been devastated and threatens to fall apart.

NOTES

1. See Patricia Blake, "This Is the Winter of Moscow's Dissent," *New York Times Magazine*, March 24, 1968, p. 126.

2. For an extremely interesting psychoanalytic interpretation of the "new man" and his place in Russian culture, see Alain Besançon, *Le tsarévich immolé* (Paris, 1967), pp. 145–61.

3. I. Kon, "Razmyshleniia ob amerikanskoi inteligentsii," *Novyi mir*, 1968, No. 1, pp. 190–91.

4. A. D. Sakharov, "Thoughts on Progress, Peaceful Coexistence, and Intellectual Freedom," *New York Times*, July 22, 1968, p. 15. For an excerpt, see p. 331.

5. I do not mean to imply that the present situation parallels that of the nineteenth century at any given moment—the 1840's, say, or the 1860's or the 1890's —but, rather, that there are points of resemblance to all of these and that there will continue to be such resemblances as long as the two basic factors of nineteenth-century alienation have their analogies in the present: namely, a repressive regime and a sensitive, estranged intelligentsia.

6. "Vernost, edinstvo, ubezhdennost," *Literaturnaia gazeta*, May 29, 1968, p. 3.

7. There is no logical or consistent legal pattern to the arrests and punishments. Fame and renown are apparently fairly effective shields against reprisals, though certainly far from foolproof.

8. Interesting in this connection is a series of articles on the Chinese cultural revolution by A. Zhelokhovtsev, "Kulturnaia revoliutsiia s blizkovo rasstoiianiia (zapiski ochevidtsa)," *Novyi mir*, 1968, Nos. 1, 2, 3. In decrying the shabbiness and drabness, the heaviness of Chinese life, the lack of privacy, the over-the-shoulder tics, Zhelokhovtsev sounds extraordinarily like an American visitor describing his reactions to life in the Soviet Union.

9. See *Literaturnaia gazeta*, May 8, 1968, p. 1; also, "Ideologicheskaia borba," *Literaturnaia gazeta*, June 26, 1968, p. 5.

10. See Konstantin Shteppa, *Russian Historians and the Soviet State* (New Brunswick, N.J.: Rutgers University Press, 1962), pp. 276–85; Cyril E. Black, *Rewriting Russian History* (New York: Vintage, 1956); John Keep, *Contemporary History in the Soviet Mirror* (London: Allen & Unwin, 1964).

11. V. Kardin, "Legendy i fakty," *Novyi mir*, 1966, No. 2, p. 239.

12. "Legendarnoe ne zacherknut," *Literaturnaia gazeta*, April 26, 1966, p. 2. The letter is also signed by F. Petrov, a Party member since 1896!

13. The Archpoet was a perhaps legendary figure reputed to have been the founder of the order of wandering poets, or Goliards, in twelfth- and thirteenth-century western Europe. Many poems praising drunkenness and lechery and denouncing the hypocrisy and secret vices of official monasticism were ascribed to him. (See Helen Waddell, *The Wandering Scholars* [London: Constable, 1927].) On Pushkin and Barkov, see S. Monas, *The Third Section: Police and Society in Russia under Nicholas I* (Cambridge, Mass.: Harvard University Press, 1961), pp. 197–228.

14. "A. Solzhenitsyn i dukhovnaia missiia pisatelia," *Grani* (Frankfurt-am-Main), No. 64 (1967), pp. 116–45, and No. 65 (1967), pp. 100–128.

15. For American reactions to the appearance of Solzhenitsyn's book, see George Siegel's article in *Dissent*, X, No. 2 (Spring, 1963), 188; and S. Monas, "Ehrenburg's Life, Solzhenitsyn's Day," *Hudson Review*, XVI, No. 1, 112–21.

16. For a discussion of two central qualities of old Russian culture—two values which that culture enhanced and which Professor Weidlé feels have disappeared from Soviet culture, but which I believe to be very much alive in Solzhenitsyn's *Ivan Denisovich* and "Matriona's House"—see Wladimir Weidlé, "Russkoe kulturnoe nasledie," *Vozdushnie puti* (New York), 1967, No. 5, pp. 115–39.

17. In the brief sketch "Lake Segden" (*Tetrad*, No. 7), a different Solzhenitsyn appears. The tone is more militant and angry, the irony far less subtle. We are reminded that the sketch comes from Solzhenitsyn's notebooks and was published without his permission. There is something too overtly indignant about it, too much written with the clenched fist. Yet it is essential Solzhenitsyn: "matriotic" rather than patriotic in its nationalism—identifying Russianness with an order of nature and landscape rather than with an order of government. Indeed, it describes an aspect of the latter order violating the former. The bureaucrats have fenced off the wild, feminine landscape of Lake Segden to rape her as they will, while excluding others from access to the magic place. It evokes powerful feelings from deep in Russian culture: the familial situation of the corrupt father imprisoning and abusing the mother/sister; invasion of the land by foreigners; the violation of socialist equality; the corruption of a pure and natural place by infidels.

18. See A. Tertz, *Fantastic Stories* (New York: Pantheon, 1963), pp. 169–214.

19. For a fuller discussion of "Graphomaniacs" (in the collection *Fantastic Stories*), see S. Monas, "From Between the Floorboards: The Voice of Abram Tertz," *Massachusetts Review*, III, No. 3 (Spring, 1962), 592–97.

20. Leo Strauss, *Persecution and the Art of Writing* (Glencoe, Ill.: Free Press, 1952).

21. See, *e.g.*, his "Canonization" and "The Ecstasy."

22. Yosif Brodsky, "Glagoly," *Stikhotvoreniia i peomy*, ed. G. Stukov (Washington, D.C.: Inter-Language Literary Associates, 1965), p. 72.

23. Brodsky, "Ryby zimoi," *Stikhotvoreniia i poemy*, p. 25.

24. Brodsky, "Bolshaia elegiia Dzhonu Donnu," *Stikhotvoreniia i poemy*, p. 130. For this poem, I have used the excellent translation by George Kline, *Tri-Quarterly*, Spring, 1965, pp. 87–92; other translations are the author's.

25. Brodsky, "Yevreiskoe kladbishche okolo Leningrada," *Stikhotvoreniia i poemy*, p. 54. For a slightly different rendition of these lines, see George Reavey's translation of the full poem on p. 454.

26. Brodsky, "Shestvie," *Stikhotvoreniia i poemy*, p. 165.

Socialist Legality on Trial

STEPHEN M. WEINER

The various political trials that have taken place in the Soviet Union in recent years have rattled skeletons in closets that the Soviets would prefer to keep sealed in silence. Since 1953, the regime has consciously sought to repudiate the excesses of Stalinist arbitrariness and to proclaim the dominance of a new rule of Soviet law under the rubric of socialist legality. The attempt has been viewed with greater or lesser degrees of skepticism by Western observers. But whatever success these efforts may have achieved to date has been placed in peril by the recent recurrence of trials obviously dominated by political considerations and almost inevitably accompanied by references to the purges of the Stalin era.

Yet, despite the ease of comparison, it is important to remember that the Soviet Union of 1968 is not the Soviet Union of 1937. This simple truism suggests the need to examine the differences between the trials now and then and not merely to dwell on the similarities.

Aside from the actual conduct of the proceedings, there is at least one significant difference between the political trials of the 1960's and those of the Stalin era. This is the response of the Soviet citizenry itself to the legal proceedings. The purge trials of the 1930's, while generating a good deal of criticism abroad, were received with passivity within the Soviet Union. Not so the recent trials of writers. Although at first, with the Siniavsky-Daniel trial, critical response was confined to well-known and hence relatively insulated intellectuals, the most recent trials have produced letters of protest and petitions signed by the famous and the not-so-famous, by authors and artists, by academicians from all disciplines, by *aspiranty*, and even by the chairman of a collective farm.[1] Resistance to political domination of the criminal process has now become a common and insistently articulated concern of a very wide spectrum of the intelligentsia.

The rise of this new "legal" literature, the product, for the most part, of persons not trained in law, is principally a political phenomenon: it indicates the development of a new and increasingly vocal popular opinion not reluctant to criticize official policies and to demand reform. Its ultimate legal significance, however, depends largely on its ability to assess adequately the weaknesses of the Soviet criminal system and to propose methods of protecting that system from political domination. The concern of this article is to examine the legal analyses that appear in this new literature and to determine the degree to which the nonlawyer writers understand the workings of the Soviet legal system.

THE MAIN LINES OF PROTEST

Three distinct attitudes emerge from the general denunciations of the trials. First is the simple proposition that the trials were not conducted fairly because they were politically predetermined, that they represent in starkest terms the subordination of the legal process and the protection of law to political demands:

> The essence of these trials lies in the fact that people have been tried for their convictions, in violation of their fundamental civil rights. . . .
> We know that many Communists abroad and in our country have repeatedly expressed their disapproval of the political repressions of recent years. We ask the participants in the consultative meeting to consider fully the peril caused by the trampling on the rights of man in our country.[2]

> In the course of recent years, ominous symptoms of a restoration of Stalinism have appeared in our social life. This appears most clearly in the repetition of the most terrible acts of that epoch—in the organization of cruel trials of persons who dared to defend their dignity and freedom of mind, who presumed to think and to protest. . . . We have no guarantees that, if we allow this to happen in silence, the year 1937 will not return once more.[3]

These writers stress the law's subordination to politics, but they do not examine the law itself. Their focus is the desirability of political freedom, not the legal means of attaining it. In short, they do not engage in any real legal analysis. Their underlying assumption appears to be that legal improvement cannot occur until there is political change. But since political change does not seem to be imminent, their statements, while politically significant, are of no relevance in an attempt to reform the legal system. Some of the other petitioners, however, have undertaken an examination of the operating legal system and have sought out methods of improving its effectiveness and independence without relying on the precedent condition of radical political reformation.

A second distinctive critical approach to the recent trials is taken by those who argue that existing procedural norms are adequate but were distorted in application. These writers engage in a three-step process of analysis. First is the assertion of the fact that violations of law occurred during the various trials:

From what we know about this trial [Ginzburg-Galanskov], it has become clear to us that it was conducted with gross violations of the correct legal norms.[4]

. . . this entire trial was conducted under conditions that involved repeated violations of socialist legality.[5]

At this point, they catalogue the irregularities. Pavel Litvinov and Larisa Bogoraz-Daniel, in discussing the Ginzburg trial, report the use of false evidence given by Dobrovolsky; the hamstringing of defense counsel and defense witnesses; the fact that witnesses were forced to leave the courtroom after testifying, in violation of Article 283 of the R.S.F.S.R. Code of Criminal Procedure; and the observation that, despite the requirement of an open trial, "the courtroom is filled with specially selected people—officials of the KGB and volunteer militia—[who] make noise, laugh, and insult the accused and the witnesses."[6]

Podiapolsky decries the illegally long pretrial detention[7] and the closed nature of the trial, including the issuance of special passes for admittance.[8] Others note the lack of press coverage of the trial despite the requirement of publicity and its important function of educating the masses.[9]

Despite this checklist of procedural violations, the writers in this second group, at the next stage of their analysis, accept as valid the official legal ideology of socialist legality, taking the position that presently operative norms of Soviet law are just and for that reason ought to be obeyed. Ironically, this group is, in a sense, close to the legal theoreticians who write in established Soviet journals of law: both groups expose violations as the appropriate counterpoint to demands for strict observance of procedural norms. The two differ principally with respect to what they consider to be the source of the violations: the established writers, working within the system, discuss the low educational level of legal workers, while the new critics intimate a more fundamental, political cause. Both assume that, in any criminal trial, justice will result from a proper application of the procedural norms.

The acceptance of socialist legality is evident when one turns to the third stage of analysis: the proposed solution to the legal distortions of the trials. The writers insist on an annulment of the sentences, since they were "handed down under conditions which involved criminal violations of socialist legality,"[10] and on a retrial "under conditions of full publicity, in conformity with all the proper legal norms, and in the presence of representatives of the public."[11] The ultimate effectiveness of the proposed solution turns on the adequate resolution of two problems. The first is whether or not the political system will refrain from interfering directly in legal processes. Like the first set of petitioners referred to above, Litvinov, Podiapolsky, and other critics in this group would undoubtedly consider political reform of paramount importance. But unlike the first, this second group of protesters, in accepting the validity of socialist legality, must also be assuming that fair trials are possible within the present political context. Thus, the second problem—the real problem posed by their point of view—is whether, if the regime did refrain from conscious and deliberate interference with the legal process, the existing norms would then be adequate to provide for fair trial with an effective defense. The question, put very simply, is whether the violations that occurred during the recent trials were solely the result of express, but secret, regime direction or whether there is something in the norms themselves that permits, or indeed requires, political direction as a normal course.

THE NORMS OF SOCIALIST LEGALITY

Most Soviet procedural norms are either formal or contextual. The formal comprise the framework within which the investigation and trial take place; the contextual govern attitudes and approaches toward participants and evidence within the framework of the process. The formal norms are most easily instituted in legislation and most obvious in violation: *i.e.*, the order of examination, the oral and public nature of the proceedings, the language used, the specific rights of the participants. By Western standards, the "Fundamentals of Criminal Procedure of the U.S.S.R." provide an adequate set of these norms. But, while these formal rules are critically important in providing the basis for a fair trial, the adequacy of defense really turns on the contextual norms: *i.e.*, the degree of truth to be established, the presumption of innocence, the burden of proof, the role of confessions, and the relationship between the defense counsel and the accused. A brief examination of these norms in Soviet procedure will indicate the degree to which they serve in theory to protect the defendant.

Objective truth

Soviet criminal procedure, as is now generally recognized, is concerned with arriving at objective truth.[12] The feasibility of a court's ascertaining objective truth derives from Marxism's theory of man's capacity for acquiring direct knowledge of events in the real world. Requiring objective truth serves to protect the innocent defendant under the rationale that truth is an adequate protection and that, if the truth is known, a Soviet court will not convict an innocent person or acquit a guilty one.

A corollary of the theory of objective truth is that anything less than such truth allows arbitrariness to enter into the process. Thus, the present emphasis on objective truth in Soviet legal theory has been accompanied by a repudiation of the principle of "maximum probability"—attributed to Vyshinsky[13]—which has been interpreted to mean that a court can establish only the maximum probability of a fact, not its certainty.[14] "Maximum probability" is currently viewed as a means of justifying arbitrariness and as a major source of violations of legality under Stalin.

It seems improbable that any court, even a Marxist one, would be institutionally capable of achieving objective truth. The significance of the stress on such truth, however, lies in its exhortative function. The maintenance of such a high standard should help to raise the level of judicial inquiry and to orient the court away from the laxity that exists at the trial level of all systems.

The requirements of objective truth should, therefore, protect the defendant in two ways. The first is through the direct link between knowledge of the truth and protection of the innocent. The second is through the need to provide devices in the trial procedure that tend toward realization of the truth. For the most part, these devices, such as the burden of proof and the right to counsel, help the defendant but can be justified in terms of the integrity of the process in achieving truth. Thus, the protection of the defendant is not dependent on the individual judge's attitude toward the defendant but on the obligation of the judge to fulfill the ultimate task of the process—to establish the truth. If this norm influences trial conduct in fact as well as in theory, the defendant is procedurally as well as normatively protected.

The presumption of innocence

This is one of the key procedural concepts for guaranteeing a fair defense. The presumption itself is difficult to define precisely. In practice, it seems to operate principally as the basis for a number of other procedural protections, particularly the burden of proof. Put most simply, perhaps it, too, serves an exhortative function, requiring the court to treat the defendant as innocent and thereby assuring the effective realization of his other procedural rights.

Under Stalin, the status of the presumption of innocence was unclear. While Vyshinsky did not contest its applicability, some commentators felt it to be invalid at trial because of the prior screening through which suspects passed[15] and opposed extending it to earlier stages of the process.[16] Others clearly asserted its validity and denied any legal significance to pretrial determinations of guilt.[17]

Since 1953, most commentators have verbally accepted the relevance of the presumption of innocence to Soviet procedure, but there has been great reluctance to incorporate it explicitly into the procedural codes. Professor M. S. Strogovich, among others, advocated introducing a precise formulation of the presumption into the 1958 Fundamentals. Prevailing opinion, however, was to the contrary.

Two types of argument were presented in opposition to Strogovich. On the one hand, some felt that, while the principle was valid, there were already sufficient procedural safeguards to protect the accused and inclusion of the presumption would be "purely declaratory" and "could only serve to disorient the personnel of the investigation and of the court."[18] On the other hand, others rejected the validity of the principle and could not see any sense in a formula that would require presuming clearly guilty persons to be innocent. As one of the delegates to the Supreme Soviet put it during the discussion of the draft 1958 Fundamentals, "The absurdity of such a state of affairs from the viewpoint of common sense is beyond dispute. The only thing that passes understanding is why this is not clear to the . . . theoreticians."[19]

This statement expressed a view long held in Soviet legal thinking. Professor Strogovich, on the other hand, has attempted to distinguish between the conclusions of the prosecutor before the trial, which have no juridical significance except insofar as he can dismiss the case, and the attitude of the judge at trial.[20] It is the judge who must be objective, and, for Strogovich, objectivity requires a presumption of innocence at trial.

The Fundamentals represent something of a compromise, but proceduralists are generally satisfied that they express the presumption of innocence indirectly, if not in explicit language. Article 7 reads: "No person may be found guilty of a crime and subjected to a criminal penalty except by sentence of the court." The presumption also finds support in Article 14, which forbids shifting the burden of proof to the defendant.

There has been some disagreement on this point. When Strogovich, writing in *Literaturnaia gazeta*, reiterated his contention that Article 7 of the Fundamentals expresses the presumption, an assistant prosecutor, Filimonov, challenged this interpretation, claiming that the preliminary investigation decides guilt and the court merely determines the degree of punishment. Filimonov, however, was repudiated in turn by Strogovich, by a writer in *Izvestia*, and by A. Gorkin, Chairman of the Supreme Court of the U.S.S.R. Thus, Strogovich's opinion now appears to represent the dominant procedural view.[21]

The burden of proof

As with the presumption of innocence, the status of the burden of proof under Stalin was not consistently favorable to an adequate defense. Usually, the burden of proving innocence was not regarded as resting on the defendant. A most notable exception, however, was Vyshinsky's theory that the burden shifts to the defendant in certain circumstances:

> The rules of the transference of *onus probandi* [burden of proof] should be formulated in this sense only: (a) the proof of circumstances corroborating the accusation is the duty of the prosecutor; (b) the proof of circumstances refuting the accusation is the duty of the accused.[22]

Following Stalin's death, Vyshinsky's concept was resolutely rejected, principally, as A. A. Piontkovsky put it, because of the danger that it would "place the accused in an extremely unfavorable procedural position, for in a number of cases the accused is unable by his own means to prove his contentions even if they are correct."[23] Piontkovsky also noted the contradiction between Vyshinsky's view and Article 111 of the 1923 R.S.F.S.R. Code of Criminal Procedure, which required the investigator to ascertain all factors both exonerating and convicting the defendant.

Piontkovsky represents the current general view that there is an absolute requirement not to place the burden of proof on the accused. This attitude found legislative acceptance in 1958, in Article 14, paragraph 2, of the Fundamentals: "The court, the procurator, the investigator, and the person conducting the inquiry have no right to shift the obligation of proof to the accused."[24]

There is thus no longer any question of the burden of proof resting on the accused. The principal question still dividing commentators is whether the burden, or "obligation," of proof lies on the prosecutor alone or on the prosecutor and the court.

The different points of view on this question may stem from differing interpretations as to the meaning of the "obligation" of proof. The concept may be defined as the obligation to persuade the trier of fact as to guilt or innocence. Because of Article 14, the burden cannot be on the defendant. Therefore, it follows from this definition that the obligation must be with the prosecutor to prove the defendant's guilt. Only the prosecutor runs the risk of losing his case if the court is not persuaded that the defendant is guilty. If, however, the obligation is merely construed as the duty to go forward with evidence, this, in Soviet and continental judicial procedure, is the task of all the trial participants, including the court itself.

The latter point of view finds support in the requirement of Article 14, paragraph 1, that the prosecutor as well as the court should adduce evidence tending toward acquittal as well as evidence toward conviction. Paragraph 1 of Article 14 suggests that the proper definition of "burden" in paragraph 2 of the same article is not the obligation to prove the truth of the accusation but, rather, the duty to present evidence *concerning* the truth of the accusation. From this interpretation follows the position that there is no peculiarly prosecutorial function in the process. This is the argument of M. A. Cheltsov, who denies the existence of an adversary procedure in Soviet criminal trials and finds the prosecutor's function to be principally that of supervising the legality of the proceedings in the name of truth.[25] By stressing the similarity of the roles of the prosecutor and the court, Cheltsov's view ties the burden-of-proof rule into the general demand for objective truth. If objective truth is in fact achieved, the operation of Cheltsov's theory should affect the position of the defendant no differently from a rule putting the burden of proof on the prosecutor alone.

The role of confessions

Post-Stalin jurists have attacked Vyshinsky's view that, in cases of conspiracy, criminal association, and counterrevolutionary organizations, confession by the accused was sufficient evidence for conviction. Vyshinsky's thesis was also implied legislatively in Article 282 of the 1923

R.S.F.S.R. Code of Criminal Procedure, applicable at all trials: when a defendant acknowledged his guilt at an early stage of the trial, the court could waive further examination and pass directly on to the final pleas.

The current view is that the confession is only "one form of evidence, which, like any other form, is subject to the most painstaking verification by means of a thorough investigation of all the rest. The confession of the defendant cannot, therefore, be taken as conclusive proof for handing down a verdict of guilty."[26]

Post-Stalin legislation has introduced three modifications underscoring this view. First, the ban on the use of force or threats to elicit a confession, which appeared in Chapter 11 of the 1923 R.S.F.S.R. Code of Criminal Procedure ("Presentation of the Accusation and Interrogation"), was moved into the section entitled "General Principles" in the 1958 Fundamentals (Article 14) and into "Fundamental Provisions" in the 1960 R.S.F.S.R. Code (Article 20). The language of the new provision is prefaced by a general "it is forbidden . . ." rather than, as previously, by a list of the specific legal officers to whom the prohibition applied. Second, the earlier provisions designating the confession as only one of various forms of evidence—a provision that Vyshinsky's theory partially ignored—has been carried over into Article 17 of the Fundamentals and Article 71 of the R.S.F.S.R. Code. But the new provisions add the further specification that no evidence can have a predetermined value for the court, the investigator, or the person conducting the inquiry. Third, Article 282 of the 1923 Code has been abolished.

The role of defense counsel

The presence of counsel representing the interests of the defendant is usually considered a crucial guarantee of the effectiveness of other defense rights. Since 1958, Soviet legislation has provided for the presence of defense counsel from the time the preliminary investigation ends and the defendant is presented with the materials of the case. There was considerable pressure prior to the enactment of the Fundamentals for admitting defense counsel to participation during the whole of the preliminary investigation, but this proposal was rejected in 1958 and has since been voiced only occasionally.[27]

The presence of counsel should aid the defendant, but whether it does or not depends largely on the relationship between attorney and client. A purely passive lawyer may be as ineffective as none at all. There has been no official definition in Soviet legal literature of the proper relationship between counsel and defendant, and, in the absence of any authoritative pronouncement, two opposing points of view have developed. Some consider the defense counsel to be "the aide of the court," with the primary function of assisting the court in determining the objective truth. While such an interpretation might not be detrimental to an innocent defendant, it would operate to deny the right of effective counsel to persons who may actually be guilty but refuse to acknowledge guilt. Proponents of the "aide" theory maintain that the counsel has the right to evaluate the evidence and present his own view to the court, even if he disagrees with his client.[28]

The opposing view is expressed in the slogan "the defense counsel defends." Adherents of this position reject the "aide" theory on the apparent ground that it allows elements of subjectivism to enter into the relationship between client and counsel: that is to say, once the defense counsel is freed of obligation to represent the defendant, he may act according to his own subjective opinion, which could result in damage to the defendant's case if the counsel's judgment of the truth is erroneous. For proponents of the "defense" theory, the criminal process is an adversary procedure in which the opposition of prosecution and defense enables the court to establish the truth. The defense counsel, they maintain, cannot act as judge or prosecutor; he has no right to interpose his own opinion about the guilt of his client in contradiction to the defendant's plea.[29] This view has recently been stated in the pages of *Izvestia*,[30] which may suggest at least semiofficial endorsement.

THE ROOT PROBLEM

The foregoing survey supports those who have been demanding retrial of the cases of Ginzburg, Galanskov, Bukovsky, and others—but only up to a point. There seems to be reasonable justification for concluding that the formal and contextual norms of Soviet criminal procedure, as outlined above, provide at least the basis for fair trial, and, to this degree, the invocation of socialist legality by the protestors against the recent trials is a legally appropriate and politically intelligent—though somewhat ironic—strategy. But there is the further question of whether the protesters have pushed their legal analysis sufficiently far to be able to assume safely that retrial in conformity with the norms of socialist legality would assure a just solution. While socialist legality does perhaps bar overt or direct political interference with the criminal process and gross violations of the procedural norms, it is not adequate to eliminate the political predetermination of the outcome of criminal trials. This arises from yet another set of norms not discussed by the critics of the recent trials: *i.e.*, the norms governing the judges' decision-making.

The specific criterion required by Soviet law for deciding a case is "on the basis of law in conformity with socialist legal consciousness." Socialist legal consciousness (*pravosoznanie*) is the generally applicable guide to judicial decision-making, including the resolution of the question of guilt or innocence.

One element of socialist legal consciousness is socialist legality. But socialist legality has marked deficiencies as a consistently adequate criterion. In essence, socialist legality is the demand that laws be obeyed. It assumes that existing statutes, both procedural and substantive, are just and consequently should be followed unswervingly in judicial practice.

Where socialist legality fails as a criterion is precisely in trials such as

those of Siniavsky and Daniel, of Bukovsky, and of Ginzburg *et al.* The
regime chose to prosecute under statutes broad in scope and vague in
definition. Socialist legality requires obedience to the law, but it does not
explain the circumstances in which a particular law is or is not properly
applicable. This failing forces the judge to look elsewhere than the statutes for guidance on the question of whether a given statute governs a
certain pattern of established facts.

Socialist legal consciousness, however, goes beyond socialist legality.
It directs the judge toward an objective standard, because legal consciousness is assumed to be not a personal but a collective understanding of the
laws. This objective standard embraces socialist democratism and humanism, proletarian internationalism, and the *partiinost* underlying Soviet law and giving rise to the principle of socialist legality.[31] Socalist
legal consciousness, in short, requires the interpretation of Soviet laws
in the light of their assumedly objective ideological underpinnings.

Besides the words of the statutes themselves, there is only one source
for an objective understanding of the ideological purposes of the law:
the Party. Socialist legal consciousness as a criterion for decision-making
directs the judge to look to *Party policy* in determining the propriety of
applying a particular statute to a particular fact situation. This is so even
when the Party has not explicitly indicated its desire as to the outcome
of a particular case. Thus, socialist legal consciousness provides the mechanism by which the political demands of the Party, clothed in ideological
garb, can impinge on the conduct of a trial. Where a statute is sufficiently broad and ambiguous facts can be established, the court, in applying the political preferences of the regime, may interpret the facts
to find guilt without necessarily violating the procedural rights that are
guaranteed the defendant.

The facility with which political demands can impinge on criminal
trials is a function of the Party's monopoly of ideological interpretation,
the activeness of the judge during the proceedings, and the role of socialist legal consciousness in guiding judicial decisions. In continental
European procedure, the court is equally active and guided by concepts
equivalent to legal consciousness; however, in the non-Communist political systems where such procedure is used, there is no single authoritative source defining legal consciousness. It is the existence of such a
source in the Soviet Union that constitutes the greatest single institutional weakness of the legal system.

The Demand for Constitutionality

Some of the literature engendered by the recent political trials seems
to rest, at least implicitly, on the foregoing legal analysis. The hallmark
of this body of writing is its dependence not on specifications of procedural violations but on the criterion of "constitutionality."

Perhaps the most forthright statement of this position is Bukovsky's final statement at his own trial.[32] The defendant attacked Article 70 of the R.S.F.S.R. Criminal Code, under which he was charged, as being in violation of Article 125 of the U.S.S.R. Constitution insofar as it was being applied to infringe on guaranteed constitutional freedoms. Article 70, declared Bukovsky, "is subject to too wide an interpretation" when it is employed to suppress peaceful political demonstrations.

Bukovsky's speech is significant in two respects. First, it contains the demand that a Soviet statute be measured against the Soviet Constitution. Yet Soviet judges do not have the power to declare a statute unconstitutional. Indeed, the very concept of constitutionality, until the recent trials, has been irrelevant in serious legal discourse. This fact suggests the second significant aspect of Bukovsky's speech, and perhaps its underlying strategy: Bukovsky is, in effect, proposing constitutionalism as the appropriate criterion for judicial decision-making in lieu of Party policy.

Similarly, P. Grigorenko, criticizing the Khaustov and Bukovsky trials, writes:

> Obviously, if declarations that Soviet law is unbiased, just, and humane have any real worth whatever, if Article 112 of the Constitution of the U.S.S.R., which says that judges are independent and responsible only to the law, has any reality, the Supreme Court must put into effect the basic law of the socialist state [the Constitution of the U.S.S.R.], remit illegal sentences, and take measures to prevent a repetition of similar acts in the future.
>
> In the contrary event, it will be clear that the Supreme Court, as one of the basic organs of power, is taking a direct part in the attack on the constitutional rights of citizens and masking that participation with lofty words about justice, impartiality, and humanitarianism. Such an eventuality would give citizens the right to defend the Constitution by all available means: first of all, by the full exposure of the anticonstitutional acts of all government organs, especially the illegal sentences of the courts.[33]

Bukovsky's and Grigorenko's proposed solution to the dilemma of Soviet criminal procedure is certainly not beyond criticism. Its principal weakness is its potential for reducing itself to merely another equivalent of the formula of socialist legality—*i.e.*, instead of statutes, the Constitution ought to be obeyed—without resolving the problem of interpretation inherent in that formula. Constitutional provisions are as subject to a variety of analyses as are statutes, and the determination of the proper interpretation in a given situation will still depend ultimately on the ideological orientation of the individual judge.

Nonetheless, even within the present political context, Bukovsky's approach may achieve some measure of success, precisely because it is directed to the individual judge. By arousing popular opinion under the banner of constitutionalism, the followers of this approach may be able to limit conscious and deliberate intervention by the regime in criminal cases and, in so doing, free the judge from his dilemma of ideological dependence arising from obedience to socialist legal consciousness. Even though the Constitution may be subject to varying interpretations, it comes surrounded by a rhetoric of democratic principles that may influence the decisions of individual judges. The rhetoric may not lead the judge to declare statutes unconstitutional, since that power lies beyond his institutional competence. But the rhetoric may influence him to apply his own standards and conceptions of fundamental freedoms, and, as a result, he may decline to apply restrictive statutes to situations that merit constitutional protection.

The Bukovsky-Grigorenko strategy appears to be aimed at preventing conscious manipulation of the legal system by the political and at substituting for the Party's authoritative ideological interpretation of statutes an individualistic sense of justice based on a myth of constitutionalism. Bukovsky and Grigorenko have thus suggested what seems to be at least a feasible and partially effective solution to the institutional weakness of the Soviet legal system. In the final analysis, the ability of the Soviet system to produce a strong and independent judiciary *without* radical political change may depend on the gradual development of this type of mythical restraint on political power.

NOTES

1. See Document 16.
2. Document 32.
3. Document 27.
4. Document 30.
5. Document 26.
6. Document 7.
7. The defendants were held in custody for a year prior to trial, whereas Article 97 of the R.S.F.S.R. Code of Criminal Procedure places an outside limit of nine months on such detention.
8. Document 26.
9. Document 28.
10. Document 26.
11. Document 30.
12. See M. S. Strogovich, *Materialnaia istina i sudebnye dokazatelstva v sovetskom ugolovnom protsesse* (Material Truth and Judicial Evidence in Soviet Criminal Procedure) (Moscow: Izdatelstvo Akademii Nauk S.S.S.R., 1955), p. 19; M. A. Cheltsov, *Sovetskii ugolovnyi protsess* (Soviet Criminal Procedure) (4th ed.; Moscow: Gosiurizdat, 1962), p. 122.
13. A. Ya. Vyshinsky, *Teoriia sudebnykh dokazatelstv v sovetskom prave* (The Theory of Judicial Evidence in Soviet Law) (3rd ed.; Moscow: Gosiurizdat, 1950), pp. 196–201.
14. A. A. Piontkovsky and V. M. Chkhikvadze, "Ukreplenie sotsialisticheskoi zakonnosti i nekotorye voprosy teorii sovetskovo ugolovnovo prava i protsessa" (Strengthening Socialist Legality and Several Questions of the Theory of Soviet Criminal Law and Criminal Procedure), *Sovetskoe gosudarstvo i pravo* (hereafter SGP), 1956, No. 4, p. 33.
15. M. A. Cheltsov, *Ugolovnyi protsess* (Criminal Procedure) (Moscow: Gosiurizdat, 1948), discussed in R. D. Rakhunov, "Soviet Justice and Its Role in Strengthening Legality," *Kommunist*, 1956, No. 7, in *Current Digest of the Soviet Press* (hereafter CDSP), VIII, No. 40 (1956), 7.

16. N. N. Poliansky, "K voprosu o prezumptsii nevinovnosti v sovetskom ugolov-nom protsesse" (Toward the Question of the Presumption of Innocence in Soviet Criminal Procedure), *SGP*, 1949, No. 9, p. 57.

17. M. S. Strogovich, "Nekotorye voprosy teorii sovetskovo ugolovnovo protsessa" (Some Questions on the Theory of Soviet Criminal Procedure), *SGP*, 1958, No. 8, p. 22.

18. See J. Hazard and I. Shapiro, "The Soviet State and Its Citizens," Part I of *The Soviet Legal System* (Dobbs Ferry, N.Y.: Oceana Publications, Inc., 1962), pp. 85–86.

19. Deputy B. S. Sharkov, quoted in Leon Lipson, "Socialist Legality: The Mountain Has Labored," *Problems of Communism*, 1959, No. 2, pp. 17–18.

20. M. S. Strogovich, "Nekotorye voprosy teorii sovetskovo ugolovnovo protsessa."

21. The various stages of this controversy were reported in *CDSP*, XVI, No. 37, 33–35; No. 39, 23–24; No. 48, 21–22. Filimonov did not take the attack lightly. Feeling that *Izvestia's* article was particularly scurrilous, he sued the newspaper and the author for libel, but lost. After the libel trial, *Izvestia* claimed that "the essence of the dispute itself became the subject of the court hearing" (*CDSP*, XVI, No. 51, 24).

22. A. Ya. Vyshinsky, *Teoriia sudebnykh dokazatelstv v sovetskom prave*, p. 244.

23. A. A. Piontkovsky, "Some Questions of Soviet Jurisprudence," *Izvestia*, May 1, 1957, in *CDSP*, IX, No. 8 (1957), 31.

24. The Draft of the Fundamentals that appeared in June, 1958, had the fol-lowing as its Article 13: "The responsibility of proving the guilt of the accused rests with the prosecutor" (*Sotsialisticheskaia zakonnost*, 1958, No. 6, in *CDSP*, X, No. 33 (1958), 6).

25. M. A. Cheltsov, *Sovetskii ugolovnyi protsess*, p. 93.

26. "For the Complete Eradication of the Harmful Consequences of the Cult of the Individual in Soviet Jurisprudence," *SGP*, 1962, No. 4, p. 3, in *CDSP*, XIV, No. 21 (1962), 8; V. A. Boldyrev, "O kodifikatsii respublikanskovo ugolov-novo i ugolovno-protsessualnovo zakonodatelstva" (On the Codification of Repub-lican Criminal and Criminal Procedure Legislation), *SGP*, 1958, No. 7, p. 96.

27. N. Chetunova, "The Right to Defend," *Literaturnaia gazeta*, September 20, 1966, p. 2, in *CDSP*, XVIII, No. 38 (1966), 18.

28. M. A. Cheltsov, *Sovetskii ugolovnyi protsess*, p. 104.

29. E. D. Sinaisky, "Osnovnye voprosy zashchity v ugolovnom protsesse" (Basic Questions of the Defense in Criminal Procedure), *SGP*, 1961, No. 5, p. 71; M. S. Strogovich, *Kurs sovetskovo ugolovnovo protsessa* (Course on Soviet Criminal Procedure) (Moscow: Izdatelstvo Akademii Nauk S.S.S.R., 1958), p. 134.

30. O. Chaikovskaia, "The Lawyers," *CDSP*, XV, No. 12 (1963), 27–28.

31. G. A. Zlobin, *Pravosoznanie v sovetskom obshchenarodnom gosudarstve* (Legal Consciousness in the Soviet All-People's State) (Moscow: Izdatelstvo "Znanie," 1963), pp. 16–17.

32. Document 2.

33. Document 1.

Turmoil in the Ukraine

GEORGE LUCKYJ

For several years after Stalin's death in March, 1953, the literary scene in the Ukraine showed little sign of ferment. Even the most notable literary work of that time, Oleksandr Dovzhenko's *The Enchanted Desna*, published in 1954, was starkly conventional both in style and in content. In the late 1950's, a number of young poets, such as Lina Kostenko, created something of a stir among fellow intellectuals. Not until the present decade, however, did their voices come fully into the open.

The reasons for the relative absence of dissent and originality in the works of Ukrainian writers in the 1950's are not difficult to fathom. Perhaps nowhere had Stalinism wrought such devastation in the arts and sciences as in the Ukraine. The wholesale liquidation of Ukrainian writers, scholars, critics, and artists in the 1930's struck fear into the hearts of the Ukrainian intelligentsia. Nor were they the only victims of Stalinist terror: the peasantry, which to this day comprises the bulk of the Ukrainian nation, and even the local Communist leadership were severely affected by it. In Russia, the intelligentsia emerged after the death of Stalin, if not intact, at least viable and strong enough to express a measure of indignation and dissent. In the Ukraine, however, the intellectuals, haunted by the stigma of "nationalism," were in a state of spiritual paralysis. The native Communists, under strong pressure from Khrushchev (who had been their boss in the critical period 1938–49), were enlisted in the Party and government apparatus, but clearly as junior partners. Their role as defenders of Ukrainian cultural and political autonomy, played in the past by Ukrainian Party leaders such as Shumsky and Skrypnyk, had come to an end. Indeed, there was no longer anyone in Kiev with enough power or prestige to oppose either the continuing Russification of the Ukraine or the theories aimed at "merging" the Russian and Ukrainian languages.

The Ukrainians did not, however, remain utterly quiescent. De-Stalinization had induced some re-examination of their recent past, and the partial rehabilitation of writers and scholars who had perished in the 1930's raised some lively questions in the minds of the younger generation. Not the least important of these questions related to the belated-

52

ness and incompleteness of the Ukrainian rehabilitation process. In Russia, the publication of formerly proscribed works began in the mid-1950's (Isaak Babel, Edvard Bagritsky, Yuri Olesha, Sergei Yesenin); it did not reach a similar crest in the Ukraine until the mid-1960's (Hryhory Kosynka, Yevhen Pluzhnyk, Mykola Zerov, Oleksa Slisarenko). Undoubtedly, those responsible for cultural policy in the Ukraine were very cautious. Nevertheless, the books that were recovered from oblivion managed to convey a great deal of the richness of the literature that had flowered in the 1920's. It is true that some of the leading writers of that era, notably Mykola Khvylovy, author of the slogan "away from Moscow,"[1] were not even rehabilitated. But those who were must have, in some measure, provided the impetus for the upsurge in the literature of the 1960's. A freer discussion of Ukrainian history and folk culture also stimulated the search for a national identity.

THE POETS OF THE 1960's

The Ukrainian literary figures of the 1960's (*shestidesiatniki*) are not outright nationalists. To be sure, some of their works, and especially those which have succeeded in revitalizing and enriching the Ukrainian literary language, appeal to national sentiment. Yet the main impact of the "young poets" in the Ukraine today, like that of the writers in the 1920's, is on a universal aesthetic plane. To say that their protest is expressed in human rather than national terms simply because the latter are still taboo is to misunderstand the nature of modern Ukrainian literature. The Ukrainian writers of the 1960's, like other writers in other lands, are reluctant to let their involvement in national politics take precedence over their concern with the human condition.

At the same time, Ukrainian literature has traditionally been preoccupied with purely national issues, too. Writers like Taras Shevchenko (1814–61), while quite capable of transcending national issues, had to devote most of their energies to challenging Tsarist encroachments on Ukrainian political and cultural freedom. Yet, whenever conditions improved, such writers tended to drift away from politics and return to their concern with general human problems.

The Soviet regime in the Ukraine was established as a result of a three-cornered fight between the nationalists, the Ukrainian Communists, and the Russian Communists. Although the latter were in control, they made considerable concessions to Ukrainian national demands from about 1922 to 1932. The Ukrainian literary revival of that period, a product of these concessions, is often identified as one of great nationalist vitality. This is true only to the extent that nationalism is a part of any emerging culture. While some intellectuals (especially Khvylovy's group) were interested in political power, others (the Futurists, the Neoclassicists, and the *Lanka* group) were genuine "fellow travelers." But, despite the clear distinctions which existed between them, these groups were indiscriminately lumped together by the Communists and liquidated in the 1930's.

There are several links between intellectual life in the Ukraine in the

1920's and the 1960's. Like the writers of the 1920's, the "modernist" poets of the 1960's cannot be described as a purely nationalist phenomenon, for they are concerned with the restoration of freedom wherever it is denied, not just in the Ukraine. National sentiment is prominent in some poets (Ivan Drach, Mykola Vinhranovsky), but others voice greater concern for universal social justice and individual freedom. Indeed, most established writers may sympathize with the authors of underground documents, but they hesitate ·to take up the burdens of national political protest. Still, the functions of "overt" writers and underground intellectuals, though separate, are complementary in that both groups are striving for a greater measure of human liberty.

Voices from the Underground

During my visit to the Soviet Union in 1964, I witnessed the fire at the library of the Ukrainian Academy of Sciences in Kiev, on May 24. Standing in a crowd of rather apathetic spectators, I was struck by the magnitude of the blaze (it was still burning the next day). When no word about this disaster appeared in the local press, I talked to some Ukrainian writers who told me that they thought the fire was an act of sabotage, but they had no answer as to who might be the saboteur. Not until nine months later did I come upon an answer in a report smuggled out of the Ukraine and published abroad.[2] It was one of the first such documents to reach the West.

According to this document, the official Soviet legal finding was that the fire was an act of arson committed by a librarian named Pohruzhalsky. The court found that his motives were personal, arising from a disagreement with the chief librarian. Adjudged emotionally unbalanced, he was sentenced to ten years' imprisonment.

The document rejects this official version of the incident as a travesty of justice. It claims that the fire was engineered by the KGB (the books and archives destroyed were concerned with Ukrainian folklore, literature, and history, including the archives of the Central Rada, the anti-Soviet government in 1918–19). This tragic loss, the document charges, was part of a continuing plot—originally devised by Stalin and furthered by his successors—to destroy the Ukrainian national heritage in order to Russify the country more easily. "Ukrainians," the document goes on, "do you know what was burned? A part of your mind and soul was burned."[3] Despite its emotional tone, and whether or not it is accurate in every detail, this underground document joins a good many others in attesting to a fundamental bitterness and disaffection among the Ukrainian intelligentsia.

The same document relates that on May 22, 1964, two days before the fire, a student demonstration was held in front of the Shevchenko monument in Kiev to protest the banning of festivities on the anniversary of the poet's burial. In this connection, it is fitting that today's Ukrainian dissenters are turning for inspiration to the historic figure of Taras Shevchenko. Revered by his countrymen as a martyred prophet as well as a writer, this nineteenth-century poet has become the focus of pent-up national feelings. Until fairly recently, Soviet authorities made a pretense of respect for Shevchenko, even if, at the same time, they editorially mutilated and tendentiously misinterpreted his works. In 1964, however, their tactic obviously changed. In March of that year, two months before the ban on festivities in his honor, a stained-glass window commemorating the 150th anniversary of his birth was removed from the entrance hall of Kiev University and destroyed.[4] The window, which had depicted the poet as the champion of a downtrodden Ukraine, was the work of a group of artists headed by Opanas Zalyvakha, who was later arrested and deported to Mordvinia.

How great an influence Shevchenko has on contemporary intellectual life in the Ukraine may be seen from another publication that appeared in the West in 1965: a posthumous collection of poems and a diary by Vasyl Symonenko.[5] Since it is the main example of Soviet Ukrainian underground literature of high artistic merit, its author deserves some comment. Tragically, Symonenko died of cancer in 1963 at the age of 28, just as his talent was in full flower. A native of the province of Poltava, he had studied journalism at Kiev University and later worked as a correspondent for two papers in Cherkassy. His first volume of poetry came out in 1962. Another, *The Earth's Gravity*, was published in 1964, after his death. Symonenko was no innovator; his greatest virtue was simplicity, and he was concerned with issues first raised by Shevchenko over a century ago: justice and freedom for the Ukraine and other non-Russian nationalities (in Shevchenko's work—the peoples of the Caucasus, in Symonenko's—the Kurds) and the whole problem of the stultifying bureaucracy imposed by Moscow on subject nations.

With a vehemence equal to Shevchenko's, Symonenko castigated tyrants and pleaded for the rights of ordinary people. This vehemence, however, obliged him to write most of his work "for the desk drawer" (unlike some of his less outspoken contemporaries, such as Lina Kostenko, Ivan Drach, Mykola Vinhranovsky, and Vitali Korotych, who have written for publication and with the censors necessarily in mind). There is evidence that on the strength of his work, circulated clandestinely, and because of his untimely death, Symonenko has become the object of a cult among Ukrainian youth.

ARRESTS AND PERSECUTIONS

Thus far in the present decade, underground pleas for greater Ukrainian autonomy have prompted two separate waves of arrests—in 1961 and 1965. In 1961, the KGB uncovered allegedly secret organizations dedicated to the overthrow of Soviet power. A typical case was the "Ukrainian Union of Workers and Peasants," seven members of which were tried and sentenced in May, 1961, in Lvov. From the petitions of two of the accused, Ivan Kandyba and Stepan Virun, we can learn their side of the story.[6]

To charges that the group wanted the Ukraine to secede from the U.S.S.R., Kandyba and Virun replied that the Soviet Constitution provides for the possibility of secession. They denied that their group was a secret organization but conceded that they all subscribed to the views set forth in the "Proposed Program of the Ukrainian S.S.R.," a pamphlet written by Lev Lukyanenko, the leader of the group (who was, of course, among those sentenced to jail). Although Lukyanenko considered his argument to be based on Marxist-Leninist tenets, his "program" could hardly have appeared orthodox to the KGB: he openly criticized the Soviet Government's past and present policies in the Ukraine as a complete departure from Lenin's views. In Kandyba's words:

> [The program] criticized the nationality policy in the Ukraine during the entire Soviet period, the mass accusations of nationalism leveled at millions of Ukrainians, . . . [the] physical destruction . . . [of] thousands of political, scientific, and cultural leaders . . . , and the suppression of hundreds of Ukrainian poets and writers, historians, and artists.
> It pointed out that the political and economic rights of the Ukraine were limited, that the country was deprived of its sovereignty and denied the right of entering into diplomatic and economic relations with other states on our planet. The Ukrainian language has not become an official language; it has been removed from governmental agencies, scholarly institutions, higher and lower educational institutions, from industry, and from the social and cultural life of the nation. . . . The Ukraine has [thus] become an appendix of Russia—with two-thirds of her natural resources being transported beyond her boundaries—and the policy of great-power Russian chauvinism weighs heavily over the entire Ukrainian economy.[7]

Accordingly, Lukyanenko's program provided that the Ukraine should secede from the U.S.S.R. and become an independent socialist republic. He regarded his group as a legitimate representation of public opinion, not a secret society. It is indeed doubtful whether the "Ukrainian Union of Workers and Peasants" (or the "Ukrainian National Committee," also uncovered in 1961) was a political organization in any meaningful sense of the term.[8] Nevertheless, Lukyanenko's group represented the beginning of a protest movement aimed at securing legal guarantees of Ukrainian statehood. This movement, however small, does not reject Marxist or Leninist ideology; it merely defends the right of self-determination. Virun, in fact, charged that the regime's refusal to grant the Ukrainians this right amounted to "racism,"[9] and Kandyba asserted—not without irony—that if the secret police were going to persist in sending Ukrainians to concentration camps, such camps should be located in the Ukraine, not in the Mordvinian A.S.S.R.[10]

THE CHORNOVIL PAPERS

The second wave of arrests in the Ukraine began in the middle of 1965 and continued into 1966. In all, about 100 persons—mainly young intellectuals—were arrested, some twenty of whom were eventually tried in secret on charges of "disseminating anti-Soviet propaganda and agitation" and sentenced to terms of hard labor ranging from six months to six years. Most of them were deported to labor camps in Mordvinia.

Some of the details of these arrests and trials have reached the West through two sets of documents authored and compiled by Vyacheslav Chornovil, a young Ukrainian journalist and critic. Chornovil became involved in protest over the repressions in early 1966, when he was sent by the radio station in Kiev to cover the trial of some of the defendants in Lvov. The trial was supposed to be conducted in public but was changed to a secret proceeding when there were signs of public indignation. Nonetheless, Chornovil set about gathering information on the defendants. Summoned to appear as a witness for the prosecution, he refused to testify on the ground that the trial was not open and was therefore illegal. The Lvov court indicted him for "refusal to testify," then changed the charge to allow prosecution under the "propaganda and agitation" clause—but in May, 1966, the indictment was overturned by the Ukr.S.S.R. Supreme Court.

Following these events, Chornovil wrote a devastating account—supported by as much documentation as he could obtain—of the illegal practices and procedures employed by the KGB and the judicial authorities in the course of the arrests, investigations, and trials that had taken place throughout the Ukraine.[11] He sent copies to the top judicial and police authorites and—separately—to the Chairman of the CC-CPUkraine, P. Ye. Shelest, enclosing with the latter copy an appeal for protection against further retaliation. In subsequent months, he also compiled a collection of materials written by twenty men and women (most of them from the group arrested in 1965), including biographical data, letters, diaries, petitions, poems, and notes, composed in many cases in the prison camps. Both the collection and Chornovil's petition were circulated among Ukrainian intellectuals, eventually reaching Western publishers.[12] Chornovil himself was rearrested in 1967 on a charge of possessing "anti-Soviet documents" and sentenced to three years at hard labor (later commuted to eighteen months).

From a literary point of view, the materials collected by Chornovil are of uneven quality, but some of them—especially writings by Svyatoslav Karavansky, Mykhaylo Horyn, Opanas Zalyvakha, Mykhaylo Osadchy, and Valentyn Moroz—have considerable merit as contributions to the literature of dissent.

The case of Svyatoslav Karavansky warrants special mention. Born in 1920 in Odessa, Karavansky served in the Red Army during World War II but was arrested in 1945 as a spy for the Rumanians and sentenced to twenty-five years' imprisonment. He was released in 1960 after serving fifteen years in various concentration camps. Finding it difficult to obtain permanent employment, he devoted himself to literary and linguistic studies; among other assignments, he did some translations of Shakespeare, Byron, and Kipling, compiled a dictionary of Ukrainian rhymes, and published a number of articles on linguistic matters. In 1965, Karavansky felt compelled to write letters to the Soviet authorities, and also to Wladyslaw Gomulka, protesting the Russification of the Ukraine and presenting a closely argued plea for freedom for his country. Shortly thereafter, he was arrested and—without benefit of trial—sent to a camp to complete his twenty-five-year sentence. His wife, in a moving letter to the Soviet authorities—a copy of which was sent to *L'Humanité*—asked them to execute her husband rather than keep him imprisoned forever.[13]

The other documents in the Chornovil collection are variations on two themes: Russification in the Ukraine and the denial of basic human rights to all Soviet citizens. For example, Mykhaylo Horyn deplores the absence of educational and cultural facilites for the millions of Ukrainians living in Russia, but he also laments the lot of every Soviet collective farmer, emphasizing that the deprivation of the peasant's elementary human rights has reduced him to the level of a nineteenth-century serf. In another document, a talented painter, Opanas Zalyvakha, argues the need for a national basis for art. Proud of the Ukrainian contribution to modern art (*e.g.*, the work of Oleksandr Arkhipenko), Zalyvakha states: "We all believe that love of one's country is not a crime but a citizen's sacred duty."[14] Another of the protests laments that Ukrainian participation in world science and culture has been thwarted by the Soviet regime; the author, Mykhaylo Osadchy, longs for a Ukrainian Einstein as Shevchenko once longed for a Ukrainian Washington. It is of interest that in all these protests the authors invoke the United Nations' Declaration of Human Rights (the Ukraine being a founding member).

Among the writers represented in the Chornovil collection is a young historian named Valentyn Moroz. Since the initial publication of the papers, another remarkable document by Moroz has found its way to the West. Addressed as an appeal to the Supreme Soviet of the Ukraine, this "Report from the Beria Reserve" is at once a stark exposé of the physical and moral brutality prevailing in the labor camps and a profound philosophical treatise on the struggle between despotism and individualism in society. Presumably without having read Zamiatin or Orwell, Moroz has conceived his own version of the Orwellian nightmare of 1984—complete with the "little cog" (*hvyntyk*), or programmed man. Yet he has unbounded faith in the ultimate triumph of human individuality.[15]

IVAN DZYUBA

One of the most significant documents in the Chornovil papers is the work of Ivan Dzyuba, the only one of the writers who was really well known before the recent wave of arrests and trials. A literary critic of considerable reputation, Dzyuba has also been a leader in the fight for greater intellectual freedom in the Ukraine. Born in 1931 in the Donets region, he was formerly an associate of the Ukrainan Academy of Sciences, a review editor of the magazine *Vitchyzna*, and the author of a book of literary criticism. He played a vital part in the literary discussions of the early 1960's, defending the experiments of the young poets and pleading for a thorough revision of the principles of socialist realism. In two outstanding articles, one on Hryhory Skovoroda,[16] the other on Taras Shevchenko,[17] he, more than anyone else, symbolized the new Ukrainian intellectual who was turning for inspiration to these two heroes of the past. He even sought to synthesize the contemplative and self-cognitive attitude of Skovoroda with the revolutionary program of Shevchenko; difficult as this task might appear, it was the sort of approach that appeals to today's young Ukrainian intellectuals, bent as they are on securing both national dignity and basic human rights.

In the spring of 1966, soon after the Siniavsky-Daniel trial, the *New York Times* reported the arrest of Dzyuba and another critic, Ivan Svitlychny.[18] The two were charged with smuggling out the poems and diary of Vasyl Symonenko. Dzyuba, because of his severe tuberculosis, was reportedly released in short order; Svitlychny spent several months in jail.

On September 29, 1966, the twenty-fifth anniversary of the tragedy of Babyi Yar, Dzyuba delivered a speech in which he sharply condemned anti-Semitism in the U.S.S.R., pleaded for Ukrainian-Jewish understanding, and defended the rights of both nationalities to the cultural freedom denied them by the Soviet authorities. A transcript of this eloquent speech was included in the Chornovil papers.[19]

Recently, another of Dzyuba's works has reached the West—a lengthy treatise entitled *Internationalism or Russification?*, originally submitted as a petition to the Communist authorities in the Ukraine.[20] One of the chapters first published from the treatise (Chapter VII) touches specifically on the sensitive subject of Ukrainian-Russian relations. Dzyuba puts the blame for the present discontent in the Ukraine squarely on the Russification policies of the Soviet regime, and he dismisses as nonsense the charges of "bourgeois nationalism" in the Ukraine. He considers Moscow's present oppressive policies as a direct continuation of Tsarist traditions; to him, the basic culprit was and remains Russian chauvinism, the excesses of which he amply documents. Dzyuba also raises—indirectly —perhaps the most important issue of all: the failure of the Russian nonconformist intellectuals of today to support the demands of non-Russian nationalities. Will Dzyuba's impassioned and yet remarkably scholarly plea find a response among the Kaverins, the Aksionovs, and the Solzhenitsyns? Surely the future of dissent in the U.S.S.R. depends largely on the answer to this question. Only rarely in the nineteenth century did a Russian (*e.g.*, Aleksandr Hertzen) speak out in support of Ukrainian aspirations.

Some Final Questions

On close analysis, the Ukrainian protest does not concern the Ukraine alone. Though deeply rooted in the national heritage, it takes cognizance of the whole framework of the U.S.S.R. and its allies. Ukrainian dissenters are not anti-Communist or anti-Marxist. On the contrary, they defend the legal foundation of the Soviet Union, protesting only when the rights of Soviet citizens, guaranteed by the Soviet Constitution, are cruelly violated. At the same time, the Ukrainians turn for assistance to and speak on behalf of other non-Russian nationalities (especially the Jews), who are equally oppressed. In a certain sense, Ukrainian dissent is related to the ferment that is taking place in Eastern Europe; certainly the present cultural revival among the Ukrainians in Slovakia is not without relevance to the Ukraine. Accordingly, copies of Ukrainian petitions have been sent to some East European Communists in the hope that they might be more sympathetic than the Russians. It may indeed be naïve to expect Gomulka, with his unwavering loyalty to Moscow and his antipathy for "ferment" of any kind, to respond to such pleas; but this relative lack of political sophistication on the part of some Ukrainian intellectuals does not vitiate their claim to the sympathy of foreigners who have also felt the weight of Moscow's domination. Gomulka might at least recall how *he* felt in 1956.

Although, in the U.S.S.R. at large, dissent has assumed a more open political orientation, this has been even more markedly so in the Ukraine. There is, undeniably, an ambition among the younger dissenters in the Ukraine to take an active part in governing their country as a genuinely separate republic, not as a mere administrative unit of the Soviet Union. Indeed, whatever Ukrainian intellectuals may have to say on the subject of freedom for all humanity, they are fully aware that, for them, the road to greater freedom leads through a nation-state.

The success or failure of the present protest in the Ukraine will depend on two crucial factors: the amount of support it receives from all Ukrainians and the reaction of the Soviet authorities. There is evidence that some Ukrainian writers and students openly support the rebellious intellectuals; for example, Lina Kostenko was among those who threw flowers in the path of the prisoners in Lvov, and Ivan Drach admitted at a press conference in New York that some of his friends were among those arrested. A letter of protest against the treatment of the arrested dissenters, signed by over 100 Ukrainian intellectuals, is now being circulated. Nor does such sympathy come solely from intellectuals. A petition from Ukrainian mothers objecting to the neglect of the Ukrainian language in Soviet kindergartens and a letter (unpublished) to *Pravda* by two Ukrainian miners who admit that they are afraid to speak their own language[21] are good examples of grassroots solidarity with the dissenters. Yet much wider support is necessary if their protests are to succeed. Such support, under present neo-Stalinist conditions, may be difficult to muster.

Thus far, it would appear that the Soviet authorities have remained unyielding to pressure from the protesters. (It is too early to tell if the removal of the hard-line secretary of the Ukrainian Central Committee, Andrily Skaba, in March of 1968, is a conciliatory move.) Yet, if Moscow should persist on a course that makes no concession at all to legitimate Ukrainian aspirations, it may well drive the dissidents to more radical measures of protest and more vocal demands for the complete independence of the Ukraine.

NOTES

1. Khvylovy's views were expressed in a series of pamphlets published in 1925 and 1926. Stalin objected that Khvylovy had "nothing to say in favor of Moscow except to call on Ukrainian leaders to run away from Moscow as fast as possible" (*Sochineniia* [Moscow, 1954], VIII, p. 153).

2. *Suchasnist* (Munich), 1965, No. 2.

3. *Ibid.*, p. 82.

4. *Ibid.*, 1965, No. 6.

5. Vasyl Symonenko, *Bereh chekan* (New York: Prolog, 1965).

6. *Suchasnist*, 1967, No. 12; 1968, No. 1.

7. *Ibid.*, 1967, No. 12, p. 54.

8. In the late 1930's, the NKVD also "uncovered" several secret organizations in the Ukraine that probably did not even exist.

9. *Suchasnist*, 1968, No. 1, p. 58.

10. *Ibid.*, 1967, No. 12, p. 67.

11. See Document 37 for excerpts.

12. For Chornovil's exposé and petition to Shelest, see *Voices of Human Courage: Appeals from Two Soviet Ukrainian Intellectuals to Soviet Authorities* (New York: Association for Free Ukraine, Inc., 1968). The documents he collected initially appeared in V. Chornovil (ed.), *Lykho z rozumu* (Paris: P.I.U.F., 1967), recently published in English as *The Chornovil Papers* (New York: McGraw-Hill, 1968).

13. Chornovil, *Lykho z rozumu*, p. 170.

14. *Ibid.*, pp. 78–79.

15. Originally published in *Suchasnist*, 1968, Nos. 3, 4. Translated into English in *Voices of Human Courage*.

16. Ivan Dzyuba, "Pershy rozum nash," *Literaturna Ukrayina* (Kiev), December 4, 1962. Skovoroda was a mystic philosopher and one of the many alienated intellectuals under Catherine the Great.

17. Ivan Dzyuba, "Ochystytelny i zhyvotvoryashchy vohon," *Duklya* (*Pryashiv*), 1965, No. 1.

18. *New York Times*, April 7, 1966.

19. See Document 38.

20. Chapters of the treatise first appeared in *Suchasnist*, 1968, Nos. 2, 4. The entire document has now been published under the title, *Internationalism or Russification? A Study in the Soviet Nationalities Problem* (London: Weidenfeld and Nicolson, 1968).

21. *Suchasnist*, 1968, No. 3.

Freedom of Worship and the Law

PETER REDDAWAY

In about 1950, a new genre of unofficial literature made its appearance in the U.S.S.R. At first, only a small trickle reached the outside world, and its extent and significance were therefore hard to assess. By now, documents totaling well over 300,000 words have been published in the West, often in obscure places. In view of the many references they contain, the published documents constitute only a small part of the whole; many others are being circulated by hand and are frequently attacked in the official press. Together, these documents represent a phenomenon unique in the annals of the Soviet state: the growth of an articulate and sophisticated body of Christian writing, reflecting a world view that, in the U.S.S.R., is perhaps the only widely available alternative to Marxism-Leninism.

The emergence of this new literature can be traced directly to the latest of the periodic antireligious campaigns that have swept the Soviet Union since its inception. Launched by Khrushchev in 1958 and continued—albeit in somewhat less vehement form—by his successors to this day, this large-scale campaign of militant atheism appears to have been designed to revive among the Party cadres an ideological fervor long damped by Stalin's terror, to recreate confidence in an elite body which was now reasserting its primacy over all other institutions, and perhaps even to forestall the possible emergence of broad-based opposition groups inspired by religious values or supported by wide sections of church opinion.

The campaign seems to have been futile and counterproductive; indeed, its effect has probably been only to strengthen the very dangers it set out to remove.[1] In response to the crude, often slanderous press attacks on believers, their illegal dismissals from their jobs, the forced closure and destruction of churches, the gross interference in church affairs by government organs, the submissivenes and even cooperation in these acts of many church leaders, the intensive propagation of the "revelations" of atheist defectors from religion, there came a flood of brave defenses, protests, and counterattacks, some of them composed by fairly prominent figures and some by simple believers, both young and old.

ANATOLI LEVITIN

Among the former, the most prolific is Anatoli Levitin (Krasnov). Born in 1915 and a schoolteacher by profession, Levitin was, from about 1942 to 1944, an ordained member of the "Living Church," an Orthodox group that had cooperated closely with the regime since its inception. From 1944, he was a lay member of the Patriarchal Church. In 1949, Levitin was arrested and spent seven years in concentration camps. Upon being amnestied in 1956, he became a frequent contributor to the *Journal of the Moscow Patriarchate*. Turning also to "unofficial" writing, Levitin was the first, at least among those we know, to argue strongly on the basis of the Soviet Constitution against the illegal persecution of individuals, in this case for their religious belief. In 1959, he came to the defense of a Moscow University student who was being persecuted for his adherence to the Old Believers' sect, in the following words to the authorities:

As the experience of recent years has shown, when arbitrariness begins, no one can tell where it will stop. Propagation of the principle of religious discrimination is a clear call for infringement of the Constitution, for the flouting of each and every legal norm. . . . Respect the Soviet Constitution . . . ; do not sow the seeds of religious hostility, hatred, and fanaticism, because these seeds invariably yield evil fruit.[2]

The small fraction of Levitin's writings that has reached us thus far shows him at once a Christian, a socialist, and, perhaps most important, a democrat, a man given sometimes to impetuous or tactless words—especially when addressing himself to the Patriarch—yet compulsively honest, refreshingly intelligent, and evidently oblivious to the price he has had to pay for his convictions: a life of total poverty and the perpetual threat of arrest. A strong supporter of the Orthodox monastic tradition, Levitin has several times attacked the persecution of monks. The monasteries at Pochaev,[3] Pskov,[4] and Troitse-Sergievaia Lavra, also Bishop Nestor of the Kiev Pecherskaya Lavra,[5] have all benefited from his articulate, sympathetic defense. Often, he has drawn telling comparisons between the inquisitorial methods of the present-day atheist press and those used by Beria's henchmen or by the conservative press of the nineteenth century.[6] And he has polemicized at length both with the writers of atheist apologetics and—in one of the most remarkable and unlikely conversations in Russian history—with officers of the KGB and other high Soviet officials.[7]

As early as 1960, Levitin himself, along with his friend Vadim Shavrov (see note 2), came under vicious fire in the Soviet press.[8] He replied, however, with a characteristic counterattack.[9] In 1961, he voiced another strong protest, this time against the closing of churches and the increasing illegal interference by state organs in church appointments, basing his objections on a detailed analysis of the complex relevant law.[10] He also branched out, with Shavrov, into a politically sensitive area of scholarship, writing a three-volume history of the "Living Church" movement.[11]

Schism Among Protestants

In August, 1961, there came a turning point in the Christian protest movement which Levitin probably had nothing to do with. An unofficial "Action Group" was formed in the Protestant union of Evangelical Christians, Baptists, and others (referred to as ECB); its purpose was to elect democratically a new All-Union Council (AUC) that would reject the state-inspired, antievangelical statutes and instructions that the official AUC had just imposed on the church. This "Action Group," from the start, adopted the practice of circulating in duplicated form, throughout the several-million-member ECB community, resolutions, bulletins, draft statutes, and, above all, open letters critical of the state for its persecutions and critical of the AUC for not protesting these persecutions but, instead, helping the state to carry them out. This, in other words, was the work of a pressure group, not just of a few critical individuals.

We need not analyze the group's literature here in detail, for the story of the ECB schism, with full texts of all the documents available before mid-1967, has already been published by the Reverend Michael Bourdeaux.[12] The most recent documents amply confirm his conclusions— namely, that, while the demands of the ECB reformers for a liberalization of the laws on religion, a free congress of the church, and the democratization of its statutes have achieved partial satisfaction, if only on the last point, the state, in 1966–67, resorted to tough and often terroristic methods to counter the reformers' increased lobbying, evangelism, and circulation of literature. Dramatic evidence of this new militant policy can be found in a letter written by A. I. Kovalchuk to Brezhnev that describes in harrowing detail Kovalchuk's narrow escape from death by police torture;[13] there are also two 10,000-word documents (with important appendixes), written on June 5, 1967,[14] and August 15, 1967,[15] that restate the reformers' demands and detail a multitude of outrages in homes, courts, prisons, and camps. Signed by five women, all wives of imprisoned leaders of the schismatic Council of Churches of the ECB (CCECB), a descendant of the original "Action Group," and all members of the Council of Relatives of ECB Prisoners, they also give extensive particulars about 200 ECB prisoners, whose release they beg United Nations Secretary-General U Thant to effect. As a footnote to these documents, a statement by one of the five, Mrs. Nina Yakimenkova, was reported from Moscow in December, 1967, in which she drew attention to the appeals and expressed dismay that neither U Thant nor any of the other foreign addressees had yet replied.[16]

At about the same time, not surprisingly, the AUC felt constrained to distribute abroad a statement asserting that the irresponsible CCECB was now losing what little support it had had.[17] In addition, the AUC's Unity Commission reported that some of the schismatics had returned to the fold.[18] It is hard to foresee, however, that this will happen on a large scale while the CCECB leaders remain in jail. Indeed, this circumstance, coupled with the continued refusal to meet most of their demands over the past seven years, must be putting a severe strain on the remarkable moderation and loyalty of the CCECB leadership. It would hardly be surprising if, after all the persecution, an alienation from Soviet society were setting in among some CCECB members. According to a recent Soviet report from Moldavia, for instance, "more and more [CCECB members] move from a religious to a political position, displaying direct hostility to the Soviet government."[19] If true, this situation would seem to have been provoked by the government's own fear of allowing any liberalization, even within a basically loyal church.

Dissent Among the Orthodox

To turn now to the Orthodox Church, no systematic documentation of its—in many ways analogous—unofficial literature has yet appeared, although Mr. Bourdeaux has sketched the outlines of this literature through late 1966.[20] The first flood of documents is related to the brutal police efforts, begun in 1961, to close the Pochaev monastery in the Ukraine, against the resolute wishes of the monks, local believers, and the many visiting pilgrims. The anguished protests of these people, which quickly reached the West and have so far succeeded in keeping the monastery open, would fill a full-length book.[21] Lack of space unfortunately precludes their discussion here.

But the event in the Orthodox Church that roughly corresponded to the August, 1961, formation of the ECB's "Action Group"—in raising protest above the individual or local level—occurred in the summer of 1965. At this time, a group of eight Orthodox bishops, led by Archbishop Yermogen, then of Kaluga, submitted a petition to the Patriarch Aleksii asking him to call an assembly (*pomestnyi sobor*) of the church: such a forum could reject the uncanonical decisions of the 1961 Assembly of Bishops, which had been steam-rollered through, as Yermogen recounted in 1967, on twenty-four hours' notice (probably at the state's instigation). These decisions had proved to have a baneful influence on local church life, facilitating increased control by state organs.

The legal aspects of this and subsequent Orthodox protests are too complex to analyze here in detail.[22] They involve contradictions between canon law and state laws, between state laws and the Constitution, and between state laws and the *de facto* procedures long permitted by the authorities, as well as the problem of whether certain official instructions and clarifications of the law were secret, semisecret, or public. Briefly, canon law provides for the parish priest to have extensive control over the administration of parish affairs; the key Soviet legislation of 1929 is not clear on whether or not he necessarily loses this control, the protesters asserting that he does not, other observers citing a (semisecret?) instruction of 1931 to the contrary. In any case, the church's *pomestnyi sobor* of 1945 adopted a statute fully in accord with canon law in this respect, and, for sixteen years, the state did not object, a fact providing circumstantial evidence in support of the protesters' interpretation.

In 1961, however, the Assembly of Bishops passed a statute reflecting more explicitly the alternative interpretation: it asserted that the parish *dvadtsatka*, the group of at least twenty parishioners that signs the parish's contract with the local authorities, would henceforth be the parish administrative body in place of the general assembly of all parishioners (provided in the 1929 law). The state did not now incorporate these changes in its own laws but began to capitalize on them through secret circulars and instructions to the local representatives of its Council on Russian Orthodox Church Affairs (CROCA), as well as through the commissions that were set up in 1963 or 1964 and attached to the local soviets to help the CROCA representatives in their policing work. One of the secret circulars, which has become public outside the U.S.S.R.,[23] urges these administrators to get "suitable" people onto the *dvadtsatka* (annulling previous contracts if necessary) and to keep its size down to twenty members (contrary to the 1929 law) so that the great majority of parishioners, including the clergy, would be disenfranchised.

THE STATE VERSUS THE CHURCH

This was the situation that prompted the action of the eight bishops as well as the subsequent vigorous protest of the two priests N. I. Eshliman and G. P. Yakunin in their petitions to the Patriarch, the Episcopate, and President Podgorny at the end of 1965.[24] There is a remarkable similarity of approach between the letter by Eshliman and Yakunin to Podgorny and that of the Baptists Kriuchkov and Vins to Brezhnev[25] eight months earlier, but, in content, the former is notably less radical. It does not ask for the abolition of the 1929 law as contrary to the constitutional principle of separation of church and state but merely urges its clear enforcement; and it documents eight areas in which state officials are seriously infringing the law in their desire to control almost every aspect of church life, including, for example, the appointment and removal of clergy and bishops, the closing of parishes, the registration of baptisms and other rites, and so on.

When the Patriarch responded to Yakunin and Eshliman by suspending them and they declined to retract their accusations, he told the bishops: "The distribution of all kinds of 'open letters' and articles must definitely be stopped."[26] By May, however, Levitin had already joined the debate in vigorous support of the two priests,[27] and so, too—although from a very moderate position—had a well-known Moscow priest, Father

Vsevolod Shpiller.[28] Levitin has not claimed any credit for the Yakunin-Eshliman stand, although it would be surprising if their systematic analysis of infractions of the law owed nothing to him. It is at least clear that he and Yakunin knew each other by early 1965. In any event, an anonymous Moscow priest, clearly a friend of Yakunin and Eshliman, also came to their support at this time with a powerful letter.[29]

The pain and dislocation caused by the post-1961 *dvadtsatka* arrangements, when ruthlessly exploited by officials of the local CROCA (after 1966, CAR: Council on the Affairs of Religions), are vividly reflected in two further sets of documents. One set concerns the diocese of Kirov, far to the northeast of Moscow, where Christians who had been petitioning the authorities intensively for several years took up the cause of Yakunin and Eshliman, focusing in particular on the scandalous activities of their own local Bishop Ioann (who regularly boasted of his KGB role!). The detail in these documents is relentless, stressing even the criminal destruction of architectural treasures.[30]

The other set concerns Father Shpiller's Nikolo-Kuznetskii parish in Moscow.[31] Here, a dubious individual became *starosta* (churchwarden), dissolved the *dvadtsatka*, and had a bogus one elected in its place. The new *starosta* dictated church policy, disregarding Father Shpiller's authority even in such matters as confession and communion. For this, in December, 1966, Father Shpiller laid a ban on him until such time as he should repent. The local authorities further assisted the *starosta* by illegally refusing to allow parishioners to add their signatures to the church contract and thus become members of the *dvadtsatka*—a body that the 1929 law (Article 31) explicitly says can be of unlimited size. They also refused numerous requests for permission to hold a general parish assembly, at which the hated *starosta* would have been voted out. In reply, the determined parishioners appealed to the procurator to urge the local soviet to permit an assembly in accordance with the law. The outcome of the struggle is as yet unknown.

ARCHBISHOP YERMOGEN

With the exception of a brief letter of March, 1967, from a conservative Moscow priest who disliked Levitin's outspokenness,[32] the final set of documents available at present comes from Archbishop Yermogen, an elderly prelate (born in 1895).

After leading the delegation to the Patriarch in 1965, Yermogen acquiesced to the Patriarch's request that he retire to the Zhirovitsy monastery, but it was agreed that he would stay there only until a new see fell vacant. In November, 1967, he complained to the Patriarch that this condition of their agreement had not been met. A month later he received an answer explaining that he had not been considered a suitable candidate for vacant sees owing to the "complications" which had invariably arisen in his dioceses in the past. To this Archbishop Yermogen replied (in February, 1968) that a ban of this kind could be imposed only by a church court and that it therefore violated canon law.[33] He also reiterated what Yakunin and Eshliman had written of him earlier: that, when he was Bishop of Tashkent, he had prevented the closing down of any churches in the diocese and had even built a new cathedral. And he added instances of his opposition to illegalities in his subsequent dioceses of Omsk and Kaluga.

In his first letter to the Patriarch, written in November, 1967, as well as in a "Historical Memorandum on Canonical and Juridical Matters" written in December, 1967 (entitled "On the Occasion of the Fiftieth Anniversary of the Restoration of the Patriarchate"),[34] Yermogen raised other highly important—and less personal—matters. Not having, as far as we know, publicly supported Yakunin and Eshliman in the past, he now demonstrated his proximity to them by reiterating some of the main themes of their protest:

> The local officials of the Council (CAR) also do not give written expla-
> nations, and their oral explanations suffer from contradictions and often
> conflict with the current legislation. Naturally, a situation in which they
> do not give a citizen the chance to know the laws he must observe, or do
> not answer his communications on matters directly affecting his activity,
> or, even worse, instead of answering his communication, deprive him of
> the job he holds, cannot be considered normal.[35]

More important still, Yermogen analyzed the history of canon law in order to demonstrate the canonical correctness of the procedures decided at the *pomestnyi sobor* of 1917–18 for setting up the synod, electing the bishops and the Patriarch, and calling church assemblies every three years. He then pointed out how all these procedures had since been neglected, with very serious results, including the unwarranted degree of CAR interference in church life that developed subsequently. He appealed for a new assembly at which the procedures decreed in 1917–18 could be reinstated in place of the uncanonical and ill-defined procedures contained in the church's 1945 and 1961 resolutions; he noted further that the ECB Church held triannual congresses, a practice adopted in 1963 in response to the pressure of ECB reformers. Yermogen also stressed the immense importance of the succession to the ninety-year-old Patriarch Aleksii, a matter similarly stressed by Levitin and others who feared that a rigged election—rather than a legitimate canonical election —could lead to schism in the church.

Yermogen's views are impressive for both their historical perspective and their immediate relevance. They also carry the moral authority of a man considered outstanding as pastoral bishop and as scholar. Much could depend on how he exercises this authority in future.

So much for the ECB and the Orthodox churches. What about dissent in other faiths and denominations? It would seem, in fact, that there is almost none, although, among the Jews and the Uniates (Ukrainian

Catholics), some voices, still barely audible, have been raised. Documents of dissent about the persecution of Judaism have apparently reached the outside world, but these have not been published, at least as yet, for reasons of discretion. And the several million Uniates, suppressed or forcibly converted to Orthodoxy in 1946, have begun to resurface; they even held an illegal congress in 1965.[36] Encouragement for them may now come from their 300,000 brethren across the Czechoslovakian border, who have recently emerged in dramatic fashion and demanded self-determination,[37] clearly implying that they may revert to Rome after their period of forced subjugation to Moscow.

Such, then, are the dimensions of the known religious dissent, although it should be noted that the texts inevitably lose much force when translated and abridged. In particular, the great scale of the protests is lost: some of the documents available or referred to contain dozens, even hundreds of signatures. Thus they do not convey to the reader the sense of isolation, defenselessness, even panic transmitted by certain documents from the Soviet literary milieu. Exceptions here are some of the Pochaev documents and the latest ECB letters (see Document 43), sent to foreign as well as Soviet addressees—always a sign of greater desperation. In most cases, the religious groups appear to have relatively few real enemies, except among officialdom, while most of their neighbors view them in a neutral or sympathetic light. The ECB, indeed, not only proselytize generally but can also take the offensive against the professional atheists, sometimes deliberately visiting atheist lectures in order to heckle the speakers.[38] It is also interesting to note the lack of self-consciousness with which, in an unofficial document,[39] three young Baptist men from the Poltava region of the Ukraine protest to Brezhnev about the local Party's overbearing refusal of Christian burial to their father, a lifelong Communist who adopted Christianity shortly before his death: it appears not to worry them that they give the clear impression that they themselves are Christians.

RISE OR DECLINE?

We must now ask: How large is the religious minority in the Soviet Union? Furthermore, is it likely to grow and to increase its influence, and, if so, in what sections of society?

Granted that statistics must be approached with caution, it is nevertheless interesting that a recent figure derived from Soviet sources indicates that fifty-eight million people in the U.S.S.R. practice some religion, while an experienced American source, Dr. Paul Anderson, suggests sixty-four million,[40] and Levitin often refers to a fifth of the population, *i.e.*, nearly fifty million. How many believe without publicly practicing is, of course, impossible to determine.

As for the growth or decline of religion in the Soviet Union, such factors as industrialization, urbanization, the scientific revolution, career considerations, and the partially compromised image of the churches, due in some degree to state infiltration and control, might all be expected to encourage decline. On the other hand, the arid emptiness of Marxism-Leninism, never widely accepted outside Party circles, and the lack of a forum in which to discuss any other philosophies tend to send those who are in search of new ideals toward religion.[41] Attempts to dress up the official ideology as a religion-substitute by giving it some spiritual and aesthetic appeal have never met with success. Further, nearly half the Soviet population still lives in the countryside, where—as in many of the towns—widespread poverty and a severe lack of cultural amenities persist.

More positively, religion is a unifying factor that permeates both the popular culture and much of the intellectual culture, and, as post-Stalin society strives to de-atomize itself, the churches become again, for some people, attractive forums for the breaking down of class barriers. Such people, moreover, increasingly recall that, for all their past sins, the churches did resist most of the state's demands—at the cost of many martyrs—that they held on grimly through the Stalinist terror and showed their patriotism in World War II, only to undergo, after 1958, a new series of repressions, perhaps minor by contrast with the 1930's but still testing. Thus, while the present regime's lack of moral legitimacy is becoming increasingly evident as a result of its partial re-enthronement of Stalin and other actions, the moral standing of the churches is tending to rise. Finally, the current tide of religious dissent, which assists the latter process perhaps more than anything else, has a firm and even growing social base, firmer indeed, in certain ways, than that of the literary and intellectual dissent. For naturally enough, the most vocal religious dissenters, often acting also on behalf of others more vulnerable than themselves, tend to be pensioners or housewives, an expanding social group in Soviet society. Many such people have little to lose, and they also have the time to write petitions, to organize protests, and to travel and lobby the authorities.

On balance, these circumstances seem favorable to the growth of religion. But is this likely to occur in two seminal sections of society: among the young and the "creative intelligentsia"? The most important point about the latter is that the central theme of its dissent, the demand for justice and legality, is identical with that of the religious dissent. For, as we have seen, religious protesters ask, above all, for legality, both within the churches and in the state's relations with them. Moreover, Levitin and Talantov in particular also see and stress that legality for believers involves an equal degree of legality for everyone else. Thus the two dissents have a common central concern.

RELIGION AND THE INTELLIGENTSIA

At a more personal level, however, many of the religious dissenters—Yakunin, Eshliman, Yermogen, Talantov, Levitin, Shpiller—are revealed by their writings to be bona fide members of the intelligentsia, while many of the key figures in the creative intelligentsia are also religious.[42] Among the latter, one need mention only Solzhenitsyn,[43] Siniavsky, Brodsky, Soloukhin, and Galanskov. Even more important, perhaps, the literary pantheon of much of the intelligentsia is dominated by deeply religious writers of the near or distant past: Pasternak, Akhmatova, Tsvetaeva, Zabolotsky, Dostoevsky, to mention only some of those whose writings are permeated with religious feeling and values, even if these do not always relate to a particular church. All this helps to explain how Svetlana Alliluyeva came to be baptized and how religious views—while sometimes, perhaps, of a superficial nature—are no longer unusual among the creative intelligentsia and in some circles are even fashionable.

As for concrete links between the religious and intellectual dissents, we should note first that the sociopolitical underground journal *Phoenix 1966* contains a systematic account of the Pochaev monastery persecutions, with an introduction by its editor, Yuri Galanskov, in which he denounces the senseless and unconstitutional repressions and praises the resistance of the monks.[44] At Galanskov's trial in January, 1968, Levitin appeared as a witness, perhaps because one of his open letters had been found in Galanskov's apartment,[45] and one of Galanskov's codefendants was Aleksei Dobrovolsky, who may be called a religious writer[46] and who in 1966 had also belonged to the organizing committee of an anti-Stalin demonstration.[47] Another sociopolitical underground journal from Moscow, *The Magazine of Socialist Democracy*, contains a long article by Levitin[48] as well as a reprint of an article called "Communism and Religion," originally published in 1923 in *Molodaia gvardiia*. Its author, a Swedish Communist, argued that Christians wanting to build socialism should be admitted freely to the Party, a body whose purpose is not to conduct antireligious agitation. Levitin's broad interests also led him to join Larisa Daniel, Dr. Pavel Litvinov, and others in one of the most radical protests provoked by the Galanskov-Ginzburg trial. Their purpose was to denounce the series of political prosecutions and to draw attention to the desperate plight of the country's "several thousands of political prisoners."[49]

More disturbing still, however, for a regime that fears a political opposition inspired by religious belief, must have been the discovery in Leningrad of an "All-Russian Social-Christian Union for the Liberation of the People." This group, based in Leningrad University and reportedly with offshoots in Tomsk and Irkutsk, proposed a parliamentary democracy in which the Orthodox Church would evidently become re-established. The anxiety of the regime at this phenomenon was apparent in the severe sentences—ranging up to fifteen years at forced labor—imposed at trials in late 1967 and March–April, 1968, on twenty members of the group, almost all under thirty years of age.[50]

But *direct* links between the religious dissent and the intellectual dissent appear, not surprisingly, to be few. Intellectuals take part in the former and religious people in the latter, but not many dissenters as yet can afford the luxury of more than one public cause. A recent document explained why:

> As regards links between the activities of believers and the intelligentsia, the intelligentsia acts separately. There are no links, since the church believes the faith must not be mixed with politics. All the protests are made on questions of faith, because if politics were brought in, the authorities would exploit this, and there might be a new wave of persecution on the grounds that the church was using its freedom for political ends.[51]

Turning finally to the interest in religion specifically among young people, the evidence of the regime's deep concern about a section of youth is now extensive. The growth of ECB Sunday schools, for example, helped to provoke the new persecution wave of 1966–67, as did, even more perhaps, the mass baptisms of young people, many of student age.[52] Indeed, the ECB reform movement has been dominated by the younger generation.[53] Of the 171 ECB members in prison in August, 1967 (whose ages we know), over half were in their twenties and thirties. There is also no lack of young men wanting to enter the Orthodox priesthood. Finally, we may note a report that unites several of our themes, that when the poet Anna Akhmatova died, in March, 1966, memorial services were held in several churches in Moscow and Leningrad. A feature of the principal service, in Leningrad, was the presence of several thousand members of the younger generation.[54]

In conclusion, it is worth quoting one of the most realistic Soviet atheist writers, Galina Kelt, who said in an article written in 1965:

> It was enough to open God's buildings during the war for many of yesterday's atheists suddenly to turn up in church. And today we are again lulling ourselves with: "many believers in our country have left the church and religion." This is self-deception . . . the closure of parishes does not turn believers into atheists. On the contrary, it strengthens people's attraction to religion and, in addition, embitters their hearts.[55]

How many people would turn up in church if real religious freedom suddenly arrived? The only answer is: no one knows. Without doubt, however, the new persecutions, which are fortunately no longer backed by Stalinist terror, have hardened the resolve of religious people to press for legality. As we have seen, most believers restrict themselves to religious dissent, but a growing minority of the more politically minded seem to feel a need for wider-based dissent and even opposition.

The religious dissent has already achieved much toward moderating the persecution and the state interference in internal church affairs. It is therefore difficult to foresee a decline in its current level of activity unless the regime makes very large concessions. Indeed, as the spiritual vacuum of Soviet life becomes more intolerable, religious dissent, along with other forms of social defiance, might well increase in both scope and intensity.

Notes

1. See in particular the richly documented article by Bohdan Bociurkiw, "Religion and Soviet Society," *Survey* (London), July, 1966, in which Soviet views to this effect are quoted.

2. From an open letter by Levitin to the editors of *Moskovskii Komsomolets*, with a copy to Khrushchev: for text, see Arkhiepiskop Ioann San-Frantsisskii (ed.), *Dialog s tserkovnoi Rossiei* (hereafter *Dialog*) (Paris: Ikhthus, 1967), pp. 21–29. The letter was prompted by the newspaper's attack on Zhenia Bobkov, the expelled student, who had also been the target of an earlier press attack. On that previous occasion Bobkov had been defended by Vadim Shavrov, the thirty-five-year-old son of Mikhail Yurevich Shavrov, an atheist highly regarded by Levitin. For Vadim Shavrov's mention of Bobkov, see *Grani* (Frankfurt), No. 63 (1967), pp. 97–110.

3. See Arkhiepiskop Ioann San-Frantsisskii (ed.), *Zashchita very v SSSR* (hereafter *Zashchita very*) (Paris: Ikhthus, 1966), pp. 21–25, 87.

4. *Ibid.*, pp. 32–62.

5. *Dialog*, pp. 35–41, 32.

6. E.g., *ibid.*, pp. 112–13; *Zashchita very*, p. 25.

7. See Document 46 and *Zashchita very*, pp. 88–101. For his polemics with atheists see *Dialog*, pp. 87–113, and *Grani*, No. 65 (1967), pp. 157–88, and No. 66 (1967), pp. 206–37.

8. *Nauka i religiia* (Moscow), 1960, No. 5, pp. 32–37. Another harsh attack appeared later in the same journal, 1966, No. 10, pp. 25–26.

9. *Dialog*, pp. 43–69.

10. *Ibid.*, pp. 103–9.

11. One volume, "Ocherki po istorii russkoi tserkovnoi smuty," has reached the West and has appeared in *Novyi zhurnal* (New York), Nos. 85–88 (December, 1966–September, 1967).

12. See his *Religious Ferment in Russia: Protestant Opposition to Soviet Religious Policy* (London, 1968); also his article "Reform and Schism," *Problems of Communism* (Washington), 1967, No. 5, pp. 108–18; and the article by Bourdeaux and Reddaway "Soviet Baptists Today: Church and State and Schism," *Survey* (London), No. 66 (January, 1968), pp. 48-66.

13. *Religion in Communist-Dominated Areas* (hereafter *RCDA*), VI, No. 15–16 (August, 1967), 127–33. For a more accurate translation, see Howard-Johnston and R. Harris (eds.), *Christian Appeals from Russia* (London: 1969).

14. See *RCDA*, VII, No. 3–4 (February, 1968), 23–40.

15. *Possev*, October 20 and 27, 1967; and P. Reddaway, "The Inexorable Persecution of the Soviet Protestants," *Times* (London), December 12, 1967. For full text, see Document 42 and Howard-Johnston and Harris, *Christian Appeals from Russia*.

16. *Daily Telegraph* (London), December 20, 1967. More recently, another document has become available in the form of an appeal made to the Soviet authorities in February, 1968, by the Kiev ECB community expressing fear for the life of the imprisoned CCECB leader, G. P. Vins, at the hands of a brutal labor-camp administration. See Document 43; the full text appears in *Possev*, 1968, No. 7, pp. 5–6.

17. *RCDA*, VII, No. 3–4 (February, 1968), 41–43.

18. *Bratskii vestnik* (Moscow), 1967, No. 5, pp. 17–18.

19. *Kommunist Moldavii*, 1967, No. 12, p. 66, translated in *Research Materials on Religion in Eastern Europe* (Geneva), I, No. 15, 1.

20. Michael Bourdeaux, *Problems of Communism*, 1967, No. 5, pp. 114–18. Mr. Bourdeaux has since prepared a systematic work, *Patriarchs and Prophets: Persecution of the Russian Orthodox Church*, to be published by Macmillan in 1969. To

date, by far the best collection of documents (with commentaries) is in Italian: *Chiesa e Società* 4, *URSS: Dibatitto nella Communità Cristiana* (Milan: Jaca Book, 1968).

21. See *Possev*, November 16, 1962, May 8, 1964, January 7, 1965, August 13 and 20, 1965, January 7, 1967, 1968, No. 5, pp. 8–9; *Zashchita Very*, pp. 63–87; and *Vestnik zapadnoevropeiskoi eparkhii* (Geneva), 1967, No. 1–2. A summary of events up to 1966 by the monastery's Spiritual Council is included in the underground journal *Phoenix* 1966, in *Vestnik russkovo studencheskovo Khristianskovo dvizheniia* (Paris—hereafter *Vestnik*), No. 84 (1967), pp. 39–69, and is to appear in English in Bourdeaux, *Patriarchs and Prophets*.

22. The best analysis is by Bohdan Bociurkiw, "Church-State Relations in the USSR," *Survey*, No. 66 (January, 1968), pp. 4–32. This is an abridged version of a still more richly documented conference paper.

23. *Vestnik*, No. 83 (1967), pp. 3–6; partially translated in M. Bourdeaux, *Religious Ferment in Russia*, pp. 14–16.

24. Texts in *Grani*, No. 61 (1966), pp. 122–89; full English translation in *St. Vladimir's Seminary Quarterly* (New York), Vol. X, Nos. 1–2. The petition of the eight bishops, not otherwise available, is quoted in the Eshliman-Yakunin submission to the Episcopate.

25. Text in Bourdeaux, *Religious Ferment in Russia*, pp. 105–13.

26. For partial translations of the documents on this episode, see *RCDA*, V, Nos. 15–16 (1966), 126–29. Texts in *Russkaia mysl* (Paris) August 25, 1966.

27. See Levitin's article "Liuboviu i gnevom" (With Love and Anger), *Russkaia mysl* (Paris), July 7, 1966; also his article of August, "Slushaia radio" (Listening to the Radio), *Possev*, September 23 and October 1, 1966.

28. See Father Shpiller's letter of March, 1966, to Metropolitan Nikodim, in *Rossiia i vselenskaia tserkov* (Brussels), 1966, No. 4, and 1967, No. 1, pp. 57–84; also his letter of January, 1967, to Archbishop Vasilii of Brussels in *Vestnik zapadnoevropeiskovo patriarshevo eksarkhata* (Paris), No. 58 (1967).

29. *Vestnik*, No. 81 (1966), pp. 5–17.

30. Letter of June, 1966, from twelve Kirov Christians to the Patriarch, in *ibid.*, No. 82, pp. 3–20; extracts from open letter of November, 1966, by Boris Talantov, *ibid.*, No. 83, pp. 29–64, which documents persecutions in addition to those listed by Yakunin and Eshliman. Later documents on developments in the Kirov diocese have just become available. Together with the earlier documents, they give a unique picture of the situation as it has evolved since 1960. The longest of these later documents, written by the prolific Talantov in April, 1968, appears in abridged form as Document 47. This document provides interesting testimony to the solidarity between the religious dissent and the protests of the radical intelligentsia against the recent trials of writers, as well as to the important role, in various contexts, of foreign radio stations such as the BBC.

31. See Levitin's article of December, 1966, "Kaplia v mikroskope," *Vestnik*, No. 83 (1967), pp. 7–28, which reproduces several documents; also the appeal addressed by the legal *dvadtsatka* of the parish to Kosygin in February, 1967 (Document 45), and other documents in Bourdeaux, *Patriarchs and Prophets*.

32. See *Dialog*, pp. 9–13.

33. For Russian text of this and the Patriarch's answer see *Vestnik*, Nos. 87–88 (1968), pp. 8–14. For Yermogen's original complaint see *ibid.*, No. 86, pp. 61–65 (translated in *RCDA*, Vol. VII, Nos. 9–10 [May, 1968]).

34. *Vestnik*, No. 86 (1967), pp. 66–80 (translated in *RCDA*, Vol. VII, Nos. 9–10 [1968]).

35. *Ibid.*, p. 63. Doubtless it was this spirit that led to personal attacks on Yermogen in his Tashkent days. See *Pravda Vostoka* (Tashkent), July 10 and September 3, 1960.

36. *Molod Ukrainy*, November 12, 1965. The people who organized this congress are here called *pokutniki*, but they appear to be Uniates.

37. *RCDA*, VII, No. 7–8 (April, 1968), 78.

38. *Nauka i religiia*, 1967, No. 11, p. 83.

39. See Document 44.

40. David Powell, "The Effectiveness of Soviet Anti-Religious Propaganda," *Public Opinion Quarterly*, Fall, 1967, where Anderson is quoted.

41. See P. Reddaway, "The Search for New Ideals in the USSR: Some First-Hand Impressions," in W. C. Fletcher and A. J. Strover (eds.), *Religion and the Search for New Ideals in the USSR* (New York: Praeger, 1967), pp. 83–90.

42. See the important but by no means exhaustive articles by Zinaida Shakhovskaia, "The Significance of Religous Themes in Soviet Literature," in Fletcher and Strover, *ibid.*, pp. 119–29; and Albert Todd, "The Spiritual in Recent Soviet Literature," *Survey*, No. 66 (January, 1968), pp. 92–107.

43. See, in particular, his little known "Molitva," *Vestnik*, No. 81, p. 22. "Underground" writing with religious content not mentioned by Shakhovskaia and Todd include the poems of A. Nadezhdina in *Vestnik*, No. 78 (1965), p. 37, and No. 85 (1967), pp. 50–56; of Anon. in *ibid.*, No. 81, pp. 23–28; of L. Ryzhov in *ibid.*, No. 85, pp. 57–8; of A. Yaskolda in *Grani*, No. 64 (1967), pp. 112–13; of L. Sergeyev in *ibid.*, No. 66 (1967), pp. 153–54; of A. Galich in *ibid.*, No. 68, pp. 7–8; and the essays of I. Ruslanov in *ibid.*, No. 68, pp. 157–89.

44. See Document 48 and note 21, *above*.

45. See *Possev*, 1968, No. 4, p. 9. Levitin stated at this trial that he had no idea how his articles got abroad.

46. See his essay "The Interrelationship of Knowledge and Faith," *Grani*, No. 64 (1967), pp. 194–201, translated in *Problems of Communism*, XVII, No. 5 (1968), 79–82.

47. See *Possev*, September 16, 1966.

48. *Ibid.*, 1968, No. 5, pp. 47–55. Levitin materials not mentioned elsewhere in this paper include an entertaining autobiographical essay and two statements of 1966 about his work as a night watchman and the official harassment he was undergoing, all in *Possev*, January 7, 1967; and the collection of his articles *Kampf des Glaubens* (Bern: Schweitzerisches Ost-Institut, 1967).

49. See Document 32. Levitin also signed another radical protest organized by, among others, Aleksandr Yesenin-Volpin (Document 30).

50. *Possev*, 1968, No. 12, pp. 13–14.

51. *Possev*, 1968, No. 5, p. 8.

52. See M. Bourdeaux, *Religious Ferment in Russia*, Chap. 6. A letter from a group of young Orthodox Church members to Orthodox leaders abroad reports a definite but not yet large influx of the younger generation into the church. See *Vestnik zapadnoevropeiskoi eparkhi* (Geneva), 1967, No. 1–2, pp. 10–12. For a compilation of evidence from the Soviet press see D. Konstantinov, "Orthodoxy and the Younger Generation," in Fletcher and Strover, *Religion and the Search for New Ideas in the USSR*, pp. 24-34.

53. For some statistics, see the article by A. I. Klibanov and L. N. Mitrokhin, "Rasskol v sovremennom baptizme," *Voprosy nauchnovo ateizma* (Moscow), III (1967), 105.

54. See *Vestnik*, No. 80 (1966), pp. 49–51.

55. *Komsomolskaia pravda*, August 15, 1965.

PART TWO

Documents

I. The Moscow Trials of 1967

The documents in this section are related to the trials of Viktor Khaustov (February, 1967) and Vladimir Bukovsky, Vadim Delone, and Yevgeni Kushev (September, 1967). Documents 1 and 3 are letters written by Piotr Grigorenko and Pavel Litvinov protesting the unconstitutional manner in which the trials were conducted. Document 2 is Bukovsky's final statement in court at the end of his trial.

1. Petition by P. Grigorenko

December, 1967

To: Chairman of the U.S.S.R. Supreme Court, A. F. Gorkin
Procurator General of the U.S.S.R., R. A. Rudenko

Our people and progressive society everywhere have just observed the half-century jubilee of the Great October Revolution.

Almost immediately after that, the fiftieth anniversary of Soviet law was observed. On that date our press published a series of laudatory articles in which, in particular, it was affirmed that Soviet law is the most just, the most unbiased, and the most humane in the world.

My own experience literally cries out against these assertions. Nevertheless, I have decided to base my assumptions on them and not on my personal experience. For that reason, I am addressing this letter to you.

Not long ago, I learned that on February 16, 1967, the Moscow Municipal Court sentenced a Moscow worker, Viktor Khaustov, to three years' deprivation of freedom under Article 190-3 of the Criminal Code of the R.S.F.S.R.

This article and two others (Articles 190-1 and 190-2) were enacted by the Presidium of the Supreme Soviet of the R.S.F.S.R. without the knowledge of the broad masses of the people, under the label of "the struggle against hooliganism."[1]

One of these three provisions, Article 190-2, has met with no objection at all from the people.[2] If there actually had been widespread acts of disrespect to the seal and the flag of the Soviet Union in the country, there are obviously several other measures directed toward the suppression of that evil.

The other two sections of Article 190 are a different matter.[3] Leading members of our society, when they learned that these provisions had been enacted into law, immediately declared that they were unconstitutional because they could be used for the suppression of the freedoms proclaimed in Article 125 of the Constitution of the U.S.S.R.—freedom of speech, of the press, of assembly, meetings, and demonstrations, and also the greatest weapon of the working class: the right to strike.

However, competent state organs denied such a possibility. It was stated that it was not a question of the suppression of the enumerated freedoms and of the right of the working class to strike but, rather, of assuring that these rights would not be employed for the purpose of venomous slander against Soviet society and the state structure, for the violation of public order, or for the disruption of work in industrial enterprises, transport, government offices, and institutions.

The trial of Khaustov demonstrated the flimsiness of these explanations. Even in the highly subjective conduct of the judicial investigation, it was established beyond any doubt that Khaustov took part in a very small, peaceful demonstration during which the standards of public order were carefully observed and that disturbed no one—neither the movement of public transportation, nor passersby, nor the work of enterprises, offices, and institutions.

Furthermore, the demonstrators, striving to avoid any kind of excess, did not offer any resistance even when they were exposed to an unprovoked hooligan attack. And the attack made upon them was precisely hooligan in character. How else can one label an incident in which unknown people, without any warning, hurl themselves upon peaceful demonstrators and commit outrages of physical violence? The fact, as established at the trial, that the attackers were members of the Komsomol operations group and employees of the KGB not only does not make the attack legitimate but makes it even more bestial. In truth, why was it necessary to break up the demonstration by using KGB personnel not wearing their uniforms and members of the Komsomol operations group without armbands?[4] Why was it necessary to attack and to use physical force instead of peacefully asking the demonstrators to disperse?

You will agree that the attack, more than anything else, resembled a provocation. It looked as if the intent was to provoke the demonstrators into resistance in order to organize later a big trial of "hooligans." The fact that the militia [uniformed police], and later the court, sided with the attackers is evidence of that supposition.

The facts adduced at the trial with all persuasiveness confirm that the actions of the accused did not constitute a crime. Despite that, he was charged under the sections of the Criminal Code mentioned above. The court did not even note that Khaustov had no previous record of criminal prosecution, that upon finishing high school he began working in a factory and labored there loyally for ten years, and that he is the only bread-winner in his family.

On the basis of all that has been said, one can conclude that the trial was not criminal in nature but political. Khaustov was convicted, not for disturbing public order, but because he had certain personal views on events that were taking place, and because he did not keep silent when he saw responsible officials of government organs suppressing the legal rights of Soviet citizens. More specifically, he was tried for participating in organizations and conducting demonstrations of protest against illegal arrests.

The political character of this trial was exposed with even greater force when, in September, 1967, three other participants in this very demonstration—Bukovsky, Delone, and Kushev—were brought to trial after seven months' detention in solitary confinement for investigation by the KGB. The authorities were not able to charge any of these men even with the ludicrous charge that had been brought against Khaustov, namely, that he had hit someone with one of the fallen wooden placards that the attackers had been trying to pull away from him.

This time, everything was different. Delone and Kushev had offered no resistance whatsoever and, at the first request, had gone to the police station. Bukovsky, indeed, conducted himself in such a way that the attackers at the demonstration did not even notice him. Despite the fact that he left the square later than all the other demonstrators, no one even tried to detain him. In a completely senseless and ridiculous fashion, he was arrested a week later in his apartment and charged under Article 190-3. Obviously, one cannot hide an already committed violation of public order in a desk drawer or between the pages of a book.

Like the trial of Khaustov, that of Bukovsky and his two comrades was, in fact, conducted behind closed doors and with unacceptable violations of the rights of the accused. By his numerous interjections and warnings and also by calling a recess in the middle of the final statement of the defendant Bukovsky, the judge prevented the latter from exercising his right of defense. The court paid no attention to Bukovsky's statement—refuted by no one—concerning the crude violations of legality that had taken place during the period of his investigative detention.

And the sentence itself! For the very same actions for which the court sentenced Bukovsky to the highest penalty under the law—three years in a forced-labor camp—his two comrades were only put on probation. One naturally asks, why? An acquaintance with the course of the trial does not leave the slightest doubt about this matter. Bukovsky was sentenced because he defended himself, and because he refused to recognize the right of the organs of the KGB to engage in uncontrolled and illegal interference in the personal lives of citizens. Delone and Kushev were "encouraged" to "express remorse," even though they had not committed any criminal act.

Proceeding from the above, as a citizen of my country entitled to all its rights and dutybound to observe unswervingly its basic law, the Constitution of the U.S.S.R., I demand of the Supreme Court of the Soviet Union:

That it review the cases of Khaustov and Bukovsky-Delone-Kushev, remit the illegal sentences, and free the accused;

That it explain to all the lower courts that participation in gatherings, meetings, demonstrations, and strikes is not to be tried under Article 190-3, and that only disturbances of public order consequent to them [should be tried];

That it use the cases cited by me as precedents to show that in these given instances the disturbers of public order were not the demonstrators but those who attacked them;

That it publish these judicial commentaries not in legal publications but in the mass-circulation press.

Obviously, if declarations that Soviet law is unbiased, just, and humane have any real worth whatever, if Article 112 of the Constitution of the U.S.S.R., which says that judges are independent and responsible only to the law, has any reality, the Supreme Court must put into effect the basic law of the socialist state [the Constitution of the U.S.S.R.], remit the illegal sentences, and take measures to prevent a future repetition of similar acts.

In the contrary event, it will be clear that the Supreme Court, as one of the basic organs of power, is taking a direct part in the attack on the constitutional rights of citizens and masking that participation with lofty words about justice, impartiality, and humanitarianism. Such an eventuality would give citizens the right to defend the Constitution by all available means; first of all, by the full exposure of the anticonstitutional acts of all government organs, including, especially, the illegal sentences of the courts.

P. Grigorenko

Moscow, G-21, Komsomolsky Prospekt
Building 14/1, Apt. 96, Telephone G-6-27-37

Notes

1. Articles 190-1, 190-2, and 190-3 were enacted as supplements to the R.S.F.S.R. Criminal Code by decree of the Presidium of the R.S.F.S.R. Supreme Soviet dated September 16, 1966. See *Vedomosti R.S.F.S.R.*, No. 38 (1966).—Ed.

2. Article 190-2 makes an act of disrespect to the flag or the seal of the Soviet Union a specific crime.—Ed.

3. Article 190-1 deals with the preparation and dissemination of "falsehoods derogatory to the Soviet state and social system." Article 190-3 prohibits the "organization of, as well as participation in, group activities that grossly violate public order, involve clear disobedience to the lawful orders of the authorities, or entail disruption of the operation of transport, state and public enterprises, or institutions." The maximum penalty under both provisions is three years' deprivation of freedom.—Ed.

4. The Komsomol operations group (*druzhinniki*) is composed of young men who work as auxiliary police in maintaining public order. They are required to wear identifying armbands when on duty.—Ed.

2. *Final Trial Statement by V. Bukovsky*

September 1, 1967

I want to express my gratitude to my defense counsel and to my comrades.

When preparing for this trial, I expected that the proceedings would completely reveal all the motives for the actions that are charged and that the court would deal with the legal analysis of the case. [But] the court has done nothing of the kind. It has engaged in character defamation. Besides, whether we are good or bad is irrelevant to the case.

I expected the prosecution to present a detailed analysis of the "disturbance" we made in the square—who hit whom, who stepped on whose foot. But this did not follow either. The prosecutor says in his speech: "As I see it, the danger of this crime lies in its insolence."

JUDGE: Defendant Bukovsky, why do you cite the speech of the prosecutor?

BUKOVSKY: I need it, and so I cite it. Do not interfere with my statement. Believe me, it is hard enough for me to speak, though outwardly my speech proceeds smoothly.

So the prosecutor considers our actions insolent. But I have here before me the text of the Soviet Constitution [which says]: "In accordance with the interests of the workers and with the aim of strengthening the socialist system, citizens of the U.S.S.R. are guaranteed by law . . . the right of street processions and demonstrations." Why is such an article included? For May Day and October demonstrations? But it is not necessary to include such an article for demonstrations that are organized by the government; it is clear that no one will disperse these demonstrations. We do not need freedom "pro" if there is no freedom "anti." We know that protest demonstrations are a powerful weapon in the hands of workers, and they are an inalienable right in all democratic states. Where is this right denied? I have before me the newspaper *Pravda* of August 19, 1967, carrying a report from Paris. In Madrid, there was a trial of the participants in a May Day demonstration. They were tried under a new law, recently passed in Spain, that provides for imprisonment from one and a half to three years for participation in demonstrations. I see a disturbing likeness between Fascist Spanish and Soviet legislation.

JUDGE: Defendant, you are comparing things that cannot be compared: the actions of the rulers of Spain and those of the Soviet state. In court, the comparison of Soviet policy with the policies of foreign bourgeois states is intolerable. Stay closer to the substance of the indictment. I object to the abusiveness of your words.

BUKOVSKY: And I object to your infringement of my right of defense.

JUDGE: You do not have the right to express anything you wish. In court proceedings, all must submit to the presiding officer.

BUKOVSKY: But you do not have the right to interrupt me. I have not departed from the essence of my case. On the basis of Article 243 of the Code of Criminal Procedure, I demand that my objection be entered in the record of proceedings.[1]

JUDGE (*to the secretary*): Enter it please.

BUKOVSKY: The prosecutor made unsubstantiated statements. But more of this later. Not one of those who spoke here produced evidence of a gross violation of the peace in Pushkin Square, except for a single witness. But is it really worth mentioning him if his name is Bezobrazov?[2]

JUDGE: Defendant, stop this intolerable tone. What right do you have to insult a witness? And you talk as if you are addressing a public meeting. Address the judge.

BUKOVSKY: But I do not insult him [the witness].

Let me examine the essence of the case. Persons in civilian clothes, without armbands, called themselves *druzhinniki,* but only by their actions could one know that they were *druzhinniki. Druzhinniki* play a positive, serious role in the battle against crime—against thieves, hooligans, and so forth—at which time they always wear armbands. A basic rule of the *druzhinniki* requires that armbands be worn. And there is no directive that gives the *druzhinniki* the right to break up political demonstrations. Incidentally, in regard to the directive, does it exist? It is not a law, but if it is compulsory and if it is sufficient to refer to it in court —it *was* applied, after all, because people were detained on the basis of it—then it must be made public in court on the strength of a person's right to speak up in court. The directive in my case requires that *druzhinniki* wear armbands in the course of their duties. But they didn't even show us their documents. When the *druzhinnik* Kleimenov, who appeared here as a witness, ran up to me, he cried: "What filth are you displaying? Now you'll get it in the eye."

Without a doubt, all this had been planned earlier; the people at the square knew about our demonstration beforehand. Indeed, militiaman Gruzinov did not appear to notice any violation of public order in the square and did not approach the demonstrators until some person in civilian clothes gave the order to seize one of us. Perhaps this person was a *druzhinnik?* No. How could an experienced militiaman recognize a *druzhinnik* if he was not wearing an armband? So who could this man have been? Just why did Gruzinov carry out the request of one private citizen to seize another who had not disturbed the peace? Obviously, he had been previously instructed, and evidently his instructions were sufficiently specific.

Colonel Abramov of the KGB arrived at the square certainly not as a private citizen. It is not likely that he was out for a stroll, which is not one of his habits. Wrongfully, the court did not call him as a witness, for he could have told things about the case no less important than the statements of the other witnesses.

Note that so far I have not used the word, but it seems that this was a *provocation.* In fact, what else could one call it? Imagine that, on May 1, you are walking along the street carrying May Day slogans and some citizen in civilian clothes, without an armband, takes the slogans away from you. It is clear here—excuse the expression—that he may get it in the neck. Yes, in the neck. Wasn't that just what the *druzhinniki* counted upon, and wasn't that why Colonel Abramov appeared at Pushkin Square? Wasn't it in order to arrive at the exact moment when there appeared to be grounds for a criminal case? These are the interesting words that Colonel Abramov uttered when Delone was brought to *druzhinniki* headquarters: "Delone, if we had not stopped that demonstration in time, you, a young poet and an intelligent young man, would have found yourself in prison with thieves and hooligans."

And why was it necessary to make so many searches? Why search a violator of public order? Was it to take from him the means whereby he had created the disturbance? There was nothing to be moved from our houses—we brought everything to the square. What was there to look for—cobblestones that we were supposed to throw? Well, it might be understandable if only our premises had been searched, but the premises of the witnesses and those of the bystanders were also searched [*enumerates their names*]. Why was this done? One can understand that searches facilitate investigation, finding other participants, and so forth. It is unthinkable, however, that such a large number of searches should be made because of a disturbance of the peace in a square. Why are photographs shown to us for the identification of persons who were not connected with the demonstration? All this is understandable only if the searches are being conducted by the KGB.

In our country, the organs of state security play a police role. What democracy can there be to speak of when we are being watched? Let them catch spies! Why are we being questioned about our acquaintances, about what we were doing two or three years ago, and so forth? I recognize the important role of the KGB in the fight for state security. But what is their business in this case? There were no external enemies involved here. Perhaps they had internal ones in mind. There were no grounds for the interference of the state security organs, but let's take a look at how our case was handled. Why did they have to drag it [the investigation] out for a period of seven months? And by the way, why did they put us at once in investigatory isolation cells of the KGB? I won't distract the court's attention by describing the conditions in the isolation cell block—but there certainly is a difference. In the isolation cell block there are two or three of us in a cell, whereas in ordinary prison cells there are seven to eight persons. If you have to stay there several months, it has its effects on a person's mental state. Moreover, there are altogether different rules regarding food and parcels. Why did they have to drag the case out for seven months? I see only one explanation: to trump up some means of covering over the traces of this unseemly business. When it finally became impossible to keep on stalling, the proceedings about us were made so secret that nobody would be able to penetrate [them] and convince himself of their illegality. Although the investigation of our case was started by the prosecutor's office, the order for my arrest was signed by the KGB Captain Smelov. By the fourth month, our case had been transferred from the prosecutor's office to the KGB. This is a violation of procedure: Article 125 of the Code of Criminal Procedure of the R.S.F.S.R. specifically defines the sphere of the KGB's competence. There is no Article 190 there. Moreover, on the same day that the decree on the introduction of this article was adopted, another decree was adopted whereby Article 125 was supplemented by the instruction that cases falling under Article 190 have to be examined by the prosecutor's office. Now, if the KGB found that our case contained grounds for an investigation under Article 70, then it had the right to start the investigation. But what was it required to start from? A presentation of charges. This it did not do. Perhaps there was no investigation under Article 70? Yes, there was. Judging from the interrogation of the witnesses, such an investigation was conducted. And, in this case, there is a document proving that the investigation did take place—an order terminating the investigation under Article 70. You cannot terminate something that had not been started. [*Lists the violated clauses of the Code of Criminal Procedure.*]

JUDGE: Defendant Bukovsky, this is of no interest to us; keep closer to the indictment. What relevance does everything you are saying have, essentially, to the resolution of your case?

BUKOVSKY: I have already said that you have no right to interrupt me. The significance is quite simple. Do you think it was easy for me, in the isolation cell, to realize that I was being accused, and the investigation conducted, under Article 70? Because this was not made known to me. It is precisely these unlawful actions of the KGB that the prosecution is trying to cover up by attempting, without proof, to support charges under Article 190 of the Criminal Code.

There have been breaches of the law in the conduct of the investigation, and it is my duty to speak out about them, so now I am speaking out.

We demonstrated in defense of legality. It is incomprehensible why the office whose responsibility it is to safeguard the rights of citizens sanctions such actions by the *druzhinniki* and the KGB.

Now I have to explain our slogans. The demonstration was conducted with a slogan demanding the freeing of Galanskov, Dobrovolsky, Lashkova, and Radzievsky. But they have not even been convicted yet.

What if it turns out that they are not guilty? In fact, Radzievsky has already been released from custody. Then where is the criminality of our demonstration?

Now, as to our second slogan. We did not come out against laws. We demanded the abrogation of the decree of September 16 and the revision of Article 70 of the Criminal Code. Was this really an illegal action on our part? We protested against an unconstitutional decree. Was this really an anti-Soviet demand? Not we alone find the decree unconstitutional. A group of representatives of the intelligentsia, among them Academician Leontovich, the writer Kaverin, and others, have presented a similar demand to the Presidium of the Supreme Soviet of the U.S.S.R.

Isn't the Constitution the basic law of our country? I shall read the full text of Article 125:

> In conformity with the interests of the working people, and in order to strengthen the socialist system, the citizens of the U.S.S.R. are guaranteed by law:
> a) freedom of speech;
> b) freedom of the press;
> c) freedom of assembly, including the holding of mass meetings;
> d) freedom of street processions and demonstrations.
> These civil rights are ensured by placing at the disposal of the working people and their organizations printing presses, stocks of paper, public buildings, and streets—

Yes, streets, citizen prosecutor!

> . . . communications facilities and other material requisites for the exercise of these rights.

Now, about Article 70. We demanded its revision because it is subject to too broad an interpretation. Here is the text:

> Agitation or propaganda carried on for the purpose of subverting or weakening Soviet authority, or of committing certain especially dangerous crimes against the state, or circulating, for the same purpose, slanderous fabrications which defame the Soviet state and social system, or circulating, preparing, or keeping, for the same purpose, literature of such content shall be punished by deprivation of freedom for a term of six months to seven years, with or without additional exile for a term of two to five years, or by exile for a term of two to five years.

Article 70 contains such heterogeneous things as agitation and propaganda aiming at the commission of particularly dangerous state crimes and, on the other hand, slanderous statements against the social system. The range of penalties is also too wide—from half a year to seven years. In the Scientific-Practical Commentary, this article is divided into fourteen points. It would seem that revision of the article ought to follow this guideline, making the penalties more specific, too.

This would lessen its arbitrary nature. True, Article 190 represents a certain step in this direction. One can see a certain tendency toward revision, but this is not enough to make it [Art. 70] completely compatible with Article 125 of the Constitution.

JUDGE: Defendant Bukovsky, we are lawyers here, and all those present in the courtroom have also been through grammar school. We realize that you have just now been exposed to problems of the law and have become interested in them. We applaud this interest, but it is unnecessary to discuss them at such length here. Understand: we must decide the question of your guilt or innocence, decide your fate. Possibly you will enter Moscow University as a student of law. There, at the seminars, you shall discuss these questions on a higher level.

BUKOVSKY: No, I won't enter. And I object to the prosecutor accusing us of legal illiteracy and a lack of seriousness. No, I do know the laws, and I speak of them seriously. If, however, what I am speaking about is so well known, it is even more incomprehensible why the prosecutor sees criticism of the law as a crime.

The preamble of Article 125 of the Constitution says:

> In conformity with the interests of the working people, and in order to strengthen the socialist system, the citizens of the U.S.S.R. are guaranteed by law . . .

It is completely clear that neither legally nor grammatically is it possible to interpret this preamble as meaning that the freedoms listed in this article, including the freedom of meetings and demonstrations, are permitted only on condition that they be exercised with the aims mentioned in this preamble.

Freedom of speech and of the press is, first of all, freedom to criticize. Nobody has ever forbidden praise of the government. If there are, in the Constitution, articles about freedom of speech and of the press, then have the patience to listen to criticism. In what kinds of countries is it forbidden to criticize the government and to protest against its actions? Perhaps in capitalist countries? No, we know that in bourgeois countries Communist parties exist whose purpose it is to undermine the capitalist system. In the U.S.A., the Communist Party was suppressed. However, the Supreme Court declared that the suppression was unconstitutional and restored the Communist Party to its full rights.

JUDGE: Bukovsky, this does not have any relevance to the accusations in your case. You must understand that the court is not competent to decide the questions you are talking about. We must not judge the laws; we must execute them.

BUKOVSKY: You are interrupting me again. You know it is hard for me to talk under any circumstances.

JUDGE: I declare a five-minute recess.

BUKOVSKY: I did not ask for one. I will soon end my final statement. You are destroying the continuity of my final statement.

(*The proceedings resume following the recess.*)

JUDGE: Defendant Bukovsky, continue your final statement, but I warn you that if you continue to criticize the laws and the activities of the KGB instead of giving an explanation about the case in hand, I must interrupt you.

BUKOVSKY: You must understand that our case is very complicated. We are accused of criticizing the laws. This gives me the right and the basis for raising these fundamental critical questions in my final statement. But there is also another aspect; the question of honesty and civic integrity. You are judges. You are supposed to embody these qualities. If you actually embody honesty and integrity, you will render the only possible verdict in this case—a verdict of "not guilty." I understand that this is very difficult:

PROSECUTOR (*interrupting*): I direct the attention of the court to the fact that the accused is abusing his right to make a final statement. He criticizes the law, discredits the activities of the organs of the KGB, and he is beginning to insult you—a new criminal act is being perpetrated here. As a representative of the prosecution, I must stop this, and I call upon you to require the defendant to talk only about the substance of the charges against him. Otherwise, one might listen endlessly, here, to speeches containing all kinds of criticism of the laws and of the government.

JUDGE: Defendant Bukovsky, you have heard the prosecutor's remarks. I will permit you to speak only on the substance of the indictment.

BUKOVSKY (*to the prosecutor*): You accuse us of trying, by our slogans, to discredit the KGB, but the KGB has so discredited itself that we have nothing to add.

(*To the court*) I shall speak about the charges. But, what the prosecutor would like to hear from me he will not hear. There is no criminal act in our case. I absolutely do not repent having organized this demonstration. I find that it accomplished what it had to accomplish, and, when I am free again, I shall again organize demonstrations—of course, in complete accordance with the laws as before. I have finished my statement.

NOTES

1. This article stipulates: "In the event that any person participating in the judicial examination objects to actions of the person presiding, such objections shall be entered in the record of the judicial session."—ED.

2. The word *besobraze* means outrage or disorder.—ED.

3. *Statement by P. M. Litvinov on the Trial of V. Bukovsky*

October 3, 1967

I regard it as my duty to bring the following to the knowledge of the public:

On September 26, 1967, I was summoned by the KGB (Committee of State Security) to appear before Gostev, a KGB official, at 2 Derzhinsky Square, Room 537. Another official of the KGB, who did not give his name, was present during our conversation.

After this talk was over, I wrote it down immediately and as fully as I could remember, because I am certain that it clearly revealed tendencies that should be made public and that cannot but alarm our progressive society and the world in general. The text of the conversation follows. I vouch for the accuracy of the substance of what was said between the KGB official and myself.

GOSTEV: Pavel Mikhailovich, we have knowledge that you and a group of other persons intend to reproduce and distribute the minutes of the recent criminal trial of Bukovsky and others. We warn you that if you do, you will be held criminally responsible.

I: Irrespective of my intentions, I cannot understand what the criminal responsibility for such action might be.

GOSTEV: The court will decide that. We only wish to warn you that if such a record should be disseminated in Moscow or other cities, or should appear abroad, you will be made responsible for it.

I: I know the laws well, and I cannot imagine what particular law would be violated by the compilation of such a document.

GOSTEV: There is such a law—Article 190-1. Take the Criminal Code and read it.

I: I know the article very well and can recite it from memory. It deals with slanderous fabrications which would discredit the Soviet social system and regime. What kind of slander could there be in recording the hearing of a case before a Soviet court?

GOSTEV: Well, your notes will be a biased distortion of the facts and a slander of the court's actions, as would be proved by the agency competent to handle such cases.

I: How can you possibly know this? And, in general, instead of conducting this senseless talk and starting a new case, you yourself should publish the record of this criminal trial and, in this way, kill the rumors circulating in Moscow. Yesterday I met an acquaintance, and she told me such a lot of nonsense about the trial that it was simply disgusting to listen to it.

GOSTEV: And why do we need to publish it? It is an ordinary criminal case of disturbance of the peace.

I: If so, it is all the more important to give information—to let all the people see it's really an ordinary case.

GOSTEV: *Vecherniaia Moskva* of September 4, 1967, gives all the information about the case. All that has to be known about the trial is reported there.

I. In the first place, too little information is given; a reader who had heard nothing previously about the case would simply not understand what it was all about. In the second place, it [the newspaper report] is false and slanderous. Rather, the editor of *Vecherniaia Moskva*, or the person who provided such information, should be charged with slander.

GOSTEV: Pavel Mikhailovich, this information is entirely correct. Remember that.

I: It says that Bukovsky pleaded guilty. Yet I, who was interested in this case, know perfectly well that he did not plead guilty.

GOSTEV: What does it matter whether he pleaded guilty or not? The court found him guilty: so he *is* guilty.

I: I am not talking now about the court's decision; nor did the newspaper have it in mind. Confession of guilt by a defendant represents a completely separate judicial concept. Furthermore, the newspaper states that Bukovsky in the past committed antisocial acts of hooliganism. One may consider his actions what one pleases, but they cannot be called acts of hooliganism.

GOSTEV: Hooliganism means disturbance of the peace.

I: Does that mean that any disturbance of the peace is hooliganism? For example, anybody who crosses the street in the wrong place is already a hooligan?

GOSTEV: Pavel Mikhailovich, you are not a child. You understand perfectly what we are talking about.

I: And, in general, it would be a good idea to tell more about Bukovsky: for example, how was he arrested while reciting poetry in Maiakovsky Square, was brought to the police station, and beaten up.

GOSTEV: That is not true. It could not be.

I: His mother said so.

GOSTEV: Who cares what she said?

I: She did not tell it to me—I do not know her—but to the court, and nobody interrupted her or accused her of slander.

GOSTEV: She should, rather, have told you how she was summoned and warned about the conduct of her son. We can summon your parents, too. And, in general, Pavel Mikhailovich, keep this in mind: *Vecherniaia Moskva* has printed all that the Soviet people should know about this case; this information is completely true; and we warn you that if either you or your friends, or anybody else, makes this record public, you specifically will be held responsible for it.

I: This is interesting. You are talking about responsibility before the law, and the law stipulates that the person who commits a certain action is responsible for it.

GOSTEV: You can avert it.

I: Yet you failed to explain to me what constitutes the danger and punishability of such an action.

GOSTEV: You understand very well that such a record can be used by our ideological enemies, especially on the eve of the fiftieth anniversary of Soviet power.

I: But I do not know of any law that would prohibit the dissemination of a nonsecret document only because it might be misused by somebody. Much critical material from Soviet papers could also be misused by someone.

GOSTEV: It should be clear to you what we are talking about. We are only warning you, and the court will prove the guilt.

I: I have no doubt that it will. The trial of Bukovsky makes that clear. And how about my friend Aleksandr Ginzburg? Is he imprisoned for the same kind of actions that you are warning me about?

GOSTEV: Well, you will learn what he did when he is put on trial. He will be acquitted if he is innocent. Could you possibly think that, in the fiftieth year of Soviet power, a Soviet court would make a wrong decision?

I: Then why was Bukovsky's trial closed to the public?

GOSTEV: It was not.

I: Yet it was impossible to get in.

GOSTEV: Those who had to get in got in. There were representatives of the public, and all the seats in the hall were taken. We did not intend to rent an auditorium for this case.

I: In other words, the public nature of legal proceedings was violated.

GOSTEV: Pavel Mikhailovich, we have no intention of arguing with you. We simply warn you. Just imagine if people should learn that the grandson of the great diplomat Litvinov is busy with such doings—it would be a blot on his memory.

I: Well, I do not think he would blame me. Can I go?

GOSTEV: Please. The best thing for you to do now would be to go home and destroy everything you have collected.

I know that a similar kind of conversation was conducted with Aleksandr Ginzburg two months before his arrest.

I protest against such actions by the State Security Agency, which are tantamount to undisguised blackmail.

I am asking you to publish this letter so that, in case of my arrest, the public will be informed about the circumstances which preceded it.

P. M. LITVINOV
Assistant to the Chair of Physics
Moscow Institute of Sensitive Chemical Technology
Moscow, 8 Aleksei Tolstoy St., Apt. 78

II.

The Ginzburg-Galanskov Trial

The documents in this section pertain to the trials of Yuri Galanskov, Aleksandr Ginzburg, Aleksei Dobrovolsky, and Vera Lashkova. Most of these documents are petitions, letters, and declarations protesting the arrests and the conduct of the trials, as well as certain inequities of the Soviet legal system in general. One of the most noteworthy in this category is Document 16, a letter from a collective-farm chairman in Latvia, addressed to Politburo member Mikhail Suslov. A dedicated Communist, Yakhimovich had once been described in Komsomolskaia pravda *(October 30, 1964) as "a man who worries more about the* kolkhoz *than about himself," and excerpts from his private diary were given wide prominence. (For his subsequent fate, see p. 359.)*

Also included in this section are open letters to the editors of various Soviet newspapers and to the Board of Directors of the Union of Journalists (Documents 15, 19, 20, 21, 22, and 23), denouncing the Soviet press for its meretricious reports on the judicial proceedings. "A Letter to an Old Friend" (Document 4) is from the White Book *compiled by Ginzburg on the Daniel-Siniavsky trial. In his final statement to the court (Document 10), Ginzburg refers to this essay. The remaining documents are Galanskov's final court statement and the defense summations presented by his lawyer, D. P. Kaminskaia, and Ginzburg's lawyer, B. A. Zolotukhin.*

4. From the White Book Compiled by A Ginzburg: "A Letter to an Old Friend" (Author Unknown)

. . . The Siniavsky trial was the Soviet regime's first open political trial in which, from beginning to end, from the preliminary investigation to the final plea, the accused admitted no guilt and accepted the sentence like men. The accused were both about forty—the optimal age for a political trial, the first such trial in over four decades. No wonder it attracted the attention of the whole world.

This was the first political trial since the time of the Right SR's, the legendary heroes of revolutionary Russia. Only, the SR's walked out of the courtroom without arousing the pity, contempt, fear, and incredulity of the world.

You and I have endlessly sickening memories of the *"mea culpas,"* "testimonies," and "confessions" of the heroes tried in the 1930's, of the secret trials that have been kept so hidden from our society. You know they were real, not science fiction. The government does not wish to reveal its "secret," which everyone knows, because the confessions belonged not only to those involved, but to the government itself. At the Twentieth and Twenty-second Party Congresses, confessions were in fact made—forced to be sure, but confessions nonetheless.

There were no notorious confessions in this trial. It was the first trial without that criminal "quality" so redolent of the Stalin era not just in the courts but in every institution, in every communal apartment.

If this trial had taken place twenty years ago, Siniavsky and Daniel would have been shot in some MGB basement or placed on the interrogative "conveyor belt," where the interrogators were rotated but the accused man remained standing for hours and days on end until his will was broken and his mind deranged. Or else serums would have been administered to suppress the will, another horrible practice of the trials in the 1930's. Or else there wouldn't have been an open trial at all; the accused would just have been shot in the corridor. . . . And the bouquet of charges would have been quite different: treason, destruction, terror, sabotage, according to Article 58 [of the former Criminal Code].

Why weren't such charges "woven" into this trial? Changes take place, time passes. It must be remembered that Siniavsky and Daniel wrote their first things in 1956, right after the Twentieth Party Congress. Siniavsky and Daniel believed in the truth of what had just been said. They believed in it and began to reinforce it [in their writings]; Siniavsky's and Daniel's stories couldn't be condemned by the Twentieth and Twenty-second Congresses even from the point of view of "socialist realism" (as Aragon and other Western Communists well understood).

It must be remembered that Siniavsky and Daniel were the first to take up the battle after almost fifty years of silence. Their example is a great one, their heroism indisputable.

Siniavsky and Daniel broke the sickening tradition of *"mea culpas"* and "confessions". . . . [They] were able to keep the discussion within the realm of science fiction and the grotesque; they denied all charges of anti-Soviet activities, past or present, demanding the respect due freedom of creativity and freedom of conscience. This was the great principle of the trial. Siniavsky and Daniel behaved courageously, firmly, but carefully, their every sentence deliberate, avoiding the net spread not so much by the prosecutor as by the presiding judge. . . .

In point of fact, why is it that Siniavsky and Daniel are anti-Soviet rather than the prosecutor who, when queried by Siniavsky, stated that he would not have published such stories [as theirs] in the homeland! Who offers the greater threat to Russia?

Siniavsky and Daniel denied the charges of anti-Soviet activities. And well they might. Such writings as theirs can only be beneficial. Just think, old friend! In the courage of Siniavsky and Daniel, in their nobility and their victory, there is a drop of our blood, our sufferings, our battle against humiliation and lies, against murderers and traitors of all sorts. What is slander? You and I remember the Stalin era—the concentration camps on an unprecedented, super-Hitlerian scale, Auschwitzes without ovens, where millions perished. We know the corruption, the bloody corruption of those in power who, having repented, to this day do not want to tell the truth, even about the Kirov case. For how long? Can there be a point where the truth about our past life becomes slander? I submit there cannot.

I submit that the concept of slander cannot be applied to Stalinist times. The human brain is incapable of comprehending the crimes that were committed.

Better to keep the trial within the limits of purely literary discussion, as Siniavsky suggested. Calmer to conduct a discussion about direct speech, the author's view, the grotesque, science fiction. Much calmer, for sure.

I, personally, am no advocate of the satiric genre, no advocate of the satiric trend in literature, but I acknowledge its equality, its permissibility, its feasibility. It seems to me that our experiences preclude our use of the grotesque genre, or of science fiction. But neither Siniavsky nor Daniel saw the rivers of blood you and I saw. They, of course, can make use of the grotesque and the fantastic.

Arzhak-Daniel's story "This Is Moscow Speaking," with its exceptionally successful Gogolesque subject, "Open-Murder Day," could not realistically be placed next to the stenographic reports of the Twenty-second Party Congress, with what was revealed there. For we have had not one "open-murder day" but twenty years of open murders.

No, better to keep within the limits of purely literary discussion. But the presiding judge, L. Smirnov, the most prominent judge in the Soviet Union (by this alone, one can estimate just how thoroughly on the defensive the authorities were at the start of the trial) preferred another course—to pronounce sentence for antirevolutionary agitation, "to go the limit" permitted by the relevant article of the Criminal Code. Siniavsky got seven years; Daniel, five.

Why was this trial honored with the presence of the Chairman of the Supreme Court? First of all, to simulate democracy. Secondly, Smirnov had to establish a method of approach to such cases for the future, to set a "standard" in order to avoid the mistakes made by Saveleva when she tried Brodsky in Leningrad.[1] If Saveleva had been on the Siniavsky-Daniel case, she would have bullied the accused and not allowed them to utter a word. . . .

The trial, which the press assured us was marked "by the full observance of all procedural norms," was, in fact, conducted in crudest violation of those norms. If, in order to justify the severity of the sentence, it was necessary for *Pravda* (February 22) to turn to Lenin's declarations at the start of the Revolution, then that in itself is a falsification. The entire world has changed since then, not just the dogmas on Soviet law intended for short-term application.

It was not only for the benefit of the West that Smirnov conducted the trial in an imitation of democracy. For all his many colleagues throughout the vast territory of the Soviet Union, the trial was an academic exercise, an educational seminar, a practical lesson to be used in testing young judicial aspirants. And the theme of the examination—how to imitate democracy. But the need—indeed the compulsion—to copy democracy also says a lot.

Siniavsky and Daniel were convicted because they were writers and for no other reason. For, a man who has looked at the Stalin era and told about it truthfully cannot be convicted of slander.

No less classical was the charge (harped on by Kedrina and quoted from her newspaper article during the trial) of Siniavsky's anti-Semitism. Anti-Semitism, no less! But that charge stank so horribly that Smirnov ordered it not to be included in the court records. Now there's a familiar motif. Just when Stalin's statement in the 1930's about anti-Semitism being the worst form of nationalism was being widely cited, Stalin's henchmen murdered Mikhoels.[2] Yet the consequence of this case was not only silent protest but open protest—an event unprecedented since 1927—the demonstrations of December 5, 1965, at the Pushkin monument in which both university students and teachers participated.

In short, the court could make no case for the guilt of Siniavsky and Daniel. The confession of the accused is too vital an element in Soviet justice. Without it, there are, somehow, no victory wreaths for the court members, the prosecutor, and the witnesses for the prosecution.

Siniavsky and Daniel, however, have etched their names in gold letters for their fight in the cause of freedom of conscience, freedom of creativity, and freedom of individuality. Their names are inscribed forever.

While we're on the subject of gold letters, the witness for the prosecution Vasilev emotionally recalled those seventy-three writers killed in the war, at the front, whose names are carved on the marble slab at the Central House of Writers. He heaped blame on Siniavsky and Daniel in the name of these writers.

If a witness for the defense had been allowed at the trial, he would have defended Siniavsky and Daniel in the name of the writers who were tortured, killed, or shot, who starved or froze to death in Stalin's concentration camps.

Pilniak,[3] Gumilev,[4] Mandelshtam,[5] Babel,[6] Voronsky,[7] Tabidze[8]—hundreds of names comprise this terrible martyrology. These dead men, these victims of an era, who would have brought glory to the literature of any country, raise their voices in defense of Siniavsky and Daniel.

At the Twenty-second Party Congress, it was promised that all the victims of Stalin's arbitrary rule would be posthumously rehabilitated and their names inscribed on an obelisk.[9] Where is that obelisk? Where is the marble slab in the Union of Writers on which the names of those who perished in Stalin's time were to have been engraved in gold letters? There are three or four times as many of these names as those on the marble slab mentioned by the witness for the prosecution.

CONCLUSION

The Siniavsky and Daniel case is the first open political trial in which those charged under Article 58 did not acknowledge their guilt.

Siniavsky and Daniel stood their ground; apparently pharmacology, that notorious aid in trial preparations of the 1930's, as well as the famous conveyor belt and the techniques for producing exhaustion that used to play such a role in judicial practice were not used in this case. Siniavsky and Daniel did not deny their authorship; they simply set aside and rejected the nonliterary charges.

Neither "truth serums" nor "conveyor belts" were employed in this case. And so it became apparent that there are people in the Soviet Union who can defend the truth of their position and accept an unjust sentence without flinching. It was writers who were being judged here, but Siniavsky and Daniel defended their literary credentials with honors.

The trial was important in one other detail: Siniavsky and Daniel made no effort to "embroil" or drag their friends into the whirlpool of events. The absence of inhumane techniques of psychological persuasion left them free to fight, and they were victorious.

A few more notes.

"The Eminent" (to use a title from classical literature) L. Smirnov courageously made his way through the literary debris. Here, he had occasion to supplement his education with a special terminology, to enrich himself with an understanding of direct speech, dialogue, the rules of the grotesque and of satire. It would seem that Smirnov might have understood that literature is not a simple matter, that even literary criticism is not a simple matter, and that the theory of romanticism significantly differs from judicial theory. Why is it that engineers are called in to plan how ditches should be dug, but, in literary matters, no special knowledge, no qualified expertise is required? Why can anyone at all pass judgment [on literature]—not only pass judgment but pronounce sentence in the most literal, physical sense—whereas, in ditchdigging, the amateur's opinion is not enough? Why? Smirnov needed literary experts and academician Vinogradov only to establish the identity of Siniavsky-Tertz and Daniel-Arzhak, to confirm officially that which neither of the accused had tried to conceal. And why the anonymity of the experts? The members of the court were known, the names of the witnesses for the prosecution were known, only the names of the experts were hidden from the public. Why this maidenly modesty, so glaringly inappropriate? Is it possible the experts were ashamed to be participating in this type of trial and thus reserved their right of secrecy—of keeping their contribution secret? In any case, here are the names of the experts: academician Vinogradov (chairman), Prokhorov, Dimshits, Kostomarov, and others. And [the experts on] death recommendations: S. Antonova, A. Barto, B. Suchkova, and academician Yudina.

Smirnov missed a golden opportunity to place all responsibility on the shoulders of the experts and to preserve his good name in the eyes of the International Association of Jurists, which is now cursing its vice-president from all sides for his arbitrary ruling. The court had only to put to the experts the following questions:

1. Can the genre of the grotesque contain slander of the state (citing the open-court trials)?

2. Can the genre of science fiction contain slander of the system (citing the open-court trials)?

Having received the answers to those questions, the court could have divested itself of moral responsibility, and academician Vinogradov and his associates would have had to cringe under the indignation of society in the event of a positive reply, or to reply in the negative and confirm the victory of Siniavsky and Daniel.

Smirnov didn't want either answer. Because attention to the literary aspect would have been a victory for Siniavsky, he did not put literary questions to the anonymous experts. Or perhaps it never occurred to the presiding judge that expertise could be used in that way.

Pravda writes in indignation that the Western press compares Siniavsky and Daniel with Dostoevsky and Gogol.[10] It was not the Western press but the Soviet critic Zoia Kedrina who, in commenting on Siniavsky's "Liubimov" and Daniel's "This Is Moscow Speaking" in an article published in *Literaturnaia gazeta* not long before the trial,[11] discussed at length the fact that, while their genres had much in common with the genres of Kafka, Dostoevsky, and Gogol, Siniavsky and Daniel did not quite reach that level. Such was the frank purport of her article. And it gives such a brilliant account of the dazzling "This Is Moscow Speaking" that the reader automatically thinks: If Daniel has not reached the level of Gogol, the gap is very, very small.

The flowering of the fantastic genre throughout the world draws attention to the work of Siniavsky and Daniel. But it seems that fantasy just won't do. What would have happened to Ray Bradbury if he had lived in the Soviet Union? How many years would he have received? Seven? Five? Exile or not?

Every writer wants to be published. Is it possible the court did not understand that the possibility of publication is as necessary to the writer as air?

How many have died unpublished? Where is Platonov? Where is Bulgakov? Bulgakov has had one-half of his works published, Platonov one-quarter. Yet they were the best writers in Russia. Usually it is enough to die to be published, but Mandelshtam was deprived even of that.

How can a writer be condemned for wanting to publish his works? And if a pseudonym is necessary, let there be pseudonyms—it's no disgrace. What other way is there?

No, Siniavsky and Daniel are not double-dealers but fighters for freedom of creativity, freedom of speech. To accuse them of double-dealing is itself the purest form, the worst form, of double-dealing. No one has the right to call someone sitting in jail a double-dealer.

In this trial, wholly predetermined as it was, there is one curious fact: Siniavsky and Daniel were charged under only one article of the Criminal Code, *i.e.*, "harboring, producing, and disseminating" [anti-Soviet propaganda], or what used to be called "counterrevolutionary agitation" under Article 58, paragraph 10. Siniavsky and Daniel were not charged under paragraph 11 (on "organization"), though one wonders what kept that flower from unfolding.

It was not just the committee of experts who attracted attention by their anonymity. The Secretariat of the Writers' Union of the U.S.S.R. signed its impertinent and offensive letter in *Literaturnaia gazeta* without listing the names of Secretariat members.[12] Why the camouflage? The tone of the letter was undignified and offensive. One would like to know who was personally responsible. In any event, I will name the staff of the Secretariat of the Writers' Union: Fedin, Tikhonov, Simonov, Voronkov, Smirnov, Sobolev, Mikhalkov, Surkov.

Pravda's editorial takes us back to the worst period of Stalinism. Consider the entire tone of the editorial, all those arguments quoting Lenin, the quotations worn out from constant use in the Stalin years on Kautsky, on capitalist democracy, on the democracy of a proletarian dictatorship—in short, all the sophistry we mastered so well over forty years. Practical examples of that sophistry are sufficiently vivid in our memories. . . .

The sentence in the Siniavsky-Daniel case plunges Soviet society once more into an atmosphere of terror and persecution.

The Soviet government has done little enough for the rapprochement of East and West. An action such as the Siniavsky-Daniel trial can only destroy what bond there is.

It seems to me we are sick with the same old disease Piotr Dolgorukov described so aptly over 100 years ago:

Many of our compatriots say: "There's no need to tell the truth about Russia to a foreigner; the sores of the fatherland should be hidden." These words, in our opinion, are completely opposed to logic, to personal dignity, to love of country, to true enlightment. Apart from the deep disgust that lies arouse in an honest and honorable man, he would need an inordinate amount of self-confidence to imagine he could fool everyone. People who want to hide and conceal their sores are like the critically ill who prefer to suffer and die rather than ask the help of a skilled doctor who could cure them and give them back their strength, refreshed and renewed. For Russia, this doctor is publicity.

NOTES

1. For a discussion of Yosif Brodsky and his poetry, see the essay by Sidney Monas, pp. 35-37.—ED.

2. Salomon Mikhailovich Mikhoels, talented actor-director of the Jewish State Theatre of the U.S.S.R. (abolished in 1949) and chairman of the wartime Jewish Anti-Fascist Committee, which raised large sums of money abroad to support the Soviet war effort. He was mysteriously murdered in January, 1948.—ED.

3. Boris Andreevich Pilniak (1894–19?) was the author of grim stories about the Civil War and the era of militant Communism. After his best novelette, *Mahogany*, appeared in Berlin in 1929 (it had been rejected for publication in the U.S.S.R.), Pilniak was removed as chairman of the All-Russian Writers' Union. He died in a concentration camp in the late 1930's or early 1940's.—ED.

4. Nikolai Stepanovich Gumilev (1886–1921), the first husband of Anna Akhmatova, was a founder of the prerevolutionary Acmeist (art-for-art's-sake) movement. He was executed in 1921 for allegedly participating in a conspiracy against the Soviet regime.—ED.

5. Osip Emilevich Mandelshtam (1892–1940) was a poet who, early in his career, was associated with the Acmeist group. Mandelshtam was sent to a concentration camp in the early 1930's, supposedly because he satirized Stalin in one of his epigrams. Some of his works were republished in the U.S.S.R. following Stalin's death.—ED.

6. Izaak Emannuilovich Babel (1894–1941) was the author of many stories, novels, and plays. In the 1930's, he was given the task of supervising collectivization in the Soviet south but recoiled at the widespread use of violence. He was removed from his post and, according to Ehrenburg, died in a concentration camp during World War II. He was rehabilitated in 1955.—ED.

7. Aleksandr Konstantinovich Voronsky (1884–1943), literary critic, editor, and writer, was a follower of Trotsky in the 1920's, expelled from the party and exiled, then released in the early 1930's. Arrested again during the "Great Purge," Voronsky is said to have died in prison.—ED.

8. Titsian Tabidze, Georgian poet and a friend of Pasternak, was liquidated in 1936 during Beria's purges of the Caucasus.—ED.

9. In his concluding speech at the Twenty-second Congress, Premier Khrushchev elaborated upon Stalin's crimes and proposed the erection of a monument in Moscow "to perpetuate the memory of comrades who fell victim to arbitrary rule" (*Pravda*, October 29, 1961).—ED.

10. *Pravda* editorial, "Socialist Democracy and the Struggle Against Ideological Subversion," February 22, 1966.—ED.

11. Zoia Kedrina, "The Heirs of Smerdiakov," *Literaturnaia gazeta*, January 22, 1966.—ED.

12. Open letter from the Secretariat of the Board of the U.S.S.R. Writers' Union, *Literaturnaia gazeta*, February 19, 1966.—ED.

5. On the Eve of the Trial: Petition of Thirty-one

To the Moscow Municipal Court
Copies to: Defense Counsel, B. A. Zolotukhin
        Chairman of the Council of Ministers of the U.S.S.R., A. N. Kosygin
        Secretary General of the CPSU Central Committee, L. I. Brezhnev

Chairman of the Presidium of the Supreme Soviet of the
U.S.S.R., N. V. Podgorny

According to rumors circulating around Moscow, the Moscow Municipal Court will hear the case of A. Ginzburg within the next few days.

Many circumstances connected with the trial of A. Ginzburg, who was arrested about a year ago, cannot fail to arouse the alarm of the public: the unprecedented duration of the twelve-month preliminary imprisonment before trial, the absence in our press of any word whatsoever about the reasons for A. Ginzburg's arrest and the prolonged investigation. Those of us who know A. Ginzburg personally do not doubt his integrity and decency. His basic interests lie in the field of culture; he has not been engaged in political activity as such. The collection of documents he compiled (which included articles from our press as well as official documents) concerning the Siniavsky-Daniel case, which so deeply disturbed our society, cannot constitute sufficient reason for his arrest and trial. This trial cannot sanitize the atmosphere of a society that not long ago witnessed mass rehabilitations of persons who had been sentenced on false charges.

The abnormal circumstances noted above compel us to ask the Moscow Municipal Court to take the case of A. Ginzburg under special consideration and to ensure the airing of public testimony, the unprejudiced selection of witnesses, and wide coverage of the trial in the press.

V. Aksionov, member of the Writers' Union
B. Akhmadulina, member of the Writers' Union
A. Babaev, member of the Writers' Union, candidate in Philological Sciences
B. Birger, artist, member of the Artists' Union
K. Bogatyrev, member of the Writers' Union
V. Veisberg, artist, member of the Artists' Union
I. M. Gelfand, corresponding member, Academy of Sciences, U.S.S.R.
Yu. Glazov, candidate in Philological Sciences
Ye. Golysheva, member of the Writers' Union
Ye. Grin, editor
A. Dobrovich, doctor
M. Zand, fellow of the Institute of the Peoples of Asia, Academy of Sciences, U.S.S.R.
V. Ivanov, Deputy Secretary of the Institute of Slavic Studies, Academy of Sciences, U.S.S.R.
M. Ivanov, member of the Artists' Union
F. A. Iskander, member of the Writers' Union
L. Keldysh, professor of Physical-Mathematical Sciences
E. Liakhovich, interpreter
P. Novikov, member of the Academy of Sciences, U.S.S.R.
N. Otten, member of the Writers' Union
A. M. Piatigorsky, candidate in Philological Sciences
I. Revzin, Doctor of Philological Sciences

Rozenfeld, professor of Biological Sciences
K. Rudnitsky, member of the Writers' Union
M. Segal, fellow of the Institute of Slavic Studies, Academy of Sciences, U.S.S.R.
Ye. Semeka, candidate in Historical Sciences
N. Stoliarova, member of the Literary Fund
T. Tsivian, candidate in Philological Sciences
I. R. Shafarevich, corresponding member, Academy of Sciences, U.S.S.R.
Yu. Edlis, member of the Writers' Union
A. Yaglom, professor of Physical-Mathematical Sciences

6. For an Open Trial: Protest of Twelve

To the Chairman of the Moscow Municipal Court
Copy to Comrade Mironov, Presiding Judge

We the undersigned, among many others, addressed a [previous] letter to you requesting that you assure us, friends of the accused Ginzburg-Galanskov-Dobrovolsky-Lashkova, the right to be present at their trial.

In spite of the announcement that the trial would be open, not a single signatory of this letter has been admitted. Numerous guards, stationed at all the approaches to the courtroom where the hearing is being conducted, let in only those who have passes. It is not known when, by what rules, and to whom these passes were issued.

The trial hearing on January 8, 1968, took place in a half-empty courtroom, while we stood outside in the cold all day, vainly hoping that perhaps you would deign to grant our request.

Proceeding from the above, we hereby register an emphatic public protest against the lawless manner in which a legally open judicial trial has been turned into a virtually closed one, and we again request that you permit all of the undersigned to enter the courtroom.

N. Gorbanevskaia	Yu. Levin
P. Litvinov	A. Shtelmakh
S. Genkin	K. Babitsky
O. Yukhnovets	V. Nikolsky
P. Yakir	P. Grigorenko
V. Telnikov	V. Timachev

[*Appended Comment*]

The collection of signatures to this protest in the vicinity of the courtroom on January 9, 1968, was interrupted by members of the KGB. Former Major-General Piotr Grigorenko was arrested at this time but was released a few hours later.

7. Open Letter by L. Bogoraz-Daniel and P. Litvinov

To World Public Opinion

The judicial trial of Galanskov, Ginzburg, Dobrovolsky, and Lashkova, which is taking place at present in the Moscow Municipal Court, is being carried out in violation of the most important principles of Soviet law. The judge and the prosecutor, with the participation of a special kind of audience, have turned the trial into a wild mockery of three of the accused—Galanskov, Ginzburg and Lashkova—and of the witnesses, an unthinkable happening in the twentieth century.

The case took on the character of the well-known "witch trials" on its second day, when Galanskov and Ginzburg—despite a year of preliminary incarceration and in spite of pressure from the court—refused to accept the groundless accusations made against them by Dobrovolsky, and sought to prove their own innocence. Evidence by witnesses in favor of Galanskov and Ginzburg infuriated the court even more.

The judge and the prosecutor throughout the trial have been helping Dobrovolsky to introduce false evidence against Galanskov and Ginzburg. The defense lawyers are constantly forbidden to ask questions, and the witnesses are not being allowed to give evidence that unmasks the provocative role of Dobrovolsky in this case.

Judge [Lev M.] Mironov has not once stopped the prosecutor, but he is allowing those who represent the defense to say only that which fits in with the case already prepared by the KGB investigation. Whenever any participant in the trial departs from the rehearsed spectacle, the judge cries, "Your question is out of order," "This has no relation to the case," "I will not allow you to speak." These exclamations have been directed at the accused (apart from Dobrovolsky), at their lawyers, and at the witnesses.

The witnesses leave the court after their examination, or, rather, they are pushed out of the court in a depressed state, almost in hysterics.

Witness Yelena Basilova was not allowed to make a statement to the court—she wanted to relate how the KGB had persecuted her mentally sick husband, whose evidence, given during the investigation when he was in a certifiable state, plays an important role in the prosecution case. Basilova was expelled from the courtroom while the judge shouted and the audience howled, drowning out her words.

P. Grigorenko submitted a request asking that he be examined as a witness, because he could explain the origin of the money found on Dobrovolsky. Galanskov gave him this money. Grigorenko's request was turned down on the pretext that he was allegedly mentally ill. This is not true.

Witness Aida Topeshkina was not allowed to make a statement to the court presenting facts to show the falsity of Dobrovolsky's evidence. Topeshkina, an expectant mother, was physically ejected from the courtroom while the audience howled at her.

The "commandant of the court," KGB Colonel Tsirkunenko, did not allow witness L. Kats back into the court after a recess, telling her, "If you had given other evidence, you could have stayed."

None of the witnesses have been allowed to stay in the court after giving evidence, although they are required to stay under Soviet law. Appeals by the witnesses on the basis of Article 283 of the Code of Criminal Procedure [the relevant article] went unheeded, and the judge said sharply to witness V. Vinogradova, "You can just leave the court under Article 283."

The courtroom is filled with specially selected people—officials of the KGB and volunteer militia—to give the appearance of an open, public trial. These people make noise, laugh, and insult the accused and the witnesses. Judge Mironov made no attempt to prevent these violations of order. Not one of the blatant offenders has been ejected from the hall.

In this tense atmosphere, there can be no pretense that the trial is objective, that there is any justice or legality about it. The sentence was decided from the very start.

We appeal to world public opinion and, in the first place, to Soviet public opinion. We appeal to everyone in whom conscience is alive and who has sufficient courage:

Demand public condemnation of the shameful trial and the punishment of those guilty of perpetrating it!

Demand the release of the accused from arrest!

Demand a new trial in conformity with all legal norms and in the presence of international observers!

Citizens of our country! This trial is a stain on the honor of our state and on the conscience of every one of us. You yourselves elected this court and these judges—demand that they be deprived of the posts that they have abused. Today it is not only the fate of the three accused that is at stake—their trial is no better than the celebrated trials of the 1930's, which involved us in so much shame and so much bloodshed that we still have not recovered from them.

We address this appeal to the Western progressive press and ask that it be published and broadcast by radio as soon as possible. We are not sending this request to Soviet newspapers, because that is futile.

LARISA BOGORAZ-DANIEL

Moscow, V-261
Leninskyi Prospekt 85, Apt. 3

PAVEL LITVINOV

Moscow, K-1
Aleksei Tolstoy St. 8, Apt. 78

8. Letter from Twenty-four Students to P. Litvinov

Moscow
January 13, 1968

Dear Pavel Mikhailovich:

Thank you and Larisa Daniel for your brave and honest letter. We are revolted to the depths of our souls by the trial, and we understand what general silence and apathy can lead to. We began to see things clearly two years ago. When Siniavsky and Daniel were convicted, we realized the crying injustice of our organs of power and the cruelty of individuals who mockingly trample upon the literary and human rights of people.

Our fathers and grandfathers were shot or died in camps; they knew all the horrors of Stalinist reaction. We can imagine how terrible it is to live surrounded by silence and fear. Therefore, the thinking generation of the 1960's calls upon all people of integrity to support these two courageous individuals by signing their names to our letter. He who keeps silent commits a crime against his conscience and against Russia. And Russia pays dearly for this with the blood of her most intelligent and talented people, from Osip Mandelshtam to Aleksandr Ginzburg. We are for the publication of Brodsky's verses, Romisov's and Zamiatin's stories, the poetry of the late Mandelshtam, and the prose of Pasternak. We are for the release of Siniavsky and Daniel; we favor a re-examination of the case of the four writers by an international tribunal in accordance with international law; we favor a severe admonition to the courts to restore the norms of socialist legality. We despise Dobrovolsky's vile treachery; he is nothing other than a Smerdiakov. We who are just emerging into life are already fed up with hypocrisy and deceit—we want truth and justice.

Only united can we succeed in accomplishing something; otherwise worse will follow: terror, reaction, innocent sacrifice. For we are responsible for all that happened in the world—after all, we are taught this by the best works of our literature. We cannot resign ourselves to the narrow-minded interpretations of Tolstoy, Chekhov, Kuprin, Blok or to the exclusion of Dostoevsky, Bunin, Tsvetaeva, Pasternak and others from the school curriculum. Our schools have produced reliable *okhranniks* [watchmen]—stupid crammers who study the history of the Party and the fundamentals of historical materialism. We cannot keep silent when demagogy, journalistic lies, and deceit are all around. We are only sorry for our parents. We request that this letter be circulated so that it may reach those who are our own age and think as we do, and so that the fate of these writers will be justly decided.

We hope that, despite everything, we are not alone and that we will hear the voices of upright people.

[*signed by twenty-four students*]

9. Appeal by Ye. Shiffers

Moscow
January 15, 1968

Colleague:

I hasten to write you this letter—an open letter to professional comrades—because something irreparable may happen. If we remain silent this time, it will not be possible for us to fall back on [the excuse of] ignorance or naivete, because I already know—having heard the BBC's radio broadcast of the letter-appeal of Larisa Daniel and Pavel Litvinov —about the illegality that is ruling your motherland and mine, the illegality of the trial of our fellow writers. This [appeal] was a cry of despair and of faith. Despair, because they [Daniel-Litvinov] handed their letter to foreign newspapers rather than trust in the integrity of our own. Faith, because they know that someone will hear and respond, and I thank them for still believing in you and me. So, our fellow citizens were convicted because that miserable fellow, Dobrovolsky, slandered himself and them, just as it used to happen to people in the years of Stalin's repressions.

Now, when you and I know these simple facts, we are faced by one question, and only one: Do we believe them?

I do not believe that the accused collaborated with the NTS;[1] [hence] their writings are not subject to the jurisdiction of a criminal court.

Perhaps you have real doubts. If so, come out with them and we will resolve them—we will demand an open re-examination of the case, with radio and television publicity in order to reach the maximum audience. This will resolve my own doubts; I must know—must know in order to live—whether my motherland is aware of this illegality, or whether she is again judging her children in ignorance, as in the not-too-distant past.

And if this is so, if the motherland knows and keeps silent, then I wish to ask that she also place me alongside those innocently convicted.

To me this action seems natural. Indeed I feel embarrassed to be signing such a letter for the first time.

YE. SHIFFERS
Director-producer

I am sending this letter to *Sovetskaia Kultura* and to personal friends.

NOTE

1. NTS stands for Narodno-Trudovoi Soiuz (People's and Workers' Alliance), a Russian *émigré* organization formed in the 1930's, with headquarters in Germany. It has since been frequently accused by the Soviet authorities of carrying on subversive activities against the Soviet Communist regime.—ED.

10. Final Trial Statement by A. I. Ginzburg

Moscow Municipal Court
January 12, 1968

I want to begin my final statement by saying I am grateful for the withdrawal of the charge of personal dishonesty against me—the charge that I, having written to Kosygin to express my view on the trial of Siniavsky and Daniel, did not send the letter to the proper address. This charge was insulting.

Next, in this trial much has been said about the NTS. No one, I think, disputes the opinion expressed by the state prosecutor concerning this anti-Soviet *émigré* organization. So I simply want to thank the state prosecutor for distinguishing us from those who killed, slaughtered, and exterminated Jews—for not making such charges against us.

And now I will pass on to the case. Earlier at this trial, on January 9, 1968, I attempted to explain the views and motives that induced me to compile the collection of materials on the case of Siniavsky and Daniel. Now I will not repeat all of that. I simply want to comment again briefly on the public reaction to the trial of Siniavsky and Daniel, on the atmosphere in which I compiled my collection, which is now pinpointed as the basis of the charges against me.

When, on the ninth of January, I tried to talk about this and compared worldwide reaction to the Siniavsky-Daniel trial with the reaction to the persecution of Greek democrats, laughter broke out in the hall—or, rather, a kind of snarling. Nevertheless, I will speak on the matter again. The prosecutor had dwelt at length on the fact that the NTS has not opposed the aggression in Vietnam. But what connection does this have with my collection of materials on the case of Siniavsky and Daniel? I can refer to the first ninety pages of the collection, which are here before us. Here, for example, is a protest signed—among others—by Norman [Mailer], who lies stricken with bayonet wounds received during the demonstration at the Pentagon against American aggression in Vietnam. In the same collection, there are protests signed by many other progressive figures of the world. The state prosecutor might be right about the attitude of the NTS toward the war in Vietnam. But this has no connection whatsoever with my collection . . . on the case of Siniavsky and Daniel, which I compiled in order to present an objective picture of the trial and world reaction to it and to ask for a review of the case.

I am accused of including in my collection materials considered by the court to be anti-Soviet. I am talking about the leaflet signed "Resistance" and about "A Letter to an Old Friend." Unfortunately, the counsel for the defense has made hardly any attempt to refute this point in the court's charge. I am forced to comment, because, if the court holds these documents to be criminal, then, in the future, no one can defend them, as happened in the case of Siniavsky's article "What Is Socialist Realism?"[1] Thus, as the compiler of the collection, I consider it my duty to talk about these two documents.

First, about the leaflet "Resistance." Its content is known to the court. The facts stated in it are true, as witnesses have confirmed—for example, Kushev. There has not been one single statement by a witness to the effect that these facts are inventions or slander. In the course of the court's examination, this leaflet has been quoted repeatedly, in particular the words: "The ferocity of the dogs only emphasizes the propensities of the trainers." The subject of the leaflet is not Soviet rule as a whole. It speaks merely of those members of KGB organs who dispersed the public meeting [in protest against the Siniavsky-Daniel trial] and then expelled forty students from the university for taking part in the meeting. These [KGB] actions seem to me to be illegal. If the court finds them lawful, then the court is answerable for its ruling. I have already explained that from my point of view the meeting in defense of Siniavsky and Daniel was completely legal; no one had a right to expel the participants from the university. Moreover, in all these actions the KGB members behaved in a rude, intolerable manner, thus placing a black stain on this honorable organization's reputation. In short, I consider that, while the leaflet may be harsh, it is directed not against Soviet rule but merely against the action of certain workers of the KGB. Besides, the leaflet contains no slander, no misrepresentation of facts; it merely reproaches those in power for a single, specific action. I ask the court to exclude this document from the anti-Soviet category.

Now about "A Letter to an Old Friend." I have already said that I don't know who the author is, but I think this person lived through the horrors of Stalin's concentration camps. He writes: "You and I—we knew Stalin's times." And the author has sharp words for that era. But this is an insufficient basis for calling the document anti-Soviet. In a speech marking the KGB's fiftieth anniversary, the KGB spokesman Andropov stated: "We must not forget that era when political adventurers assumed the leadership of our agencies." The author of "A Letter to an Old Friend" says the same thing.

Another quotation from this "Letter" has been cited: "Gorky advanced the cannibalistic slogan, 'If the enemy does not surrender, he has to be destroyed.'" In the first place, this applies to the era that I just talked about. In the second place, a critic of one writer, even a great one, is not a critic of the whole system of rule. A person who has lived through the horrors of that terrible time cannot help feeling disturbed when it suddenly seems to him that in contemporary life he sees relapses into the past, and, in this situation, it is wholly rightful for him to express his agitation in sharp terms. I maintain that "A Letter to an Old Friend" contains no slander against the Soviet system and no appeal for its overthrow, and I ask the court not to qualify this work as anti-Soviet.

Concerning the charge in the indictment that I passed on several newspaper clippings of anti-Soviet content to Gubanov, my lawyer has given a full and well-grounded argument, and I will not repeat it.

Concerning the charge that the collection I compiled on the case of Siniavsky and Daniel was handed over by Galanskov to the NTS with my knowledge, a quite convincing argument has again been made to prove that the accusation is not only unconfirmed but contradicts facts revealed in the course of the court examination.

That leaves the charge that I compiled a tendentious collection of materials on the case of Siniavsky and Daniel. I do not consider myself guilty. I acted as I did, because I was convinced I was right. My lawyer has pleaded for a just sentence for me. I know that you will convict me, because not one person charged under Article 70 has ever been acquitted. I will go off to the camp calmly to serve my time. You can put me in a prison, send me to a camp, but I am sure that no single honest person will condemn me. I ask the court only one thing—give me a sentence no shorter than Galanskov's. [*Laughter in the courtroom, and cries of* "Longer! Longer!"]

[*During Ginzburg's speech, Judge Mironov repeatedly interrupted him with reproofs.*]

NOTE

1. Siniavsky's critical essay on socialist realism, written under the pen name of Abram Tertz, was published in English translation by Pantheon Books, New York, in 1961, under the title *On Socialist Realism.*—ED.

11. *Final Trial Statement by Yuri Galanskov*

Moscow Municipal Court
January 12, 1968

I would like to begin my concluding words by stating that I do not acknowledge my guilt with regard to that part of the charges based on Article 88, Part I, of the R.S.F.S.R. Criminal Code.

There is a tape recording of my conversation with the investigating judge. In the course of this conversation, I corrected the investigator, who said that I had sold dollars. I told him then, and again assert today, that I did not want to sell dollars but to exchange them through official channels. Actually, in their testimony, both Yentin and Borisova stated that I personally had no need whatsoever to exchange dollars. It was Yentin himself who suggested that I should do this. Since I did not spend any of the money obtained as a result of the exchange, not even fifty kopeks for a meat pie, but gave everything to Dobrovolsky, I do not acknowledge my guilt under the provisions of Article 88.

Nor do I plead guilty to the charges based on Article 70 of the R.S.F.S.R. Criminal Code concerning connections with the anti-Soviet *émigré* organization NTS. Neither my testimony nor Dobrovolsky's, on which this charge is based, justifies the conclusion that I am guilty of any such offense. This is what I believe, and this is what I shall continue to believe.

The prosecution has provided here much valuable and previously unknown information about the NTS. I am aware that to the KGB authorities this information is of major interest. I, too, was interested in hearing it. In my opinion, however, the first part of the prosecutor's speech, which addressed itself to this problem, does not have any substantial bearing on the case and could not, I hope, substantially influence the court in its decision.

A charge has been made against me that, in terms of its sociopolitical implications, is frightening. However, I am not easily frightened.

Indeed, my name has long been known in the West. I am known as a poet and also because of my protest in front of the American Embassy on the occasion of the aggression committed by the U.S.A. in the Dominican Republic. First of all, however, I am not a braggart and have never sought notoriety; secondly, this fact, in itself, is in no way confirmation of a relation with any foreign anti-Soviet organization whatsoever.

I am not readily intimidated by the fact that the legal norms governing our country are now receiving more intensive attention. The Marxist potential of the Party is reasserting itself more strongly than ever before. The October Revolution, which, unlike any other revolution, has survived a period of dictatorship and has proved strong enough not to be vanquished by the dictatorship, has retained its revolutionary-proletarian nature.

Life and experience have taught me how to conserve my energies properly. I cannot, at this time, prove that I am innocent of all the charges against me, since most of them are absolutely baseless and unrelated to reality. I appeal to the court for caution in its judgments regarding Dobrovolsky, Lashkova, and myself. As to Ginzburg, his innocence is so obvious that there can be no doubt about the decision of the court in this connection.

In conclusion, I would like to mention the social problems dealt with in the journal *Phoenix*. Initially, *Phoenix* was conceived by me as a pacifistic periodical, and it was the Siniavsky-Daniel trial that played the key role in causing me to change its character.

The materials that I asked to be placed in evidence represent my point of view concerning the course of this trial. I requested that they be submitted to the CC of the CPSU and to the Ideological Commission. I believe that these organizations will be interested in these data and that they will have an effect on the future fate of Siniavsky and Daniel.

I believe that a review of this case will play a great role in confirming the immense moral potential of socialism.

12. Speech by Attorney D. P. Kaminskaia in Defense of Galanskov

Moscow Municipal Court
January 12, 1968

The indictment against Galanskov is based on two articles: Article 70 and Article 88, Part One, of the R.S.F.S.R. Criminal Code. I would like to begin with a discussion of those charges based on Article 70.

These charges can be divided into two basic parts:

1. Galanskov's participation in the compilation of a collection of material on the Siniavsky-Daniel case and Galanskov's compilation of the journal *Phoenix*.

2. Facts giving the prosecution grounds to charge Galanskov with maintaining contact with the anti-Soviet *émigré* organization, the NTS.

To begin with, I would like to analyze the facts and circumstances pertaining to the first part of the charges.

The prosecution claims that Galanskov, together with Ginzburg, tendentiously selected materials on the Siniavsky-Daniel trial and arranged for the duplication of the collection as well as its transmission abroad. First of all, I deem it my duty to point out that the prosecution has no proof whatsoever that Galanskov took part in the compilation of the collection of materials on the Siniavsky-Daniel case. During the preliminary and court investigations, Ginzburg asserted that he alone compiled this collection. Beginning with his initial interrogation on January 19, Galanskov has asserted the very same thing, never altering his testimony. Not one of the witnesses interrogated refuted this fact. Defendants Lashkova and Dobrovolsky consistently maintained that the collection was compiled solely by Ginzburg with no outside assistance at all. Therefore, I ask the court to drop this charge from the indictment against Galanskov.

The charge also states that Galanskov compiled *Phoenix* with Ginzburg's help and made four copies of it with Lashkova's help. In the opinion of the prosecution, this journal contains five "criminal" articles. In other words, the prosecution believes that Galanskov's compilation of this journal is itself criminal and that five of the many documents are criminal, namely:

·"An Open Letter to Sholokhov," written by Galanskov himself.

The article entitled "The Russian Path to Socialism," attributed to academician Varga.

An article by Siniavsky entitled "What Is Socialist Realism?"

An article entitled "A Description of Events at the Pochaevsky Monastery in Our Days."

An anonymous story entitled "The Revelations of Viktor Velsky."

Whether or not Ginzburg aided Galanskov is a question that will be dealt with by Ginzburg's defense counsel. The task of Galanskov's defense counsel, in this case, is limited to analysis of the five incriminating works.

The attorneys representing Lashkova and Dobrovolsky, as well as several witnesses at this trial, have already said enough about the article "A Description of Events at the Pochaevsky Monastery in Our Days." It was consequently established that the facts discussed in the article did indeed occur. Therefore this article in no way slanders Soviet reality. It is merely a description of events that actually took place. . . .

As for Siniavsky's "What Is Socialist Realism?," the sentence passed by the Supreme Court of the R.S.F.S.R. in the Siniavsky-Daniel case deprives me of the right to discuss this work or to challenge its classification as criminal.

"The Revelations of Viktor Velsky," as published in the journal *Phoenix*, is seen as most seriously incriminating Galanskov. I would like to analyze this piece in greater detail. In the indictment, "The Revelations of Viktor Velsky" is termed an "article," a serious error that, in turn, leads to an erroneous evaluation of the work. This is a work of art in which, as in any work of art, fictitious characters act in fictitious situations. It is always important in analyzing any work of art to determine whether or not the speeches of the characters express the basic idea and pathos of the work. Some statements by the characters in this story might, for example, be interpreted as anti-Soviet. Alongside them, however, one finds other statements expressing the exact opposite views.

The story consists of two parts. The first part reveals the attitude of the protagonist toward his act of falsely denouncing some of his comrades out of an unfounded fear. The second part of the story, which is essentially allegorical philosophy, is altogether different in structure. Here is what Velsky says about himself in the second part of the story: "It is silly and shameful to read what I have written, what a tempest in a teapot has been created, and how weak and pitiful this man is. . . ." And further: "This was a vicious denial, but an ideal that made life worth living was at stake. . . . I cannot reread these pages: I think only of putting an end to my life. However, I cannot even do that—I am a coward."

These excerpts I have quoted show that the second part of the novel describes Velsky's discrediting of himself.

Furthermore, let me especially point out to the court another theme in the story—the total contempt for *émigrés*. Incidentally, this was precisely the reason this novelette could not be and was not published in any of the *émigré* publications. The character achieves his dream of finding himself in the "free world" of the West, sees its mercenary nature, and comes to understand how illusory is this freedom that he strove so hard to attain. "I [realized] the mechanization of the great political game. I had to be a paid traitor." And here is the outcome of Velsky's life: "I am finished, finished, finished. This is not a portrait or a prototype—this is simply how my life turned out. . . ."

"The Revelations of Viktor Velsky" is a complex and unusual work. One may dispute its artistic merits, but we are not engaged in a literary debate. The content and meaning of this work are as follows: an embittered, petty man committed treason, but even such a man was unable to live in exile. He preferred insanity to the treasonable well-being of Western *émigrés*. It is no accident that this work found neither an editor nor a publisher in the West. I ask the court to exclude it from the list of works deemed criminal.

A great deal has already been said in this trial about "An Open Letter to Sholokhov,"[1] which was written by Galanskov himself. It is undoubtedly possible to term this letter sharp, coarse, and erroneous. However, we must not forget that the idea of writing the letter came to Galanskov when he was in a mental hospital. This has already been established in the course of the trial investigation. This explains the exceptionally emotional quality of the letter. The letter is an answer to Sholokhov's address to the Twenty-third Congress of the CPSU. In Galanskov's opinion, the content and form of Sholokhov's address demanded a reply. I would like to remind you that Galanskov's letter was not the sole response to Sholokhov's address. The documents contain another letter addressed to Sholokhov, which was considerably more restrained and tactful. However, in essence, it offers the same type of criticism of the speech. The purpose of this trial is not, of course, to decide whether or not Sholokhov was correct in his statements. We know, however, that Galanskov considered the address inhumanitarian, unfair, and insulting. We must also remember that this letter was addressed to an individual as criticism of a single individual and is not in any way a criticism of the Soviet system as a whole. Had this "Open Letter" been limited even to the sharpest possible criticism of Sholokhov, had it not contained the general statements already quoted here, which, I cannot deny, are criminal in nature, then I would have asked the court to exclude this document from the indictment, too. Nonetheless, when Galanskov wrote this letter, he did not do so with the purpose of overthrowing or subverting the Soviet system.

Thus, I admit as criminal only two of the entire group of documents published in *Phoenix*: Siniavsky's article "What Is Socialist Realism?"—on the basis of the sentence passed by the Supreme Court of the R.S.F.S.R.—and the "Open Letter to Sholokhov," in view of the considerations cited above. However, it is altogether inadmissible to indict Galanskov under Article 70 of the R.S.F.S.R. Criminal Code on the ground that these works are anti-Soviet. To do so, the anti-Soviet intentions of the author must be proved. What did Galanskov himself say in his editorial in the journal *Phoenix* about his purpose in including Siniavsky's article in his collection? "I am including this article because of its merits as literary criticism."

The lack of any direct intent to weaken or overthrow the Soviet system precludes the possibility of classifying these actions by Galanskov under the terms of Article 70 of the R.S.F.S.R. Criminal Code, even though the inclusion of articles containing certain slanderous statements in his collection provides grounds for indictment under Article 198, paragraph 1, of the R.S.F.S.R. Criminal Code. . . .

Galanskov is also charged with having given Dobrovolsky his "Open Letter to Sholokhov," allegedly for the purpose of having copies made. I would like to call to the attention of the court the fact that, in his testimony throughout the entire investigation, Galanskov has never varied in his statements on this point. From the beginning to the end of the investigation, Galanskov has admitted that he wrote the "Open Letter" and was the editor-compiler of the journal *Phoenix*, but he has consistently denied that he gave Dobrovolsky the "Open Letter" for duplication. Galanskov has asserted that Dobrovolsky's testimony to this effect is false. Let's try to get to the bottom of this part of Dobrovolsky's testimony.

However willingly Dobrovolsky has discussed his own and, most important, others' crimes in the course of the investigation and trial, we must not forget that his testimony, like any other, must be corroborated, especially since he speaks as a defendant vitally interested in the outcome of the trial. Thus, in view of the unlimited faith that the prosecution has placed in Dobrovolsky's testimony, [we must ask that] it be checked particularly thoroughly. Frankly, I myself do not trust it. It has frequently been amended [in the course of the investigation]. He lied in his most personal letters, which were seized at the Serbsky Institute and are now offered as evidence in this trial; he lied when he wrote in his own words that he was left "alone with his faith and with God." He lied during the investigation and during face-to-face confrontations. Included in the record of the case is Dobrovolsky's first testimony given on the day of his arrest, January 19, 1967, and Galanskov's first testimony given after his arrest on the same day. Galanskov said: "I compiled *Phoenix* and I am ready to assume full responsibility for this act." What did Dobrovolsky say? "I gave Radzievsky nothing, let him answer for himself." Then, backed into a corner in a personal confrontation with Radzievsky, he altered his testimony. He said: "The 'Open Letter to Sholokhov' was given to Radzievsky not by myself but by the author, Galanskov." Dobrovolsky then described the alleged meeting between Radzievsky and Galanskov at the Lermontov monument in picturesque detail.

In both his initial and subsequent testimony, Dobrovolsky lied. He was governed by a single desire—to avoid responsibility, to transfer his guilt to someone else. This episode may perhaps be only a minor part of the charges against Galanskov, but it is extremely important for the light it sheds upon Dobrovolsky's personality.

But let us go further. In his letters to the investigating judge, Dobrovolsky declared that he had nothing to do with the case and offered to submit proof. Here, for example, is what he wrote on March 13, 1967, to the investigator, Major [Yeliseev]: "I have tried to convince you of my innocence and have suggested that you check the fingerprints on the copy of the 'Open Letter' given to Radzievsky. You refused. You are keeping me here solely on the basis of Radzievsky's testimony. It was Galanskov who gave him the letter. Radzievsky has accused me, because he is aware that I am a schizophrenic and believes that nothing will be done to me." But Radzievsky had not accused him of anything. He had stated nothing but the truth, which was subsequently confirmed, and which Dobrovolsky himself was forced to acknowledge in the end.

In the letter to his relatives that was intercepted during the court-ordered psychiatric examination, he wrote of his despair, horror, and confusion and claimed he was being detained for no reason, that he had done nothing. As was made clear, Radzievsky had never met Galanskov. There is no testimony at all confirming Dobrovolsky's assertion that it was not himself but Galanskov who gave Radzievsky the "Open Letter" for duplication. Why did Dobrovolsky give this document to Radzievsky? To have copies made? I cannot exclude the possibility that he wished to sell it eventually. It is known that Dobrovolsky sold a Solzhenitsyn story to his acquaintance [Galanskov] for five rubles. There is also another possibility. It is clear from the testimony of witnesses that Dobrovolsky wanted to put together his own anti-Stalinist collection. It is not impossible, then, that the document was procured to be used in this collection.

Thus, Dobrovolsky's testimony, the testimony of a man with a vital personal interest in the outcome of the case, has found no support whatsoever either during the investigation or in court. And, for this reason, the story of the delivery of the "Open Letter" to Radzievsky for duplication should be dropped from the list of charges against Galanskov. The same applies to the charge that Galanskov gave Radzievsky the article "The Russian Path to Socialism" for the same purpose. Not even the public prosecutor mentioned this in his statement.

I will move on to the main point in the indictment against Galanskov —the ties with the anti-Soviet *émigré* organization NTS. Indeed, where this part of the indictment is concerned, Galanskov's situation and his defense become extremely complex. The complexity is all the greater, because, at the preliminary investigation, Galanskov gave conflicting testimony on this subject. However, despite this, I believe that the accusation is not backed by adequate evidence to justify charging Galanskov with criminal connections with the anti-Soviet *émigré* organization NTS.

What evidence does the prosecution have?

First, an abundance of objective evidence: a hectograph, a coding device, money, and literature published by the NTS. This evidence was found during the preliminary investigation. The prosecution has other evidence, too: Dobrovolsky's testimony at the preliminary investigation and in court and Galanskov's testimony in the part of the preliminary investigation to which I referred before.

The prosecution has no other proof.

Let me begin with an analysis of the objective evidence—the key element in the charge. It has been revealed to the court that all of this evidence—the hectograph, the money, the coding device, and the anti-Soviet literature published by the NTS—was found in Dobrovolsky's possession. The court also knows that Dobrovolsky's testimony about his and Galanskov's relations with the NTS was given after these were found in Dobrovolsky's possession. Consequently, this evidence in itself does not incriminate Galanskov; quite the opposite. It could be used as evidence against Dobrovolsky. At the preliminary investigation, Dobrovolsky gave testimony that was the only evidence of Galanskov's guilt. I submit that, if Galanskov had not partially confirmed Dobrovolsky's testimony at the preliminary investigation, the court would have had no grounds whatsoever for accusing him of connections with the NTS.

Let us now deal with Galanskov's testimony.

In evaluating the testimony of a man accusing someone else, ascertaining the reasons for the charge is often quite easy. But understanding the reason for [false] accusation itself is always rather difficult. In legal practice we quite frequently come across this phenomenon. I do not feel it necessary to try to convince the court that it is very risky to place complete trust in such testimony. This danger has been repeatedly emphasized in instructions from higher courts stressing that the confession of the accused does not represent adequate proof of his guilt. The fact that such instructions are issued by our leading authorities again and again is proof that this problem is quite common.

What are my reasons for asserting that the testimony initially given at the investigation but repudiated by Galanskov at the end of the preliminary investigation—during the signing of the 201 items—is, as he now claims, untrue?

How does Galanskov himself explain his own behavior?

First, out of desire to help Dobrovolsky. When he was under court-ordered psychiatric observation at the Serbsky Institute, Galanskov received a note from Dobrovolsky, now on file with the other documents in this case, that read: "Brother, for God's sake, I beg you, please assume the burden of my guilt. You know I cannot go to jail now." Galanskov, as we now know, received several such notes and did indeed take the blame for Dobrovolsky's guilt.

Second, Galanskov has already described here how depressed he was after spending such a long time in prison. "I yielded to Dobrovolsky's requests after deciding that, in any case, I would be accused in connection with *Phoenix*, so I took the blame for everything myself," Galanskov said.

I am quite well aware that some may find this explanation convincing and others may not. I beg the court, however, not to forget that Galanskov is a very sick man. He suffers from a stomach ulcer which causes him great pain. The establishment of this fact by a medical commission is among the reports in the file of the case. His illness had greatly lowered his resistance and destroyed his will. Combined with the difficult circumstances of imprisonment, this surely could not have failed to have its effect. The psychiatric examination has established that Galanskov is of sound mind. Yet it is known, and certificates to this effect are included in the file, that over a period of many years he displayed serious deviations from normal behavior and was diagnosed as suffering from "schizophrenia" in the Solovev and Katsenko hospitals. Even at the Serbsky Institute, the physicians had to postpone his psychiatric examination, since, for a long time, they had difficulty in diagnosing Galanskov's mental state. Therefore, in giving this testimony, Galanskov may have wanted simply to hasten the date of the trial in order to bring an end to his physical agony. However, in case the court considers all of this unconvincing and concludes that Galanskov's testimony—which I have termed self-accusation—is the truth, I would like to discuss the case against Galanskov as seen by the prosecution.

In attesting to Galanskov's guilt, the investigation relied entirely upon Dobrovolsky's testimony. This testimony is quite extensive. Galanskov is charged with having met with the foreigner Genrikh—who, according to the investigation, is an emissary of the NTS—to whom he gave the *White Book* compiled by Ginzburg and from whom he received literature, a hectograph, money, and coding equipment. I have already mentioned that Galanskov admitted this in one of his statements. You know that Genrikh has not been located, and there is, therefore, no proof whatsoever of his affiliation with the NTS. It is known, too, that Galanskov himself does not deny meeting him. He confirms that he did meet a foreigner named Genrikh at the Kropotkinskaia subway station.

The discrepancy between the testimonies of Galanskov and Dobrovolsky is this: Dobrovolsky states that Genrikh went to meet Galanskov, while he himself did not speak to the foreigner at all; whereas Galanskov claims the opposite. Dobrovolsky presumes that the *White Book* was given to the foreigner at that meeting. He "presumes" it, precisely because only Galanskov could have told him what was or was not given to the foreigner that day; he maintains that he personally saw nothing. That is what he said in one of his statements: "I confirm, once again, that I did not witness the actual delivery, that I only presumed it [took place] because Galanskov told me about it." Dobrovolsky stated this during his confrontation with Galanskov. During that same confrontation he also said: "I do not know who delivered the *White Book*. From Galanskov's words, I understood that it either had been delivered or was to be delivered shortly." Then he went on: "I cannot say whether the *White Book* was delivered at the Kropotkinskaia subway station. That is where the meeting with the foreigner took place, but no material changed hands there." As you can see, the testimony is extremely vague

and contradictory. Galanskov himself denies that he gave the collection
of documents on the Siniavsky-Daniel case compiled by Ginsburg to anyone at any time. The prosecution has no other evidence that Galanskov
sent the *White Book* abroad.

Dobrovolsky denies that the foreigner Genrikh came to meet *him*.
However, certain aspects of the circumstances of the encounter justify
my claim that this foreigner went there to meet, not Galanskov, but
Dobrovolsky himself. Check any part of the testimony given by Dobrovolsky: he steadfastly insists that this meeting took place in October,
1966. He states, moreover, that it was on the same day as the party given
by Potashova. The investigation established the exact date of this party
as October 22. Dobrovolsky's testimony has thus been confirmed. Yet,
on the basis of Lashkova's and Ginzburg's testimony, it was definitely
established during the investigation that Lashkova did not finish the
typing of this collection before November 10, 1966. Thus, at the time
when the foreigner Genrikh came to Moscow, the collection was not
even completed. Therefore, Galanskov could not possibly have given the
Ginzburg collection of documents on the Siniavsky-Daniel case to the
foreigner Genrikh in October, 1966.

The circumstances of this meeting involve another interesting detail.
While relating his talk with Genrikh during a visit to some church,
Dobrovolsky stated: "He told me that one of my articles had been published in some journal or other. I do not remember, however, who took
this article out of the country for me. Genrikh also told me that on his
next trip he would bring me my fee." When Genrikh asked Dobrovolsky
in what currency he wanted his fee, Dobrovolsky answered: "In rubles."
I urge the court to pay careful attention to this extraordinarily important
point. It seems strange to me that Dobrovolsky does not remember precisely what article was involved if this was the only one he had sent
abroad. It is likewise strange that Dobrovolsky does not remember who
took the article out of the country, since he states that Genrikh was the
only foreigner he had encountered. It is strange that Genrikh, whom
Dobrovolsky had met by pure accident, would specifically offer him
money and would discuss his article with him. Isn't this too much to
constitute a coincidence?

Dobrovolsky maintains that there was another encounter with a foreigner named Nadia, who has been described by the investigating authorities as an emissary of the NTS. Galanskov admits that he met the foreigner Nadia, and Dobrovolsky claims that it was at this very same
meeting that *Phoenix* was delivered. Galanskov denies this. Dobrovolsky
also says that Nadia came specifically to see Galanskov. Galanskov, on
the other hand, insists that she came to see Dobrovolsky.

I realize that the court has unlimited faith in Dobrovolsky's testimony,
but I would like to remind the court that another man's fate should not
be decided solely on the basis of special sympathy for Dobrovolsky, who,
I repeat, has a vital interest in the outcome of this case. Consequently,
in choosing between the testimony of these two men, we must be im-

partial and try to find serious evidence to justify our choice. No witness has corroborated the testimony concerning the meeting with or the delivery of *Phoenix* to the foreigner Nadia. For this reason, I will return to Dobrovolsky's testimony.

In February, 1967, Dobrovolsky wrote a note to the investigator, Major Yeliseev of the KGB. In the note he wrote: "After thinking about our talk, I am ready to offer the investigating authorities an opportunity [to seize] the remaining copy of *Phoenix*. This must be done as soon as possible, because it may be sent abroad. The resolution of this problem must not be put off." In March of that same year, Dobrovolsky wrote to Yeliseev again: "At the beginning of January, Galanskov completed *Phoenix* and told me someone would be coming from abroad to pick it up." Subsequently, Dobrovolsky claimed that at the time Galanskov was arrested, *Phoenix* had not as yet been sent abroad. Dobrovolsky also maintained that, if released, he could not only find *Phoenix* but even prevent its delivery to the Grani Publishing House. It is strange that the investigators showed no interest in this and that Dobrovolsky was not asked a single question about the matter. However, soon after this, Dobrovolsky testified that he learned from Galanskov that *Phoenix* had been sent abroad. But such testimony alone is entirely inadequate when, in addition, it is full of contradictions and not corroborated by a single witness. I submit that this testimony is contradictory and, since it is not supported by any other testimony, that it cannot be used in this case as the basis of the charge that Galanskov transmitted the journal *Phoenix* to the NTS' Grani Publishing House.

Dobrovolsky holds that everything found during the search of his apartment (the hectograph, money, etc.) was given to him by Galanskov. At this point we might repeat that Dobrovolsky has a profound interest in the resolution of this question, especially since all these things were found on his own premises. The prosecution confirmed the correctness of Dobrovolsky's testimony on this matter through the interrogation of Brocks-Sokolov, who was arrested in Leningrad at the end of 1967 as an NTS courier. This interrogation not only does not convince me, it also reveals the total groundlessness of the charges against Galanskov. Brocks-Sokolov, the NTS courier, reached the U.S.S.R., according to Dobrovolsky, after Galanskov had already given him the hectograph, money, etc., and after Galanskov and Dobrovolsky had been arrested. As we know, when Brocks-Sokolov was arrested, a questionnaire to be used to obtain information on certain Soviet citizens—the writer [V.] Aksionov and others, even Galanskov—was found in his possession. His testimony makes the charges against Galanskov illogical and absurd, since it is quite clear to everyone that one would first find out about a man's convictions and then give him a hectograph and money, and not vice versa. I contend that these charges against Galanskov are obviously completely contradictory and illogical. . . .

Therefore, in summary, we can say that none of the charges against Galanskov, under the provisions of Article 70 of the R.S.F.S.R. Criminal

Code, have been proved. Of all that Galanskov has been charged with, I admit to only two items of a criminal nature: Galanskov's inclusion in *Phoenix* of his own "Open Letter to Sholokhov" and Siniavsky's article "What Is Socialist Realism?." In view of the lack of any anti-Soviet intent on his part, I appeal to the court to judge Galanskov's actions under the terms of Article 190, paragraph 1, of the R.S.F.S.R. Criminal Code.

In conclusion, let me refer once more to the charges against Galanskov under the provisions of Article 88, Part 1, of the R.S.F.S.R. Criminal Code.

First of all, I ask the court to take into consideration the fact that there has been no evidence or witness produced to confirm that these dollars belonged to Galanskov. All we know is that he gave them to Yentin to be exchanged. However, criminal liability exists even if an individual acts as an intermediary without pay. There certainly was no self-interest involved in this exchange, as witnesses Yentin and Borisova have confirmed. This was an isolated, incidental episode in Galanskov's life, not typical of his personal traits or his occupation.

Galanskov claims, furthermore, that from what Yentin told him, he believed that the exchange of currency would be handled officially, by an individual entitled to do so. The court must consider this testimony as it must all the rest, and, on the basis of its evaluation, determine Galanskov's liability under the provisions of Article 88.

Finally, a few words about the audience at this trial; I fail to understand the reason for the laughter in this courtroom when the fact that Galanskov has committed good, selfless deeds was mentioned. I do not understand why you have laughed at the statement that he is a kind man; that he visited an elderly woman, scrubbed her floor, and brought her medicine; and that he helped an acquaintance educate her children. Galanskov is extraordinary, a fine person. He wanted to fight what he believed to be unfair. Alone, he went to the American Embassy to demonstrate his protest against the aggression in the Dominican Republic. He was incapable of remaining passive.

A feeling of personal responsibility and high civic duty is basic to Galanskov. He has never sought wealth, a career, or glory. He simply wanted to see the triumph of justice.

I ask the court to remember that these young men are our children— not only because of their youth but also because they were raised in our midst. They are not indifferent to their surroundings, and, therefore, we cannot be indifferent to them. To a large extent, we bear responsibility for their errors and delusions; we have no right simply to abandon them to their fate.

NOTE

1. Document 62.—ED.

13. Speech by Attorney B. A. Zolotukhin in Defense of Ginzburg

Moscow Municipal Court
January 12, 1968

I would like to discuss another circumstance which imparts a complex moral aspect to this trial. In his indictment, the public prosecutor stated repeatedly that Ginzburg holds anti-Soviet convictions. As we know, convictions *per se* are not grounds for punishment. Furthermore, I do not believe that there is any proof that Ginzburg has ever held anti-Soviet views, either during the period of the acts for which he is being tried or earlier.

The indictment refers to testimony given by Ginzburg in 1960, when he was eighteen, in connection with the investigation of the periodical *Sintaksis*, which he edited. At that time, as a young man, he found himself in very difficult circumstances, and during the investigation he expressed certain views that he subsequently rejected and that he regarded as erroneous and incorrect long before this case arose. The procurator refused to accept Ginzburg's explanation of this matter, in which Ginzburg stated that this testimony was given after eight months of solitary confinement, after five days without food, and at a point of acute physical and moral depression. Testimony given eight years earlier, under such difficult conditions, cannot be considered serious judicial evidence. This is not proof that Ginzburg held anti-Soviet views at the time of the compilation of the material on the Siniavsky-Daniel case. Not a single one of the innumerable witnesses was able to produce evidence to support this charge either during the preliminary investigation or during the trial.

What were the motives that led Ginzburg to compile the collection of material on the Siniavsky-Daniel case?

The Siniavsky-Daniel case was the first open trial in which two writers were prosecuted because of the content of their works. There had been famous cases in the past in which writers were subjected to harsh criticism and labled anti-Soviet in connection with the content of their works. Such was the case with *The Days of the Turbines*, by [M.] Bulgakov, and *Mahogany*, by [B.] Pilniak. We remember well the affair of Boris Pasternak's novel *Doctor Zhivago*. However, not one of these writers was ever charged with a criminal offense.

The Siniavsky-Daniel trial was unusual, and that was the reason it evoked a great deal of interest on the part of Soviet and world public opinion. You recall the attention it received in our press, which devoted long articles to the case. It is entirely understandable that under such circumstances Ginzburg wanted to read the works that were the subject of the trial. He wanted to know precisely what sort of work constituted grounds for charging a writer with a criminal offense. He read those works, and, not finding them to be of a criminal nature, he then wrote a letter to Kosygin in which he explained his point of view on the matter. The letter was written before sentence was passed on Siniavsky and Daniel—the very sentence that Ginzburg had anticipated. In February, the sentence was pronounced. Even when it is a question of a simple criminal trial, every individual has the right to interpret the sentence in his own way. And, when it is a matter of a sentence that raises serious questions, I believe that even greater differences of opinion may arise. Ginzburg was among those who considered this sentence erroneous.

Here, at this trial, with no reference to Ginzburg, there has been a great deal said about the anti-Soviet *émigré* organization NTS. The dark shadow of the NTS has hovered over this entire trial. It is precisely for this reason that I deem it my duty to point out that disagreement with the decision of the court in the Siniavsky-Daniel case has been voiced by individuals whose irreproachable ideology could not be questioned by anyone. I wish to remind you of the letter in defense of Siniavsky and Daniel signed by sixty-two writers, including Chukovsky, Ehrenburg, Kaverin, and others. The authors of this letter indicated that they did not consider Siniavsky's and Daniel's activities anti-Soviet. I am saying this in order to emphasize that Ginzburg's reaction was not exceptional.

Nor did progressive public opinion in the West remain indifferent to the trial. What, then, was the reaction of those whom we justifiably consider to be the most sincere friends of our country? The collection of documents on the Siniavsky-Daniel case includes a letter from Aragon in which he voices an unfavorable opinion on the trial [defense counsel quotes the letter]. The collection includes a declaration by the Secretary General of the British Communist Party, John Gollan, in which he, too, expresses his disapproval of the trial.

Ginzburg considered the sentence unjust. In this connection, I would like to pose one general question. How should a citizen who holds such an opinion act? He might regard a matter of this sort with total indifference, or, on the other hand, he might be provoked into civic reaction. A citizen may look on indifferently as an innocent person is led off under guard, or he may come out in defense of that person. I do not know which type of behavior the court would consider preferable. I think, however, that the behavior of the person who is not indifferent is more worthy of a citizen. This is a general question that is applicable to both minor and major protests, most particularly when a person is convinced of the justice of his own opinion. I hope that even the prosecution does not question this.

Ginzburg did everything possible to help Siniavsky and Daniel. Here in court, it was justly pointed out to Ginzburg that, in this case, he should have appealed to the Supreme Court. Ginzburg failed to do so. Why? Because many appeals addressed to the Supreme Court have gone unanswered. Ginzburg assumed that, if he were able to collect all the documents on the Siniavsky-Daniel case and submit them to the higher courts, this would be the single most effective way of helping Siniavsky and Daniel. Ginzburg set to work, and, by the beginning of November, 1966, he had completed the collection.

At this point, I deem it necessary to raise the question of whether this collection is criminal and anti-Soviet in nature. I find the answer to this question in the formulation of the indictment, which terms the collection not anti-Soviet but tendentious. . . . Let us examine the collection and decide to what extent the charge may be applied to it.

The collection consists of 150 documents, divided into three main sections. The first contains material on the reaction of the Soviet and Western press; the second, a transcript of the trial itself; and the third, more on the reaction of the press and numerous letters from private citizens commenting on the outcome of the trial.

I claim categorically, taking complete responsibility for the claim, that the extracts from the Soviet press—from Moscow and elsewhere—were assembled with utmost accuracy, [given] the fact that this press reflects points of view that are diametrically opposed to Ginzburg's. Thus both points of view are represented in the collection with equal thoroughness. Can such an approach be considered tendentious? I would call it objective. I can affirm that, without exception, all documents accessible to Ginzburg were included in the collection, and I ask the court to drop the charge against Aleksandr Ginzburg that his collection of documents on the Siniavsky-Daniel case is tendentious.

Ginzburg is likewise accused of including two anti-Soviet documents among the 150 in the collection: one entitled "Resistance" and another, "Letter to an Old Friend," which allegedly impart an anti-Soviet quality to the collection. It is on the basis of this that Ginzburg is charged with anti-Soviet agitation and propaganda. Ginzburg himself explained to the court that he did not consider these documents "criminal." This is his personal point of view, which may not persuade the public prosecutor. Moreover, in court Ginzburg declared: "Even if I had considered them criminal, I would have been obliged, all the same, to include these two documents in the collection, since they reflected a type of reaction common to individual members of the intelligentsia—opinions that I would have to include since I was striving, above all, for objectivity."

Indeed, the collection offers the greatest possible variety of views. It includes materials on the need for the continued democratizing of our country, for enlarging freedom of creativity, and for strengthening the international prestige of our country. Along with these materials, Ginzburg included in his collection the leaflets "Resistance" and "Letter to an Old Friend." However, to prove Ginzburg's guilt under the provisions of Article 70 of the R.S.F.S.R. Criminal Code, it must be proved that he included these documents, which are criminal from the point of view of the court, with anti-Soviet purposes in mind—that is, with the intention of undermining and weakening the Soviet system. And even the charge itself describes the collection as tendentious, but not anti-Soviet

—for its purpose is to change the court's verdict, not to undermine the system. As to the documents themselves that are considered criminal by the court—it would be difficult to prove that their objective is to undermine or weaken the Soviet system. The inclusion of documents that contain individual criminal elements cannot be used as proof of guilt under the terms of Article 70 of the R.S.F.S.R. Criminal Code.

A question arises that perhaps there is a violation of the terms of Article 190. This would depend on how Ginzburg intended to publicize his collection. Ginzburg intended to circulate it within the R.S.F.S.R., as the prosecution insists. Ginzburg is accused of giving permission, allegedly in October, 1966, to Galanskov to pass the collection, through the NTS emissary Genrikh, to the publishers of *Grani*. The question of the delivery of the collection was exhaustively covered by attorney Kaminskaia in her defense of Galanskov. However, since this has a bearing on the charge against Aleksandr Ginzburg, I should like to review the matter.

In fact, there is only one version of the transmission of the collection [to the West]—the one based on Dobrovolsky's testimony. Dobrovolsky allegedly learned from Galanskov that the *White Book* was delivered through [NTS agent] Genrikh—but to whom specifically Dobrovolsky could not say. Dobrovolsky claims that Galanskov told him about this during a party at the home of witness Potashova. Dobrovolsky also claims that Lashkova, who typed up the collection, had worked intensively, allegedly because the courier from abroad was expected imminently. [Yet] following the completion of the typing, the documents lay untouched for two or three weeks. Dobrovolsky insisted on this fact during the preliminary hearings and repeated it during the trial.

Lashkova testified that she finished typing the collection some time in November, but not before November 10, 1966. As I have already pointed out, according to Dobrovolsky's testimony, the time of the delivery of the collection was connected with the party at Potashova's. The testimony of witness Potashova and of the defendants Lashkova and Galanskov, who attended the party, has concretely established that the party took place on October 22. Consequently, this was no less than two weeks prior to the completion of Lashkova's typing of the collection. This constitutes all the proof necessary to demonstrate that, when the foreigner Genrikh arrived in Moscow in October, 1966, the collection could not possibly have been passed to him since it was not finished. The prosecution has no other information whatsoever as to how the collection made its way abroad nor any other grounds for charging Aleksandr Ginzburg with complicity in the affair in any other capacity.

Why, then, did Dobrovolsky assert this in his testimony? I submit that he had his reasons for doing so. We must not forget that Dobrovolsky's situation at the time of his arrest was, quite simply, tragic. It was in his apartment, and only in his apartment, that [the police] found all the material evidence—hectograph, money, and NTS literature—that served as grounds for charging the defendants with having ties with the *émigré* anti-Soviet organization, the NTS. We must not forget, too, that Dobrovolsky had been previously charged with anti-Soviet activities. From the moment he is arrested, a person dreads not only the evidence of his guilt that is already known but also the extrinsic circumstances that may turn up as evidence against him. Dobrovolsky knew that he was guilty of meeting with four foreigners, disseminating NTS literature, and talking to Lashkova and Kats about the NTS. That is what Dobrovolsky was thinking about. He wanted to save himself, at any cost. This is confirmed by the note he addressed to Galanskov during his period of psychiatric observation at the [Serbsky] Institute [of Forensic Psychiatry in Moscow], in which he begged him to assume his, Dobrovolsky's, guilt. No, he did not stop at bearing false witness. The morality of this man allowed him to beg another inmate to assume the entire burden of his guilt. If he could slander even Galanskov, with whom he was well acquainted, what did he care about Ginzburg, with whom, according to his own court testimony, he had no more than a "hello-and-goodbye" relationship? Moreover, the prosecution—Dobrovolsky certainly knew— would be interested in Ginzburg and in his collection.

Thus, Comrade Judges, I believe that the testimony that Dobrovolsky gave at that time and repeated in court represents only his own suppositions, which not only are uncorroborated by anyone or anything but also contradict the materials obtained in the course of the judicial investigation.

Let us take a look at Ginzburg's testimony. He says: "I intended to submit, and did submit, this collection only to the legal authorities." One copy of the collection was actually submitted by Ginzburg to the KGB: it is lying on your table. The investigation established that Ginzburg showed one copy of the collection to Ehrenburg. Witness Stoliarova confirmed that she knew for a fact that Ehrenburg, who, as everyone knows, is a deputy to the Supreme Soviet, was shown the collection by Ginzburg. True, Ginzburg refuses to name the other deputies. However, this collection has now become a criminal issue, and Ginzburg cannot identify these individuals without their explicit agreement. And, as we all know, Ginzburg has been deprived, for the time being, of the opportunity to obtain such agreement.

Thus we see that Ginzburg's version has been confirmed, if only in part. Furthermore, during the investigation Ginzburg stated that he knew that the collection had been informally submitted to the Chairman of the Supreme Court. The prosecution, however, has not made one single attempt to verify this statement. I believe that Ginzburg personally played no role in the transmission of his collection to the West. We all know that Galina Serebriakova's manuscripts and Yevgeniia Ginzburg's memoirs, etc., have been published in the West. Witness Levitin, when asked how his articles made their way to the West, answered that he had absolutely no idea. This signifies that a person may simply not know how his works turned up in the West.

In conclusion, I would like to turn to [the charge that] Ginzburg passed to Gubanov newspaper clippings that the prosecution considers anti-Soviet. It has already been established that these clippings were in Norwegian, Danish, and Italian—languages that Ginzburg does not speak —and in French, which Ginzburg speaks very poorly. As Ginzburg testified, the clippings came into his possession accidentally, while he was gathering materials from the foreign press concerning the Siniavsky-Daniel case. His attention was attracted by a number of the newspaper articles that were clearly unrelated to the Siniavsky-Daniel case but in which the word SMOG was written in capital letters (the court had the opportunity to verify this). Unaware of the specific content of the articles and unable to figure it out, having realized that they discussed SMOG, Ginzburg gave them to Gubanov, a SMOGist. To prove the [willful] circulation of slanderous fabrications, one must prove the existence of criminal intent. The fact that Ginzburg did not know and could not have known the content of these articles is proof of the absence of such intent. Consequently, he cannot be convicted of circulating anti-Soviet materials.

In this court, witnesses Stoliarova and Pinsky have spoken of Ginzburg's honesty and decency, of his unquestionable intelligence, talent, and courage. In this court, I have the honor not to have to insist on the moral virtues of Ginzburg since, apart from whether he is a good or a bad man, I can firmly assert that he is not guilty.

In conclusion, I want to add that, in my opinion, the prosecution has not produced sufficient evidence to convict Ginzburg of anti-Soviet activities.

I request the acquittal of Aleksandr Ginzburg.

JUDGE: Does the state prosecutor wish to comment upon the defense counsel's statement?
PROSECUTOR: No.

14. For a Retrial: Letter by the Vakhtin Brothers

January 18, 1968

To: The Supreme Court of the U.S.S.R.
The Politburo, CPSU Central Committee
The Presidium of the U.S.S.R. Supreme Soviet

DECLARATION

During the last two years, several political trials have taken place in Moscow and Leningrad, beginning with the widely known case of Siniavsky and Daniel and concluding for the present with the judgment handed down against Ginzburg, Galanskov, Dobrovolsky, and Lashkova. All these trials have been held in an abnormal atmosphere of secrecy and confused and improbable journalistic sensationalism. This by itself is enough to enable the attentive observer to see clearly that, in the course of the preliminary investigation, and, later, in the course of the trial, flagrant violations of both Soviet law and constitutional norms were permitted—not to mention the impossible moral atmosphere of these trials.

We lost our father during the time of massive Stalinist repressions. He was posthumously rehabilitated. We cannot be reconciled to the thought that the terror that our country and people experienced during those terrible times of lawlessness and atrocities could occur again, even in lesser degree. Our fatherland, to which we have dedicated our lives, has endured innumerable sufferings through wars, revolutions, and the mutual extermination of compatriots. And among the most terrible sufferings of all were those caused by the lawlessness that sapped the spiritual and physical forces of our society. We cannot reconcile ourselves to the new lawlessness, for otherwise our life and work would lose their meaning and become nothing more than mere biological existence.

We demand a retrial of the cases of Siniavsky and Daniel, of Galanskov, Ginzburg, Dobrovolsky, and Lashkova, of Bukovsky, of Ogurtsov, and others. [We request that] the retrials be open and public and that they clarify both the manner in which the [original] proceedings were conducted and the essence of these cases. We demand light, clarity, and public knowledge! The right to make this demand is given to us by the very essence of the Constitution, by our understanding of our civil rights and our human dignity, and by our desire to see our fatherland great and pure—in matters big and small.

B. B. VAKHTIN
YU. B. VAKHTIN

15. Against Slander: Letter by V. M. Voronin

January 21, 1968

To the Editor-in-Chief of *Izvestia*

On January 16, 1968, your newspaper published an article by T. Aleksandrov and V. Konstantinov entitled "In the Same Harness." This article can only evoke indignation, just as the farce of the Ginzburg-Galanskov-Dobrovolsky-Lashkova trial (which the article concerns) evoked protest.

The article "In the Same Harness" is disgusting in every respect. First, it is completely unfair in that it seeks to slander publicly people who cannot rise to their own defense. The authors of the article resort to dishonorable and base methods to describe the defendants in the most repulsive terms: "swindlers," "criminals," "immoral people," etc. Who gave T. Aleksandrov and V. Konstantinov the right to act in this manner? . . . Such methods have no place in the Soviet press; they are yellow-press tactics that provoke indignation.

Second, the article staggers one with the absolute groundlessness of its allegations. There is not a single argument, fact, or piece of evidence to support even one of the assertions made by the authors in this article. We leave to the consciences of T. Aleksandrov and V. Konstantinov such unsubstantiated charges as the alleged "cheating" and "moral and political turpitude" of Ginzburg, his alleged "desire to live off society" and at the same time to "slander it," and other similarly groundless assertions. The article offers not one proof of the existence of alleged ties between the defendants and the NTS. Why was Brocks-Sokolov brought into the article? Is it possible to take as proof of such "ties" [the testimony] that "agents" of this organization told the names of the accused to Brocks and instructed him to convey packages with their photographs into the U.S.S.R.? If the court convicted the defendants on the basis of such "evidence," how can one speak of legality? And how do we treat the authors of the article, who cover up illegality? And, if there were irrefutable proofs of ties between the defendants and the NTS, why didn't T. Aleksandrov and V. Konstantinov cite them?

Third, certain facts are purposely distorted in the article, while others are ignored. Yes, as the authors say, "it was known" that this trial was being conducted from January 8 through January 12 in Moscow; however, this knowledge was not due to announcements in the Soviet press. T. Aleksandrov and V. Konstantinov fail to state that the trial was not public and open, as required by Soviet law; nor do they inform us that the "Moscovites attending the trial" were not the general public and that only "selected people" were allowed into the courtroom—those who had been given special passes. The authors of the article do not write that those Moscovites who wished to attend the trial were not given the opportunity to do so, that foreign correspondents were not allowed into the courtroom on the ground that "no seats were available" (!), that the representative of Amnesty International was refused entry. T. Aleksandrov and V. Konstantinov say not a word about these and other scandalous violations of legality and justice that were permitted in the court. There is no mention in the article of the inordinately long preliminary detention of the defendants before trial; nor is there any mention of the cynical violations of procedural norms—beginning with the denial to "objectionable" witnesses of the right to speak and the removal of witnesses from the courtroom after their testimony had been given and ending with the confiscation of notes made at the trial by, for example, Ginzburg's fiancée; etc., etc.

T. Aleksandrov and V. Konstantinov write about the "approval" with which the specially selected public greeted the pronouncement of the court's verdict, but they say not a word about the protests of both the

Soviet public and the public abroad—they are silent about the appeal of P. M. Litvinov and L. Daniel. The authors of the article, having set themselves the thankless task of slandering the accused in the eyes of society, portray them as "criminals," but they say nothing about the real offense held against them—such as A. Ginzburg's *White Book* on the trial of Siniavsky and Daniel and the journal *Phoenix 66* edited by Yu. Galanskov.

It is impossible not to evaluate all this as a deliberate attempt to delude public opinion concerning the true nature of the trial that took place in Moscow.

Whatever the motives that prompted T. Aleksandrov and V. Konstantinov to write this article, and your newspaper to publish it, the appearance of such a piece stains the honor of our press just as the conduct of the recently concluded trials stains the honor of the state and the conscience of all its citizens.

As a citizen of the country that proclaimed the slogans of freedom and justice to the whole world, I protest against the publication in your newspaper of the article by T. Aleksandrov and V. Konstantinov.

As a citizen of the R.S.F.S.R., in the name of which the disgraceful sentence was handed down, I protest against that sentence and the judicial farce that was played out in Moscow.

I demand an immediate, open, and unprejudiced re-examination of the case in the presence of the general public and foreign correspondents.

I demand the public condemnation of closed trials in which dissenters are denied their rights and the punishment of those guilty of violating the rule of law.

I demand the re-establishment of truth and justice.

V. M. VORONIN

Arzamas, Karl Marks St., Bldg. 20, Apt. 3.

16. *"The Duty of a Communist"*: From a Kolkhoz Chairman to Suslov

I do not have sufficient information to judge the degree of guilt of the persons subjected to repression, but of one thing I am firmly convinced and one thing I know—the type of trial that took place in the Moscow Municipal Court January 8–12, 1968, is causing enormous damage to our Party and to the cause of Communism, both in our country and elsewhere.

We have celebrated the glorious [fiftieth] anniversary; we pride ourselves on our achievements in economic and scientific techniques; and we ourselves, at the very time the United Nations has declared 1968 the Year of the Defense of the Rights of Man, are handing the enemies of Communism trump cards to be used against us. It is absurd!

We were naked, hungry, and destitute, but we won because we placed in the foreground the liberation of man from injustice, outrage, lack of rights, etc. And we can lose everything, despite our rockets and hydrogen bombs, if we forget the origins of the Great October Socialist Revolution.

From the time of Radischev,[1] trials of writers have always been an abomination in the eyes of progressive, thinking people. What were our home-grown leaders thinking of when they shut Solzhenitsyn's mouth, made a fool of the poet Voznesensky, "punished" Siniavsky and Daniel with forced labor, when they involved the KGB in spectacles with "foreign enemies"?

One must not subvert the confidence of the masses in the Party; one must not speculate with the honor of the state, even if a certain leader wants to end *samizdat* [underground literature]. *Samizdat* can be eliminated by only one means: by the development of democratic rights, not their violation; by observance of the Constitution, not its violation; by the realization in practice of the Declaration of Human Rights, which Vishinsky signed in the name of our state, not by ignoring it.

Incidentally, it appears that Articles 18 and 19 of the Declaration read:

> Everyone has the right to freedom of thought, conscience, and religion. . . . Everyone has the right to freedom of opinion and expression; this right includes freedom to hold opinions without interference and to seek, receive, and impart information and ideas through any media and regardless of frontiers.

You know Article 125 of our Constitution perfectly well, so I shall not quote it. I only want to recall the thought of V. I. Lenin to the effect that "we need full and true information, and truth should not depend upon the question of whom it should serve" (*Works*, 5th edition, Vol. 54, p. 446).

I believe that the persecution of young dissenters in a country where more than 50 per cent of the population are younger than thirty years of age is an extremely dangerous line—adventurism. It is not the toadies, not a public of Yes men (O Lord, how they have multiplied!), not the mama's boys who will determine our future but, rather, those very rebels, the most energetic, brave, and high-principled members of our young generation.

It is stupid to see in them the enemies of Soviet power and more than stupid to let them rot in prisons and to mock them. For the Party, such a line is equivalent to self-strangulation. Too bad for us if we are not capable of reaching an understanding with these young people. They will create, inevitably they will create, a new Party. Ideas cannot be murdered with bullets, prisons, or exile. He who does not understand this is no politician, no Marxist.

You, of course, remember the "Testament of Palmiro Togliatti." I have in mind this part of it:

A general impression has been created of foot-dragging and opposition in the matter of a return to Leninist norms that would insure, both within the Party and outside it, more freedom of utterance and discussion on questions of culture, art, and politics as well.

It is difficult for us to explain to ourselves this foot-dragging and this opposition, particularly in view of contemporary conditions, when the capitalist encirclement no longer exists and economic construction has attained enormous successes.

We have always proceeded from the thought that socialism is a system in which there exists the broadest freedom for the workers who participate in the cause, who participate in an organized way in the leadership of social life as a whole. (*Pravda*, September 10, 1964.)

Who benefits from a policy of foot-dragging and opposition? Only overt or covert Stalinists, political bankrupts. Remember: Leninism—yes! Stalinism—no! The Twentieth Congress of the Party did its work. The genie is at large and cannot be confined again! By no forces and nobody!

We are on the eve of the fiftieth anniversary of the Soviet army [February 23]. We are on the eve of the consultative meeting of the fraternal Communist parties [which opened in Budapest February 26]. Do not complicate your work for yourselves; do not darken the atmosphere in the country.

On the contrary, Comrade Podgorny [Soviet President] could amnesty Siniavsky, Daniel, and Bukovsky and could order a review of the case of A. Ginzburg and others. The Moscow Municipal Court, in this last case, permitted the grossest violations of legal procedure. Prosecutor Terekhov, Judge Mironov, and the commandant of the court Tsirkunenko should be punished in appropriate fashion, primarily for acting like idiots and abusing their power.

One cannot achieve legality by violating the laws. We will never permit anyone to prostitute our Soviet courts, our laws, and our rights. Such violators should be thrown out with a vengeance, for they are doing Soviet power more harm than all your NTS's, BBC's, and Radio Liberty's taken together.

Let *Novyi mir* again print the works of A. Solzhenitsyn. Let G. Serebriakova publish her "Sandstorm" in the U.S.S.R. and Ye. Ginzburg her "Journey into the Whirlwind." Anyway, they are known and read; it's no secret.

I live in the provinces, where for every electrified home there are ten unelectrified ones, where in the winter the buses can't get through and the mail is late by whole weeks. If information [of the trials] has reached us on the broadest scale, you can well imagine what you have done, what kind of seeds you have sown throughout the country. Have the courage to correct the mistakes that have been made before the workers and peasants take a hand in this affair.

I don't want this letter to be passed over in silence, for the cause of the Party cannot be a private cause, a personal cause, and, even less, a second-rate cause.

I consider it the duty of a Communist to warn the Central Committee of the Party, and to insist that all members of the Central Committee of the Communist Party of the Soviet Union be acquainted with the contents of this letter.

The letter is sent to Comrade Suslov with this in view.

With Communist greetings!

I. A. YAKHIMOVICH

NOTE

1. Aleksandr Nikolaievich Radishchev (1749–1802) was a philosopher and poet, a forerunner of the Decembrists. Later revolutionary democrats were greatly influenced by his writings and activities.—ED.

17. Against the Verdict: Letter by B. V. Sazonov

January 23, 1968

To: The Supreme Court, R.S.F.S.R.
The papers *Izvestia* and *Komsomolskaia pravda*
Attorneys B. A. Zolotukhin and D. P. Kaminskaia

I have familiarized myself with the speech given by Comrade B. A. Zolotukhin, defense counsel for A. Ginzburg, at the January, 1968, trial and also with the reports which appeared in the newspapers *Izvestia* and *Komsomolskaia pravda* regarding this trial. After comparing these documents, I have come to the conclusion that the above-named organs of the press misinformed the Soviet public by describing the trial in an extremely one-sided, tendentious fashion and by repeating false information that defames the character of at least several of the defendants. (I have in mind primarily A. Ginzburg, since I have not been able to acquaint myself with the documents relating to the other defendants.)

I have also familiarized myself with the appeal addressed by L. Bogoraz-Daniel and P. Litvinov to the world community. From it, I have learned that the trial of the accused persons Yu. Galanskov, A. Ginzburg, Dobrovolsky, and V. Lashkova violated several rules of the Soviet Criminal Code and that the court tried not so much to find out the true facts of the case and judge it from the viewpoint of Soviet law as it tried by every means to condemn several of the above-named persons.

All this taken together alarms me as a citizen of this country. We must have guarantees against the possibility of a repetition of the bloody events that occurred at the time of the cult of personality. An essential condition for this is public knowledge of the work of our courts, as this is vital both for public control of the courts' activities and for inculcating a spirit of lawfulness and good citizenship in the Soviet people and thus bringing about stricter observance of Soviet laws.

I therefore demand the nullification of the court's verdict in the case of Yu. Galanskov, A. Ginzburg, Dobrovolsky, and V. Lashkova and a re-examination of the case with public knowledge and in accordance with Soviet law.

B. V. Sazonov
Philosopher

18. Protest of Fifty-two Scholars and Professionals

January 27, 1968

To: Procurator General of the U.S.S.R. Rudenko
The U.S.S.R. Supreme Court

In December, 1967, letters were sent to various procuratorial and judicial offices requesting that those who wished to do so be allowed to attend the [then] impending trial of Ginzburg, Galanskov, Dobrovolsky, and Lashkova. The signers of these letters considered it their civic duty to press the authorities to make the trial public, since, in the past, our society had repeatedly been faced with flagrant violations of legality committed in court cases where the proceedings were either hidden from, or falsified to, the public. Such was the case, for example, in the trials of Siniavsky and Daniel, of Khaustov, and of Bukovsky. All these trials were declared to be public, but in reality were not. Only persons with special passes were allowed into the courtroom, and the criteria for the issuance of these passes and the person(s) who issued them are not known. In sum, a specially selected "public" was present in the courtroom, while friends and even several close relatives of the defendants were not permitted to attend.

Only through the device of keeping the public ignorant of the proceedings was the KGB able to settle accounts with the dissidents. Indeed, the accused, who acted within the framework of our Constitution and our laws and who, in several instances, used the Constitution as their defense, demanded that legality be observed but were nevertheless committed to harsh sentences without genuine evidence of their guilt. In any event, the public has no knowledge of such evidence. Only in the absence of open hearings could our press have printed reports that distorted the trial proceedings and grossly deceived readers regarding the trials' true nature. (For example, the only published notice concerning the

Bukovsky trial, in the newspaper *Vecherniaia Moskva,* informed the public that Bukovsky had admitted his guilt, although this was completely false.)

There have been no answers to the letters [mentioned above], and not one of the signers of the letters has received permission to attend the trial, which has just been completed. Furthermore, the trial of Ginzburg, Galanskov, Dobrovolsky, and Lashkova was characterized by even more scandalous violations of legality and turned out to be a repetition, in still more somber form, of the other previously mentioned trials.

All entrances to the Moscow Municipal Court Building were guarded by numerous KGB functionaries, as well as by *druzhinniki* and policemen, who refused entry to anyone who did not possess special authorization (the nature of which they stubbornly refused to disclose). During the days of the trial, the "Commandant of the Court" was Tsirkunenko, a colonel of the KGB. Characteristically, even the relatives of the defendants were not all, and not immediately, admitted to the courtroom, even though many of them carried legal summonses. Relatives of the defendants, witnesses, and other citizens were subjected to rude treatment, threats, and insults; they were photographed in order to intimidate them; their conversations were subjected to eavesdropping. Throughout the trial, constant surveillance was maintained over the relatives and close friends of the defendants with the express purpose of blackmailing them.

All this was done so that no objective information could leak out of the courtroom. For example, the wife of Galanskov and the fiancée of Ginzburg received threats that added reprisals would be taken against the defendants if accounts of the trial were written down. Unknown persons coming out of the courtroom attempted to give completely false information to foreign correspondents, who themselves had not been admitted to the court session.

Many of us were witnesses to these facts and are prepared to corroborate them.

The fact that the organization that carried out the investigation [of the accused] was constantly involved in efforts to keep the trial from being public is a mockery of justice that should not be permitted in a civilized society. No one who respects himself and his calling as a judge had the right to conduct a court hearing under such conditions. And the fact that the trial proceedings were in every way kept hidden from the public appears to be sufficient grounds for a vote of nonconfidence in the court and its verdict.

Therefore, we cannot believe either in the justice of the [court's] prosecution of the case of Ginzburg, Galanskov, and Lashkova, or in the truth or sincerity of Dobrovolsky's testimony, on the basis of which the former were alleged to have had ties with the NTS. This testimony compels us to recall the even more menacing aspects of the trials of the 1930's, when accused persons were subjected to coercion during the period of investigation and forced to admit their own guilt and that of others, with the result that millions of people were executed, tortured, or incarcerated in labor camps for decades. In this connection, it must be noted that, in this case, the accused were held in isolated confinement for investigation during an entire year, which far and away exceeds the investigatory periods stipulated under the Complete Procedural Code of the R.S.F.S.R.

It is generally known that Ginzburg compiled a collection of materials relating to the trial of Siniavsky and Daniel, which evoked a reaction on the part of both the Soviet and the world public; that Galanskov was editor of the mimeographed journal *Phoenix*, the contents of which had included, specifically, protocols of the discussion of the draft of the third volume of the *History of the Party* by old Bolsheviks and documents of the Writers' Union recording the expulsion of Boris Pasternak from the Union; and finally, that Lashkova typed these materials. These things had been done openly. They [Ginzburg and Galanskov] placed their signatures on all the manuscripts. They attempted to make these materials public so that they could circulate openly. Soviet laws do not prohibit such activity.

Do these actions of the defendants constitute a just basis for their arrest? Isn't the indictment accusing them of having ties with subversive organizations (NTS) a typical means of reprisal utilized in the days of Stalin?

Such questions naturally arise as a result of the violations of the public's right to be informed that were perpetrated during this trial. Is it not incredible that people who acted openly and supported openness were in fact judged and sentenced secretly? A court organized and acting lawfully would not only have no fear of publicity but would welcome it in every way.

We demand a retrial of the case of Ginzburg, Galanskov, Dobrovolsky, and Lashkova by a reconstituted court acting in conformity with all the norms of legal procedure and with full publicity.

We also demand that those officials guilty of gross violations of legality in this trial be brought to account.

Yu. Apresian, candidate in Philological Sciences
Afanaseva, member, U.S.S.R. Union of Journalists
L. Alekseeva, editor
K. Babitsky, linguist
S. Belokrinitskaia, linguist
K. Bogatyrev, member, Union of Soviet Writers
L. Belova, candidate in Philological Sciences; member, Union of Cinematographers
N. Vvedenskaia, candidate in Physical-Mathematical Sciences
N. Viliams, instructor, MITKhT [Moscow Institute of Precise Chemical Technology]
Ye. Vinogradova, candidate in Fine Arts
A. Velikanov, physicist
T. Velikanova, mathematician
Ye. Volkovmokaia, linguist
S. Gindikin, candidate in Physical-Mathematical Sciences

Yu. Gastev, teacher, Moscow State University
M. Grabar, lecturer, Moscow Institute of Aviation Technology
Yu. Glazov, candidate in Philological Sciences
S. Goffe, artist
P. Gaidenko, candidate in Philosophical Sciences
Yu. Gerchuk, critic; member, U.S.S.R. Union of Artists
I. Golomshtok, art historian; member, U.S.S.R. Union of Artists
R. Dobrushin, Doctor of Physical-Mathematical Sciences
V. Dybo, candidate in Philological Sciences
Yu. Davydov, candidate in Philosophical Sciences
M. Domshlak, art historian
V. Ivanov, candidate in Philological Sciences
Ye. Kopeleva, proofreader, Publications Section, State Radio Com-
mittee
G. Korpelevich, graduate Student, MGU
Kasatkin, candidate in Philological Sciences
L. Kapanadze, candidate in Philological Sciences
L. Krysin, candidate in Philological Sciences
O. Kiselev, actor
R. Minlos, candidate in Physical-Mathematical Sciences; senior scientific
worker, MGU
I. Milchuk, candidate in Philological Sciences
V. Meniker, economist
A. Ogurtsov, candidate in Philosophical Sciences
B. Poliak, candidate in Physical-Mathematical Sciences
S. Pozharitskaia, candidate in Philological Sciences
A. Piatigorsky, candidate in Philological Sciences
L. Pazhitnov, candidate in Philosophical Sciences
Sedov, candidate in Historical Sciences
N. Sadomskaia, candidate in Historical Sciences
V. Skvirsky, geographer
Ye. Semeka, candidate in Historical Sciences
M. Taniuk, director
Yu. Telesin, mathematician
M. Ulanovskaia, bibliographer
M. Feigina, historian
I. Faleeva, sociologist
B. Shragin, candidate in Philosophical Sciences
A. Yakobson, translator

Send answers to this appeal to the following address: Moscow, G-117,
Pogodin Street, House 2/3, Apt. 91, B. I. Shragin.

Additional Signatures, February 6, 1968:
N. Belogorodskaia, engineer
G. Bulatov, actor
Yu. Blumental, musician
N. Blumental, student at the Institute of Culture

P. GRIGORENKO, construction engineer; former Major-General
A. GRIGORENKO, senior technician
YU. GUBANOV, electrician
D. DANIEL, schoolboy, son of Yuli Daniel
N. YEMELKINA, civil servant
D. ZHITOMIRSKY, Doctor of Art History
A. KOSTERIN, writer
A. KAPLIN, candidate in Physical-Mathematical Sciences
M. KAZARTEV, worker
G. KRAVTSOVA, plumber
O. LEONTEVA, candidate in Art History
V. NIKOLSKY, senior engineer; physicist
A. PAVLOVA, construction engineer
S. PISAREV, scientific worker
M. PUZIKOV, engineer
I. RUDAKOV
V. TETERIN, civil servant
M. SHAPOSHNIKOV
YU. YUKHNOVETS, worker
A. KHRABROVITSKY, literary scholar
A. TSVETOPOLSKAIA, senior engineer
UTKINA, senior engineer

19. For a Truthful Press: Protest of Thirty

To: The Editor-in-Chief, *Komsomolskaia pravda*
    The Party Committee of *Komsomolskaia pravda*
Copy to the Board of the Union of Journalists

On January 18, 1968, an article by F. Ovcharenko entitled "The Lackeys" was published in the newspaper *Komsomolskaia pravda*. Each of us is acquainted with at least one of the defendants and knows the circumstances of the case, and, on this basis, we maintain that the article contains gross distortions of fact and misinforms the reader. Specifically, Ginzburg and Galanskov are depicted in a false light—as parasites. These allegations are easily refuted by the actual work histories of the accused, their character traits, and their labor books.

Much more important and dangerous is the false information given about this case. For example, the article states: "In searches of the quarters of Ginzburg, Galanskov, and Dobrovolsky, articles of espionage equipment were found—cryptographic manuals, Shapirographs (hectographs), instructions, anti-Soviet literature, leaflets." No such articles were found in the possession of Ginzburg or Galanskov, in contrast to Dobrovolsky—as is apparent from the records of the searches, copies of which not only are included in the evidence relating to the case but are also in the possession of relatives of the accused. According to F. Ovcharenko, the guilt of the accused was proved "by the testimony of a great number of witnesses . . . , by the authoritative conclusions of experts." First of all, only psychiatric experts figured in the trial, and such testimony, as is well known, determines only responsibility, not guilt. Second, however, one may treat the testimony of the witnesses; not one of them—not even Brocks-Sokolov—confirmed that there were ties between Ginzburg and Galanskov and the NTS.

We will not continue enumerating all the distortions of truth contained in the article. Enough has been said to raise a question as to the professional integrity of the author of the article "Lackeys."

We consider that such a scandalous act in the practice of journalism should be judged [in a hearing] by the Editors or by the Union of Journalists. In our opinion, the following should be invited to attend this hearing: the relatives and close friends of the defendants, the judge, the procurator, the lawyers, the witnesses (those called by both the prosecution and the defense), and the court recorder. We are certain that, if all interested parties are allowed to testify, the truth will become known, the article "Lackeys" will receive the judgment it deserves, and the newspaper will publish a retraction.

N. GORBANEVSKAIA
O. TIMOFEEVA [-GALANSKOVA]
A. S. VOLPIN
L. I. GINZBURG
S. CHUDAKOV
YE. GALANSKOVA
V. POKHODAIEV
YE. A. GALANSKOVA
T. S. GALANSKOV
A. BOLTRUKEVICH
A. TOPESHKINA
A. I. KIRIAGINA (witness at search of Ginzburg's flat, January 17, 1967)
L. KATS
S. GENKIN

G. V. GALANSKOVA
V. A. NIKOSKY
S. SHTUTINA
A. POVOLOTSKAIA
N. SVETLOVA
KARELIN
SHADRINA
SHTERNFELD
A. VIKTOROV
K. GALANSKOV
N. VIKTOROVA
A. SHTELMAKH
N. USTINOV
YE. VASILEVA
I. KAMISHANOVA
G. KAGANOVSKY

20. For a Truthful Press: Letter from Ginzburg's Mother to Komsomolskaia pravda

In your newspaper of January 18, 1968, you published an article by F. Ovcharenko entitled "The Lackeys." In this article, my son Aleksandr Ginzburg was pictured in a false light, and the circumstances of the court case against him were misrepresented. There is no need to dwell on every single part of the article where the facts were distorted— for example, the assertion that my son had been sponging off me, that he had been placed under a criminal charge in 1964, etc. I will mention only what I feel to be the most important parts.

In the four-column article, my son was constantly described as "a paid agent of the NTS" who disseminated "propaganda" materials and publications of that organization, and he was alleged to have told the court about his "activities in cooperation with the NTS."

During the trial, there was not one word about my son's receiving from anyone whatever any payment for the book of documents he compiled. The prosecutor, who had called my son "an agent of the NTS," himself admitted in court that he had made a mistake. It seems that this "mistake" also got accidentally into the text of the court's sentence; however, none of the evidence in the case, not one of the witnesses who testified, nor a single question by the prosecution even touched on this point. Anyone who was present at the trial must know this quite well—and I hope that the journalist who reported the trial proceedings was in the courtroom.

I do not know from what sources the author of the article got his information that "spying equipment" and NTS instructions and leaflets were found during the search of Ginzburg's home. In the official list compiled after the search, of which I have a copy, no Shapirographs or NTS literature and no cryptographic materials are mentioned. Nor was my son accused of anything like this during the trial.

There was nothing "unexpected" about the fact that my son refused to confess at the trial that his actions had been anti-Soviet. He did not "suddenly state this"; he asserted it from the very start of the investigation until the end of the trial.

The few examples I have cited are enough to give me the right to call the article by F. Ovcharenko slanderous and to demand its retraction.

I ask that you check the facts I have put forward, as well as other points in the article about Aleksandr Ginzburg, against the documents—the official search record and the record of the court sessions. I ask you to let me know the results of the check and to publish the retraction in the newspaper.

If the check is dishonestly carried out, or if my letter remains unanswered, I will be forced to bring charges against the author of the article and the newspaper for the slander of my son Aleksandr Ginzburg.

L. I. GINZBURG

21. For a Truthful Press: Letter from Galanskov's Wife to Komsomolskaia pravda

February 24, 1968

On January 18, 1968, *Komsomolskaia pravda* published an article entitled "The Lackeys," by F. Ovcharenko, devoted to the trial of Galanskov, Ginzburg, Dobrovolsky, and Lashkova, which ended on January 12 of this year in the Moscow Municipal Court.

I attended this trial, and I am personally acquainted with all four of the accused. I am familiar with the circumstances of the case. For these reasons, I consider it my duty, civic and personal (I am the wife of one of the accused—Yuri Galanskov), to protest the crude distortions of the facts made by the author of this article. These distortions seem all the more unacceptable in view of the fact that the author attended the trial and had the opportunity, after acquainting himself with the real state of affairs, to present an objective account of the proceedings in court.

Since I know that Aleksandr Ginzburg's mother has already written a similar letter, I shall dwell only on the elements of F. Ovcharenko's article that relate directly to Yuri Galanskov.

It is true that Yuri Galanskov is the editor and compiler of the journal *Phoenix*. From the first day of his arrest to the last day of the trial, he himself never denied this. And this was probably the only established reason for giving him such a strict sentence: seven years' imprisonment in a camp.

I would like to begin by stating that Galanskov compiled this journal alone, without any participation whatsoever by Ginzburg. The only evidence of Ginzburg's participation in the compilation of *Phoenix* was Dobrovolsky's testimony that Ginzburg had supposedly delivered a film containing the article "The Russian Path to Socialism" to Galanskov. But Galanskov testified in court that he had received this article from another person (moreover, he gave the exact name of this person). In addition, throughout the investigation and the trial, he consistently reiterated that he alone had compiled *Phoenix*.

The author of the article probably knows all this, but, nonetheless, he writes: "But the partners had new concerns . . . they were compiling a new collection with the pretentious name of *Phoenix*." As for pretentiousness, I have difficulty arguing with a person who uses such expressions as "the history of the fall of the latter-day Herostrats," "unchanging spiritual rags," etc. But I maintain that "they" did not compile the collection; it was compiled solely by Galanskov.

What kind of collection is it?

F. Ovcharenko holds that it is composed of "falsifications that have been kept in reserve."

Here are the contents of the journal *Phoenix* as presented in the record of the search that was made on January 17, 1967, in the course of which the journal was confiscated: "You May Begin" (editorial); A. Siniavsky: "What Is Socialist Realism?"; "The Revelations of Viktor Velsky"; Yu. Galanskov: "An Open Letter to Sholokhov"; "Stenographic Transcript of the Discussion of the Pasternak Affair at a Meeting of Moscow Writers"; A. Siniavsky: "In Defense of Pyramids"; "Protest by the Creative Intelligentsia"; "Discussion of the Third Volume of the History of the CPSU at the Institute of Marxism-Leninism with Old Bolsheviks Participating"; Ye. S. Varga: "The Russian Path to Socialism"; "A Letter by N. Bukharin"; Karaguzhin: "Two Stories"; O. Mandelshtam: "Two Letters"; E. Genri: "An Open Letter to the Writer I. Ehrenburg"; "Questions Put to Writer E. Genri at a Lecture 'On Neo-fascism' at Moscow State University"; G. Pomerantz: "Address to the Institute of Philosophy"; Yu. Galanskov: "Organizational Problems of the Movement for General and Complete Disarmament and Peace Throughout the World"; G. Pomerantz: "Quadrillion"; "The Interrelationship Between Knowledge and Faith: the Apologetic Experience of A. Dobrovolsky"; "A Description of Events in the Pochaevsky Monastery in Our Day"; verses by young writers; obituaries.

It would have been very obliging if, in the article, the author had named at least one piece in *Phoenix* that could definitely be called falsification. Since the author did not do so, one must assume either that he knowingly wrote lies or that he has no conception of the meaning of these works or the content of the journal *per se.*

Let us leave to the author's conscience the statement that "this ledger was sent to Paris through Genrikh, the resourceful NTS emissary." We should do so because this point in the charges is based exclusively on the testimony of the very same Dobrovolsky and is not corroborated by anyone, and also because the last lines in [Ovcharenko's] article clearly contradict the actual facts. For, the actual facts demonstrate that the journal *Phoenix* never got outside the country. Ovcharenko writes: "And Posev and Grani will burst with joy once again. They will give this material to the editors of bourgeois newspapers and journals and to the radio stations, and the latter will use them extensively in their ideological attacks on the Soviet Union."

As the author, who was present in the courtroom, should know, the prosecution did not have a single copy of *Phoenix* that had been published by Posev or any other foreign publishing house—indeed, not a copy of either the complete *Phoenix* or of any of the five articles from it that the court condemned as criminal. . . . None of these was published by Grani, Posev, or any other foreign publishing house. This was established by the court. The only exception to this was the article by Siniavsky, which had been published abroad many years before Galanskov compiled *Phoenix*. But perhaps the author has some information, if only concerning a single Voice of America, BBC, or Deutsche Welle broadcast that was devoted to any of these works that the court considers criminal in nature? It is unlikely that there were *no* such broadcasts, but, at any rate, none was mentioned in court. . . .

In the article, the author more than once uses the expression "stealthily spitting on one's country," alludes to the "secret" dispatching of materials to foreign countries, and even asserts that Galanskov and Ginzburg "maintain a conspiracy of silence with the cunning of recidivists." But aren't these emotional claims contradicted by the fact that both Galanskov and Ginzburg openly put their names on the collections they compiled? After all, even Ovcharenko himself admits that on each copy of the "complete collection of slanderous material" compiled by Ginzburg (which is, by the way, a collection of material on the Siniavsky-Daniel case; there is not a word to indicate this in the article) the following is written: "Compiled by A. Ginzburg"; and on the title page of the journal *Phoenix* one finds: "Edited by Yu. Galanskov." Isn't this too clear a violation of the "conspiracy of silence" and one that certainly does not jibe very well with the "cunning of the recidivists"?

If we judge from the content of the article "The Lackeys," it seems F. Ovcharenko considers it irrefutable that Galanskov and Ginzburg had contact with the anti-Soviet *émigré* organization known as the NTS.

But what evidence of this contact does he cite? He writes: "Their guilt has been irrefutably proven by the testimony of a large number of witnesses, by numerous documents, by material evidence, and by the authoritative conclusions of experts." Let us attempt to analyze each of these categories of "irrefutable" proof separately.

1. *"The testimony of a large number of witnesses."*

As we know, twenty-five witnesses testified in court. Not one of these witnesses gave a single piece of testimony that demonstrates, even indirectly, a link between Galanskov and Ginzburg and the NTS. As regards the witness to whom Ovcharenko devoted so much space in the article— "the young Venezuelan Nicholas Brocks-Sokolov, who arrived in the Soviet Union from Grenoble in December of last year," *i.e.*, two weeks before the trial and a year after the arrest of Galanskov and Ginzburg— even from Ovcharenko's article it is clear that Brocks had no notion whatsoever about the alleged ties between any of the defendants and the NTS. As he testified in court (I quote from the Ovcharenko article), "I recall that, at the time of Slavinsky's 'lectures,' I believed that Ginzburg, Galanskov, and Dobrovolsky were writers. In France, the newspapers report about them as if they were writers and that they had been put in prison and dealt with unjustly. . . ." By the way, this very Brocks-Sokolov, who had never set eyes on either Galanskov or Ginzburg before, was the *only* witness to express a condemnation of them. "In this trial criminals are being prosecuted for maintaining ties with the NTS," he stated. But even these words cannot serve as any kind of proof since Brocks-Sokolov himself, by his very own admission, first heard this from KGB investigators.

The second witness whose testimony is cited by Ovcharenko in his article is Kushev. I shall not analyze the part of the article that refers to his testimony since he has already done so himself in his open letter to the editor of *Komsomolskaia pravda*.[1] From this letter, it is apparent that Ovcharenko's claim that "Ginzburg and Company . . . palmed off NTS products on unwilling and unfortunate young people" slanders not only Ginzburg and Galanskov but Kushev himself as well. (It is in connection with this that Kushev's name is mentioned.)

2. *"Documents and material evidence."*

Ovcharenko writes: "During the search, spying equipment—carbon paper for secret messages, hectographs, instructions, anti-Soviet literature, and pamphlets—was found in the possession of Ginzburg, Galanskov, and Dobrovolsky." Nothing of the sort was discovered in either Galanskov's or Ginzburg's possession. This is confirmed by copies of the search records in my and Ginzburg's mother's possession. The only material evidence discovered in Galankov's possession and the only material evidence that figured in the court trial was the journal *Phoenix*. All the items that Ovcharenko enumerates in his description of "spying equipment" were found only in Dobrovolsky's possession.

3. *"The authoritative conclusions of experts."*

The only expert to appear in court was a psychiatrist. As we know, in itself, the psychiatric examination only establishes the mental state of the accused, but not his guilt or innocence in any particular crime.

These, then, comprise the "irrefutable proof."

It does not seem to me that there is any need to discourse at length as to why these "proofs" did not confirm and cannot confirm the existence of links between Galanskov and Ginzburg and the NTS. To the contrary, they testify rather that such ties did not exist. . . .

F. Ovcharenko not only reiterates throughout his entire article that Galanskov and Ginzburg were connected with the NTS; he even calls them "paid agents" of the NTS. . . . Here, Ovcharenko is no longer merely distorting the facts and proceedings of the trial; he is raising new accusations against Galanskov and Ginzburg, accusations that were not part of the sentence or even of the prosecution's bill of indictment. In court there was no reference whatsoever to "paid agents" of the NTS. The author of this article "The Lackeys" knows this. I hope he also knows that Galanskov and Ginzburg were tried under Article 70 of the R.S.F.S.R. Criminal Code—*i.e.*, for anti-Soviet agitation and propaganda —and not for participating in any anti-Soviet organization. Ovcharenko is, thus, really accusing Galanskov and Ginzburg of crimes covered by Article 72 of the R.S.F.S.R. Criminal Code—participation in an anti-Soviet organization—or even by Article 64 of the R.S.F.S.R. Criminal Code— treason to one's homeland—if one considers the NTS to be maintained by the U.S. Central Intelligence Agency. I believe that the author, in calling Galanskov and Ginzburg "paid agents" of the NTS, did not doubt that the NTS is an anti-Soviet organization, or that "paid agents" must be considered active members, or that members of an anti-Soviet organization should be tried under Article 72 and not under Article 70 of the R.S.F.S.R. Criminal Code.

To any unprejudiced person who reads Ovcharenko's article, it is clear that the proof of Galanskov's criminal activity cited in the article is patently insufficient. I, personally, have every reason to believe that F. Ovcharenko was not concerned with presenting a clear account of this political trial. He was much more concerned with simply compromising and besmirching people whose fate has evoked expressions of concern and desire to help from numerous Soviet and foreign public figures (several names are also cited in Ovcharenko's article). Unfortunately, in response to the moral challenge of these statements, F. Ovcharenko counters with only one thing—lies.

Begin with the fact that he calls Yuri Galanskov a parasite when, in fact, he was tried not at all as a parasite but as a person from a working family, a person who had worked while completing school and who was a worker at the time of his arrest. Next, Ovcharenko accuses Galanskov of self-interest. He makes him out to be a person who acted in the interest of profit; this again is a false accusation. Everyone who knew Galanskov and his way of life can corroborate the fact that he never had such leanings and that he never had a spare ruble in his pocket. Finally, he accuses Galanskov of vanity, of yearnings for fame. Is it possible that a person writing in a youth newspaper cannot even conceive that there are people who act—perhaps even rashly—out of lofty, pure motives? He might have been motivated, say, by concern over the fact that, while the decisions of the Twentieth and Twenty-second Congresses on the restoration of Leninist norms and the democratization of public life had not been officially abolished, their implementation, in any case, had been obstructed. Does one have to be connected with an anti-Soviet organization to feel concern over this, to feel the desire to act, to speak out?

But I have no intention of starting an argument with F. Ovcharenko over this question in this letter; his bias and his unscrupulousness are all too evident.

The purpose of this letter is quite different. I am sending it to the editors of *Komsomolskaia pravda*. I consider this my duty, all the more so because Yuri Galanskov is now in prison and is not only unable to file for court action against the man who has slandered him but has not even an elementary chance of defending himself against this slander or refuting it.

O. Timofeeva-Galanskova

Moscow, Zh 80
Third Golubvinsky Pereulok
Building 719, Apt. 4

NOTE

1. Document 22.—ED.

22. For a Truthful Press: Letter by Ye. I. Kushev

OPEN LETTER

To the Editors of *Komsomolskaia pravda*

On January 18, 1968, an article entitled "The Lackeys," by F. Ovcharenko, was published in your newspaper. Among the many distorted facts [it presented] regarding the trial and the personalites of the accused, one part of the article related directly to me. I quote from the text:

I repeat, Ginsburg and company not only were intoxicated with these [NTS] publications but also tried by every possible means to disseminate them. As the witness Ye. Kushev indicated in court, they palmed off NTS products on unsuspecting and unfortunate young people, former fellow students and friends.

This is a deliberate lie. Presumably, the author of the article was in court and could not help but hear my words to the effect that I did not know Ginzburg at all. He also could not have avoided hearing the single passage in my interrogation that concerned Galanskov. I reproduce it here from memory:

ATTORNEY KAMINSKAIA (Galanskov's defense counsel): Do you know anything about Galanskov's criminal activities—
I: I am well acquainted with Galanskov but know nothing about him of an incriminating nature. I know that he is the editor of the journal *Phoenix*, but I cannot judge as to the hostile character of the journal as I have not read it.

In essence, then, I corroborated in court only Dobrovolsky's and Lashkova's testimony to the effect that on my own initiative I obtained from them three brochures published by the NTS. It does not follow that they "palmed off" these brochures on me or anyone else. Moreover, I did not testify with regard to any other persons.

Thus, Ovcharenko first libels the condemned persons; second, he deliberately generalizes from a single episode; and third, he tries in an irresponsible manner to paint me as a dishonorable man.

I demand that you publish my letter with an appropriate editorial retraction, but, as I have little hope that you will do so, I am at the same time sending copies of the letter to my friends and acquaintances.

YEVGENI IGOREVICH KUSHEV

Moscow, G-99, 10 Smolensk St., Apt. 17

23. For a Truthful Press: Letter of Protest by A. Yakobson

To the Board of Directors, U.S.S.R. Union of Journalists

I address myself to your organization because it bears moral responsibility for the content of the Soviet press and, in the first instance, of the central newspapers.

I want to examine the question of the veracity of the information provided by the press regarding the case of Ginzburg, Galanskov, Dobrovolsky, and Lashkova, which was tried in the Moscow Municipal Court from January 8 to January 13, 1968. Having no firsthand knowledge of the circumstances of the trial, I attempt to draw my conclusions about it, like all citizens not present at the proceedings, solely from newspaper material.

The first press reaction to the January proceedings was a brief report in *Vecherniaia Moskva* of January 18, 1968, which said that "the court, on the basis of the testimony of the witnesses and defendants as well as the material evidence, found the persons named guilty of having had criminal communications with an exile anti-Soviet organization."

Now, it is these three items—the testimony of the witnesses, the confessions of the defendants, and the material evidence—that I propose to discuss on the basis of their representation in our press, specifically, in the article "In the Same Harness," by T. Aleksandrov and V. Konstantinov, in *Izvestia* of January 16, 1968, and in the article entitled "The Lackeys," by F. Ovcharenko, in *Komsomolskaia pravda* of January 18, 1968. Let us see whether the elucidation of these three items in the newspaper articles really leads the reader logically to the conclusion that the defendants had criminal links with an exile anti-Soviet organization.

First of all, what is said, *concretely*, about the testimony of the witnesses?

Except for the obscure mention made of Ye. Kushev in *Komsomolskaia pravda*, the only witness named turns out to be Nicholas Brocks-Sokolov, a citizen of Venezuela. In the pages of the press, he grows into the central figure of the trial, the major trump card of the prosecution. The *Izvestia* article makes him the main personage, giving him more space than the defendants. "In the Same Harness" is not only the title of the article, it is the gist and undercurrent of the entire text. The task the authors set for themselves is precisely to make the reader believe, by every possible means, that Brocks-Sokolov and the four defendants belong to the same spy organization and thus are bound together by a single "belt of the Fall" (*Izvestia*). An equally important role is given to Brocks-Sokolov by *Komsomolskaia pravda* in its efforts to argue the prosecution's case.

And what do we know about Brocks-Sokolov? We know that he was recruited by the white-*émigré* organization Narodno-Trudovoi Soiuz (NTS), that he came to the U.S.S.R. from France as a tourist and was arrested as a spy. On him was discovered a belt containing a Shapirograph (hectograph), cryptographic materials, anti-Soviet literature, and money. Brocks also had in his possession photographs of the defendants.

All this, we read in *Izvestia*, is now in the hands of the court as material evidence!

The question is: How can spying equipment belonging to Brocks, who came to our country in December of 1967, convict people who were in prison, under investigation, from January 1967 to January 1968? Why are the four accused tied with Brocks in the same ill-fated harness?

Let us try to find the answer to this question after analyzing in more detail what Brocks's mission was. It turns out that the NTS agents who recruited Brocks assured him that his role was to render assistance to the four defendants. Brocks-Sokolov readily agreed to carry out the assignment and put on the secret belt with the concealed packages, which he was to deliver to a "certain person" in Moscow, says *Komsomolskaia pravda*. From *Izvestia* we learn that the meeting was to take place in Sokolniki. Thus, it follows from the press reports that Brocks-Sokolov assumed the role of intermediary.

Perhaps the case might be clarified by the one who was to receive Brocks's packages? Who is he? What is his name? What was he supposed to do? Why is this important but barely mentioned link omitted from the chain of accusations? Didn't Brocks want to give away his partner? Absolutely not! It used to be said that a windbag is a boon to a spy. Such a spy as Brocks-Sokolov is a boon to the KGB.

The gentleman from Sokolniki, by the way, is not the only person with whom the organization that sent Brocks planned to establish connections through the same Brocks. Among the items of material evidence that were "in the hands of the court" were "letters prepared with return addresses." *Izvestia* lists these letters as taken from the same belt [and says that] "they were intended for certain persons in the Soviet Union. . . . ." "Certain persons" again! Would it not be in the interests of the prosecution to determine who they are? Or were the KGB workers unable to find the addressees from the addresses given?

But let us suppose that all the "certain persons" have really not been determined, and let us suppose that these persons were indeed going to render some unknown help to the prisoners. But this still leaves open the question: How and in what way did the underground equipment found on Brocks, and also the money, letters, and photographs, for whomever they were intended, incriminate the defendants? Why is all this cited as material evidence of the guilt not of Brocks himself but of those whom he only "knew by hearsay" (*Izvestia*)?

Now let us switch to Brocks's testimony at the trial—if it can be called testimony. . . .

At the University of Grenoble, where he studied, Brocks attended lectures given by Mikhail Slavinsky, who—*Komsomolskaia pravda* explains—is "a member of the NTS." From the mouth of Slavinsky, Brocks learns that there are in the Soviet Union "zealots for freedom" whose names are Galanskov, Ginzburg, and Dobrovolsky (*Izvestia*). That's the whole "testimony." Now I ask the reader to follow the newspaper's logic: Brocks-Sokolov declares in the Moscow Court that in Grenoble a professor praised Ginzburg and Galanskov, and Moscow ranks this professor as among the leadership of the NTS; thus, the persons he praised must also be considered "paid agents of the NTS" (*Komsomolskaia pravda*).

I consider that there were no grounds whatsoever for Brocks to appear in the January court proceedings in the role of witness—and the main witness at that, as the newspapers make clear. But, at the same time, this fellow takes upon himself the functions not only of witness but also of prosecutor and even judge. He declares in court: ". . . I was told that these are writers and that they are being prosecuted here for their ties with the NTS." Who but Brocks-Sokolov presumes to predict the court's judgment on a case involving Soviet citizens!

Under the law, incidentally, a witness does not have the right to be present in the courtroom until he gives his testimony. If an exception was made for Brocks, what was the reason for it? Moreover, had he not been present in the court before his testimony, from where could he have learned about the defendants—that they were "criminals," or anything else? All by hearsay?

The following thought arises: What was Brocks-Sokolov's true role in the January trial?

It is noteworthy that the authors' attitude toward the spy Brocks is one of great indulgence—indeed, of touching pity. At times, one detects a note of tender emotion when they talk of this "still so very young, tow-headed fellow who speaks Russian fairly well" (*Komsomolskaia pravda*). While recognizing that Brocks proved to be "up to his ears in dirt," the authors of the *Izvestia* article are quick to add: "It looks as if he got into it through naiveté and his great trustfulness toward people. . . ." Sympathetically, they quote the following from Brocks's statement in court: "I should like to say that I am sorry that I have unintentionally violated the laws of this country."

An altogether different tone is taken toward the defendants. Their biographies are painted in solid black—though one should add here that this is not true of all the defendants to the same degree, Dobrovolsky being somewhat of an exception. But toward Galanskov and Ginzburg there is no mercy. *Izvestia*, for instance, says that Ginzburg "discovered himself in swindling." *Komsomolskaia pravda* explains that, in 1960, he "was called to account for swindling and forgery of documents," spending two years in prison. [The paper adds:] "In 1964, another criminal suit was instituted against him for similar unseemly acts." It would not hurt to tell the reader that, in 1960, Ginzburg took a school examination (for students not attending lectures) on behalf of a close friend and for this purpose substituted his own photograph on the appropriate [examination] paper. This is doubtless a legal offense, but is it such a terrible moral discrediting of Ginzburg? And further, except for Ginzburg, who was ever sentenced (and when) to two years' imprisonment for a like offense? One suspects that the real, hidden motive behind the persecution [of Ginzburg] in 1960 was not connected with the forging of documents. Was it not the same the second time, in 1964?

Komsomolskaia pravda is not very much concerned about the consistency of its judgments regarding Ginzburg's and Galanskov's personalities. Let us cite some facts bearing on the responsibility of these judgments.

It is said that the defendants went about their business "with the prudence of experienced merchants." Yet, at the same time, we learn that "after getting some 50-dollar notes from Galanskov on one occasion, blackmarket operators contrived to hand over for them . . . a pack of mustard-plasters." Fine merchant!

We learn of the defendants that they "maintain a silent conspiracy with the cunning of hardened criminals." [Yet] right away it turns out that, on the title page of Galanskov's incriminating collection *Phoenix*, there appears [the inscription] "Edited by Yu. Galanskov." Also, in the compilation that constituted Ginzburg's crime and in the editions [of it] published in various countries, everywhere there appears: "Compiled by A. Ginzburg." And these are conspirators? One is tempted to repeat the words of the author Ovcharenko: "A strange dialectic emerges." The interesting thing is: for what readers were these passages intended? . . .

Now let us see how the testimony of the defendants themselves appears in the pages of the press and what confessions were included in such testimony.

Both articles quote the testimony of Dobrovolsky. We read in *Izvestia*:

"Exactly such a Shapirograph [hectograph] was given to me earlier by Galanskov," stated the defendant Dobrovolsky.

And here is *Komsomolskaia pravda*:

PROSECUTOR: What do you know about the foreign ties of Galanskov and Ginzburg?
DOBROVOLSKY: In connection with Galanskov's transfer to me of NTS literature and a Shapirograph, I became interested in where he had obtained all this. Galanskov told me that he had had a foreign connection since 1962 and had obtained it through Ginzburg.
PROSECUTOR: With what organization was this foreign connection?
DOBROVOLSKY: Galanskov told me that he had ties with the NTS.

Thus, the testimonies of Galanskov and Ginzburg remain unknown to the reader, and, from the testimony of Dobrovolsky, two things follow: In the first place, in relation to the other defendants, Ginzburg and Galanskov, Dobrovolsky appears as a witness for the prosecution, acknowledging not his own guilt but that of others. Secondly, it is revealed that the objects that served in court as material evidence of the guilt of all the defendants (the Shapirograph and the NTS literature) were found at the residence of Dobrovolsky.

The suspicion involuntarily arises: Weren't these things found *only* at Dobrovolsky's?

One begins to wonder whether there are any grounds for a case involving a group of persons. Let us ask: Why did Galanskov and Ginzburg find themselves in the same dock? Yes, *Komsomolskaia pravda* calls them "companions" and alleges that "they are compiling a new collection with the pretentious title *Phoenix*." But why *they*? Why *companions*? No evidence is cited of joint literary activity by Galanskov and Ginzburg, and, if one goes by public signature, then the compilation of the *White Book* was the work of Ginzburg and the compilation of *Phoenix* solely that of Galanskov. Might there not be testimony by the compilers themselves on this point? The author of the article in *Komsomolskaia pravda*, Ovcharenko, alludes only once to the testimony of Ginzburg and Galanskov, passing on this evidence, for some reason, in these words: "They both suddenly declared that they did not regard what they had done in collaboration with the NTS, an organization hostile to our people, as anti-Soviet activity." What does this mean? Does it mean, first, that the defendants confessed to working together and to their connections with the NTS, as Ovcharenko wants to present the affair? Or does it mean, second, that, while the defendants did not admit any anti-Soviet activity on their part—and that is all—Ovcharenko himself qualifies this activity as joint and ties it to the NTS? One cannot doubt that it is the second and not the first. The defendants simply denied the accusations; otherwise, the author of the article would certainly have cited their testimony verbatim, as he did in the case of Dobrovolsky.

Thus, in the trial, complete trust was placed in the testimony of Dobrovolsky. He received a short sentence (2 years) as compared with Galanskov (7 years) and Ginzburg (5 years). The authors of the newspaper articles try by all means to benefit Dobrovolsky by differentiating him from his co-defendants (I will not say comrades)!

Komsomolskaia pravda refers to "Ginzburg, Galanskov, and the bookbinder Dobrovolsky, who was inveigled into their company."

Izvestia consoles Dobrovolsky by saying, "One would like to think that his confession and acknowledgement of guilt in the recent trial will open his eyes and help, at last, to start him on an honest path."

As one compares all the facts of the behavior of the defendants and other circumstances, it comes to mind that the role of Dobrovolsky is analogous to the role of Brocks-Sokolov.

However, [a look at] who was present at the trial is even more revealing.

Izvestia reports: "Moscow citizens attending the trial greeted with approval the verdict of the court."

Komsomolskaia pravda says more precisely: "Moscow citizens present in the courtroom greeted the verdict with applause and cries of approval."

I am among those Moscow citizens for whom no place was found in the courtroom.

In full conformity with Soviet laws providing for open, public trial, a group of persons submitted an application to the appropriate authorities requesting permission to be present at the trial. We submitted the application ahead of time so that no excuse could be made later on the grounds of the smallness of the premises, etc.

I do not know what Moscow citizens attended the trial, although it can be surmised. I am among those Moscow citizens, as well as those non-Moscovites, who can judge the January trial only from the newspapers. One expression that was used in the newspapers was "massive misinformation." Suppose the readers should apply this to something other than the author did!

A. Yakobson
Translator

P.S. As a further detail, I wish to note one contradiction of fact between *Izvestia* and *Komsomolskaia pravda*. *Komsomolskaia pravda* quotes Brocks as testifying in the January trial: ". . . I was told that these packages contained only materials that could be of help to them [the defendants]. When I was detained, it turned out that what was there was not what they had told me."

"Yes," the author of the article, Ovcharenko, goes on to say, "the packages turned out to contain something other than what Nicholas had believed. Money, intended by no means for charitable purposes. A Shapirograph and a batch of carbon paper for cryptography. . . . Leaflets with anti-Soviet slogans. . . . And in five envelopes—which *Brocks-Sokolov was supposed to drop into a mailbox*—were *enlarged photographs of the defendants*, on the backs of which was a short text concluding with threatening demands for immediate emancipation."

From this, it clearly follows that the envelopes containing the photographs, which Brocks personally was to drop into a mailbox, could not have been in the packages, which were intended for delivery to a mysterious stranger; for, otherwise, the other—criminal—contents of these packages would not have been a secret to Brocks.

But here is the discrepancy! *Izvestia*, while maintaining, like *Komsomolskaia pravda*, that Brocks "before his arrest knew nothing about the contents of the packages," reports at the same time: "The packages, which Brocks was to hand over to a 'certain person' in Sokolniki Park in Moscow, *contained photographs* of people with whom he was not acquainted. . . ."

Can it be that these are not the same photographs referred to in *Komsomolskaia pravda* and that the people photographed are not the same? We read further in the *Izvestia* article: "Five . . . envelopes containing photographs, and the photographs are of the defendants in the dock—Ginzburg, Galanskov, and Dobrovolsky—who were known to Brocks only by hearsay."

Whom shall be believe—*Izvestia* or *Komsomolskaia pravda*?

Only one thing here is not open to question: that Brocks, the chief witness for the prosecution, "was not acquainted" with the defendants and knew about them only through "hearsay." Everything else gives rise to amazement: how Brocks-Sokolov got confused in his simple task, and how, following right after him, the authors of both articles did the same.

A. Yakobson

24. Against Barbarism in the Court: Letter
by P. Grigorenko

January, 1968

To the Members and Candidate Members of the Politburo, CPSU Central Committee

International Human Rights Year began in the U.S.S.R. with an unprecedented violation of human rights. At this very time, our motherland has been nailed to a pillory of shame in the eyes of all the world as well as of Communist society. This was done by official representatives of the government through a barbaric trial organized by organs of the KGB.

During the trial of Galanskov, Ginzburg, Dobrovolsky, and Lashkova (held January 8-12 of this year), I, like many other citizens of Moscow, paced for several hours each day in front of the court building and felt —with unsual bitterness—the injustice and shame this trial was bringing upon our country.

Yet, in spite of this, I had not intended to write you. It seemed to me that the Politburo itself, for which the interests of the *Party, motherland,* and *world Communist movement* are paramount, would find out what had transpired [at the trial] and would respond properly to world opinion. However, the mendacious articles about this trial published in *Izvestia* (No. 15712) and *Komsomolskaia pravda* (No. 13089) compel me to take up my pen.

For whom are these packs of dirty lies intended?

Certainly not for world opinion! World opinion would not believe [such lies], for it knows that this trial, though formally open, was in fact held in complete isolation from unauthorized eyes. F. Ovcharenko, writing in *Komsomolskaia pravda*, lied when he claimed that the hall was full and that workers and officials of Moscow enterprises and institutions were in attendance. Quite on the contrary, the trial was conducted in a half-empty hall and was attended precisely by those persons who had no right to be there—employees of the investigatory organs (KGB) and other persons carefully chosen by the KGB. Even the witnesses, who, by law, are required to remain in the courtroom after testifying, were dismissed from the trial despite their pleas and protests.

The KGB and the militia occupied more than just the courtroom. They literally flooded the Moscow Municipal Court Building and its environs with their agents. This was witnessed not only by us Soviet citizens but also by all the foreign correspondents who were constantly gathered around the court building—none of whom, of course, was admitted to the courtroom.

Can they really believe that such complete isolation of the trial was in the interest of the full elucidation of the truth? No, they know as well as we do that *truth does not fear the light*, [that truth] does not fear witnesses and observers. Only sordid affairs are carried out in isolation from the people, in darkness, behind closed doors. . . .

This "typical trial" is a provocation—analogous to the trials organized in the days of Yagoda, Yezhov, and Beria. The only difference is that, at that time, they [the authorities] spoke of "enemies of the people" without concretely defining their crime, whereas, nowadays, they rely on pure fabrication as the basis for an unjust sentence.

Indeed, these people were arrested for creating honest literary works that even a specially chosen court could not have deemed to be anti-Soviet. For that reason, they [the authorities] fabricated "ties with the NTS." The precariousness of the accusation can be judged from the fact that, first, the prosecutor, in a completely absurd manner, rejected those defense witnesses who would have proved dangerous to the prosecution's case, and the court approved these unfounded rejections; and second, that Brocks-Sokolov, who had no relationship, direct or indirect, to the case being tried, was brought in as a witness for the prosecution, [the story of] his notorious belt making it appear that material evidence was available.

This unwise venture has inflicted the gravest injury on the motherland. Apart from the moral-ethical, political, and juridical aspects of the case, I wish to point out, as a military specialist, that it is difficult even to estimate, on the one hand, the great number of allies lost by our country and, on the other hand, the number of potential supporters acquired by our probable enemies during this trial. Not even the fiercest of our enemies could have done us more harm. . . .

Comrade members and candidate-members of the Politburo!

It is not too late to remedy the folly committed by bureaucrats preoccupied only with their own careers and not with the interests of the motherland. Look into this case and you will be convinced that the charges were unfounded. In world public opinion, there has been no doubt of this for some time. And world public opinion will not change when confronted with an even more naked lie.

In such circumstances, the leadership of the Party and government does not have the right to pose as a disinterested observer. In my opinion, it is obliged to demonstrate to the whole world that it took no part in this provocation and that it intends to initiate measures to reverse the illegal sentences, to put an end to such dirty business, and to impose serious punishment on those who organized, prepared, and carried out this provocation, so shameful and harmful to our country.

P. GRIGORENKO

Moscow, G-21, Komsomolsky Prospekt 14/1
Apt. 96, Telephone G-64-27-37

25. Appeal of Thirteen Witnesses

To: Chairman of the Moscow Municipal Court
    Chairman of the R.S.F.S.R. Supreme Court
    Chairman of the U.S.S.R. Supreme Court
    Procurator of the R.S.F.S.R.
    U.S.S.R. Procurator General
Copies to:
    Chairman of the Presidium of the U.S.S.R. Supreme Soviet, N. V.
      Podgorny
    Chairman of the U.S.S.R. Council of Ministers, A. N. Kosygin
    Secretary General of the CPSU Central Committee, L. I. Brezhnev
    Chairman of the Presidium of the Moscow Municipal Collegium
      of Lawyers
    S. L. Ariia, Attorney
    B. A. Zolotukhin, Attorney
    D. P. Kaminskaia, Attorney
    V. Ya. Shivesky, Attorney

We, who were witnesses at the trial of Ginzburg, Galanskov, Dobrovolsky, and Lashkova (held at the Moscow Municipal Court, January 8–12, 1968), express our protest against the violation of court procedure that was allowed to take place during the trial with regard to ourselves. Article 283 of the Procedural Code of the R.S.F.S.R. states:

> Witnesses who have already been questioned must remain in the courtroom and may not leave until the end of the judicial investigation without the permission of the court. The chairman may permit already questioned witnesses to leave the hall prior to the conclusion of the judicial investigation only after hearing the opinions of the prosecutor, the defendant, and the defense lawyers or, in civil cases, the plaintiff, the defendant, and their respective representatives.

Each of us expressed his desire to remain in the courtroom after giving testimony, referring to the above-cited article of the R.S.F.S.R. Procedural Code [to affirm] that this was not only our right but, in the first instance, our obligation. Yet the Chairman of the Court (Deputy Chairman Mironov of the Moscow Municipal Court) dismissed all the witnesses, punctuating his demand that they withdraw with rude shouts. The "Commandant of the Court," KGB Colonel Tsirkunenko, was even more offensive and insulting. The demand that we leave the room was not argued [before the court] but simply justified on the basis of a lack of seats and breathing room, even though there were enough empty places.

We believe that this violation of established procedural order should be reviewed by an unbiased court.

We request that the appellate and review courts, during the processing of the appeal and also in the event of a retrial of this case, take into account the content of our declaration as testimony to one of the flagrant abuses of legality that took place during this trial.

Ye. Basilova
V. Vinogradov
A. Yepifanov
I. Kamishanova
L. Kats
Ye. Kushev

A. Levitin
S. Potashova
N. Serebriakova
G. Simonova
N. Stoliarova
A. Topeshkina
N. Ustinova

26. Protest by G. S. Podiapolsky

To the Procurator General of the U.S.S.R.

As you are obviously aware, in early January of this year (1968), the trial of Galanskov, Ginzburg, Dobrovolsky, and Lashkova, charged under Article 70 of the R.S.F.S.R. Criminal Code, was held in the Moscow Municipal Court.

And, as you are obviously unaware, this entire trial was conducted under conditions that involved repeated violations of socialist legality, as specifically set forth in the following:

1. The period of detention of the accused for pretrial investigation significantly exceeded the maximum period stipulated by existing law. This violation was apparently not caused by any special complications arising in connection with the elucidation of the facts of the case and could have no other purpose than to exert psychological pressure on the accused before the trial (which is not permissible).

2. The trial was officially declared to be open, but, in fact, this was not the case. It was necessary to show passes to enter the courtroom, and even the closest relatives of the accused were allowed to enter only after humiliating delay and after the trial had begun.

This violation of public access to the trial certainly cannot be justified by any ridiculous references to a lack of space; it could have had no other purpose than to avoid the very publicity that would have precluded the subsequent violations of legality and procedural rules that took place during this trial and that obviously were planned in advance.

3. An incomplete list of the violations committed during the trial is as follows: Defense witnesses were ejected by the court for no reason and were not heard out; testimony given on behalf of the defendants was rudely interrupted by the judge and not entered into the record; and,

after testifying, witnesses were immediately turned out of the courtroom, even though existing procedural laws require that witnesses remain in court until the end of the session. The "listeners" in court, consisting for the most part of disguised KGB agents, mocked the defendants and defense witnesses; yet not once did the judge call them to order. The members of the court had not the slightest intention of objectively reviewing the evidence relating to the case and obviously pursued the sole objective of judging the accused on other charges. Because of this, the clearly false testimony of defendant Dobrovolsky, which contradicted that of all the other defendants and which (as far as it is possible to surmise) he gave as a result of having been worked over during the year-long investigations, was accepted as irrefutable proof of the other defendants' guilt. On the other hand, defense arguments, which unquestionably proved the groundlessness of certain accusations, were simply ignored by the court.

The experience of previous trials of this nature indicates that those who organized this trial in such a manner could not have been unaware that the result of all these violations would be to discredit Soviet law in the eyes of society and do inestimable damage to the prestige of our state both within the U.S.S.R. and abroad.

In accordance with what I have set forth, I appeal to you to do the following:

1. To carry out a complete and detailed examination of all the violations and abuses that took place at the aforementioned trial, with the purpose of disclosing their full extent and exposing the true criminals.

2. To hold an open trial of those guilty of these abuses under Article 69 of the R.S.F.S.R. Criminal Code, since the crimes committed during the Galanskov trial are specified in this article—to wit, activity directed toward the undermining of a state organ (the Soviet court as an organ of socialist legality); activity that has as its goal the weakening of the Soviet state (by doing damage to its moral prestige); and activity involving the exploitation of a state institution (the Moscow Municipal Court).

3. To annul the sentence in the Galanskov case, since it was handed down under conditions that involved criminal violations of socialist legality and that were absolutely incompatible with an objective examination of the case; and to conduct a new and open trial in conformity with existing procedural norms—or, at least, to annul the sentence.

4. To increase the procurator's surveillance of the activities of our courts so that future illegal actions, which cast shame on our state, will not be permitted.

G. S. PODIAPOLSKY

Moscow, G-351,
Yartsevskaia Street 18, Apt. 27

27. *Rebirth of Stalinism? Letter by I. Gabai, Y. Kim, and P. Yakir*

To the Leaders of Art, Science, and Culture in the U.S.S.R.

We the signers of this letter, turn to you with words of deep alarm for the fate and honor of our country.

In the course of recent years, ominous symptoms of a restoration of Stalinism have appeared in our social life. This appears most clearly in the repetition of the most terrible acts of that epoch—in the organization of cruel trials of persons who dared to defend their dignity and freedom of mind, who presumed to think and to protest.

Of course, the repressions have not reached the scale of those [earlier] years. But we have sufficient grounds to fear that, among the officials of state and Party, there are a number of people who would like to reverse the course of our social development. We have no guarantees that, if we allow this to happen in silence, the year 1937 will not return once more.

We will not soon again be able to see Andrei Siniavsky and Yuli Daniel, condemned to long years of suffering solely because they dared to write about things that they considered to be true.

Quite young people—Viktor Khaustov and Vladimir Bukovsky—have been torn away from life for a period of three years. Their entire "crime" consisted in publicly expressing disagreement with the draconic laws and punitive measures that once again pillory our country.

The action of the kangaroo court that tried them was an example of cynical illegality and perversion of the facts.

The recent trial of four young people exceeded all bounds in trampling upon human rights. Even A. Vyshinsky might have envied the organization of that trial. He, at least, extorted confessions of a sort and statements by witnesses. Prosecutor Terekhov and Judge Mironov did not even need to go through the empty formality of presenting proof. Yuri Galanskov, physically a very sick man, was sentenced to seven years of hard labor. The sole and less than circumstantial proof of his guilt was the deposition of an ignoble and craven person, A. Dobrovolsky. Aleksandr Ginzburg was sentenced to five years of hard labor in the face of all the testimony of the witnesses and the material evidence.

Even the life of Aleksei Dobrovolsky, who played the ill-omened role of a Kostomarov[1] at that trial, has been damaged. If he has even a shred of conscience, thirty pieces of silver are far from a sufficient recompense for the contempt and rejection that await this slanderer. For this moral mutilation of Dobrovolsky—a scoundrel who destroyed his comrades and slandered them out of vile self-interest—our punitive organs also bear the largest share of responsibility.

The extent of the guilt of Vera Lashkova consisted in the fact that she typed several texts that the court considered to be of a criminal character. And, in the prevailing conditions of our country, as the experience of others condemned under the criminal statutes (L. Rendel, A. Marchenko, and others) shows, she will pay very dearly for that offense—through a notation in her passport and loss of the right to live and study in Moscow.

The atmosphere surrounding the trial was one more link in the chain of illegality. The official organs shamelessly misinformed the Western Communist press. It was announced on the day the trial began that it had not yet been scheduled. The Deputy Chairman of the Moscow Municipal Court, Mironov, when questioned about it a few days before the trial, said that the case had not yet been referred to the Municipal Court.

People trying to enter the courtroom were subjected to outright blackmail and a contemptuous disrespect for human dignity. The taking of photographs, relentless shadowing, the checking of documents, eavesdropping on conversations—this is far from a complete list of the phenomena that marked the memorable days of the star-chamber proceedings in the case of Ginzburg and his co-defendants. Perhaps the most frightening thing about it was that, among the spies, there were some quite young people—young men and girls. Instead of engaging in serious study, they engaged in eavesdropping; instead of attempting to realize and comprehend something, they made denunciations—and, from the viewpoint of the KGB, this informing presumably represented the very epitome of youthful morality in contrast to the "immorality" of Ginzburg, who dared to intervene on behalf of people sentenced without being guilty.

You are, of course, familiar with the letter of L. Bogoraz-Daniel and P. Litvinov.[2] With full responsibility, we declare: Every line in that letter is not only the truth; it is only the smallest part of the truth about the unprecedented outrages and mockery of the accused. The organization of the trial and the conduct of the judge, whose responsibility demands complete impartiality, in effect deprived the accused of their right of self-defense, and the bestial hooting of what was called "the public" created an atmosphere of moral indignation against them. In the courtroom, people sat turning the pages of newspapers, or they dozed, waking up only to clamor for severer sentences.

The authorities once again organized a so-called public trial by exploiting the basest traits of specially chosen people with the logic of drumheads, an impudent indifference to the fate of others, and a mindlessness that demanded neither information nor an analysis of the facts.

While, in the courtroom, the hysterical women and the Black Hundreds[3] dozed or mocked the accused, out in the corridor, and, later, outside in the cold, the people who constituted the real public milled about: friends and relatives of the accused, people who did not know them but wished to know the truth—writers, artists, students, teachers.

For the uninformed, the central organs of the press concocted falsifications that were either direct lies or tendentiously selected facts. Those who pretend to the role of ideological preceptors have neglected something very important: "It is essential to take not single facts but the whole complex of facts bearing upon the question under examination, *without a single exception*, since otherwise the suspicion—and a wholly justified suspicion—inevitably arises that the facts have been selected or chosen arbitrarily, that, instead of an objective nexus and interrelationship, . . . a subjective concoction is perhaps being offered for the justification of a dirty business. That, after all, occurs . . . more often than it would seem." Those are the words of V. I. Lenin (XXX, p. 351).

The inhuman lynching of intellectuals is the logical culmination of the atmosphere of recent years in public life. The naive hopes for a thorough cleansing of our public life that were instilled in us by the decisions of the Twentieth and Twenty-second Congresses have not borne fruit. Slowly but surely, the process of restoring Stalinism goes on. In this process, chief reliance is being placed on our own passivity, our short memory, and the bitter fact that we are accustomed to an absence of freedom.

Here are some of the milestones of the rebirth of Stalinism in recent years:

1. The name of J. V. Stalin has been cited from the highest platforms in a wholly positive context. The newspapers have written about the applause that has greeted the mention of his name. They have not written that this was frequently the applause of people with a servile hunger for a strong personality, people who want to justify their own conduct in the not too distant past, or people suffering from remnants of perverted nationalistic feelings.

For how long was it necessary to pervert human nature to the point where it could applaud the murderer of hundreds of thousands of people, the organizer of tortures and torments?

2. This might perhaps be explained by a desire to treat history objectively. Of course, an objective attitude toward a hangman is also a fact of moral pathology, but one could still understand it.

But, for some reason, there is not enough objectivity to permit telling the truth about the major political leaders of the first decade of Soviet power. It would, after all, be possible, without violating the proper bounds of Party discussion, to say honestly of various persons that they did not organize terroristic actions, did not engage in espionage, and did not sprinkle broken glass into foodstuffs. It would, after all, be possible to relate also what they accomplished while in their high positions. But the great Civil War services of the People's Commissar for National Minorities J. V. Stalin remain with us to this day, alongside the unrelieved wrecking activities of the then People's Commissar for the Armed Forces and Chairman of the Revolutionary Military Council, L. D. Trotsky.

3. As a consequence of all this, the term "cult of personality" has all but been banned from our press. Artistic and scholarly works in which Stalin and the crimes of the Stalinist period are subjected to criticism are either not approved or, if already set up in type, are not printed (the memoirs of B. Vannikov, L. Slavin's book on Marshal Yegorov, the frontline diaries of K. Simonov, the memoirs of Ye. Ginzburg, and many, many others). Matters have gone so far that the powerful ideological official Fedoseev has recommended that the term "cult of personality" be used only with reference to Latin American dictators or Mao Tse-tung.

4. Not one democratic beginning has been carried through to completion. To the present day, the literary or artistic taste of the hanger-on still has the force of law for the writer, artist, director, reader, viewer. In the cinema archives, films that would do great honor to our art are rotting. Wonderful paintings lie neglected in cramped studios and attics. Room is found in literature only for the low-grade productions of a Kochetov or a Smirnov—especially those glorifying J. V. Stalin—and only a favored few have been able to read Solzhenitsyn's *Cancer Ward*.

The attempt to stop the so-called *samizdat*, or uncensored literature, is doomed to fail. Had there been no *samizdat* in Russian literature, we should have lost Radishchev's novel, [Griboedov's[4] play] *Woe from Wit*, and many of Pushkin's poems. And, even in our time, the solicitude of a group of readers for the unpublished word will preserve for better times the true facts about the thought and creativity of our contemporaries. The hangers-on can do nothing about it! The Zhdanovs pass into oblivion, but the work of an Akhmatova[5] conquers generation after generation.

Sensing this, the punitive organs resort to outright forgeries, as was the case in the absurd attempt to link the compiler of the book on the trial of Siniavsky and Daniel with the *émigré* organization NTS.

In the social sciences, the pernicious and unilateral dictates of political expediency continue to be imposed. For the scholar, to deviate from the truth means death; yet our contemporary historians, philosophers, and economists are compelled to do it every day. If, by chance, a particle of the truth finds its way into print, the authors begin to be persecuted. Examples are well known.

5. The Crimean Tatar nation has only recently been rehabilitated. But the Soviet public knows little of this, just as it does not know that this people, against whom an enormous great-power crime was committed, still cannot return to its homeland. And those who attempt to do so are sent back or subjected to acts of repression.

6. What is most demeaning is that constant surveillance, in all its forms, has become part of the daily life of a large number of Soviet citizens.

There are only a few examples from our public life.

Once more, we remind you: silent connivance with the Stalinists and the bureaucrats who are deceiving both the people and the leadership, stifling every sign, every complaint, every protest, leads logically to the very worst result—illegal reprisals against human beings.

Under these conditions, we appeal to you people of creative labor, people in whom our nation places its unlimited trust: raise your voices against the imminent danger of new Stalins and Yezhovs. The fate of future Vavilovs and Mandelshtams is on your conscience.

You are the heirs of the great humanistic traditions of the Russian intelligentsia.

You have before you the example of the courageous behavior of the contemporary progressive intelligentsia of the West.

We understand that you are placed in such conditions that, each time you are called upon to fulfill your duty as citizens, it requires an act of courage. But, after all, there is no other choice; either courage or cowardly complicity in foul deeds, either the acceptance of risks or alliance with the Vasilevs and Kedrins, either sacrifice or joining the ranks of the yellow hack-writers of *Izvestia* and *Komsomolskaia pravda*, who consider it morally justifiable to slander publicly the people whom they have helped to lynch.

We want only a little: that our people should have the moral right to protest the six-month imprisonment of M. Teodorakis.[6]

And, for this to happen, only a little more is needed: to bring about the return from long-term imprisonment of our unjustly condemned fellow citizens.

We remind you once more: languishing in the cruel conditions of hard-labor camps are people who dared to think. The silence of each one of you will be a step toward another trial of a Daniel or a Ginzburg. Slowly, with your silent consent, a new 1937 may arrive.

ILYA GABAI
Pedagogue, editor

Moscow, A-55, Novolesnaia Street, Bldg. 18, Block 2, Apt. 83. Office telephone, B-3-10-39

YULI KIM
Teacher

Moscow, Riazansky Prospekt, 73, Apt. 90, Office telephone, G-9-71-18

PIOTR YAKIR
Historian

Moscow, Zh-280, Avtozavodskaia Street, Bldg. 5, Apt. 75. Home telephone, Zh-5-21-15

NOTES

1. Nikolai Ivanovich Kostomarov (1817–85), Russian historian and writer, was a founder and one of the leaders of the secret Society of Cyril and Methodius (Taras Shevchenko was also a member). Arrested when the society was discovered by the Tsarist police, Kostomarov "conducted himself in a cowardly fashion and swore fealty to the autocracy" (*Bolshaia Sovetskaia Entsiklopediia* [2d ed.; Moscow, 1953], XXIII, 128).—ED.

2. Document 7.

3. The Black Hundreds was an ultrareactionary, anti-Semitic organization sponsored and supported by the Tsarist secret police.—ED.

4. Aleksandr Sergeevich Griboedov (1795–1829), diplomat and playwright, was best known for his comedy *Woe from Wit.*—ED.

5. Anna Andreevna Akhmatova (1888–1966) was an eminent poetess. For further identification, see Biographical Notes, p. 463. Kopelev's eulogy at her funeral appears on pp. 426-28.—ED.

6. Teodorakis, a famous Greek composer, was imprisoned by the Greek junta in 1967 and exiled to one of the Aegean islands.—ED.

28. *Protest by Twenty-four Intellectuals*

To: Secretary General L. I. Brezhnev
    Prime Minister A. N. Kosygin
    President N. V. Podgorny
    Procurator General R. A. Rudenko
    Attorneys
    Editors of *Izvestia, Komsomolskaia pravda, Literaturnaia gazeta, Moskovskii komsomolets*

The signers of this letter are deeply disturbed by the circumstances surrounding the trial of Y. Galanskov, A. Ginsburg, A. Dobrovolsky, and V. Lashkova and by the course of the trial and its outcome. It is no secret that this judicial proceeding has attracted the attention of society.

Moreover, in the course of the hearings, no information concerning them was made public. The trial, though officially declared open, in fact took place behind closed doors. It is fully understandable that this gave rise to an atmosphere of suspicion, alarm, and mistrust. The articles that appeared in *Izvestia* and *Komsomolskaia pravda* after the trial only increased this mistrust. The peremptory and, at the same time, strangely nervous tone of the newspaper articles, which were in the nature of a psychological attack on the trusting reader; the murkiness of the argumentation arising from an obvious lack of precise facts; the gravity of the accusations and their diffuseness; the formal openness of the trial and its actual secrecy—all this, taken together, appeared most unseemly.

It seems as though the press was unable to ascertain a sufficient number

of concrete facts that were clearly and incontrovertibly proved. It seems
that the court, which pronounced such severe sentences on two of the
four defendants, conducted itself in a manner that seriously breached
the standards of Soviet jurisprudence. All this evokes alarm in us.

All this also evokes understandable misgivings among friends of our
country abroad and, at the same time, gives our ideological enemies
unnecessary grounds for portraying the state of our society and our
democracy in an unfavorable light.

The fact that several "open" criminal trials dealing with political
affairs have taken place within a comparatively short period and in substantially similar conditions calls forth gloomy associations. The shameful trials of the 1930's, which have not been and will not be erased from
our memory, were also conducted "openly," yet—as we now know—
tendentiously and unscrupulously, even claiming justification in the
theory of "sharpening class struggle."

Must we now, after living through fifty years of Soviet power, actually be witnesses [again] to the mobilization of the hypocritical methods of the past? We insist on a new, fully public, and strictly objective
court examination fully conforming to Soviet legality.

We insist on this in the interests of truth and legality, in the interests
of the reputation of the Soviet state, and in the name of justice and
humanity.

VASSILI AKSIONOV, writer
PAVEL ANTOKOLSKY, poet
BORIS BALTER, writer
BORIS BIRGER, artist
VLADIMIR BOINOVICH, writer
FAZIL ISKANDER, writer
KAMIL IKRAMOV, writer
VENIAMIN KAVERIN, writer
YURI KAZAKOV, writer
NAUM KORZHAVIN, poet
VLADIMIR KORNILOV, poet
FEDOT SUKHOV, critic

SERGEI LARIN, critic
LEV LEVITSKY, critic
NOVELLA MATVEEVA, poet
OLEG MIKHAILOV, critic
VALENTIN NEPOMNIASHCHI, critic
KONSTANTIN PAUSTOVSKY, writer
YURI PILIAR, writer
GRIGORI POZHENIAN, poet
MIKHAIL ROSHCHIN, writer
BENEDICT SARNOV, critic
FELIKS SVETOV, critic
MARIA YUDINA, pianist

29. Yu. Piliar's Retraction

[On April 24, 1968, Literaturnaia gazeta published the following statement of retraction, said to have been received by the Secretariat of the
Moscow Writers' Organization from Yu. Piliar, one of the signers of
the protest of twenty-four intellectuals printed above as Document 28.
—ED.]

To the Secretary of the Board of Directors of the Moscow Writers'
Organization

I was able to acquaint myself for the first time with the full text of
the letter [of twenty-four intellectuals] only at the offices of the secretariat of the Moscow division. Until then, I simply had not read the
whole letter and, consequently, had not grasped its true meaning, specifically with respect to its evaluation of the Soviet court, with which
I categorically disagree. I consider my action in signing that letter to
have been thoughtless at the very least, and I am ashamed of my gul-
libility.

The fact that some dishonest persons, without asking the permission
of the signers, disseminated abroad that document, which was addressed
to Soviet leaders, makes me indignant. Now, having acquainted myself
with the full text of the document, I cannot help but express my condemnation of the organizers of the whole venture, who thus abused
the confidence of a whole group of writers. In any case, I never gave
anyone permission to use my name in any questionable declarations
[to be publicized] outside the borders of my country.

In view of the foregoing, I withdraw my signature from that letter.

Yu. Piliar

30. Petition of 170

Copies to:
Procurator General of the U.S.S.R., Comrade Rudenko
Supreme Court, R.S.F.S.R.
President of the Presidium of the Supreme Soviet of the U.S.S.R.,
N. V. Podgorny
President of the Council of Ministers of the U.S.S.R., A. N. Kosygin
Secretary General of the CPSU Central Committee, L. I. Brezhnev
Attorneys Ariia, Zolotukhin, Kaminskaia, Shveisky

We have familiarized ourselves with the letter written by Larisa Bogoraz-Daniel and Pavel Litvinov regarding the trial of Yuri Galanskov,
Aleksandr Ginzburg, Aleksei Dobrovolsky, and Vera Lashkova.[1] We
agree completely with the authors of the letter, and we consider it our
duty to make the following declaration.

From what we know about this trial, it is clear to us that it was conducted with gross violations of the correct legal norms.

Though represented as an open trial, the proceedings, in fact, took
place behind closed doors. Admission to the courtroom was by special
permission and was restricted to an audience specially selected with a
view to bringing about the moral isolation of the accused. The noise

and shouts of this public, the insults hurled at the accused and the witnesses, the mockery of the [defendants'] relatives—all this was designed to create an atmosphere of "public indignation." At the same time, not one of the friends of the accused, not one representative of the public interested in an impartial court examination was admitted to the trial. Those who gathered daily at the court building in hopes of learning something about the course of the trial were subjected to coarse treatment and provocations at the hands of the *druzhinniki*, militiamen, and unknown persons in civilian clothes. All those present were repeatedly photographed, and their conversations were subjected to constant eavesdropping. Immediately after testifying, the witnesses were rudely ejected from the courtroom, although, according to the law, witnesses are required to remain present until the conclusion of a court examination.

Numerous facts likewise indicate that the trial itself was of a flagrantly tendentious character. From the very beginning, the court sided with the prosecution. Questions put by the defense counsel were frequently ruled out as having no relevance to the case; the accused and their counsel were required to keep strictly within the framework of the indictment and were not allowed to use materials bearing on the case as a whole, whereas the prosecutor was allowed full scope. Since none of the witnesses supported the basic points of the indictment, their interrogation was reduced to an empty formality: twenty-five witnesses were interrogated in the course of a single day; they were sometimes cut off halfway through a sentence; and they were not allowed to appeal to the bench. Quite unexpectedly, Nicholas Brocks-Sokolov was called in as a witness, although his evidence had no relevance whatsoever to the case. Evidently it was calculated that his very presence at the trial would confuse the public.

This tendentious court handed down an equally tendentious verdict. The judgment fully satisfied the demands of the prosecutor, notwithstanding the fact that Galanskov, Ginzburg, and their counsel convincingly refuted all the fundamental charges of the indictment. The sentences handed down with respect to Galanskov and Ginzburg are either completely groundless or rest upon the testimony of Dobrovolsky, which was supported neither by the accused nor by the witnesses. On the contrary, all the evidence of an incriminating nature and the material evidence—NTS literature, money, and the Shapirograph found at his place—testify only against Dobrovolsky himself, on whom the court imposed a much lighter sentence. The impression arises that Dobrovolsky played a shadowy role in this trial and received a shorter term as his reward.

The conduct and outcome of the trial cause us great alarm. Several times already during the last few years, patent violations of legality and of the required public nature of court proceedings have occurred during political trials (the Siniavsky-Daniel case, the Khaustov case, the Bukovsky case, and others) and have become increasingly flagrant and obvious from case to case. In the last trial, these violations assumed a character of complete arbitrariness. No one can feel secure so long as this is not stopped and denounced.

We insist that the case of Galanskov, Ginzburg, Dobrovolsky, and Lashkova be re-examined under conditions of full publicity, in conformity with all the proper legal norms, and in the presence of representatives of the public chosen from among the signers of this letter. We likewise insist that those responsible for having organized this trial and thus discrediting Soviet justice receive just punishment.

(Enclosed: The Open Letter of L. Bogoraz-Daniel and P. Litvinov, "To World Public Opinion").

AVRAMENKO, mathematician
G. D. AVRUTSKY, engineer
N. I. AZAROVA, candidate in Philological Sciences
YU. AIKHENVALD, poet-translator
I. M. AKSELROD, instructor
A. ALEKSANDROVA, student, Pedagogical Institute
S. D. ALBANOV, architect (Magadan)
T. BAGROVNIKOVA, technician
T. BAEVA, student, Historical Archives Institute
M. YA. BERZINA, junior scientific worker
A. A. BRIANDINSKAIA, mathematician
YA. P. L. VASILEVSKY, mathematician
L. F. VASILEV, lawyer
YU. VISHNEVSKAIA, bookstore clerk
O. VOLKOVA, scientific worker
A. VOLOTSKAIA, junior scientific worker
A. S. VOLPIN, candidate in Physical-Mathematical Sciences
G. GABAI, teacher
I. GABAI, editor
YU. GENDLER, lawyer (Leningrad)
S. GENKIN, mathematician
V. GERLIN, teacher
V. A. GERSHOVICH, mathematician
V. NIKIFOROV, engineer
T. NIKOLAEVA, candidate in Philological Sciences
T. NIKOLSKAIA, student, Leningrad University
NOVIKOVA, instructor, technical school
B. OGIBENIN, candidate in Philological Sciences
V. A. PAVLINCHUK, junior scientific worker
L. G. PAVLOVSKAIA, engineer
A. PLOMNER, pensioner
A. POVOLOTSKAIA, editor
G. PODIAPOLSKY, geologist
M. POZDNIAK, engineer
G. POMERANTZ, library worker

V. PONOMAREV, physics (Kharkov)
A. POPOV, geologist
S. POTAPOVA, student, Pedagogical Institute
N. PRIADKINA, *student*, Textile Institute
N. RAPP, Doctor of Physical-Mathematical Sciences
(Kharkov)
YU. RAPP (Kharkov University)
A. RAPPAPORT, pedagogue
B. M. RATNOVSKY, engineer
B. A. REZNIKOV, physicist
YE. GILEROVA, teacher
G. GLADKOVA, editor
YU. GLAZOV, candidate in Historical Sciences
M. GLAZOVA, candidate in Philological Sciences
V. GOLOMIDOV, student, Institute of Culture
R. YA. GOLDIN, engineer
N. GORBANEVSKAIA, engineer-translator
A. V. GRIB, candidate in Chemical Sciences
V. V. GRIKOVICH, engineer
V. N. GRISHIN, mathematician
M. YE. DEZA, candidate in Phys.-Math Sciences
DZEBOEVA, biologist
B. DOMNIN, mathematician
N. DOROKHOVA, secretary-typist
G. G. DURMAN, scientific worker
B. Y. YEFIMOV, office worker
L. M. YEFIMOVA, instructor
YE. ZHIGUNOV, editor
ZAVELSKY, economist
YU. ZAKS, engineer-chemist
L. ZIMAN, pedagogue
K. KH. ZIMINA, architect
B. ZYBOK, student, Medical Institute
V. ROMANOV, bibliographer
I. G. ROMANOVA, teacher
V. RUBIN, candidate in Historical Sciences
M. RUBINA, candidate in Biological Sciences
V. SAVNIKOVA, worker, Likhachov plant
A. SAMBOR, radio journalist
V. L. SVECHINSKY, architect (Magadan)
D. M. SEGAL, linguist
V. A. SERGEEV, engineer
M. SERGIENKO, student
V. A. SIPACHEV, chemist
M. SLONIM, student, Moscow University
T. I. SMIRONOVA, musical instructor, kindergarten
YE. V. SMORODINOVA, engineer

V. B. Sokhransky, engineer
Ye. Starikov, engineer (Kaliningrad)
A. Starostin, physicist
Ye. L. Stepanov, librarian
G. Superfin, student, Tartusk University
Ye. Surits, translator
B. Sushko, laboratory assistant
T. Sushko, chemist
V. I. Tatarsky, Doctor of Physical-Mathematical Sciences
A. Ivanov, historian
V. V. Ivanov, engineer, candidate in Technical Sciences
V. S. Imshennik, senior scientific worker
A. Kanaev, geologist
M. Kaplan, geologist
L. Kats, librarian
G. Kashina, geologist
L. Kvachevsky, engineer-chemist (Leningrad)
A. I. Kibalchich, architect
A. Kim, physician
Yu. Kim, teacher
D. A. Kirtnits, Doctor of Physical-Mathematical Sciences
Yu. I. Kiselev, artist
Ye. Kolesnikov, engineer
G. Kopylov, candidate in Physical-Mathematical Sciences (Dubna)
V. R. Kormer, engineer
A. Korkhov, office worker
I. Korkhova, economist
S. Korytnaia, critic
G. Krapiviansky, deputy-director of art school
V. A. Krasin, economist
A. G. Krasina, technician
I. Kristi, mathematician
Yu. Telesin, mathematician
V. Telnikov, pedagogue
V. Timachev, geologist
A. Topeshkina, editor
V. Tupitsyn, mathematician
V. Turchin, Doctor of Physical-Mathematical Sciences
K. F. Turchin, junior scientific worker
I. V. Uspensky, candidate in Biological Sciences
I. Fadeeva, geologist
L. Fedorov, engineer
Sh. N. Feldman, senior scientific worker (Sverdlovsk)
L. M. Finkelshtein, instructor, history of music
G. Freidin, translator
V. Fridman, engineer (Leningrad)
B. Khazanov, mathematician

M. Kharitonov, editor
A. Khrabrovitsky, specialist in literature
V. Tsyplakov, student, Energy Institute
Chilikina, instructor
V. Shakhsuvarov, engineer
Shevtsova, candidate in Economic Sciences
T. Kuznetsova, airport employee
V. Lebedev, editor
Ye. Lebedeva, journalist
A. E. Levitin (Krasnov), religious writer
Yu. K. Lekomstev, candidate in Philological Sciences
T. Loginova, student, Pedagogical Institute
V. Luchkov, physiologist
M. Luchkova, engineer
I. G. Makarevich, student, Institute of Cinematography
I. R. Maksimova, editor
A. Marchuk, artist
M. Meerson, student, Moscow University
Yu. Metlin, geophysicist (Leningrad)
V. Milashevich, engineer-hydrologist
Z. Mirkina, translator
V. A. Mikhailov, engineer
A. Muchink, mathematician
G. Natapov, mathematician
N. Shiriaeva, bibliographer
B. I. Shlifshtein, engineer-economist
I. Kh. Shmain, mathematician
A. A. Shtelmakh, engineer
S. Shtutina, engineer
A. Shuster, physicist
V. Shchadrin, physicist
V. Shcheglov, mathematician
G. Shchedrovitsky, candidate in Philosophical Sciences
V. Edelman, physicist
G. Edelman, mathematician
K. O. Erastov, translator
T. D. Erastova, mother of six children
A. Yulikov, student
I. Yakir, student, Historical-Archives Institute
P. Yakir, historian
R. Yakir, engineer
A. Yakobson, translator

Note

1. Document 7.—Ed.

31. Petition by Forty-six Residents of Novosibirsk

To: Procurator General of the U.S.S.R. Rudenko Supreme Court, R.S.E.S.R.

Copies to:

Chairman of the Presidium of the Supreme Soviet of the U.S.S.R., N. V. Podgorny

Secretary General of the Central Committee of the CPSU, L. I. Brezhnev

Attorneys B. Zolotukhin, D. Kaminskaia

Editorial Office of *Komsomolskaia pravda*

The absence from our newspapers of coherent and complete information on the substance and course of the trial of A. Ginzburg, Yu. Galanskov, A. Dobrovolsky, and V. Lashkova, convicted under Article 70 of the Criminal Code of the R.S.F.S.R., has disturbed us and led us to seek information from other sources—namely, foreign Communist newspapers. What we have been able to find out has caused us to doubt that this political trial was conducted with due regard for the norms required by law, such, for instance, as the principle of open trial. This causes us alarm.

Our sense of civic responsibility prompts us to declare most emphatically that we consider the holding of what have in effect been closed political trials impermissible. We are alarmed at the fact that, behind the actually closed doors of the courtroom, illegal proceedings have taken place and unfounded sentences based on illegal accusations have been handed down. We cannot permit the judicial machinery of our state to slip from the control of the general public and [thus] plunge our country again into an atmosphere of judicial tyranny and lawlessness. We therefore demand that the verdict of the Moscow Municipal Court in the case of Ginzburg, Galanskov, Dobrovolsky, and Lashkova be annulled, that the case be retried in fully public hearings with scrupulous observance of all legal norms, and that the evidence be unfailingly publicized in the press.

We also demand that those guilty of having infringed the public nature of the court proceedings and the judicial norms guaranteed by law be legally called to account.

G. P. Akilov, candidate in Physical-Mathematical Sciences
S. L. Andreev, engineer
R. L. Berg, Doctor of Biological Sciences
Yu. Borisov, Doctor of Physical-Mathematical Sciences
I. S. Alekseev, candidate in Philosophical Sciences
L. G. Borisova, graduate student
I. Basserman, graduate student

YE. B. VISHNEVSKY, junior scientific worker
L. VIACHESLAVOV, graduate student
A. V. GLADKY, Doctor of Physical-Mathematical Sciences
M. M. GROMYKO, Doctor of Historical Sciences
I. Z. GOLDENBERG, instructor
F. A. DREIZIN, candidate in Philological Sciences
B. YE. ZAKHAROV, candidate in Physical-Mathematical Sciences
G. ZASLAVSKY, candidate in Physical-Mathematical Sciences
K. ILICHEV, intern
E. S. KOSITSYNA, teacher
KULAKOV, candidate in Physical-Mathematical Sciences
A. V. KLORIN, engineer
L. A. LOZOVSKY, engineer
D. B. LIKHACHEVA, junior scientific worker
V. F. MENSHIKOV, graduate student
B. YU. NAIDORF, teacher
R. NAKHMANSON, candidate in Physical-Mathematical Sciences
S. I. POLITKO, systems worker
V. S. PERTSOVSKY, teacher
B. I. PRILOUS, senior laboratory assistant
S. ROZHNOVA, graduate student
N. V. REVIAKINA, candidate in History
SOKOLOV, candidate in Physical-Mathematical Sciences
B. YE. SEMIACHKIN, junior scientific worker
N. A. TOPESHKO, engineer
YE. TITOV
L. A. TRISHINA, assistant in the Department of General Linguistics, Novosibirsk State University
A. I. FET, Doctor of Physical-Mathematical Sciences
A. M. FRIDMAN, candidate in Phys.-Math. Sciences
N. N. FILONENKO, graduate student
I. V. KHRIPLOVICH, candidate in Phys.-Math. Sciences
I. N. KHOKHLUSHKIN, junior scientific worker
F. A. TSELNIK, engineer
M. I. CHEREMISINA, candidate in Philology; senior scientific worker
A. V. SHABAT, candidate in Physical-Mathematical Sciences
A. M. SHALAGIN, engineer
E. SHTENGEL, junior scientific worker
G. S. YABLONSKY, junior scientific worker
V. A. KONEV, candidate in Philosophy

32. Open Letter of Twelve to World Communist Leaders

[In February, 1968, a "consultative conference" of Communist and Workers' parties, which took place in Budapest, decided to convene a formal world Communist meeting. Originally scheduled to be held in Moscow in November—December, 1968, the meeting was postponed, as *a result of the Soviet invasion of Czechoslovakia, until June, 1969. The following letter of protest against the recent trials was forwarded to the conference presidium by registered airmail, and a copy was simultaneously addressed to the Central Committee of the CPSU.—*Ed.]

To the Presidium of the Consultative Conference of Communist Parties in Budapest

A series of political trials have been conducted in our country in recent years. The essence of these trials lies in the fact that people have been tried for their convictions in violation of their fundamental civil rights. Precisely as a result of this, the trials have been conducted with gross violations of legality, the major one being the absence of public information.

The people no longer wish to submit to such illegality, and this has led to indignation and protests, which have been growing from trial to trial. A great number of individual and collective letters have been sent to various judicial, governmental, and Party organs, all the way up to the Central Committee of the Communist Party of the Soviet Union. These letters have gone unanswered. Instead, the reply to those who have protested most actively has been discharge from their work, a summons from the KGB, threats of arrest, or, finally—the most shocking form of reprisal—forcible confinement in a mental hospital. These illegal and inhuman actions can produce no positive results; on the contrary, they increase tension and give rise to further indignation.

We believe it our duty to point out also that several thousands of political prisoners, about whom almost no one knows, are in camps and prisons. They are kept in inhuman conditions of forced labor, on a semistarvation diet, exposed to the arbitrary actions of the [prison] administration. Even after they have completed their sentences they are subjected to extrajudicial and frequently illegal persecution—restrictions on their choice of a place of residence and administrative surveillance, which places free men in the position of exiles.

We also call your attention to the fact of discrimination against small nations and the political persecution of people who are struggling for national equality, which is particularly clear in the case of the Crimean Tatars.

We know that many Communists abroad and in our country have repeatedly expressed their disapproval of the political repressions of recent years. We ask the participants in the consultative meeting fully to consider the peril caused by the trampling on the rights of man in our country.

ALEKSEI KOSTERIN
Writer

Moscow, Malaia Gruzinskaia Street, Building 31, Apartment 70.

LARISA BOGORAZ
Philologist

Moscow, V-261, Leninsky Prospekt, Building 85, Apartment 3.

PAVEL LITVINOV
Physicist

Moscow, K-1, Aleksei Tolstoi Street, Building 8, Apartment 78.

ZAMIRA ASANOVA
Physician

Uzbek Soviet Socialist Republic, Fergana Oblast, Yangi Kurgan settlement.

PIOTR YAKIR
Historian

Moscow, Zh-180, Avtozavodskaia Street, Building 5, Apartment 75.

VIKTOR KRASIN
Economist

Moscow, Belomorskaia Street, Building 24, Apartment 25.

ILYA GABAI
Teacher

Moscow, A-55, Novolesnaia Street, Building 18, Block 2, Apartment 83.

BORIS SHRAGIN
Philosopher

Moscow, G-117, Pogodin Street, Building 2/3, Apartment 91.

ANATOLI LEVITIN-KRASNOV
Religious writer

Moscow, Zh-337, Third Novokuznetskaia Street, Building 23.

YULI KIM
Teacher

Moscow, Zh-377, Riazansky Prospekt, Building 73, Apartment 90.

YURI GLAZOV
Linguist

Moscow, V-421, Leninsky Prospekt, Building 101/164, Apartment 4.

PIOTR GRIGORENKO
Construction engineer, former Major-General;

Moscow, G-21, Komsomolsky Prospekt, Building 14/1, Apartment 96.

33. *Petition of Ninety-five Mathematicians*

March 9, 1968

To: The Minister of Health, U.S.S.R.
    The Procurator General of the U.S.S.R.
Copy to:
    Chief Psychiatrist, City of Moscow

We have learned that the prominent Soviet mathematician and well-known specialist in the field of mathematical logic Aleksandr Sergeevich Yesenin-Volpin has been forcibly, without prior medical examination and without the knowledge or consent of his relatives, placed in Psychiatric Hospital No. 5, Stolbovaia Station, 70 kilometers from Moscow.

The forcible commitment of a talented and entirely ablebodied mathematician to a hospital for seriously disturbed mental patients and the conditions in which he finds himself as a consequence of the very nature of the institution subject him to severe mental trauma, are injurious to his health, and abase his personal dignity.

Proceeding from the humanitarian aims of our legislative organs and, even more, of our public health services, we consider this fact a flagrant violation of medical and legal norms.

We request that you intercede immediately and take the necessary steps to enable our colleague to [resume] work under normal conditions.

P. S. NOVIKOV, member, U.S.S.R. Academy of Sciences; Lenin Prize winner

I. M. GELFAND, corresponding member, U.S.S.R. Academy of Sciences; Lenin and State Prize winner

LAZAR LIUSTERNIK, corresponding member, U.S.S.R. Academy of Sciences; State Prize winner

ANDREI MARKOV, corresponding member, U.S.S.R. Academy of Sciences

DMITRI MENSHOV, corresponding member, U.S.S.R. Academy of Sciences; State Prize winner

S. P. NOVIKOV, corresponding member, U.S.S.R. Academy of Sciences, Lenin Prize winner

I. R. SHAFAREVICH, corresponding member, U.S.S.R. Academy of Sciences; Lenin Prize winner

VADIM ARNOLD, Lenin Prize winner; professor; Doctor of Physical-Mathematical Sciences

ANATOLI VITUSHKIN, Lenin Prize winner; professor; Doctor of Physical-Mathematical Sciences

ALEKSANDR KRONROD, State Prize winner; professor; Doctor of Physical-Mathematical Sciences

YURI MANIN, Lenin Prize winner; Doctor of Physical-Mathematical Sciences

N. M. MEIMAN, State Prize winner; professor; Doctor of Physical-Mathematical Sciences

Professors/Doctors of Physical-Mathematical Sciences:

F. F. BOKSHTEIN
D. A. BOCHVAR
V. A. YEFREMOVICH
LIUDMILA KELDYSH
A. A. KIRILLOV
V. A. KONDRATEV
A. G. KUROSH
YE. M. LANDIS
A. M. LODSHITS

A. YA. POVZNER
N. B. ZBOLINSKY
I. I. PYTETSKY-SHAPIRO
F. P. PALAMODOV
YU. M. SMIRNOV
S. V. FOMIN
G. Z. SHILOV
A. M. YAGLOM
I. M. YAGLOM

Doctors of Physical-Mathematical Sciences:

M. S. Agronovich
A. V. Arkhangelsky, assistant professor

V. Ponomarev, senior scientific worker
Ya. G. Sinai, senior scientific worker

Candidates in Physical-Mathematical Sciences:

B. G. Averbukh, assistant professor
B. M. Alekseev, assistant professor
L. M. Balakina
T. M. Baranovich, assistant professor
L. Vassalygo
N. M. Beskin
Blinchevsky
N. M. Brushlinskaia
N. Vvedenskaia, senior scientific worker
A. D. Venttsel, assistant professor
T. D. Venttsel, assistant professor
F. Ya. Vetukhovsky
Ye. Vinburg, assistant professor
L. Volevich, senior scientific worker
Ye. Vul
S. Gindikin, scientific worker
V. L. Golov
M. I. Grabar, assistant professor
S. A. Kabakov
K. V. Kim
N. Kh. Konstantinov, senior scientific worker
L. A. Kronrod, assistant professor
A. N. Kryzhkov

A. L. Krylov
O. S. Kulagina, senior scientific worker
V. Levchenko
A. L. Lund
R. A. Minlos, senior scientific worker
K. A. Mikhailova
A. L. Onishchik, assistant professor
V. P. Orevkov
B. Poliak, senior scientific worker
A. Skobeev
M. A. Smoliansky
V. M. Tikhomirov, assistant professor
L. Tutubalin, assistant professor
L. Flitman
D. V. Fuks, senior scientific worker
Yu. I. Khmelevsky, assistant professor
L. L. Tsinman
A. Chernavsky
Z. Ya. Shapiro
I. Sharygin
V. A. Yankov

Candidates in Technical Sciences:

L. Ya. Kelperks

S. A. Panov

Candidate in Sciences: G. Tiurina, senior worker

Candidate in Pedagogical Sciences: Yu. A. Shikhanovich

Others:

K. Babitsky, junior scientific worker
F. L. Varpakhovsky, lecturer
N. Viliams, instructor
Yu. A. Gastev, instructor
Ye. Ye. Glusburg, junior scientific worker
A. Gvozden, junior scientific worker

I. G. Kristi, engineer
V. V. Kun, junior scientific worker
G. S. Podiapolsky, junior scientific worker
V. S. Osaulenko, junior scientific worker
V. K. Finn, engineer
G. E. Chekin, junior scientific worker
G. A. Shestopal, senior instructor

We request that a reply be sent to the name of any of the signers of this letter at the following address: Moscow, 234 Leninskie Gory, The Lomonosov Moscow State University, Mechanical-Mathematical Department.

34. Retraction by Fifteen Mathematicians

Radio Moscow Broadcast in English to Eastern North America, 0010 Moscow time, March 26, 1968:

Some time ago, U.S. newspapers, including the *New York Times*, published a letter said to have been received from a group of professors of Moscow University in connection with the placing of mathematician Yesenin-Volpin in a mental hospital.

The U.S. papers were obviously out to make political capital of this. Radio Moscow today received a letter from the Moscow University professors referred to in the *New York Times*. We bring you the full text of this letter:

Some time ago, we, professors of mathematics at Moscow University, signed a letter in connection with the commitment of mathematician Yesenin-Volpin [to a mental institution]. The letter was addressed to Soviet medical and judicial bodies and expressed our concern over the conditions in which Yesenin-Volpin was being held and over the fact that his hospitalization had not been properly agreed upon with his family. Later, we were pleased to hear that he had been transferred to another hospital more suited to his case. At the same time, we were highly indignant to learn that the letter had come into the hands of persons to whom it had not been addressed, and that it had been published by some foreign newspapers and broadcast by foreign radio stations. Unfortunately, the foreign press and radio did not stress the fact, of which we have long been aware, that for many years Yesenin-Volpin has been under the observation of psychiatrists and has many times been placed in mental hospitals. This attempt to distort the real meaning of the letter, which was prompted by concern for a colleague, a sick man but a capable mathematician, cannot but arouse our indignation.

[The letter is signed by Professor/Doctor of Mathematics Kurosh, Alternate Members of the Soviet Academy of Sciences Liusternik and Menshov, and twelve other university faculty members.]

35. Petition of 121

To: The General Secretary of the CC-CPSU, L. I. Brezhnev
   The Chairman of the U.S.S.R. Council of Ministers, A. N. Kosygin
   The Chairman of the Presidium of the U.S.S.R. Supreme Soviet, N. V. Podgorny
   The Chairman of the U.S.S.R. Supreme Court, A. F. Gorkin
   The Procurator General of the U.S.S.S., R. A. Rudenko
Copies to:
   The Editors of *Pravda, Izvestia, Komsomolskaia pravda, Literaturnaia gazeta, and Vechernaia Moskva*
   Attorney A. Zolotukhin

Shocked by the injustice of the trial of Aleksandr Ginzburg, we are addressing this appeal to you.

On the basis of the materials of which we have knowledge concerning the trial, it is clearly evident that A. Ginzburg was prosecuted on account of the collection of documents he compiled on the Siniavsky-Daniel case, even though the verdict of "guilty" was based on his [alleged] ties with the NTS—which were not proved by anyone or anything. This impression is strengthened by the articles appearing in our newspapers, which, at the very least, misinform the public by distorting the facts established at the trial. The unsubstantiated accusations regarding [collusion with] a certain anti-Soviet organization were evidently made in order to defame the compiler of the collection of documents on the Siniavsky-Daniel case.

It is impossible to regard this as anything other than an attempt to revive the methods applied in the trials of 1937.

The essence of the trial was obscured by facts that were irrelevant to the case, such as the sudden appearance, a year after the start of the investigation and several days before the trial, of a Venezuelan citizen armed with "material evidence."

We see the case of A. Ginzburg as a direct continuation of the trial of Siniavsky and Daniel.

We completely subscribe to the contention of Attorney B. A. Zolotukhin that the collection compiled by A. Ginzburg is neither criminal nor biased in nature.

Everything that we know about this trial gives us the right to request an immediate review of the case of A. Ginzburg.

N. Adamian, member, Union of Soviet Writers

I. Andronov, member, Union of Soviet Artists

Ye. Andronov-Leontovich, Doctor of Physical Sciences

Yu. D. Apresian, candidate in Philological Sciences

P. I. Afanaseva, librarian, People's Assessor

M. Arapov, linguist

K. Babitsky, linguist

S. Belokrinitskaia, linguist

M. Berkenblit, junior scientific worker, Institute of Problems of the Transmission of Information, U.S.S.R. Academy of Sciences

V. N. Bovsheverov, Chief of Laboratory, candidate in Physical-Mathematical Sciences

Bozhovich, candidate in Art History

Bodnova, junior scientific worker, Institute of Chemical Physics, U.S.S.R. Academy of Sciences

M. Bongard, Chief of Laboratory, Institute of Chemical Physics, U.S.S.R. Academy of Sciences

Yu. Bregel, candidate in Historical Sciences

I. K. Bunina, senior scientific worker, Institute of Slavic Studies, U.S.S.R. Academy of Sciences

N. G. Vainberg, mathematician

Garlinskaia, member, Union of Cinematographers

I. M. Gelfand, corresponding member, U.S.S.R. Academy of Sciences

V. P. Golyshev, translator

Ye. M. Golysheva, member, Union of Soviet Writers

M. I. Grabar, lecturer, Head of Mathematics Department, Moscow Institute of Aviation Technology

Gurvich, senior scientific worker, Institute of Atmospheric Physics, U.S.S.R. Academy of Sciences

A. Ye. Gurvich, Professor/Doctor of Biological Sciences, Gamalei Institute of Epidemiology and Microbiology

Davidovskaia, engineer-electrician

L. A. Diky, senior scientific worker, candidate in Physical-Mathematical Sciences

Dinaburg, engineer-mathematician, Institute of Chemical Physics, U.S.S.R. Academy of Sciences

Yu. Dombrovsky, member, Union of Soviet Writers

Dybo, candidate in Philological Sciences

T. Yelizarenkova, candidate in Philological Sciences

N. Yerofeeva, architect

A. K. Zholkovsky, junior scientific worker, Moscow State Pedagogical Institute of Foreign Languages

V. V. Ivanov, chief, Structural Typology Section, Institute of Slavic Studies, U.S.S.R. Academy of Sciences

M. Ivanov, member, Union of Soviet Writers

O. V. Zanchenko, mathematician

N. Zorkaia, candidate in Art History

ZUBKOVSKY, junior scientific worker, Institute of Atmospheric Physics, U.S.S.R. Academy of Sciences

I. S. ZYKINA, chemist

M. I. KAGANOV, Professor/Doctor of Physical-Mathematical Sciences

Z. KAGANOVA, junior scientific worker, mathematician

V. N. KADANSTEV, engineer

KAZAKOV, engineer-electrician

M. A. KALLISTRATOVA, candidate in Physical-Mathematical Sciences

KAMENOMOSTSKAIA, candidate in Physical-Mathematical Sciences, Institute of Chemical Physics, U.S.S.R. Academy of Sciences

KANEVSKY, engineer-mechanic

L. KASATKIN, candidate in Philological Sciences

I. KEDER-STEPANOVA, candidate in Biological Sciences, senior scientific worker, Institute of Problems of the Transmission of Information, U.S.S.R. Academy of Sciences

L. KELDYSH, Professor/Doctor of Physical-Mathematical Sciences

YE. KOBASOVA, electrician

S. A. KOBALEV, candidate in Biological Sciences, senior scientific worker, Moscow State University

A. KON, junior scientific worker, Institute of Atmospheric Physics, U.S.S.R. Academy of Sciences

L. KOPELEV, member, Union of Soviet Writers

V. KORNILOV, member, Union of Soviet Writers

K. M. KUK, translator

L. KRYSIN, linguist

A. P. LABUT, senior engineer, Moscow State University

YU. LEVITANSKY, member, Union of Soviet Writers

M. A. LEONTOVICH, member, U.S.S.R. Academy of Sciences

I. S. LIPKINA, engineer

M. LORIE, member, Union of Soviet Writers

G. LIUDMIRSKAIA, instructor

A. S. MARCHUKOV, mathematician

MEDVEDOVSKAIA, mathematician

I. MELCHUK, candidate in Philological Sciences

A. G. MESHNOVSKY, Doctor of Physical-Mathematical Sciences, Institute of Theoretical and Experimental Physics

A. F. MILLER, candidate in Physical-Mathematical Sciences

S. MIKHAILOVA, engineer

I. MOKARIK, mathematician

S. MOROZOV, architect

MOSTOVAIA, mathematician, junior scientific worker, Institute of Chemical Physics, U.S.S.R. Academy of Sciences

D. MURAVEV, editor, Iskusstvo publishing house

YE. MURINA, art historian

N. NAUMOV, member, Union of Soviet Writers

S. P. NOVIKOV, corresponding member, U.S.S.R. Academy of Sciences

L. OSTROVSKAIA, architect

N. D. Otten, member, Union of Soviet Writers

L. Ye. Pinsky, member, Union of Soviet Writers

M. P. Petrov, junior scientific worker

M. Podolskaia, candidate in Philological Sciences

K. M. Pokrovskaia, physicist

V. Poliakov, member, Union of Soviet Writers

Posviansky, mathematician

M. A. Provotrova, engineer

A. V. Rabinovich, mathematician

I. Revzin, Doctor of Philological Sciences

Reznik, engineer

S. Reznikov, architect

V. M. Rodionov, Doctor of Biological Sciences, Institute of Biomedical Chemistry, U.S.S.R. Academy of Sciences

N. I. Romanova, mathematician

I. Rubanova, candidate in Art History

Yu. G. Rudoi, physicist

P. Riazantseva, film writer

D. Samoilov, member, Union of Soviet Writers

V. Sannikov, candidate in Philological Sciences

A. Simonov, writer

I. Simolon, scientific worker, Institute of Silicate Chemistry, U.S.S.R. Academy of Sciences

V. V. Smolianinov, junior scientific worker, Institute of the Problems of the Transmission of Information, U.S.S.R. Academy of Sciences

Ye. M. Smorgunova, linguist

Yu. N. Sokolov, geophysicist

I. Soloviova, member, Union of Soviet Writers

B. V. Sukhotin, candidate in Philological Sciences

V. I. Tatarsky, Doctor of Physical-Mathematical Sciences, senior scientific worker, Institute of Atmospheric Physics, U.S.S.R. Academy of Sciences

A. Timofeevsky, film writer

L. Ya. Timoshenko, member, AAP

T. I. Tovstukha, junior scientific worker, Institute of Automatics and Telemechanics, U.S.S.R. Academy of Sciences

V. N. Toporov, candidate in Philological Sciences

M. R. Tulchinsky, candidate in Historical Sciences

V. Khinkis, member, Union of Soviet Writers

Khodorovich, junior scientific worker, Institute of the Russian Language, U.S.S.R. Academy of Sciences

T. Tsivian, candidate in Philological Sciences

L. M. Chailakhian, candidate in Biological Sciences, Institute of Problems of the Transmission of Information, U.S.S.R. Academy of Sciences

I. K. Chukovskaia, member, Union of Soviet Writers

B. Churganova, linguist

M. L. Shik, candidate in Biological Sciences
V. Shitova, member, Union of Soviet Writers
I. Ye. Shifrin, physicist
V. V. Shmidt, candidate in Physical-Mathematical Sciences, senior scientific worker, Institute of Metallurgy, U.S.S.R. Academy of Sciences
A. A. Shteinberg, member, Union of Soviet Writers
A. I. Shub, physicist
S. M. Epshtein, senior laboratory worker, Zoological Institute, U.S.S.R. Academy of Sciences
K. Yusina, mathematician
A. Yaglom, Professor/Doctor of Physical-Mathematical Sciences

36. Protest by Grigorenko's Wife

January 23, 1968

To: Comrade L. I. Brezhnev, CC of the CPSU
Comrade Gorkin, the U.S.S.R. Supreme Court
The Procurator General, Comrade Rudenko
The President of the Academy of Medical Sciences, Comrade Blokhin

From Zinaida Mikhailovna Grigorenko, Party member; 2nd Komsomolsky Pereulok 14, Apt. 96, Tel. G-6-27-37

Declaration

At the request of Attorney Kaminskaia, my husband, Piotr Grigorevich Grigorenko, was to appear in the Moscow Municipal Court as a witness in the trial of Ginzburg, Galanskov, *et al.* The Chairman of the court, Mironov, turned down the request, citing as his reason a certificate issued by Mental Health Clinic No. 1, Leningrad District, attesting that my husband is mentally unbalanced.

This certificate is false; in December, 1965, a decision by the VTEK [Medical Board for the Determination of Disability] confirmed his sanity; his case was removed from the files, and, since then, he has not [even] been called in for consultation. A document to this effect was presented to the court.

In full possession of his health, P. G. Grigorenko is employed as a foreman at the SU-2 [a division of the Moscow Building Trust] and also heads a Party school in the capacity of propagandist. There are twenty people in his group, thirteen of them Communists and seven non-Party members.

It turns out, then, that, in one place, my husband serves as a political leader, while, in another, he is regarded as mentally disturbed. What is this—a mistake? No, it is a violation of legality, which has been going on for more than four years.

On February 1, 1964, Grigorenko—a Major-General and Candidate in Sciences—was arrested and charged with anti-Soviet activity. Yet, his case was not investigated, and, instead, he was sent to the Serbsky Institute, where he was found to be mentally disturbed. On the basis of that finding, he was sent to a Leningrad prison-hospital for compulsory treatment.

When I asked precisely when my husband had lost his sanity—since I had never noticed it—I was told by the investigators, Lt. Colonel[s?] Kuznetsov and Kantov, that my husband's political views and his dissemination of them rendered him socially dangerous. I was also informed by the [other?] investigators—lawyers—that he would be kept in the [army] reserve in the status of a sick person, retaining his rank and pension.

From Party sources, I learned that there is a regulation that mentally ill people temporarily have to relinquish their Party cards, which are restored to them after recovery. What, then, happened next?

By Khrushchev's order of August 29, 1964, my husband was demoted to the rank of private and expelled from the Party as mentally unbalanced.

All the patients in the hospital received sickness benefits—except my husband. The law was observed with regard to murderers and rapists. Two of the inmates—Lt. Col. Shevchenko, who had knifed his daughter, and Lt. Col. Burkovsky, who had shot three men—were retired into the reserve, also keeping their ranks and pensions.

On April 29, 1965, my husband was discharged from the hospital as a Group-2 invalid. For ten months this Group-2 invalid, a disabled war veteran, was refused both his pension and a position. He was forced to go to work as a loader.

In December, 1965, by a decision of the VTEK of Mental Health Clinic No. 1, Leningrad District, my husband was certified to be mentally healthy and his case removed from the files. But this was not followed by the restoration either of his Party card or of his military rank, or of the pension he had earned by thirty-four years of honorable military service. Wounded a number of times, he has not been certified, to this day, as a disabled war veteran.

The entire story that I have related here is nothing but a gross miscarriage of justice. I consider it a prelude to new repressions against my husband. I am filled with horror, the more so because, during the years of the personality cult, I lost my first husband, my sister, and my brother-in-law, in addition to having been myself subjected to repressions.

As a Communist and as a citizen of the Soviet Union, I demand an end to the illegal acts against my husband and my family and to the persecution of my children and myself. I demand the complete restoration of my husband's rights as a Party member and citizen and the reinstatement of his military rank.

III. The Nationalities Problem

The documents below are a very small yet representative sample of all the available material concerned with aspects of the nationalities problem in the U.S.S.R. Documents 37 and 38 reflect the struggle waged by Ukrainian intellectuals for national as well as human rights in general. Document 38 also addresses itself to the persecution of Jews. (For other references to Soviet anti-Semitism, see Documents 67, 75, and 76.) Documents 39 and 40 deal with the suppression of the rights of Crimean Tatars. For a description and analysis of recent developments in the Ukraine, as well as for references to other compilations on this subject, see the article by George Luckyj on pp. 52-61.

37. Essay by V. Chornovil

January 17, 1968

Copies to:
   The Procurator General of the Ukrainian S.S.R.
   The Chairman of the Supreme Court, Ukrainian S.S.R.
   The Chairman of the Committee of State Security, Council of Ministers, Ukrainian S.S.R.

I do not beg anything of you: numerous inquiries, depositions, complaints, and entreaties have foundered against the cold wall of your indifference. . . . [*The author lists a number of prominent personalities who had petitioned the authorities—to no avail—for open trials for Ukrainian intellectuals charged with alleged anti-Soviet activities.*]
   You are indifferent to human tragedies, to the demoralizing impact of fear, which creeps like a cold serpent into many a Ukrainian home. Your only concern, allegedly, is to see that the law is upheld. Therefore, let us take a look at what is now going on in the Ukraine from the point

of view of socialist legality. There is ample evidence, today, from which to draw proper conclusions.

I submit my opinions not because I have any hope of alleviating the plight of the individuals who were sentenced and imprisoned. You have taught people not to foster any such naive hopes. However, failure to express one's views about what is happening would indicate silent participation in the willful abuse of socialist legality.

RELAPSE INTO TERROR—OR JUSTICE?

The Soviet court should not be engaged in the revival of terror. Its mission is to administer just punishment for crimes and to re-educate. Every first-year law student learns about the humaneness of Soviet law. The law states: "When applying the measures of criminal punishment, the court not only punishes the offender but also endeavors to correct and re-educate him" (*The Statute on the Judicial System of the Ukr.S.S.R.*, Article 3). In the past few years, there has been emphasis on the widest possible participation of the community in the re-education of those who break laws (people's courts, release on bail, people's procurators and advocates at the court investigation, etc.). Article 20 of the Code of Criminal Procedure of the Ukr.S.S.R. not only guarantees that court investigations be conducted in public (except in significant, clearly defined cases); it also aims at increasing the educational role of trials by stressing the indispensability of holding them on the premises of enterprises, construction sites, at *radhosps* (state farms) and *kolhosps* (collective farms), with people's procurators and advocates participating. "The law guarantees a thorough, complete, and objective investigation of the circumstances of the case and provides for the punishment of interrogators, judges, and other individuals who try to bring about the conviction of a defendant or to intimidate a witness through force, threats, or blackmail." The law clearly defines the legal procedures that protect the rights of the suspect or the accused, guarantee respect for his dignity, and give him an opportunity to prove his innocence. Finally, and most important, the law obliges the investigative organs, the prosecution, and the court "to determine the circumstances that contributed to the commission of the crime, and to take steps through appropriate organs to remove them . . . widely utilizing the help of the community in revealing and removing the reasons and circumstances that lead to the commission of crimes" (Article 23, Code of Criminal Procedure, Ukr.S.S.R.). . . . .

I will base my comments concerning [recent] breaches of such elementary requirements of justice on various materials, the majority of which I enclose:

[*Here the author lists sixteen items, consisting of single documents or collections of documents pertaining to the arrests, trials, searches, etc., that he is protesting.*]

What Is Not Punishable Under Article 62 of the Criminal Code of the Ukrainian S.S.R.

In conformity with the interests of the working people, and in order to strengthen the socialist system, the citizens of the U.S.S.R. are guaranteed by law: (a) freedom of speech; (b) freedom of the press; (c) freedom of assembly, including the holding of mass meetings; (d) freedom of street processions and demonstrations. (Article 125 of the Constitution of the U.S.S.R.)

Agitation or propaganda carried on for the purpose of subverting or weakening Soviet authority, or of committing certain especially dangerous crimes against the state, or circulating for the same purpose slanderous fabrications that defame the Soviet state and social system, or circulating, preparing, or keeping, for the same purpose, literature of such content shall be punished by deprivation of freedom for a term of six months to seven years, with or without additional exile for a term of two to five years, or by exile for a term of two to five years. (Article 62, paragraph 1, Criminal Code of the Ukr.S.S.R., Section on "Especially Dangerous State Crimes.")

The court, procurator, interrogator, and investigative organs are under obligation, within the realm of their competence, to initiate action in each instance in which indications of a crime are disclosed. (Article 4, Code of Criminal Procedure, Ukr.S.S.R.)

The very talented painter O. Zalyvakha; the art critic B. Horyn; the psychologist M. Horyn; the lecturers at Lutsk Pedagogical Institute V. Moroz and D. Ivaschenko; the teacher from Ivano-Frankovsk, M. Ozerny; the student of Kiev Medical Institute Ya. Hevrych; the Kiev researchers I. Rusyn and O. Martynenko; the laboratory technician at Kiev University Y. Kusnetsova; the pensioner from Theodosia M. Masyutko; and others—all were sentenced under Article 62 of the Criminal Code of the Ukr.S.S.R. Yet this currently popular Article is unconstitutional. The Supreme Soviet should either annul it or make it more specific. In its present version, Article 62 completely contradicts the freedoms that are guaranteed to Soviet citizens in the Constitution of the U.S.S.R.

If anyone criticizes current nationality policies for their departure from Leninist norms, then he (even if mistaken) has every right to do so, according to the Constitution of the U.S.S.R. However, according to the Criminal Code of the Ukr.S.S.R., the same individual can be deported to a labor colony, his criticism having been interpreted as "propaganda carried on for the purpose of subverting or weakening Soviet authority." If, under Stalin, anyone thought of criticizing the personality cult—or, under Khrushchev's rule, his love of reorganization could this not have been interpreted (indeed it was!) as "the dissemination of

slanderous fabrications that discredit Soviet national and social order"?
It seems possible to apply the charge of "slanderous fabrications" to all
statements that do not coincide with official directives.

The practices of recent months corroborate these suppositions. Judges
stretch this elastic article of the code like an accordion—each one inter-
prets to his own liking the concept of "anti-Soviet." (In Ivano-Frankovsk, ancient aphorisms, the use of the word *"vatra"* [bonfire], and
Shevchenko's poems were considered anti-Soviet.) Because he had in
his possession several photocopies of books, Yaroslav Hevrych was sentenced to five years in a labor colony. In the case of the teacher Ozerny,
the authorities confiscated a copy of Akras' *History of the Ukraine*,
which had passed Tsarist censors, the magazine *Zhinocha Dolya*
[Women's Fate], and an apolitical book by the modernist Pachovsky,
Ukrainian Bohemia (these books are in the open stacks of libraries).
. . . M. Horyn was sentenced to six years and O. Zalyvakha to five years
in a hard-labor camp, while I. Svitlychny and O. Kosiv were released
without being tried—although the charges were the same against all of
them. Where is the logic?

The law must be formulated clearly, and, according to Article 4 of
the Code of Criminal Procedure for the Ukr.S.S.R., no crime should be
left unpunished. If the current trials are being held for the purpose
of terrorizing the population, but with a sincere aim to keep within the
letter and spirit of the law, then, having said "a," it is necessary to say
"b." It is necessary to imprison immediately those who gave Hevrych,
Martynenko, or Ozerny the books they had. After spending six to seven
months in the care of the KGB, these people will in turn tell where they
received the books and will receive the appropriate "lawful" five to six
years of hard labor, and so on. . . . It is also necessary to go after anecdotes—after all, many of them are clearly "slanderous fabrications" that
"defame the Soviet . . . social system." Trials resulting from the use
of anecdotes, which are so popular among the townsfolk, will greatly
alleviate the housing crisis in large cities. . . .

When I refused to testify at the secret trial in Lvov on April 16, I was
told that I was to appear in court to answer to a charge under Article
172 of the Criminal Code of the Ukr.S.S.R. (refusal to give evidence).
The decision in itself was illegal since I merely refused to give evidence
at an illegal secret trial. However, even this did not satisfy the irate Procurator Antonenko and Judge Rudyk. They changed their own ruling,
and on April 19 charged me under Article 62 of the Criminal Code
of the Ukr.S.S.R. The managers of justice were not in the least concerned by the lack of evidence of my "anti-Soviet" activities (aside
from the trifling testimony given by Osadchy, not corroborated by witnesses or myself); they understood very well the nature of Article 62.
. . . True, on May 17, the Supreme Court of the Ukr.S.S.R. revoked
this illegal charge—probably only because, as yet, there had been no
orders "from above" to place the next group of "anti-Soviet agitators
and propagandists" behind bars.

V. I. Lenin was not an all-forgiving humanitarian. However, even in those strained times, when there were exploiting classes in the country, when there were enemies on all sides, Lenin could afford to abolish the death penalty in 1920. Under him, the "Cheka" (Soviet secret police) tracked down those who rose in armed rebellion against Soviet order or were preparing to take up arms, but it did not hunt for convictions. Lenin did not order Sukhanov thrown into prison for his anti-Marxist book; instead, he entered into polemics with him. Even Stalin, before he dared to break Leninist norms of social order, was not afraid of anti-Soviet literature. In 1928, the Leningrad publishing house Pryboi published many copies of a book written by a White *émigré*, V. Shulhyn, entitled *The Year 1919*, which overflowed with bitter malice against the Revolution and expressed hope for a change in the Soviet order. The book was republished from a foreign edition without the slightest abridgement. A short foreword stated that Shulhyn was "an extreme right nationalist and monarchist," "a crude anti-Semite," and that he propagated "zoological policies of nationalism" (we add: he was not only the inspirer of pogroms against the Jews but also an inveterate hater of Ukrainians). It was stated that the book was useful for wide circulation because it would enable the reader to see the enemy at close range and would help fight chauvinism. And then, with no further comment or explanation, the floor was given to Shulhyn.

[*There follow several anti-Soviet quotations from Shulhyn's work.*]

When copying quotations from this book, I wrote after each quotation: "Leningrad, 1926." I was concerned lest comrades from the KGB might arrive to carry out another search, confiscate my notes, and charge me under Article 62 of the Criminal Code of the Ukr.S.S.R. with malicious fabrications against Soviet order and against Lenin, or even accuse me of great-power chauvinism. . . . Such fears are not groundless. After all, somewhere in the Kiev Oblast KGB office they are holding my notebook filled with quotations from works of various writers and a bibliography of foreign Ukrainiana. That notebook does not contain one sentence of which I am the author. While making notes in passing, I did not know when and in what context I would use the material (or even whether I would use it at all, but the KGB is firmly convinced that all this material was for use in "anti-Soviet propaganda and agitation," for "undermining," "weakening," and "disseminating slanderous fabrications." Otherwise, the KGB would not hold onto the book for six months, along with [other seized materials including] fifty-five old editions of books and even a complete set of a Ukrainian journal from the year 1900.

In 1926, Stalin was not beset by fear that everyone who read V. Shulhyn's book would become an inveterate monarchist bent on destroying Soviet rule. Ten years later, he suspected his closest companions of treason and ordered them to be shot. Twenty years later, this was called the personality cult. Ten years have passed since then, and, suddenly, an old familiar note is heard in the public addresses of some of our leaders. In a speech to members of the Ukrainian Academy of Sciences, Comrade Shulzhenko, Deputy Chairman of the Committee for State Security, Council of Ministers, Ukr.S.S.R., . . . asserted that all oppositional moods and activities in our country are the direct result of bourgeois propaganda and the work of bourgeois intelligence services. Presumably, if a magic wand could be waved and the bourgeois world suddenly ceased to exist, paradise would reign. In the villages, everyone would rejoice over the fate of an individual who has no passport and is thus bound to the *kolhosp* for life. In the cities, Ukrainians would take pride in the fact that they have become turncoats without kin or nation. No one would suffer embarrassment on behalf of democracy while throwing into the ballot box an unread slip of paper listing a name designated by the *obkom* or *raikom*. . . .

The Deputy Chairman of the KGB made one more disclosure to the Kiev members of the Academy. It seems that reading a book that contains an undercurrent of veiled criticism of our regime is enough to cause an individual who lacks a firmly established ideological outlook to develop anti-Soviet attitudes. This naturally leads to the conclusion that it is necessary to protect people from reading troublemaking books by every possible means, even by sentencing them to prisons and labor colonies. But, what happens then to the Marxist thesis that social existence (and not hostile books) determines consciousness? . . .

Marxism-Leninism undoubtedly is stronger than bourgeois ideologies. However, while people in the Soviet Union are brought to trial for reading books published in the West, our books and newspapers, with their harsh criticism of capitalism, bourgeois nationalism, and current policies of capitalist countries, are easily obtainable (even through the mail) in the U.S.A., Canada, and a number of other foreign countries. In Kiev, we publish a special newspaper exclusively for Ukrainians abroad, *Visti z Ukrainy* [News from the Ukraine], which may not be read here in the Ukraine because it contains specialized truth—only for export. Is it possible that non-Marxists have mastered even better than our own leaders the Marxist-Leninist thesis that states that revolutions and socio-economic changes are not exportable, that ideas take root in new ground only when social, economic, and political conditions are ripe for them, that to forbid the propagation of ideas means to add strength and attractiveness to them? . . .

How "Especially Dangerous State Criminals" Are Exposed

The inviolability of the homes of citizens and privacy of correspondence are protected by law. (Constitution of the U.S.S.R., Article 128.)

Unlawful search, unlawful eviction, or other acts committed by an official that infringe upon the inviolability of a citizen's dwelling are punishable by deprivation of freedom. (Article 130, Criminal Code, Ukr.S.S.R.)

Violation of the secrecy of correspondence by an official is punishable by corrective labor. . . . (Article 131, Criminal Code, Ukr.S.S.R.)

The work of the KGB is simpler than that of the militia. A hooligan or a murderer hides, but an "especially dangerous state criminal" gets up on a platform at an evening commemorating an anniversary (for example, Shevchenko's) and speaks. Later, he walks down the street with his friends, quietly, not glancing back. An informer may walk almost alongside them and listen to all that is being said. If, on orders from the KGB, "the especially dangerous" individual is dismissed from his job . . . [and] he does not cry or repent but instead continues his "dangerous talk," then it becomes necessary to take more serious measures against him. The most modern techniques come to aid. It is not difficult to make arrangements at the post office, the telegraph and telephone office. Ask any telegraph or telephone employee—someone will tell you in strictest confidence how correspondence and conversation are monitored. . . .

If the "especially dangerous" person lives on a top floor (which is usually the case), then he suddenly notices that the attic, which was always open in the past, is now sealed, and he is not allowed to go up even for his private belongings that are stored there. Or he is assigned to new quarters, and, during the night, he hears a banging on the wall of a room where there is no one living. Or, in a students' dormitory, he discovers under his bed a set of metal "whiskers" with a metal extension through the window (this was found under the window of M. Plakhotnyuk, a student at Kiev's Medical Institute).

Thus, a new dweller is found in your home. He hears everything: whom you speak to and what you say, what you whisper to your wife. . . . If you discover the presence of this "unregistered lodger"—life becomes hell. You weigh every word, become uncommunicative and irritable. You become accustomed to speaking in whispers, to glancing over your shoulder while walking, to showing your fist to people who brazenly take your photograph as you walk with your friends. . . . Sometimes you make mistakes and insult a decent person because you mistake him for an informer. Meanwhile, your dossier is being filled. . . .

Confrontations and Interrogations
of the Accused and of Witnesses

The court, procurator, investigator, and person conducting the inquiry shall not have the right to shift the obligation of proof to the accused. It shall be prohibited to solicit the accused's testimony by force, threats, or any other illegal measures. (Article 22, Code of Criminal Procedure, Ukr.S.S.R.)

Interrogation of the accused, except in special cases, should be conducted in the daytime. (Article 143, Code of Criminal Procedure, Ukr.S.S.R.)

The accused, if he so desires, is to be given the right to write his deposition in his own hand. . . . (Article 145, Code of Criminal Procedure, Ukr.S.S.R.) (The same applies to witnesses—Article 170, Code of Criminal Procedure, Ukr.S.S.R.)

At the request of relatives or close friends of the arrested, *visits with the prisoner* may be permitted by the investigation officer or the procurator. (Article 162, Code of Criminal Procedure, Ukr.S.S.R.)

It is not necessary to jam fingers between doors, to push needles under fingernails, to slap faces in order to force a person to consider his acts a terrible crime and even to admit to the interrogator everything that the latter needs for his previously planned scheme. It is sufficient to lock a man up for long months in a stone sack with bars, subject him to a *parasha* [privy] and other attributes of prison life, deny him any visitors for six months, harp several hours every day on the need for him to feel great guilt, and finally reduce him to such a state that when his wife comes to visit he does not immediately recognize her. As a result of moral terror, threats, and promises (which are all forgotten at the trial), any necessary evidence can be extorted from an individual. . . .

The following is a dialogue between the judge and the teacher Ozerny from the trial in Ivano-Frankovsk:

JUDGE: "You told the witness that you read it (a manuscript of an article dealing with the burning of the library of the Academy of Sciences, Ukr.S.S.R., in Kiev). At the interrogation, you said that you took it from your briefcase and gave it to the witness. Did you give it to him, or did you merely mention it? Which testimony is true?"

—"That which I am giving here at the trial."

—"Why did you not say this at the interrogation?"

—"At the interrogation, I was so weary that at times I signed even things with which I disagreed. I was interrogated for eleven hours and then for ten hours."

—"Was there a break?"

—"For dinner." (Eleven hours plus ten plus dinner—twenty-four hours. And what about Article 143 of the Criminal Code, Ukr.S.S.R.?)

—"Were you tired?" (Naive question. . . . The judge should be subjected to interrogations without sleep and rest. Perhaps he too would admit that the trial he was conducting was anti-Soviet. . . .)

—"Yes, I told the interrogator that I did not give the documents to Malarchyn. I got tired and signed whatever was written. I was interrogated forty-six times. This time I was questioned for six hours and forty-eight minutes. My testimony given here is true. I also told that to the interrogator. He tired me out to such a degree that I said, write whatever you like. I signed. . . ."

[*Other examples follow.*]

The following facts are revealing about the methods used in conducting preliminary investigations: . . .

—In order to produce moral shock and obtain the necessary evidence, the investigative officers stooped to searching the intimate lives of the accused and the witnesses, although the details had no bearing on the case. . . . In Ozerny's case, certain unsavory implications were made about alleged intimate relations between the accused and a witness. . . . [In another case,] the interrogators Rybalchenko and Rapota convinced L. Horbach that she and Osadchy used to kiss in doorways, although Horbach barely knows Osadchy. . . . As can be seen from the complaint to the Procurator General of the U.S.S.R. made by the wife of Yu. Daniel, Moscow investigative officers blackmailed witnesses in a similar way.

—Olha Worbut, a student of Kiev University, who was arrested for a few days at the beginning of September, was forced to undress and to undergo the humiliating experience of a body search. Nothing was found. Naturally—nothing was expected to be found, but a "confession" was obtained, and the soul of a human being was incurably offended. This same procedure was periodically repeated in the cell of each prisoner.

—Thanks to an "understanding" warden and a "sympathetic" neighbor in an adjacent cell, M. Zvarychevska received three notes from M. Horyn and even one from the outside, from Olha Horyn. The notes [urged confession]. . . . Eventually it became apparent that . . . the notes were composed in one of the KGB offices by a handwriting expert. . . .

One could cite similar facts endlessly. As a result of such experiences and prolonged imprisonment, the weaker souls eventually collapse. I would prefer not to believe the rumors to the effect that food given the prisoners contains drugs that cause the individual to become apathetic and agreeable to every suggestion. As a matter of fact, secret trials give rise to such rumors. Even Horyn's counsel raised his arms in a gesture of hopelessness as his client repented, took blame for everything that had happened or not happened, and even refused the private interview with his counsel that was guaranteed him by law. It was as if he was saying, "I have no secrets from the investigative officer." You see what friendships develop after spending seven months behind bars. . . .

The Trial

Violations of procedural norms at the trial

A copy of the indictment and the notice of the summons to trial are to be given to the defendant for signature no later than *three days* before the trial. *All other persons* are to be informed of the trial *within the same time limit.* (Article 254, Code of Criminal Procedure, Ukr.S.S.R.)

Documents used as evidence in the case *should be examined or announced* at the trial. These actions may take place either on the initiative of the court or as a result of *appeals made by the participants in the trial* at any time during the trial. (Article 214, Code of Criminal Procedure, Ukr.S.S.R.)

The *verdict of guilty* may not be based on assumptions. (Article 227, Code of Criminal Procedure, Ukr.S.S.R.)

The preliminary or court investigation is considered one-sided and incomplete in any case where individuals whose evidence has an essential bearing on the case were not questioned. . . . (Article 268, Code of Criminal Procedure, Ukr.S.S.R.)

The verdict is considered not to correspond to the factual circumstances of the case . . . if, in the presence of contradictory evidence that has an essential bearing on the conclusions of the court, *there is no indication in the verdict* why the court accepted certain evidence and disregarded other evidence. (Article 389, Code of Criminal Procedure, Ukr.S.S.R.)

Finally, after some five to eight months, the creaky vehicle of the preliminary investigation has reached the trial. It has reached the trial in spite of numerous violations of preliminary investigation procedures already mentioned above. These violations "did not come to the procurator's attention," they were not reported by the "lawyer," and the protests of witnesses (and perhaps also those of the accused) remained "a cry in the wilderness."

Yet, it would seem that justice has nothing to fear. On the contrary, the code recommends that "the determining role of trials" be more emphasized and that trials receive the widest publicity (Article 20, Code of Criminal Procedure, Ukr.S.S.R.). To the presiding officer of the trial, it is recommended "that the necessary educational level of the trial be maintained" (Article 260, Code of Criminal Procedure, Ukr.S.S.R.). Do you think, however, that the trial of the Lutsk Pedagogical Institute lecturers was held in the largest hall of the institute, in the presence of a full auditorium of students and lecturers? Only a few of them were lucky enough to hear the charges against Ivaschenko and Moroz. The selection of the audience for the trial of Ozerny in Ivano-Frankovsk was conducted even more carefully. . . .

Do you think that large notices were posted in the creative organizations of Kiev, Lvov, and Ivano-Frankovsk, calling for everyone to come to the trials, to listen, and to be convinced by the integrity of the judges not to make the same mistakes as the Horyn brothers, Zalyvakha, Hevrych, Martynenko, Masyutko? Of course not. All other trials following Ozerny's were conducted behind closed doors. In order to prevent uninvited guests, even the closest relatives of the accused were sometimes not informed. . . .

[*Here the author goes on to relate cases in which the court either failed to call "undependable" witnesses to testify or nullified their testimony. For example:*] A person not so rich in knowledge as the chief of the Kiev Oblast Court, Matsko, or Procurator Kovalenko would surely be surprised by the following phrase included in the verdict passed on Yaroslav Hevrych: "The testimony of witnesses Pronyuk and Horska to the effect that they did not pass anti-Soviet materials to Hevrych is to be disregarded, inasmuch as it does not coincide with the testimony of Hevrych and the material evidence." After spending a few months in the care of the KGB . . . . an individual says "yes" and is believed. Another person is free and, probably, for this reason is not acceptable [as a witness] . . . According to Article 369 of the Code of Criminal Procedure, the verdict "does not correspond to the factual circumstances of the case" because "it does not state why the court took into consideration some evidence and disregarded other evidence." The crude and mocking tone often used by the judge and the procurator toward the defendants and the witnesses must also be considered a direct violation of procedural norms. . . . [*There follow numerous examples of taunts and insults directed by the procurator or judge at witnesses and defendants in different trials. The author also cites statements betraying the severely limited expertise of court officials in cultural matters.*]

The secret trial

The examination of the case in all trials in the U.S.S.R. is public, insofar as the law does not provide for exceptions. The accused is guaranteed the right to defense. (Constitution of the U.S.S.R.)

In accordance with Article 91 of the Constitution of the Ukr.S.S.R., *the examination of all cases in all courts of the Ukr.S.S.R. must be public,* insofar as the law does not provide for exceptions. (Statute of the Judicial System of the Ukr.S.S.R., Article 11.)

Openness of the court examination: The court inquiry in all trials must be public, except in cases where this would affect the protection of state secrets. A closed trial also is allowed on the recommendation of the court in cases where the crime was committed *by a person under 16 years of age,* in *sex crimes,* and in other crimes where the aim is to prevent the revelation of *details of intimate relations between individuals* who are participants in the case. . . . Courts should *widely promote the practice of holding trials directly in enterprises,* on building sites, in *radhosps* and in *kolhosps,* in the presence of people's procurators and people's advocates. (Code of Criminal Procedure, Ukr.S.S.R., Article 20.)

The verdict must be revoked in all cases where the court has violated the requirements of the code concerning public trial. . . . (Code of Criminal Procedure, Ukr.S.S.R., Article 370.)

Each person accused of committing a crime has the right to be considered innocent until such time as his crime is established in a legal manner *by means of a public trial* at which he is guaranteed all opportunities for defense. (Universal Declaration of Human Rights adopted by the United Nations, Article 11.)

Article 20 of the Code of Criminal Procedure of the Ukrainian S.S.R. is understandable even by elementary-school children. There is no indication in this clause that any other laws or instructions exist that would give more scope for secret trials. Then, why were Zalyvakha, Hevrych, Hed, Menkosh, Kuznetsova, Martynenko, Masyutko, Rusyn, and others tried in secret? All of them were of age, they had not committed sex crimes, and there was no need to bring in intimate details of their private lives. None of them had passed on any military or technical secrets to foreign intelligence services (that is, if data about the number of Ukrainian and Russian schools in the Republic, about the language of instruction in schools of higher learning, and about the number of books that are published in the Ukr.S.S.R. in Russian and in Ukrainian have not been relegated to the ranks of state secrets). On the other hand, when the spy Penkovsky was tried, the widest publicity was given to the trial, and the stenographic report was published in a large number of copies. The concern there was with passing secret materials [to foreigners]—here, with books that are available to everyone abroad. However, here they seem to have become the superbomb that the instigators of secret trials fear like fire. . . .

We have only meager information about the secret trials in Ternopil and Ivano-Frankovsk (there is a rumor going about that Zalyvakha categorically denied his guilt). For this reason, I will give a more detailed account of how justice reigned in Kiev and Lvov.

On March 9–11 (?), Hevrych was tried by the head of the Kiev Oblast Court, Matsko, the Assessors Yarko and Zahorodny, and Procurator Komashechenko (I did not have enough time to note the "lawyer's" name, but he played no role). Justice began from the point where no one, not even relatives, were notified of the trial. So, on the first day, Comrade Matsko had peace. On March 10, the witnesses were called, and, thus, some people found out about the trial. (Couldn't they have held a secret trial without witnesses? No one would have even known about it. . . .) Hevrych's friends and acquaintances, his colleagues from the Pedagogical Institute, having got hold of Matsko, began asking him under what law Hevrych was being secretly tried. Militia and plainclothesmen ejected the excessively inquisitive citizens from the court halls so that they would not obstruct justice. Some were pulled by the sleeve, some pushed by the shoulders. . . . However, the people did not scatter; instead, disregarding even the comrades in plainclothes and dispensing with the usual piety, they began to speak about the illegality [of the trial]. In order to get rid of them, an announcement was made that sentence would be pronounced the following day at two o'clock (as we know, the law requires that the sentence always be read in public). As might have been expected, the high court lied: sentence was pronounced at eleven o'clock in the morning. . . . But Comrade Matsko miscalculated somewhat. At eleven o'clock, a few dozen [of Hevrych's friends] were gathered in front of the building anyway. They watched as a large group of people, in almost ceremonial step, marched past them into the courthouse. With great respect the militia and plain-clothesmen guarding the door allowed these people through. Sentence was passed within ten minutes, but only a few of [Hevrych's friends] could get into the courtroom. There was "not enough room" for them. All the benches, except the last one, were occupied by the [other] unexpected "friends" of the accused who had been led in so ceremoniously. . . .

Only three "outside" individuals were permitted into the courtroom to hear the sentence pronounced, and these were tightly encircled by the attending "citizenry." Even these three, however, caused problems for the bosses of justice. Probably believing that the sentence was not a secret because, in "all cases, it is to be pronounced in public" (Article 20, Code of Criminal Procedure), the poets Lina Kostenko and Lubov Zabashta decided to record it. The "citizenry" forcibly took away their notes from them. . . .

Either we are the greatest hypocrites in the world, or we have a sufficiently short memory to forget today what we fiercely supported yesterday. When Lenin's norms of justice, after being dragged through the mire, were proclaimed anew, it seemed that all kinds of "troikas" and closed trials of individuals, whose only crime probably was that their minds were capable of thinking, had disappeared forever. It is possible that we so greatly exaggerated our expectations? . . .

THE CONTEMPTIBILITY OR STUPIDITY OF THE ACCUSATIONS AND HARSH SENTENCES

Any punishment assigned by the court that, even though it is within the bounds of the appropriate article of the Criminal Code, is nevertheless obviously unjust in its magnitude is considered inappropriate to the severity of the crime and to the condemned person. (Article 372, Code of Criminal Procedure, Ukr.S.S.R.)

Let us now look at the over-all production of the "justice machine" in the Ukraine during recent months.

The following sixteen persons were sentenced to various terms in corrective labor colonies: (1) Ivashchenko—lecturer in Ukrainian literature at the Pedagogical Institute in Lutsk: two years. (2) Moroz—lecturer of history at the Pedagogical Institute in Lutsk: four years. (3) Ozerny —teacher of Ukrainian and German at Ripkovska High School, Ivano-Frankovsk Oblast: six years (the Supreme Court commuted this sentence to three years). (4) Hevrych—fifth-year student at the Kiev Medical Institute: five years (the Supreme Court commuted this sentence to three years). (5) Kuznetsova—laboratory worker in the University of Kiev: four years. (6) Martynenko—engineer from Kiev: three years. (7) Rusyn—employee in a Kiev research institute: one year. (8) Masyutko—retired, resident of Theodosia: six years (of this, three years in "isolation"). (9) Zalyvakha—artist from Ivano-Frankovsk: five years. (10) Hed—laborer, student of evening courses in Lvov: three years. (11) Menkosh—employee of a fashion enterprise in Lvov: two-and-a-half years. (12) Horyn, Mykhaylo—research worker in the Institute of Labor Psychology in Lvov: six years (of this, three years in a labor colony). (13) Horyn, Bohdan—art critic, employed at the Museum of Ukrainian Art in Lvov: four years. (14) Osadchy—lecturer at Lvov University: two years. (15) Zvarychevska—employee of Lvov Oblast Archives: eight months. (16) Hryn—degree candidate, research worker at the Institute of Geophysics, Academy of Sciences, Ukr.S.S.R. Kiev: two years. . . .

[*The list continues with the names of those on probation and those released after temporary incarceration.*]

The homes of dozens of people were searched and their books, letters, diaries, and personal notebooks were confiscated. Hundreds were interrogated (the interrogations continue). Through KGB intervention (indirect), many people lost their jobs and were punished administratively. . . .

Up to now, we have spoken mostly about the violation of procedural norms in conducting trials and investigations; what the defendants were accused of we mentioned only in passing. I will now deal with this in greater detail. . . .

What is the basis of the accusations? Let us quote some phrases from the [Ozerny trial] in Ivano-Frankovsk: "facts about refusal to attend political training," "misuse of the works of Shevchenko," "use of the word *vatra*," "football-grandstand conduct," etc. . . .

After eliminating all these and similar "crimes," we are left with [the charge that] several articles were read or mentioned to friends by Ozerny: "On the Occasion of Pogruzhalsky's Trial," "Ukrainian Education in a Chauvinistic Vise," "An Address by the Pope," "A Reply from the Cultural Workers of Canada (and the U.S.A.?) to the Cultural Workers of the Ukraine," a short work by Ozerny himself, which he did not circulate, and an anecdote or fable of his about supply shortages under Khrushchev. [At the trial] . . . these articles were *mentioned only by name.* Can a title itself (for example, "On the Occasion of Pogruzhalsky's Trial") indicate that an article is anti-Soviet? If there were no closed sessions of the court (and such were not mentioned), how could the court know that such or such an article was anti-Soviet? Or did they simply take the procurator's word for it? . . . Can one sentence people for reading official addresses (by the Pope or a president of a foreign country), even if they are ideologically foreign to us? . . .

At the Ivano-Frankovsk trial, it was not proved that Ozerny actively circulated this material. Mentioned only was the fact that he asked a friend to retype the article "On the Occasion of Pogruzhalsky's Trial" and the Pope's address (as a matter of fact this address was broadcast by the Vatican station, which is not jammed here, so it was heard by thousands). . . . His cited "flights of fancy" and drunken conversations hardly constituted "agitation and propaganda carried on with a view to undermining or weakening Soviet order" or the commission of "especially dangerous state crimes." Nor can one seriously speak about "dissemination or preparation of literature of such content." The only thing left is "possession." So why six (or even three) years in a labor colony?

[*In similar detail the author enumerates the charges brought against Hevrych, Masyutko, and Karavansky, denouncing the severity of their punishment. Karavansky was not even given a trial; he was sent to a camp to complete a twenty-five year term for a previous offense, for which he had served fifteen years.*]

FINAL THOUGHTS—WHERE ARE WE HEADING?

. . . . Communism is the highest flowering of the spiritual world of each individual. A man is not a soulless automaton or a robot who can live by a defined program. He considers each program with his brain and his heart. The meeting of thoughts, the contest of views, the crossing of ideas—that is the lever that always has and always will drive mankind forward. The greatest material saturation, without the unfettering of thought and will, is not Communism. It is merely a large prison with a higher ration for the prisoners.

Even in Communism men will suffer. This will be the suffering of the ever-striving intellect. Even in Communism there will be conflicts, often tragic. These will be conflicts between the spirit and the deed. Yet, the conflicts will be resolved not by compulsion and force but by the healthy mind of the unfettered personality. It is this kind of society about which great minds have dreamed.

Today in our land, it has been proclaimed that Communism, through some *fata morgana*, has become a reality and that "the present generation of Soviet people will live in Communism" (Program of the CPSU). Thus, the same Communist society will contain student Ya. Hevrych, once he returns from the camps, and Judge Matsko, who sent him there for reading books; translator Karavansky (if he survives the camps) and the procurator who sent him to finish his twenty-five-year sentence; critic Svitlychny's sister and the KGB investigation officer from Donetsk who said to her, "We shot too few of you in our time"; Masyutko and the "experts" and procurator Sadowsky, who told lies about Masyutko. . . . Under this kind of Communism, there may still be camps for people who hold divergent views, as well as secret trials and the KGB—that highest synod in matters of heterodoxy. It may be that our generation will live in a *proclaimed* Communism—just as we now live in a *proclaimed* sovereign republic, have *proclaimed* freedoms and *proclaimed* socialist justice. Several times in the past, history has disproved the Jesuit motto, "the end justifies the means." One cannot build a just society by means of terror and the stifling of social impulses in people. The dialectics of history are inexorable, and unworthy means disgrace the end; what is obtained becomes a rachitic shadow of what was planned.

It is quite possible that, in themselves, Comrade Matsko from the Kiev Oblast Court and Comrade Koval from the Kiev KGB are not predatory and bloodthirsty people. . . . Maybe, in the depths of their souls, they do not find it very pleasant to take part in such unpopular cases. . . . But they justify the bad taste in their mouths (if they have it) in terms of the categorical directive "from above" and the soldier's readiness to act with cruelty in the interests of the state. They do not stop to think that in maintaining order by means of prisons and camps, in not hesitating to violate laws, they undermine the fundamentals of the Soviet system and make a travesty of the people's dream of the most just society in the world. . . .

Today, the KGB dislikes very much to have its deeds compared with those of its predecessors of the 1930's. At that time, supposedly sense-less and groundless accusations were made against people, prisoners were tortured, "troikas" passed sentences without detailed investigation, etc. . . . For some reason, everyone associates Stalin primarily with the year 1937, when all known Party leaders were put in prison. Actually, the terror began much earlier. . . . At least concerning the Ukraine, it is possible to speak of a tendency toward serious violation of socialist justice starting at the end of the 1920's. First, with the spread of col-lectivization, came the arrest of that part of the intelligentsia (mostly from the villages) that had supported the UNR (Ukrainska Natsio-nalna Rada—Ukrainian National Council) during the Revolution but that eventually had become completely loyal to the Soviet government and had joyfully welcomed the Ukrainization proclaimed by the Party. People were easily convinced of this group's guilt, once they had been reminded of its old sympathies. Then, the authorities took care of a group of famous scholars (Yefremov, Hermayze, etc.) who, while not veiling their opposition, had not carried on any organized struggle against the Soviet government but, instead, had worked toward the de-velopment of Ukrainian culture. The NKVD fabricated the SVU (As-sociation for the Liberation of the Ukraine), and, through promises and threats, obtained "confessions" [concerning its activities] from the scholars (though not from all). Then, they conducted a public show trial of the leaders of a nonexistent organization. . . . Next, they turned their attention to members of the intelligentsia who, although not Party members, had stood firmly on Soviet positions (Vyshnya, Kurbas, Yalovy, etc.) They accused people of the most idiotic things the NKVD could dream up. After the tragedy of December 1, 1934 [Kirov's assassination], the terror was intensified. The number of ar-rests among the Party-affiliated creative intelligentsia increased. By 1937, Ukrainian learning and culture were already bled white. [Mean-while] . . . arrests had begun among Party workers, who, a few years previously, had been glorifying the activity of the NKVD. The climax was reached in 1937: then the informer, the defendant, and the investigator were all imprisoned in the same cell. . . . At first, the NKVD did not use torture, or, if they did, it was of a sporadic, amateurish nature. The initial means of torture were lack of sleep, hunger, inhuman prison conditions, and threats. However, beginning in mid-1937, "enemies of the people" were literally tortured—it was officially permitted. . . . The bloody cleaver reached the point where it felled those who had wielded it: the "Yezhovites" (followers of Yezhov) murdered the "Yagoda-ites" (followers of Yagoda), the "Beria-ites" (followers of Beria) murdered the "Yezhovites". . . .

A look into the past shows what happens when arbitrariness and lack of principles are once allowed in the activities of the investigative and judicial organs. Today, a search is conducted in someone's home without a warrant, some pre-Revolutionary editions are confiscated as being "anti-Soviet," there is no answer to the complaint; tomorrow, with the help of highly paid "experts," the authorship of an article will be attributed to someone seeing it for the first time; the day after tomorrow, an "organization" will be fabricated and completely innocent people will be punished. . . .

Some party leaders have taken a suspicious stand. Instead of interfering with the illegal acts of the KGB and ending the arbitrariness, they have worked on public opinion in the most unscrupulous manner, hand in hand with the KGB's secret informers. Shortly after the arrests, allegations were heard from sources high and low concerning nationalistic organizations, American dollars, printing houses, even arms. The lies grew obvious, and so, for a switch, there came stories of massive anti-Soviet agitation and propaganda. This was at the time when the investigations were in progress and, according to Soviet law, the accused were not yet to be considered guilty. As early as November of last year, the First Secretary of the CC-CPUkraine, P. Shelest, promised Rusyn's wife, who chanced to see him at a reception, that no one would be unjustly punished, that the accused would be tried in open courts with the greatest publicity, and that the press would provide coverage. Yet, in late March 1966, just before the beginning of the Twenty-third CPSU Congress, Rusyn, Kuznetsova, and Martynenko were tried behind closed doors in complete secrecy. In his report to the Twenty-third Congress of the CPUkraine [in March 1966], P. Ye. Shelest named Ivan Drach as one of the best young poets of the Ukraine; but the KGB major in charge of security during the Lvov secret trials assessed the work of the poet in somewhat different terms: "So you are Drach? Why do you write all kinds of trash instead of educating people! You even protect anti-Soviets. That rabble should be hanged!" What should one believe today: the words of the First Secretary of the CC-CPUkraine or the deeds of writer-procurators and majors of the KGB who are also "literary critics"? Who is thrown behind bars in the Ukraine these days? Those on trial belong to a generation that grew up under Soviet government and that was educated in Soviet schools, in Soviet institutions of higher learning, and in the Komsomol. People who are being tried as bourgeois nationalists do not even remember the bourgeois order that their forebears endured with bitterness on their own rich land. And no one has thought of looking for a deeper cause [of unrest] than the tiresome nonsense about the effect of bourgeois ideology and bourgeois nationalism.

Honored comrades, who needs that "bourgeoisie" except you yourselves to back up your old formula, which is supposed to replace honest thinking and a courageous search for ways to achieve justice? The police methods of mental prophylaxis were powerless and will remain so if any unsolved problem—particularly the nationality problem—continues to be ignored. Again and again it will be necessary to imprison those who stubbornly refuse to call white that which is black. It will be necessary to stifle human consciences [altogether] instead of relying on people with a developed sense of honor. . . . And, later, it will be necessary to rehabilitate people once more and to acknowledge that truth for which they sacrificed their youth. History always clarifies things. . . .

In a situation where the condemnation of Stalin's despotism and rapacious methods is final and irrevocable (no matter what some helplessly cruel people would like), . . . experiments with silencing and terrorizing represent an infamous and historically irresponsible course. With all conviction, I say that this course, in its essence, is anti-Soviet. Therefore I write.

VYACHESLAV CHORNOVIL

Vyshhorod,
Kiev Oblast,
"Berizky"

38. *Babyi Yar Address by I. Dzyuba*

September 29, 1966

There are events, tragedies, the enormity of which make all words futile and of which silence tells incomparably more—the awesome silence of thousands of people. Perhaps we, too, should keep silent and only meditate. But silence says a lot only when everything that could have been said has already been said. If there is still much to say, or if nothing has yet been said, then silence becomes a partner to falsehood and enslavement. We must, therefore, speak and continue to speak whenever we can, taking advantage of all opportunities, [for they] come so infrequently.

I want to say a few words—one-thousandth of what I am now think-ing and what I would like to say here. I want to address you as men—as my brothers in humanity. I want to address you Jews as a Ukrainian —as a member of the Ukrainian nation to which I proudly belong.

Babyi Yar is a tragedy of all mankind, but it happened on Ukrainian soil. And, therefore, a Ukrainian has no more right to forget it than a Jew has. Babyi Yar is our common tragedy, a tragedy for both the Jew-ish and the Ukrainian nation.

This tragedy was brought on our nations by fascism.

Yet one must not forget that fascism neither begins nor ends in Babyi Yar. Fascism begins in disrespect to man and ends in the destruc-tion of man, in the destruction of nations—though not necessarily in the manner of Babyi Yar.

Let us imagine for a moment that Hitler had won, that German fas-cism had been victorious. One can be sure that the victors would have created a brilliant and "flourishing" society that would have attained a high level of economic and technical development and made the same scientific and other discoveries that we have made. Probably the mute slaves of fascism would eventually have "tamed" the cosmos and flown to other planets to represent humanity and earthly civiliza-tion. Moreover, this regime would have done everything in order to consolidate its own "truth" so that men would forget the price they paid for such "progress," so that history would excuse or forget their enormous crimes, so that their inhuman society would seem normal to people and even the best in the world. And then, not on the ruins of the Bastille but on the desecrated, forgotten sites of national tragedy, thickly choked with sand, there would have been an official sign: "Dancing Here Tonight."

We should therefore judge each society not by its external technical achievements but by the position and meaning it gives to man, by the value it puts on human dignity and human conscience.

Today, in Babyi Yar, we commemorate not only those who died here. We commemorate millions of Soviet warriors—our fathers—who gave their lives in the struggle against fascism. We commemorate the sacri-fices and efforts of millions of Soviet citizens of all nationalities who unselfishly contributed to the victory over fascism. We should remem-ber this so that we may be worthy of their memory and of the duty that has been imposed upon us by the countless sacrifices of human lives, hopes, and aspirations that were made.

Are we worthy of this memory? Apparently not, since even now var-ious forms of human hatred are found among us—[including one] we call by the worn-out, banal, and yet terrible [name], anti-Semitism. Anti-Semitism is an "international" phenomenon. It has existed and still exists in all societies. Sadly enough, even our own society is not free of it. Perhaps there is nothing strange about this—after all, anti-Semitism is the fruit and companion of age-old barbarism and slavery, the foremost and inevitable result of political despotism. To conquer it—in entire societies—is not an easy task, nor can it be done quickly. But what is strange is the fact that no struggle has been waged here against it during the postwar decades; what is more, it has often been artificially nourished. It seems that Lenin's instructions concerning the struggle against anti-Semitism are forgotten in the same way as his precepts regarding national development of the Ukraine.

In Stalin's day, there were open and flagrant attempts to use prejudices as a means of playing off Ukrainians and Jews against each other—to limit the Jewish national culture on the pretext of Jewish bourgeois nationalism, Zionism, and so on, and to suppress the Ukrainian national culture on the pretext of Ukrainian bourgeois nationalism. These cunningly prepared campaigns wrought damage on both nationalities and did nothing to further friendship between them. They only added one more sad memory to the harsh history of both nations and to the complex history of their relationship.

We must return to these memories not in order to open old wounds but in order to heal them once and for all.

As a Ukrainian, I am ashamed that there is anti-Semitism here, as in other nations; that those shameful phenomena we call anti-Semitism —[and which are] unworthy of mankind—exist here.

We Ukrainians must fight against all manifestations in our midst of anti-Semitism or disrespect toward the Jews. . . .

You Jews must fight against those in your midst who do not respect the Ukrainian people, the Ukrainian culture, the Ukrainian language—against those who unjustly see a potential anti-Semite in every Ukrainian.

We must outgrow all forms of human hatred, overcome all misunderstandings, and by our own efforts win true brotherhood.

It would seem that we ought to be the two nations most likely to understand each other, most likely to give mankind an example of brotherly cooperation. The history of our nations is so similar in its tragedies that, in the Biblical motifs of his "Moses," Ivan Franko recreated the story of the Ukrainian nation in terms of the Jewish legend. Lesia Ukrainka began one of her best poems about the Ukraine's tragedy with the line: "And you fought once, like Israel. . . ."

Great sons of both our nations bequeathed to us mutual understanding and friendship. The lives of the three greatest Jewish writers—Sholom Aleykhem, Itskhok Peretz, and Mendele Moykher-Sforim—are bound up with the Ukraine. . . . The brilliant Jewish publicist Vladimir Zhabotinsky fought on the Ukrainian side in the Ukraine's struggle against Russian Tsarism and called upon the Jewish intelligentsia to support the Ukrainian national liberation movement and Ukrainian culture.

One of Taras Shevchenko's last civic acts was his well-known protest against the anti-Semitic policies of the Tsarist government. Lesia Ukrainka, Ivan Franko, Boris Hrinchenko, Stepan Vasylenko, and other leading Ukrainian writers well knew and highly valued the greatness of

Jewish history and of the Jewish spirit, and they wrote of the suffering of the Jewish poor with sincere sympathy.

Our common past consists not only of blind enmity and bitter misunderstanding—although there was much of this, too. Our past also shows examples of courageous solidarity and cooperation in the fight for our common ideals of freedom and justice, for the well-being of our nations.

We, the present generation, should continue this tradition and not the tradition of distrust and reserve.

But, sadly enough, there are a number of factors which are not conducive to letting this noble tradition of solidarity take firm root.

One of these factors is the lack of openness and publicity given to the nationalities question. As a result, a kind of "conspiracy of silence" surrounds the problem. The attitude in socialist Poland could serve as a good example for us. We know how complicated the relations between Jews and Poles were in the past. Now there are no traces of past ill-feeling. What is the "secret" of this success? In the first place, the Poles and the Jews were brought closer together by the common evil of the Second World War. But we, too, had this evil in common.

Secondly—and this we do not have—in socialist Poland, relations between nationalities are the subject of scientific sociological study, public discussion, inquiries in the press and literature, and so on. All this creates a proper atmosphere for successful national and international enlightenment.

We, too, should care about and exert ourselves—in deed rather than just in word—on behalf of this kind of enlightenment. We must not ignore anti-Semitism, chauvinism, disrespect toward any nationality, a boorish attitude toward any national culture or national language. There is plenty of boorishness in our midst, and, in many of us, it begins with the rejection of ourselves—of our nationality, culture, history, and language—even though such a rejection is not always voluntary nor is the person involved always to be blamed.

The road to true and honest brotherhood lies not in self-oblivion but in self-awareness, not in rejection of ourselves and adaptation to others but in being ourselves and respecting others. The Jews have a right to be Jews and the Ukrainians have a right to be Ukrainians in the full and profound, not merely the formal, sense of the word. Let the Jews know Jewish history, Jewish culture, and the Yiddish language and be proud of them. Let the Ukrainians know Ukrainian history, the Ukrainian culture and language and be proud of them. Let them also know each other's history and culture and the history and culture of other nations, and let them know how to value themselves and others—as brothers.

It is difficult to achieve this—but better to strive for it than to shrug one's shoulders and swim with the current of assimilation and adaptation, which will bring about nothing except boorishness, blasphemy, and veiled human hatred.

With our very lives, we should oppose civilized [forms of] hatred for mankind and social boorishness. There is nothing more important for us at the present time, because, without such opposition, all our social ideals will lose their meaning.

This is our duty to millions of victims of despotism; this is our duty to the better men and women of the Ukrainian and Jewish nations who have urged us to mutual understanding and friendship; this is our duty to our Ukrainian land in which we live together; this is our duty to humanity.

39. An Appeal from Representatives of the Crimean-Tatar People to the People of the World

June 21, 1968

In 1944, our entire people was slanderously accused of treason to the Soviet homeland and was forcibly moved from Kiev.

[At that time] all grown men were at the front, and able-bodied old men and adolescents were in the labor army. In a single day, on May 18, approximately 200,000 defenseless women, children, and invalids were driven from their homes without warning by NKVD troops. They were put onto trains and taken to reservations under guard. Marshal Voroshilov was in charge of this operation. We were transported to [Soviet] Central Asia in closed train cars. We had almost no food or clothing, and the trip lasted about three weeks. At the end of the war, the men returning from the front were also sent there. About half of our entire people perished during the very first years as a result of the inhumane deportation and the unbearable conditions under which we lived. Simultaneously, our national autonomy was abolished, our national culture was crushed, our monuments were destroyed, and the graves of our ancestors were defiled and removed from the face of the earth.

During the next twelve years, we lived as exiles. We were subjected to discrimination, and our children, even those who had been born in exile, were branded as "traitors." Slanderous literature, which is still read by Soviet people, was published against us.

Following the Twentieth Congress of the CPSU, our people were released from exile, but the accusation of treason against our homeland was not lifted, and, as before, we were not allowed to return to the Crimea. From 1957 to 1967, we sent hundreds of thousands of collective and individual letters to the CC of the CPSU and to the Presidium of the Supreme Soviet of the U.S.S.R. demanding an end to this injustice. On several occasions, after persistent requests, representatives of our people in Moscow were received by Party and government leaders Mikoyan, Georgadze, and Andropov. Each time, we were promised a prompt resolution of the Crimean-Tatar question, but, instead, we were subjected to more deportations, dismissals from work, and expulsions from the Party.

Finally, on September 5, 1967, the Presidium of the Supreme Soviet of the U.S.S.R. issued a decree that absolved us from the charge of treason. Nonetheless, we were not named Crimean Tatars but, rather, "citizens of the Tatar nationality who previously lived in the Crimea." In so doing, the decree legalized our exile from our homeland and abolished our existence as a nation. After its publication, several thousand people traveled to the Crimea but once more were forcibly expelled. The protest that our people sent to the CC of the CPSU remained unanswered, as did the protests of representatives of the Soviet public who supported us.

The authorities' only reply was persecution and court actions. Beginning in 1959, over 200 of the most active and courageous representatives of our people were sentenced for terms ranging up to seven years, even though they had always acted within the framework of the Soviet Constitution. Recently, the repressions directed against us have become particularly intense. On April 21, 1968, in the city of Chirchik, troops and the militia dispersed Crimean Tatars who had gathered to celebrate the birthday of Lenin and arrested over 300 persons. In May, 800 representatives of our people arrived in Moscow for the purpose of presenting the CC of the CPSU with a letter demanding that our people be permitted to return to the Crimea. On May 16 and 17, almost all these representatives were arrested and sent to Tashkent under guard. Simultaneously, in Tashkent, four representatives of our intelligentsia were sentenced to various terms of imprisonment. Every day, people are summoned to the local KGB organs, where blackmail and threats are used in an attempt to dissuade us from returning to our homeland.

We have been slanderously accused of wishing to return to the Crimea in order to oust those presently living there. This is not true. We are a peaceful people and have always lived in peace together with the multinational population of the Crimea. It is not we who are threatening anyone—it is rather that *we* are constantly threatened by national destruction.

The thing that is being done to us has a very specific name: GENOCIDE.

In the course of our struggle, we have collected more than three million signatures on letters sent by our people to the Soviet government. This means that every adult Crimean Tatar has signed at least 10 of these letters. But the appeal of 300,000 persons repeated 10 times has been in vain. Not a single Party or government agency has ever answered us, nor has any Soviet newspaper ever mentioned our struggle.

This is why we appeal to the people of the world.

We appeal to all peoples of the Soviet Union, as a small independent people appeals to fraternal peoples.

We appeal to all peoples of the world and, first and foremost, to those that have experienced national inequality and oppression.

We appeal to all people of good will in the hope that you will assist us.

HELP US RETURN TO THE LAND OF OUR FATHERS!

This letter is signed by representatives of the Crimean-Tatar people, who have a mandate, in the name of the people, authorizing them to struggle for the return to the homeland by all legal means:

ZAMLIRA ASANOVA, physician	Bekobad
ROLLAN KADIEV, theoretical physicist	Samarkand
RESHAT BAIRANOV, fitter	Melitopol
MURAT VOENYI, construction worker	Tashkent
ZORA KHALILOVA, teacher	Namangan
MUSTAFA IBRISH, engineer	Tashkent
ELDAR SHABANOV, driver	Bekobad
AISHE BEKIROVA, teacher	Bekobad
RAMAZAN MURATOV, worker	Bekobad
MUSTAFA KURKIN, driver	Uzbek S.S.R.
ILIAS UMEROV, mechanic	Akkurganskii Region
LENARA GUSOINOVA, engineer	Bekobad
IVAN GUNGUROV, engineer	Begovat
MURZA MAMUTOV, teacher	Begovat
REMZA VOENNYI, physician	Begovat
EDEM ISLIAMOV, physician	Begovat
ENVER VSLILIAEV, physician	Begovat
ANIDA KERIMOVA, housewife	Sovetobad
FIKRET ISLIAMOV, engineer	Sovetobad
AKHSEIT SEITMEMETOV, engineer	Margolan
ASAN AFUZOV, instructor	Fergana
D. KASAEV, teacher	Fergana
NURFOT MURKHAS, engineer	Tashkent Oblast
S. TARKHAN, electrician	Chirchik
Z. EMIROVA, student	Chirchik
D. ISLIAMOVA, feldsher	Chirchik
ASANOV, chief of supply section	Chirchik
R. ABDULTAROV, driver	Chirchik
R. ABZATOV, driver	Chirchik
S. IZIDINOV, technician	Chirchik
M. EDEMOV, lathe operator	Chirchik
ABDULAMINOV, electrician	Chirchik
SELIMA AKIMOVA, pensioner	Samarkand
ARIF KEMAL, pensioner	Samarkand
AIDER YAKUBOV, student	Samarkand
AIDAZ YAKUBOV, student	Samarkand
MEMOTOV, [illeg.], pensioner	Samarkand
MEMOTOVA, pensioner	Samarkand

[illegible], worker	Samarkand
SHAIPOVA, employee	Samarkand
USEIN ABIBULLAEV, pensioner	Samarkand
KHATIDNA ABIBULLAEVA, housewife	Samarkand
EMIR-ASAN KHAFAZ, blacksmith	Samarkand
DZHAFAR BOLAT, pensioner	Samarkand
SIPP-AGIA ADILLA, housewife	Samarkand
V. ISMAILOV, instructor	Samarkand
D. MALAIDTNEV, engineer	Samarkand
FATIMA YAZDZHELEVA, teacher	Samarkand
RUSTOM SIM-ARIF, carpenter	Samarkand
MUSTAFA KONSUL, designer	Samarkand
SARIA YAGIAEVA, engineer	Samarkand
LENNARA AZAMATOVA, teacher	Samarkand
AMNIE AZAMATOVA, pensioner	Samarkand
USEIN AZAMATOV, pensioner	Samarkand
ROMZI KAISOROV, warehouse manager	Samarkand
DLIAPER IRIKH, driver	Samarkand
OSMAN DADOI, welder	Samarkand
EMIR-ULIN DADOI, grinder	Samarkand
NURI SEITVELIEV, cabinetmaker	Samarkand
EDINO OSMANOVA, worker	Samarkand
SEIT-ABDI YAKUBOV, driver	Samarkand
RUSLAN EMINOV, construction worker	Samarkand
ISMAIL YAZTSDZHIEV, bricklayer	Bulungur
IZZET EMIRSALIEV, mechanic	Tashkent
SOIRAN KHALILOV, technician	Fergana
AIDOR BARIEV, tractor driver	Chirchik
APVER AMETOV, driver	Kirgiz S.S.R.
AKKII KHALILOV, projectionist	Gulistan
ABLAZ ABDURMANOV, mechanic	Kitab Settlement
VIDUI SMEDALEV, feldsher	Andizhan
GOMER BAEV, engineer	Novorossiisk
DYARA KOSSE, instructor	Margelan
REZA ULIFOV, worker	Tashkent
MEDINE KARALIEVA, painter	Angrep
EBAZER SEIDAMIEV, mold filler	Begovat
ALI SAMEDINOV, crane operator	Begovat
ZIPUR IBRALIEV, machine operator	Bekobad
DELIAVER RESHIDOV, driver	Begovat
IDRIS ASANOV, driver	Begovat
YUNUS VEISOV, worker	Bekobad
FERA SAMIDINOVA	Bekobad
ZAKIDE KUDUSOVA, teacher	Bekobad
MUPIRE ABLIALIMOVA, weaver	Leninabad
KHALIL ABRAIMOV, machine operator	Begovat
KADYR BILIALOV, machinist	Begovat

TOKHTAR-GAZY RUSTEMOV, construction worker	Bekobad
NURI DIBAKH, electrician	Leninabad
D. SULEIMANOV, driver	Begovat
REFAT SULEIMANOV, machinist	Begovat
ROBIIA SETTAROVA, teacher	[illegible]
MURTAZA KHALILOV, barber	Begovat
REMAT ALTI, driver	Begovat
SERVER BEKIROV, driver	Begovat
AMET AKHCHIL, carpenter	Begovat
VLAFER VESIEV, carpenter	Bekobad
NARIMAN BORANGAZIEV, driver	Begovat
FAKHRY ISMAILOV	Fergana
M. SAROPIKA	Kzyl-Orda
LEPURA BELIALOVA	Samarkand
ISMAIL ISMAILOV	Novorossiisk
SHEIT BEKIROV	Samarkand
SH. IBRAIMOVA	Samarkand
ZEKKI MUZHDABAYEV	Samarkand
GALINA SMIRNOVA	Samarkand
ENVER AMETOV	Kirgiz S.S.R.
IIALIN KURTAMETOV	Samarkand
ROSHAT SEITUMEROV	Chirchik
F. KHALILOV	Chirchik
KHIRUF ISMAILOV	Chirchik
OSMAN MAMUTOV	Bekobad
IZZET ABLIAZOV	Bekobad
MEDZHIT YAGIAEV	Leninsk
SERVER ISMAILOV	Leninsk
ABDURAKHMAN ADILOV	Alti-[illegible]
GUNKHASH KASAEVA	Fergana
BASIR RAMAZANOV	Fergana
MAMEDI RAMAZANOV	Fergana
SERPOR ABDULLAEV	Kuvasai

40. *P. G. Grigorenko on Tatar Rights*

On the evening of March 17, 1968, the representatives in Moscow of the Crimean Tatars held a party in honor of the seventy-second birthday of the progressive Soviet writer A. Ye. Kosterin. Because of serious illness, Comrade Kosterin could not attend, but his wife, Vera Ivanovna Kosterina, and his closest friend, retired Major-General P. G. Grigorenko, were present. Addressing the gathering on behalf of his colleagues, one of the representatives spoke as follows:

Comrades! I have the honor, in the name of all the Moscow representatives of the Crimean Tatars, to extend congratulations, on the occasion of his 72nd birthday, to one of the more progressive writers of our times, a great friend of our people, one of Russia's best sons, a revolutionary—Aleksei Yevgrafovich Kosterin. On behalf of the sixty representatives in Moscow, who represent more than a half million Crimean Tatars, I thank Comrade Kosterin for everything he has done for our people and for other minority peoples whose rights have been violated by the evil forces of the country. [*Loud applause.*] Comrade Kosterin held out a helping hand to us in a time of cruel repressions against the representatives of our people, who demanded recognition of the Crimean Tatars' soverign rights—first of all, the right to a homeland—and in a time of grim struggle by our people for the right to exist. We shall never forget this! [*Loud applause.*]

Twenty-four years ago, when freight cars were taking away from the Crimea—their native land—women, children, and white-haired old men heartbroken with despair; when tens of thousands of our compatriots were dying in reservations from hunger and disease; when our compatriots were being imprisoned only because they took measures to try to save their people from national extinction and to return them to their homeland—we had the right to ask: "Russia, have you no conscience? Are there none among your sons who will say that a crime is being committed? Why do they, by their indifference, pander to your infamous deeds?"

Now we can say: "Yes, there are!" A. Ye. Kosterin and those who share his democratic views are the embodiment of Russia's conscience. The help that they have extended to our people brings to our national movement a new momentum that will considerably ease our struggle and hasten the time when progress will triumph.

I am certain that the greatness of Russia will indeed be measured by the number of such persons as Aleksei Yevgrafovich Kosterin.

In the name of all the representatives of the Crimean Tatar people, I wish a speedy recovery and many happy returns of the day to Comrade A. Ye. Kosterin. [*Loud applause.*]

[*Former Major-General P. G. Grigorenko delivered the following speech in response.*]

Dear comrades! My closest friend, Aleksei Yevgrafovich Kosterin, who, as you know, is at this moment confined to the hospital with a serious attack of thrombosis, requested his wife, Vera Ivanovna, and myself to represent him at this evening's affair. For me, this is a great honor. I am especially touched by the fact that he charged me with expressing his and my mutual views regarding the struggle of the Crimean Tatars to preserve thier national autonomy.

Aleksei Yevgrafovich, who was born and raised in the northern Caucasus, where there are many nationalities, was able to observe from childhood the cruel nationalistic oppression of the smaller nations, the national dissensions and enmity constantly stirred up by the oppressors, the repulsive chauvinism of a great power. Suffering cruelly from the realization that his nation had assumed the role of an oppressor of "aliens," he decided that he, as a Russian patriot, would devote his entire life to the struggle for national equality, for friendship among the peoples. He has never in his entire life been unfaithful to that youthful pledge.

Three years spent in a Tsarist jail not only did not break his revolutionary spirit but hardened it. Liberated by the February Revolution, he completely immersed himself in the work of organizing and educating the peoples of the northern Caucasus. Even when this area was captured by the "Whites," he did not abandon these peoples. He organized the partisan movement in the mountains and himself participated in it until the "Whites" were driven from the Caucasus.

After the Civil War the problem of equal nationality rights remained uppermost in his Party work as well as in his creative literary activities.

Only once did the protesting voice of writer Aleksei Kosterin fall silent. This happened during the time of the barbaric banishment of the Povolozhye Germans, the Kalmyks, and the smaller nations of the northern Caucasus—of your people, the Crimean Tatars—from their native lands. It happened because there was no possible way for his voice to make itself heard. For he himself was at that time behind the barbed wire of the Stalin-Beria labor camps.

But the nightmare of seventeen years in labor camps did not break him. As soon as he became free again, he immediately raised his voice boldly and firmly in defense of the "smaller and forgotten ones."

I will not speak of his current struggle. You know of it as well as I. He has put his warm heart—the heart of a real Bolshevik-Leninist—totally into the struggle to re-establish the nationality policies of Lenin. Unfortunately, the strain has been more than his heart could bear. But we all believe that this is temporary and that the day is not far off when his voice will be heard again—loud and clear. [*Loud applause. Cries of* "Long years of life and health to our best friend!"]

What shall I say in conclusion? What can be said that would give a general portrait of the man? This is not easy, but still I will try.

This is a Bolshevik-Leninist, a revolutionary in the highest sense of the word.

This is a true humanist, one who gave all the strength of his great soul to the defense of small nations and peoples, to the struggle for equal nationality rights, to the friendship of all peoples.

This is a wonderful and original writer, one who carries on the best humanistic traditions of Russian literature. It is a pity that life did not permit the talent of this writer to unfold fully. Even now, his works are hardly ever published, and this, as you know, cannot help but affect the creative productivity of a writer.

This is also a remarkable father, a person who, by making his own life an example, raised such a daughter as Nina Kosterina. You know, surely, that Nina's diary, published in editions numbering millions and in almost all languages—on a level with *The Diary of Anne Frank*—serves the cause of the struggle against fascism in all its facets, the cause of the struggle among peoples, and the development of humanistic ideas and traditions.

Such is Aleksei Kosterin, the man whose seventy-second birthday we are honoring today.

Allow me now to express briefly Kosterin's and my views regarding the actual problems of your movement.

It will soon be a quarter of a century since your people were expelled from their homes and driven from the land of their ancestors into reservations where living conditions were such as to presage the inevitable destruction of the entire Crimean Tatar nation. Yet, to spite their enemies, this hardy, work-loving people overcame all and survived. After losing 46 per cent of their number, they gradually began to regain strength and resumed the struggle for their national and human rights.

This struggle has resulted in some gains. The system of forcible resettlement and exile has been ended, and the political rehabilitation of the Crimean Tatar people has been effected. This latter step, however, was taken with various reservations that did a great deal to detract from the act itself. Most important, the great mass of the Soviet people, who had been widely informed at one time that the Crimean Tatars had sold out the Crimea, was never told that this "sellout" was nothing but a figment of the imagination. But, the worst irony was yet to emerge—namely, the fact that the very edict that effected the political rehabilitation of the Crimean Tatars simultaneously legalized the liquidation of that nation. For now, you see, there are no Crimean Tatars, only "Tatars who at one time lived in the Crimea."

This single fact should be convincing evidence that your struggle has not only fallen short of its goals but, in a certain sense, has taken you a few steps backward. You were formerly subjected to repressions as Crimean Tatars, but, since the "political rehabilitation," it seems that there is no such nation. The nation has disappeared, but discrimination remains. You did not commit the crimes for which you were driven from the Crimea; yet you are not permitted to return there.

What basis is there for placing your people in a position of such inequality? Article 123 of the U.S.S.R. Constitution reads: "Any direct or indirect restriction of the rights . . . of citizens on account of their race or nationality is punishable by law."

Thus, the law is on your side. [*Lengthy applause.*] But despite this, your rights are being violated. Why?

We think the main reason for this lies in the fact that you underestimate your enemy. You think that you are dealing only with honest people. This is not so. What happened to your nation was not the work of Stalin alone. And his accomplices not only are still alive but hold responsible positions. They are afraid that, if you are given back what was unlawfully taken from you, they may, in time, be called upon to answer for their participation in such arbitrary rule. [*Wild applause.*] Therefore, they are doing everything possible to prevent you from succeeding in your struggle. After all, if everything is kept as it is, then it gives the impression that there was no lawlessness in the past.

You have chosen tactics that help them preserve this state of affairs. You address yourselves to the leadership of the Party with meekly written pleas, which pass through the hands of those who are against your struggle for national equality. And, since your pleas concern matters for which there are no indisputable, hard and fast rules, they are presented to persons who are bound to declare them doubtful, debatable issues, and, thus, your case becomes enmeshed in judgments and opinions that have nothing to do with the basic problem.

For instance [one hears such arguments as]: "There is no room in the Crimea for settling the Tatars." "If the Tatars move, there will be no one left in Central Asia to do the work." "The Crimean Tatars already feel at home where they are. Besides, they do not represent an independent nation; so those of them who wish to live in a Tatar republic should go to the Tatar A.S.S.R." "It would cost a lot of money to resettle them." And so on.

All these claims, as well as many other arguments advanced by the enemies of your national revival, are not worth an empty eggshell. But as long as you *request*—and "weighty" arguments are brought forward against your requests—your case is not moving forward, or it is even moving backwards. In order to put a stop to this abnormal situation, you must learn that *what is prescribed by law should not be requested; it should be demanded!* [*Wild applause, cries of* "Right!"]

Start to demand! And demand not bits and pieces but everything that was unlawfully taken away from you—the re-establishment of a *Crimean Autonomous Soviet Socialist Republic!* [*Wild applause.*]

Do not limit your activity to the writing of petitions. Strengthen your demands by all means that are available to you under the Constitution—make good use of the freedom of speech and of the press, of meetings, street processions and demonstrations.

A newspaper is put out for you in Tashkent, but the persons who put out this paper do not support your movement. Take the newspaper away from them. Elect your own editorial board. If they prevent you from doing this—boycott the newspaper and start another of your own. A movement cannot develop normally without its own press.

In your fight, don't lock yourselves into a narrow nationalist shell. Form contacts with all progressive persons of other nationalities in the Soviet Union, first of all those nationalities among whom you live—Russians, Ukrainians, the nationalities that have been and continue to be subjected to the same indignities as your people.

Don't consider your case to be inner-governmental. Seek help from the whole of progressive society and from international organizations. There is a specific name for what was done to your people in 1944. It is *genocide*, pure and simple—"one of the gravest crimes against humanity" (B.S.E., Vol. 10, p. 441).

The convention adopted by the U.N. General Assembly on December 9, 1948, included in the category of genocide "acts committed with intent to destroy, in whole or in part, a national, ethnic, racial, or religious group as such" by any of various methods and, specifically, "by deliberately inflicting on the group conditions of life calculated to bring about its physical destruction in whole or in part. . . ." Such acts—*i.e.*, "genocide"—are, from the viewpoint of international law, crimes condemned by the civilized world, for which the chief culprits and their accomplices are liable to punishment under law. So you see, international law is also on your side. [*Wild applause.*] If you cannot obtain a solution of the problem within the country, you have a right to appeal to the U.N. and the international tribunal.

Stop begging! Take back that which was taken from you unlawfully! [*Wild applause; in a single outburst of emotion, those in the audience jump up from their seats shouting* "Crimean A.S.S.R.!"] And remember, in this just and noble struggle, you must not allow your opponents to snatch with impunity the fighters who are in the foremost ranks of your movement.

There have already been a series of trials in Central Asia in which fighters for equal rights for the Crimean Tatars have been sentenced unlawfully and on false grounds. Right now in Tashkent, a trial of a similar nature is being prepared for Mamed Enver, Yuri and Savri Osmanov, and others.

Do not permit judicial reprisals to be carried out against these people. Demand and obtain for them an open trial, come to it in great numbers, and do not permit the court to be filled with specially selected spectators.

And, finally, Aleksei Yevgrafovich has asked me to tell you that he has received many congratulatory letters and telegrams from the Crimean Tatars. He cannot answer them at the present time and therefore wishes me to convey his deepest and most sincere thanks to all who sent him words of greeting and congratulation. He promises that in the future he will devote all his efforts to the struggle for full and equal rights for all nations, for sincere friendship between all the peoples of the world.

I raise my glass in honor of all brave and inflexible fighters for national equality, to one of the most outstanding warriors on this front, the writer and Bolshevik-internationalist Aleksei Yevgrafovich Kosterin, and to the health of the Crimean people! To our future meeting in Crimea, dear friends, on the territory of a re-established and reborn Crimean Autonomous Soviet Socialist Republic!!! [*Wild applause; toasts are drunk to A. Kosterin, the friendship of all peoples, a future meeting in Crimea, and to the Russian and Ukrainian peoples represented by comrades A. Ye. Kosterin and P. G. Grigorenko. Singing of the songs* "Port-Arthur," "Shompol," *and others.*]

IV. Religious Dissent

As in the preceding section, the materials presented in this section are only a small sample of the relevant material that has reached the outside world. Documents 41 through 45 provide specific illustrations of the official persecution and illegal interference in the affairs of the Orthodox and Evangelical-Baptist Churches in the Soviet Union. Document 46, from the voluminous writings of A. E. Levitin (Krasnov), discusses, among other matters, collusion of certain ecclesiastical officials in the implementation of the policies of the state. The last two documents attest to the repressive measures of the regime and also offer evidence of the emerging link between intellectual and religious dissent in the U.S.S.R. For a comprehensive analysis of these and many other relevant documents, see Peter Reddaway's article on pages 62-75.

41. Petition by P. S. Overchuk

June 10, 1967

To the Procurator of Ukr.S.S.R., Citizen Glukh, Kiev
Copies to the Council of Relatives of Evangelical Christian-Baptist Prisoners in the U.S.S.R.
From prisoner Pavel Semenovich Overchuk, born 1932, sentenced by the Kiev District Court September 24, 1966.

COMPLAINT

I, a believer of the Evangelical-Baptist faith, have been sentenced to two years and six months' deprivation of freedom in an ITK [corrective labor camp] of normal regime under Article 138, paragraph 2, of the Criminal Code of the Ukr.S.S.R. In fact, [however,] I was sentenced because of my religious convictions. Together with all my convicted fellow-believers, I disagree with the action taken [against us] by the investigatory and judicial organs. In violation of Article 16 of the Criminal Code of the Ukr.S.S.R. (which requires that justice be assured on the

214

basis of the equality of all men before the law regardless of national, racial, or religious affiliation) and in complete contradiction to the facts, [these organs] falsely made a criminal case against us under articles of the Criminal Code of the Ukr.S.S.R., brought us to trial, and convicted us. [They] acted not on the basis of Soviet law but from the position of atheists aiming at the forcible suppression of religion in our country.

The president of the court, Matsko, convincingly demonstrated that —quite apart from the law—the organs of the KGB, as well as the militia, the procurator's office, and the courts, have special instructions under which they act (*i.e.*, in sentencing believers unlawfully).

We of the Evangelical-Baptist faith have been convinced over and over again that, in fact, the faithful are being treated not in accordance with the laws of our country or with generally accepted international laws but in accordance with secret (unpublished) instructions that permit all sorts of persecutions and even the physical destruction of believers.

In our places of detention, my fellow-believers and I have been restricted in every possible way only because of our faith. When I was in ITK-65, Kiev Oblast, with five other fellow-believers (V. N. Zhurilo, V. N, Filaretov, V. N. Dongar, I. T. Koptilo, and N. K. Velichko), we turned in a petition to the MOOP [Ministry for the Protection of Social Order] of the U.S.S.R. asking permission—in accordance with an existing statute regulating the rights of prisoners—to perform the Christian ceremony of the Breaking of Bread, which is an integral part of the Evangelical-Baptist religion and obligatory for all church members. [However], instead of [recognizing] this basic religious need of ours, the labor-camp directorate of the MOOP, Ukr.S.S.R., without forwarding our petition to Moscow, [sent back] an irresponsible answer of its own in letter No. 1/2-141-o of March 24, 1967, signed by the deputy director of the political department of the labor-camp directorate of the MOOP, Ukr.S.S.R., N. Volokhov. The gist of his answer was as follows: "The complaint has been taken into consideration and has been rejected. At the same time, we want to make it clear to you that the practice of religious ceremonies in the ITK is categorically forbidden." What makes this answer irresponsible is that there is no reference to any relevant stipulation in our country's legislation that denies the minimal satisfaction of the religious needs of believers in places of detention. . . .

On April 19, 1967, I was told by the commander of the ITK that I had no right to believe in God or to pray to God. I replied that such statements flouted the law, that I was a believer and could not live a single day without praying to my God, who is the creator of the entire universe and of all living creatures.

Various threats were made by the administration of ITK-21. They told me that other people—*i.e.*, imprisoned labor-camp workers—would be watching me and would . . . eavesdrop on every word I said to anybody about God and that, if I worshipped God, I would be severely punished. I declared that it was not necessary to set spies after me, for I was willing to admit right away that I had prayed to God while at liberty, as well as in prison and in ITK-21, and that, if I had not done so [in the first place], I would be a free man instead of being here.

On April 26, 1967, my seventy-one-year-old mother (whose husband died at the front) and other relatives came to see me. I went to the division guard, I. P. Chelnokov, with a request for permission to receive a general visit and a food parcel, but he told me that no visits could be granted to a person who prays to God. I replied that, through no fault of my own, I had not had a visit for five months and had not received food parcels for three months despite the fact that as a prisoner under a normal regime I was entitled to have both a general visit and a food parcel once every two months; and [I pointed out that] it is nowhere stipulated that a person who prays to God may not receive visitors.

The guard's reply was that he had consulted with the procurator, who told him that they [the camp administration] had the authority to deprive me of all rights because I prayed to God in the barracks . . . in the presence of other prisoners. I replied that I had been placed in these conditions and that there was no place where I could pray to God without other prisoners seeing me. [I added], however, that if they gave me another more convenient place, I would use it. Again, the division guard told me that I must not pray and threatened that, unless I stopped doing so, instead of being allowed a visit, I would be put in the *shizo* [disciplinary isolation cell]. If this did not help, they would put me in a cellblock (prison regime) where I would not be permitted any correspondence or visits, where I would be allowed to receive [only] one food parcel every six months, and where I would be denied the opportunity of buying food products in the [camp] shop, would be subjected to hard physical labor, and would receive a reduced food ration. I would not be released [from the cellblock] until the end of my term, and, if even this [treatment] did not help, they would cut out my liver, and I would be forced to act as the administration of ITK-21 demanded —*i.e.*, to stop praying to God. . . .

After all these threats, I. P. Chelnokov went to the commander of ITK-21, Lieutenant-Colonel D. I. Mechkan, and I was then summoned in also. With the senior official (N. K. Kryachko, the political representative), the division guard, and others present, Mechkan declared that my request to receive a visit was denied and that [instead] he would sentence me to the *shizo* for having prayed to God in my barracks. . . . [He said] that they [the camp authorities] were in possession of statements from those delegated to watch me, revealing that I had continued to pray morning and night. I answered that it was not necessary to spy on me and watch me, that I had said from the start that I was a believer, and that I would go on praying to God regardless of all threats, as I had been doing up till then. [I told Mechkan that] the administration of ITK-21 was the first [penal authority] to prohibit my praying to God and, what is more, to punish me for it. In prison, as well as in

ITK-65, nobody had ever forbidden me to pray to God since I had the legal right to do so.

[I pointed out that] I had not exactly chosen the place where I prayed . . . and that I had no other more convenient place. If, however, the camp commander would suggest a more suitable place where I would not be seen by other prisoners, I would use it. Mechkan said, "Go and pray in the toilet." I answered that I had feelings of human dignity and was not going to pray in such a place, and, furthermore, that such statements insulted my religious feelings and did him no honor as a commandant appointed to educate people. After this, Lieutenant-Colonel Mechkan said that they [the camp authorities] had their own laws and would force me to obey them—*i.e.*, to stop praying to God. Then I signed . . . a resolution that put me in the *shizo* for ten days. The resolution said that I was being put there because I prayed to God and talked about God to other prisoners. Thus, instead of [permitting] the visit which had been due me for five months, they put me in the *shizo*, where I spent Easter and the May Day holiday (from April 26 to June 5, 1967). . . .

It may be asked whether such acts have stopped me from praying to God. On the contrary, I value all the more the divine gifts of air and light, and I have witnessed the baseness of the atheistic campaign, which is not an ideological struggle with believers but is deliberately designed to destroy them physically. . . .

All that has been pointed out here clearly demonstrates that the actions of the fanatically inclined atheists of ITK-21 administration are unlawful, discriminatory, and nothing short of genocidal.

For confirmation of the justness of my complaint, ask to see the resolution concerning my internment in the *shizo* and you will learn of the arbitrary acts of the ITK-21 administration.

I request that you issue instructions:

1. to strike my penalty (*shizo*, ten days) [from the record, because] it was illegally imposed;

2. to give me, like other prisoners, the opportunity to make use of the privileges accruing to those who have completed one-third of their sentence, because I have not violated regulations;

3. to allow me the opportunity, in accordance with the existing statute, to receive visits and food parcels like all other prisoners;

4. to grant me the privilege of buying sugar, margarine, and other products in the [camp] shop, like all prisoners under a normal regime;

5. to allow me the privilege of corresponding freely with close relatives, to which all prisoners under a normal regime are entitled.

I ask you to inform me of the action you take at the following address: Dnepropetrovsk Oblast, Solonenski Region, Village of Appolonovka, Box YaE 308/21.

Imploringly yours, the prisoner—

P. S. OVERCHUK

42. Appeal by Five Baptist Women

August 15, 1967

To the United Nations Secretary-General, U Thant
Copies to: The U.N. Commission on Human Rights
The International Commission of Jurists
The President of the U.S.S.R. Council of Ministers,
A. N. Kosygin

From the Council of Relatives of Prisoners Belonging to the Evangelical Christian and Baptist Church (ECB) in the U.S.S.R.

Dear Mr. Secretary-General:

The Council of Relatives of ECB Prisoners in the U.S.S.R. is forced to turn to you once more because, under the U.N. Charter, you are appointed to protect the fundamental rights of man, irrespective of nationality, race, or religion.

All our petitions to the government of our country have been in vain.

In our country, freedom of religion has been openly proclaimed, but, for more than forty years, we have been unable to enjoy it in reality. Our church history is one of constant oppression and persecution. Our older people were, formerly, the children of prisoners and now are the mothers and fathers of prisoners. . . .

At the present time, more than 200 believers have been convicted, and new court cases are in preparation. Meetings of believers of unregistered congregations are dispersed by the militia, and believers are fined for attending prayer meetings. ECB believers in the U.S.S.R. are placed in the position of being forced to act against their own consciences or being persecuted.

We consider it necessary to call your attention to the following facts:

1. *Dispersal of prayer meetings; confiscation of private houses and church premises.*

All congregations seeking to be registered legally . . . have been refused registration by the authorities concerned. The congregations have been declared illegal, and unlawful physical measures are being taken against them. In order to prevent any religious service from being held by unregistered congregations, their church premises are being confiscated, as are, also, the private residences of believers if services are held in them.

Churches have been confiscated in the following towns: Cheliabinsk, Podolsk in the Moscow region; Frunze, Odessa, Kharkov, Vladivostok; Gomel, Yasinovka village (Lvov Province), Barnaul; Zhitomir; Brest, Krivoi Rog; Dedovsk (Moscow region), and Izmail.

In 1965, at Podolsk, a private house belonging to V. V. Kuznetsova was confiscated because religious meetings had taken place there. All petitions for the return of the house have been unavailing.

At Barnaul, militiamen and auxiliary police, choosing a time when the owners of the house were not at home, arrived by car, cut their way through the door, carried out all the household effects, and demolished the house with a bulldozer.

Religious meetings of unregistered congregations are being dispersed by the militia and auxiliary police. For example, at Slutsk (Minsk region) on February 13, 1966, believers kneeling in prayer were disturbed by the noisy entrance of several dozen militiamen and police. They began shouting menacingly, "Get up! Stop!" Then an order was given: "Take them one by one and drag them into the motorcars!" The believers were driven to the militia headquarters, and eleven people were convicted by a hurriedly convened court and sentenced to fifteen days' imprisonment for attending a religious meeting. . . .

Similar events are occurring in very many places. . . . In Kiev alone, there have been eighty-five cases of ten- to fifteen-day arrests for this [same] reason.

Besides all this, administrative measures have been taken against believers for holding and participating in religious meetings. Fines of 10–15 rubles have been mercilessly and indiscriminately imposed on large families and pensioners. Many of the latter have been fined 50 rubles, which is sometimes almost double their monthly pension. . . .

2. *Denial of the right of Christian parents to bring up their children according to their own convictions; interrogation of children of Christian parents by agents of the procurator's office.*

Complete violation of parental rights has become a common phenomenon in our days. No one recognizes the right of believing parents to educate their children according to their own convictions. Christian parents are openly told that they must not "inculcate religion in their children"; they are given threatening warnings that, if they disobey, "society" has the right to take any measures necessary to safeguard the children's minds against "religious poison."

These words are translated into deeds. The courts deprive people of their parental rights; children are taken away and sent to boarding schools to be educated.

For example, at Kazan in 1962, Nina, the twelve-year-old daughter of the Christian Repin family, was taken away from them. This case was reported in an article entitled "Pirates from the Prayer House," which appeared in the newspaper *Volzhskaia kommuna* (Kuibyshev, May, 1962). . . . The fact that the crime against these believers was not kept secret but was publicized in newspapers (with invented additions about "coercion of conscience," "compulsion," etc.) reveals how deeply endemic illegality has become and how those who perpetrate it have lost all sense of justice—a fact more terrible than the injustice itself.

In the village of Dubrovy, in the upper Dvina district, Vitebsk region, the Sloboda family became converted to God. . . . The local atheists arrived in a fury. At the *kolkhoz* meeting in April, 1966, it was decided to take the Sloboda children away from their parents. A few days later, a car drove up to the school where the children, Galia (eleven) and Shura (nine), were pupils. A policeman and several people in civilian clothes took the children directly from the classroom, and, although the frightened children began to scream, they were quickly bundled into the car. Their father, who was working a short distance away, heard the screaming and came running to rescue his children. He was pushed away while heartbreaking cries came from the car. The father held onto the car, but they beat his hands. The *kolkhoz* driver of the car said later that the children screamed the whole way to Vitebsk and that, unable to bear it, he had driven the car at top speed. When they stopped en route, the elder girl jumped out of the car and started to run, but she was caught and forced back into the car. When they arrived at Vitebsk, the exhausted children had stopped screaming but were weeping quietly. Their parents wrote several times to Moscow, but the children were not returned to them. . . .

Another method is also used to try to set children against their believing parents and to persuade them to go to boarding school: they are tempted with gifts and promises of interesting journeys. This was done by one Moiseev who came from Moscow to Perm and introduced himself as an author. He went around to the schools where children of Christian parents were being taught and tried to persuade them to go to Moscow with him. He promised them a carefree life and all kinds of good things. "At home," he said, "you have to help your mothers and look after your younger brothers and sisters. There, you will only learn and have fun."

Children of Christian parents all over the country are being interrogated for the purpose of obtaining information against their parents and other believers. The children are required to answer such questions as: "Do you go to church?"—"Do many children attend the service?"— "Who leads the service?"—"Do visitors come?"—"Who are they?"— "Are separate children's meetings held?," etc.

The interrogation is usually carried out by the staff of the procurator's office. Legally minors can be questioned only in the presence of their parents. This provision is completely ignored, as shown by the following cases:

. . . In August, 1966, at Zhitomir, two teachers from School No. 17 came to the home of the Shimansky family, who are believers, and took away Katia Shimanskaia, a fifth-grade pupil, to the Pioneer Palace under the pretext that she had to attend some kind of meeting that was being held there. There, she was met by the investigator of the town procurator's office and was questioned in a separate room. . . .

In July, 1965, at Rostov, Sasha and Seriozha Bublik were interrogated by the investigator of the procurator's office. Sasha was nine years old, and Seriozha, eight. The questioning lasted three hours. . . .

In Leningrad, on July 3, 1967, the investigator of the procurator's office of Vsevolozhsky district interrogated Galia Kuiavskaia (twelve). When the girl came to the school for her books, she was taken to the headmaster's room, the door was locked, and she was then questioned.

In the same town, on July 5, 1967, Seriozha Kleimenov (fourteen) was questioned. Neighbors of the Kleimenovs lured Seriozha to their flat, and, after he had entered, the door was immediately locked behind him. Seated in the room were the investigator of the Vsevolozhsky district procurator's office and Belokopytova, a teacher from the school. The hysterical and terrified boy was then interrogated. . . .

3. *Trials of ECB believers.*

Apart from arrests of believers at prayer meetings, at their places of work, and in their homes, they are also being seized on public highways without warrants of arrest from the the procurator's office. This violates not only the "Agreement on Human Rights" (Article 19) but also the basic law of our own country, the Constitution of the U.S.S.R., Article 127. Only after the arrests have been made are warrants issued by the procurator's office. . . .

Relatives of persons who disappear in this way find them in prison only after long search.

As stated earlier, 200 ECB believers are imprisoned at the present time. The charges against them are as follows: (1) organizing (holding and taking an active part in) illegal meetings; (2) circulating religious literature; and (3) recruiting minors.

Contrary to all logic, prayer meetings of unregistered congregations are declared to be illegal. The attempt is made to prove that these meetings disturb public order. As unregistered congregations are deprived of their churches, the meetings have to be held in the private homes of believers. In those instances where such private homes have been confiscated (because services were held in them) or where no home large enough to accommodate all members of the congregation is available, meetings are held in the woods.

Meetings that are held in private homes cannot in any way disturb public order; neither can religious services held in the woods, for the simple reason that the woods are not a public place.

The presence of children of Christian parents at divine services is labeled indoctrination of minors. If a preacher exhorts believers to educate their children along religious lines, he may also be accused of encouraging the proselytization of children. . . .

Trials of ECB believers bear little resemblance to normal court proceedings. No effort is made in these trials to prove the charges brought against the accused. The court in no way goes to the heart of the case or tries to solve it. The accused have no rights, no one pays any attention to their arguments, and all their petitions are turned down without explanation. Only in rare cases are the accused permitted to complete their defense pleas. The judges are more interested in seeing that the trials should have an "educative influence on the community"—*i.e.*, should predispose the people against believers—than they are in examining the facts of the actual cases before them.

On November 29-30, 1966, in the Municipal Court of Moscow, a judicial action was instituted against the chairman of the ECB Council of Churches, G. K. Kriuchkov, and the Council's secretary, G. P. Vins.

The court failed to summon seventeen witnesses, including the principal prosecution witnesses, on the basis of whose testimony the indictment had been drawn up. The accused, Kriuchkov and Vins, had requested that these persons be present at the trial. Kriuchkov stated,

> All the accusations against Vins and myself are based on what the witnesses Grigorovsky and Shveikin heard from Zakharov and Khrapov, and not on firsthand information. Accordingly, I ask that Zakharov and Khrapov be summoned so that they themselves may testify. Otherwise, it will be a case of somebody saying something, another person hearing it, and a third person hearing it from the second. The charges have been built up on the basis of hearsay evidence at third hand.

The request was refused, the procurator declaring that the summoning of these witnesses would take a long time, that he was very busy, had no time, and was hurrying to another court case. Strange reasons for refusal! The procurator is in a hurry and has no time to examine the details of the case, and the court is in a hurry, too. With such haste, a completely innocent person may be sent to be shot.

On the first day of the trial, the court session lasted from 10 A.M. to 9 P.M. It was evident that an attempt was being made to sap the strength of the accused and weaken them to a point where they would be physically incapable of carrying on their own defense. At 7 P.M., the questioning of Vins began, but he declared that he was too exhausted and could not concentrate on the court's questions and asked that the cross-examination be adjourned to the following day. The court, however, was in a hurry and decided to start cross-examination immediately. This was conducted with atheists present in the courtroom, the latter behaving abominably. Every answer Vins gave was greeted with noise, laughter, and shouting, with the result that it was sometimes impossible for him to give complete answers to the questions. The court obviously encouraged such conduct in the hall, and it was only after energetic protests from the relatives of the accused that some semblance of order was restored the following day.

On the second day, the court sat from 10 A.M. to 1 o'clock the following morning. When Kriuchkov was directed to make his defense plea, he asked for an adjournment of the court on the ground that it was necessary for him to redraft his speech because of the nonappearance of the seventeen witnesses. He also pleaded that extreme exhaustion was breaking his concentration. The court refused Kriuchkov's request and, in spite of the late hour, directed him to proceed with his plea, warning him that, if he did not comply, the court would give its verdict without hearing his defense at all.

The verdict was given at 1 A.M.; Kriuchkov and Vins were both sentenced to three years' imprisonment.

An analysis of indictments [in cases involving believers] shows that all believers have been sentenced solely for their religious convictions.

For example, the indictment in the case of V. A. Golub, N. I. Butkov, and A. N. Balatsky, dated March 23, 1966, and signed by the procurator of the town of Lugansk, stated:

> Golub, Balatsky, and Butkov, in their sermons at prayer meetings held twice or three times a week, constantly try to inspire, both in adult members of the church and in minors of school age whom they have attracted, a belief in God and in the blessings of the world to come. They also preach that life on earth is temporary and passing and must be lived in accordance with what the Bible teaches—namely, that all things are lawful but all things are not expedient. . . .

Butkov, Balatsky, and Golub were all condemned to four years' imprisonment. . . .

The verdict handed down against G. K. Kriuchkov and G. P. Vins on November 30, 1966, stated:

> The Court Board on Criminal Cases has established that the document "Answers to those who object to the ministry of the Organizing Committee brethren" contains the following assertion: "But there is a limit to man's obedience to human authority. We have very many biblical, evangelical, and historical examples in which true ministers of God do not allow any human authority to deprive them of the right to do God's will." The same document asserts: "Undoubtedly, if the law of our country should ever prohibit us from believing in God and from serving Him truly, then many Christians will go, as before, into the catacombs, to the stake or to be eaten by wild animals, or anywhere, simply in order to inherit God's Kingdom."

. . . . In order to be able in some way to justify their lawless actions against believers, the authorities resort to lies and slander.

The Organizing Committee for the Convocation of an ECB Congress, elected by many believers to organize a congress, addressed a single request to the government of our country asking permission to hold an ECB congress. The request was lawful and was plainly and clearly formulated.

As we have mentioned, this request was answered with arrests. However, the members of the Organizing Committee and believers continued to petition the government concerning the congress. This also was lawful.

Because many believers and congregations had rejected the AUCECB as a religious center, the believers asked the members of the Organizing Committee to take over the spiritual guidance of these congregations, and, in 1965, a Council of ECB Churches was elected from among the members of the Organizing Committee. The Council of ECB Churches continued to apply to the government for permission to hold a congress, as the Organizing Committee had done.

The right of a religious center to exist is conferred by its election by the believers. The authorities were notified of the election of the Council of ECB Churches, and copies of the declarations of ECB congregations were also sent to them. But, in spite of the unquestioned election of the Council of Churches by the believers, the ministers of the Council of Churches were subsequently persecuted for "operating illegally."

According to the principle of the separation of church and state, the state organs are required to recognize a religious center elected by the believers, whatever its composition. To recognize means not to persecute, not to repress, and—obviously—not to interfere in the spiritual activity of the religious center. What the believers requested of the government was lawful and absolutely clear: (1) to give permission for a congress; and (2) not to repress the Council of Churches elected by the believers.

However, in order to give a semblance of legality to the unlawful actions taken against believers, the Council of Churches, and the congregations supporting them, a campaign of slander was organized. The chairman of the Council on Religious Affairs of the U.S.S.R. Council of Ministers, V. A. Kuroedov, speaking through the pages of *Izvestia*, alleged that the Council of ECB Churches, "having highhandedly declared itself to be the religious center of all Baptists," demanded that "the government remove the legally acting religious center—the AUCECB—and appoint the Council of ECB Churches in its place."

Undoubtedly, if the Council of ECB Churches had, in fact, ever addressed to the authorities a request of the sort described by V. A. Kuroedov, the request would certainly have been granted, for the "removal" of particular ministers by the Council on Religious Affairs and the "appointment" of others in their place is not such an uncommon action. The facts proclaim this. But, when the believers declared that they wanted to solve their own internal religious questions by themselves in a free democratic congress, and that they themselves wanted to elect the ministers of the spiritual center without any outside interference, . . . [the entire press] began, as by command, to say that the Council of Churches and the congregations guided by it were demanding that government bodies interfere in church affairs (!!!) and were insisting on a ban on atheism in the schools, etc.

4. *Detention conditions of ECB prisoners.*

The general situation is that ECB prisoners are forbidden to have a Bible in camps and prisons. The Bible is the first necessity of every believer, and the ban against it is not, in all probability, part of the [official] rules for the camps.

ECB prisoners are forbidden to pray in the camps and prisons. Pavel

Overchuk, in the camp of Dnepropetrovsk Province . . . , was placed in the punishment cell on April 26, 1967. His mother arrived the same day for a visit but was told by the camp commander that her son had been put in the punishment cell and deprived of visits and food parcels for six months because he prayed morning and evening and spoke about Christ.[1] . . .

In spite of the rules of the camps, believing prisoners have been deprived of the right to correspond with relatives and friends. Any letters containing religious phrases are withheld. . . .

According to Article 142, paragraph 2, of the Criminal Code of the R.S.F.S.R., the maximum punishment should be three years' imprisonment, but, in the present circumstances of the ECB churches in our country, many believers are spending long years behind barbed wire.

N. P. Khrapov (Tashkent) became a believer when he was twenty-one, and he was at once sentenced to twelve years. After twelve years in prison, he was freed. However, he was soon condemned again for his belief, this time to twenty-five years in prison, though he was rehabilitated after five and a half years. In 1960, he was condemned for the third time (seven years) and was rehabilitated in 1964. Thus, of his thirty-two years as a Christian and member of the ECB Church, Khrapov has spent twenty-two years in camps and prisons. Now he has again been sentenced, to five years. . . .

In January, 1964, in the prison of the town of Barnaul, Nikolai Kuzmich Khmara was tortured to death. No one says that this horrible murder was done on instructions from Moscow. It was the arbitrary act of the local authorities. But the local authorities always sense exactly what policy has been adopted by the central authorities with respect to believers.

In the summer and autumn of 1966, eighteen trials of ECB believers took place. At the time of these trials, terrible lawlessness occurred throughout the whole country. Prayer meetings were broken up with incredible cruelty, believers were brutally beaten, and everywhere there were arrests. Such was the result of the tone set by Moscow.

In 1964, in Nikolaev, the believer Kucherenko was arrested. Two days after the arrest, his dead body was delivered to his wife.

On March 30, 1967, in the town of Novo-Boiarka, Kiev Province, a prayer meeting took place in the home of N. P. Shelestun. On April 2, Shelestun was summoned to the Boiarka police station and was beaten up in the commandant's office. He was told: "Tell the others that the same fate awaits them." . . .

In 1963, the believer A. I. Kovalchuk was under investigation in the Rovno prison. In a few months, he was turned into an invalid. Bleeding profusely and with a crushed gall bladder, he was transferred from the prison to the hospital and set free. Now Kovalchuk has been arrested again, and his relatives have not even been told where he is. . . .

The facts about persecutions that have been mentioned here are only a fraction of everything that is going on. We intercede with you, Mr. U

Thant, to organize a committee to investigate the cases of the condemned believers. We beg you to do everything possible to secure: (1)
religious freedom; (2) the right of parents to bring up their children
until they are of age. . . .

Signed on behalf of the Council of Relatives of Prisoners by the following members of the Council:

LIDIA MIKHAILOVNA VINS, Ul. Soshenka 11B, Kiev
NINA PETROVNA YAKIMENKOVA, D. Desna 84, Leninskii Raion, Moscow
   Oblast
ALEKSANDRA KOZOREZOVA, Ul. Krasnyi put 47, Omsk
YELIZAVETA ANDREEVNA KHRAPOVA, Ul. Baiskinskaia D. 53, Tashkent
KLAVDIIA VASILEVNA KOZLOVA, Ul. Moskovskaia D. 20, Yoshkar-Ola

NOTE

1. See Document 41.—ED.

43. Open Letter by the Evangelical Christians and Baptists in Kiev

February 25, 1968

In 1963, our Kiev community of Evangelical Christians and Baptists,
together with the other communities [of believers in Kiev], authorized
one of our members, preacher Georgi P. Vins, to represent us in the Organizing Committee of the All-Union ECB Congress (now termed the
Council of Churches of the ECB [CCECB]). As a member of this committee and later as its secretary, G. P. Vins was commissioned by the
believers to submit petitions to the central authorities, as well as to ensure the reform of the spiritual ministry to all ECB communities
throughout the country. . . .
   Nevertheless, no sooner was G. P. Vins elected to this office than he
suffered persecution of various kinds—slander, attacks in the press, insults, threats of arrest, summonses to the procurator's office, etc. Nor
was he the only one to suffer persecution. His wife was dismissed from
her job with a compromising statement in her work record, so that, up
to now, she has been unable to enjoy the constitutional right to work.
His daughter was terrorized at school.
   In May, 1966, G. P. Vins was arrested in the reception room of the
Central Committee of the CPSU, where he had been sent as a delegate
by the CCECB to submit a petition addressed to L. I. Brezhnev requesting that the All-Union delegation of ECB believers, arrested on May

17, 1966, be released and received. On November 29–30, 1966, G. P. Vins and CCECB representative G. K. Kriuchkov were sentenced by the Moscow City Court to three years' imprisonment in a normal corrective labor camp, under Article 142, paragraph 2, of the Criminal Code of the R.S.F.S.R., notwithstanding the fact that the court failed, in fact, to prove them guilty of any of the crimes of which they had been accused. . . .

In February, 1967, G. P. Vins was sent to serve his sentence in one of the camps of the Perm region, but, in the summer of the same year, he was transferred to another camp. (His address is P.O. Box 2040 A, Taly Postal District, Kizel, Urals.) The conditions under which he is being kept in the new camp indicate the real reason for his transfer and the intentions of the responsible authorities.

The Kiev ECB community possesses reliable information as to the intent of certain agencies to liquidate Georgi Petrovich Vins by means of camp conditions. Vins has now been reduced to a state of complete physical exhaustion. Violating the existing regulations of the Ministry of Public Order governing the treatment of prisoners in camps,, the authorities made Vins, a member of the building brigade, walk five to six miles every day under guard to his place of work and back, over rugged, mountainous terrain (10 to 12 miles daily in all). Although an engineer by profession, he was employed as a manual hauler, dragging logs from the forest for the construction of railway buildings.

Because of all this, Vins in October, 1967, contracted an infection from which he has so far not recovered and that, combined with excessive work, has reduced him to complete exhaustion and caused him to develop heart disease. In addition, boils have appeared all over his arms and body. Sometimes he has fainted at work or on his way there. Nevertheless, his serious state of health has not exempted him from work. Eventually he contracted an inguinal hernia, . . . but, even after this, he was still forced to do hard physical labor despite the fact that this would completely destroy his health and endanger his life.

Because of continuous threats from certain quarters to destroy Vins and the obvious intent to carry them out, we believers, as well as Vins himself and his relatives, distrust any surgical intervention that might be carried out on the camp premises. . . .

According to the regulations, Vins should be released before serving his full sentence, since he has never infringed camp rules. The camp administration recommended him for early release, but the Taly administrative commission refused to grant it. This fact also reveals that Vins is being discriminated against for his religious convictions, and, in the light of all the above, our fears for Vins's life have increased. . . .

1. We consider the transfer of G. P. Vins to a job suited to his present state of health absolutely essential. If this is not done, our fears will be confirmed that he is being liquidated wittingly and with the sanction of the authorities.

2. We request that a government commission be set up to investigate

the treatment of G. P. Vins in camp, as well as the conditions under which all other ECB believers are detained, since several of those sentenced for their faith in God are facing death in labor camps.

3. Once more, we bring before the Procuracy of the U.S.S.R. the question of reviewing the cases of Vins and of all other imprisoned ECB believers in order that they may be rehabilitated.

We pray to our Heavenly Father that He may give you wisdom. We ask all ECB believers to increase their prayers for brother Vins and all those fulfilling their mission in bondage.

On behalf of the 400 ECB believers of Kiev
[*signed by 176 members*]

44. Letter by the Brothers Butenko

March 26, 1967

To the General Secretary of the CC-CPSU, Comrade L. I. Brezhnev

From the sons of the deceased Aleksei Butenko (Anatoli, Sergei, and Leonid), residing at the following address: Mirgorod, Poltava Oblast, Shimatskaia St., House 24.

DECLARATION

We, the sons of our dear dead father, Aleksei Vasilievich Butenko, bring to your attention the illegal acts of the local authorities, who have deprived us of our family right to fulfill the last wish of our dear dead father regarding the burial of his body. This has left on our young hearts a deep wound that cannot be salved and can never be cured.

The authorities added to our already great sorrow by not allowing us to fulfill the request of our father. He was a member of the CPSU for twenty-five years, but, while seriously ill, he turned to God, became a Christian, and requested that he be buried as a believer.

His testament was written with his own hand, with his own personal signature. But the local officials, acting without any authorization and without any feeling, tore our mother's hands from the coffin (there is a photograph of this), put the coffin into an automobile, and took it off in a direction completely different from the one we would have taken.

At the cemetery, they did not even allow all the relatives to take their leave of our loved one. Moreover, when our mother was paying her last respects, they held the lid of the coffin over her head, and she had to push it up with her hand in order to finish saying farewell.

Having still not allowed us to bury the coffin, they began to herd the believers back to the car. They began to hurl insults and wave their hands, forced everyone into the car, and drove to the militia station.

Thus, we fulfilled our last duty to our father. And he was an honorable, dedicated man who had been awarded the badge of honor.

ANATOLI, SERGEI, and LEONID BUTENKO

45. *Petition by Moscow Parishioners*

February 17, 1967

To the Chairman of the Council of Ministers of the U.S.S.R., Aleksei Nikolaevich Kosygin

From members of the administrative council ("*dvadtsatka*") and parishioners of the Orthodox parish of Nikolo-Kuznetsky Church, Vishniakovsky Pereulok, Moscow.

PETITION

Dear Comrade Chairman,

Allow us to address you in the final but firm hope that you will protect us from the arbitrary administrative measures of those officials in authority who, even in this fiftieth jubilee year of our state, carry out their official dealings with us with a mere pretense of legality instead of in accordance with Soviet law. . . .

We are no alien body within our state or society. Neither do we desire to become such. Not just by words but by deeds, both during and after the Second World War, believers have testified and continue to testify to their loyalty to our Socialist Fatherland—the common Fatherland of all citizens, nonbelievers and believers alike. For this reason, we most strongly protest against restrictions on our rights, which are guaranteed by the laws of our country.

The present law on religious communities of April 8, 1929, is perhaps a little outdated; it was passed at a time when some religious communities and their leaders often held reactionary views. Yet even this law . . . guarantees us certain rights, which, though very limited, are, nevertheless, clearly defined, thus assuring us a definite status within the legal framework of the state. . . .

Because we were extremely dissatisfied with the way in which the executive committee of our parish of St. Nicholas—an important Moscow church often visited by foreign church leaders and well known abroad—was conducting its business, we, the members of the administrative council of the parish, or so-called *dvadtsatka*, and other members of the above-mentioned parish have repeatedly petitioned the Executive Committee of the Workers' Representatives of the Kirov District of Moscow, as well as the Moscow representative of the Council for Religious Affairs of the U.S.S.R. Council of Ministers, requesting permission to hold a general meeting of the parishioners to examine our complaints about the [parish] executive committee and to elect a new executive committee. We based our appeal on Articles 12 and 13 of the Instructions of the Ministry of Justice and the Ministry of the Interior of 1923, which guarantee the right of believers to hold meetings. The first petition to the Executive Committee of the Kirov District of Moscow, a copy of which was sent to the Moscow representative of the Council for Religious Affairs, was issued on August 19, 1966; the second, on the same subject, on September 9, 1966; the third, also on the same subject, on November 24, 1966. The petitions were signed by seventeen of the twenty members of the *dvadtsatka* (including the members of the auditing commission) and by 170 regular parishioners, whose addresses were given.

No reply to any of these petitions has been received . . . although, by law, an answer should be issued within one month.

In protest against the executive committee (consisting of church warden S. I. Pliashkevich and treasurer Ya. P. Popov) for arbitrary behavior without precedent and abuse of its position—and especially for its refusal to submit the accounts of parish funds, which are at its complete disposal, for due auditing—all the members of the auditing commission have handed in their resignations. The Executive Committee of the Kirov District of Moscow and the representative of the Council for Religious Affairs were informed of this step.

Since our petitions remained unanswered, on November 16, 1966, we sent a complaint to the Public Procurator of the City of Moscow, reporting the Kirov District Executive Committee's violation of the law with the connivance of the representative of the Council for Religious Affairs. . . . The Public Procurator alone has replied, writing (on November 25, 1966) to inform us that he had forwarded our complaint to the Council for Religious Affairs with instructions to notify us of any decision taken. . . .

Having illegally prevented a general meeting of all our parishioners, the secretary of the Kirov District Executive Committee and the Moscow representative of the Council for Religious Affairs issued authorization, on December 16, 1966, for a meeting in the church of a new *dvadtsatka* that had suddenly materialized, consisting of the executive committee (churchwarden Pliashkevich and treasurer Popov), together with several persons it had engaged for work in the church and a number of other persons about whom so little is known that we cannot even say whether they belong to our faith.

At the same time, the churchwarden informed the members of the real *dvadtsatka*, who had long been registered as such with the Kirov District Executive Committee, that he and the secretary of the Executive Committee, with the agreement of the representative of the Council for Religious Affairs, had "dismissed" them from the *dvadtsatka*. This organization of a false *dvadtsatka* is an incredibly arbitrary act. The removal of legally registered members of the existing *dvadtsatka* is a crass violation of the rule of law. . . .

Dear Comrade Chairman, we realize that all governmental and national administrative decrees, instructions, ordinances, statutes, and laws dealing with the Orthodox Church and other religious communities are aimed at limiting the activities [of these institutions] to matters of their own organization and administration. But they do not restrict the internal independence of our church or of other religious communities; they safeguard the right to observe ecclesiastical and canonical laws within the bounds of internal church life; they do not restrict our freedom to administer our financial resources and any state property allotted for our use, provided that we strictly observe all the requirements of the law; they protect members of religious communities from all possible forms of coercion and administrative duress in the organization of their internal affairs. We very much appreciate the general aim and spirit of existing legislation on religious bodies, even though in many respects it may be outdated.

Thus, it was with a feeling of special satisfaction that we recently read in the newspaper *Izvestia* (No. 204, 1966) a statement of the Chairman of the Council for Religious Affairs of the U.S.S.R. Council of Ministers:

The ideological struggle against religion must not violate the rights of believers. A series of decisions of the Party and government very clearly point out the inadmissibility of [arbitrary] administrative measures. . . . Strict observance of the laws on religious cults is equally incumbent upon religious organizations and local government bodies.

Yet, even as *Izvestia* prints this declaration . . . for the whole world to see, here in Moscow, in the Church of St. Nicholas, the exact opposite of what is officially declared is taking place, as we have just set out in detail. . . .

By their interference in the internal affairs of our religious community, the local authorities distort and profane the entire meaning and spirit of Soviet legislation on religious cults. And all of this goes on with the knowledge and connivance of that very same Council for Religious Affairs of the Council of Ministers. . . .

We now have no other recourse than to appeal to you, the Chairman of the Council of Ministers of the U.S.S.R., for the protection of our violated rights. Dear Aleksei Nikolaevich, we respectfully ask you to issue authoritative instructions requiring the Council for Religious Affairs of the Council of Ministers, which is subordinate to your authority, and the Executive Committee of the Kirov District of Moscow to respond to our petition by finally granting permission for the convocation of a general meeting of members of the parish of St. Nicholas. . . .

If possible, would you kindly inform us of the steps taken by your department at this address: A. P. Krushinskaia, Apt. 19, 9 Tatarskaia St., Moscow.

Yours very respectfully,

The *dvadtsatka* of the parish
of St. Nicholas, Moscow

[*There follow* 170 *signatures of members of the* dvadtsatka *and parishioners.*]

46. A. E. Levitin on Freedom of Religion and Freedom of Atheism

May 30, 1965

Face to Face

In Moscow, on May 21, 1965, I met with representatives of anti-religious circles in a room of the Zhdanov District Soviet Executive Committee, on Taganka Square. Members of a variety of organizations participated in the meeting. There were two important officials of the KGB, the managing director of the State Political Publishing House, the assistant director of the monthly *Nauka i religiia* [Science and Religion], the assistant director of the House of Scientific Atheism, representatives of the Obkom [regional Party committee], a representative of the Council for the Affairs of the Orthodox Church, and the secretary of the Zhdanov District Soviet Executive Committee.

My writing activity was the subject of discussion at this meeting, although a number of general questions were also dealt with. Since the contents of the discussion are of definite interest to readers, it is published together with some brief commentary.

Major Shitikov (*representative of the KGB*): Anatoli Emmanuilovich! We would like to have a friendly talk with you and would like to ask you several questions. Several representatives of society are here. By the way, next to you is Aleksei Alekseevich Trushin [of the government's Council for the Affairs of the Orthodox Church, since reconstituted as the Council for Religious Affairs], whose name must be familiar to you.

Levitin: I'll answer all your questions with pleasure.

Shitikov: We know very well, Anatoli Emmanuilovich, that you publish your articles by any means you can and with unusual persistence. If any evidence is needed, here it is: you know Gleb Pavlovich Yakunin well. He states—

LEVITIN: It's not necessary [to go on]. I know.

SHITIKOV: Oh, he told you. A citizen left his briefcase in a telephone booth. It was brought to the police; in the briefcase, they came upon your article.

LEVITIN: Who was it?

SHITIKOV: You want to know? Ivan Petrovich Nedoshivin, who lives in the Izmailovskii [district of Moscow].

LEVITIN: Never heard of him.

SHITIKOV: You are leading your typists into error by saying that your articles are very good. . . .

LEVITIN: I know you have my typists under surveillance.

SHITIKOV: . . . Anatoli Emmanuilovich! You're a citizen of Moscow; you live in this hero-city. You ought to know the laws and obey them, but, instead, your actions contradict all the generally accepted rules of conduct.

LEVITIN: I'm already fifty years old. (*Voices:* You are not fifty yet.) That makes no difference, it's a round number. In fifty years, I have formed unshakable and clear convictions. I express them in my articles. I write the truth. You yourselves don't say that there is anything untrue in my articles. I protest against the barbarous persecution of religion, as expressed in the destruction of churches and the humiliation of believers. I protest against a policy that reduces the church to the scum of the earth while Comrade Trushin, who is present here, is the dictator of the Moscow Church. He, a non-believer and a Communist, assigns and removes priests as he pleases. (It should be understood that this statement applies to the whole existing order, not just to Trushin.) All this is contradictory to every existing principle and even to Stalin's Constitution. I protest against it in the articles that I have disseminated, that I am disseminating, and that I will continue to disseminate in accordance with my right of free speech. By the way, Russian literature has always defined the word "citizen" as someone who fights for and upholds the truth, not as someone who crawls on his belly before the authorities. I'm not afraid of anything. I have never been afraid—and that's especially true now, at fifty years of age, as I approach the limit beyond which any kind of threat becomes ineffective.

SHITIKOV: No one is threatening you. We want to talk to you as a comrade.

A CITIZEN—(*unknown to me*), *sitting at the end of the table; he seems to be a representative of the regional committee:* Anatoli Emmanuilovich! You have a very prepossessing appearance.

LEVITIN: Thank you.

UNKNOWN CITIZEN: The impression you make is a sympathetic one. But that surprises me. Your articles create a completely different impression. They are thoroughly evil and odious. You take single facts and generalize from them. You say that this is the policy of both the Party and the government, and you allege that some arrangement has been made for a forcible fight against religion. If your articles should fall into the hands of our enemies, they certainly could make use of them. But what you say isn't true. You surely know that the Party has fought against such distortions, and that Khrushchev repeatedly protested against them.

LEVITIN: That reminds me of Stalin's admirers, who always refer to Beria when speaking of violence and say that Stalin had nothing to do with it. In my opinion, the answer lies with the leader himself. If the leader doesn't know what's going on, that's even worse. That means he's a bad leader and ought to be replaced. (*Voices*: Which was done.) Incidentally, Stalin never said that people must be annihilated, nor did he say anything clearly to the contrary. Now, as to the point that my articles might perhaps be misused by someone. Here in front of me hangs a portrait of Lenin. It would of course be ridiculous if I, as a believer, pretended to be like Lenin. However, you know that Lenin himself wrote several times that his articles on differences within the Party might be used by the enemy—he was aware of it, but he wrote anyway. Certainly he knew that his speeches at the Tenth and Eleventh Party Congresses, in which he dealt with bureaucratic distortion, might be exploited by the enemy. Nevertheless, he gave those speeches.

ROMANOV (*assistant director of the House of Atheists*): Anatoli Emmanuilovich! Your "literary works" can hardly be called such. They are full of unmitigated evil. In your letter to Nikodim, you write, for example: "I wonder how I would have arranged my life if I were an atheist . . ."—and add that you would have been an opportunist. You say that followers of atheism are crooks with their outlook of "You die today, but I—not till tomorrow." And you also say that one derives the same benefit from propagating atheism as from spreading syphilis. Now, isn't that intolerable! You hate the atheists, you slander them, you tear open an abyss between atheists and believers. You humiliate all of us. Judging from your articles, you hate fascism. But it was basically non-believers who defeated fascism and who have just celebrated the twentieth anniversary of their victory over fascism. You can't deny that.

LEVITIN: I didn't mean to insult anyone. If anybody's feelings are hurt, please accept my apology. I wrote about rigid atheism. Luckily, not all atheists are that unbending. Furthermore, in my letter to Nikodim, I gave examples of those who, having become atheists, were good and honest people (*i.e.*, in particular, Mikhail Yurevich Shavrov, the father of my friend Vadim.) As a whole, in fact, rigid atheism is really Nietzscheism, not Communism. Why should we worry about generations that will be living a hundred years from now when brambles are growing out of our bodies? You must not forget the circumstances in which my articles were written: they were written at a time when believers were being baited and persecuted, were being dragged in the dust and forced to sit with gags in their mouths, unable to say anything.

ROMANOV: However, you consider it necessary to apologize for yourself here.

LEVITIN: I apologize for the form, not the substance—for what is called an unparliamentary approach.

GRIGORIAN (*assistant director of the monthly* Nauka i religiia): I like your articles. I like them because of their wide range of views. That's why I'm astonished that you've been attacking atheism so much lately. You know that there are different forms of atheism. Atheism, as you are well aware, developed over the course of centuries. Originally it sprang from the core of the church itself, in the form of heresies, and, by now, it has taken different forms. In this respect, I'm your ally on some issues. You wrote extensively on the monks of Pochaev. May I call to your attention that I heard about the shocking things going on in Pochaev earlier than you did, and that I also did more to stop them. Right at the time, I telephoned and also spoke to the CC about it. And you certainly know that our journal has recently attacked that odious woman Allah Trubnikova. I myself have many friends among the believers. But the point is that one has to be unbiased toward atheism.

LEVITIN: I know, you've held to an honorable course in the fight against religion, and once you had Shamoro suggest that we both meet. I shall meet with you with great pleasure. As for my being unbiased, let me ask you: have you read my article on Khrushchev?

GRIGORIAN: I've read it.

LEVITIN: Can you think that my attitude toward Khrushchev is biased?

GRIGORIAN: Oh, as for that article—you speak about an honest and truthful *Rus* [Russia]. On all that, I fully agree with you. I also want such a *Rus*. But why do you identify it with the church? We all know quite well what the Orthodox Church is like.

LEVITIN: I don't identify it with the church.

ROMANOV: Yes, you do. You state directly that the Holy *Rus* is preserved only in the church.

LEVITIN: I also mention your collaborator.

GRIGORIAN: Yes. You treat him as if he had one foot in the Holy *Rus*. We'll talk about that later.

CHERTIKHIN (*director of the Political Publishing House*): Anatoli Emmanuilovich! I am the director of the Political Publishing House. You never discuss the brochures we publish. Why not? Haven't you read them? Knowing you, I can hardly believe it. You obviously prefer to argue with your pupil, Duluman.

LEVITIN: And with Ilichev.

CHERTIKHIN: Anatoli Emmanuilovich! I don't want to talk to you in comradeship. I am not a comrade of yours, of course.

LEVITIN: Quite.

CHERTIKHIN: I want to address you as a former colleague of mine. I'm a Candidate of Sciences. You also prepared to become a candidate. A scientist has to write about the field in which he is trained. You, however, have aspired with unusual aplomb to fields of knowledge that are completely beyond your capacity. You deal with what you call "philosophical matter," though there is no such term. You write in your articles that modern science can make ingenious discoveries but cannot develop a complete image of the world. You write that the [United Nations] Declaration of Human Rights, adopted by the delegates of Eisenhower and Churchill, is the basis of socialism.

LEVITIN: This I did not write.

ROMANOV: I quote from the letter to Nikodim: "It is necessary to give wide publication to the Declaration in order to bring Soviet legislation and the structure of Soviet daily life into correspondence with it. That is the basis of socialist democracy."

LEVITIN: That's quite another thing, to speak of socialist *democracy*. What can actually be meant by democracy [in Soviet Russia] when the most important and principal document that has been signed and ratified [in the U.N.] has not only not been put into practice here but has not even been published?

CHERTIKHIN: You confuse and make fools of people, Anatoli Emmanuilovich! We cannot tolerate that.

LEVITIN: My honored colleague! Above all, don't make a Kazan orphan of yourself, and don't play the role of the insulted. From the way you're talking, one would think that you sit in Novo-Kuzminki and print your articles in editions of 20 copies, while I print millions of copies. In my letter to Nikodim, I cite the answer I gave to the camp's executive commissioner when he suggested that I become an "informer": If people don't tell the truth, you must prove them false; but if they do tell the truth, you have to concur with them."

VOICES: We know, we read it.

LEVITIN: Suppose I write an untruth. It is easier for you, as director of the Political Publishing House, to disprove it than for anyone else. Thousands of people read your publications.

ROMANOV: Tens of millions.

LEVITIN: All the better. Then why don't you refute me?

CHERTIKHIN: We are not disposed to.

LEVITIN: Then why did you get upset? And why did you come here?

CHERTIKHIN: It was an opportunity [to talk], just as we said.

TRUSHIN: When he [Levitin] understood that the authorized representative of the Council for Orthodox Church Affairs was here, he suddenly attacked me, calling me a dictator of the Moscow Church. (*Laughter. A voice:* "Like the 'ober-procurator.'[1]") There's no truth in it, of course. Everyone knows that our actions are strictly within the law. At the last meeting of [Council] representatives, this was given special stress. The fact is that Anatoli Emmanuilovich has lost touch with reality. Priests whose registration we have withdrawn come to him [to protest]. There are priests who violate the laws, and those we dismiss. But can we dismiss them when Levitin doesn't like it? Anatoli Emmanuilovich believes them. That's why he never gives us any explanations [when we ask]. I receive many letters, but I always answer them.

ROMANOV: Has Anatoli Emmanuilovich ever contacted you?

TRUSHIN: Never, though all the doors are open to him: the House of Scientific Atheism, as well as all the editors and offices. [*To Levitin:*] Why, then, do you choose to distribute your work in such a clandestine manner?

LEVITIN: Apparently not very clandestine. You all know my articles. Incidentally, where did you get them?

SHITIKOV: That's what we're explaining to you, Anatoli Emmanuilovich.

TRUSHIN: Perhaps you are now working as a stoker [as you say]. But that's only a pretext. One can't live on 35 rubles.

SHITKOV: And also pay the typists.

GRIGORIAN: Anatoli Emmanuilovich! Let me speak to you as one journalist to another. When you get information, you have to check it out, first of all, and [you're supposed to] publish it only after you've notified one official. You often publish information that's six months old, about situations that long since have been rectified.

LEVITIN: These are nothing but words. Give me facts.

ROMANOV: It's a fact that you write on all aspects of public life in your articles. And it's a fact that in every article you write about the personality cult. Everybody has already forgotten about it. Is it necessary to bring it up?

GRIGORIAN: No, one must write about the cult of personality so long as its residue exists.

SHITIKOV: Anatoli Emmanuilovich! You said that you have disseminated, are disseminating, and will continue to disseminate your articles. You also called our Constitution the Stalin Constitution. It may perhaps be Stalin's, but it's still in force. You are well acquainted with the Article that allows all citizens to disseminate antireligious propaganda and that restricts religious preaching to special houses and special people. Apart from the Constitution, other legislation exists that has to be respected. Of course, nobody can forbid you to write about whatever you want, but if you continue to distribute your work in the same way you have been, you not only will run up against us—you will also run up against another public institution, which will confront you with Article 162, dealing with the transaction of illegal business.

LEVITIN: All of that is your affair; mine is writing. Yours is to react to it.

SHITIKOV: Now to the second question: about your work. You insist that you need to work as a teacher. But that's in direct contradiction to your convictions. In our society, the school is separated from the church, and all education is built on an antireligious foundation.

LEVITIN: How do you see my convictions involved here? Of course, I will never say anything antireligious, but I love teaching people grammar and Russian literature. In more than twelve years of teaching, I have educated an uncountable number of people. They all know literature now, but I didn't discuss religion with them.

ROMANOV: In your "Evolution of Anti-Religious Thought," however, you tell how one time you couldn't communicate with a class until the pupils understood you were a believer.

LEVITIN: Now, what's wrong with that? I've never made a secret of it.

GRIGORIAN: Anatoli Emmanuilovich! You should devote yourself to scientific work. For the present, the best thing for you would be to write a bibliography.

CHERTIKHIN: Anatoli Emmanuilovich! You know about atheism better than anyone else. We need a bibliography on atheism. Pay: 150 rubles.

LEVITIN: I am compelled to remind you of a phrase from one of my articles. 'Don't buy, and you won't bully; don't bully, and you won't buy." (*Voices:* "Nobody intends either to bully or to buy.")

LEVITIN: Besides, the pay of 150 rubles is too low.

CHERTIKHIN: But, since you say you're a teacher, it's nearly the same [pay].

LEVITIN: No, it's not the same: one means teaching people to read; the other, helping the atheists.

GRIGORIAN: No, for Anatoli Emmanuilovich, work must of course be selected with due regard for his convictions.

SECRETARY OF THE DISTRICT EXECUTIVE COMMITTEE: Anatoli Emmanuilovich, when I met with you a few months ago, we spoke about your finding a job. We're glad that you found a situation right away. And, since then, I have read approximately 40 per cent of everything you've written. We will see that you get a job that will correspond better to your education. Permit me to speak on your behalf and to defend your interests. And I hope that we will never meet again.

LEVITIN: Thank you. (*Levitin shakes hands with both the secretary and Grigorian and bows to the others.*)

SHITIKOV: Oh, Anatoli Emmanuilovich, we didn't answer one of your questions—namely, where we got your publications. From your readers— they bring them to us.

LEVITIN: So much the worse for my readers.

In 1949, during my imprisonment in the Lubianka, Dr. S. V. Gruzinov, an elderly physician from Moscow, was with me in cell No. 33. Once, he began to read a very long and sentimental poem out loud. (I don't remember the author). The poem told about a girl who was sentenced to death by burning, and, after she was burned, her silhouette rose again out of the ashes. "This represents the free word," moralized the author. The doctor read the poem and smiled. So did I. It really sounded ridiculous, this grandiloquent liberal oratorio on the "almighty free word" spoken in a dark, ill-smelling cell crammed with eight men who were afraid to speak of anything frankly, even among themselves. (I, in this sense, was an exception, thanks to my natural indiscretion.)

And yet, the free word nevertheless did rise again and has shown once more how powerful it is. There is evidence of its power in the above discussion. Indeed, what significance can there be in the writings of a former schoolteacher who holds no official position, writings that he distributes among his friends? All these pennings are nothing but words—"little shells of words"—as Maiakovsky said. But the fact is that they are the free words of a free man to whom fear and profit are alien. And, thus, nine solid old men dwell upon these words, nearly learn my articles by heart, know them almost better than I do myself, and come together to confer with each other on the subject.

The free word is that powerful. The liturgy of the Orthodox Church uses the term "The Sun of Truth," but the free, true word is the sun's ray!

During the above discussion, B. T. Grigorian spoke of the need to distinguish among various forms of atheism. On this point I fully agree with him. At the time when atheists acted as inquisitors (from 1957 to 1964), I hurled irate words at them. If anyone among them (as, for example, Duluman) was offended, let me recall the old Russian proverb: "Birching is no torment if science is furthered." It is another thing to speak of honorable atheists who honestly wish to understand religious problems and who suggest a dialogue on an equal footing with believers.

There are such atheists nowadays, and, in the future, they will obviously play an even greater role. One can have a serious and sincere discussion with them, respecting them as honest people and comrades, without, of course, retreating one iota from one's own convictions. Incidentally, the conversation [I planned] with B. T. Grigorian, which took place the next day [after the meeting] and went on for nearly five hours, convinced me of this.

The conversation was not that of diplomats but, rather, a most down-to-earth, man-to-man talk between two writers pressing their opinions in a free and unrestrained manner. It brought back vividly to mind my student days, when, strolling through the town, I had just such witty (and also witless) conversations with comrades.

The establishment of full, as opposed to imaginary, freedom of religion in our country would destroy the artificial barriers between atheists and believers and would leave room for that atmosphere of friendship and collaboration in which they could search for the truth together.

The struggle for freedom of religion, for freedom of atheism, and for full freedom of conscience is the olive branch that I stretch out to my friends—believers and atheists.

I intended to finish here, but, after some consideration, I feel that my appeal to fight for freedom of atheism may astonish many people, while others may consider it demagoguery.

Yet, no—this is not demagoguery, it is the truth of life. For, in our society, atheism is not free, any more than religion is free. The situation of atheism at present strongly recalls the situation of the Orthodox Church in prerevolutionary Russia.

Orthodoxy, as is well known, was, at the time, the official ideology.

Any disputes over that ideology were categorically prohibited. "In our society a priest is an unfortunate person; one must not argue with him," wrote V. S. Soloviev. The church was under compulsion and, therefore, not free.

Atheism is not free in the Soviet Union, because it, too, is under compulsion; it is obligatory and not open to discussion. (One can conclude this even from the above discussion, since all the participants were convinced that a believer could not possibly be a teacher.)

Therefore, the struggle for religious freedom is also a struggle for the freedom of atheism—because methods of compulsion (direct or indirect) compromise atheism, depriving it of all ideological meaning and all spiritual fascination.

And therefore: Long live free religion and free atheism!

A. E. Levitin

Note

1. The administrative head of the Orthodox Church in Tsarist times.—Ed.

47. Declaration by B. V. Talantov[1]

April 26, 1968

To the U.S.S.R. Public Prosecutor

From Citizen Boris Vladimirovich Talantov, Uritsky St., 12,
Apt. 1, Kirov

Complaint

On May 31, 1967, the newspaper *Kirovskaia pravda* printed an article by O. Liubovikov ("No Punches Pulled") that contained libelous assertions, coarse threats, and baseless insults directed against me. . . .

The following incidents led to the appearance of the article by O. Liubovikov.

In August, 1966, twelve believers in Kirov Province (including myself) forwarded to Moscow . . . an open letter addressed to Aleksii, Patriarch of Moscow and of All Russia.

Basically, the letter gave a description of the unworthy acts of the local Bishop Ioann calculated to disrupt church life. The believers, accordingly, requested the Patriarch to remove Bishop Ioann forthwith. Incidentally, the letter mentioned that the local civil authorities, between 1960 and 1964, had unlawfully and forcibly closed down forty churches in the Province of Kirov (53 per cent of the total), set fire to the ikons and ikonostases in these churches, looted the material valuables, and completely demolished some of the churches. . . .

Following on this letter, I wrote a second letter, to the editors of *Izvestia*, entitled "The Soviet State and the Christian Religion."

In connection with the aforementioned letters, I was summoned on February 14, 1967, to the Kirov KGB office, where it was suggested to me that I should officially disclaim having signed the "Open Letter of the Kirov Believers," which had become known abroad. In a written declaration, . . . I confirmed the authenticity of my signature under the "Open Letter" and stated that I was ready to prove that the contents of both letters were true but that I had absolutely no idea how the "Open Letter of the Kirov Believers" got abroad.

On the very same day, an official of the KGB removed from my flat my professional files, consisting of synopses of various philosophical works with my notes on them. The KGB officials promised to return the files after inspecting them, but they have so far failed to keep this promise.

Later, on February 15, I learned from a BBC broadcast that . . . the Metropolitan Nikodim in London had declared the "Open Letter" to be another anonymous communication and therefore quite untrustworthy. . . . As an Orthodox Christian, I was extremely indignant about this statement by Metropolitan Nikodim since I was convinced from earlier correspondence with the Moscow Patriarchate that the Metropolitan could have had no doubts about the authenticity of the letter. On March 22, therefore, I sent a letter to Patriarch Aleksii refuting Metropolitan Nikodim's assertion about the anonymous nature of the "Open Letter of the Kirov Believers" and confirming the authenticity of its contents.

In addition to myself, seven other citizens of the city of Kirov signed the "Open Letter." At the beginning of April, they were individually called before the Kirov City Council in connection with the letter. The interrogations there were conducted by the Council secretary, L. Ostanina, who described me as "a dangerous person with foreign connections" and threatened anyone who signed such a letter in future with imprisonment. Despite the threats, all the persons confirmed that they had signed the "Open Letter" voluntarily and deliberately, and four of them (including E. M. Khaliavina) sent a letter, on May 20, to Patriarch Aleksii confirming that they had knowingly signed the "Open Letter" . . . and pointing out that the local authorities in Kirov Province were continuing as before to persecute believers and were refusing to open churches that had previously been illegally closed.

At the same time, KGB officials kept intimidating certain believers who had appealed for a second church to be opened in Kirov City, accusing them of being in league with me, a "dangerous political criminal." Finally, a lecturer in the Polytechnic Institute, where I had worked in 1955–1958 as a teacher of higher mathematics, publicly called me an "enemy of the people" in the style practiced in Yezhov's time. . . .

As is proved by the closed court trials of A. Siniavsky and Yu. Daniel in February, 1966, and of Yu. Galanskov, A. Ginzburg, A. Dobrovolsky, and V. Lashkova in January, 1968, and by the appeal of P. Litvinov and L. Daniel to the Soviet and international public . . . , the state security organs and the courts of law in our country are, even today, behaving in a fashion that is arbitrary and unlawful. . . .

I, therefore, deem it my duty to lodge a determined protest against the arbitrary way in which court trials are nowadays held *in camera*, against the persecution of people for their beliefs, and against the inhuman confinement of political prisoners in prisons and camps. . . .

[To return to] the article "No Punches Pulled," most of it is devoted to the "Open Letter of Kirov Believers to Patriarch Aleksii." . . . In the "Open Letter," the Kirov believers complained not about Soviet laws but about the arbitrary and illegal action of the local authorities in open violation of existing laws. *Good laws in any country do not, of themselves, guarantee legality and law and order. Only if there is control by the public over the activities of judicial and administrative bodies can legality and law and order be ensured.* . . . Nowhere have believers been condemned on the grounds of their belief in God. They have usually been charged with hooliganism, with parasitism, with fictitious political offences (spying, foreign connections), with infringing the laws on religion, etc. . . .

We have no law that punishes people for believing in God; yet doctors, teachers, engineers, and even ordinary workers and employees have been dismissed and are still being dismissed "at their own request," or for some such formal reason, as soon as it becomes known that they attend church and take part in religious ceremonies. . . .

We have no law that punishes people for believing in God; yet many articles have been and are being published in national and local newspapers that openly declare the teaching of religion by parents to their children to be a crime. . . .

Believers from the illegally closed church-communities in Kirov Province have frequently complained of being unlawfully persecuted for their faith to the U.S.S.R. Public Procurator and the U.S.S.R. Supreme Court, to N. S. Khrushchev, L. Brezhnev, A. Mikoyan, A. N. Kosygin, and N. Podgorny, and to all the national newspapers. The local authorities have, in every case, reacted to the complaints by acts of repression of one kind or another against the complainants.

Finally, the persecutions suffered by believers and the severe punishment meted out to them by the courts are mentioned in the complaint lodged by the Evangelical Christians and Baptists with the United Nations and broadcast by the BBC on December 16, 1967.[2] The facts described in this complaint, as well as those described in my letter to *Izvestia*, prove irrefutably that *in the U.S.S.R. Christian believers are social pariahs.* At the present time, they are deprived even of the limited rights that were extended to them in the latter years of the Stalin regime. . . .

In the "Open Letter of the Kirov Believers," it was stated that, in Kirov Province, in the period from 1960 to 1963, churches were closed down "by arbitrary and forcible action." But O. Liubovikov, in an effort to prove the unprovable, alleges that the churches that were closed down "had no revenues; the clergy refused to serve in those churches and betook themselves elsewhere."

This is a falsehood, which is spread everywhere abroad by Metropolitan Nikodim and which carries conviction only abroad since Russian believers are unable either to travel abroad or to send a letter there refuting this falsehood. . . . It was not the priests who refused to serve in the closed churches but the provincial officials of the Council for the Affairs of the Russian Orthodox Church (Smirnov, Medvedev, Liapin) who, by committing scandalously arbitrary actions, deprived the priests in question of their registration and refused to register anyone afresh. The churches that were closed down had adequate revenues, and, when they were shut down, their money balances accrued to the state treasury. . . .

In the city of Kirov itself—which in Stalin's time had two churches—the Serafimov and the Fedorov—the City Council, at the end of 1962, closed down the Fedorov Church, which had large revenues, and, despite the protests of believers (complaints addressed to N. S. Khrushchev were signed by a total of 5,000 people), blew it up quite unnecessarily in the beginning of 1963. As already mentioned, the City Council and the state security organs, in early 1967, frightened the activist believers of Kirov with threats of imprisonment for petitioning to have a second church opened. In the Serafimov Church, today the only one left in Kirov, the accommodation is terribly cramped, and elderly believers are consequently unable to attend Divine service on feast days. . . .

Following the example of Metropolitan Nikodim, O. Liubovikov, in his endeavors to cover up the arbitrary behavior that led to the closing down of the churches, asserts an untruth and accuses me of slandering the social structure of the U.S.S.R. But incontestable facts cannot be refuted. The only way to raise the prestige of the authorities is to correct the mistakes committed in the past toward believers and to restore the situation to normal. That is what we believers are attempting to achieve. . . .

I do not deny that I have always protested against the forcible implantation of nihilistic atheism. [But] I absolutely repudiate the unsubstantiated allegation made by O. Liubovikov that I have transgressed any Soviet laws. . . .

Nowadays, people who openly defend their religious and philosophical convictions, and who criticize the arbitrary and illegal actions of the authorities, are charged without justification with being in illegal communication with the bourgeois West. In Yezhov's day, they were accused of imaginary espionage; nowadays, they are accused of being linked with the NTS and the CIA. . . . Such an accusation, however, is quite unconvincing. People in our country are not parrots who can only repeat what is said in the West. Practical experience of daily life generates new thoughts and new ideas in their heads and stimulates scientific progress. Marxism-Leninism is undergoing a practical testing not in the West but in the U.S.S.R. It is, therefore, only in the U.S.S.R. that it can be given a scientifically based critical assessment. On one point, we believing Christians, on the strength of fifty years' experience of life in a socialist society, have become convinced that the widely propagated teaching in our country about the rise and decay of religion is erroneous. Our belief derives from actually living in a socialist society and is not based on bourgeois propaganda from the West. Accordingly, we Christian believers suggest to the atheists in our country that we start an open and friendly discussion on the problems that interest us, as is being done in certain socialist states. . . .

Ideas cannot be conquered by violence. . . .

B. V. TALANTOV

NOTES

1. For fuller text see Michael Bourdeaux, *Patriarchs and Prophets: Persecution of the Russian Orthodox Church,* to be published by Macmillan in 1969.—ED.

2. For excerpts from this complaint, see Document 43.—ED.

48. *Galanskov on Religious Persecution*

The following is Yu. Galanskov's introductory note to "Description of Events in the Pochaevsky Monastery" published in Phoenix 1966 *and referred to in Document 12.*—ED.

In their cruel and senseless battle against Christianity, the antireligious authorities have tried various violent methods of reprisal against believers and clergymen. Having proclaimed constitutional freedom of conscience, the authorities have formally announced the necessity of fighting religion with atheistic propaganda; they have resorted to administrative reprisals and the physical destruction of clergymen and the more active believers.

The process of smothering the Russian Orthodox Church began almost immediately after the Revolution, and, in that process, both the laws and the elementary norms of human morality have been trampled upon.

Clergymen have been arrested and shot, and believers put into camps. Churches have been closed down and destroyed. The antireligious terror has severely weakened the Russian Orthodox Church but has not completely destroyed it. At the same time, in the face of international opinion, it has been necessary to observe at least outwardly the legal guarantees of freedom of religion.

Finding themselves unable to crush the church by antireligious terror, the authorities have more and more frequently resorted to administrative-legal pressures, at the same time trying to corrupt the church from within by planting antireligious agents within church institutions.

"Description of Events in Pochaevsky Monastery in Our Day," by an anonymous author, has been widely distributed recently in many typewritten copies, and it persuasively documents for us the selfless opposition of a handful of legally defenseless people, dedicated to the service of God and morality, against the inhumanity and cruelty of a state machine bent on their destruction.

V. Writers and Censors

The documents in this section tell the remarkable story of Aleksandr Solzhenitsyn's demand (Document 49) for the total abolition of the Glavlit (Main Administration for Literary Affairs and Publishing) and the ensuing campaign of harassment launched against him by the regime. Documents 51–55 and 58–60 are Solzhenitsyn's own defense of his actions as he confronted the officials of the Writers' Union and their threats, intimidation, and abuse. Documents 50, 56, and 57, on the other hand, illustrate the support he has received from other prominent literary figures in the Soviet Union in their common quest for relaxation of the stringent censorship imposed upon them by the regime. Document 61, Svirsky's address to the Writers' Union, is an all-encompassing attack on the censorship to which all Soviet cultural activities are subjected, and, finally, Document 62 is an impassioned defense of underground literature and writers written by Yuri Galanskov in 1966.

49. Solzhenitsyn to the Fourth Congress of Soviet Writers

May 16, 1967

To the Presidium and the delegates to the Congress, to members of the Union of Soviet Writers, and to the editors of literary newspapers and magazines:

Not having access to the podium at this Congress, I ask that the Congress discuss:

I. The no longer tolerable oppression, in the form of censorship, that our literature has endured for decades and that the Union of Writers can no longer accept.

Under the obfuscating label of *Glavlit*, this censorship—which is not

245

provided for in the Constitution and is therefore illegal, and which is nowhere publicly labeled as such—imposes a yoke on our literature and
gives people unversed in literature arbitrary control over writers. A survival of the Middle Ages, the censorship has managed, Methuselah-like,
to drag out its existence almost to the twenty-first century. Of fleeting
significance, it attempts to appropriate to itself the role of unfleeting
time—of separating good books from bad.

Our writers are not supposed to have the right, are not endowed with
the right, to express their cautionary judgments about the moral life of
man and society or to explain in their own way the social problems and
historical experience that have been so deeply felt in our country. Works
that might express the mature thinking of the people, that might have a
timely and salutary influence on the realm of the spirit or on the development of a social conscience are proscribed or distorted by censorship on
the basis of considerations that are petty, egotistical, and—from the national point of view—shortsighted. Outstanding manuscripts by young
authors, as yet entirely unknown, are nowadays rejected by editors solely
on the ground that they "will not pass." Many members of the [Writ-
ers'] Union, and even many of the delegates at this Congress, know how
they themselves have bowed to the pressures of the censorship and made
concessions in the structure and concept of their books—changing chapters, pages, paragraphs, or sentences, giving them innocuous titles—just
for the sake of seeing them finally in print, even if it meant distorting
them irremediably. It is an understood quality of literature that gifted
works suffer [most] disastrously from all these distortions, while untalented works are not affected by them. Indeed, it is the best of our literature that is published in mutilated form.

Meanwhile, the most censorious labels—"ideologically harmful," "de-
praved," and so forth—are proving shortlived and fluid, changing before
our very eyes. Even Dostoevsky, the pride of world literature, was at one
time not published in our country (still, today, his works are not published in full); he was excluded from the school curriculum, made unacceptable for reading, and reviled. For how many years was Yesenin considered "counterrevolutionary"?—he was even subjected to a prison term
because of his books. Wasn't Maiakovsky called "an anarchistic political
hooligan"? For decades the immortal poetry of Akhmatova was considered anti-Soviet. The first timid printing of the dazzling Tsvetaeva[1] ten
years ago was declared a "gross political error." Only after a delay of
twenty to thirty years were Bunin,[2] Bulgakov,[3] and Platonov[4] returned to
us. Inevitably, Mandelshtam, Voloshin,[5] Gumilev, and Kliuev[6] will follow in that line—not to mention the recognition, at some time or other,
of even Zamiatin[7] and Remisov.[8]

· A decisive moment [in this process] comes with the death of a trouble-
some writer. Sooner or later after that, he is returned to us with an "explanation of [his] errors." For a long time, the name of Pasternak could
not be pronounced aloud; but then he died, and, since then, his books
have appeared and his verse is even quoted at ceremonies.

Pushkin's words are really coming true: "They are capable of loving only the dead."

But the belated publication of books and "authorization" [rehabilitation] of names does not make up for either the social or the artistic losses suffered by our people as a consequence of these monstrous delays and the suppression of artistic conscience. (In fact, there were writers in the 1920's—Pilniak, Platonov, Mandelshtam—who called attention at a very early stage to the beginnings of the cult [of personality] and the peculiar traits of Stalin's character; but these writers were silenced and destroyed instead of being listened to.) Literature cannot develop in between the categories of "permitted" and "not permitted," "about this you may write" and "about this you may not." Literature that is not the breath of contemporary society, that dares not transmit the pains and fears of that society, that does not warn in time against threatening moral and social dangers—such literature does not deserve the name of literature; it is only a façade. Such literature loses the confidence of its own people, and its published works are used as wastepaper instead of being read.

Our literature has lost the leading role it played at the end of the last century and the beginning of this one, and it has lost the brilliance of experimentation that distinguished it in the 1920's. To the entire world, the literary life of our country now appears immeasurably more colorless, trivial, and inferior than it actually is—[or] than it would be if it were not confined and hemmed in. The losers are both our country—in world public opinion—and world literature itself. If the world had access to all the uninhibited fruits of our literature, if it were enriched by our own spiritual experience, the whole artistic evolution of the world would move along in a different way, acquiring a new stability and attaining even a new artistic threshold.

I propose that the Congress adopt a resolution that would demand and ensure the abolition of all censorship, open or hidden, of all fictional writing and that would release publishing houses from the obligation to obtain authorization for the publication of every printed page.

II. The duties of the Union toward its members.

These duties are not clearly formulated in the statutes of the Union of Soviet Writers (under "Protection of copyrights" and "Measures for the protection of other rights of writers"), and it is sad to find that for a third of a century the Union has not defended either the "other" rights or even the copyrights of persecuted writers.

Many writers have been subjected during their lifetime to abuse and slander in the press and from rostrums without being afforded the physical possibility of replying. More than that, they have been exposed to violence and personal persecution (Bulgakov, Akhmatova, Tsvetaeva, Pasternak, Zoshchenko,[9] Platonov, Aleksandr Grin,[10] Vassili Grossman). The Union of Writers not only did not make its own publications available to these writers for purposes of reply and justification, not only did not come out in their defense, but, through its leadership, was always

first among the persecutors. Names that adorned our poetry of the twentieth century found themselves on the list of those expelled from the
Union or not even admitted to it in the first place. The leadership of the
Union cravenly abandoned to their distress those for whom persecution
ended in exile, labor camps, and death (Pavel Vasilev, Mandelshtam,
Artem Vesely,[11] Pilniak, Babel, Tabidze, Zabolotsky,[12] and others). The
list must be cut off at "and others." We learned after the Twentieth
Party Congress that there were more than 600 writers whom the Union
had obediently handed over to their fate in prisons and camps. However,
the roll is even longer, and its curled-up end cannot and will not ever be
read by our eyes. It contains the names of young prose-writers and poets
whom we may have known only accidentally through personal encounters
and whose talents were crushed in camps before being able to blossom,
whose writings never got further than the offices of the state security service in the days of Yagoda, Yezhov, Beria, and Abakumov.

There is no historical necessity for the newly elected leadership of the
Union to share with its predecessors the responsibility for the past.

*I propose that all guarantees for the defense of Union members sub-
jected to slander and unjust persecution be clearly formulated in paragraph 22 of the Union statutes, so that past illegalities will not be
repeated.*

If the Congress does not remain indifferent to what I have said, I also
ask that it consider the interdictions and persecutions to which I myself
have been subjected.

1. It will soon be two years since the state security authorities took
away from me my novel *The First Circle* . . . , thus preventing it from
being submitted to publishers. Instead, in my own lifetime, against my
will and even without my knowledge, this novel has been "published" in
an unnatural "closed" edition for reading by an unidentified select circle.
My novel has [*thus*] become available to literary officials but is being
concealed from most writers. I have been unable to obtain open discussion of the novel within writers' associations and to prevent misuse and
plagiarism.

2. Together with this novel, my literary papers dating back fifteen to
twenty years, things that were not intended for publication, were taken
away from me. Now tendentious excerpts from these papers have also
been covertly "published" and are being circulated within the same circles. The play *Feast of the Conquerors*, which I wrote in verse from
memory in camp, where I went by a four-digit number and where, condemned to die by starvation, we were forgotten by society, no one outside
the camps coming out against [such] repressions—this play, now left far
behind, is being ascribed to me as my very latest work.

3. For three years now, an irresponsible campaign of slander has been
conducted against me, who fought all through the war as a battery commander and received military decorations. It is being said that I served
time as a criminal or surrendered to the enemy (I was never a prisoner-

of-war), that I "betrayed" my country and "served the Germans." That is the interpretation now being put on the eleven years I spent in camps and in exile for having criticized Stalin. This slander is being spread in secret instructions and meetings by people holding official positions. I vainly tried to stop the slander by appealing to the Board of the Writers' Union of the R.S.F.S.R. and to the press. The Board did not even react, and not a single paper printed my reply to the slanderers. On the contrary, slander against me from rostrums has intensified and become more vicious within the last year, making use of distorted material from my confiscated papers, and I have no way of replying.

4. My novel *Cancer Ward* . . . , the first part of which was approved for publication by the prose department of the Moscow writers' organization, cannot be published either by chapters—rejected by five magazines —or in its entirety—rejected by *Novyi mir*, *Zvezda*, and *Prostor*.

5. The play *The Reindeer and the Little Hut*, accepted in 1962 by the Sovremennik Theater, has thus far not been approved for performance.

6. The screen play *The Tanks Know the Truth*; the stage play *The Light that Is in You*; [a group of] short stories entitled *The Right Hand*; the series *Small Bite*—[all these] cannot find either a producer or a publisher.

7. My stories published in *Novyi mir* have never been reprinted in book form, having been rejected everywhere—by the Soviet Writer Publishers, the State Literature Publishing House, and the Ogoniok Library. They thus remain inaccessible to the general reading public.

8. I have also been prevented from having any other contacts with readers [either] through public readings of my works (in November, 1966, nine out of eleven scheduled meetings were cancelled at the last moment) or through readings over the radio. Even the simple act of giving a manuscript away for "reading and copying" has now become a criminal act (ancient Russian scribes were permitted to do this five centuries ago).

Thus my work has been finally smothered, gagged, and slandered.

In view of such flagrant infringements of my copyright and "other" rights, will the Fourth Congress defend me—yes or no? It seems to me that the choice is also not without importance for the literary future of several of the delegates.

I am, of course, confident that I will fulfill my duty as a writer under all circumstances—even more successfully and more unchallenged from the grave than in my lifetime. No one can bar the road to truth, and, to advance its cause, I am prepared to accept even death. But may it be that repeated lessons will finally teach us not to stop the writer's pen during his lifetime?

At no time has this ennobled our history.

A. I. SOLZHENITSYN

NOTES

1. Marina Tsvetaeva (1892–1941) was a poetess whose verses are distinguished by their spontaneity and complex sound effects. Tsvetaeva emigrated in 1922, returned to the Soviet Union in 1939, and two years later, under attack as a "formalist," committed suicide. She has since been rehabilitated.—ED.

2. Ivan Alekseyevich Bunin (1870–1953), poet, novelist, and short-story writer, was a critic of the Soviet Union, from which he fled shortly after the Bolsheviks seized power. In 1933, Bunin became the first Russian writer to receive the Nobel Prize for Literature.—ED.

3. Mikhail Afanasevich Bulgakov (1891–1940) was a postrevolutionary satirist who directed his barbs at, among other targets, the October Revolution itself. His play *The Crimson Island* (1928) was a direct attack on Soviet censorship. His most famous work, *The Master and Margarita*, recently appeared in the Soviet Union in doctored form and was published in New York (Harper & Row) in 1967.—ED.

4. Sergei Fiodorovich Platonov (1860–1933), a historian of international repute, in 1920, helped to negotiate the Riga Peace Treaty between the Soviet Union and Poland. In 1930, during a general purge of historians, he was charged with illegal possession of state archives, imprisoned for a year, and then exiled to Kuibyshev, where he died.—ED.

5. Maksimilian Aleksandrovich Voloshin (1877–1931), symbolist poet, author of *Mute Demons* (1919) and *Poems of the Terror* (1924).—ED.

6. Nikolai Alekseievich Kliuev (1887–1937) was a poet whose subject was the Russian peasant. A member of the Socialist Revolutionary party, Kliuev spoke out against the collectivization of the Russian countryside and was arrested in the early 1930's and sent to a concentration camp, where he died.—ED.

7. Yevgeni Ivanovich Zamiatin (1884–1937) wrote the novel *We* (1924), a biting satire of a totalitarian state, which is believed to have inspired Orwell's novel *1984*. Zamiatin was permitted to leave Russia in 1931 and died in Paris six years later.—ED.

8. Aleksei Mikhailovich Remisov (1877–1958), novelist and essayist, was vehemently anti-Bolshevik. After the October Revolution, Remizov fled to France, where he remained until his death.—ED.

9. Mikhail Mikhailovich Zoshchenko (1895–1958) was a humorist and short-story writer who was immensely popular during the 1920's and 1930's. In 1946, he was attacked by Zhdanov for his story "The Adventures of a Monkey," which allegedly satirized the Soviet people and political system. He was expelled from the Writers' Union and remained in obscurity for a long time, publishing only a few insignificant items before his death.—ED.

10. Aleksandr Grin (Grinevsky) (1880–1932) was the author of fantasies somewhat in the manner of Edgar Allan Poe.—ED.

11. The novelist Artem Vesely (1899–1939) was a political commissar attached to the Red Army during the Civil War. His works draw historical parallels between the October Revolution and the peasant uprisings of the seventeenth and eighteenth centuries.—ED.

12. Nikolai Alekseevich Zabolotsky (1903–58) was a poet who was at first influenced by Western modernists and later followed in the tradition of the Russian classical poets. In the 1950's, Zabolotsky warned his colleagues that the "thaw" would be of short duration and would be followed by reprisals.—ED.

50. *Antokolsky to Demichev*

To Comrade P. N. Demichev, Secretary of the CPSU Central Committee

Dear Piotr Nilych!

Like other delegates to our Congress, I too have received the famous letter written by Aleksandr Isaevich Solzhenitsyn, and it has perturbed me, as it has several other comrades.

As an old writer and a Communist, I feel obliged to share my feelings with you.

I consider Aleksandr Solzhenitsyn a writer endowed with rare talent, a rising hope of our realistic literature, an heir to the great and humanistic traditions of Gogol, Leo Tolstoy, and Aleksei Maksimovich Gorky. We ought to cherish such contributors to our culture. Criticism of those works of Solzhenitsyn that have been published has shocked me because it is biased, unjust, and unconvincing.

The ban of Solzhenitsyn's manuscripts, described in detail in his letter, strikes one as an incredible occurrence unworthy of our socialist society and our Soviet state. It is all the more dreadful in view of the fact that the same thing happened several years ago to the manuscript of the second part of the novel by the late Vassili Grossman.

Is it possible that such reprisals against the manuscripts of our writers are threatening to become a custom sanctioned by law in our country?

This cannot and must not happen!

Such savagery toward works of art is incompatible with our fundamental laws and unthinkable in any normal human community.

If Solzhenitsyn's works contain controversial and unclear elements, if political mistakes have been discovered in them, they should be submitted to the public for open discussion. Writers have many opportunities to do this.

I have worked in the field of literature for fifty years. I have written many books and lived out my life, a life full of vicissitudes. I have experienced periods of burning anxiety for the fate of our entire literature, and sometimes for various comrades: Bulgakov, Pasternak, Titsian Tabidze—I recall the names of those who were close to me.

Having lived out my life, I would never have thought that such anxiety would recur in the evening of my days and on the eve of the great and glorious anniversary!

If a Soviet writer is compelled to turn to his fellow writers with a letter like Solzhenitsyn's, this means that we are all morally responsible to him and to our own readers. If he cannot tell his readers the truth, then I too, old writer that I am, have no right to look my readers straight in the eye.

PAVEL ANTOKOLSKY

51. *Solzhenitsyn to Writers' Union*

September 12, 1967

To the Secretariat of the Board of the Union of Writers of the U.S.S.R.
—All Secretaries

Even though supported by more than a hundred writers, my letter to the Fourth Congress of the Union of Writers has been neither published nor answered. The only thing that has happened is that rumors are being spread in order to assuage public opinion. These rumors—highly uniform and evidently coming from a centralized source—aver that *Cancer Ward* and a book of [my] stories are being printed. But, as you know, this is a lie.

In a conversation with me on June 12, 1967, [some of the] secretaries of the Board of the Union of Writers of the U.S.S.R.—G. Markov, K. Voronkov, S. Sartakov, and L. Sobolev—declared that the Board of the Union of Writers deemed it a duty to refute publicly the base slander that has been spread about me and my military record. However, not only has this refutation failed to materialize, but the slanders continue; at instructional meetings, at activist meetings, and at seminars, a new batch of fantastic nonsense is being disseminated about me—[e.g.,] that I have run off to the Republic of Arabia or to England (I would like to assure the slanderers that it is, rather, they who will be doing the running). Prominent persons persistently express their regret that I did not die in the camp, that I was liberated. (Incidentally, immediately following *Ivan Denisovich*, the same regret was voiced. This book is now being secretly withdrawn from circulation in [public] libraries.)

These same secretaries of the Board promised at least to "examine the question" of [approving] publication of my latest novel, *Cancer Ward*. But, in the space of three months—one-fourth of a year—no progress has been made in this direction either. During these three months, forty-two secretaries of the Board have been unable to make an evaluation of the novel or to make a recommendation as to whether it should be published. The novel has been in this same strange and equivocal state—no direct prohibition, no direct permission—for over a year, since the summer of 1966. While the journal *Novyi mir* would now like to publish the story, it lacks the permission to do so.

Does the Secretariat believe that my novel will silently disappear as a result of these endless delays, that I will cease to exist, and that [therefore] the Secretariat will not have to decide whether to include it in or exclude it from Soviet literature? While this is going on, the book is being read avidly everywhere. At the behest of the readers, it has already appeared in hundreds of typewritten copies. At the June 12 meeting, I apprised the Secretariat that we should make haste to publish the novel if we wish to see it appear first in Russian, that under the circumstances we cannot prevent its unauthorized appearance in the West.

After the senseless delay of many months, the time has come to state that, if the latter does happen, it will clearly be the fault (or perhaps the wish?) of the Secretariat of the Board of the Union of Writers of the U.S.S.R.

I insist that my story be published without delay.

SOLZHENITSYN

52. Secretariat Meeting with Solzhenitsyn

Proceedings of a Session of the Secretariat of the Union of Soviet Writers

September 22, 1967

The session was attended by approximately thirty secretaries of the Union of Writers and by Comrade Melentiev of the Cultural Department of the Central Committee. K. A. Fedin was chairman. The session, which discussed letters written by Solzhenitsyn, started at 1:00 P.M. and ended after 5:00 P.M.

FEDIN: I have been shaken by Solzhenitsyn's second letter. His claim that things have come to a standstill seems to me to be without foundation. I feel that this has been an insult to our collective. By no means is three and a half months a long time to spend examining his manuscript. I have sensed something in the nature of a threat [in the letter]. This strikes me as offensive! Solzhenitsyn's second letter seems to urge us to take up his manuscripts in all haste and to publish them immediately. The second letter continues the line of the first, but the first letter spoke more concretely and with more fervor about the fate of the writer, while the second, I feel, was offensive. Where do we stand with regard to the complex question of publishing Solzhenitsyn's things? None of us denies that he is talented. [Yet] the tenor of the letter veers in an impermissible direction. His letter is like a slap in the face; it is as if we are reprobates and not representatives of the creative intelligentsia. In the final analysis, he himself is slowing down the examination of the question with these demands. I did not find the idea of literary comradeship in his letters. Whether we want to or not, today we must get into a discussion of Solzhenitsyn's works, but it seems to me that generally speaking we should discuss the letters.

[*Solzhenitsyn requests permission to say a few words about the subject of discussion. He reads a written statement.*]

It has become known to me that in preparation for the discussion of *Cancer Ward,* the secretaries of the Board were instructed to read the play *Feast of the Conquerors,* which I myself have long since renounced; I have not even read it for ten years. I destroyed all copies of it except the one that was confiscated and that has now been reproduced. More than once, I have explained that this play was written not by Solzhenitsyn, member of the Union of Writers, but by nameless prisoner Sh-232 in those distant years when there was no return to freedom for those arrested under the political article, at a time when no one in the community, including the writers' community, in either word or deed spoke out against repression, even when such repression was directed against entire peoples. I now bear just as little responsibility for this play as many other authors bear for speeches and books they wrote in 1949 but would not write again today. This play bears the stamp of the desperation of the camps in those years when man's conscious being was determined by his social being and at a time when the conscious being was by no means uplifted by prayers for those who were being persecuted. This play bears no relationship whatsoever to my present works, and the critique of it is a deliberate departure from a businesslike discussion of the novel *Cancer Ward.*

Moreover, it is beneath a writer's ethics to discuss a work that was seized in such a way from a private apartment. The critique of my novel *The First Circle* is a separate matter and should not be substituted for a critique of the story *Cancer Ward.*

KORNEICHUK: I have a question to put to Solzhenitsyn. How does he regard the licentious bourgeois propaganda that his [first] letter evoked? Why doesn't he dissociate himself from it? Why does he put up with it in silence? How is it that his letter was broadcast over the radio in the West even before the Congress started?

[*Fedin calls upon Solzhenitsyn to reply. Solzhenitsyn replies that he is not a schoolboy who has to jump up to answer every question, that he will deliver a statement like the others. Fedin says that Solzhenitsyn can wait until there are several questions and then answer them all at the same time.*]

BARUZDIN: Even though Solzhenitsyn protests against the discussion of *Feast of the Conquerors,* we shall have to discuss this play whether he wants to or not.

SALYNSKY: I would like Solzhenitsyn to tell us by whom, when, and under what circumstances these materials were removed. Has the author asked for their return? To whom did he address his request?

[*Fedin asks Solzhenitsyn to answer these questions. Solzhenitsyn repeats that he will answer them when making his statement.*]

FEDIN: But the Secretariat cannot begin the discussion until it has the answers to these questions.

VOICES: If Solzhenitsyn wants to refuse to talk to the Secretariat at all, let him say so.

SOLZHENITSYN: Very well, I shall answer these questions. It is not true that the letter was broadcast over the radio in the West before the Congress: it was broadcast *after* the Congress closed, and then not right away. Very significant and expressive use is made here of the word "abroad," as if it referred to some higher authority whose opinion was very much cherished. Perhaps this is understandable to those who spend much creative time traveling abroad, to those who flood our literature with sketches about life abroad. But this is alien to me. I have never been abroad, but I do know that I don't have time enough left in my life to learn about life there. I do not understand how one can be so sensitive to opinion abroad and not to one's own country, to pulsing public opinion here. For my entire life, I have had the soil of my homeland under my feet; only *its* pain do I hear, only about *it* do I write.

Why was the play *Feast of the Conquerors* mentioned in the letter to the Congress? This is apparent from the letter itself: in order to protest against the illegal "publication" and dissemination of this play against the will of the author and without his consent. Now, concerning the confiscation of my novel and archives. Yes, I did write several times, beginning in 1965, to protest this matter to the Central Committee. But, in recent times, a whole new version of the confiscation of my archives has been invented. The story is that Teush, the person who was keeping my manuscripts, had some tie with another person who is not named, that the latter was arrested while going through customs (where is not mentioned), and that something or other was found in his possession (they do not say what); it was not something of mine, but it was decided to protect me against such an acquaintanceship. All this is a lie. Teush's friend was investigated two years ago, but no such accusation was made against him. The items I had in safekeeping were discovered as a consequence of [police] surveillance, wiretapping, and an eavesdropping device. And here is the remarkable thing: barely does the new version [of the confiscation] appear than it crops up in various parts of the country. Lecturer Potemkin has just aired it to a large assemblage in Riga, and one of the secretaries of the Union of Writers has passed it on to writers in Moscow, adding his own invention—that I supposedly acknowledged all these things at the last meeting at the Secretariat. Yet not a single one of these things was discussed. I have no doubt that I will soon start getting letters from all parts of the country about the dissemination of this version.

VOICE: Has the editorial board of *Novyi mir* rejected or accepted the novel *Cancer Ward?*

ABDUMOMUNOV: What kind of authorization does *Novyi mir* require to print a story, and from whom does it come?

TVARDOVSKY: Generally, the decision to print or not to print a particular thing is a matter for the editorial board to decide. But in the situation that has developed around this author's name, the Secretariat of the Union must decide.

VORONKOV: Not once has Solzhenitsyn appealed directly to the Secretariat of the Union of Writers. After Solzhenitsyn's letter to the congress, some of the comrades in the Secretariat expressed the desire to meet with him, to answer questions, to talk [with him] and offer assistance. But, after the letter appeared in the dirty bourgeois press and Solzhenitsyn did not react in any way, . . .

TVARDOVSKY [*interrupting*]: Precisely like the Union of Writers!

VORONKOV: . . . this desire died. And now the second letter has come. It is written in the form of an ultimatum; it is offensive and disrespectful to our writers' community. Just now, Solzhenitsyn referred to "one of the secretaries" who addressed a party meeting of Moscow writers. I was that secretary. [*To Solzhenitsyn*]: People were in a hurry to inform you, but they did a bad job of it. As to the confiscation of your things, the only thing I mentioned was that you had admitted at the last meeting that the confiscated items were yours and that there had been no search made of your house. Naturally, after your letter to the Congress, we ourselves asked to read all your works. But you should not be so rude to your brothers in labor and writing! And you, Aleksandr Trifonovich [Tvardovsky], if you consider it necessary to print this story and if the author accepts your corrections, then go ahead and print it yourself; why should the Secretariat be involved?

TVARDOVSKY: And what happened in the case of Bek?[1] The Secretariat was also involved then and made its recommendations, but, all the same, nothing was published.

VORONKOV: What interests me most of all, now, is the civic person Solzhenitsyn: Why doesn't he answer the malicious bourgeois propaganda? And why does he treat us as he does?

MUSREPOV: I have a question, too. How can he possibly write in his letter: "Prominent persons persistently express regret that I did not die in the camp"? What right does he have to write such a thing?

SHARIPOV: And by what channels could the letter have reached the West?

[*Fedin asks Solzhenitsyn to answer these questions.*]

SOLZHENITSYN: What other things have been said about me? A person who, right now, occupies a very high position publicly declared that he is sorry he was not one of the triumvirate that sentenced me in 1945, that he would have sentenced me to be shot then and there! Here [at the Secretariat] my second letter is interpreted as an ultimatum: either print the story, or it will be printed in the West. But it isn't *I* who presents this ultimatum to the Secretariat; life presents this ultimatum to you and me both. I write that I am disturbed by the distribution of the story in hundreds—this is an approximate figure—in hundreds of typewritten copies.

VOICE: How did this come about?

SOLZHENITSYN: My works are disseminated in one way only: people persistently ask to read them, and, having received them to read, they either use their spare time or their own funds to reprint them and then give them to others to read. As long as a year ago, the entire Moscow section [of the Writers' Union] read the first part of the story, and I am surprised that Comrade Voronkov said here that they didn't know where to get it and that they asked the KGB. About three years ago, my "short stories" or poetry in prose were disseminated just as rapidly; barely had I given them to people to read when they quickly reached various cities in the Union. And then the editors of *Novyi mir* received a letter from the West from which we learned that these stories had already been published there.[2] It was in order that such a leak might not befall *Cancer Ward* that I wrote my insistent letter to the Secretariat. I am no less astonished that the Secretariat could fail to react in some way to my letter to the Congress before the West did. And how could it fail to respond to all the slander that surrounds me? Comrade Voronkov used here the remarkable expression "brothers in writing and labor." Well, the fact of the matter is that these brothers in writing and labor have for two and a half years calmly watched me being oppressed, persecuted, and slandered, . . .

TVARDOVSKY: Not everyone has been indifferent.

SOLZHENITSYN: . . . and newspaper editors, also like brothers, contribute to the web of falsehood that is woven around me by not publishing my denials. I'm not speaking about the fact that people in the camps are not allowed to read my book. It was banned in the camps, searches for it were conducted, and people were put in punishment cells for reading it even during those months when all the newspapers were loudly acclaiming *A Day in the Life of Ivan Denisovich* and promising that "this will not happen again." But, in recent times, the book is secretly being withdrawn from libraries outside [the camps] as well. I have received letters from various places telling me of the prohibition against circulating the book; the order is to tell the readers that the book is in the bindery, that it is out of print, or that there is no access to the shelves [where the book is kept], and to refuse to circulate it. Here is a letter recently received from the Krasnogvardeiskii Region in the Crimea:

> In the regional library, I was confidentially told (I am an activist in this library) of an order that your books be removed from circulation. One of the women workers in the library wanted to present me with [a copy of] *A Day* as a souvenir, since the library no longer needs it, but another woman immediately stopped her rash girlfriend: "What are you doing, you mustn't! Once the book has been assigned to the Special Section, it is dangerous to make a present of it."

I am not saying that the book has been removed from *all* libraries; here and there it can still be found. But people coming to visit me in Riazan were unable to get my book in the Riazan Oblast Reading Room! They were given various excuses, but they did not get the book. . . .

The circle of lies becomes ever wider, knowing no limits, even charging me with having been taken prisoner and having collaborated with the Germans. But that's not the end of it! This summer, in the political education schools, *e.g.*, in Bolshevo, the agitators were told that I had fled to the Republic of Arabia and changed my citizenship. Naturally, all this is written down in notebooks and is disseminated a hundred times over. And this took place not more than a few miles from the capital! Here is another version. In Solikamsk (PO Box 389), Major Shestakov declared that I had fled to England on a tourist visa. This is the deputy for political affairs—who dares disbelieve him? Another time, the same man stated: "Solzhenitsyn has been *forbidden* to write officially." Well, at least here he is closer to the truth.

The following is being said about me from the rostrums: "He was set free ahead of time, for no reason." Whether there was any reason can be seen in the court decision of the Military Collegium of the Supreme Court, Rehabilitation Section. It has been presented to the Secretariat. . . .

TVARDOVSKY: It also contains the combat record of Officer Solzhenitsyn.

SOLZHENITSYN: And the expression "ahead of time" is used with great relish! After the eight-year sentence, I served a month in deportation prisons, but, of course, it is considered shameful to mention such a petty detail. Then, without being sentenced, I was permanently exiled. I spent three years in exile with that eternal feeling of doom. It was only because of the Twentieth Congress that I was set free—and this is called "ahead of time!" The expression is so typical of the conditions that prevailed in the 1949–53 period: If a man did not die beside a camp rubbish heap, if he was able even to crawl out of the camp, this meant that he had been set free "ahead of time"—after all, the sentence was for eternity and anything earlier was "ahead of time."

Former Minister Semichastny, who was fond of speaking on literary issues, also singled me out for attention more than once. One of his astonishing, even comical, accusations was the following: "Solzhenitsyn is materially supporting the capitalist world; else why doesn't he claim his rights [*i.e.*, collect his royalties] from someone or other for his well-known book?" Obviously, the reference was to *Ivan Denisovich*, since no other book of mine had been published [at that time]. Now if you knew, if you had read somewhere that it was absolutely necessary for me to wrest the money from the capitalists, then why didn't you inform me about it? This is a farce: whoever collects fees from the West has sold out to the capitalists; whoever does not take the fees is materially supporting them. And the third alternative? To fly into the sky. While Semichastny is no longer a minister, his idea has not died; lectures of the All-Union Society for the Dissemination of Scientific Information have carried it further. By way of example, the idea was repeated on July 16 of this year by Lecturer A. A. Freifeld at the Sverdlovsk Circus. Two thousand persons sat there and marveled: "What a crafty bird, that Solzhenitsyn! Without leaving the Soviet Union, without a single kopek in his pocket, he contrived to support world capitalism materially." This is indeed a story to be told at a circus.

We had a talk on June 12, right here, at the Secretariat. It was quiet and peaceful. We seemed to make some progress. A short time passed, and suddenly rumors were rampant throughout all of Moscow. Everything that actually took place was distorted, beginning with the fabrication that Tvardovsky had been shouting and waving his fist at me. But everyone who was there knows that nothing like that took place. Why these lies, then? And, right now, we are all simultaneously hearing what is said here, but where is the guarantee that after today's meeting of the Secretariat everything will not be distorted again? If you really are "brothers in writing and work," then my first request is that when you talk about today's session, don't fabricate and distort things.

I am one person; my slanderers number in the hundreds. Naturally I am never able to defend myself, and I never know against whom I should defend myself. I wouldn't be surprised if I were declared to be an adherent of the geocentric system and to have been the first to light the pyre of Giordano Bruno.[3]

SALYNSKY: I shall speak of *Cancer Ward*. I believe that it should be printed—it is a vivid and powerful thing. To be sure, it contains descriptions of diseases in pathological terms, and the reader involuntarily develops a phobia about cancer—a phobia that is already widespread in our century. Somehow this [aspect of the book] should be eliminated. The caustic, topical-satirical style should also be eliminated. Another negative feature is that the destinies of almost all the characters are connected with the camp or with camp life in one form or another. This may be all right in the case of Kostoglotov or Rusanov, but why does it have to be applied to Valim, to Shulubin, and even to the soldier? At the very end, we learn that he is no ordinary soldier from the army, that he is a camp guard. [Still] the basic orientation of the novel is to discuss the end of the difficult past. And now a few words about moral socialism [a concept expounded in the novel]. In my opinion, there is nothing so bad about this. It would be bad if Solzhenitsyn were preaching *a*moral socialism. If he were preaching national socialism or the Chinese version of national socialism—that would be bad. Each person is free to form his own ideas on socialism and its development. I personally believe that socialism is determined by economic laws. But, of course, there is room for argument. Why not print the story, then? [*He subsequently calls upon the Secretariat to issue a statement decisively refuting the slanders against Solzhenitsyn.*]

SIMONOV: I do not accept the novel *The First Circle* and I oppose its publication. As for *Cancer Ward*, I am in favor of publishing it. Not everything in the story is to my liking, but it does not have to please everyone. Perhaps the author should adopt some of the comments that have been made, but, naturally, he cannot adopt all of them. It is also our duty to refute the slander about him. Further, his book of stories should be published. The foreword to the latter book would be a good place in which to publish his biography, and, in this way, the slander would die out of its own accord. Both we and he himself can and must put an end to false accusations. I have not read *Feast of the Conquerors*, nor do I desire to do so, since the author doesn't wish it.

TVARDOVSKY: Solzhenitsyn's position is such that he cannot issue a statement. It is we ourselves, the Union, who must make a statement refuting the slander. At the same time, we must sternly warn Solzhenitsyn against the inadmissible, unpleasant way in which he addressed the Congress. The editorial board of *Novyi mir* sees no reason why *Cancer Ward* should not be printed, naturally with certain revisions. We only wish to receive the Secretariat's approval or at least word that the Secretariat does not object. [*He asks Voronkov to produce the Secretariat's draft communiqué which was prepared back in June. Voronkov indicates that he is in no hurry to produce the communiqué. During this time voices are heard:* They still haven't decided. There are those who are opposed!]

FEDIN: No, that isn't so. It isn't the Secretariat that has to print or reject anything. Are we really guilty of anything? Is it possible, Aleksandr Trifonovich, that you feel guilty?

TVARDOVSKY (*quickly, expressively*): I?? No.

FEDIN: We shouldn't search for some trumped-up excuse to make a statement. Mere rumors don't provide sufficient grounds for doing so. It would be another matter if Solzhenitsyn himself were to find a way to resolve the situation. What is needed is a public statement by Solzhenitsyn himself. [*To Solzhenitsyn:*] But think it over, Aleksandr Isaevich— in the interest of *what* will we be publishing your protests? You must protest above all against the dirty use of your name by our enemies in the West. Naturally, in the process, you will also have the opportunity to give voice to some of the complaints you've uttered here today. If this proves to be a fortunate and tactful document, we will print it and help you. It is precisely from this point that your acquittal must proceed, and not from your works or from this bartering as to how many months we are entitled to examine your manuscript—three months? four months? Is that really so terrible? It is far more terrible that your works are used there, in the West, for the basest of purposes.

[*Approval is expressed by members of the Secretariat.*]

KORNEICHUK: We didn't invite you here to throw stones at you. We summoned you in order to help you out of this trying and ambiguous situation. You were asked questions, but you declined to answer. By our works, we are protecting our government, our Party, our people. You have sarcastically referred here to trips abroad as if they were pleasant strolls. We travel abroad to wage the struggle. We return home from abroad worn out and exhausted, but with the feeling of having done our duty. Don't think that I was offended by the comment concerning travel sketches. I don't write them. I travel on the business of the World Peace Council. We know that you suffered a great deal, but you are not the only one. There were many other comrades in the camps besides you. Some were old Communists. From the camps, they went to the front. Our past consists not of acts of lawlessness alone; there were also acts of heroism—but you didn't notice the latter. Your works consist only of accusations. *Feast of the Conquerors* is malicious, vile, offensive! And this foul thing is disseminated, and the people read it! When were you imprisoned? Not in 1937. In 1937, *we* went through a great deal, but nothing stopped us! Konstantin Aleksandrovich was right in saying that you must speak out publicly and strike out against Western propaganda. Do battle against the foes of our nation! Do you realize that thermonuclear weapons exist in the world and that, despite all our peaceful efforts, the United States may employ them? How then can we, Soviet writers, not be soldiers?

SOLZHENITSYN: I have repeatedly declared that it is dishonest to discuss *Feast of the Conquerors*, and I demand that this argument be excluded from our discussion.

SURKOV: You can't stop everyone from talking.

KOZHEVNIKOV: The long time lapse between the receipt of Solzhenitsyn's letter and today's discussion is, in fact, an expression of the *seriousness* with which the Secretariat approaches the letter. If we had discussed it at the time, while the impact was still hot, we would have treated it more severely and less thoughtfully. We ourselves decided to find out just what kind of anti-Soviet manuscripts these were, and we spent a good deal of time reading them. The military service of Solzhenitsyn has been confirmed by relevant documents; yet we are not now discussing the officer but, rather, the writer. Today, for the first time, I have heard Solzhenitsyn renounce the libelous depiction of Soviet reality in *Feast of the Conquerors*, but I still cannot get over my first impression of this play. For me, this moment of Solzhenitsyn's renunciation of *Feast of the Conquerors* still does not jibe with my perception of the play. Perhaps this is because in both *The First Circle* and *Cancer Ward* there is a feeling of the same vengeance for past suffering. And, if it is a question of the fate of these works, the author should remember that he is indebted to the organ that discovered him. Some time ago, I was the first to express apprehension concerning "Matriona's House."[4] We spent time reading your manuscript, which you did not even venture to give to any editorial board. *Cancer Ward* evokes revulsion from the abundance of naturalism, from the surfeit of all manner of horrors. All the same, its basic orientation is not medical but social. . . . And it is apparently from this that the title of the work is derived. In your second letter, you demand the publication of your novel, which still requires further work. Is such a demand worthy of a writer? All of our writers willingly listen to the opinions of the editors and do not hurry them.

SOLZHENITSYN: Despite my explanations and objections, despite the utter senselessness of discussing a work written twenty years ago, in another era, in an incomparably different situation, by a different person—a work, moreover, that was never published or read by anyone and that was stolen from a drawer—some of the speakers have concentrated their attention on this very work. This is much more senseless than, say, at the First Congress of Writers, rebuking Maksim Gorky for "Untimely Thoughts" or Sergeev-Tsensky for the *osvagovskie* correspondence,[5] which had been published a good fifteen years earlier. Korneichuk has stated here that "such a thing has never happened and will not happen in the history of Russian literature." Precisely!

OZEROV: The letter to the Congress proved to be a politically irresponsible act. First of all, the letter reached our enemies. It contained things that were incorrect. Zamiatin was put in the same heap together with unjustly repressed writers. As regards the publication of *Cancer Ward*, we can make an agreement with *Novyi mir* that the thing may be printed only if the manuscript is corrected and the corrections are discussed. There remains some other very important work to be done. The story is uneven in quality. There are good and bad points in it. Most objectionable is the penchant for sloganeering and caricatures. I would ask that quite a number of things be deleted, things that we simply do not have time to discuss now. The philosophy of moral socialism does not belong merely to the hero. One senses that it is being defended by the author. This cannot be permitted.

SURKOV: I, too, have read *Feast of the Conquerors*. The mood of it is: "be damned, the whole lot of you!" The same mood pervades *Cancer Ward* as well. Having suffered so much, you had a right to be angry as a human being, Aleksandr Isaevich, but, after all, you are also a writer! I have known Communists who were sent to camps, but this in no measure affected their world view. No, your story approaches fundamental problems not in philosophical terms but in political terms. And then there is [the reference to] that idol in the theater square, even though the monument to Marx had not yet been erected at that time.

If *Cancer Ward* were to be published, it would be used against us, and it would be more dangerous than Svetlana's memoirs. Yes, of course, it would be well to forestall its publication in the West, but that is difficult. For example, in recent times I have been close to Anna Andreevna Akhmatova. I know that she gave [her poem] "Requiem" to several people to read.[6] It was passed around for several weeks, and then suddenly it was printed in the West. Of course, our reader is now so developed and so sophisticated that no measly little book is going to alienate him from Communism. All the same, the works of Solzhenitsyn are more dangerous to us than those of Pasternak: Pasternak was a man divorced from life, while Solzhenitsyn, with his animated, militant, ideological temperament, is a man of principle. We represent the first revolution in the history of mankind that has changed neither its slogans nor its banners. "Moral socialism" is a philistine [*burzhuaznyi*] socialism. It is old and primitive, and (*speaking in the direction of Salynsky*) I don't understand how anyone could fail to understand this, how anyone could find anything in it.

SALYNSKY: I do not defend it in the least.

RIURIKOV: Solzhenitsyn has suffered from those who have slandered him, but he has also suffered from those who have heaped excessive praise on him and have ascribed qualities to him that he does not possess. If Solzhenitsyn is renouncing anything, then he should renounce the title of "continuer of Russian realism." The conduct of Marshal Rokossovsky and General Gorbatov is more honest than that of his heroes.[7] The source of this writer's energy lies in bitterness and wrath. As a human being, one can understand this. [*To Solzhenitsyn:*] You write that your things are prohibited, but not a single one of your novels has been censored. I marvel that Tvardovsky asks permission from us. I, for example, have never asked the Union of Writers for permission to print or not to print. [*He asks Solzhenitsyn to heed the recommendations of* Novyi mir *and promises page-by-page comments on* Cancer Ward *from "anyone present."*]

BARUZDIN: I happen to be one of those who, from the start, has not been captivated by the works of Solzhenitsyn. "Matriona's House" was already much weaker than the first thing [*One Day in the Life of Ivan Denisovich*]. And *The First Circle* is much weaker, so pitifully naive and primitive are the depictions of Stalin, Abakumov, and Poskrebyshev. But *Cancer Ward* is an antihumanitarian work. The end of the story leads to the conclusion that "a different road should have been taken." Did Solzhenitsyn really believe that his letter "in place of a speech" would be read [from the rostrum of] the Congress? How many letters did the Congress receive?

VORONKOV: About 500.

BARUZDIN: Well! And would it really have been possible to get through them in a hurry? I do not agree with Riurikov: it is proper that the question of permission be placed before the Secretariat. Our Secretariat should more frequently play a creative role and should willingly advise editors.

ABDUMOMUNOV: It is a very good thing that Solzhenitsyn has found the courage to repudiate *Feast of the Conquerors*. He will also find the courage to think of ways of carrying out the proposal of Konstantin Aleksandrovich [Fedin]. If we publish his *Cancer Ward*, there will be still more commotion and harm than there was from his first letter [to the Congress]. Incidentally, what's the meaning of "sprinkled tobacco into the eyes of the Rhesus monkey—just for the hell of it"? Why the "just for the hell of it"? This is against our entire style of narration. In the story, there are the Rusanovs and the great martyrs from the camp—but is that all? And where is Soviet society? One shouldn't lay it on so thick and make the story so gloomy. There are many tedious passages, turns, and naturalistic scenes—all these should be eliminated.

ABASHIDZE: I was able to read only 150 pages of *Cancer Ward* and therefore can make no thoroughgoing assessment of it. Yet I didn't get the impression that the novel should not be published. But I repeat, I can't make a thorough assessment. Perhaps the most important things are farther on in the book. All of us, being honest and talented writers, have fought against embellishers even when we were forbidden to do so. But Solzhenitsyn tends to go to the other extreme: parts of his work are of a purely essayist, exposé nature. The artist is like a child, he takes a machine apart to see what is inside. But genuine art begins with putting things together. I have noticed him asking the person sitting next to him the name of each speaker. Why doesn't he know any of us? Because we have never invited him. The proposal of Konstantin Aleksandrovich was correct: let Solzhenitsyn himself answer, perhaps first of all for his own sake.

BROVKA: In Belorussia, there are also many people who were imprisoned. For example, Sergei Grakhovsky was also in prison for twenty years. Yet he realized that it was not the people, not the Party, and not Soviet power that was responsible for illegal acts. The people have already seen through Svetlana's notes—that fishwife twaddle—and are laughing at them. But before us stands a generally acknowledged talent, and therein lies the danger of publication. Yet, you feel the pain of your land, even to an extraordinary degree. But you don't feel its joys. *Cancer Ward* is too gloomy and should not be printed. [*Like all preceding and subsequent speakers, he supports Fedin's proposal that Solzhenitsyn himself speak out against the Western slander concerning his letter.*]

YASHEN: The author is not tortured by injustice; he is, rather, poisoned by hatred. People are outraged that there is such a writer in the ranks of the Union of Writers. I would like to propose his expulsion from the Union. He is not the only one who suffered, but the others understand the tragedy of the time better. The hand of a master is discernible in *Cancer Ward*. The author knows the subject better than any physician or professor. As for the siege of Leningrad, he now blames "still others" besides Hitler. Whom? We don't know. Is it Beria? Or today's outstanding leaders? He should speak out plainly. (*All the same, the speaker supports Tvardovsky's decision to work on the story with the author,* [remarking that] *it could then be shown to a limited number of people.*)

KERBABAEV: I read *Cancer Ward* with a feeling of great dissatisfaction. Everyone is a former prisoner, everything is gloomy, there is not a single word of warmth. It is downright nauseating to read. Vera offers the hero her home and her embraces, but he renounces life. And then there is [the remark] "twenty-nine weep and one laughs"—how are we to understand this? Does this refer to the Soviet Union? I agree with what my friend Korneichuk said. Why does the author see only the black? Why don't I write about the black? I always strive to write only about joyful things. It is not enough that he has repudiated *Feast of the Conquerors*. I would consider it courageous if he would renounce *Cancer Ward*. Then I would embrace him like a brother.

SHARIPOV: I wouldn't make any allowances in his case—I'd expel him from the Union. In his play, not only everything Soviet but even Suvorov is presented negatively. I completely agree: let him repudiate *Cancer Ward*. Our republic has reclaimed virgin and disused lands and is proceeding to score one success after another.

NOVICHENKO: The letter with its inadmissible appeal was sent to the Congress over the head of the formal addressee. I approve Tvardovsky's stern words that we should decisively condemn this kind of conduct. I disagree with the principal demands of the letter: it is impossible to let everything be printed. Wouldn't that also mean the publication of

Feast of the Conquerors? Concerning *Cancer Ward*, I have complicated feelings. I am no child, my time will come to die, perhaps in an agony like that of Solzhenitsyn's heroes. But then the crucial issue will be: How is your conscience? What are your moral reserves? If the novel had been confined to these things, I would have considered it necessary to publish it. But there was the base interference in our literary life—the caricatured scene with Rusanov's daughter, which is not congruent with our literary traditions. The ideological and political sense of moral socialism is the negation of Marxism-Leninism. All these things are completely unacceptable to us, to our society, and to our people. Even if this novel were put into some kind of shape, it would not be a novel of socialist realism but only an ordinary, competent work.

MARKOV: This has been a valuable discussion. [*The speaker notes that he has just returned from Siberia, where he spoke before a mass audience five times.*] I must say that nowhere did Solzhenitsyn's name create any particular stir. In one place only was a note submitted to me. I ask your forgiveness, but this is exactly the way it was written: "Just when is this Dolzhenitsyn [sic!] going to stop reviling Soviet literature?" We await a completely clear answer from Solzhenitsyn to the bourgeois slander; we await his statement in the press. He must defend his honor as a Soviet writer.

As for his declaration with regard to *Feast of the Conquerors*, he took a load off my mind. I view *Cancer Ward* in the same light as Surkov does. After all, the thing does have some worth on some kind of practical plane. But the social and political settings in it are utterly unacceptable to me. Its culprits remain nameless. What with the excellent collaboration that has been established between *Novyi mir* and Aleksandr Isaevich, this story can be finished, even though it requires very serious work. But, of course, it would be impossible to put it into print today. So what next? [Let me suggest some] constructive advice: That Aleksandr Isaevich prepare the kind of statement for the press that we talked about. This would be very good just on the eve of the holiday.[8] Then it would be possible to issue some kind of communiqué from the Secretariat. All the same, I still consider him our comrade. But, Aleksandr Isaevich, it's your fault and no one else's that we find ourselves in this complicated situation. As to the suggestions concerning expulsion from the Union— given the conditions of comradeship that are supposed to prevail, we should not be unduly hasty.

SOLZHENITSYN: I have already spoken out against discussion of *Feast of the Conquerors* several times today, but I shall have to do so again. In the final analysis, I can rebuke all of you for not being adherents of the theory of development, if you seriously believe that in twenty years' time and in the face of a complete change in all circumstances, a man does not change. But I have heard an even more serious thing here: Korneichuk, Baruzdin and someone else mentioned that "the people are reading *Feast of the Conquerors*," as if this play was being disseminated. I shall now speak very slowly; let my every word be taken down accurately.

If *Feast of the Conquerors* is being widely circulated or printed, I solemnly declare that the full responsibility lies with the organization that had the only remaining copy—one not read by anyone—and used it for "publication" of the play during my lifetime and against my will; it is this organization that is disseminating the play! For a year and a half, I have repeatedly warned that this is very dangerous. I imagine that there is no reading room there, that one is handed the play and takes it home. But at home there are sons and daughters, and desk drawers are not always locked. I had already issued a warning before, and I am issuing it again today!

Now, as to *Cancer Ward*. I am being criticized for the very title [of the story], which is said to deal not with a medical case but with some kind of symbol. I reply that this symbol is indeed harmful, if it can be perceived only by a person who had himself experienced cancer and all the stages of dying. The fact is that the subject is specifically and literally cancer, [a subject] which is avoided in literature, but which those who are stricken with it know only too well from daily experience. This includes your relatives—and, perhaps soon, someone among those present will be confined to a ward for cancer patients, and then he will understand what kind of a "symbol" it is.

I absolutely do not understand why *Cancer Ward* is accused of being antihumanitarian. Quite the reverse is true—life conquers death, the past is conquered by the future. By my very nature, were this not the case, I would not have undertaken to write it. But I do not believe that it is the task of literature, with respect to either society or the individual, to conceal the truth or to tone it down. Rather, I believe that it is the task of literature to tell people the real truth as they expect it. Moreover, it is not the task of the writer to defend or criticize one or another mode of distributing the social product or to defend or criticize one or another form of government organization. The task of the writer is to select more universal and eternal questions, [such as] the secrets of the human heart and conscience, the confrontation between life and death, the triumph over spiritual sorrow, the laws in the history of mankind that were born in the depths of time immemorial and that will cease to exist only when the sun ceases to shine.

I am disturbed by the fact that [some] comrades simply did not read certain passages of the story attentively and hence formed the wrong impressions. For example, "twenty-nine weep and one laughs" was a popular camp saying addressed to the type of person who would try to go to the head of the queue. Kostoglotov comes out with this saying only so that he may be recognized, that's all. And, from this, people draw the conclusion that the phrase is supposed to apply to the entire Soviet Union. Or the case of "the Rhesus monkey." She appears twice [in the story], and, from the comparison, it becomes clear that this evil person who spills tobacco in people's eyes is meant to represent Stalin specifically. And why the protest over my "just for the hell of it"? If "just for the hell of it" does not apply, does that mean that this was normal or necessary?

Surkov surprised me. At first, I couldn't even understand why he was talking about Marx. Where does Marx come into my story? Aleksei Aleksandrovich, you are a poet, a man with sensitive artistic taste; yet, in this case, your imagination played a dirty trick on you. You didn't grasp the meaning of this scene. Shubin cites Bacon's ideas and employs his terminology. He says "idols of the market," and Kostoglotov tries to imagine a marketplace and in the center a gray idol; Shubin says "idols of the theater," and Kostoglotov pictures an idol inside a theater—but that doesn't work, and so it must be an idol in a theater square. How could you imagine that this referred to Moscow and to the monument to Marx that had not yet even been built? . . .

Comrade Surkov said that, only a few weeks after [Akhmatova's] "Requiem" had been passed from hand to hand, it was published abroad. Well, *Cancer Ward* (Part I) has been in circulation for more than a year. And this is what concerns me, and this is why I am hurrying the Secretariat.

One more piece of advice was given to me by Comrade Riurikov—to repudiate Russian realism. Placing my hand on my heart, I swear that I shall never do it.

RIURIKOV: I did not say that you should repudiate Russian realism but, rather, your role as it is interpreted in the West.

SOLZHENITSYN: Now, concerning the suggestion of Konstantin Aleksandrovich. Well, of course I do not welcome it. Publicity is precisely what I am relentlessly trying to attain. We have concealed things long enough—we have had enough of hiding our speeches and our transcripts under seven locks. Now, we had a [previous] discussion of *Cancer Ward*. The Prose Section decided to send a transcript of the discussion to interested editorial boards. Some likelihood of that! They have hidden it; they barely agreed to give me, the author, a copy. As for today's transcript, Konstantin Aleksandrovich, may I hope to receive a copy?

Konstantin Aleksandrovich asked: "What interest would be served should your protests be printed?" In my estimation, this is clear: the interest of Soviet literature. Yet it's strange that Konstantin Aleksandrovich says that I should resolve the situation. I am bound hand and foot and my mouth is closed—how am I to resolve the situation? It seems to me that this would be an easier matter for the mighty Union of Writers. My every line is suppressed, while the entire press is in the hands of the Union. Still, I don't understand and don't see why my letter was not read at the Congress. Konstantin Aleksandrovich proposes that the fight be waged not against the causes but, rather, against the effects and against the furor in the West surrounding my letter. You wish me to print a refutation—of what, precisely? I can make no statement whatsoever concerning an unprinted letter. And, most important, my letter contains a general part and a personal part. Should I renounce the general part? Well, the fact is that I am still of the same mind as I was then, and I do not renounce a single word. After all, what is the letter about?

VOICES: About censorship.

SOLZHENITSYN: You haven't understood anything if you think it is about censorship. This letter is about the destiny of our great literature, which once conquered and captivated the world but which has now lost its standing. In the West, they say the [Russian] novel is dead, and we gesticulate and deliver speeches saying that it is not dead. But, rather than make speeches, we should publish novels—such novels as would make them blink as if from a brilliant light, and then the "new novel" would die down and then the "neo–avant-gardists" would disappear. I have no intention of repudiating the general part of my letter. Should I, then, declare that the eight points in the personal part of my letter are unjust and false? But they are all just. Should I say that some of the points [I protested about] have already been eliminated or corrected? But not one of them has been eliminated or corrected. What, then, can I declare? No, it is you who must clear at least a little path for such a statement: first, publish my letter, issue the Union's communiqué concerning the letter, and indicate which of the eight points are being corrected. Then I will be able to make my statement, willingly. If you wish, you can also publish my statement today concerning *Feast of the Conquerors*, even though I neither understand the discussion of stolen plays nor the refutation of unprinted letters. On June 12, here at the Secretariat, I was assured that the communiqué would be printed unconditionally. and yet, today, conditions are posed. What has changed [the situation]?

My book *Ivan Denisovich* is banned. New slanders continue to be directed at me. You can refute them, but I cannot. The only comfort I have is that I will never get a heart attack from this slander because I've been hardened in the Stalinist camps.

FEDIN: No, this is not the proper sequence. You must make the first public statement. Since you have received so many approving comments on your talent and style, you will find the proper form, you can do it. Your idea of our acting first, then you, has no sound basis.

TVARDOVSKY: And will the letter itself be published in this process?

FEDIN: No, the letter should have been published right away. Now that foreign countries have beat us to it, why should we publish it?

SOLZHENITSYN: Better late than never. So nothing will change regarding my eight points?

FEDIN: We'll see about that later.

SOLZHENITSYN: Well, I have already replied, and I hope that everything has been accurately transcribed.

SURKOV: You should state whether you renounce your role of leader of the political opposition in our country—the role they ascribe to you in the West.

SOLZHENITSYN: Aleksei Aleksandrovich, it really makes me sick to hear such a thing—and from you of all persons: an artist with words and a leader of the political opposition. How does that jibe?

[*Several brief statements follow, demanding that Solzhenitsyn accept what was said by Fedin.*]

VOICES: Well, what do you say?

SOLZHENITSYN: I repeat once again that I am unable to provide such a statement, since the Soviet reader would have no idea what it is all about.

NOTES

1. A novel by Aleksandr Bek was reportedly first approved, then rejected, for publication in the May, 1968, issue of *Novyi mir.*—ED.
2. Four prose poems by Solzhenitsyn were published in *The New Leader*, January 18, 1965.—ED.
3. A sixteenth-century philosopher, burned by the Inquisition for disputing a number of ecclesiastical dogmas, including the concept of a geocentric universe.—ED.
4. An English translation appeared in *Encounter* (London), May, 1963.—ED.
5. Gorky's column "Untimely Thoughts," which appeared in the paper *Novaia zhizn* (Petrograd) during 1917–18, criticized the Revolution as "premature" and warned that Lenin's policies could result in a return to "barbarism" and "oriental despotism." Sergeev-Tsensky also expressed initial misgivings about the Revolution, though, in time, he wrote with growing optimist of the Soviet era.—ED.
6. The poem was dedicated to the memory of Stalin's victims; it appeared in the Soviet Union in heavily censored form.—ED.
7. General Gorbatov's memoirs appeared in English under the title *Years of My Life* (New York: Norton, 1967).—ED.
8. A reference to the fiftieth anniversary of the October Revolution.—ED.

53. *Zimianin on Solzhenitsyn* et al.

[*The following remarks were made by M. V. Zimianin, Editor-in-Chief of* Pravda, *during a private meeting with Soviet journalists at Leningrad in October, 1967.*—ED.]

Recently there has been a great deal of slander in the Western press against several of our writers whose works have played into the hands of our enemies. The campaign by the Western press in defense of [Valeri] Tarsis ceased only when he went to the West, where it became evident that he was not in his right mind.

At the moment, [Aleksandr] Solzhenitsyn occupies an important place in the propaganda of capitalist governments. He is also a psychologically unbalanced person, a schizophrenic. Formerly he had been a prisoner and, justly or unjustly, was subsequently subjected to repressions. Now he takes his revenge against the government through his literary works. The only topic he is able to write about is life in a concentration camp. This topic has become an obsession with him. Solzhenitsyn's works are aimed against the Soviet regime, in which he finds only sores and cancerous tumors. He doesn't see anything positive in our society.

I have occasion to read unpublished works in the course of my duties, and, among them, I read Solzhenitsyn's play *Feast of the Conqueror*. The play is about repressions against those returning from the front. It is genuine anti-Soviet literature. In the old days, people were even imprisoned for works of this kind.

We obviously cannot publish his works. Solzhenitsyn's demand that we do so cannot be honored. If he writes stories that correspond to the interests of our society, then his works will be published. He will not be deprived of his bread and butter. Solzhenitsyn is a teacher of physics; let him teach. He very much likes to make public speeches and often appears before various audiences to read his works. He has been given such opportunities. He considers himself a literary genius.

Among the other names that come up quite often in the Western press, one must not forget [Yevgeni] Yevtushenko and [Andrei] Voznesensky. We have beautiful poetry and a great many poets who write wonderful poems. But, in the West, they basically recognize only these two, because they find in their works passages worth using in their propaganda. We, of course, cannot consider the works of these poets to be anti-Soviet like those of Solzhenitsyn. They write good patriotic works, too. They are not that young any longer, although everyone thinks of them as being young; their works, however, lack the necessary political maturity. That is why they sometimes play into the hands of our enemies. I know them and have spoken with them about this. But they also consider themselves geniuses.

Take Yevtushenko. Recently, during a closed meeting, he was criticized by [Sergei] Pavlov, the Secretary of the Central Committee of the VLKSM (Komsomol). So Yevtushenko replied in words that were four times more powerful, ten times more powerful. He made fun of Pavlov in a poem. In this way, he branded him forever.

Then there is the tale of Voznesensky. Last year he went to the U.S.A.; he read his poetry there before large audiences. He had a great success and also profited financially. He was getting ready to go on a tour of American cities again this year. His trip was already arranged; it was publicized in the U.S.A., and his visa was reserved at the American Embassy. At this time, the war in the Middle East broke out. Our relations with the U.S.A. deteriorated. The Board of Administration of the Writers' Union clearly hinted to Voznesensky that it would be better for him not to go to the U.S.A. at that time. Simultaneously, the administration told the American Embassy that the poet was ill.

What did Voznesensky do? I came to the office on Monday morning and glanced through my mail. There was a letter from Voznesensky accusing the Writers' Union. I telephoned him at home. I was told that he had left and that his destination was unknown. I telephoned the Central Committee. They answered that they, too, had received a letter from Voznesensky and that they also had telephoned him at home but had not been able to locate him. One day went by, then another. No Voznesensky. Then suddenly I learned that the BBC had broadcast Voznesensky's letter to *Pravda*. He did not appear until a week later. Apparently he had been sitting it out at a *dacha* on the outskirts of Moscow. I invited him to come and see me. He denied having given the letter to Western journalists.[1]

I told him that he might get off with a reprimand the first time, but, if he ever did it again, he would be ground to dust. I myself would see to it that not a trace of him remained.

Some thought that we should have published his letter and given him an answer. But why make this sordid story a topic of general discussion?

NOTE

1. Voznesensky also openly condemned the Soviet literary bureaucrats for their "boorish," "provocative," and "mendacious" interference in literary affairs (*Problems of Communism*, September–October, 1968, p. 55).—ED.

54. *Writers' Union to Solzhenitsyn*

November 25, 1967

[Letter] No. 3142
To: Comrade A. I. Solzhenitsyn

Dear Aleksandr Isaevich!
At the meeting of the Secretariat of the Board of the Union of Writers of the U.S.S.R. on September 22 of this year, at which your letters were discussed, in addition to sharp criticism of your act, the comrades expressed the well-intentioned thought that you should have sufficient time to reflect carefully on all that was discussed at the Secretariat and only then make a public statement clarifying your position on the anti-Soviet campaign surrounding your name and your letters that has been launched by hostile foreign propaganda. Two months have passed.
The Secretariat would like to know what decision you have reached.

Respectfully,
N. VORONKOV

(On behalf of the Secretariat)
Secretary, Board of the Union
of Writers of the U.S.S.R.

55. *Solzhenitsyn to Writers' Union (2)*

December 1, 1967

[There are a number of things] I am unable to understand from your (letter) No. 3142 dated November 25, 1967:
1. Does the Secretariat intend to defend me against the slander (calling it unfriendly would be an understatement) that has been going on without interruption for three years in my homeland? (New facts: On October 5, 1967, at a very crowded assemblage of listeners at the House

of the Press in Leningrad, the editor-in-chief of *Pravda*, Zimianin, repeated the tiresome lie that I had been a prisoner of war, and he also tried the old trick used against those who have fallen from grace in announcing that I am a schizophrenic and that my labor-camp past is an obsessive idea. The MGK [Ministry of State Control] also set forth new false versions to the effect that I allegedly "tried putting together in the army" either a "defeatist" or a "terrorist" organization. It is incomprehensible why the military collegium of the Supreme Court did not detect this in my case.)

2. What measures did the Secretariat take to nullify the illegal ban on the use of my published works in libraries and the censorship decree prohibiting any mention of my name in critical articles? (*Voprosy literatury* applied this ban even to . . . a translation of a Japanese article. At the University of Perm, sanctions were invoked against a group of students who sought to discuss my published works in their academic review.)

3. Does the Secretariat wish to prevent the unchecked appearance of *Cancer Ward* abroad, or does it remain indifferent to this menace? Are any steps being taken to publish excerpts from the novel in *Literaturnaia gazeta* and [to publish] the whole novel in *Novyi mir*?

4. Does the Secretariat intend to appeal to the government to join the International Copyright Convention? Doing so would enable our authors to obtain reliable means of protecting their works from foreign pirating and shameless commercial competition.

5. In the six months since I sent my letter to the [Writers'] Congress, has circulation of the unauthorized "edition" of excerpts from my papers been discontinued, and has this "edition" been destroyed?

6. What measures has the Secretariat taken to return to me these papers and the novel *The First Circle*, which they impounded, apart from giving public assurances that they already had been returned (Secretary Ozerov, for instance)?

7. Has the Secretariat accepted or rejected K. Simonov's proposal to publish a volume of my stories?

8. Why is it that, to date, I have not received for my perusal the September 22 stenographic report of the meetings of the Secretariat?

I would be very grateful to have an answer to these questions.

A. SOLZHENITSYN

56. Tvardovsky to Fedin

January 7–15, 1968

Dear Konstantin Aleksandrovich:

After our ninth discussion on the same subject, I am writing to tell you how I feel about Solzhenitsyn's letter to the Secretariat.

This is not an official report to the First Secretary of the Board of the

U.S.S.R. Union of Writers, although I by no means wish to divorce my profound respect for Fedin the writer from the respect I owe to his duties and titles. But I shall try, without all the formal conventions, to talk to you directly, as if we were face to face at your country home or elsewhere.

I shall begin with the main point: whom and what are we really discussing when we refer to the still-unresolved question of Solzhenitsyn? This is a question that provides food for incessant interpretations and reinterpretations in literary circles and elsewhere, interpretations that do not reflect favorably on the leadership of the Union of Writers.

Scarcely anyone will deny that, as a personality, Solzhenitsyn has stood out with striking clarity against the general literary landscape and that this writer attracts both warm adulation and particularly cruel dislike. Let us, for the moment, not ignore the question of which side prevails but simply agree on the fact that the dispute itself is evidence—at the very least—of the commanding stature of this writer.

Indeed, an outstanding aspect of Solzhenitsyn's literary career that cannot be easily minimized is the fact that, although he made his debut when already a mature and full-grown man, his first effort displayed a remarkably original mastery of his craft. The review of *Ivan Denisovich* by K. I. Chukovsky, an experienced critic and writer who cannot, as they say, be easily deceived, was entitled "A Literary Miracle." S. Ya. Marshak, who is now dead but whose literary judgments were equally authoritative, published an article in *Pravda* in which he praised *Ivan Denisovich* as "accurate and true-to-life." In *Izvestia*, K. M. Simonov greeted the appearance of Solzhenitsyn, who he said was a new and remarkable literary talent.

There is no need to enumerate all the well-known and less well-known writers here and abroad who warmly and enthusiastically greeted the first story by this new writer. I shall name only two: you and M. A. Sholokhov.

Your high evaluation of this manuscript by a then-unknown author played a major part in Solzhenitsyn's fate. In my letter to the First Secretary of the CC, CPSU (at that time Khrushchev), urging that *Ivan Denisovich* be published, I referred in particular to your praise of the manuscript. As is well known, *Ivan Denisovich* was published with the knowledge and approval of the Central Committee of the CPSU. At that time, Sholokhov also spoke with warm approval of *Ivan Denisovich* and asked me to convey his congratulations to the author of the story. . . .

There were, it is true, also some adverse reactions to Solzhenitsyn's appearance on the literary scene; some ascribed his immense success wholly to the sensational nature of the subject matter of his book, which is set in a forced-labor camp. For instance, one of the leaders of the Union of Writers predicted that "In three to five months this little story will be forgotten." However, it was not forgotten. In a short time, "this little story" had brought its author extraordinary, ever-increasing popularity, both in our country and abroad, and his name—whether we like it or not—has acquired worldwide fame. He is acclaimed as one of the greatest writers of the present day. No one who has spent time abroad or who has followed the foreign press will contradict this. . . .

The most significant ideological and literary works of recent years owe much to Solzhenitsyn. This is not a question of imitation but simply of inspiration. The author's own innate truthfulness, which does not fear the complexities of life but goes boldly forward to disclose them, has had an influence on readers incomparably greater than that of the "single-season" fiction that smooths over and impoverishes reality according to the latest prescribed formula.

When I spoke earlier of the sharply divergent attitudes toward Solzhenitsyn in literary circles, I did not mean to attribute the hostility toward him solely to envy of his great success, since such envy is inevitable in any sphere of art. The heart of the matter is that a certain number of our writers prefer to write in the old way—because it is easier and they are more accustomed to it. But these writers cannot help but see that our readers no longer want to read things written in the old way—and this is true even of those readers who are most sharply critical of Solzhenitsyn. In short, he has greatly complicated our literary life.

I hope the foregoing will not be misunderstood as an assertion that Solzhenitsyn is completely without defects; I do not see him as the ideal writer, one who cannot be criticized or who has no weaknesses. But we have already spoken on this subject.

It is most urgent now to understand that Solzhenitsyn concerns us not simply as a writer—however highly we may evaluate him—but because, symbolically, he stands at the crossroads of two opposing tendencies in the social consciousness of our literature, one striving to go back, the other to go forward in accordance with the irreversible historical process. That this is precisely the situation is revealed by the many months that we have devoted to discussion of the Solzhenitsyn affair in the long series of expanded, closed, and open sessions in the Secretariat.

I must say bluntly that the nature of these discussions does no honor to the Secretariat or to any of those on whom, as a Chekhov character put it, "everything depends." The unproductive and baseless nature of this whole "affair" can be traced, first, to the fact that all attention, indignation, and condemnation has been directed toward the letter that Solzhenitsyn sent to the delegates of the Congress of Writers. The form of the letter is really deserving of condemnation—here, I agree with everyone else. But, however bad the form may be, one cannot simply, on this basis, exclude the contents of the letter as if it did not exist. The contents of the letter concisely and accurately represent a point of view, and I do not recall a single attempt to refute any one of the statements contained therein or to label them as false, mendacious, selfish, or harmful to Soviet literature as a whole. Why is this? The simple reason is that, on the whole, the arguments are irrefutable. As for me, I would subscribe to them with all my heart. And you know I am by no means alone in holding this opinion. Until now, I have neither written nor signed any of the "documents" concerning Solzhenitsyn's letter, since I think that all the questions that the letter raises should be solved normally by collective discussion in the Secretariat.

You also know that I have repeatedly stated in your presence here, as well as in the Secretariat—as has been recorded—and in the Central Committee, my feelings about censorship and about the personal fate of Solzhenitsyn. I have, in fact, spoken out more sharply than Solzhenitsyn himself. . . .

Another misfortune is caused by the hopeless attempts to solve the problems created by Solzhenitsyn's letter "secretly," despite the fact that the Solzhenitsyn affair has acquired immense social and political significance, . . . has received international publicity, and has caused many literary debates, which continue to this day even far outside literary circles. It is impossible to solve this "question of questions"—which involves not only the Union of Writers but Soviet literary life in general—by "secret" means. How useless it is to mark time, how fruitless our arguments are in secret sessions, and how depressing is our silence outside! The leadership of the Union of Writers seems incapable of making a decision, so how can it emerge and face a large audience directly or publish an article in the press in order finally to close the Solzhenitsyn "affair"? It is obvious that Solzhenitsyn, on the other hand, in presenting his case to the Union of Writers, is ready at any time to speak before an audience or to publish a defense in the press; whereas the Union of Writers is incapable of either condemning or rejecting his claims, of saying anything publicly, because it cannot, in the last analysis, count on the support or sympathies of either its readers or its writers. . . .

What is particularly saddening is the position that you have recently adopted concerning this "affair." You argue that Solzhenitsyn first must offer a rebuff to the West, which has launched an unbridled anti-Soviet campaign in the press and on radio in connection with his letter to the Union of Writers. Otherwise, you will not publish [his book of stories], which, incidentally, has been published not only in all the bourgeois countries but also in all the other socialist countries.

You refuse to protect Solzhenitsyn, a member of the Union of Writers, from the widespread fabrications concerning his past. In other words, not only are the contents of his letter to be ignored, but Solzhenitsyn himself is to be left to suffer political ostracism, despite the absolutely undisputed substance of his letter. To hear that you, Konstantin Aleksandrovich, a great Russian writer, a friend of Gorky and a follower of his tradition of leadership in literature, have agreed to such terms is strange and incomprehensible. How can you associate yourself with the proposal made by Sholokhov, whose letter says in effect: "Don't let Solzhenitsyn write"? It would be especially lamentable for you to associate yourself with the author of *And Quiet Flows the Don* after the notorious literary-political speeches he made, in which he so debased himself in the eyes of his readers and admirers. And, in general, it is sad that you have joined

Sholokhov in this matter, instead of setting an example of an artistic attitude that is worthy of you and alien to petty bureaucratic considerations; it is also sad that you tend to share the position of those comrades in the Secretariat whose dislike of Solzhenitsyn is not surprising.

Above all, the ... istent demand that Solzhenitsyn should express "his attitudes," that he should "give a rebuff," etc., as an essential condition for his further literary and public career seems strange coming from such a person as you. These conditions are obviously reminiscent of the long-condemned and rejected practice of exacting a confession from a writer or drawing "a line of demarcation." Such "confessions" and "lines of demarcation," like those that recently appeared in *Literaturnaia gazeta*, signed by G. Serebriakova, A. Voznesensky, etc., do us immense harm by giving rise to the concept that our writers are morally and ethically un-discriminating, deprived of a sense of their own dignity, or wholly dependent upon "instructions" or "demands" (which, incidentally, are one and the same thing). Do you really think that such confessions are to the advantage of the Union of Writers? Do they strengthen its authority? I cannot believe that. . . .

It is absurd to think that the solution of this whole Solzhenitsyn controversy could depend on a single secret "piece of paper"! That is the level to which we have been reduced! A piece of paper—one or two pages long—has become more important for us writers than a novel 600 pages long—a novel that is already prepared for publication and that might become, according to a majority of those who have read the manuscript, the treasure and the pride of our literature today. Is it possible that this piece of paper is more important than the fate of a writer whose remark-able talent is not disputed even by his fiercest antagonists? . . .

I want to say something about *Cancer Ward*. . . . I think that, essentially, we are even more interested in the publication of this novel than in its author. It is not only that a significant work is being criminally concealed from a large number of Soviet readers but also that, at the same time, the novel is being distributed by the thousands to those "meticulous readers" in the West. . . .

The first eight chapters of *Cancer Ward* were being prepared for the January issue of *Novyi mir*; then publication plans were suspended. *Cancer Ward* is but one in a whole list of great and valuable works that have been held up (although not banned), such as *A Hundred Days of the War*, by K. Simonov; *The New Appointment*, a story by A. Bek; a work by Ye. Drabkina devoted to the final years of Lenin's life, called *The Winter Crossing*. I could list many more. Publication of *Cancer Ward*, which, in itself, would be a literary event, would unblock the traffic jam that has formed, as on a road when the leading truck breaks down. This would be of indisputable benefit to Soviet literature in its present crisis—to be blunt—in its present extremely unhappy stage. It would remove the atmosphere of gloomy "silence," as well as the serious misunderstandings, the lack of clarity, the pointless waiting. . . .

And all this now depends entirely on you, Konstantin Aleksandrovich.

The Secretariat, of course, would support you if you took a stand in support of publication—even with all the necessary reservations. You would only have to say what has already been said in the Secretariat during the discussions of *Cancer Ward*. In other words, I call upon you to return to the "communiqué" that was signed by me, edited by you, and then suddenly rescinded because of your present attitude on the question. This document is in the files of the 'Solzhenitsyn affair," and I shall not cite it in its entirety because I have detained you enough without that, although I have not said even a tenth of what I should.

Here, then, are my concrete proposals, the implementation of which, in my opinion, would even now be advantageous in every sense:

1. *Literaturnaia gazeta* should immediately publish extracts from *Cancer Ward* with a footnote saying "this novel is to be published in full in *Novyi mir*."

2. The Soviet Writer publishing house should be instructed to prepare an anthology of Solzhenitsyn's works for printing, with a foreword that would give, *inter alia*, the biography of the author.

3. This foreword should be published in *Literaturnaia gazeta* or *Literaturnaia Rossiia* with appropriate footnotes. . . .

I am not so naively optimistic as to think that, after hearing my advice, you will suddenly burst into tears and change your point of view concerning the "Solzhenitsyn affair." But I do not doubt that, in time, you will change your point of view, simply because changing circumstances will force you to.

"But what can I do?" This was your reply to me when I reproached you for the injustice of deliberately placing impossible demands on Solzhenitsyn. This happened at the session where we were sitting together! I do not remember what I said then, but I do remember your words, that you showed confusion, dissatisfaction with yourself and with all of us. Only one thing can be done now: to act according to your own conscience and intelligence. . . .

Thank God the times are past when only a "wagging finger" was needed to decide the specific problems of art or science, ignoring the opinions of the people who work in these specific fields. Whether we are bad or good, it is up to us and to no one else to decide the problems of literature. We should not now be waiting for direct "instructions." Instructions will not come, and that is a step forward, one that, in past times, we would not have dreamt possible. We should make use of our progress by discarding our fears, without, of course, releasing ourselves from our responsibility.

In general, we do not know which is the more dangerous: to choose a course of action that may prove erroneous or to take no action at all for fear of making a mistake. In war, making a decision, even if it is erroneous, is preferable to waiting irresolutely.

Moreover, you know as well as I that the history of world literature contains no case in which the persecution of a man of talent—even by talented men—was crowned with success. But, in our case, in the long run, it is better to make a mistake by publishing than to avoid mistakes (if they could be avoided!) by banning a novel. In the present situation, I consider that, for you, the real danger is that you may seal a shameful decision with your signature or—just as shameful—that you may make no decision at all in the "Solzhenitsyn affair."

I know you, Konstantin Aleksandrovich, as a writer, and I have known you from my early youth. . . . I have heard much about you from S. Ya. Marshak, who is now dead, and from others who knew you in Leningrad. They all said that Fedin is an honorable man, a man capable of standing up to defend what is right and to come to the aid of a comrade. . . . But now I am compelled to say some cruel things to you, which perhaps will offend you, but I have already said them at our recent meeting concerning this "case." You know that the dog who barks does not bite. I am a blunt person, and perhaps I not infrequently do myself harm by lacking restraint. . . .

The sharpness of my retorts to you at our last meeting with P. Markov and K. Voronkov was caused by the irritation—which I find incomprehensible—with which you speak of A. I. Solzhenitsyn. It is impossible to speak in such a way of a man and a writer who has paid for every page and every line as none of us has who are now judging him and wrangling over how to deal with him. He has endured the supreme trials of the human soul—war, imprisonment, and a lethal illness. And now, er so successful a debut in the literary world, he has had to bear other rials, including political pressure, surreptitious literary ostracism, direct slander, the banning of any mention of his name in the press, and so on. Frankly speaking, what is the point of using for an indictment against him papers that were taken from him by "special methods," including the manuscript of a play written more than twenty years ago in the hell of a forced-labor camp, a play written by Prisoner Sh-232, a man without a name, and not by A. Solzhenitsyn, whom we know as a member of the Union of Writers? This play was then reproduced in countless copies so that people might study it as allegedly the latest work of the writer!

Yes, I condemn the form of his "letter," but I cannot in all humanity cast stones at him, because I understand the depths of despair that compelled him to take that step.

On the third day of sitting at my desk writing this letter, I received a telephone call from the State Literary Publishing House. A voice said: "In your article on Marshak, which is to be published in the fifth volume of your complete works, you mention the name Solzhenitsyn. . . . We have our instructions." Of course, I refused to exclude the mention of Solzhenitsyn although this might threaten the publication of the fifth volume. Is it not amazing that such things can happen!

I am ending my letter, as I have already said, without much hope of a favorable outcome. Perhaps some of what I have written is incorrect and some is controversial. But I had to write for the sake of my duty and my conscience.

I do not expect a reply from you, because I know that you have little time, and because it is not the reply that interests me: the reply should be the resolution of the "Solzhenitsyn affair," which we have awaited these many months.

We must bring this affair to an end, my dear Konstantin Aleksandrovich.

With unchanging respect and with the very best wishes.

Yours,

TVARDOVSKY

57. Kaverin to Fedin

January 25, 1968

OPEN LETTER

To Konstantin Fedin:

We have known each other forty-eight years, Kostia. We were childhood friends. We have the right as friends to judge one another. It is more than a right, it is an obligation. Your former friends have pondered more than once what motives could have prompted your behavior in those unforgettable events in our literary life that strengthened some of us but transformed others into obedient bureaucrats far removed from genuine art.

Who doesn't remember, for example, the senseless and tragic history of Pasternak's novel, which did a great deal of damage to our country? Your involvement in that affair went so deep that you were forced to pretend that you didn't know of the death of the poet who had been your friend and had lived alongside you for twenty-three years. Perhaps the crowd of thousands that accompanied him, that carried him on outstretched arms past your house, was not visible from your window. How did it happen that you not only did not support *Literaturnaia Moskva*, an anthology that was indispensable to our literature, but crushed it?[1] After all, on the eve of the meeting of 1500 writers in the cinema actors' building, you supported its publication. With an already prepared and dangerously treacherous speech in your pocket, you praised our work without finding even a trace of anything politically undesirable in it.

This is far from everything, but I do not propose in this letter to summarize your public activities, which are widely known in writers' circles. Not without reason, on the seventy-fifth birthday of Paustovsky, [the mention of] your name was greeted with complete silence. After the banning of Solzhenitsyn's novel *Cancer Ward*, which had already been set in type by *Novyi mir*, it will not surprise me if your very next appearance before a wide audiences of writers is received with whistles and footstamping.

Of course, your position in literature should have prepared us to some degree for this staggering fact. One must go very far back to discover the very first point at which the process of spiritual deformation and irreversible change began. For years and years, it went on beneath the surface and did not come into any striking contradiction to your position —a position that at times, although one could not exactly approve of it, could somehow be explained in historical terms. But what is pushing you along that path *now*, with the result that once again our literature will suffer gravely? Don't you understand that the mere act of publishing *Cancer Ward* would relieve the unprecedented tension in the literary world, break down the undeserved distrust of writers, and open the way for other books that would enrich our literture? A. Bek's superb novel, which was first authorized and then forbidden although unconditionally approved by the best writers in the country, just lies there in manuscript form. So do the war diaries of K. Simonov. One could scarcely find a single serious writer who does not have in his desk a manuscript that has been submitted, deliberated upon, and prohibited for unclear reasons that exceed the bounds of common sense. Thus, behind the scenes of the imaginary well-being proclaimed by the leadership, a strong, original literature is growing—the spiritual treasure of the country that it (the country) urgently and keenly needs. Don't you see that our tremendous historical experience demands its own embodiment [in literature] and that you are joining forces with those who, for the sake of their own well-being, are trying to halt this inevitable process?

But let's return to Solzhenitsyn's novel. There is now no editorial board or literary organization where it is not being said that [Georgi] Markov and [Konstantin] Voronkov were *for* the publication of the novel and that the typesetting was broken up only because you spoke out decisively against it. This means that the novel will remain in thousands of (separate) pages, passing from hand to hand and selling, it is said, for a good sum of money. It also means that it will be published abroad. We will be giving it away to the reading public of Italy, France, England and Western Germany; that is to say, the very thing that Solzhenitsyn himself repeatedly and energetically protested against will occur.

Perhaps there can be found in the leadership of the Writers' Union people who think that they will be punishing the author by giving his book away to foreign publishers. They will punish him by [giving him] a worldwide notoriety that our opponents will use for political ends. Or do they think that Solzhenitsyn will "mend his ways" and begin to write in another way? This is ridiculous in reference to an artist who is a rare example, who persistently reminds us that we are working in the literary tradition of Chekhov and Tolstoy.

But your path has still another meaning. You are taking upon yourself a responsibility, apparently without realizing its immensity and significance. A writer who puts a noose around the neck of another writer is one whose place in the history of literature will be determined not by what he himself may have written but by what was written by his victim. Perhaps, without even suspecting it yourself, you will become the focus of hostility, indignation, and resentment in literary circles.

This can be altered only if you find in yourself the strength and courage to repudiate your decision.

You undoubtedly understand how difficult it is for me to write you this letter. But I do not have the right to keep silent.

V. KAVERIN

NOTE

1. Two volumes of the anthology *Literaturnaia Moskva* appeared in late 1956 and early 1957. See Hugh McLean and Walter N. Vickery (eds.), *The Year of Protest—1956* (New York: Vintage Russian Library, 1961), for translations of most of the contents.—ED.

58. *Solzhenitsyn to* Literaturnaia gazeta

April 21, 1968

I have learned from a news story published in *Le Monde* on April 13 that parts of my novel *Cancer Ward* are being printed in various Western countries, and that the publishers—Mondadori (Italy) and The Bodley Head (England)—are already fighting over the copyright to this novel since the U.S.S.R. does not participate in the Universal Copyright Convention—despite the fact that the author is still living!

I would like to state that no foreign publisher has received from me either the manuscript of this novel or permission to publish it. Thus, I do not recognize as legal any publication of this novel without my authorization, in the present or the future, and I do not grant the copyright to anyone. I will prosecute any distortion of the text (which is inevitable in view of the uncontrolled duplication and distribution of the manuscript) as well as any unauthorized adaptation of the work for the cinema or theater.[1]

I already know from my own experience that all the translations of *One Day in the Life of Ivan Denisovich* were spoiled by haste. Evidently the same fate awaits *Cancer Ward* as well. But besides money, there is literature.

A. SOLZHENITSYN

NOTE

1. Before this letter was published in *Literaturnaia gazeta*, on June 26, 1968, it had already appeared in *L'Unità* (Rome), on June 4. In the latter version, this sentence reads as follows: "All distortions of the text (which are inevitable in view of the uncontrolled duplication and distribution of the manuscript) are harmful to me; I denounce and forbid any arbitrary adaptation of the work for the cinema or theater."

59. *Solzhenitsyn to Writers and Newspapers*

April 18, 1968

To: The Secretariat of the Union of Writers of the U.S.S.R.
   The journal *Novyi mir*
   Literaturnaia gazeta
   Members of the Union of Writers

At the editorial offices of *Novyi mir*, I was shown the [following] telegram:

IMO177. Frankfurt-am-Main. Ch 2 9 16.20. Tvardovsky. *Novyi mir*. This is to inform you that the Committee of State Security, acting through Victor Louis, has sent one more copy of *Cancer Ward* to the West, in order thus to block its publication in *Novyi mir*. Accordingly we have decided to publish this work immediately—*The editors of the journal* Grani.

I should like to protest against both the publication [of the work] in *Grani* and the actions of V. Louis, but the turbid and provocative nature of the telegram requires, first of all, the clarification of the following:

1. Whether the telegram was actually sent by the editors of the journal *Grani* or whether it was sent by a fictitious person (this can be established through the international telegraph system; the Moscow telegraph office can wire Frankfurt-am-Main).

2. Who is Victor Louis, what kind of person is he, of what country is he a citizen? Did he really take a copy of *Cancer Ward* out of the Soviet Union, to whom did he give it, and where else are they threatening to publish it? Furthermore, what does the Committee of State Security have to do with this?

If the Secretariat of the Writers' Union is interested in establishing the truth and stopping the threatened publication of *Cancer Ward* in Russian abroad, I believe that it will help to get prompt answers to these questions.

This episode compels us to reflect on the terrible and dark avenues by which the manuscripts of Soviet writers can reach the West. It constitutes an extreme reminder to us that literature must not be brought to a state in which literary works become a profitable commodity for any scoundrel who happens to have a travel visa. The works of our authors must be printed in their own country and must not become the plunder of foreign publishing houses.

SOLZHENITSYN

60. *Solzhenitsyn to Writers' Union Members*

To the Members of the Union of Writers of the U.S.S.R.

Almost a year has passed since I sent my unanswered questions to the Writers' Congress. Since that time, I have written to the Secretariat of the Union of Writers and have been there three times in person. Nothing has changed to this very day: my archives have not been returned, my books are not being published, and my name is interdicted. I have urgently informed the Secretariat of the danger of my works being taken abroad, since they have been extensively circulated from hand to hand for a long time. Not only did the Secretariat not assist in the publication of *Cancer Ward*, which had already been set up in type at *Novyi mir*, but it has stubbornly acted against such publication and even hindered the Moscow prose section from *discussing* the second part of the story.

A year has passed and the inevitable has happened: recently, chapters from *Cancer Ward* were published in the [London] *Times Literary Supplement*. Nor are further printings precluded—perhaps of inaccurate and incompletely edited versions. What has happened compels me to acquaint our literary community with the contents of the attached letters and statements, so that the position and responsibility of the Secretariat of the Union of Writers of the U.S.S.R. will be clear.

The enclosed transcript of the Secretariat's meeting of September 22, 1967, written by me personally, is of course incomplete, but it is absolutely accurate and will provide sufficient information pending the publication of the entire transcript.

SOLZHENITSYN

Enclosures:
1. My letter to all (forty-two) secretaries of the Writers' Union dated September 12, 1967.
2. Transcript of the session of the Secretariat, September 22, 1967.
3. Letter from K. Voronkov, February 25, 1967.
4. My letter to the Secretariat, December 1, 1967.

61. *Speech by G. Svirsky*

January 16, 1968

Two years ago, the Moscow writers informed comrade Demichev, Secretary of the Central Committee, of the difficulties facing social literature. As the activities report of the Party committee stated, censorship had become inexplicably powerful: the works of Soviet writers were being either proscribed or mutilated. Comrade Demichev agreed that no one could live and work under such conditions. "We are going to correct them," he promised.

And what has happened? Has the censorship been brought back within legal bounds? Does it now concern itself only with military and state secrets? Not at all!

Cruel and unsparing as a flood, it has invaded all social literature. The Writers' Union has tried to save at least some books by great artists—Solzhenitsyn, Bek, and others. So what? The opinion of the writers' collective means nothing today. Figuratively speaking, the Writers' Union has been engulfed by the flood, like the city of Kitezh.[1] Only the spires emerge above the floodwaters of the censorship. . . .

An official act of the government gave our collective farms the right to decide for themselves what they would plant and cultivate. Economic reform is underway in industry. Many people are being called on to take part in public life. Only the Writers' Union stands outside this natural and healthy process.

Every writer has his conscience as a citizen. The Communist writer also has a Party conscience. He must answer for what he writes. But the right of answering to the people for what he writes has been taken from him. The writer is humiliated, stripped of the one essential thing—the right to make his inner thoughts and feelings known to the people and to speak responsibly without the intervention of a pseudo-secret authority that has arrogated to itself the right to decide everything for him, striking out whatever it pleases. The sociological writer, today, feels that he is a second- or third-class citizen. He is crushed by a life without the protection of law, crushed by the militant primitivism of the censorship authorities.

But is all this perhaps not true? Do the censorship authorities perhaps have the right to do what they are doing? Let us examine things calmly, on the basis of fact. Calmly and thoughtfully.

In Leningrad the play *Dion* was prohibited; in Moscow it was authorized.[2] The film *Before the Tribunal of History* was authorized in Moscow and Leningrad but prohibited in Gorky and some other cities and towns. One of the Moscow literary reviews was forbidden to mention the name of Solzhenitsyn, even in an article devoted to Soviet literature abroad. But an editorial office in a neighboring street was permitted to do so. [*Stir in the hall.*]

In the last few decades, V. Pomerantsev's best stories have been cut out of his books. Concerning one of them, for example, the official conclusion was that it "discredited the Soviet procuracy." A few months later, the same story appeared in the semiofficial review of the procuracy of the U.S.S.R., *Socialist Legality*. (*Noise in the hall.*)

Arbitrary action on the part of the decision-making authorities has become customary. Thus, Simonov's and Ordynsky's film *If Your Home Is Dear to You* is enthusiastically received by moviegoers but is banned for the Army. And M. Shatrov's play *The Bolsheviks* has never been officially authorized; yet it is being performed without the permission of *Glavlit*.[3]

The uncontrolled manipulation of texts and the elimination of whole chapters have become the rule. Let anyone start talking to any writer about the censor's whims, and one will soon be interrupted with: "That's nothing! Take me, for example. . . ." (*Laughter in the hall.*)

When one hears about all this, and even more when one experiences it oneself, one involuntarily thinks of the tank attack described by Tvardovsky:

Lying in the trench. . .
The heart breaks at the thought
Of being crushed blindly
The tank, after all, cannot see. . .

But is *Glavlit* really so deaf and blind? Or does it perhaps see very clearly those whom it crushes beneath its wheels? Is some rule followed as to what is authorized, and what prohibited? What targets are placed under fire—annihilating fire at times?

Solzhenitsyn hasn't been printed for years; that is a known fact. Nor have the works of [Yevgeniia] Aksionova-Ginzburg, or of other Communists who came out of Beria's jails and recounted what they had endured. This was a shameful decision—and, as time has shown, a stupid one.[4]

The Communists of Western parties often say today that Aksionova-Ginzburg's book has proved to be the most effective weapon against the book of the renegade Svetlana Allilueva. In an attempt to protect her father, Svetlana Allilueva asserts that it was not he but the system that was to blame—the Soviet Communist system.[5] To judge by the Western press, the book by Aksionova-Ginzburg, a Communist, refutes Allilueva's slander. The image of the Bolshevik woman portrayed in Aksionova-Ginzburg's book—a woman who, as the Italian newspaper *L'Unità* writes, even in the camps, kept her "faith in man, in the Party, and in the indestructible force of Leninist truth"—this image struck the Western reader and, for many, neutralized to a great extent the harmful influence of Allilueva's writings. Nearly every newspaper and journal in Europe testifies to this: the French Communist journal *La Nouvelle Critique*, the Italian journal *Rassegna Sovietica*, the Austrian Communist review *Tagebuch*, and some ten other Communist, socialist, and even bourgeois publications. The British Communist paper *Morning Star*, in particular, devoted an article to Aksionova-Ginzburg under the title, "The Heroism of a Soviet Woman." The article unequivocally states: "Every Communist must read this book." The German magazine *Der Spiegel* published a picture of Yevgeniia Ginzburg with the caption "Faithful to the System."

And in our country? What didn't they say [here] about Aksionova-Ginzburg when, to the author's own surprise, her book appeared in the West! With what sarcasm Semichastny spoke of her in one of his speeches! We could not even weigh such a book as this soberly. . . . Moreover, even today, when everyone knows what importance the work of the communist writer Aksionova-Ginzburg has assumed, it is still prohibited here. . . .

And what do they expunge from the books that *are* published, your books and mine? They put the branding iron to anything that seeks to eliminate the deadly consequences of the personality cult, sometimes even to indirect mention that the personality cult once existed. *Glavlit* did not even permit the dramatist M. Chatrov, in his work *The Bolsheviks*, to bring on stage such Bolshevik Party figures as Kollontai, Yenukidze, Petrovsky, and others. . . . In demanding that Comrades Yenukidze and Petrovsky be eliminated from the play, Nazarov, Deputy Chief of *Glavlit*, invoked the charges made against them in 1937. Nothing could sway *Glavlit*, not even an article in *Pravda*, the central organ of our Party, in which these revolutionaries were described as loyal Leninists.

Glavlit's most dreaded enemy has become the appeal to the word of truth. Here is the freshest example, from November, 1967. In the anthology *Day of Poetry*, written in Georgian, the censors categorically ruled out these lines, which crowned a composition by the highly talented Georgian poet Mikhail Kvilividze:

> Everything will be repaid, both Good and Evil . . .
> And one word will be enough,
> One just, courageous word,
> To justify a whole life!

How they must hate the truth to prohibit these lines!

What do they tell writers, both Communist and outside the Party, when these writers attempt to defend their works? What do they tell them when there is nothing substantive to object to? They say: "This is not the time!" "Circumstances do not permit it!" "You must wait!" "Wait a while!". . . .

And so it is that we sometimes wait. We wait a year, two years, ten years.

But it suddenly becomes apparent that not everything is banned. Not all writers are advised to "wait." On the contrary, a considerable amount of prose and poetry directly related to the personality cult of Stalin is not only not banned but printed in huge editions and thrust into the firing line. For example, *The Creation of the World*, Vol. 2, a novel by Zakrutkin, was authorized and published in the magazine *Oktiabr*, Nos. 6 and 7, 1967.

"Do not touch Stalin," the positive hero says in a menacing voice to an opponent of Stalin—and Zakrutkin does not correct the hero's statements. "We know why Stalin has stuck in your throats. . . . Because he defends Lenin's ideas and thwarts all attempts to betray Lenin. . . . That is precisely the reason you fear Stalin as you fear fire." One would say that Zakrutkin knows nothing of the Party documents on the struggle against Trotskyism, of the fact that this struggle was led by the Central Committee, and that it was Ordzhonikidze who delivered the report "on the opposition" at the Fifteenth Congress. He gives a single man credit for the defeat of the opposition. But what, then, about everything the Party has said of Stalin? After all, this [Zakrutkin's book] is something published not in the 1930's but today, in 1967.

V. Zakrutkin answers this question in advance, and he answers it unequivocally. "Who knows," muses Dolotov, Zakrutkin's hero, thinking of Stalin in a melancholy, touching way, "perhaps the prisons, the exile, the solitude of the *taiga*, the cold and the hunger—all that he endured—truly hardened his soul, made him brusk and coarse, but he is loyal and devoted to Lenin like a soldier! With all his strength and determination, he defends the teaching of Lenin against the opposition riffraff and watches over the purity and discipline of the Party."

And so, to believe Zakrutkin, there was no Twentieth Congress. For him, it was nothing but a bad dream, as they say. . . .

Do many of you know the young poet F. Chuev? As a poet, he has as yet done nothing to enrich literature. All we know is that he is being sponsored by someone on the Komsomol Central Committee and that that person has, in particular, recommended him for a trip abroad. But now Chuev has shown his political face: he has begun to write about Stalin. And to write in such a way that various organizations have had to turn their attention to him right away. In a section of the Army, an officer has been severely punished by the party for distributing Chuev's verse.

Has Chuev quieted down? No! He has been going around to various institutions causing scandals by reading his verses, in which this central theme serves as the refrain: "Put Stalin back on his pedestal!"

For the fiftieth anniversary of the October Revolution, Chuev was awarded a government decoration—the medal "for distinction in work." That, then, is how Chuev has distinguished himself! . . .

Kaverin has not distinguished himself. Bek has not distinguished himself. That is why they have not been rewarded. But Chuev has distinguished himself! Who will take responsibility for the fact that the Central Committee has been led into error? Who, specifically, just *who* are the mentors of this Red Guard in the Writers' Union—and in the publishing houses?

When all is said and done, are we going to answer for the cadres who are being reared among us?

When people try to evade criticism of survivals of the past, they sometimes say: "You must not stir up the past," you must not "reopen wounds" or "rub salt in the wound," and so on.

But these very people—V. Zakrutkin, S. Smirnov, F. Chuev, and their ilk—are the ones who are "reopening wounds" and "stirring up the past," thereby drawing the irritated attention of the public to the past and tearing people away from their current concerns.

Lenin said that one must not lie, even to one's enemies. Here at home, people lie to friends. How people have lied these past few years! They lied about Pasternak, about Solzhenitsyn, about Voznesensky, about Yevtushenko, about Yevgeniia Ginzburg, about Bulat Okhudzhava. They lied by saying that these writers were not patriots, that they were encouraging backward elements. What haven't they lied about? We have gotten so used to lies that sometimes we do not even worry about a semblance of truth. And we have drawn writers themselves into this lying—they are forced to tell untruths, to lie in the name, as the saying goes, of a higher discipline. . . .

I know that irresponsible elements are going to start trumpeting—for the *n*th time—that the writers, especially those of Moscow, demand so-called freedom of the press for everyone, from monarchists to anarchists. Look, what more do you want?

So, then, is the old Bolshevik Drabkina, who worked with Lenin, an anarchist? Her memoirs, *The Winter Crossing*, which were unanimously approved by our Party organization, are being endlessly withheld. Or what about A. Bek, author of *The Volokolamsk Highway*; is he perhaps a monarchist? Then, how are we to brand those who howl about our literature?

Yes, we demand freedom! But not freedom outside the Party, the Party of which we are the flesh and blood. The Party's interests are our interests. We demand to be freed from the perversions of the Party line brought about with impunity by the militant cliquists. Ideological subversion by foreign enemies of our country has become more frequent in recent times. . . . Now it is our own home-grown reactionaries who are being used as weapons. They are being eagerly quoted abroad. Their position could not jibe better with the enemy's contention that the perversions of the period of the Stalin personality cult are organically inherent in the Communist system. The enemy has understood that there is no more terrible or more explosive idea in the world than the assertion—above all, when it appears in certain Soviet books—that Stalin was a faithful Leninist, that he always defended Lenin's ideas. This archslanderous thought is a real goldmine for our enemies, because, today, they tie it in with the great tragedy of the Chinese people, with the countless murders of Communists perpetrated under the slogans: "Long live Mao Tse-tung! Long live Stalin!"

We call ourselves internationalists. Yet, in what a position we are putting our comrades—the Communists of Italy, France, and the rest of the world—who have to defend us before their readers, who are informed from every source! . . .

In 1954, I wrote a novel called *State Examination*. It is about the fate of cybernetics between 1949 and 1953, about the courage of the scientists who defended science against insult, about the scientists who, in the end, launched Sputnik.

For thirteen years now, this book has not been allowed to appear. Even though it was given the imprimatur of the Soviet Writer Publishing House, it has been withheld by the censor—withheld like so many other books exposing the daily arbitrariness of officialdom. Who answers for it? No one! The propaganda office of the Central Committee says: "Ask the publishing house!" The publishing house points the finger at *Glavlit*. . . .

The elimination of books that discuss issues is a particularly dangerous symptom. It means that people who think are not needed. In an arbitrary system, anyone who thinks is a potential heretic.

Architects are familiar with the concept of the "Jesuit style." The outer wall of a church is extended to the upper story, but only as a false wall for decorative purposes. What lies behind the wall is completely different from what one would expect at first glance.

This Jesuit style, inherited from years gone by, is not always overcome in our ideological work. Moreover, it is not always possible to eliminate it since the very organic structure of the arts administration has remained unchanged. Outside—a decorative façade: righteous speeches, promises, citations. But behind them, behind the façade—*Glavlit*, ideology's open secret; *Glavlit*, which has been given unheard-of rights; *Glavlit*, which more often than not is incompetent, but which is always vested with the right to ban. Why does this style, so long discredited, still exist? One has the impression that *Glavlit* often misinforms the Central Committee's Politburo, using quotations taken out of context, statements by anti-heroes, etc. . . .

I wish to address this anguished question to my comrades: When will the barriers in the path of literature that studies life be lifted?

Perhaps we have made enough concessions to the interdictors who have disgraced the lofty name of Communist; the time has come to wage war against those who give no thought to their people or to the international Communist movement and who damage our country's dignity and prestige. (*Applause.*)

G. Ts. Svirsky

(Stenographic account)

Notes

1. According to the legend on which the Rimsky-Korsakov opera *The Invisible City of Kitezh* was based, the mythical city was inundated but could still be seen shimmering below the surface of the water.—Ed.

2. Written by Leonid Zorin, the play recounts the relationship between the Roman Emperor Domitian and two writers, Dion and Publius, with allusions to present-day Soviet literary life. The play opened in November, 1965, and was closed down in March, 1966.—Ed.

3. The play is one of a trilogy specially prepared for the Sovremennik Theater—where it is still running—to celebrate the fiftieth anniversary of the 1917 Revolution. Its central concern is an argument among Bolsheviks in the early years of their power as to whether it would be morally right to institute a reign of Chekist terror against the enemies of the Revolution; the losers fear that terror might become a way of life.—Ed.

4. Yevgeniia Semionovna Ginzburg, *Journey into the Whirlwind* (New York: Harcourt, Brace & World, 1967).—Ed.

5. ". . . of course I disapprove of many things, but I think that many other people who still are in our Central Committee and Politburo should be [held] responsible for the same things for which he alone was accused. And, if I feel somewhat responsible for those horrible things, killing people unjustly, I feel that responsibility for this was and is the Party's, the regime's, and [that of] the ideology as a whole" (*New York Times*, April 27, 1967).—Ed.

62. *Galanskov on Sholokhov*

In his speech to the Twenty-third Congress of the Union of Soviet Writers [March, 1966], Delegate M. Sholokhov stated:

I would like to say a few words concerning the writer's place in public life. Today, the question posed by Maksim Gorky rings from former times for the writers of the whole world: "Whose side are you on, masters of culture?" . . .

[Later] at the same Congress, in connection with the Siniavsky-Daniel affair, Mr. Sholokhov said:

Some people, protecting themselves with words about humanism, deplore the severity of the sentence. I see here delegates who are Party members in the Soviet Army. How would they have acted if traitors had been found in their midst? Our soldiers know very well that humanism is by no means gibberish. And another thing: if these young people with black consciences had lived in the memorable 1920's, when people were judged not in law courts but by revolutionary tribunals—oh, what a different punishment would have been handed the accused! Yet here they speak of the "severity of the sentence."

All this insane vulgarity was met with enthusiastic applause. . . . It might very well be that the laws of a military tribunal are severe. And let us assume that, in "our battles" for humanism, we have learned nothing more than the fact that "humanism is by no means gibberish." But what was the speaker getting at? Maybe Mr. Sholokhov cannot envision the Soviet government as anything other than a military encampment and would like to picture Siniavsky and Daniel, in their turn, as spies who have suddenly made their way into one of the barracks, namely the Union of Soviet Writers. . . .

Yes, in the "memorable 1920's," any "leaders of revolutionary consciousness" would have been shot without a word. These men, however, were tried not by a military tribunal but by an ordinary civil law court, and they haven't been shot (as they would have been in the memorable 1920's and the even more memorable 1937). They have simply relinquished their personal freedom for five and seven years [respectively], because they dared to exercise creative independence in their literary work and tried to publish their works abroad! While, in contemporary Russia, creative freedom and the freedom to publish are guaranteed in words, in fact, all that is guaranteed is the mockery of freedom by police and bureaucrats.

Mikhail Sholokhov . . . is still speculating upon the revolutionary humanistic concepts of Party, nation, and Soviet man, at a time when the "revolutionary-humanistic concepts of the Party" have ceased to be humanistic, when the people have been reduced to a bestial condition, and the mythical Soviet man has had no more success than Soviet power. . . . That Sholokhov thinks of Russia as a monolithic territory in which all people belong, from birth, to a military department based on serfdom, that, in his imagination, the Union of Soviet Writers is a unit in this territory—this is understandable. However, what is absolutely incomprehensible is how Siniavsky and Daniel qualify as traitors. For, Siniavsky and Daniel never registered in Sholokhov's territory and never pledged allegiance to its military laws. They never bowed before its military-police apparatus, which, to this day, stifles freedom in Russia. . . .

You, citizen Sholokhov, are no longer a writer. Once you were an average novelist, but you have long since ceased to be even that; now you are an ordinary political demagogue. . . . It is hard to take your writing seriously when you say:

> A very strange picture evolves when a writer writes one thing at home and has something entirely different published abroad. He employs the same Russian language, but, in one case, he uses it to mask himself, while, in the other, he uses this same language with rabid ill will, with hatred for all that is Soviet, for all that is dear to us, for everything sacred. . . .

Is it possible to imagine a greater travesty on the Russian language than this? Could one insult it further? Could one lose the spirit of that language any more completely? . . . I strongly urge you, Mr. Sholokhov, not to use the Russian language to say the revolting things you do—or you may lose not only all your readers but your bosses as well. . . . The Siniavsky-Daniel trial showed that the Russian literary intelligentsia has separated into two camps and that the absolute majority of this intelligentsia stands in the camp of creative freedom. Had it not been for the weight of government pressure, the scales would have tipped the other way, and Siniavsky and Daniel would have been carried out of the court in triumph. . . .

In any country where basic democratic freedoms are actually upheld and not merely paid lipservice, people would have demanded the release of the accused and would have protested the government's action openly. Had the case occurred in a democratic society, a number of literary figures would have left the Union of Soviet Writers in protest and perhaps have established a rival union—for instance, a Union of

Russian Writers. But, in our country, people wrote plaintive letters asking the leadership for permission to defend freedom and justice, acting as though they were some kind of criminals. So far this is still the protest of slaves, but it is a protest nevertheless. So far there is still slavery, but at least there is a movement afoot to defend freedom and justice. . . .

Unfortunately, there are people in the West who, like the respected secretary of the European Writers' Union, Giancarlo Vigorelli, think that Soviet underground literature, "if it exists at all, is no more than an occasional manuscript, some leaflets, etc.," and that "it has no significance." [They believe] that the main literary products are published in the "light of day" by the official organizations.

Vigorelli should know his subject better before he talks about it. The Union of Soviet Writers and the official publishing organizations of contemporary Russia are instruments of atrophy for the writer and his literature; they ruin taste and stupefy the reader. Literature, after all, is the most specific, concrete, and available way of learning about the world. It is the most effective means of developing feelings and shaping points of view. . . . Fortunately for Russia, and quite naturally, today's Russians do not read their contemporary native literature. Or, if they read it, they do so with great selectivity; otherwise stupefaction and atrophy of feelings would have become general. As basic fare, Russians read native and foreign classics and current foreign literature in translation. Only since 1960 have we begun to read Pasternak widely, as well as Akhmatova, Tsvetaeva, Khlebnikov, Mandelshtam, Bulgakov, etc. Such reading has come about not thanks to but, rather, despite the Union of Soviet Writers and the official publishing societies; [the literature has been circulated] almost illegally, in fear of administrative and moral reprisals and often under the threat of legal repercussions. It may interest you to know that the typescript production of the best examples of contemporary Russian literature has reached unprecedented proportions since 1960. It is this kind of underground literature—*i.e.,* literaure not published openly, ranging from the unpublished writers of the 1920's through the works of Siniavsky and Daniel—that has had the most significant meaning in our national culture. Conversely, the output of the official publishing trade, with the possible exception of an occasional volume, has had no part whatsoever in the awakening of our national conscience, nor any positive significance in our culture. And if anyone in the West is under the misapprehension that the creativity of Yevtushenko or Voznesensky has had an influence on the development of the new Russian literature, they are deeply mistaken. [Such work] is all so very insignificant and of such doubtful value that one wonders whether anything at all of worth [gets into print], or whether we can hope that something of value will appear in the future. Personally, I think that true works of literature will continue to escape organizations like the Writers' Union and official publications so long as freedom of expression, freedom of the press, and freedom of organization are not re-established. . . . Until such time, literature can develop only outside of the Union and the publishing agencies—in other words, underground. I see no other possibility. In today's Russia, only dishonest literature can develop in "the light of the day"—meaning phony literature such as the writing of Mikhalkov, who openly stated, "It is good to have security forces to protect us from people like Siniavsky and Daniel." . . . Such literature—with the "Mikhalkovs" at the helm—relies on the organs of the KGB to "protect" it from any manifestation of creative freedom, and any significance it has at all is only negative. . . .

Literary Russia today is like a Sleeping Beauty who has just awakened from an ideological trance without yet having had time to clear her eyes. So the Secretary of the European Writers' Union declares, "Don't pay any attention to her; the main thing is the literary swindlers and speculators with their victories in print." But life itself played a trick on Vigorelli. The underground activity of Siniavsky and Daniel (leading to their arrest, which, in turn, sparked widespread protest from European leftist intellectuals) forced the Secretary to come to Moscow and defend this very activity (the significance of which he had denied). Yes, our right hand is still in shackles while the left shows the scars of handcuffs. For the present, the work of Siniavsky and Daniel is the work of the left hand only. But it will yet be possible in Russia to read with amazement true works of art—including future works of Siniavsky and Daniel, if their talent survives in the camps, which are not as they were in Stalin's day. . . .

Comrade Sholokhov, you never led the fight against tyranny, and now you are defending [tyranny's] successors. I, on the other hand, have always defended the just against tyranny and tyrants. But if you really wish to "support and develop" antityrannical criticism in fact as well as in words, I'll chance it and count on your help. When my modest contribution to the development of such criticism meets with lack of support, with bureaucratic and police obstacles, the way Siniavsky's did when he wrote his superb article "On Socialist Realism," I shall count on your extraordinarily exaggerated authority as a great prize winner, because I have nothing else to depend on. For, in today's Russia, there are no free organizations, no free press, no free court. In contemporary Russia, everything is left to the power of the state. I, of course, must rely on you, but I think that maybe I shouldn't put too much faith in you, and therefore I shall affix a pseudonym at the bottom of this document instead of my own name. But what pseudonym shall I choose? I never thought about it before. Well, I will just sign,

Yu. Galanskov

Go ahead, laugh at me for this. But, you know, the "pseudonym" is somehow more comfortable. You see, because of poor health, I have to avoid all bureaucratic and judicial reprisals. Yes, and my mother's health is too poor for it also. And then there is the question of losing job and study opportunities—though I am aware, of course, that all citizens of my country are constitutionally entitled to work and to receive an education, and I am an honest citizen of Great Russia—I hope you personally believe that. And then there is the Mordvinian camp where, by the way, Siniavsky is, and where, despite his brilliance and his talent as a writer and literary critic, there is no chance for him to exercise either of these gifts. Do you know that in the Mordvinian camp a writer has to do the same hard labor as any ordinary criminal, on half-starvation rations? That one is allowed, after completing half his sentence, to receive additional food packages twice a year, but no more often? And that the package is limited to five kilograms [11 pounds]? That's very clever and humane, isn't it? Especially when we know only one thing about humanism—that it is "by no means gibberish"? Imagine—in the Mordvinian camp, as in all other prisons and camps for political prisoners, there is no possibility of involving oneself in problems of national culture or politics, the war in Vietnam, or revisionism, disarmament, and peace. If I tell you that I am an avowed social pacifist, you will understand that I don't wish any violence. By the way, I am also an underground writer—meant in the sense of a human underground, the sense in which Dostoevsky expressed it. I recommend that you read him. Do you know what an underground author is? A social pacifist, not an underground millionaire. He doesn't even own a typewriter, let alone money. An underground writer works like a common laborer for a piece of bread and peers about, fearful that someone might disturb him. And really, the devil knows what this government is going to do. You yourself must be able to understand that it is difficult to be an underground author—especially one who composes an essay about a highly respected but stupid prize winner who is threatening to stunt the flowering of the national culture, setting Russia's development back several decades. Finally—an underground author is, beyond any question, a citizen of Russia and a man of honor, and that's why he cannot just stand by and watch the humiliation of his country and her finer sons.

Incidentally, I give you the address of my pseudonym: Moscow, Zh-180, 3rd Golutvinsky Lane, House 7/9, Apt. 4.

YURI TIMOFEEVICH GALANSKOV

VI. In Defense of Czechoslovakia

Anatoli Marchenko appears to be one of the most fascinating young dissidents to appear within the past few years. A worker by birth, he spent six years in a labor camp—an experience that he describes in My Testimony (recently published in the West). In Document 63, written less than a month before the Soviet invasion of Czechoslovakia, Marchenko avows his support for the Czecholovak reform program and condemns the attempts of the Soviet government and press to conceal the true nature of events in that country from the public. Documents 64 and 65 are protests in defense of Marchenko, who was arrested on July 29, 1968.

Document 66 also appeared before the invasion, while Documents 68 (excerpted from an issue of Chronicle of Current Events, an underground journal), 71 and 72 decry the Soviet occupation of Czechoslovakia. Document 67 describes the arrest of six participants in an August 25, 1968, demonstration in Moscow's Red Square. As this book goes to press, two trials are known to have taken place as a result of these protests: The first, an open one, was held in Moscow in early October, 1968; three defendants were punished by exile (ssylka) to remote regions of the country (Pavel Litvinov—five years, Larisa Bogoraz-Daniel—four years, and Konstantin Babitsky—three years), and two to imprisonment (Vladimir Dremliuga—three years, and Vadim Delone—two and a half years). The final court statements of Litvinov and Mrs. Daniel appear as Documents 69 and 70. The second trial, held secretly in Leningrad, in December, 1968, resulted in three prison sentences (Lev Kvachevsky—four years, Yuri Gendler—three years, and Anatoli Studentkov—one year) and three confinements to an insane asylum. Among the victims of the latter was Viktor Feinberg, mentioned in Document 67. For further information on punitive actions taken against these and other protesters, see Section VIII, Reprisals, and the Biographical Notes at the end of the book.

63. *Letter by A. Marchenko*

July 22, 1968

To: *Rude pravo, Literarni listy, Prace*
Copies to: *L'Humanité, L'Unità, Morning Star*, BBC

OPEN LETTER

At the recently concluded session of the Supreme Soviet of the R.S.F.S.R., all the deputies dwelt upon one question: the events in Czechoslovakia. The deputies unanimously supported the CPSU Central Committee Plenum on this question and also unanimously approved the Warsaw letter of the five Communist parties to the Central Committee of the Communist Party of Czechoslovakia. They approved and supported the entire policy of the Party and government on this question.

If Communists [wish to] endorse this policy as a model of proper Marxist-Leninist policy in relations between fraternal parties, that is their business and a matter of their party conscience. But here at the session, this policy was unanimously endorsed by the deputies to the R.S.F.S.R. Supreme Soviet who [supposedly] express the opinion of the voters, *i.e.*, of the people, the overwhelming majority of whom—including myself—are not Communists.

Even before *Izvestia* had had time to reach the entire population with its reports on the work of the [Supreme Soviet] session, the paper suddenly launched a campaign in its succeeding issues in support of the decisions adopted by the session on behalf of "all" the people and "all the workers." I have my opinion in this regard and would like to avail myself of the right, guaranteed me by the Constitution, to express my opinion and stand on this question.

I am closely (as far as this is possible in our country) following the events in Czechoslovakia, and I cannot look calmly and indifferently upon the reaction that these events are evoking in our press. For half a year our newspapers have been trying to misinform public opinion in our country and, at the same time, to misinform public opinion abroad on our people's attitude toward these events. The newspapers represent the position of the Party leadership as the position—even the unanimous position—of all the people. All Brezhnev had to do was to pin the labels of "imperialist intrigue," "menace to socialism," "offensive by antisocialist elements," etc., on the current developments in Czechoslovakia, and, in a flash, the entire press and all resolutions began chorusing these expressions, even though, today, just as a half year ago, our people essentially do not know the real state of affairs in Czechoslovakia. Workers' letters to the newspapers and the resolutions of mass meetings are only repetitions of prepared formulas handed down from "above" and are not expressions of independent opinion based on a knowledge of concrete facts. Obedient voices repeat after the Party leadership: "The waging of a resolute battle to preserve the socialist order in Czechoslovakia is not only the task of the Czechoslovak Communists, it is our common task as well"; or "I support the conclusions of the Plenum on the necessity of waging the struggle for the cause of socialism in Czechoslovakia," etc. (*Izvestia*, No. 168).

The authors of these letters and declarations probably did not even ask themselves why decisions concerning the struggle for socialism in Czechoslovakia are being made by a CC Plenum of the CPSU. It probably did not occur to them that our appeal to the "healthy forces" in Czechoslovakia might possibly be an appeal to antigovernment elements and an incitement to armed attack on the legal government. They probably did not realize that the words "this is our task" could mean, at the very least, political pressure on a sovereign nation and, at the worst, possible intervention by our troops in the Czechoslovak Socialist Republic. It is probable, too, that the authors of these letters, in endorsing the policy of the CC-CPSU, did not realize that this policy is strikingly reminiscent, for example, of the U.S. policy in the Dominican Republic, which was denounced a hundred times in our press.

On the basis of articles in the Czechoslovak press, Western radio reports, and the few facts that have been reported in our press, I believe that the C.S.R. has been making genuine progress toward the development of a healthy society. [There is] a struggle of ideas and opinions, freedom to criticize, an attempt to implement in practice the declared ideals of socialism that up to now have everywhere existed only in the form of slogans or promises for the distant future. This is why the Warsaw letter of the five Communist parties and the decisions of the CC Plenum of the CPSU, unanimously supported by our press, have evoked a feeling of outrage and shame in me.

In view of all the talking we have done about the need for a people to decide its own fate, just why is the fate of the Czechs and Slovaks being decided not in Prague but, rather, in Warsaw and Moscow? What leads Brezhnev and Ulbricht to believe that they can make a better assessment of the situation in Czechoslovakia than Dubcek and the Czechs and Slovaks themselves?

I do not believe either the mythical imperialist plots against the C.S.R. or the [alleged] "offensive of internal forces of reaction." I don't think that even the authors of these myths believe them. . . .

Are our leaders really disturbed by what is happening in the C.S.R.? In my opinion, they are not merely disturbed, they are scared—not because what is happening poses a threat to socialist development or to the security of the Warsaw Pact nations, but because the events in the C.S.R. could undermine the authority of the leaders of these nations and discredit the very principles and methods of government that are currently dominant in the socialist camp.

One might ask what could be more horrible and scandalous than Chinese Communism. Every day our newspapers expose the bloody Chinese terror, the ruin of the economy, the theoretical errors of the Chinese Communist Party, etc. The Chinese leaders reply in kind. There is no longer any question of [normal] cooperation between recent brothers and great peoples. Yet no meeting or plenum of the CC-CPSU has adopted a resolution on the need to defend the cause of socialism in China, nor has there been any discussion of the responsibility of the fraternal parties toward their own peoples or toward the people of China, who have been drowning in blood for several years now. To be sure, the Communist Party of China has not relinquished the reins of government. But what of it? Are the results of this government better than the prospects offered by a free, democratic development in the C.S.R.? Is the open hostility of the Chinese CP toward our nation better than friendly relations with the present Czechoslovak government?

Yet our leaders do not remind the Chinese leadership that we liberated China from Japanese militarism and do not lay claim, on that basis, to the role of defender of the Chinese people against internal reaction. We do not appeal to "healthy forces" and "true Communists" in China with promises "that Communists and all Soviet people, in fulfillment of their international duty, will lend those forces all manner of aid and support!" (Speech by N. V. Podgorny at the third session of the R.S.F.S.R. Supreme Soviet on July 19, 1968, in *Izvestia*, No. 168.) However, our Chinese brothers who are being physically destroyed probably need this aid more than the "true Communists" in the C.S.R., who not only are free and secure but also enjoy the same freedom of speech as all citizens. With respect to China our leaders take the position of detached observers, and there has been no joint initiative, such as that of Party Committee Secretary V. Prokopenko, Brigade Leader Akhmatseev, and Candidate of Sciences Antosenkov (*Izvestia*, No. 168), to offer "all-out" aid to the Chinese people. Can it really be that our sense of collective responsibility is less aroused by the bloody terror that the Central Committee of the Chinese Communist Party has unleashed against its own people than by the basically peaceful development of democracy in Czechoslovakia? How can one explain such a contradictory reaction?

In my opinion, the first explanation is that we dare not talk to China from a position of strength, whereas from force of habit we permit ourselves to speak to Czechoslovakia in domineering tones.

No less important is the fact that despite Chinese hostility toward the CPSU, China's internal policy strengthens rather than undermines the position of the CC-CPSU within our own country. "In China there are public executions; in our own country, none!" our press rejoices (see Chakovsky's "Answer to a Reader," *Literaturnaia gazeta*).[1] Compared with the regime in China, our present regime is not one of terror but merely one of suppression—it is almost liberal, almost as much so as [the Russian regime] in the nineteenth century. But if Czechoslovakia should really succeed in organizing democratic socialism, then there would be no justification for the absence of democratic freedoms in our country, and then, for all we know, our workers, peasants, and intelligentsia might demand freedom of speech in fact and not merely on paper.

What the Warsaw letter really meant is "we cannot allow" and has nothing at all to do with a mythical threat to socialism in Czechoslovakia.

Our leaders have voiced concern about the "true Communists" who supposedly were being slandered and subjected to "moral terror" by Czechoslovak antisocialists who had seized the machinery of propaganda (one would think that there had been an armed seizure of the postal, telegraph, and radio services in Prague). But, somehow, they forget to mention that these Communists themselves have had the opportunity to refute these slanders publicly. To be sure, the justifications uttered by Dr. Urvalek, the former Chairman of the Supreme Court of the C.S.R., for example, sound unconvincing—but how does this have anything to do with antisocialists? He [Urvalek] said all that he wanted to say and all that he could say. It is understandable [however] why our leaders hasten to intercede for the likes of Urvalek and Novotny: the precedent of making Party and government leaders personally responsible before the people is a dangerous and contagious one. What if our own leaders should suddenly be required to account for deeds that have shamefully been termed "errors" and "excesses" or, still milder and more obscure, "difficulties experienced in the heroic past" (when it was a matter of millions of people unjustly condemned and murdered, of torture in KGB dungeons, of entire peoples declared to be enemies, of the collapse of the nation's agriculture, and similar trivia)? . . .

In their Warsaw letter to the Czechoslovak CP, the five parties . . . proposed the use of all means available in the arsenal of the socialist nations to combat "antisocialist" forces. It is too bad that the fraternal parties were not more specific—that they did not say concretely what kind of means: Kolyma? Norilsk? Khunviiny? "Open" courts? Political concentration camps and prisons? Or merely conventional censorship and nonjudicial reprisals such as discharging people from their jobs?

And, in the face of the situation that has developed, we still are offended that Czechoslovakia has demanded the withdrawal of Soviet troops from its territory! Indeed, after our pronouncements and resolutions, and the presence of our military units on C.S.R. soil, these are no longer the troops of an ally; they are a threat to a nation's sovereignty.

In this letter, I should also like to express my own stand on these events, which disagrees with the "unanimous" support of the decisions of the CC-CPSU Plenum. The newspaper campaign of recent weeks has aroused in me the apprehension that this may be paving the way for intervention under any pretext that may arise or be artificially created.

I would like to remind the authors of the letters and the participants in the meetings and gatherings supporting the policy of the CC-CPSU that all of the so-called errors and excesses in our nation's history took place amid stormy, sustained applause turning into an ovation—amid shouts of unanimous approval by our highly conscientious citizens. It turned out that obedience was the most cherished civic virtue.

And I should also like to recall more remote historical events: how the valorous Russian Army, having freed the peoples of Europe from Napoleon, just as valorously drowned the Polish uprising in blood. Davydov, the Russian hero of the War of 1812, was prouder of his feats in the reprisals against the Polish patriots than in the patriotic war.

I am ashamed for my country, which is once more assuming the shameful role of gendarme of Europe.

I would also be ashamed for my countrymen if I believed that they were truly unanimous in supporting the policy of the CC-CPSU and the government with respect to Czechoslovakia. But I am confident that this is not the case, and that my letter is not the only one—such letters are [just] not published in our country. In this case, too, the unanimity of our citizens is being created artificially through the violation of the same freedom of speech that is being upheld in the C.S.R.

But even if I were the only one with this opinion, I still would not renounce it, for it is the dictate of my conscience. In my estimation, conscience is a more reliable guide than the constantly changing line of the CC and the resolution passed by various assemblies in keeping with the fluctuations of this general line.

Permit me to tender my admiration and sympathy for the process of democratization in your country.

A. T. MARCHENKO

U.S.S.R., Aleksandrov, Vladimir Oblast
Novinskaia St., Bldg. No. 27

NOTE

1. See Document 86.—ED.

64. In Defense of Marchenko: Petition

To the Prosecutor of Timiriazevskii Region, City of Moscow

We have learned that, on the morning of July 29, our friend Anatoli Tikhonovich Marchenko was detained by the militia on a suspected identity-card violation (Article 192-1, Criminal Code of the R.S.F.S.R.) and is being held in a pretrial detention cell at the sixty-fourth station [otdeleniie].

We consider this detention illegal for the following reasons:

1. In this case, there was no identity-card violation, because Anatoli Marchenko departed from Aleksandrov, where he lives, on the eve of July 27 (this can be corroborated by his landlady in Aleksandrov) and did not even spend the three days in Moscow that are allowed under the law.

2. Even though, formally, this is Marchenko's third detention, the first two warnings were, in fact, also illegal: in the first instance, Marchenko had undergone one and a half months of hospital treatment and was suffering the aftereffects of an operation. In the second instance, he was detained on the very day he arrived in Moscow; he had been invited to attend a literary evening at the Central House of Writers.

3. Even if there really had been a case of identity-card violation, this would be no reason to hold him in a pretrial detention cell, since such a violation is not by nature a dangerous crime; it endangers no one, and there is no reason to believe that Marchenko would have sought to evade investigation: he is employed and has a fixed place of residence.

In addition to the foregoing, we also wish to point out that a search was made of the apartment of L. Bogoraz [Daniel], where Marchenko was staying in Moscow and where he was keeping his personal papers. During the search, not only Marchenko's [legal] papers and medical records but also his private files—personal letters; protest letters concerning the situation in camps for political prisoners; replies to these letters from official sources; rough drafts; synopses of the works of Marx, Engels, Plekhanov, and Lenin; articles from politicoeconomic journals; and articles pertaining to literary criticism—were confiscated. Such confiscation of documents can have no relation whatsoever to an identity-card violation.

Also confiscated were papers and a book belonging to L. Bogoraz personally; these were in her own briefcase.

All these things go to show that the charge of identity-card violation lodged against Anatoli Marchenko is merely a pretext for political reprisals against a man who is known to our society as the author of a documentary book on political camps, the author of a number of protests against the treatment of political prisoners in our nation.

We demand the immediate release of Anatoli Marchenko and an investigation into the circumstances of his detention.

P. LITVINOV
P. GRIGORENKO
I. RUDAKOV
I. BELOGORODSKAIA
L. BOGORAZ [DANIEL]

[Return address:]
Moscow, V-261, Leninskii Prospekt,
Bldg. No. 85, Apt. 3

65. *In Defense of Marchenko: Protest*

CITIZENS!

On July 29, 1968, Anatoli Marchenko was arrested in Moscow. We, his friends, consider it our duty to tell what preceded and caused his arrest.

Anatoli Marchenko is a worker. He is thirty years old. He spent six of these years—from 1960 to 1966—in political camps and prisons. He learned firsthand what a camp in the post-Stalin era is like: he emerged deaf, suffering from bleeding intestines and severe headaches. During these six years, he thought of how he would write about all he had seen once he was released from the camp. In 1967, he wrote a book entitled *My Testimony*. "Today's Soviet camps for political prisoners are just as horrible as those under Stalin," he wrote. "Some things are better, others are worse. It is essential that these things be known by everyone—by those who want to know the truth, but who instead are fed on slick, mendacious newspaper articles; and by those who do not want to know, who close their eyes and ears so that someday, after emerging cleansed from this filth, they may again justify themselves [with the words] 'My God, but we knew nothing about it. . . .'"

After Marchenko completed his book, he was once again in danger of arrest. Several times KGB agents detained him and told him that he wouldn't "get away with this book." But Marchenko continued to do everything in his power to inform everybody about the situation political prisoners were in: he appealed to newspapers, to writers, to scientists, and to the Red Cross. His last letter before his arrest was sent to the Czechoslovak newspapers. "It is understandable why our leaders hasten to intercede for the likes of Urvalek and Novotny," he wrote. "The precedent of making Party and government leaders personally responsible before the people is a dangerous and contagious one. What if our own leaders should suddenly be required to account for deeds that have shamefully been termed 'errors' and 'excesses' . . .?" On July 29, the letter was transmitted to the Czechoslovak Embassy in Moscow, and, on the very same day, Marchenko was arrested.

Marchenko's enemies have many ways to sentence him to a new term under any false pretext. They can do this secretly or slander him in the newspapers. They can deprive him of defenders or intimidate them. We, his friends, have only one way of helping him: publicity. May as many people as possible know of his courageous struggle and his new arrest.

If you do not want to put up with this tyranny in the future, if you understand that Marchenko has been fighting for all of us and that all of us must fight for Marchenko, we ask you to defend him in the way that you yourselves deem necessary.

LIUDMILA ALEKSEEVA (Tel. 258-70-34)
LARISA BOGORAZ [DANIEL] (Tel. 134-68-93)
VIKTOR KRASIN (Perevo pole, Shkolnaia St., 44)
PAVEL LITVINOV (Tel. 299-38-05)

You may write or telephone any of us if you wish additional information.

66. *In Defense of Czechoslovakia: Declaration*

To THE COMMUNISTS OF CZECHOSLOVAKIA
To ALL THE CZECHOSLOVAK PEOPLE

Dear Friends!

The Soviet Party-government leadership, alarmed by . . . political events in your country, has recently made a number of pronouncements and has undertaken actions that have been assessed by the overwhelming majority of the world community, including the Communist community, as an attempt at interference in the internal affairs of Czechoslovakia. Fear has even been and is being expressed that the ruling circles of our nation are planning—assuming that the development of events appears to be unfavorable from their point of view—to use the armed forces to halt such a development.

This is furthered by the unobjective and one-sided reporting on the events in Czechoslovakia, with which those among our people who think for themselves cannot agree.

We Soviet Communists, knowing full well the mood of our people, its love of peace, and its feeling of genuine friendship for your people, consider such fears unfounded. A Party-government leadership that would start a war in Europe, and particularly a war against a friendly socialist country, would quickly be discredited and would lose the confidence of the people.

Observing the activities of the new leadership of the Communist Party of Czechoslovakia, we feel more and more admiration for its courageous, wise, and uncompromising struggle to re-establish the Party's prestige, which was lost as a result of the unwise policies of its previous leaders. We have the greatest respect for and confidence in the Communists of Czechoslovakia, in its working people, and in all socialist forces in your nation.

A. YE. KOSTERIN
P. G. GRIGORENKO
SERGEI P. PISAREV
I. A. YAKHIMOVICH
V. A. PAVLICHUK

67. *Letter by Natalia Gorbanevskaia*

August 28, 1968

To: The Editors-in-Chief of *Rude pravo, L'Unità,* the *Morning Star,* the *Times, Neue Zürcher Zeitung,* the *New York Times,* the *Washington Post,* and all the newspapers of the world that publish this letter

I urge you to print in your newspaper my letter about a demonstration in Red Square in Moscow on August 25, 1968, since I am the only participant who is currently at liberty.

Those who took part in the demonstration were Konstantin Babitsky, linguist; Larisa Bogoraz-Daniel, philologist; Vadim Delone, poet; Vladimir Dremliuga, worker; Pavel Litvinov, physicist; Viktor Feinberg, art critic; and I—Natalia Gorbanevskaia, poet.

At noon, we sat down on the parapet on Lobnoe Mesto and unfurled banners proclaiming: "Long live a free and independent Czechoslovakia!" (in the Czech language); "Shame on the occupiers!"; "Hands off the C.S.S.R.!" [Czechoslovak Socialist Republic]; and "For your and our friendship!" Almost immediately, whistles were heard from all corners of the square, and plainclothes agents of the KGB came running toward us. They had been on duty in Red Square awaiting the departure of the Czechoslovak delegation from the Kremlin.

As they ran up to us, they shouted, "These are all dirty Jews [*zhidy*]!" and "Beat the anti-Soviets!" We sat quietly and offered no resistance. They tore the banners from our hands and beat Viktor Feinberg in the face until the blood flowed, breaking some of his teeth. Pavel Litvinov was beaten on the face with a heavy bag.

A small Czechoslovak flag was ripped from my hands and destroyed. They shouted: "Get out of here, you scum!" We remained seated.

After several minutes, some automobiles approached, and everyone except me was pushed into them. I had my three-month-old son with me, and, for this reason, they did not seize me immediately. I remained on the parapet of Lobnoe Mesto for about 10 minutes. [Then] I was beaten up in a car.

My baby also was taken to the police station, and I was not allowed to nurse him for more than six hours. Arrested with us were several persons from the surrounding crowd who had expressed sympathy for us. They were released late that evening.

All who had been detained were searched that night under charges of "group activities in flagrant violation of public order." One of us, Vadim Delone, had earlier been given a suspended sentence, under the relevant article [190-3] of the Criminal Code of the Russian Republic, for participation in a demonstration on January 22, 1967, in Pushkin Square.

After the search, I was released, apparently because I must care for my children. But I continue to be summoned to give evidence. I refused to give evidence about how the demonstration was organized and carried out since it was peaceful and did not violate public order. But I did give testimony about the arrest and illegal actions of those who seized us, and I am ready to testify about this to world public opinion.

My comrades and I are happy that we were able to take part in this demonstration and that we were able, even briefly, to break through the sludge of unbridled lies and cowardly silence and thereby demonstrate that not all the citizens of our country are in agreement with the violence carried out in the name of the Soviet people.

We hope that the people of Czechoslovakia have learned or will learn about this. The belief that the Czechs and Slovaks, when thinking about the Soviet people, will think not only about the occupiers but also about us gives us strength and courage.

NATALIA GORBANEVSKAIA

Moscow, 13/3 Novopeschanaia St., Apt. 34

68. *Czechoslovakia and the U.S.S.R.* (*from* Chronicle of Current Events)

Issue No. 3
August 31, 1968

On August 21, 1968, the troops of five Warsaw Pact nations launched a perfidious and unprovoked attack on Czechoslovakia. This aggressive act of the U.S.S.R. and its allies was sharply condemned by world public opinion.

Now let us discuss problems in our country that are in one way or another connected with the Czechoslovak situation.

The facts show that, even under conditions that practically preclude the possibility of resistance, the struggle to implement the principles of humanism and justice continues unabated. [*An account of the Marchenko affair follows.*]

On July 30, Valeri Pavlichuk died. He had been a young physicist in the city of Obninsk. One of the most active civic workers and Communists in the city, a talented scientist and teacher, he had been expelled from the Party and discharged from his job for disseminating publications that were not officially authorized [*samizdat*]. But this had not broken his spirit. Shortly before his death, he wrote an open letter to A. Dubcek in which he proclaimed his solidarity with the new political policy of the Czechoslovak Socialist Republic, seeing in it an example of genuine socialist construction free of dogmatism and hypocrisy.

Even before the invasion of the Czechoslovak Socialist Republic, Czech newspapers began to disappear from the bookstands, and, after the invasion, *L'Humanité*, *L'Unità*, *Morning Star*, *Borba*, *Rinascità*, and other publications were no longer available. Regular jamming of foreign radio broadcasts commenced. The press and the airwaves were monopolized by our propaganda.

On August 24, in Moscow's October Square, a citizen shouted out something against the invasion of Czechoslovakia and was fiercely beaten by unidentified persons in civilian clothing. Two of them pushed him into a car and drove off, while a third remained standing beside another car. Outraged eyewitnesses demanded that the militia detain this participant in the beating. All the militia did was check his identification. Numerous cases are known of people failing to show up, out of principle, at meetings held for the purpose of unanimously approving the entry of our troops into the Czechoslovak Socialist Republic. There were also instances when people found the courage either to abstain from voting or to vote against approval. Such was the case at meetings held at the Institute of the International Workers' Movement, the Institute of the Russian Language, in one of the departments at Moscow State University, at the Institute of World Economics and International Relations, at the Institute of Philosophy, and at the Institute of Radio Engineering and Electronics.

Leaflets protesting the occupation of Czechoslovakia are being circulated quite widely throughout Moscow. The text of one such document is given below:

LET US THINK FOR OURSELVES

The Central Committee and the majority of the members of the Communist Party of China as well as the Communist parties of Albania, Indonesia, North Korea, and the so-called parallel Communist parties—Japan, India, and Australia—maintain that "bourgeois revisionism" and outright counterrevolution reign in the U.S.S.R., that the CPSU, by unmasking the Stalin cult and not recognizing Mao's genius, "has betrayed the ideals of the dictatorship of the proletariat," that the Soviet press is slandering China, and so on.

What if one of our zealous successors to Stalin and Beria were suddenly to decide to call upon the Chinese, Albanian, and other brethren for assistance? What if their tanks and parachutes were suddenly, in the middle of the night, to appear on the streets of our cities? And what if their soldiers—in the name of saving and defending the ideals of Communism, as they understand them—were to begin arresting the heads of our Party and government, closing down newspapers and radio stations, and shooting at those who dared resist?

Not only the overwhelming majority of Czech and Slovak Communists but also all the Italian, French, British, Swedish, Norwegian, as well as the Rumanian and Yugoslav Communists—in short, a great majority of Communists throughout the entire world, including the leaders of seventy-eight out of ninety parties that, to date, have supported the CPSU in its quarrel with the Chinese CP—are convinced that it is precisely Czechoslovakia that, since January, 1968, has genuinely begun to implement the ideas of Marx; they are convinced that there is not a word of truth in all our writings about the "counterrevolutionary threats" and "revisionist degeneration" in Czechoslovakia.

But what if these Communists in foreign countries—and there are many of like mind in Hungary, Poland, G.D.R., and Bulgaria—are convinced that the CC of the CPSU is committing serious political errors, that the aftermath of the Stalin cult in our country has not only not been eliminated but is instead being sharply renewed, and that this is exemplified by the unprovoked military invasion of a peaceful socialist country? What if they decided to "save" us and to impose upon us, with the help of tanks, cannons, and parachute landings, the kind of socialism to which they subscribe? What if, on the streets of our cities, Yugoslav, Rumanian, Czechoslovak, or G.D.R. tanks and propagandists with submachine guns were to appear and to tell us that this was nothing more nor less than fraternal aid and an expression of proletarian solidarity?

Let us think about all of these things. Let us think: Who is really helped and who is injured by all that happened on August 21? . . .

· Reports have been received on events occurring in other cities throughout the nation. In Leningrad and in the cities of the Baltic republics, leaflets condemning the invasion of Czechoslovakia have been distributed. In Tartu, a student was arrested for writing a protest on the wall of a cinema. . . .

On August 1 and 2, four persons were arrested in Leningrad: Gendler, legal consultant; Lev Kravchevsky, chemist; Yevgeni Zhazhenkov, engineer; and Nikolai Danilov, lawyer. Under an illegal pretext, their homes were searched and allegedly anti-Soviet literature was confiscated. The true reason behind the arrest was the fact that they tried to write a letter concerning Czechoslovakia. Most of the arrested had previously been subjected to repression. . . . [*An account of the August 25 demonstration in Red Square follows.*]

Leo Tolstoy wrote: "Thoughts about what one of our actions may mean to peace in general cannot serve as a guide to our deeds and actions. Man has been given another guide, and this guide is infallible —man is guided by his conscience. When he follows his conscience, he knows without question that he is doing what he must." From this follows the moral principle and the guide to action: "I cannot remain silent."

This does not mean that everyone who sympathizes with the demonstrators must follow them into the square, and it does not mean that every moment is suitable for demonstrations. It does mean that everyone who thinks like the heroes of August 25 must, following the dictates of his own mind, choose the proper time and form of protest. There are no general formulas. Only one thing is generally understood: "sensible" silence may lead to folly—to the restoration of Stalinism. Following the trial of Siniavsky and Daniel in 1966, not a single act of tyranny and coercion by the authorities has escaped public protest or reproof. . . . This is a valuable precedent and the beginning of the self-liberation of the people from degrading fear and participation in evil.

Let us recall Hertzen's words: "Nowhere do I see free people; thus I cry out, Stop! Let us begin by liberating ourselves."

69. Final Trial Statement by Larisa Bogoraz-Daniel

Moscow
October 11, 1968

I am obliged to begin my final plea with what I said at the start: Many of my relatives have not been allowed into the courtroom, and none of my friends. However, there are many people here who are not known to the defendants. This is a breach of procedure.

In my final legal plea, I was not able to speak of my attitude toward the invasion of Czechoslovakia. I shall just speak of my motives. Why, disagreeing with the policy of my government, did I not content myself with my notification to my place of work instead of going to Red Square?[1]

JUDGE: Do not speak of your beliefs. That has nothing to do with the court.

MRS. DANIEL: I have to speak of my motives, since this question was asked of me.

I did not act on impulse. I thought about what I was doing and fully knew what the consequences might be. I do not consider myself a public person, still less a political one. There was much that I had to suppress within myself to do what I did—my general inertia and disgust at public exhibition. I am fond of my freedom and value life. I would have preferred not to do what I did but, rather, to give anonymous support to other people who think the way I do and have greater weight in our society.

I thought some of our public personages might speak out publicly, but they did not. I was faced with the choice of acting on my own or keeping silent. For me to have kept silent would have meant joining those who support the action with which I did not agree. That would have been tantamount to lying.

I do not consider my way of belief the only right one, but, for myself, it is the only one. It was all the meetings and items in the press telling of uniform support that caused me to say openly that I was against the action. If I had not done this, I would have had to consider myself responsible for the error of our government. Feeling as I do about those who kept silent in a former period, I consider myself responsible.

PROSECUTOR: The defendant has no right to speak of things that have nothing to do with the accusation and no right to speak of the actions of the Soviet government and people. I demand that defendant Bogoraz be denied the right to continue with her final plea.

DEFENSE COUNSEL: The defendant is explaining her motives. The court must take them into account before rendering its verdict.

JUDGE (*to Mrs. Daniel*): This is my third reprimand to you. You are trying to speak of your beliefs.

MRS. DANIEL: So far, I have not touched on my beliefs in the Czechoslovak question. I thought a great deal before I went to Red Square. There were reasons against it, above all, the utter futility of my act. But, for me, the results were not what mattered, only my attitude on this question.

I do not admit myself guilty, but have I any regrets? To some extent, I do.

I regret very deeply the fact that with me on this bench is a young man whose personality is still unformed. I am speaking of [defendant Vadim] Delone, whose character may be crippled by being sent to a prison camp. The rest of us are adults. I regret, too, that the gifted and honest scholar Babitsky will be torn away from his work.

VOICE FROM COURTROOM: Speak about yourself.

(*The judge calls the court to order and instructs Mrs. Daniel to speak only about her own case.*)

MRS. DANIEL. (*to the judge*): Perhaps you would like me to show you the notes for my final plea before I deliver it. . . . The prosecutor ended his summation by suggesting that the verdict will be supported by public opinion. I, too, have something to say about public opinion. I do not doubt that public opinion will support this verdict, as it would approve any other verdict. We will be depicted as social parasites and outcasts and people of alien ideology.

Those who do not approve of the verdict, if they should state their disapproval, will also find their way here.

I know the law, but I also know it in practice. And therefore, today, in this my final plea, I ask nothing of this court.

NOTE

1. Mrs. Daniel had written to the administration of her place of employment on August 21, the day after the invasion of Czechoslovakia, that she considered herself on strike.—ED.

70. *Final Trial Statement by Pavel Litvinov*

Moscow
October 11, 1968

I will not take your time by going into legal details; the attorneys have done so. Our innocence of the charges is self-evident, and I do not consider myself guilty. At the same time, that the verdict against me will be "guilty" is just as evident to me.

I knew this beforehand, when I made up my mind to go to Red Square. Nothing has shaken these convictions, because I was positive that the employees of the KGB would stage a provocation against me. I know that what happened to me is the result of provocation.

I knew that from the person who followed me. I read my verdict in his eyes when he followed me into the Metro. The man who beat me up in Red Square was one I had seen many times before. Nevertheless, I went out into Red Square.

I shall not speak of my motives. There was never any question for me whether I should go to Red Square or not. As a Soviet citizen, I deemed it necessary to voice my disagreement with the action of my government, which filled me with indignation.

I knew my verdict as I signed the protocol at the police station, in which it was stated that I had committed a crime under Article 190.

"You fool," said the policeman, "if you had kept your mouth shut, you could have lived peacefully." He had no doubt that I was doomed to lose my liberty. Well, perhaps he is right, and I am a fool.

The act of which we are accused is not considered by the law a grave crime. Therefore, taking us into custody was unlawful. Surely they could not have thought we would run away after what we did.

The pretrial investigator, too, acted as though everything was a foregone conclusion. He collected only those facts that he considered necessary.

Nobody asked me whether I believed in the opinions I expressed. But if I did believe in them, the count under Article 190, Section One, on spreading willful lies, would have to be dropped automatically. I not only believed, but I was convinced.

The indictment is too abstract. It does not say what, in actual fact, was subversive to our social and state systems in the slogans we displayed. The formulation of our crime in the pretrial investigation was more concrete.

The prosecutor also says that we were against the policy of the Party and government but not against the social and state system. Perhaps there are people who consider all our policies and even our political errors as the logical outcome of our state and social system. I do not think so.

I do not think that the prosecutor himself would say this, for he would then have to say that all the crimes of the Stalin era resulted from our social and state system.

As for the trial itself, the official procedures were violated. Our friends were not allowed in. My wife gained admission only with great difficulty. There are people here who surely have less right to be here than our friends.

The prosecutor reversed the sense of Article 125 of the Constitution. He said that liberties are to be used if they work in the interests of the state. However, it is in the interests of socialism and of the toilers that people are given these rights.

(*The prosecutor interrupted to complain that this argument was not relevant.*)

This *is* relevant. Who is to judge what is in the interest of socialism and what is not? Perhaps the prosecutor, who spoke with admiration, almost with tenderness, of those who beat us up and insulted us. . . .

This is what I find menacing. Evidently, it is such people who are supposed to know what is socialism and what is counterrevolution.

This is what I find terrible, and that is why I went to Red Square. This is what I have fought against and what I shall continue to fight against for the rest of my life.

71. Yevtushenko on the Invasion

[*The following is the text of a telegram reportedly sent by Yevgeni Yevtushenko to Premier Kosygin and CPSU General Secretary Brezhnev on August 21, 1968.*]

I don't know how to sleep. I don't know how to continue living. All I know is that I have a moral duty to express to you the feelings that overpower me.

I am deeply convinced that our action in Czechoslovakia is a tragic mistake and bitter blow against Soviet-Czech friendship and the world Communist movement. It lowers our prestige in the world and in our own eyes. It is a setback for all progressive forces, for peace in the world, and for humanity's dreams of future brotherhood.

Also, it is a personal tragedy for me, because I have many personal friends in Czechoslovakia and I don't know how I will be able to look into their eyes if I should ever meet them again.

I also feel that it is a great gift to all reactionary forces in the world and that we cannot foresee the consequences of this action.

YEVGENI YEVTUSHENKO

72. Petition by P. G. Grigorenko and I. Yakhimovich

February 28, 1969

To the Citizens of the Soviet Union!

The campaign of self-immolation begun by Prague student Jan Palach on January 16, 1969, as a protest against interference in the internal affairs of the Cz.S.S.R. is not abating. Another live torch, the latest so far, burned in St. Wenceslas Square in Prague on February 21.

This protest, which has taken so horrible a form, is addressed primarily to us, the Soviet people. It is the unsolicited and completely unjustified presence of our troops that calls forth such anger and despair among the Czechoslovak people. Not in vain has Jan Palach's death aroused the entire working people of Czechoslovakia.

We all bear some part of the guilt for his death and for the deaths of other Czechoslovak brothers who have committed suicide. By approving the armed forces' intervention, by justifying it, or by simply remaining silent, we contribute to the continued burning of live torches in the squares of Prague and other cities. The Czechs and the Slovaks have always considered us their brothers. How, then, can we permit the word "Soviet" to become, for them, synonymous with the word "enemy"?

Citizens of our great country!

The greatness of a country lies not in the might of its armed forces brought down upon a numerically small, freedom-loving nation but in the moral strength.

Shall we then continue to look on in silence while our brothers perish?

It is now clear to all that the presence of our troops in the territory of the Cz.S.S.R. is based neither on the defense of our fatherland nor on the interests of the countries of the socialist community.

Is it possible that we lack the courage to admit that a tragic mistake has been made and to do everything in our power to correct it?! It is our right and our duty!

We call on all the Soviet people to use every legal means, without taking hasty and ill-considered action, to bring about the withdrawal of Soviet troops from Czechoslovakia and the renunciation of interference in her internal affairs! Only thus can the friendship between our peoples be restored.

Long live the heroic Czechoslovak people!
Long live Soviet-Czechoslovak friendship!

PIOTR GRIGORENKO
IVAN YAKHIMOVICH

VII. Stalinism Redivivus?

The themes touched upon by the authors of the following documents
are also found in the preceding sections—*violations of legality, censorship, persecution of religious and ethnic minorities, and, of course, the
over-all problem of freedom and justice in Soviet society*—but the dominant motif here is "Stalinism," *a term that has come to represent all
the enduring ills of the Soviet system, all the iniquities and evils that
stand in the way of achieving a more humane social and political order.
"Stalinism" is the all-embracing symbol for the sufferings and privations
of the recent past (Document 73) as well as for the tyrannies of the
distant past and distant countries (Document 74). It is evoked not only
by the more radical dissenters but also by writers and journalists in good
standing with the regime and by members of the technological elite as
high-ranking as the physicist A. D. Sakharov (Document 76). All told,
then, the documents below may be said to represent the quintessence of
the case of the dissenters versus the regime.*

73. Letter by Lidia Chukovskaia

February, 1968

To the Editor of *Izvestia*

NOT EXECUTION, BUT THE THOUGHT AND THE WORD

(On the Fifteenth Anniversary of Stalin's Death)

In our day, one trial follows another. Under one pretext or another—
be it in undisguised, concealed, or partially concealed form—the spoken
and written word is under condemnation. They condemn books written
at home and published abroad. They condemn a journal printed in our
land but not on a press. They condemn a collection of documents exposing the lawlessness of courts. They condemn the cry from the Square

in defense of those who have been arrested. The word is being persecuted as if to give new truth to the old axiom Leo Tolstoy was wont to
use: "The Word is Deed." Indeed, the word must truly be the deed if,
for the word, people are sentenced to years of confinement in the prisons
and camps, if it takes whole years and even decades for the great poetry
and great prose, . . . so vital to everyone, to break forth into the light.
I would say that we need them as much as we need bread—in fact,
because of their piercing truth, we need them more than bread. And it
is perhaps because the true word cannot ring out and become a book and
through the book [reach] the soul of man, or because the true word has
been forcibly driven inward and abandoned—perhaps this is why the
artificiality, the falseness, and the stiffness of the other words, the ones
that *are* published and *do* reach the reader, are felt so acutely.

Not long ago I chanced upon a single short verse in a magazine. I
was greatly disturbed by it. Although insignificant in itself, it expresses
a kind of thought and feeling that is today very widespread but very
false. It begins with the heart-rending question:

> Can the enormous bill from days gone by
> Really have been paid off?

and it ends on a comforting note:

> That long bill has been wept over
> And paid back with interest.

The consoling conclusion—this is what disturbed me. Today we need
consolation least of all. What we need most is an examination of the
past to awaken our memory and arouse our conscience. If we are to
believe the author, despite all that has happened, everything, thank God,
is in order on our moral balance sheet: we have made ends meet. So
what is there left to talk about?

But there *is* something to talk about. Today, the human dignity of
the writer and the fruitfulness of his work are determined by his attitude
toward the Stalinist period of our history, which has sunk its claws into
our present.

There are accounts that are inevitable and yet irredeemable. When
we discuss our recent past, it is blasphemy to write about paid-up accounts. What price list do you use to pay for Norilsk and Potma, Kar-
aganda and Magadan, for the dungeons of the Lubianka and Shpaler-
naia? How and with what can you pay for the suffering and death of
one innocent man—and there were millions of them! *How much do you
pay per head?* And who has the right to say: "The account is settled"?
It is probably better if we do not total up the account! It is utterly impossible for anyone to pay up such an account for the simple reason that
mankind has not learned how to resurrect the dead.

And who will pay for the betrayed faith of the people in the magic words: "In our country, no one is imprisoned without just cause"? For the belief that, if Ivan Denisoviches are behind bars, they must indeed be enemies? It must be recognized that the provocation machines—radio, meetings, newspapers—functioned so magnificently in the past, so efficiently and smoothly, that, in some cases, even decent people became fierce persecutors of the innocent. Wives renounced their husbands, children their fathers, and the closest friends turned from one another. But these people, the betrayers, were also victims of a sort—victims of the organized lie. Can't we apply to them the words uttered in other times: "Well, you martyrs of dogma, you are also victims of the age!"?

How can one pay for the mass, organized destruction of the soul, the debauchery of the pen, the dissipation of the word? If it were indeed possible to pay, there would seem to be only one way: through complete, unvarnished candor. But the words of truth have suddenly been stilled, and the Stalinist butchery is once more enshrouded with a curtain of fog that thickens before our very eyes.

The thirst after the most basic, elementary justice goes unslaked. Certificates are issued to the wives of those who perished, stating that their husbands were arrested without cause and have been posthumously rehabilitated in the absence of evidence of crime. This is fine. The same certificates—concerning the absence of evidence of crime—are also issued to those prisoners who had the good fortune to survive. Excellent. They have returned. But where are those who were the cause of all this suffering? Those who invented the evidence of crime on the part of millions of people? Those who fabricated one fantastic story after another under the label of "Case under Investigation?" Those who gave the order to vilify the condemned in the newspapers? Who are these people? Where are they, and what are they doing today? Who, at any time or any place, has totaled up their crimes, which they committed with impunity, methodically, calmly, day after day, year after year? And what kinds of certificate have ever been issued to *them,* to these criminals—and by whom?

Evidently, they were not issued such certificates by anyone. Otherwise, it would not happen that the person in charge of the publication of poetry is guilty of the death of poets; that, at a solemn meeting, the presidium is graced by a writer who chiefly wrote denunciations; that a pension for just deeds is received by a gray-haired, venerable old man who, in the past, was responsible for the murder of Vavilov[1] or Meierhold.[2] . . . Oh, how the fog has enveloped us!

The poem states that there has been weeping over the bill. To be sure, oceans of tears have been shed. But they have been shed in secrecy, on the pillow. There is a Railroader's Day, a Flier's Day, a Tanker's Day, but where is the Day of Mourning for Innocent Martyrs? Where are the common graves, the monuments bearing the names of those who perished; where are the cemeteries that relatives and friends, bearing wreaths and bouquets of flowers, could come to visit on Memorial Day and openly weep? And finally, where are the lists of names of those who ordered the denunciations, of the people who carried out the orders, of those who. . . . But enough of this! At the graveside, silence and sorrow are more fitting.

I do not speak of revenge, I do not advocate a tooth for a tooth. I have no desire for vengeance. I speak of social rather than criminal justice. I say this because, even though the informers, the executioners, and the provocateurs richly deserve the death penalty, our people do not deserve to be fed on executions.

Let clear thought and precise words rather than new executions grow forth from the death of the innocent. Bolt by bolt, I want a thorough examination made of the entire machine that transformed a person in the prime of life into a cold corpse. I want *it* to be sentenced. Publicly. We must not write off the bill of the past with the comforting stamp "Paid in Full." Rather, we must earnestly and meticulously unravel the web of cause and effect, strand by strand, and analyze it. Millions of peasant families, labeled "*kulaks*" or "*kulak* hirelings," were driven north to their doom. Millions of city-dwellers were labeled "spies," "saboteurs," and "wreckers" and were sent to prison or to the camps, or, in some cases, were simply executed. Entire peoples were accused of treason and were banished from their homes and sent to alien lands.

What led us to this unprecedented misfortune? To this complete defenselessness of people before the machine that attacked them? To this unheard-of fusion of the state security organs, which were breaking the law every minute of the day and night; the prosecution organs, which were created to uphold the law but which became monstrously blind for years; and, finally, the newspapers, which, instead of adhering to their duty to defend justice, monotonously hurled slander at the persecuted in a planned, mechanized way—the newspapers, which turned out millions upon millions of lying words about imaginary "unmasked," "hardened," "vile" enemies of the people who were in the pay of foreign intelligence? When and how did this happen? This compound was unquestionably the most dangerous of all chemical combinations ever known to science. How was it possible? Finding the answer to the question entails an enormous amount of work for the historian, the philosopher, and the sociologist—but, most of all, for the writer. This is our major task today, a task that cannot be postponed. It is urgent. We must call upon young and old to make a courageous evaluation of the past, so that our road to the future will be more brightly lit. The present trials over the word would never have come to pass if this work had been done in good time.

The destruction of the truthful word, after all, also stems from the accursed Stalin days. And this was one of the darkest deeds committed over the decades. During the Stalin era, the loss of the right to independent thought closed the door to doubt, to question, and to the cry of anguish and opened it to self-assured, shameless, widely publicized, highly repetitious lies. The constantly repeated lies kept the people from knowing what was happening to their fellow citizens in their own country—some did not know because they were unsophisticated or naive, while others really did not want to know. Whoever knew or guessed what was happening was doomed to silence through fear of instant death—it was not the fear of some kind of unpleasantness at work, or of unemployment or hardship, but fear of simple physical extermination.

This goes to show what a great honor was bestowed on the word in those days: they even killed for it.

. . . I have said that from the graves of those who perished there should spring not new executions, not the execution of the executioners, but rather clear thought. . . .

Out of all this talk of "it's over and done with," one simple, clear thought grows forth naturally. The thought has been known to all since the beginning of time, but we shall all have to perceive and assimilate it new. A century ago, Hertzen[3] repeated it day after day in his *Kolokol* [The Bell]: without the free word, there are no free people; without the independent word, there can be no mighty nation capable of internal change. "Resounding, candid speech alone can satisfy man," Hertzen wrote. "Only the spoken conviction is sacred," Ogarev[4] wrote. To them, silence was a synonym for slavery, for the "bowed head." Hertzen wrote of the "conspiracy of silence." "Muteness supports despotism."

The trials in recent years and recent months have evoked a resounding rebuff from people of various ages and occupations. The intolerance toward present-day infractions of the law reflects the painful indignation that people feel against themselves for being as they were yesterday and against the oppression of the past. Over the young shoulders of today's defendants, we of the older generation see rows of [human] shadows. Behind the lines of the manuscript that deserves to be printed but is not, we see the faces of the writers who did not live to see their manuscripts turned into books. And behind today's newspaper articles, we see those hooting heralds of the executions of yesterday.

"Liberation of the word from censorship"—such was one of the mottos of Hertzen's *Kolokol*. The *Kolokol* was published for the last time 100 years ago, in 1868. A century ago! Since then, censorship has become less conspicuous but all-pervasive. Without resorting to the red pencil, censorship has dozens of ways of burying an objectionable manuscript alive.

May it come to pass that the word will be liberated from all shackles, whatever they be called. May muteness perish—it has always supported despotism.

And may the memory remain eternal, indestructible, in spite of the supposedly settled account. Memory is one of man's most precious treasures. Without memory there can be neither conscience nor honor, nor can the mind function. A great poet is memory personified. I cite the lines of the poet who did not want to part with memory either in this world or beyond the threshold of death.

Because even in blessed death I am afraid
To forget the rumbling of the "Black Marias,"

To forget the banging of the hateful door,
And how the old woman wailed like a wounded beast.

The memory of the past is a reliable key to the present. Are we to
tear up the bill, to allow the past to become overgrown with the weeds
of reservations and stupidity? Never!

Even if our memories failed us, today's trials over the word and the
dry crackle of the newspaper articles would convey to us the noxious
fumes of the past.

But today is today, not yesterday. The "conspiracy of silence" is at
an end.

LIDIA CHUKOVSKAIA

NOTES

1. Nikolai Ivanovich Vavilov (1887–1943), a noted Russian plant geneticist, was
exiled for opposing the theories of Lysenko and died in a concentration camp.—ED.

2. Vsevolod Emilievich Meierhold (1874–1942) was an outstanding *avant-garde*
theatrical director. After the October Revolution, he joined the Communist Party
and staged a number of plays noted for their impressive mass scenes. Accused of
"formalism" in the mid-1930's, Meierhold refused to submit to Party dictates, for
which he was arrested in 1939, following the complete suppression of his theater.
He died in a concentration camp.—ED.

3. Aleksandr Ivanovich Hertzen (1812–79), revolutionary, writer, philosopher,
was founder and coeditor of the famous literary journal *Kolokol* (The Bell), which
was printed in England and smuggled into Russia. His most famous work is *From
the Other Shore*, his brilliant and far-ranging autobiography.—ED.

4. Nikolai Platonovich Ogarev (1813–77), a revolutionary publicist and poet,
was coeditor (with Herzen) of *Kolokol.*—ED.

74. Letter by Lev Kopelev

[*The following letter appeared in the Viennese journal* Tagebuch, *the
cultural-political organ of the Austrian Communist Party (issue of
January–February, 1968). An introductory note states that the letter
was sent in reply to a* Tagebuch *correspondent who had written to Kopelev posing "some questions that have troubled observers of recent
works of Soviet literature."*—ED.]

November–December, 1967

IS THE REHABILITATION OF STALIN POSSIBLE?

With great anxiety, dear friend, you write about certain recent Soviet
publications that, as you put it, have made an "extremely unpleasant"
impression on you. To be precise, it is a question of the article by [G.
A.] Deborin and [B. S.] Telpukhovsky in *Voprosy istorii KPSS* [Prob-

lems of the History of the CPSU], No. 9; the memoirs of K. Voroshilov, which appeared in *Oktiabr*, No. 10; the novels by V. Zakrutkin and
V. Kochetov (*Oktiabr*, Nos. 6 and 10, respectively); the reportage of
V. Kochetov "City in Uinform," which appeared as a book, and a poem
by S. Smirnov, which appeared in *Moskva*, No. 10.

You think you discern in all these writings, different though they are
in theme and genre, the expression of one and the same stubborn tendency, *i.e.*, the desire to rehabilitate Stalin. It is quite natural that you
should be not only saddened but seriously disturbed by the fact that,
after everything that has become known in the last fourteen years and
in the face of numerous documents and the memories of millions of
people, publicists and writers are still to be found who take it upon
themselves to ignore the resolutions of the Twentieth, Twenty-second,
and Twenty-third Party congresses and who consider themselves qualified to maintain that, while Stalin may have committed "some mistakes," his work was, by and large, still progressive and necessary for our
country and the international workers' movement.

You want to know my opinion. I shall try to answer your questions
as exactly and briefly as I can.

I think you are right to condemn as sharply as you can these utterances of incorrigible "servants of the cult of Stalin." Still, I hope that
their efforts will prove vain and your fears exaggerated. How can I hope
for this? On the basis of the following considerations.

The defenders of Stalin appeal to objective historical truth. Was it
not Stalin who led the Party and state in the years of industrialization
and the Second World War, in the years of undoubted successes and
victories? They appeal to historical objectivity and cite the weighty
subjective factor of the raising of new generations in the spirit of socialist patriotism and respect for the revolutionary tradition. They consider
themselves duty-bound to maintain that Stalin was an outstanding
statesman, that his work benefited socialism and our mother country,
etc.

If, however, in accordance with the principles of Marxist historical
science, one juxtaposes these attempts at rehabilitation with all the facts
that have become known in the interim, if one takes into account the
true, and not the imaginary, effect on the intellectual and moral consciousness of youth, then one must clearly recognize that efforts of this
sort can only have consequences diametrically opposed to the intentions of even the most well-meaning exponents of rehabilitation.

The rise and development of the notorious [Stalin] cult during the
1930's and 1940's was the result of many objective and subjective
preconditions:

a. Millions of people were convinced that our country was an isolated fortress besieged by mortal enemies. Consequently, they considered extreme centralization, accompanied by iron discipline, both essential and justified.

b. The successes achieved in industrial and cultural construction were remarkable against the background of world economic crisis and accelerating fascism, and they provided an argument for those who maintained that all the difficulties and sacrifices were only coincidental or the result of sabotage while all the achievements, on the other hand, were the results of the genius-like leadership of the "coryphaeus of all knowledge."

c. General confidence in the press and the state bureaucracy—but first and foremost in the organs of state security, the office of the Procurator General, and the courts—was so great that most people resisted their doubts and the lessons of their own experience even when heroes and leaders were declared overnight to be traitors, spies, and enemies of the people, when history was ceaselessly turned upside down, when heroic deeds that he had never accomplished were ascribed to Stalin and crimes of which they were innocent were charged to his opponents.

d. This blind trust was further accentuated by mass persecutions, which evoked anxiety and fear in some and, in others, strengthened the belief that cunning enemies were everywhere and, consequently, that any hesitation, any doubt of the exactitude of Stalin's words and deeds, or even any leniency in dealing with those who hesitated and doubted constituted direct support for the enemy.

e. During the war and after it, all these objective and subjective preconditions underwent, let us say, both a natural and an artificially engendered intensification. Take myself, for example. I was among those who came to love Stalin, and to love him honestly, during the war. He was the head of our state and of our army. He embodied our faith in our own strength, our hope of victory, our love of all we were fighting for and were ready to die for. We ascribed to him all the virtues we saw in our best people. We believed the myth of the great, all-knowing leader because we wanted to have such a leader; we ourselves had created this myth—some consciously, others unconsciously—and we were convinced of its reality, or quasi reality. Beyond that, we were convinced that it was an absolute historical necessity, for we believed that victory was impossible without an unlimited authority and unlimited faith.

It took many years and two Party congresses, it took this perspective to enable us to re-evaluate our historical experience, and it took the new facts that came to light after 1953, the new knowledge of the past and present as they really were, before we finally grasped what a repulsive "naked emperor" we had clothed in our blind faith and fanaticism and how dearly this had cost our country and the international workers' movement.

Twenty—or even ten—years ago, in ignorance of the facts or in an effort to ease one's mind with dialectical sophistries, one could simultaneously support socialism *and* Stalin; quite honestly, one could praise the achievements of the land of the Soviets and believe in the wisdom of Stalin's policy.

That is no longer possible today.

After everything that became known at the Twentieth and Twenty-second Party congresses, after the publication of the hitherto secret documents of Lenin, after the publication of the eyewitness testimony of hundreds of old Communists, the mythology of the cult of Stalin has been destroyed once and for all.

1. Today it is generally known and has clearly been proved that Stalin's tyrannical and unprofessional intervention in the administration of agriculture during the years 1929–33, as well as in the postwar period, led to extended famines and to the destruction of the economic foundations not only of the individual peasant farms but also of collectivized agriculture.

2. Today it is generally known and has been proved that with Stalin's knowledge, indeed at his command, hundreds of thousands of people, including the overwhelming majority of the commanding officers and generals of the Red Army and the majority of the experienced and trained leaders of industry, were arrested, exiled, murdered, and tortured to death in the years 1935–40. In those years, more Communists were confined in Stalin's prisons and camps than in all the capitalist and fascist countries taken together. Among those shot and condemned as enemies of the people were the overwhelming majority of the delegates to all past Party congresses, the majority of the delegates to the immediately preceding Seventeenth Party Congress of 1934 and of the Central Committee members elected by it, and the overwhelming majority of the members and functionaries of all the Union Republic governments and of all *oblast* and *raion* Party committees.

3. Today it is generally known and has been proved that Stalin attempted to turn the 1939–41 nonaggression pact with Germany into a treaty of friendship; that, in official documents and speeches, he called the enemies of Hitler imperialist aggressors; and that he in fact forbade all antifascist propaganda.

4. Today it is generally known and has been proved that Stalin, a man who was pathologically suspicious and who even distrusted his oldest and most loyal friends and comrades-in-arms (*e.g.*, Yenukidze,[1] Ordzhonikidze,[2] Postyshev,[3] Tukhachevsky,[4] and others), naively and for quite incomprehensible reasons placed full confidence in the friendship of Hitler, whom he trusted so much that he even set aside numerous warnings that reached him through various channels, ignored the reports of all his agents, and thus condemned our army to its worst defeats and the entire country to frightful losses and sacrifices.

5. Today it is generally known and has been proved that after the war, with Stalin's knowledge and at his command, millions and millions of people were subjected to repressive acts of the most severe kind. Entire peoples—the Volga Germans, the Kalmuks, the Chechens, the Balkars, the Ingushi, the Karachais, and the Crimean Tatars—had their homelands stolen from them and were exiled as nations, as national communities. The overwhelming majority of Soviet citizens who had

been taken prisoners of war, as well as of those who had been inmates of fascist concentration camps, were condemned for "high treason." Their tragic fate is embodied in the figure of Ivan Denisovich of Solzhenitsyn's novel.

6. Today it is generally known that Stalin was the one who inspired the defamatory witch-hunt against Yugoslavia and who strove to transplant the methods of the Beria terror, of lies and provocations, to Poland, Bulgaria, Hungary, Rumania, and Czechoslovakia.

These are the reasons why the exculpation of Stalin would be tantamount to the defamation of socialism. Today, Stalin can still be defended only by incredibly stupid and naive persons from the ranks of those bureaucrats, in retirement or grown gray in the service, whose thoughts run along the same lines as those of the anecdotal character of Dostoevsky: ". . . if there is no God, what sort of a Captain can I be?"; or by completely conscienceless, cynical partisans of the jesuitical principle "The end sanctifies the means," who are unable to grasp the fact that Stalin's "means" themselves constitute a negation of the end that is adduced to justify them.

Today, to attempt to rehabilitate Stalin, to act as if there had never been a Twentieth or a Twenty-second Party Congress and as if the documents that have come to light were still unknown, to spread fairy tales about Stalin's virtues and lies about his loyalty to Lenin, as Zakrutkin and Kochetov are busy doing—to do these things is nothing other than to furnish the enemies of Communism with propaganda weapons, to play ideologically into their hands, and to instill, in youth, cynicism and hypocrisy, civic apathy, and a contemptuous disbelief in those very ideas to which the restorers of the cult pay lipservice.

It follows that articles, memoirs, poems, and literature of this sort, quite regardless of the subjective intentions of the authors, objectively damage our country and our Party, strengthen our opponents, and disarm or repel our friends.

Still, the experience of history shows that ideological censorship only harms the healthy forces of cultural and literary development—harms them just as does any sort of administrative repression of literary or scientific works. I am, consequently, convinced that it would not be permissible to demand the prohibition or destruction of the works named above, or of others like them, or to impose penalties or restrictions of any sort on their authors. To do so would be to apply their own methods against the latter-day heirs of the Stalin cult, to apply Stalinism under another name.

What is needed is something else. An objective and critical investigation of such restorationist tendencies in literature, to be undertaken not only in our country but also in the press of fraternal Communist parties, would significantly lessen the damage that these works cause and might thus forestall an expansion of efforts with a similar intent. The partisans and restorers of the Stalin cult fear nothing more than the free expression of opinion, publicity, concrete historical truth, and competent Marxist criticism.

We should not prevent either Deborin or Kochetov, or others like them, from writing and publishing anything they have a mind to. And we should also not hinder those who wish to criticize them. This is the only way to set bounds to the accelerating activity of the rehabilitators of Stalin. Limits, however, must be set. Our country needs to defend itself—for the sake of all our friends and for the sake of socialism throughout the world.

Yours,

Lev Kopelev

NOTES

1. Avel Sofronovich Yenukidze (1877–193?), an old Bolshevik, was repeatedly arrested and exiled for his revolutionary activities. After the Revolution, Yenukidze became secretary of the All-Russian Central Executive Committee of the Soviets. He was shot without trial during the purges of the 1930's.—Ed.

2. Although the Bolshevik leader Grigori Konstantinovich Ordzhonikidze (1886–1937) sided with Stalin throughout the intra-Party struggle of the 1920's, Stalin never completely trusted him. His sudden death may have been the direct result of his efforts to save victims of Stalin's purges.—Ed.

3. Pavel Petrovich Postyshev (1888–1940), an old Bolshevik, was replaced by Khrushchev as Central Committee secretary in 1938 and later executed. At the Twentieth Party Congress, Khrushchev disclosed that Postyshev had been condemned on false evidence.—Ed.

4. Mikhail Nikolaevich Tukhachevsky (1893–1937), a famed Soviet general, was a Red Army commander in the Civil War and the 1920 war against Poland. In 1935, he became one of the first five marshals of the Soviet Union but was relieved of his command two years later on charges of Trotskyism and conspiring with foreign powers. He was executed, after a secret trial, at the outset of a sweeping purge of the Red Army and has recently been rehabilitated.—Ed.

75. Address to the Institute of Philosophy in Moscow by G. Pomerantz

I would like to speak of the moral aspect of personality in the life of the historical collective. In order to clarify immediately what I will be speaking against, I will begin with some verses by Korzhavin:

Today we sing your praises
And we have good reason,
Founder of a powerful state,
Prince of Moscow, Ivan Kalita.

In appearance quite repulsive,
Base at heart, but that's not the point,
The creative path you chose
Turned out to be historically progressive. . . .

I won't go on—the second stanza is the most important. The model may be applied to anyone—even to Genghis Khan. "In appearance quite repulsive, base at heart, but that's not the point": he brought backward peoples, including the Russians, the blessings of an advanced Chinese culture. Therefore, let us erect a monument to Genghis Khan. And such a monument has been erected—in the Chinese People's Republic.

Let us see how the model parodied by Korzhavin works when applied to two academic examples. Once there were two emperors, one in India, the other in China—Ashoka and Chin Shih Huang-Ti. Both had a progressive task before them, the unification of the country. Ashoka was not equal to his progressive task. He succumbed to false pity, false humanism. I would like to give that humanism a more precise description. I can't, because in those distant times there were no petty bourgeois. Otherwise I would, of course, have called that humanism petty bourgeois. Ashoka succumbed to false humanism and could not distinguish progressive wars from reactionary ones. Having barely conquered his realm, he put his sword in its scabbard, refused to take part in any war, and, instead of sending his armies abroad, began sending out his Buddhist priests, who carried reactionary religious opiates to the workers of neighboring countries: "Don't take another life, don't take that which doesn't belong to you, don't lie," etc.

But Chin Shih Huang (the suffix "Ti" is a title similar to The August) was a true humanist. If an enemy did not surrender, he destroyed him; if he did surrender, he destroyed him. True, Chin Shih Huang did not like the word "humanism" (in Chinese it sounds like "zhen"), and he ordered all books that dealt with "zhen" burned, as well as all other books except works on agriculture, military affairs, and magic. Bookish intellectuals concerned with "zhen" were rounded up, incinerated in latrines, or subjected to other disgraceful deaths. There proved to be 400 such intellectuals in all. It was a layer that had not yet managed to spread; so Chin Shih Huang's job was comparatively simple.

Having purged the country of false humanism, Chin Shih Huang united China and established a single Chinese state on solid principles: for withholding information, death; for denouncing [others], promotion or other encouragement. The great constructions of ancient China were built, including the Great Chinese Wall, which still stands today. (They went on building and rebuilding it, but the foundation was laid by Chin Shih Huang.)

This wonderful state system had only one drawback: it was impossible to live under it. Even Chin Shih Huang, the creator of the system, could not stand it; he succumbed to the professional disease of progressive figures—persecution mania. Nor could the people stand it. The son of Chin Shih Huang was nearly dethroned. After several years of upheaval, the Han dynasty was established, having rehabilitated intellectuals and education. Since that time, the Chinese have called themselves Han, but, for 2,100 years, Chinese emperors refrained from don-ning military garb. Only recently have semimilitary jackets returned to fashion.

Chin Shih Huang was no mere ignorant tyrant. He was acting on the basis of a highly developed scientific theory. The origins of that theory apparently went back to Mo Ti, the inventor of the principle "all for the people" (it was on this basis that his followers abolished art and science as incomprehensible to the people). Shang Yang gave the theory a sterner character, replacing the vague term "people" with the more precise "state." In the name of the state, it was proposed that all archaic institutions—the family, for example—be destroyed, lest family ties interfere with loyalty to the sovereign. Han Fei wrote a brilliant treatise in which man in the hands of the government was compared to a stick of wood in the hands of the artisan. The treatise has survived and been translated into English and French, and excerpts of it can be found in any copy of UNESCO's *Classics of the East*. Han Fei did not compare man to a machine simply because there were no machines then. Actually, he can be considered the forerunner of cybernetics.

And so, both emperors were utopians. Ashoka because he saw in man only a spiritual being, Huang because he saw in man a machine that could be programmed with the help of reward and punishment. Within a schematic framework, the first utopia obviously has to be called reactionary, and the second progressive, because Ashoka relied on religion— as we know, always and everywhere a reactionary force—while Chin Shih Huang relied on scientific theory.

And then they both died and turned to dust; and, from Chin Shih Huang, we have the Great Chinese Wall, while, from Ashoka, only the inscription carved in stone: "I, Emperor Ashoka, did battle with the realm of Kalinga and became convinced that 100,000 men would have to be killed, and my heart shuddered."

I am not contending that walls don't have to be built. But I am contending, and completely seriously, that the memory of the shattered heart of Ashoka is a thing without which no people can survive.

The theoretical model parodied by Korzhavin is based on two premises: (1) man's moral aspect has no great meaning; and (2) progress will solve everything.

Both assumptions can be refuted. There exists not only a sequence of facts but a sequence of moral positions that tradition cannot do without. There is the sequence of the slaughtered, the decapitated, the executed, who, having accomplished nothing, have only their moral attitude to pass on to their descendants. The slaughtered Gracchi arose again in France after 2,000 years, and their moral stance, having taken hold of minds, became a force when the revolution began. Neither the Girondists nor the Jacobins were rooted in the soil of justice, but their decapitated shadows arose again in the communes of 1871, and the shadows of the communes rose up during the storming of the Winter Palace. In recognition of this heritage, the Soviet government called a liner in the Baltic fleet *Marat*. . . .

I move to the second point. What is progress? If we set aside the value judgments, then the real substance of progress is differentiation. An amoeba differentiated itself, and the many-celled organism came into being; but with differentiation came death. The amoeba is deathless in a sense: it divides into two, and both halves go on living (if they are not destroyed). But somatic cells, having gone beyond germ cells that preserved their immortality at the expense of all the rest, are mortal from the moment of birth and cannot but die. In this way, progress is linked with certain losses.

It is the same in society. Primitive collectives are amazingly stable, but civilizations have fallen one after another. Therefore, not every differentiation is good, only that differentiation which does not lead to disintegration, to the "joint destruction of the embattled classes." Only that differentiation is good in which the integrating factors—memory, ideas, forms, institutions—are reorganized and renewed. Any differentiation, any progress will loosen the old integrating factors. But if they are not renewed what takes place is what used to be called in the old days "moral decline," and the development no more deserves to be called progressive than does progressive paralysis.

Montaigne said: "Simple peasants are excellent people; philosophers are excellent people; evil lies in half-education." He meant, of course, moral half-education. The peasant is tied to a system of taboos, a system not unlike the tribal system. This system of taboos—the moral experience of the collective—guards the individual incapable of reasoning as a moral being. The philosopher is an intellectually and morally developed man. In ancient times, it was said: "The wise man does not need law, he has reason." Or again in the age-old words, "Love God and do as you wish." But to be half-educated is to be what is called in the Bible "a boor." A boor is a man enlightened just enough not to fear breaking taboos, but not enough to reach moral truth through his own mind and experience. As a result of progress, boorishness has become a very severe problem in the twentieth century. The peasant masses were torn out of the patriarchal situation in which patriarchal taboos held firm, and they were urbanized. Where development was especially rapid—in the countries of central Europe, which were latecomers to the path of progress and were hurrying to catch up and overtake—the growth of boorishness was particularly appalling. It threatened the very existence of European civilization.

To what extent was this inevitable? To get the answer, let us compare two neighboring countries, Germany and Denmark. In both countries, the same symbolic [moral] system—in which the highest values were tied to the symbols of "Christ," "the immortal soul," and so forth and so on—was formally observed. In both countries, the development of capitalism took place. Denmark, it is true, did not have as an additional burden the unification of the country.

The attention of the Danish intelligentsia was directed solely toward the enlightenment of the people, not toward the "training of soldiers to fight the hereditary enemy." Back in Hans Christian Andersen's time, Pastor Grundvik set up the first winter universities of culture, where the peasants were introduced to all the riches created by the human mind; thus the Danish peasant, having ceased being patriarchal, could become educated. But, in Germany, what developed was the phenomenon that emerged in the 1930's—a violent petty bourgeoisie.

When those rabid petty bourgeois occupied Denmark, the fascist commandant gave a routine fascist order: "All Jews must register and wear yellow stars." A routine order. But then the fairy tale began. The King and Queen of Denmark went out for a walk sporting yellow stars. In half an hour, all Copenhagen was sporting them, and, in several hours, the whole country. While Hitler's men were figuring out what to do in this situation, all the legitimate wearers of yellow stars were headed in boats for Sweden. . . .

I hope that I have convinced you and that you have also reached my conclusion: not all progress is good, and not all progress is "progressive." On the basis of what has been said, let us try to reach an evaluation of an historic figure or personality who, today, has been made an object of silence, but whom I want to call by name: Josef Vissarionovich Stalin.

I want to pose two questions. First, was Stalin a progressive figure? And second, where is his spirit, his outlook, leading us?

In order to answer the first question, we must clearly identify that special mandate which the historical figure must fulfill, his personal obligation. Stalin was given power on certain conditions, and, until he made his power absolute, those conditions could not be ignored. He could not [choose] *not* to bring about industrialization and the collectivization of agriculture; he could not [choose] *not* to concern himself with the defense of the country. Anyone designated Secretary General would have tackled the same problems. Therefore what is important is not what Stalin did but how well he did it. Pretty badly, I venture to say. On the credit side, his only achievement was industrialization; all the rest is on the debit side. Collectivization was handled in such a way that, to this day, people have to leave Moscow and go out and harvest potatoes. . . . As to how Stalin prepared the country for war, you can read Nekrich's recently published book.[1] Stalin literally beheaded the army on the eve of the battle.

But that isn't the whole story. Aside from the written mandate—the program of the Party—Stalin obeyed unwritten mandates, borne by the wind. As he strengthened his power, those unwritten mandates played a greater and greater role in his activities. First of all, there was the mandate Lenin called "the Asiatic." You probably remember Lenin's article "In Memory of Count Heiden": "The serf who is enslaved is not at fault, but the serf who cannot live without a master is a lackey and a boor" (*kholui i kham*). (Correction from the floor, "A lackey and a slave": *kholui i kholop*.) One could also quote another of Lenin's favorite phrases: "A pitiful nation of slaves." Centuries of Tatar rule and serfdom left a rather stifling tradition of lackeying and boorishness. The Revolution upset that tradition, but, on the other hand, it uprooted masses of peasants from their accustomed stations, turned whole layers of patriarchal people into masses without the old foundations and without much mastery of the new ideology. Those masses didn't seek a deepening and strengthening of freedom—they didn't even understand what it was for, individual freedom. They wanted masters and order. Such was Stalin's mandate number two.

The third mandate was the mandate of decapitated religion. The peasant believed in God, and, in the Spas icon or in Our Lady of Kazan, he found an object of love and selfless devotion (the selfish motives of religious feeling I am inclined to relate to mandate number two). It was explained to the peasant that there was no God, but that did not extinguish religious feelings. So Stalin gave the workers a god, an earthly god, of whom it could not be said that he did not exist. He existed in the Kremlin, and occasionally he would appear on the tribune and wave his hand. He would take care that not a single hair fell from a worker's head. He was the railroad worker's, the athlete's, the ballerina's best friend.

The feeling that gave Stalin his mandate number three was in itself a pure one. The children expressed it best.

> I'm just a little girl,
> I can dance and sing.
> I haven't seen Stalin,
> But I love him just the same.

The word "Stalin," here, easily becomes a symbol of an all-good, all-powerful, omniscient being, the source of all perfection, or, as they used to say, "the inspiration of our victories." It is only a matter of degree.

How could Stalin have realized three such mandates simultaneously—or is our scheme too complex? Well, Stalin had a special talent for hypocrisy, and, evidently, even for self-deception. And history is filled with examples of dual and ambiguous historical personalities. . . .

I venture to make a comparison, . . . a degrading comparison, with an uncrowned figure, with Azev. Azev was the leader of the militant organization in the Socialist Revolutionary Party and an agent of the secret police. In his capacity as an SR, he organized the murder of his immediate superior in the secret police, the Minister of Internal Affairs, von Plehve. Other acts of terror were successfully carried out under Azev's leadership.

This primitive example suggests an approach, or the model for an approach, to the much more complex question of evaluating Stalin's personality. Azev carried on activities that could be viewed as services for the Revolution, or at least for the SR Party. All the same, the provocateur as such deserves no praise; therefore, the question as applied to Stalin can be formulated thus: Was Stalin not only ideologically (that is, in words alone) but morally, with all his being, on the level of the movement of which he was a part? If so, then, during that [early] period, he might have been of some worth. Or was the truth what Lenin wrote in his will, that "J. V. Stalin is a morally foreign body in the leadership of the party"? If so, then he simply claimed and held onto a place belonging to someone worthier, with the help of intrigue and terror. Then, on the whole, he was harmful, even if, in individual instances, he was able to make the right decisions.

In seeking an answer to this question, one could collect, note down, and study all the testimony of Stalin's contemporaries—about his exile in 1917, etc. Something has been done along these lines, but too little, and the issue remains open.

I move on to the next question. Where is Stalin's spirit leading us? Some comrades have held onto the impression of their youth, when they rose up as soldiers to the dagger-fire of machine guns with the words, "For the Homeland, for Stalin!" In 1943, I myself cried "For the Homeland, for Stalin, forward!" In 1943, "for Stalin" meant against Hitler. History gave us no better choice. It put a whole generation in the position of Pangloss, to whom the officer gave the choice of being hanged or going to the front. No matter how Pangloss objected that neither alternative corresponded to his choice, the officer remained adamant. In real life, this was not at all funny. Ehrenburg tells in his memoirs how, in 1937, Nikolai Ivanovich Bukharin went off to Paris, without asking permission or saying anything to anybody, and wandered the streets there for several days, breathing the air of freedom. He returned to Moscow knowing pretty much what was in store for him, but he couldn't stay away. Logic would have forced him to expose Stalin, but Stalin had already managed to seize power in his fatal grasp; and to beat Stalin would have meant to beat the Soviet system; yet the Soviet system was one of the most powerful obstacles in the path of fascism. Not that Stalin didn't like Hitler—perhaps he did—but the logic of the system was stronger than Stalin's will. Because of Hitler, it was impossible to perform the surgical operation necessary to cure the Soviet system. Bukharin was forced to keep silence—and later, to speak.

That's how it was a quarter of a century ago, but *now* "for Stalin" does not mean against Hitler, against fascism. Hitler is *kaputt*, and Stalin is dead and unmasked. For better or worse, an unmasked idol cannot be masked again. We could pass some kind of a resolution, but it wouldn't be any more effective than Nicholas I's resolution on the complaint of a landowner whose daughter married without his consent: "The marriage is annulled. The girl will be considered a virgin." Stalin, having turned into a despot and a murderer, can never again be worthy of respect, let alone love. Knowingly to restore respect for Stalin would be to establish something new—to establish respect for denunciation, torture, execution. Even Stalin didn't try to do that. He preferred hypocrisy.

To restore respect for Stalin would mean to raise up a moral monster beside our banner. As yet, that has never been done. Abominations have been committed, but the banner has stayed clean. On it is written: "An association in which the free development of each is the condition for the free development of all." Marx, Engels, Lenin have stood beside that banner—all people with human weaknesses, but people. All people of whom it could be said, to use Marx's favorite phrase, "I am a man, and nothing human is alien." Stalin can no longer stand next to them. That would be to sully the banner with mud. One has to be able to separate Stalin as a symbol of the antifascist war from the meaning of the war itself. . .

The threat of nihilism, of ideological vacuum, is frightening to some. But immature cultures cannot fill a vacuum. They fall like houses of cards. One of the most important reasons for the [present] vacuum is the conflict between religious and scientific world views. A thousand years of mankind's moral development was coded into what are called the world religions. The scientific world view shook the world religions loose, but it couldn't create images of moral beauty compared to Buddha or Christ. Obviously that is the job not of science but of poetry, and the process, which cannot be directed, is a very long process—a century long, perhaps even many centuries long. Therefore, from Red Guard attacks on religion, the world Communist movement has moved with the force of events to another form of contact with religion—*to the dialogue*, about which so much has been written in *Problems of Peace and Socialism*.[2] It seems to me that a dialogue with [other] world cultures, which have to their credit the art of Bach, Rubens, and Dante, is a worthier course to take than restoration of the cult of a despot and murderer. By means of the dialogue, we can enlist the strength of the entire intelligentsia and bring to the people genuine enlightenment, genuine meaning—the meaning of a culture that does not have to be mixed up with either atheistic or religious symbols. This will be an authentic culture, an authentic edification—one of the best ways out of the contemporary "vacuum."

NOTES

1. A reference to the work of the historian A. M. Nekrich, 1941: 22 *iiunia* (Moscow: Academy of Sciences, 1965), which was severely critical of Stalin's role on the eve of the German attack on the U.S.S.R. The book has been censured and withdrawn from circulation.—ED.

2. Formerly the Cominform journal, now the mouthpiece of the pro-Moscow Communist parties.—ED.

76. Sakharov on Freedom

An extreme expression of the dangers of modern social development is the growth of racism, nationalism, and militarism, and, in particular, the rise of demagogic, hypocritical, and monstrously cruel police dictatorships. Ranking first are the regimes of Stalin, Hitler, and Mao Tse-tung, followed by a number of reactionary regimes in smaller countries (Spain, Portugal, the United Arab Republic, Greece, Albania, Haiti, and several Latin American countries).

All these tragic phenomena have as their source the struggle of self-ish interest groups, the struggle for unlimited power, the suppression of intellectual freedom, the dissemination among the people of emotional and intellectually simplified mass myths for the Philistine (in Germany—the myth of race, land, and blood, the myth of the Jewish menace, anti-intellectualism, and the concept of "*Lebensraum*"; in the. U.S.S.R.—the myth of intensifying class struggle and proletarian infallibility, upheld by the cult of Stalin and by the exaggeration of contradictions in the capitalist countries; in China—the myth about Mao Tse-tung, extreme Chinese nationalism, and a resurrected concept of "*Lebensraum*," anti-intellectualism, rabid antihumanism, and certain prejudices of peasant socialism).

The usual pattern [of dictatorship] involves the resort to demagogy, storm troopers, and Red Guards in the first stage, and [the entrenchment of] a terrorist bureaucracy—with reliable "cadres" of the type used by Eichmann, Himmler, Yezhov, and Beria—at the height of the deification of unlimited power. The world will never forget the book-burnings in the squares of German cities; the hysterical, cannibalistic speeches of the fascist "leaders"; and their even more cannibalistic secret plans for annihilating and enslaving whole peoples, including the Russians. The Fascists achieved a partial realization of these plans during the war they unleashed, annihilating prisoners of war and hostages, burning villages, and carrying out a criminal policy of genocide (the main blow of genocide fell on the Jews in the war period, but the policy evidently also had a certain provocation aim, especially in the Ukraine and in Poland).

We will never forget the trenches many kilometers long filled with corpses, the gas chambers, the SS dogs and fanatical doctors, the compressed piles of women's hair, the suitcases with gold teeth, and the fertilizers in the form of "products" from the factories of death.

Analyzing the reasons for Hitler's rise to power, we have not forgotten the role of German and international monopoly capital; neither have we forgotten the criminally sectarian, dogmatically narrow policies of Stalin and his comrades-in-arms, setting Socialists and Communists against one another.

Fascism in Germany lasted twelve years. Stalinism in the U.S.S.R. lasted twice as long. Although they have many common characteristics, there are also certain differences. Stalinism was a much more refined type of hypocrisy and demagogy, relying not on an open, cannibalistic program like Hitler's but on a progressive, scientific, and socialist ideology popular among the workers. This provided a very convenient screen for deceiving the working class and for lulling the vigilance of the intellectuals and other rivals in the struggle for power; [it was coupled] with the insidious and sudden use of the mechanism of a chain reaction of torture, execution, and denunciation, intimidating and making fools of millions of people, the majority of whom were neither cowards nor fools. As a consequence of the "specific" character of Stalinism, a terrible blow was struck at the Soviet people and at its most active, capable, and honest representatives. No less than 10 to 15 million Soviet people perished—in the torture chambers of the NKVD from torment and execution; in camps for exiled *kulaks* and so-called semi-*kulaks* and members of their families; in camps "without the right of correspondence" (these were, in fact, prototypes of the Fascist death-camps, where, for example, mass machine-gun shootings of thousands of prisoners took place because of "overcrowding" or on "special orders"); in the mines of Norilsk and Vorkuta, from cold, hunger, and exhausting work; on countless construction sites, in lumber camps, or on canal-building projects; or simply on the transportation trains, in the boarded-up railway wagons, and in the flooded holds of the "ships of death" on the sea of Okhotsk, when whole peoples were being resettled (the Crimean Tatars, the Volga Germans, the Kalmyks, and many Caucasian peoples).

The temporary bosses were replaced (Yagoda, Molotov, Yezhov, Zhdanov, Malenkov, and Beria), but Stalin's inhuman regime remained just as fierce and, at the same time, dogmatically narrow and blind in its cruelty. The destruction of military and engineering cadres before the war, [Stalin's] blind faith in the "reasonableness" of his brother-in-crime Hitler, and other sources for the national tragedy of 1941 have been treated very well in Nekrich's book, in the notes of Major-General Grigorenko, and in a number of other publications—and these cases in point are far from the only examples revealing the [Stalinist] combination of crime, criminal narrow-mindedness, and shortsightedness.

Stalinist dogmatism and isolation from real life were especially evident in the countryside—in the policy of unrestrained exploitation of the agricultural sector through extortionist state purchases [of farm produce] at "symbolic prices,"[1] combined with almost serflike enslavement of the peasantry, with the deprivation of the collective farmer's right to use the basic means of mechanization, and with the appointment of *kolkhoz* chairmen on the basis of obsequiousness and sly resourcefulness. The consequence is apparent in the massive destruction of the [rural] economy and of the whole way of life in the country—[damage] which is difficult to rectify and which, in accordance with the law of "communicating arteries,"[2] has also undermined industry.

The inhuman character of Stalinism was clearly evident in the repressions against war prisoners who had survived Fascist imprisonment and were then thrown into Stalinist camps; in the antiworker "decrees"[3]; in the criminal resettlement of whole peoples condemned to a slow death; in the vulgar, animalistic anti-Semitism peculiar to the Stalinist bureaucracy and the NKVD (and Stalin personally); in the Draconian laws on the protection of socialist property (five years for "a bag of grain," etc.), which mainly served as one of the means to satisfy the demand of the "slave market"; and in the Ukrainophobia that characterized Stalin. . . .

The writer is very aware of those ugly phenomena in the area of human and international relations that are engendered by the egotistic principle of capital when it does not feel the pressure of socialist, progressive forces; he feels, however, that progressive people in the West understand this even better than he does and are struggling with such problems. Thus, the writer concentrates his attention on what he sees before his eyes and on what, in his view, hinders progress on the global problem of overcoming divisiveness, as well as in the struggle for democracy, social progress, and intellectual freedom.

Our country has now entered the path of self-purification from the obscenity of "Stalinism." "Drop by drop we are squeezing the slave out of ourselves" (to quote A. P. Chekhov); we are training ourselves to express our own opinions without looking to the higher-ups or fearing for our very lives.

The beginning of this path, one that has been difficult and far from straight, appears to date back to N. S. Khrushchev's report to the Twentieth Congress of the Communist Party of the Soviet Union. This bold speech, which took Stalin's former associates in crime by surprise, as well as a number of accompanying measures—the liberation and rehabilitation of hundreds of thousands of political prisoners, the steps taken toward restoration of the principles of peaceful coexistence, and the moves made toward the revival of democracy—makes us value the historic role of N. S. Khrushchev very highly, despite the number of regrettable mistakes of a voluntarist nature that he committed in later years and despite the fact that Khrushchev, having held a number of rather important posts while Stalin was alive, was certainly one of his accomplices.

The unmasking of Stalinism is far from over in our country. It is, of course, absolutely necessary that *all* [relevant] authentic materials be published (including the NKVD archives) and that nationwide investigations be carried out. It would enhance the international authority of the CPSU and the ideal of socialism if Stalin, the murderer of millions of Party members,[4] were to be excluded symbolically from the CPSU— as was contemplated in 1964 but "for some reason or other" called off —and if the victims of Stalinism were to be politically rehabilitated.

The influence of neo-Stalinists on our political life must be limited as much as possible. Here we are forced to bring up the issue of one individual. One of the most influential representatives of neo-Stalinism is now the head of the scientific department of the Central Committee of the CPSU, S. P. Trapeznikov. The leadership of our country and our people ought to know that the position of this undoubtedly intelligent and shrewd man, whose views and principles are very consistent, is basically a Stalinist one (*i.e.*, it represents, in my opinion, the interests of the bureaucratic elite), and it differs radically from the hopes and aspirations of the largest and most active part of our intelligentsia (which express, I believe, the true interests of *all* our people and of progressive mankind). The leadership of our country ought to understand that, as long as such a man (if I am not mistaken in my evaluation of his views) exercises any influence, there can be no hope of strengthening the position of the Party leadership among the scientific and artistic intelligentsia. A hint of this was given in the last election to the Academy of Sciences of the U.S.S.R., when S. P. Trapeznikov was blackballed by a considerable majority—but the hint was not "understood" by the leadership. We are not discussing the professional or personal qualities of Comrade S. P. Trapeznikov, about which I know very little, but rather his political line. I base my previous remarks on secondhand information; thus, in principle, I cannot exclude the possibility that all this may be completely contrary to fact (although I consider it highly improbable). In that more pleasant circumstance, I would ask forgiveness and retract everything that I have written above.[5]

In recent years, elements of demagogy, violence, cruelty, and baseness have again taken hold of a great country that had embarked on the path of socialist development. I am speaking, of course, about China. One cannot read without pain and horror about the mass infection of antihumanism being spread by the "great helmsman" and his comrades-in-arms—about the Red Guards who, according to the Chinese radio, "jump for joy" during public executions of "enemies of the ideas" of Chairman Mao. In China, the idiocy of the cult of personality has assumed monstrous, grotesque, tragicomic forms, carrying to absurdity many of the characteristics of Stalinism and Hitlerism. But this absurdity has become an effective means of making fools of tens of millions of people and destroying and murdering millions of the more honest and more intelligent of these people. The full picture of the tragedies that have befallen China is not clear. At any rate, it cannot be regarded apart from the internal economic difficulties in China since the failure of the great-leap-forward adventure, or apart from the struggle for power among various groups, or apart from the foreign political situation—the war in Vietnam, the divisiveness in the world, the insufficient and belated character of the struggle against Stalinism in the U.S.S.R.

The split in the world Communist movement is often considered to be the greatest damage caused by Maoism. This, of course, is not so. The split is the consequence of a "disease" and, to a certain extent, points the way to overcome it. In the presence of "disease," formal unity would represent a dangerous and unprincipled compromise that would eventually lead the world Communist movement to a dead end.

The crimes of the Maoists against the rights of man have gone too far; indeed, the Chinese people are more in need of a unity of world democratic forces to defend *their* rights than of a unity of world Communist forces, with its Communist masters as conceived in the Maoist sense, to combat the so-called imperialist danger somewhere in Africa or Latin America or in the Near East.

The threat to intellectual freedom is a threat to the independence and value of the human personality, a threat to the meaning of human life.

Nothing threatens freedom of personality and the meaning of life as much as war, poverty, and terror. However, there are also very serious indirect dangers, only somewhat more removed. One of these dangers is the stultification of man (the "gray mass," according to the cynical definition of bourgeois futurology) through "mass" culture, entailing a deliberate or commercially motivated lowering of its intellectual level and content, emphasis on entertainment or utilitarianism, and carefully protective censorship.

Another danger is linked to the problems of education. The system of education under government control, the separation of the school from the church, universal free education—all this represents a great achievement on the path of socialist progress. But there is another side to everything. In this case, it is the superfluous unification that has spread to teaching itself, to the curriculum—especially in such subjects as literature, history, social studies, geography—and to the system of examination. One cannot help but see the danger in unwarranted reliance on authority, in a narrowing of the framework for discussion and the intellectual boldness of conclusions, at an age when the formulation of [the student's] convictions is taking place. In old China, the system of examinations for jobs led to intellectual stagnation and canonization of the reactionary aspects of Confucianism. It is very undesirable to have anything similar in modern society.

Modern technology and mass psychology have provided all sorts of new opportunities for managing the criteria, behavior, aspirations, and convictions of the popular masses. This means management not only by means of information based on the theory of advertising and mass psychology but also by means of more "technical" methods such as have been described in the foreign press. Examples are biochemical control of the birth rate, biochemical control of psychic processes, and radio-electronic control of psychic processes. In my view, we cannot wholly reject these new methods, we cannot impose a ban in principle on the development of science and technology; but we must clearly understand the terrible danger—fundamental to human values and to the very meaning of life—that lurks in the [potential] abuse of technical and biochemical methods and methods of mass psychology. Man must not be turned into a chicken or a rat, as in certain famous experiments that attempted to induce "electronic pleasure" from electrodes inserted into

the brain. Also involved is the problem of the ever-increasing use of tran-
quilizers and stimulants, authorized or unauthorized narcotics, and so
on.

Also, we must not forget the very real danger that [Norbert] Wiener
wrote about in his book *Cybernetics*—the absence in cybernetic tech-
nique of stable human criteria. The tempting, unprecedented power
accessible to mankind—or, even worse, to one or another group of a divided mankind—through the use of the wise counsels of future intellectual aids, artificial "thinking" automatons, may turn into a fatal trap, as
Wiener emphasizes; these counsels may turn out to be incredibly insidious, pursuing, not human goals, but the solution of abstract problems
transformed in the artificial brain in some unforeseen way. Such a danger will become completely real in a few decades if human values and,
primarily, freedom of thought are not reinforced in this period and if
divisiveness is not liquidated. Let us return to the dangers and demands
of the present day—to the necessity for intellectual freedom, which
would give the people and the intelligentsia the opportunity to control
and publicly examine all actions, intentions, and decisions of the ruling
group. . . .

Both Marx and Lenin always emphasized the depravity of the bureaucratic system of government as the antithesis of a democratic system.
Lenin said that every cook should learn how to run the government.
Today the multiplicity and complexity of social phenomena, the dangers
confronting mankind, have grown immeasurably, and it is therefore all
the more important to insure mankind against the danger of dogmatic
and voluntarist mistakes, which are inevitable when problems are decided by the "cabinet method," with the secret advice of "shadow
cabinets."

It is no coincidence that censorship problems (in the broad meaning
of the word) have been one of the central questions in the ideological
struggle of recent years. Here is a quotation from the progressive [Amer-
ican] social scientist, L. Coser:

> It would be absurd to attribute the alienation of many avant-garde au-
> thors of the nineteenth and twentieth centuries solely to the battle with
> the censors; yet one may well maintain that these battles contributed in no
> mean measure to such alienation. To these authors, the censor came to
> be the very symbol of the philistinism, hypocrisy, and meanness of bour-
> geois society. . . . Many an author who was initially apolitical was drawn
> to the political left in the United States because the left was in the fore-
> front of the battle against censorship. The close alliance of avant-garde
> art with avant-garde political and social radicalism can be accounted for,
> at least in part, by the fact that they came to be merged in the mind of
> many as a single battle for freedom against all repression. . . . (Quoted
> from I. Kon, in *Novyi mir*, 1968, No. 1.)

We all know the passionate and profoundly reasoned appeal dealing
with this question [of censorship] by the outstanding Soviet writer
A. Solzhenitsyn. A. Solzhenitsyn, G. Vladimov, G. Svirsky, and other

writers who have spoken out on this theme have clearly demonstrated how incompetent censorship aborts the living soul of Soviet literature—indeed, the same thing applies to all the other manifestations of social thought—causing stagnation, dullness, and a complete absence of any fresh and profound ideas; for profound ideas come about only through discussion in the face of objections, only when there is a potential possibility of expressing not just true but also dubious ideas. This was quite clear even to the philosophers of ancient Greece, and there is hardly anyone today who doubts the fact. Yet, after fifty years of undivided rule over the minds of a whole country, our leadership seems to fear even a hint of such discussion. Here we must touch on the shameful tendencies that have emerged in recent years.

We will mention only a few random examples, without attempting to present the whole picture. Once more censorship has been intensified, crippling Soviet artistic and political literature. Scores of profound and brilliant works have not been able to see the light of day—including the best works of A. Solzhenitsyn, which are executed with great artistic and moral force and which contain deep artistic and philosophical generalizations. Isn't this a disgrace?

Widespread indignation has been aroused by the law adopted by the Supreme Soviet of the R.S.F.S.R. as a supplement to the Criminal Code —a law that directly contradicts the civil liberties proclaimed in our Constitution.[6]

The trial of Daniel and Siniavsky, which was condemned by progressive public opinion at home and abroad (from Louis Aragon to Graham Greene) and which has compromised the Communist system, has not yet been reviewed. The writers themselves are languishing in a camp of severe regimen and are being subjected (especially Daniel) to harsh humiliations and ordeals.[7] . . .

A party employing such methods of persuasion and education can hardly pretend to the role of spiritual leader of mankind.

Isn't it a disgrace to hear a speech at a Moscow Party conference by a President of the Academy of Sciences of the U.S.S.R. who either was too intimidated or too dogmatic in his views?[8] Is it not disgraceful that there has been a recurrent backsliding into anti-Semitism in personnel policy? (One might add that, in the highest bureaucratic elite of our government, the stench of narrow-minded anti-Semitism has never fully disappeared, even after thirty years.) Isn't it a disgrace that the Crimean Tatars, who lost about 46 per cent of their population (mainly children and old people) in the Stalinist repressions, continue to be restricted in their rights as a people?[9]

Is it not most disgraceful and dangerous of all that attempts have been made, directly and by means of keeping silent [about the past], to rehabilitate Stalin, his henchmen, his policies, and his pseudosocialism of terroristic bureaucracy—a socialism of hypocrisy and ostentatious growth, at best a quantitative and one-sided growth accompanied by the loss of many qualitative characteristics?

Although all these disgraceful developments do not approach the horrible scale of the crimes of Stalinism—coming closer in scope to the sadly notorious McCarthyism of the "cold war" era—Soviet society cannot fail to be extremely alarmed and disquieted; we must be vigilant in the face of even insignificant evidences of the possible emergence of neo-Stalinism in our country.

We are certain that world Communist public opinion also reacts negatively to all attempts to revive Stalinism in our country, since [such a revival] would be a terrible blow to the attractive force of Communist ideas throughout the globe.

Today, the key to progressive reconstruction of the state system in the interests of mankind lies in intellectual freedom. This has been understood, particularly in Czechoslovakia; without a doubt, we must support their [the Czechs'] daring initiative, which is of great import to the fate of socialism and of all mankind (we must support them both politically and, in the first stage, by increasing economic aid).

The censhorship situation (*Glavlit*) in our country is such that mere "liberal" directives will hardly help correct it once and for all. What are needed are very far-reaching organizational and legislative measures— for example, the enactment of a special law on *press and information*, which would clearly and cogently define what may or may not be done, and which would place the attendant responsibility in the hands of people who are competent and who are controlled by public opinion. It is very important to increase the exchange of information on an international scale in every way possible (press, tourism, etc.); it is also very important to get to know ourselves better, not to stint on funds for sociological, political, and economic research and investigation—which should not be *exclusively* government-controlled programs (in the latter case, we might succumb to the temptation of avoiding "unpleasant" themes and problems).

NOTES

1. Sakharov is referring here to so-called confiscatory prices, far below market levels, which were paid to *kolkhozes* for compulsory deliveries of produce.—ED.

2. Connections between the anterior, interior, and posterior areas of the brain. The expression appears to be a simile for the Party's unbroken chain of command within the industrial complex.—ED.

3. Between 1938 and 1940, the Soviet government promulgated a series of decrees that stipulated severe punishments for workers who either left their jobs without permission or were guilty of unexcused absences from work for as little as twenty minutes at a time. The penalties ranged from deprivation and reduction of pay to imprisonment. The harshest provisions of these decrees have since been repealed. (See Ann Kahl, "The Worker," *Problems of Communism*, 1965, No. 2.—ED.)

4. More than 1.2 million members of the CPSU—half of the entire Party—were arrested in the years 1936–39 alone. Only 50,000 were freed—the rest were tortured during interrogation, were shot (600,000), or perished in camps. Only a few of those rehabilitated were permitted to work in responsible positions; even fewer were

able to participate in the investigation of crimes of which they had been witnesses and victims. In recent times, there have been frequent appeals "not to pour salt into the wounds." Such appeals usually come from those who have no wounds whatsoever. Actually, only a thorough analysis of the past and its consequences for the present will allow us to wash away all the blood and dirt that soiled our banner. In discussions and in literature, the idea is sometimes advanced that the political evidences of Stalinism were a "superstructure" on top of the economic base of an anti-Leninist "pseudosocialism," leading to the formation of a special class in our country—the bureaucratic "nomenclature" elite, which appropriated the fruits of social labor with the help of a complex chain of open and hidden privileges. I cannot deny that there is a certain amount of truth (incomplete in my opinion) in this approach—in particular, it explains the tenacity of neo-Stalinism. But a complete analysis of this train of ideas is beyond the scope of the present article, which is mainly concerned with a different aspect of the problem.—SAKHAROV

5. Sergei P. Trapeznikov is an expert on agriculture. Since 1965, he has been head of the Department of Sciences and Educational Institutions of the Central Committee of the CPSU. He is known for his pro-Stalinist views and his close personal ties with Brezhnev.—ED.

6. A September, 1966, addition to Article 190 penalizing "group activities that grossly violate public order."—ED.

7. At the present time, the majority of political prisoners are being kept in a group of camps of the Dubrovlag in Mordvinia (including criminals, there are approximately 30,000 prisoners). According to available information, since 1961, the regime in this camp has been continuously more cruel, and the "staff" left over from Stalinist times has assumed even more authority than before. (In all fairness, it must be admitted that recently a certain improvement has been reported; let us hope that this change will remain in effect.) The restoration of Leninist principles of public control over places of imprisonment would no doubt be highly advisable. No less important would be a complete amnesty for political prisoners (and not that "token" amnesty which was announced for the fiftieth anniversary of the October Revolution, reflecting the temporary victory of rightist elements in our leadership), as well as a review of all the political trials that have evoked doubts among progressive people.—SAKHAROV

8. Speech by M. Keldysh, *Pravda*, April 1, 1968.—ED.

9. The problems of nationalities will continue to be a cause of unrest and dissatisfaction unless *all* existing deviations from Leninist principles are recognized and analyzed, and unless a firm course for correcting all the errors is adopted.—SAKHAROV

VIII. Reprisals

The measures taken by the Soviet authorities against some of the signatories of the protest documents are vividly described in the documents below. Document 77 is a stenographic report on a trade-union meeting held to determine the fate of a woman teacher, V. M. Gerlin, who had signed a protest against the trial of Galanskov et al. (see Document 30). Evidently transcribed by one of the participants and then sent abroad, the notes present a remarkable picture of the personal courage and intellectual integrity of a woman pitted against the organized onslaught of doctrinaire apparatchiki and turncoats and of the few who raised their voices in her defense. Documents 78, 79, and 80, excerpted from Chronicle of Current Events, provide information on the reprisals taken against various individual dissenters. Documents 81 and 82 were written by I. A. Yakhimovich, whose audacious letter of protest (Document 16) led to his dismissal from his post as kolkhoz chairman, expulsion from the Party (interestingly enough, over the protests of his local Party organization and thus in violation of the Party's own regulations), cancellation of his identity card, which made it impossible for him to find any other employment, police surveillance, and, finally, arrest. While still at liberty, he was active in behalf of Czechoslovakia (Documents 66 and 72) and political freedom in general. His last letter (Document 82) was written on March 25, a few hours before he was carted off to jail. Similar actions have been taken against the dissident Piotr Grigorenko, as is vividly described in Document 83. The last seven items in this section (Documents 84–90) are articles selected from the Soviet press. Together, they convey the flavor of the antidissident campaign being waged by Soviet officialdom.

77. "Shame on You, Comrades": The Voice of a Teacher

April 16, 1968

CHAIRMAN: This trade-union meeting must decide on the question of dismissing V. M. Gerlin, a literature teacher in the upper grades, who does not deserve our confidence with respect to her ideological and political views.

A. V. Novozhilova: The trial of the four young writers occurred at the beginning of January, 1968. They were engaged in genuine anti-Soviet activity. Their degree of guilt varied, but the charge against them was proved by irrefutable facts. They were found to possess a printing device, dollars as well as Soviet money, and anti-Soviet literature. In addition to his anti-Soviet activity, the accused Ginzburg even had his articles published abroad. These four were arrant anti-Soviets, and they received well-deserved punishment. Their trial was not completely open, but then, what importance does that have when the issues are so clear? They could not be permitted to make their anti-Soviet statements in the presence of Soviet people; they could not be permitted to force our people to listen to such slander. Perhaps there were other reasons why no one from the street was allowed to walk into the courtroom. But we don't have to know all the reasons. We must trust our institutions and not be suspicious of them. After the court's decision, Litvinov and Bogoraz-Daniel delivered a slanderous diatribe to the foreign press that contained anti-Soviet demands—a plea for freedom for defendants and for condemnation of the Soviet court which tried them. Several unstable members of the intelligentsia consented to join in sending this dirty letter to the West. Their signatures were added to those of Litvinov and Bogoraz-Daniel. A group of ideologically unstable people, they chose to defend recognized criminals. Our teacher, Gerlin, was among those who signed this letter. She is attempting to be at one and the same time a defender of anti-Soviet people and a teacher of literature. Such duplicity is intolerable. A person who wavers or doubts cannot be a guide in our ideology, cannot be a teacher, and cannot work in our schools.

V. M. Gerlin: Everything that is now happening to me is already familiar. I was condemned behind my back in 1949, condemned . . . only because I am the daughter of a man who was shot in 1937. Today I am being condemned once again, or, more accurately, I have already been condemned behind my back, since a Party conference and the local trade-union committee have already made a decision without even bothering to hear my side. The decision of this meeting is preordained; the collective has to support an already adopted decision, and it is for this purpose alone that you are gathered. . . . I am not afraid of this—things have been even worse. But I must discuss my actions and my reasons for them.

I became an orphan at the age of seven; my father, a Communist, was shot, and my mother was sentenced to eight years in prison for associating with an enemy of the people. She did not live long after having been rehabilitated. I was arrested when I was nineteen years old. My institute unanimously denounced me, together with two other "enemies," who have since been rehabilitated and today are teachers of Marxism. When I, too, returned to Moscow after being rehabilitated, there were a great many people who were ashamed to look me in the eye. These people simply accepted my guilt, never daring to question the decision of their superiors. Before branding somebody else a criminal, all who are living witnesses to the years 1937 to 1947 should remember the mass meetings that were held in those years and the demands made then for the shooting of Tukhachevsky and I. Yakir.[1] Thousands of guiltless people were accused," unmasked," and compelled to expose so-called anti-Soviet organizations, which allegedly existed even among children in kindergartens. I know that these were violations of the law. And I know that it is important for the honor of our state that the letter of the law be observed, since the *spirit* of the law is expressed in the *letter* of the law. For us, history is not in textbooks, not in dead pages—history is in our blood. We must feel a personal responsibility for history, and we must, therefore, not be indifferent to violations of the law; we must sound the alarm every time we believe that the law of the Soviet state has not been precisely observed, since, on a statewide scale, legality and only legality is a means to justice. I do not understand people who lack civic courage, people who are not interested in justice or in the honor of our country. Just and lofty ideas find fulfillment only in just methods of application. Civil agitation to correct injustice is not only my right but my obligation—that was the motive for my act of signing the letter. My major objective was to protest the illegality of the court procedures.

Now, about the letter itself. I did not sign and would not sign the appeal made by Litvinov and Bogoraz-Daniel that was addressed to world opinion outside the U.S.S.R. I appealed only to state and judicial officials. I do not consider it proper for me to appeal over the heads of Soviet officials to world public opinion. In condemning me for being antisocial, you, for some reason, introduced quotations only from that letter by Litvinov and Bogoraz-Daniel, although my signature is on a different letter. My letter was directed (I emphasize once again) to the Supreme Court, Comrades Brezhnev, Kosygin, Podgorny, and to the lawyers of the accused. There is not a word in it about appeal to the foreign press. The demands made in this letter are sharply divergent from those of Litvinov and Bogoraz-Daniel. I do not ask that the accused be freed, but only that their case be reconsidered "with genuine observance of all judicial norms including an open trial," and punishment of those persons who are truly guilty of violating legality—that is, the Moscow Municipal Court. The letter I signed does not raise the issue of the guilt of those tried; I do not take up this question in general. I am not competent to do so, since I cannot assume the functions of a court. But—once again—the exact and honorable observance of the law should interest every conscientious person. Every criminal, murderer, and lawbreaker in a legally constituted state, and most especially in a Soviet state, must be tried strictly according to the law, with strict observance of the law, and without any violation of the law.

Voice from the hall (the mathematics teacher, N. N. Nozhkina):

And you think anti-Soviet persons should be tried according to the law?

GERLIN: Yes, anti-Soviet people, even war criminals.

NOZHKINA: But they are our enemies! How is it possible to defend our enemies? They want to harm us, but we should observe the laws! We can't allow that! They wouldn't grant us the same privileges.

GERLIN: Shame on you! Your words are not only unworthy of a teacher, they are unworthy of an even moderately reflective person. I do not want to forgive our enemies but to judge them according to the law, and only according to the law. Our law is sufficiently strong and firm to punish any person who violates it, without resorting to injustice. And if we do not observe the laws of our own country, how will we distinguish ourselves from our enemies? You are essentially invoking the lynchings and punishments of '37! Where is the guarantee that, having illegally condemned the guilty today, the same court will not condemn the innocent tomorrow?

NOZHKINA: We cannot judge criminals with justice! That would mean exonerating them all!

GERLIN: To condemn the guilty and exonerate the innocent is the meaning of law. A person who doesn't understand such obvious things should go through a course in elementary political theory.

NOZHKINA: What does the fate of some criminals matter to you, how does it affect you?

GERLIN: I am not raising the question of their fate. I am talking only about observance of the laws in a lawful state. But to continue. The people who were ordered to expel me and who have already made that decision want to listen to nothing and understand nothing; they condemn me by repeating insistently one phrase from the letter I signed: "We fully support the authors [Litvinov and Bogoraz-Daniel] of the letter." But what does it mean to "fully support" Litvinov and Bogoraz-Daniel? In reading the letter, I understood, and still understand, this phrase in only one sense: we support the position of civic anxiety and alarm which resounds in the letter written by Litvinov and Bogoraz-Daniel. In other respects, the letter I signed is in conflict with that of Litvinov: it makes different demands and addresses different people. If the letters were in agreement, a new text with different demands would have made no sense, and it would have been enough to say "we fully support Litvinov and Bogoraz-Daniel." I agree that the phrase "we fully support" is susceptible to two interpretations. If I had composed the letter, or had the opportunity to edit it, I would not have allowed such carelessness in phrasing. The phrase either should not be there or should have read precisely: we share the concern of Litvinov and Bogoraz-Daniel over the violation of Soviet laws in a recent political trial. I insist, in returning to this matter, that the comrades bear in mind my explanation of this "criminal" phrase and take my interpretation and evaluation into account.

Comrades, I am not afraid of what will happen to me. Things were even worse for me in the past. I am thinking today not only of myself but of you. Because of you, I do not want a repetition of the situation in 1949. But what is happening now speaks for itself: this meeting, held after the decision to discharge me was made, confirms the sense of injustice that prompted me to sign the letter. Consider which is more important—a slovenly or even untruthful phrase contradicted by the actual contents of the letter or the purity and sacredness of Soviet law, without which our state is unthinkable. . . .

NOVOZHILOVA: Why don't you want to admit that the Soviet government could have valid reasons, which it is not obliged to divulge to anyone, for not admitting just anyone to the courtroom?

GERLIN: The law itself stipulates the occasions when a trial may be closed to the public. But, since 1956, you and I and everyone must understand how dangerous it is to hold secret trials. Has history taught you, a historian, nothing? Penkovsky's trial was transmitted over television, and no one questioned the legality of an open trial in that case.

EIDLIN (history teacher): Do you think the accused were guilty of being anti-Soviet?

GERLIN: I have already said that I cannot answer this question, since I am not a judge. Is it possible that you have not yet understood what is and what is not relevant to this matter?

SOMEBODY: Why did you appeal to the "Voice of America" and the BBC?

GERLIN: I appealed to our government and judicial bodies. I am not responsible for what is broadcast on the BBC.

VOICE: But the BBC transmitted it.

GERLIN: The BBC, but not me. I am not the BBC.

ANDREEV (vocational teacher): Why do you always say "we," "we"? Who are these "we"? What organization are you representing?

GERLIN: I said "we" with only one meaning: we citizens (and that includes you) should be attentive to what happens in our country. I signed the letter, and I am responsible for my signature.

ANDREEV: Who gave you the letter to sign?

GERLIN: I do not consider that an ethical question, and I will explain why. Since I am being driven from my job because I signed the letter (and just for signing, without having given it to anyone else to sign), then the person who gave the letter to me would be subject to still greater persecution. These people did not wish to do anything bad, nor did they do anything bad, and I will not burden their fate. . . .

CHAIRMAN: Who wishes to speak?

(*Three minutes of complete silence.*)

SAVELEV (drawing teacher, deputy director of the pedagogical division): Valeria Mikhailovna has spoken about humanity, about respect for mankind. Her feelings are well known to me. But there is something else that is not familiar to me: what does this children's collective have to do with what we have been discussing? But here's what I have learned. Until recently, nobody in the school knew or talked about such poets as Andrei Bely, Sasha Cherny, Akhmatova, or Gumilev. And now? Students who are not in her [Gerlin's] classes ask about these poets. Where have they learned about them? From children in her literature course. Nobody talked about these poets or read their verses before, but now they are read and reprinted. Why? They are even printed on the school's [mimeograph] machines. Why don't they just use what is in the library? Where did this unhealthy heightened interest come from? . . .

VOICE: Who signed first, you or your husband?

GERLIN: I did. . . .

NOZHKINA: If this trial had been held according to the legal norms, what would you have said then?

GERLIN: I would have said that justice had triumphed.

NOZHKINA: How can one pin you down? . . .

VOICE: Why do you feel this indignation about political matters? You haven't written about criminal matters.

GERLIN: You're mistaken, I have written on criminal matters, but they didn't hound me from my job for that. . . .

ANDREEV: In effect, she signed the letter from Litvinov and Bogoraz-Daniel. Her letter was nothing more than an addition to Litvinov's letter. Aren't there any people other than you in this union who are honorable? Do you think you are the most honorable? Don't we have our own newspapers and institutions? But you didn't turn to them. That means that you have trampled on the very Soviet laws of which you speak. You didn't say who gave you the letter. You're only saying what's to your advantage. You're not telling the truth in saying that you were not the first to sign. You were one of the first.

GERLIN: The signatures are in alphabetical order.

ANDREEV: And you are making a mistake when you speak about Soviet legality. If you received an appeal, you should have sent it to the proper place.

GERLIN: But I sent it to the Soviet government!

ANDREEV: And then, you also declare that Litvinov's letter is a contribution to democracy. You tell us here that you didn't give out the keys to your apartment while your husband says he did. Look, I keep my keys in my pocket, but where are yours? You are not telling the truth, you are opposing the Soviet state. We chose our judges so that we can have confidence in them, but you demand that they be punished. The letter was written from beginning to end by an anti-Soviet hand. Even among Party members there are some dishonorable people. Who told you about the decision of the Party meeting?

GERLIN: I ascertained this "government secret" myself: there was a Party meeting and, after that, a local committee meeting, which made the decision to fire me. It is obvious that this committee is not the first to meet.

ANDREEV: Once again, you don't want to reveal the dishonorable people for whom you are covering up. Who told you about the meeting?

GERLIN: I have already explained.

ANDREEV: A person who signed such a letter cannot work at our school.

OSIPOVA: We all know and understand that the vocation of a teacher involves definite obligations. We all know Valeria Mikhailovna. She is a good teacher. We have to act properly, not crudely. I cannot help believing her explanations; I must take them into account. We must also respect the motives that prompted Valeria Mikhailovna. In reality, she feels strongly about the issue of legality, and she has a right to. Even if she made a mistake in not attributing the necessary importance to the first phrase in the letter—why must we punish her for one mistake? I want to make the following analogy. Lenin, in speaking against great-power chauvinism and nationalism in general, said that, while we must forgive nationalism in the oppressed nations, we must not forgive the chauvinism of the dominant powers. If our colleague erred, then her mistake is understandable. And it is necessary not to punish but to understand her. She did not sign the letter sent out by Litvinov and Bogoraz-Daniel—she signed a letter to the chief organs of the Soviet state. We must not ignore this fact. Let us first consider the matter, and then decide.

L. P. SEMEROVA: We are faced with a very complicated situation. The hand of the enemy is apparent in Poland and in Czechoslovakia. The ideological struggle has grown particularly intense. Valeria Mikhailovna says that she is grieved about the laws and about human justice. The fate of the accused matters less to her than the manner and process by which the judgment was formulated. How can a Soviet person talk this way? When all this is transmitted abroad, it aids the hand of the enemy. We call on people to correct shortcomings, but why write letters? Why collect signatures? Why make this known to the entire world? These letters sully our state and our laws. Valeria Mikhailovna's words reveal that she thinks that she alone understands well and analyzes well and that other people do not understand! . . . If a teacher does not have confidence in the righteousness of the state, he cannot be an educator. Pouring out filth in letters is forbidden. And why is there any need to talk about the past? It has already been evaluated, and there is no reason to bring it up again.

OGORODNIKOV (physical-education teacher): Alla Leonidovna said something here about chauvinism. For shame! What has this got to do with nationality!?

OSIPOVA: You misunderstood me!

OGORODNIKOV: Perhaps I misunderstood you, but all the same! Alla Leonidovna is incorrect. Valeria Mikhailovna is trying to disown Litvinov's letter. But it doesn't work! It is impossible to disown one and sign the other. That is very clear. There are only two sorts of propaganda. Everything that is beneficial to Western propaganda is hostile to ours. Her political laxity makes Valeria Mikhailovna an untrustworthy teacher. I distrust her politically.

N. YE. SMIRNOVA (literature teacher): I have heard many things here that must be refuted. First of all, why have almost all the comrades who spoke talked about the Litvinov and Bogoraz-Daniel letter? Valeria Mikhailovna did not sign that letter. She has convincingly demonstrated, facts in hand, that she had taken a different position from Litvinov and Bogoraz-Daniel, that her letter was addressed to the proper Soviet authorities, and that the motives that produced it were truly civic. A person takes a responsible step not because of fame or profit; he takes that action which his conscience as a citizen prompts him to take. If Valeria Mikhailovna did, in fact, make a mistake in not attributing the required meaning to the first phrase of Litvinov's letter, which has provoked such agitation here, she has explained this matter convincingly enough. . . .

VASILEVA (teacher in the primary grades): Comrades, I, as a Communist, must declare bluntly that Valeria Mikhailovna signed a document of indisputably anti-Soviet content. Those comrades who are now discussing the letter of Litvinov and Bogoraz-Daniel are behaving correctly. . . . We must discuss not only the slovenly formulation of the letter but, out of our sense of responsibility, the anti-Soviet content of this letter. Why did 220 persons sign such a letter? What is this, an expression of personal outrage? And you are trying to tell us that this is not offensive! Nor have you considered the complicated international situation, which is most important to us as ideologically experienced teachers. Comrades, I do not trust Valeria Mikhailovna to educate children!

EIDLIN: I understand Valeria Mikhailovna. Her fate was not an easy one. But was she perhaps the only one who went through all that? Just yesterday, oppressed by her terrible story, I told it to my father. And I learned, unexpectedly, that my father had also suffered from the cult. He suffered in 1952. I never knew about this: I did not live with my father and did not see him. Although he suffered, he talked agitatedly about those who write dirty letters about our country to our enemies. My father educated me to be politically conscious and firm. But what have we here? Precisely the opposite: We have someone who is politically weak, which, to be quite frank, leaves me unmoved about her fate. . . .

V. I. NAGORNAIA (physical-education teacher): We made a mistake. At the local committee meeting, we made a decision without having listened to Valeria Mikhailovna. She is right—this should not have happened. We do not judge an act—we judge a person. What we deal with is not just paper but a person, and one must not only be able to read a paper, one must know how to listen to a human being. I knew nothing about the letter, I had no opinion before today. Today, I have listened to a person. I cannot doubt her. You think to yourself, why is it that this trial has provoked such distress, why have people been accused of violating the law? No one has answered this question for me. Why can't these facts be published? Perhaps then it would all be clear. . . . And then . . . some people talk about Valeria Mikhailovna's "literary circle." It has been meeting for less than a year. That is a short time to have caused the alleged changes in the children. The literary group could not corrupt the children. Besides, aside from literature, we have other subjects. There is physical education. And I, a teacher of physical education, say: I also educate, so you must remove me, too, then everyone. . . .

NOZHKINA: I am not convinced that Valeria Mikhailovna came to defend justice. This is a strange kind of justice. Alla Leonidovna and Valentina Leonidovna talked about her here, but they did not convince me. They did not convince me! If Valeria Mikhailovna herself were right, she should be able to convince me. Your opponents here have convinced me, but not you. I don't believe in your system of legality. The main thing, Valeria Mikhailovna, is that these events were a personal affront to you. . . . Your signature was a defense of people you do not know. Should one defend criminals? What kind of justice is this? It is just to condemn criminals, but you defend them. . . .

INGEROV (director of the school): None of you, comrades, was uncertain about who would defend Gerlin. This matter must be taken into consideration. The list of defenders is not accidental, nor is it accidental that we could predict which names would be on it. It is time for these comrades to think about themselves. Where will such a position lead them? The collective does not wish to work with those who defend that view. Valeria Mikhailovna's speech should be discounted. The first and second letters are one and the same thing! It is useless to use tricks and traps! The same thing! It does not extricate you, it deceives no one! Valeria Mikhailovna has been quietly contemptuous of us all. Why did she say that everything was decided earlier? These statements and the statements of her defenders are all pitiful attempts. None of their little ways deceive us, it is useless to hint and hedge. . . . Not one genuinely thoughtful person spoke up in Valeria Mikhailovna's defense. . . . Today, the chief question, comrade-defenders, is what attitude you intend to take from now on. We cannot permit you to follow a double policy. You have no right to introduce doubts into sixteen-year-old minds. A group was formed [around Gerlin] that is rushing unscrupulously to defend its comrades. Can we be sure that a [true] Soviet situation will be restored with Valeria Mikhailovna's departure? We unequivocally warn these comrades. Let them consider the matter first, then vote. We consider this a political matter. Valeria Mikhailovna should have been discharged earlier. . . . A politically unreliable person should not be allowed to teach our children. . . .

CHAIRMAN: Valeria Mikhailovna, you do not have the civic qualities and integrity that you have talked about. You are apolitical in many matters. The comparison with the cult of personality is itself an indication of great political ignorance. People who have a clear conscience and genuine civic feelings are completely secure. Why don't I feel exposed to danger? I have a clear conscience.

A motion has been made to ask the OMK to discharge V. M. Gerlin according to Article 48 of the KZOT, Code of Labor Law on the request of the trade-union organization.

The voting results were as follows: out of a total of forty-two persons, five were opposed to dismissal, two abstained. In the OMK, the vote was slightly different: two or three against dismissal and one abstention.

GERLIN: I am very ashamed. I am so ashamed that I cannot raise my eyes. I am ashamed, ashamed for you, comrades. Because you cannot hear and understand, you cannot think, because many of you have shown yourselves to be even more unprincipled than I thought you were.

NOTE

1. Both Marshal M. N. Tukhachevsky and General I. Ye. Yakir of the Red Army were tried in secret and executed in 1937.—ED.

78. *Trials in Leningrad (from* Chronicle of Current Events)

April 30, 1968

Between March 14 and April 5, seventeen Leningrad intellectuals went on trial in the Leningrad Municipal Court. Prosecutor Guseva and Judge Isakova, Deputy Chairman of the Leningrad Municipal Court, took part in the trial.

All of the defendants were charged with violation of Articles 70 and 72 of the R.S.F.S.R. Criminal Code. The crux of the charge was participation in the All-Russian Social-Christian Union for the Liberation of the People.

Here is a brief description of the Union's program: The establishment of a democratic order in which the chief of state should be elected by all of the people and should be responsible to the parliament. The chief organ of control—a synod composed of representatives of the clergy—should have "veto" power with respect to the chief of state and the parliament. Land—the property of the state—is to be allocated to private individuals or collectives. Exploitation is prohibited; hired labor is permitted only on a parity basis. Enterprises should be, for the most part, the property of workers' collectives, and the main enterprises such as transportation, electronics, etc., should be government-owned. The fundamental principle of the economy is to be individualism.

The Union's regulations are as follows:

Strict secrecy and the division of the membership into "troikas" [groups of three], with each person knowing the senior member and the second person in his troika. In addition, each person should recruit new members and establish new troikas in which he becomes the senior member. The members do not know the head of the organization. If necessary, they can contact him in writing through the senior member of their troika.

In practice, the organization (the Union) was solely engaged in (1) the recruitment of new members and (2) the dissemination of literature. (In the course of searches, books and [hand] copies of books by [Milovan] Djilas, [Nikolai A.] Berdiaev, Vl. Solovev; [Georg von] Rauch's *History of Soviet Russia*; Tibor Merai's *Thirteen Days That Shook the Kremlin*—an account of the events in Hungary in 1956; Gorky's *Untimely Thoughts*; etc., and even [Yevgeniia S.] Ginzburg's *Krutoi Marshrut* (Into the Whirlwind) were confiscated.)

The organization was formed sometime in 1964. By mid-1965, it had about ten members. During this period, although the KGB office in Leningrad already knew of the organization's existence, it did not stop its activities but instead permitted them to develop and expand. (In court, the state's witness Aleksandr Gidoni stated that, in 1965, he had informed the KGB about the organization and was advised by the KGB to continue his contacts with the members).

Between February and March, 1967, about sixty persons were arrested or detained in Leningrad, Tomsk, Irkutsk, Petrozavodsk, and elsewhere.

In November, 1967, the Leningrad Municipal Court tried four leaders of the organization under the terms of Articles 64, 70, and 72 and sentenced them as follows:

Vladimir Ogurtsov: translator from Japanese into Russian, thirty years old, sentenced to fifteen years;

Mikhail Sado: orientalist, thirty years old, thirteen years;

Yevgeni Vagin: literary critic at Pushkin House publishers, twenty years old, ten years; and

Averochkin: lawyer, twenty-eight years old, eight years of confinement in a severe-regimen corrective-labor colony.

The trial took place between March 14 and April 5, 1968. There was no essential difference between the defendants and the state witnesses, but only those who had recruited others for the organization were actually put on trial. All of the accused pleaded guilty, acknowledging the points in the indictment, but they did not all repent their actions (in particular, Ivoilov, Ivanov, Platonov, and Borodin.)

Here is a list of the convicted men. The two figures at the end of each item are the length of sentence given and, in parentheses, the sentence demanded by the prosecutor:

1. Viacheslav Platonov. Born 1941. Orientalist. 7 years (7).

2. Nikolai Ivanov. Born 1937. Literary historian, Leningrad State University instructor: 6 (7).

3. Leonid Borodin. Born 1938. Director of school in Luzhskiy region, Leningrad District: 6 (6).

4. Vladimir Ivoilov. Economist (Tomsk). Leningrad State University graduate: 2 (2).

5. Mikhail Konosov. Born 1937. Mechanic for Leningrad Gas System. Student by correspondence of the Gorky Institute of Literature: 4 (5).

6. Sergei Ustinovich. Born 1938. Graduate of Leningrad State University: 3 years 6 months (4).

7. Yuri Buzin. Born 1936. Engineer. Agricultural graduate: 3 (4).

8. Valeri Nagorny. Born 1948. Engineer at *LITMO* (Institute of Precision Mechanics and Optics): 3 (4).

9. Aleksandr Miklashevich. Born 1935. Engineer. Agricultural Institute graduate: 3 (3).

10. Yuri Baranov. Born 1938. Engineer. Graduate of a motion-picture engineering institute: 3 (4).

11. Bochevarov. Born 1935. Graduate of Leningrad State University: 2 years 6 months (3).

12. Anatoli Sundarev. Born 1939. Translator. Leningrad State University graduate: 2 (2).

13. Antoli Yevlev. Born 1937. Chemist. Leningrad State University graduate: 2 (3).

14. Vladimir Veretenov. Born 1936. Chemist. Leningrad State University graduate: 2 (3).

15. Olgerd Zobak. Born 1941. Mechanic at the Leningrad Institute of Precision Mechanics and Optics: 1 year 2 months (on the basis of time served in the course of the preliminary investigation) (1 year).

16. Oleg Shuvalov. Born 1938. Leningrad Institute of Precision Mechanics and Optics: 1 year 2 months (on the basis of time already served) (1 year).

17. Stanislav Konstantinov. Librarian: 1 year 2 months (on the basis of time already served) (1 year).

The violations of legality during this trial were just like those in the Moscow trial:

1. In the case of some of the accused, the limits for confinement under guard were exceeded.

2. Admission to the courtroom was by special passes to an [allegedly] "open" trial (which took place in a half-empty courtroom).

3. Most of the witnesses were removed from the courtroom immediately after testifying.

It is also not clear why the heads of the organization were tried separately, or why they were charged under the provisions of Article 64 (treason) as well as under Articles 70 and 72. Was the program compiled by them considered a "conspiracy to seize power"? If so, then the procedures used are clearly illegal. In this case, all sorts of violations of legality could have transpired during the trial of the four defendants since there was no press coverage of the trial until it had ended; it was obviously a completely closed trial.

It is reliably known that no one was charged with maintaining ties with NTS, or with engaging in [illegal] currency transactions, or with harboring a weapon.

79. *The Novosibirsk Signatories* (*from* Chronicle of Current Events)

June 30, 1968

In Novosibirsk, the basic idea of the reprisals has been to purge the *Akademgorodok*—*i.e.*, the institutes of the Siberian Department of the Academy of Sciences and the University—of those people who had signed the Novosibirsk letter. [Document 31]. This aim has been pursued in various ways, such as by persistently urging people to leave "on their own initiative," offering some of the teachers at the Physical-Mathematical School a job and an apartment in Novosibirsk proper, or by outright threats. Thirty-six-year-old R. Sagdeev, Corresponding Member of the Siberian Department of the Academy of Sciences, has proposed to "drive them all out of the *Akademgorodok*" and "make them unload pig iron." According to rumors, Academician Trofimchuk, Corresponding Member Dmitri Beliaev, Corresponding Member Slinko, and chief university Vice-Chancellor Yevgeni Bichenkov are especially active in the persecutions. On the initiative of Corresponding Member Valentin Avrorin, Dean of the Humanities Department of Novosibirsk State University, the university's department of mathematical linguistics, several of whose instructors signed the letter, has been shut down. The Philological Division of the Humanities Department of the Novosibirsk State University and the Division of Northern Languages and Siberian Linguistics at the Institute of Philosophy, History, and Literature of the Siberian Department of the Academy of Science are apparently also in jeopardy.

At a meeting of the Moscow Division of the Union of Artists, three members—Boris Birger, Yuri Gerchuk, and Igor Golomshtok—were condemned verbally, but no reprisals were taken against them. Then the presidium of the board was convened, but these three as well as five members of the presidium who could be counted upon to vote against sanctions were not informed of the meeting. Boris Birger and these five presidium members fortunately learned about the meeting and turned up there; as a result, the projected expulsion of all three was not passed.

When the newspapers—in particular, *Literaturnaia gazeta* and *Literaturnaia Rossiia*—carried articles asserting that it was not fitting for a member of the Writers' Union to sign [such] letters, several writers—including Vassili Aksionov, Yevgeni Yevtushenko, and Vladimir Tendriakov—reputedly visited the Secretariat of the Writers' Union and declared, in the name of 100 (according to other versions: 120 or 150) members of the Union, that, if even a single signatory was expelled from the Union, they would all resign.

Veniamin Kaverin is said to have made a similar declaration in behalf of himself, Pavel Antokolsky, Konstantin Paustovsky, and Kornei Chukovsky.

At the Russian Language Institute, the actions of eleven scientific associates who signed letters concerning the trial were discussed. Lev Skvortsov, a thirty-two-year-old Candidate in Philological Sciences, was the most outspoken in condemning them. His approximate words were: "I know that there is an anti-Soviet organization in Moscow and that its headquarters is in our Institute." Lev Skvortsov was one of the unpublicized "experts" brought in to analyze the authors' texts in the Siniavsky-Daniel case (the official expert, it is known, was Academician Viktor Vinogradov). Skvortsov was also an expert during the investigation of the Galanskov *et al.* case, but the results of his analysis were not presented in court because they were conjectural. It is said that the conclusions of his analysis were that the *Letter to an Old Friend*, for example, was written jointly by Galanskov and Ginzburg, even though it is apparent to the naked eye—without the application of either stylistic or textual analysis—that it was written by a person of another generation. In the judgment of the court, *Letter to an Old Friend* was an anti-Soviet document. It was also declared to be such in the final indictment. It is clear, then, how dangerous it is to be accused of being the author of this work.

The "Church" Group in Maiakovsky Square

At six o'clock, on the evening of June 17, 1968, three young English people attempted to distribute a leaflet demanding freedom for Soviet political prisoners in Maiakovsky Square in Moscow. The young people —Janette Hammond, aged twenty, John Curswell aged twenty-one, and Vivian Broughton, aged twenty-five—were detained by representatives of the state security organs and expelled from the Soviet Union the following day. They are members of the youth organization known as "Church." This organization was created a year ago. Its membership is made up of Christian radicals, Marxists, and anarchists. It is known for its numerous street demonstrations against American aggression in Vietnam. In January, following the Moscow trial, its members organized a six-hour demonstration at the Soviet Embassy in London.

The "Church" group's leaflet is in no way anti-Soviet in nature. Both the statement by Bertrand Russell and the words of the authors of the leaflet express the sympathy and concern of friends of our country with respect to the repressive measures used in the Soviet Union against freedom of speech and conscience. The leaflet opens with pictures of Yuri Galanskov and Lord Bertrand Russell and the appeal: "Freedom for Galanskov!," "Freedom for the Baptists!," "Freedom for All Political Prisoners in the U.S.S.R.!" The leaflet presents brief histories of five political prisoners: Andrei Siniavsky, Yuli Daniel, Yuri Galanskov, Aleksandr Ginzburg, and Vladimir Bukovsky; it describes the persecution of Christian Baptists in the U.S.S.R. It includes an excerpt from the appeal "To the People of the World" by Larisa Bogoraz-Daniel and Pavel Litvinov [see Document 7], as well as a statement by Bertrand Russell. The following is a slightly abridged version of this statement:

> In the West, there is a group of influential people who are always ready to condemn maliciously any event in the Soviet Union and, at the same time, to boast of the "freedom" and "democracy" that the so-called free world supposedly enjoys. Such people live in a black-and-white world and are unable to appreciate things as they are. In the West, those of us who have for many years fought against the Cold War in all its forms have welcomed the great changes that have taken place in the Soviet Union during the past fifteen years, changes that are unquestionably in the direction of greater happiness and freedom. This remarkable development is menaced by the mockery of justice that just took place in Moscow. The injustice of the court action even prompted the organ of the Communist Party of Great Britain to publish its own critical commentaries on this trial. I believe that the case of these Soviet writers should be retried by an "open" court.

Still earlier, on June 6, near the Arbat subway station, Roger de Bie, representative of the Flemish Committee to Assist Eastern Europe, circulated a petition calling for the liberation of political prisoners and containing pictures of the prisoners. Bie was also detained and expelled.

On June 23, Larisa Bogoraz-Daniel and Pavel Litvinov made the following statement:

> We are deeply moved by the courageous act of the three English youths who openly spoke out in defense of human rights in our country. Several months ago, we became convinced that our protest had met with a [favorable] response on the part of leading cultural figures in Europe and America. This provided great moral support for us. Now, on the basis of the action of the Flemish and the English, we see with joy that progressive youth in the West also understands the meaning of our struggle.

The News in Brief

At Mordvinian Camp No. 11, Vadim Gaenko, a Leningrader sentenced to four years under Articles 70 and 72 for connections with an illegal Marxist circle and the journal *Kolokol* (The Bell), lost his fingers while operating a machine tool.

In May, Yuri Galanskov and Aleksandr Ginzburg arrived in Mordvinian Camp No. 17. Their address is Mordvinian A.S.S.R., Potma Station, Ozernyi Subdivision, P. O. Box ZhKh 385/17a. From the first day of their arrival, they were put to work sewing gauntlets for special work clothing. After a time, Yuri Galanskov was sent to the camp hospital to undergo examination for stomach ulcers. Also under hospital care, and member of a construction brigade, is Aleksei Dobrovolsky. His address is Mordvinian A.S.S.R., Potma Station, Lavas Subdivision, P. O. Box ZhKh 385/3.

On May 12, Aleksandr [Yesenin-] Volpin was released after spending three months in psychiatric hospitals.

On May 16, Ilia Burmistrovich, a mathematician and candidate in Physical-Mathematical Sciences, was arrested in Moscow. The investigation is being conducted by KGB organs and, as might be expected, the charge is violation of Article 190-1 of the [R.F.S.F.R.] Criminal Code. Evidently, the specific substance of the charge is underground publishing activity. Reportedly copies of works by Siniavsky and Daniel, a stenographic account of their trial, Gorky's *Untimely Thoughts,* and copies of works by Tsvetaeva, Platonov, Kipling, Joyce, and others were found in his possession.

In late 1967 and in 1968, the following were released from Mordvinian political camps upon completing their sentences:
Aleksandr Potapov from the city of Lipetsk. Former secretary of Komsomol Committee. Article 70. Leaflets with anti-Khrushchev contents. Served five years;
Veniamin Ioffe from Leningrad. Articles 70 and 72. Illegal Marxist circle. Published the journal *Kolokol.* Served three years;
Valeri Smolkin from Leningrad. Same charge and sentence.

Since the start of the investigation, Irina Zholkovskaia has been trying to have her marriage to Ginzburg registered. The KGB told her that this question would be resolved by the court that tried Ginzburg. On February 19, she met with Judge Mironov, who told her that this matter did not depend on him since the case had been appealed to the R.S.F.S.R. Supreme Court.

80. Reprisals Against Individual Protesters (*from* Chronicle of Current Events)

Although the full extent of the reprisals against the protesters is not yet known, the following list indicates the kinds of action the Soviet regime has been taking.
1. Vladimir Dremliuga, worker, and Konstantin Babitsky, linguist and art critic, who participated in the August 25, 1968, demonstration in Red Square against the Soviet intervention in Czechoslovakia, were

sentenced, respectively, to three years of imprisonment and three years of exile in the Omsk region.

2. The following individuals were expelled from the Party:

B. Birger, artist (also demoted from membership to candidate-membership in the Union of Artists)

L. Belova, candidate in Philological Sciences and Member, Union of Cinematographers

P. Gaidenko, candidate in Philosophical Sciences (also dismissed from job; Party membership reinstated . . . severe reprimand substituted for expulsion)

A. Ogurtsov, candidate in Philosophical Sciences

L. Pazhitnov, candidate in Philosophical Sciences (also dismissed from job at Institute of Art History)

F. Suchkov, critic

Valentin Nepomniashchi, critic

V. A. Pavlenchuk, junior scientific worker (expelled from the Party . . . for underground publishing activity. The Kaluga Oblast Party Committee revoked his security clearance, and he was dismissed from his job because of a "reduction in manpower." The Party organization at the Physics and Power Institute was dissolved because it protested that the City Party Committee had violated Party regulations in expelling him.)

E. S. Kositsyna, teacher (also dismissed from job "at her own request")

S. Rozhnova, graduate student

G. S. Yablonsky, junior scientific worker (also attacked in pogrom letter written by Yu. Shpakov in the newspaper *Sovetskaia Rossiia*)

S. V. Fomin, professor of Physical-Mathematical Sciences

N. Naumov, writer

V. M. Rodionov, Doctor of Biological Sciences, U.S.S.R. Academy of Sciences

M. R. Tulchinsky, candidate in Historical Sciences; editor, Nauka Publishing House (later reinstated by the Party Control Committee attached to the CC-CPSU. Severe reprimand substituted for expulsion from the Party.)

3. In addition, the following individuals were dismissed from their jobs:

A. M. Piatigorsky, candidate in Philological Sciences, Institute for Asian Peoples (He was a member of the organizing committee for a conference in Estonia but was not given permission to attend. When he went "on his own," he was dismissed for absenteeism.)

Yu. Glazov, candidate in Historical Sciences (dismissed at request of the Learned Council)

N. Viliams, instructor

M. Grabar, lecturer

V. Meniker, economist, Institute for Economics of the World Socialist System

I. Kamyshalova, typist

N. Ustinova, typist

Yu. Aikhenvald, poet-translator, teacher of language and literature (Dismissed from job under Article 49 of Labor Code. Reinstated after appeal in court.)

V. Gerlin, teacher (Dismissed from job under the provisions of Article 49 of Labor Code. Reinstated after appeal in court. [See Document 78.])

B. Y. Yefimov, office worker (reinstated)

V. Savenkova, worker

I. Kristi, mathematician, Institute of Theoretical and Experimental Physics

R. L. Berg, Doctor of Biological Sciences, Institute of Molecular Biology, Siberian Department, Academy of Sciences

A. V. Gladky, Doctor of Physical-Mathematical Sciences, Institute of Mathematics, Siberian Department, Academy of Sciences and Novosibirsk University

F. A. Dreizin, candidate in Philological Sciences

B. Yu. Naidorf, teacher

V. S. Pertsovsky, teacher

M. I. Cheremisina, candidate in Philology

E. Shtengel, junior scientific worker

Aleksandr Kronrod, State Prize Winner, Professor/Doctor of Physical-Mathematical Sciences

L. A. Kronrod, assistant professor

Yu. A. Shikhanovich, candidate in Pedagogical Sciences

A. Ye. Gurvich, professor/Doctor of Biological Sciences

L. Krysin, linguist (expelled from Editorial Collegium of *Russkaia rech* and *Prepodavanie russkovo yazyka v shkole*)

D. Muravev, editor (appeal for reinstatement denied)

4. The following individuals were expelled from the Komsomol:

A. Kon, junior scientific worker

N. I. Romanova, mathematician

A. Aleksandrova, student (also expelled from Pedagogical Institute)

V. Luchkov, physiologist

K. Ilichev, intern

M. Luchkova, engineer

5. The following individuals received severe Party reprimands:

Yu. Davydov, candidate in Philosophical Sciences

Boris Balter, writer

Yuri Piliar, writer

Mikhail Roshchin, writer

I. S. Alekseev, engineer

L. G. Borisova, graduate student

V. A. Konev, candidate in Philosophy

A. V. Arkhangelsky, assistant professor

I. Andronov, member, U.S.S.R. Union of Artists

6. The following individuals were subjected to other reprisals:

A. I. Fet, Doctor of Physical-Mathematical Sciences (demoted to junior scientific worker)

D. M. Segal, linguist (defense of dissertation postponed indefinitely)

A. Volotskaia, junior scientific worker (defense of dissertation postponed indefinitely)

Sergei Larin, critic (expelled from the Union of Journalists)

Yu. Gerchuk, critic (expelled from the Union of Artists)

I. Golomshtok, art historian (demoted from membership in the Union of Artists to candidate-membership status for six months).

81. Letter by Yakhimovich:
"A Spectre Is Haunting Europe"

One has to reach a state of horror and panic to attack one's allies, to attack Soviet people. And indeed, did not these people—Pavel Litvinov, Larisa Bogoraz-Daniel, and others—support the Soviet government? Did they not support the Communist Party of Czechoslovakia? Perhaps they supported France, Salazar, or the military junta in Greece?

No! The Stalinists feel the ground slipping out from under them; they know the fatal hour proclaimed by history is nigh. This is the panic of the doomed. This is the panic of living corpses. But be vigilant. They have powerful modern weapons in their hands. They have the reins of authority in their hands. These are unreliable hands. These are the hands of criminals. Communists throughout the world, stop them before it is too late!

We know the fate that awaits Pavel Litvinov and [his] comrades.

We know what the accusations will be like—they will be false accusations, dirty accusations.

This is not merely guesswork on my part, I know this from my own experience. On September 25 of this year, five persons came to my apartment and conducted a search based on the suspicion that I had robbed the Yurmala Municipal *Gosbank* [State Bank] of 10,000 rubles. But they searched for and confiscated political literature and everything related to the events in Czechoslovakia, even *Pravda* and *Izvestia*, since I had inserted comments on certain statements. You can be sure that they will now "find" grounds for the direct interference of the KGB organs and for [my] arrest.

An investigator asked me why I had not worked for such a long time (since April 1 of this year). I was fired while on leave (because of a letter written to M. A. Suslov at the Central Committee). They refuse to give me a residence permit to live with my family. As anyone knows, in the U.S.S.R., without a residence permit, you can't even get a job as a janitor, nor can you get admitted to a single health clinic. How much hypocrisy it takes—when you know upon whose orders and why all these things were done—to ask an unemployed man the question: Why aren't you working? If all our newspapers are filled with slander, if they slander the fraternal Communist Party of the Czechoslovak Socialist Republic, then what does it take to slander some former collective-farm chairman or other?

Whether they wish it or not, those Communist parties that support the CPSU in its gross errors are doing the latter [the CPSU] a disservice. They are, in fact, weakening our country, since they are strengthening the adventurist elements in the leadership and weakening the healthy, progressive elements.

WE REPEAT: COME TO YOUR SENSES!
WE REPEAT: HANDS OFF THE C.S.R.!
WE REPEAT: FREEDOM FOR POLITICAL PRISONERS!
WE REPEAT: LENINISM—YES! STALINISM—NO!

I. A. YAKHIMOVICH

Former chairman of the Yauna Gvarde collective farm in Kraslavskii Region. Yurmala City—10, Latvian S.S.R., 18, Buldori Pereulok.

82. *On the Eve of Arrest: I. Yakhimovich*

Moscow
March 25, 1969

The days of my liberty are numbered. On the eve of imprisonment, I appeal to people whose names are sealed in my memory and my heart —hear me out! . . .

I am compelled to talk about myself because soon a flood of lies and hypocrisy will come out of the court. I am compelled to talk about myself because my fate is the fate of my people and my honor is their honor.

I am accused, under Article 183 of the criminal code of Latvia, of spreading false fabrications deliberately slandering the Soviet state and social system. The maximum sentence is three years' deprivation of freedom. . . .

Bertrand Russell: You are a philosopher, so perhaps you can see more quickly what the accusations are founded on. . . . What laws have I broken? The Constitution of the Latvian Soviet Socialist Republic and the Declaration of Human Rights allow one to write and distribute things, and to demonstrate, etc. . . . Whom does my freedom threaten, and why is it essential to take it away from me?

Comrade Alexander Dubcek: When seven people went out onto Red Square on August 25 [1968] with the slogans "Hands Off Czechoslovakia" and "For Your Freedom and Ours," they were beaten until they bled; they were called "anti-Soviet slanderers," "yids," and the like.

I could not be with them, but I was on your side, and I shall always be on your side as long as you serve your people honestly. "Remain firm, the sun will rise again. . . ."

Aleksandr Isaevich [Solzhenitsyn]: I am happy that I had the opportunity to read your works. May "the gift of the heart and the wine" be yours. Pavel [Litvinov] and Larisa [Daniel]: We welcomed your gladiator-like courage. "Hail, Caesar, we who are about to die salute you." We are proud of you. . . .

Peasants of the Young Guard Collective Farm: I worked with you for eight years. That is long enough to get to know a person. Judge for yourselves, and may your judgment serve the truth. Don't let yourselves be deceived.

Workers of Leningrad, Moscow, and Riga, dockers of Odessa, Liepai, and Tallinn: To save the honor of his class, the worker Valdimir Dremliuga went to Red Square to say "No" to the occupiers of Czechoslovakia. He was thrown into jail. . . . Who will help a worker if not another worker?

Comrade Grigorenko, Comrade Yakir: You are hardened fighters for truth. May life preserve you for the just cause. . . .

I address myself to people of my own nationality—to the Poles, wherever they are living and wherever they work. Do not keep silent when injustice is being done!

Poland is not yet lost while we still live.[1]

I address myself to Latvians, whose land has become my homeland, whose language I know as I know Polish and Russian. Do not forget that in the labor camps of Mordvinia and Siberia are thousands of your fellow countrymen! Demand their return to Latvia. Watch carefully the fate of everyone deprived of freedom for political reasons.

Academician Sakharov: I heard your "Reflections." I regret that I did not manage to write to you. The debt is mine.

Communists of all countries, Communists of the Soviet Union: You have one lord, one sovereign—the people. But the people is made up of living persons, of real lives. When human rights are violated, especially in the name of socialism and Marxism, there can be no two positions. Then your conscience and your honor must command.

Communists to the fore! Communists to the fore!

Above all, it is dangerous for Soviet power when people are deprived of their freedom because of their convictions, for it will not be long before it, too, loses its freedom.

The strong of this world are strong because we are on our knees.

Let us arise!

NOTE

1. This is the first line of the Polish national anthem.—ED.

83. Police Provocation: A Letter from Grigorenko to Rudenko

December 4, 1968

To: Comrade R. A. Rudenko, Procurator General of the U.S.S.R.

On November 19 of this year, a search was made of my apartment, lasting from 7 A.M. to 7 P.M.

I will not go into the fact that the person nominally in charge of this operation did not have the slightest comprehension of procedural rules or even of elementary politeness; he is a man accustomed to deciding arbitrarily the fate of persons placed in his hands. This can be substantiated by those who witnessed the behavior and actions of Justice Councillor Berezovsky, Investigator for Especially Important Affairs of the Procurator's Office of the Uzbek S.S.R. I was not obliged to endure his boorish conduct for too long a time. By way of protesting the illegal actions of those conducting the search, I refused to take further part in it half an hour after it had begun. Accordingly, I shall mention only the basic violations for which those conducting the search were alone responsible.

1. The search was made on the basis of a warrant issued by Justice Councillor Berezovsky. . . . The warrant was endorsed by Malkov, Procurator of the City of Moscow. It stated that, during the investigation of the case of Bariev and others, it had been established that documents containing slanderous fabrications against the Soviet governmental and social order were found in the apartment of P. G. Grigorenko.

I affirm, and I am prepared to bear full responsibility for this affirmation, that no evidence whatsoever of the existence of such documents was presented to Procurator Malkov. This is because, first, there is no "case of Bariev and others"; and second, there have never been, nor could there be, any documents containing slanderous statements against the Soviet governmental and social order that could be linked even indirectly with the name of Bariev and his comrades.

What, then, *is* involved here?

It is a case of ordinary *police provocation* against people who take up the fight against the tyranny of the authorities. You surely know that, on April 21 of this year, in the Chirchik City Park of Culture and Rest, the Uzbek police . . . attacked a peaceful festive gathering of Crimean Tatars commemorating the birthday of the founder of the Soviet state and the initiator of Crimean-Tatar national autonomy—V. I. Lenin. Completely unsuspecting and peacefully strolling people, dancing and singing national and revolutionary songs, as well as amateur actors staging theatrical performances were subjected to high-pressure blasts of cold water and chlorine emulsion, which threw them to the ground, ruined their clothes, and inflicted indelible moral and psychological damage. Then the police clubs went into action. The whole idea behind this was to goad the outraged people into defending themselves and then to charge them with resisting the authorities. But the people displayed unbelievable restraint and did not respond to the provocation. [Instead] they staged a peaceful protest demonstration against the humiliation to which they had been subjected. As a result, over 300 persons were arrested. Of this number, twelve—most of whom had not participated in the gathering and were arrested in their homes—were subsequently tried and *convicted* of "disturbing public order."

Aider Bariev, a tractor driver, who managed to avoid arrest, flew to Moscow the same day, and, on the morning of April 22, he sent to the Office of the Procurator of the U.S.S.R. a telegram describing in detail the Chirchik events—this unprecedented encroachment on *human rights* and infringement of the norms of *human ethics*. Naturally, he did not express himself in polite terms. In the simple language of a workingman, he called a spade a spade. He stayed on in Moscow as the authorized representative of the people who had sent him, making fruitless visits to the institutions headed by you and to other state and social organizations. Using every available means, he and other representatives of his people tried to obtain punishment of the Chirchik hoodlums and an end to the unlawful judicial persecution of the victims of the Chirchik pogrom. You made no response to the telegrams and letters of Bariev or to the collective appeals of all the representatives of the Crimean-Tatar people in Moscow at that time. Not once did you or any of your deputies receive any of these representatives, nor did you even try to get to the bottom of their complaints. . . . You, as the supreme guardian of Soviet law, were not touched by the fact that people were rounded up like wild animals on the streets of the capital of our homeland and forcibly transported, under brutal conditions, to hateful places of administrative exile. You, a jurist and an expert in the law, were not even swayed by the fact that these were not merely individuals but people's representatives—*i.e.*, citizens who did not have the right to decide to leave without the consent of those who had sent them. You passed over this fact just as you passed over the tragedies involving individuals who, trying to be worthy of the trust placed in them, resorted to desperate measures, such as jumping out of the windows of a rapidly traveling train, in order to escape from their police escorts and continue to carry out the mandate imposed on them by their people.

As soon as Bariev was replaced in Moscow by another person, he returned to Chirchik and was put under arrest. This [arrest] was based [in part] on the above-mentioned individual and collective letters from representatives of the Crimean-Tatar people, which had been sent to various Soviet institutions, including the Procurator's Office of the U.S.S.R., social organizations, and various representatives of Soviet society. It was also based on communications sent back from Moscow by the people's representatives. . . . According to the rulings handed down by individuals like Berezovsky, all these documents contained slanderous statements against the Soviet state and social order. I shall not attempt to explain here how a document containing a true description of an actual happening can somehow be transformed into something slanderous. I shall merely confine myself to asking you several questions that have a direct relationship to such fabrications.

I ask you, as the supreme defender of Soviet law, whether anyone has the right to make a person criminally answerable for writing a complaint to you, a complaint that you did not find time to examine and the facts of which you did not verify!

I ask you: Is it possible, even by the wildest stretch of the imagination, to ascribe the bloody battle in Chirchik to a violation of public order and not to a gross police provocation aimed at providing grounds for severe reprisals against a people justly struggling for national rebirth? . . .

So much for legal justification for searching my apartment. If it were only a matter of the issue at hand, I would not go on any further. But I must add that I am not clear—or, rather, I am completely in the dark—as to your personal role in both the Chirchik affair itself and the court trials of Crimean Tatars that took place following the September 5, 1967, ordinance of the Supreme Soviet of the U.S.S.R., as well as in the trials that are now being prepared. The illegal and often flagrantly provocative nature of these trials is so obvious that one marvels that this cannot be seen by a jurist of international standing, a person who is at pains to teach the entire world how to combat crimes against mankind!

2. Having established the utter lack of connection between myself and the Uzbek matters, let us attempt to determine the real reason this search was carried out and who deemed it necessary. An exhaustive answer is provided by the composition of the "investigating" group and the official-departmental-agency affiliation of the person who actually directed the search. In addition to Berezovsky, *seven* KGB agents and three "witnesses"—also state security agents—were present at the search. And so, for one official of the Uzbekistan Procurator's Office—take note of this—there were *ten* Muscovites, not counting those who barred entry to the house from the street. And all of them were from the KGB. The search was also directed by a KGB agent—Aleksei Dmitriyevich Vragov. This was all I was able to find out about him through Berezovsky. Vragov himself refused to reveal not only his position but also his place of work, even though he was required by law to inform me of both. It was this half-obscure, quasi-official person, then, who directed the search. It was directly from him that Berezovsky received his instructions. It was he that was empowered to decide such debatable matters as whether or not to confiscate this or that document. It was he who directed the activities of the other KGB agents during the search. The only thing that Berezovsky, the nominal head of the search, did

was to dictate the titles of the documents assembled by the KGB agents to the agent of the same organ who was writing up the protocol [of search].

Thus, the search was made by the KGB, which used the "Bariev case" as a pretext and connived with the investigator in charge of that case. It marked the conclusion of yet one more stage in the relations between the KGB and myself. As you know, the first stage ended with my release from the most terrible prison in the Soviet Union—the so-called special psychiatric hospital—where I was "placed" by the KGB, which was frustrated in its attempt to produce any justification for my arrest and to elicit an "open-hearted confession" from me. The next stage began two or three months after my release, when the KGB organs, without any provocation on my part, once again took an interest in me. For more than three years, I have been subjected to continuous surveillance: constant, round-the-clock trailing of myself, members of my family, and my visitors; uninterrupted observation of my apartment by visual and other means; the tapping of my telephone; inspection of my correspondence; and the confiscation of some of my letters. Twice during these years, my apartment has been secretly searched. I complained of all these actions in a letter addressed to Yu. V. Andropov, chief of the KGB. As is usually the case in our country, I received no answer. The only thing that happened was that the police-spy surveillance became less obvious. . . . It is evident that some new provocations are being planned for me, and I do not intend to await them passively.

I am a Communist, and, as such, I detest with all my soul organs of illegal force and tyranny based on caste. In our country, these organs include the organization created by Stalin and today called the KGB. . . . I conceal from no one my hatred for this organization. I consider it to be hostile to the people, and I shall fight for its early liquidation by all legal means available to me. Therefore, I do not wish to enter into any kind of relations with it, and I do not recognize its right to interfere in my life and in my social activity. This parasitic organization, which devours limitless quantities of the people's wealth while taking away their best sons and causing irreparable moral damage, must disappear from our society forever, and the sooner the better.

I have long known that the courts and the organs of the procuracy stand in a relationship of subordination to the KGB. If this requires illustration, the search conducted in my apartment is extremely revealing. The procuracy organs in this case were mere errand boys. They can continue to perform this little-esteemed role in the future, but not with respect to me. By my life, by my participation in the defense of the homeland, by virtue of the blood I have spilt for it, and by virtue of my Communist convictions, I have won the right to consider myself a co-master of my country and an equal member in the family of Soviet peoples. I am entitled to tread my native soil freely, without police-spy surveillance, to defend my convictions freely, and to enjoy all the rights vested in me as a citizen of the U.S.S.R. by the Soviet Constitution and the Universal Declaration of Human Rights. No one—least of all such an organization as the KGB—has the right to deprive me of these rights. Moreover, the procuracy organs have an obligation to help citizens fight for their legal rights and not to help organizations that are attempting to rob them of these rights.

3. After all the foregoing, it only remains to be seen just why the representatives of this organization for which I have so little esteem came [to my apartment], what they wanted from me, what they are fighting against now and—it would seem—in the future. Let us attempt to find the answer by analyzing the confiscated material.

The fact of the matter is that the confiscated materials had nothing to do with "slanderous fabrications" and did not conform to the stipulations in the search warrant. What was confiscated were all my typewritten and handwritten documents, letters, and notes. There was nothing slanderous and certainly nothing anti-Soviet in any of them. They contained anti-Stalinist materials and open statements of protest against violations of Soviet law by the authorities, against judicial tyranny, and against continuing acts of discrimination and genocide directed at the Crimean Tatars, the Volga Germans, and certain other small national groups.

This is what was confiscated:

Numerous letters, both individual and collective, addressed to me by Crimean Tatars and embodying the *cris de coeur* of a suffering and disenfranchised people; and materials pertaining to the popular movement of the Volga Germans to regain their national rights.

Copies of my letters to the Politburo of the CC-CPSU, including those relating to the arbitrary acts committed against me personally (illegal expulsion from the Party, demotion from general to private, deprivation of deserved pension) and those exposing judicial tyranny and the falsification of history to the benefit of renascent Stalinism.

A handwritten copy of a brochure by Academician Sakharov and my review of this brochure.

All the works of that tireless fighter against Stalinism, the writer-Bolshevik, participant in the revolutionary movement since 1912, and member of the Bolshevik party since 1916, who spent three years in Tsarist prisons and seventeen years in Stalinist torture chambers and death camps on Kolyma: Aleksei Yevgrafovich Kosterin.

A manuscript assembling and analyzing all the facts that had come to my knowledge pointing to the implementation, after the October (1964) Plenum of the CC-CPSU, of a concealed but firm policy directed toward a *rebirth of Stalinism.*

Notes on open court trials (criminal in form, political in substance) of Crimean Tatars who participated in the movement for national equality and of freethinking people in Moscow (the trials of Daniel-Siniavsky, Khaustov, Bukovsky, and others; the trial of Galanskov-Ginzburg and others).

Biographical data on those sentenced for a Red Square demonstration against the invasion of Czechoslovakia by Soviet troops and against the spilling of brotherly blood by Soviet soldiers and Czechoslovak citizens.

The manuscript of a work by Academician Varga entitled "The Russian Road to Socialism."

A copy of a letter by a group of Soviet intellectuals (Artsimovich, Kapitsa, Kataev, Leontovich, Plisetskaia, Sakharov, Chukovsky, and others) to the Twenty-third Congress of the CPSU, expressing alarm at trends toward a rebirth of Stalinism.

A copy of a letter written by twenty-three persons, all children of Communists who were barbarically annihilated by Stalin (Yakir, Petrovsky, Antonov-Ovseenko, Berzin, Yenukidze, Bukharin, Vavilov, Piatnitsky, and others), voicing [similar] concern over trends toward a rebirth of Stalinism and a glossing over of the crimes committed by Stalin and his henchmen, and also recalling the decision of the Twenty-second Congress to erect a monument in Moscow to the victims of Stalinism.

Translations from Czechoslovak newspapers (The "Two Thousand Words" manifesto, Smrkovsky's speech over the Czechoslovak radio, etc.).

A list of persons subjected to Party and administrative reprisals for having signed various documents protesting violations of Soviet law and of elementary human rights by the courts, the procuracy, and the KGB.

A typewritten text of the Universal Declaration of the Rights of Man, published in the U.S.S.R. in a tiny edition and only for the use of jurists.

A typewritten text of the (unpublished in the U.S.S.R.) Pacts on Rights adopted by the U.N. General Assembly two years ago, the Pact on Social and Economic Rights and the Pact on Political Rights. . . .

Notes on all speeches made at the funeral of writer A. Ye. Kosterin.

Among the literary works confiscated were Anna Akhmatova's "Requiem," dedicated to those who suffered in Stalin's dungeons, including her only son; a number of Marina Tsvetaeva's works not published in the U.S.S.R.; "Tanka," an unpublished poem by N. Korzhavin and a profound work on the morally corrupting influence of Stalinism; the book *My Testimony*, by A. Marchenko, describing present-day prisons for political prisoners; and a typewritten copy of Hemingway's book *For Whom the Bell Tolls*.

The foregoing list fairly comprehensively characterizes the principles on which the confiscations were based. In light of this, I hardly need add that everything that I myself had written was confiscated—even scraps of paper bearing a single word written by my hand. Thus I was deprived of the materials of my scientific work, my personal correspondence, drafts of various documents, including those that had been disseminated as well as those that had never left my desk. In general, everything that was typewritten, handwritten, or not published in the U.S.S.R. was confiscated. Clearly, if I had not, just the night before, given into other hands Korolenko's *Letters to A. Lunacharsky,* Gorky's *Untimely Thoughts,* and the verses of Osip Mandelshtam, all these would have been confiscated as well.

I had a copy of a book manuscript dealing with the start of the last war—*Notes of an Intelligence Agent* (the memoirs of Reserve Colonel V. A. Novobrantsev)—with an inscription by the author. When this book was also earmarked for confiscation, I vigorously protested . . . whereupon Justice Councillor Berezovsky, obeying Vragov's command to "Confiscate!," decided to demonstrate the book's slanders on Soviet society and government and read the following from the author's fore-word: "Stalin is dead, but the poisonous seeds sown by him continue to germinate."

After that, I refused to remain at the search any longer. But my presence wasn't really needed any more. After fewer than half of the items earmarked for confiscation had been recorded in writing, all the rest were dumped in a bag, sealed, and taken away. . . . Judge for yourself the degree to which the integrity of the bag's contents is guaranteed. All the more so since the [subsequent] unsealing of the bag, in which I refused to participate because of its utter senselessness, was performed in the presence of "witnesses" who themselves were agents of the organ conducting the search. Not a single one of the witnesses I insisted upon was summoned.

This is how legality was observed in each concrete instance. But I am not interested in this case alone. What I would like to know is the attitude of the organs of the *Soviet* procuracy toward *Soviet* law. My personal experience indicates that, in political matters, these organs are engaged solely in selecting those paragraphs [of the laws] that lend an appearance of legality to the unbridled tyranny of the authorities. But I naively assumed that, even for this, it was necessary to know the law. It turns out that this is not necessarily so. The paragraphs in question are evidently selected by "specialists" on law. The practical enforcers [of the laws] are in no way interested in the laws they enforce. They do what they are ordered to do, without investigating to see whether it is legal or not. Berezovsky came to make the search without any copy of the Criminal Code or the Code of Criminal Procedure, and only when I caught him in violation of the law with the aid of my own copies of these documents—and, even then, only in a few instances and very unwilling—did he alter his behavior. . . .

4. In conclusion, I would like to try, with your assistance, to answer one more question: *Why was all this done?*

Perhaps it was an attempt at intimidation? Not very likely. The KGB and I know each other too well for either of us to expect this kind of thing to happen.

Well, then, perhaps it was motivated by the hope of finding something that could be used to build a "case" and put me away in some remote place from which my voice would not be heard? Entirely possible, but, if so—stupid. To stage a trial based on trumped-up charges is risky these days, and to count on my really engaging in criminal activities . . . No, the KGB knows me too well to count on such a thing. I, too, have never counted on the stupidity of my enemy.

Accordingly, we're left with only one assumption—namely, they wanted to find out the nature of my present activities and, at the same time, to hinder them by depriving me of my materials and my "tools of production." The latter is borne out particularly by the fact that both my typewriters (office and portable) were taken away, despite the fact that there was no official authorization for this action. Moreover, the confiscation of typewriters . . . is so wildly arbitrary that it makes me uncomfortable even to mention it. Judge for yourself. Taking a sample of a typewriter's print requires only a few minutes. Furthermore, it should be done in the presence of the typewriter's owner. Why, then, are typewriters confiscated and hauled away? At best, to deprive the owner of the possibility of using them. And at worst? At worst—if you don't already know this, I will tell you—to prepare falsifications [to be used] against the typewriter's owner.

When I protested that I had not checked the confiscated documents, Investigator Berezovsky said: "What's the matter, are you suspicious of something?" . . . I fear that you, too, may ask the same question, and I will answer in precisely the same way that I answered Berezovsky: "I am suspicious of nothing. I am merely indicating the possibilities resulting from procedural violations. What will actually develop out of these possibilities the future will tell." But I have no desire to wait idly to see what the outcome will be. I therefore insist that all the violations of law committed against me be nullified.

Accordingly, I demand:

1. That all documents and both typewriters confiscated from me be returned immediately;

2. That all illegal actions with respect to me and my family be discontinued: police-spy surveillance, observation of my apartment both by visual means and with the aid of special apparatus, all tapping of telephone conversations, and the reading and confiscation of correspondence.

I assume that your authority and prerogatives—if I am to base myself, of course, on the law—are entirely sufficient to compel the proper persons to fulfill my demands. It is with this expectation that I shall await your reply.

I trust that you will take due cognizance of the fact that I have refrained from filing a complaint for the past fourteen days, thereby giving the "investigators" time to examine what they confiscated. Hoping that you will take this into consideration, I shall count on receiving your answer not later than the time limit of two weeks set by the Presidium of the U.S.S.R. Supreme Soviet [for responding to such requests].

P. GRIGORENKO

Moscow, G-21, Komsomolskii prospekt
Building 14, Apt. 96, Tel. 2-46-27-37

84. Report on the Ginzburg-Galanskov Trial by F. Ovcharenko (*from* Komsomolskaia pravda)

January 18, 1968

There is excitement among the sensation-hunting "specialists in the Russian question," the anti-Soviet propagandists of the White *émigré* press, the commentators of the *Deutsche Welle*, the Voice of America, and all the rest. A full complement of frantic cries has been raised about freedom, of which you readers and I have evidently been deprived. Pathetic and tearful petitions are already being tapped out in the West; committees are even being formed for the purposes of rescue and rendering material and moral assistance.

These "well-wishers" are firmly convinced that crude summary justice was meted out in Moscow to a group of talented young writers, the authors of works widely known to and loved by the people, selfless fighters for—well, for what? It is on this point that the various stories differ most. One feels that highly experienced commentators are finding it difficult to formulate a program of "young talents." Meanwhile, Yuri Galanskov, Aleksandr Ginzburg, and Aleksei Dobrovolsky, solemnly promoted to the status of writers by the bourgeois press and called nothing less than "outstanding poets and journalists," are not regarded as such in their own country. These names mean absolutely nothing to Soviet readers, since, to this day, not one of them has been credited with a single published line.

The furor was raised because the three, together with Vera Lashkova, laboratory assistant at a preparatory faculty of Moscow State University, recently landed in the dock. And here we shall have to talk about things extremely remote from literature.

Who were the people brought to trial?

A. Ginzburg is typical. A first-year correspondence student at an archives institute, he is over 30 and has not yet found a definite occupation. He has been a librarian, a machinist, a lighting technician in a theater, and a museum worker, but most of the time he was supported by his mother. He never stayed anywhere long. He either quit his jobs or was fired for absenteeism. Workers at the Moscow Sewage Purification Trust demanded that he be dismissed from the collective for anti-social behavior and violation of labor discipline. He hid a criminal in his apartment. In 1960, proceedings were instituted against him for swindling and for forging documents. He spent two years in confinement. In 1964, criminal proceedings were again instituted against him for similar unsavory activities.

The rest are much like Ginzburg. Proceedings were instituted against A. Dobrovolsky for pasting up hooligan leaflets in public toilets. Yu. Galanskov has also had repeated trouble with the militia as a violator of public order.

In short, where violation of the law is concerned, each one of them has accumulated experience; the same cannot be said of their writing.

This was what they were like yesterday. Today, under Article 70 of the Russian Republic Criminal Code, A. Ginzburg, Yu. Galanskov, A. Dobrovolsky, and V. Lashkova are being tried for crimes against the Soviet people.

Yesterday's loafers today stand accused of having criminal connections with the White *émigré* organization NTS, which has made its task the overthrow of the existing system in the U.S.S.R. and the restoration of bourgeois regimes; of receiving anti-Soviet literature from NTS and disseminating it in our country; of sending materials to the West that contain slander of our people and our homeland; and of engaging in manipulations connected with the receipt of foreign currency from abroad.

The courtroom was crowded. Those present included relatives of the accused, workers and employees in the capital, representatives of enterprises and organizations with which the defendants had been connected at different times.

The court attentively studied the facts, the testimony of the witnesses, the material evidence, and the conclusions drawn by the experts. Questions. Answers. The citation of documents. The story of the fall of these modern Herostratuses was traced step by step.

"We wanted our names to be known throughout the world," Yu. Galanskov declared in court; before his arrest, he and Ginzburg had worked at a museum.

They had oriented themselves, quite "professionally," to the world of the dollar and provocations. Galanskov and Ginzburg realized clearly what was expected from them in that world and what they had to do to hear words of approval, not only from the little provincial newspapers published by NTS but also from substantial weeklies with four-color covers.

Ginzburg, Galanskov, and the bookbinder Dobrovolsky, who was drawn into their crowd, passed from abstract declarations to energetic action. They became the paid agents of NTS, the so-called People's Labor Alliance, a White *émigré* organization that had formerly served Hitler and was now supported by the U.S. Central Intelligence Agency. They collected slanderous materials denigrating the Soviet state and social system, amassed and made copies of them, and then secretly sent them abroad to be used by the bourgeois press.

But they were working not just "for export." Through special messengers arriving in our country under the guise of tourists, they received NTS literature from abroad—pamphlets, books, and leaflets in which every line was steeped in hatred and bile, in which almost every page contained a call for terror.

Interrogation of the defendants disclosed some not unimportant details. Here is the testimony of A. Dobrovolsky:

PROSECUTOR—What do you know about Galanskov's and Ginzburg's connections abroad?

DOBROVOLSKY—When Galanskov gave me NTS literature and a Shapirograph, I asked him where he had obtained all this; he replied that he has had foreign contacts since 1962 and had established these contacts through Ginzburg.

PROSECUTOR—With what organization abroad was contact maintained?

DOBROVOLSKY—Galanskov said he was in contact with NTS.

When the homes of Ginzburg, Galanskov, and Dobrovolsky were searched, dozens of anti-Soviet publications from abroad were seized. These included the NTS program and regulations; the White Guard newspaper *Posev*, published in leaflet form; the inveterate anti-Soviet magazines *Nashi dni* and *Grani*; and works by NTS ringleaders and ideologists. The materials Galanskov had received from the bosses and passed on to Dobrovolsky and Ginzburg contained recommendations and instructions on forms and methods of struggle against the Soviet system, including armed struggle, and appeals for terrorist acts and for the organization of NTS cells in the Soviet Union. The pages of these sinister opuses were filled with such statements as: "The destruction of the Communist dictatorship in Russia will serve as a beginning for the normalization and renewal of the entire world." They were literally checkered with anti-Soviet terminology: "the Communist yoke," "liberation from Communism," etc. Ginzburg & Co., I repeat, not only ecstatically absorbed these publications, but also sought to propagandize them in every way. As the witness Ye. Kushev testified in court, they would accidently, as it were, foist these NTS products upon the unwitting young people who were their former schoolmates and acquaintances.

Among them was Vera Lashkova, who is now in the prisoners' dock. At one time, she had been attracted by the sham originality of her new acquaintances. Unstable by nature and without ever having seriously reflected on her political views, she succumbed to the sentiments of this threesome and became an accomplice in their criminal activities. She typed many copies of the materials, filled with slanderous spite, that her companions scurried about seeking out from morning till evening. She read the NTS literature palmed off on her and offered it to others. At times, Lashkova was doubting and anxious, but, upon being reassured by her employers that there was nothing reprehensible about it and with the more than generous pay she received per page, she soon calmed down. Of course, at the age of twenty-two, it is already possible to judge the nature of one's activities independently. But this simple idea did not occur to her until too late.

"I gave impermissibly little thought to facts I should have strictly weighed. Had I done so in time, everything might have been different," V. Lashkova said contritely in court.

Without detracting from the seriousness of V. Lashkova's guilt, it should, nevertheless, be admitted that her participation in the criminal game concocted by the NTS accomplices was to some extent fortuitous. The case of Ginzburg, Galanskov, and Dobrovolsky is quite different. They knew what they were doing. This is why they always maintained the strictest conspiratorial secrecy. Their NTS friends helped them do this. They set up a prearranged code for them and provided special cryptographic devices.

When the homes of Ginzburg, Galanskov, and Dobrovolsky were searched, espionage equipment was discovered—special cryptographic paper, Shapirographs, anti-Soviet literature and leaflets. All these were used when the occasion arose. The testimony of the defendant V. Lashkova is of interest in this connection.

PROSECUTOR—Did Galanskov ask you to type some sort of coded letter?

LASHKOVA—Yes, I typed a letter for him.

PROSECUTOR—Tell the court when and in what circumstances.

LASHKOVA—At Galanskov's home, I made one copy, on onionskin paper. The letter was not written to anyone in particular; at any rate, there was no address. The letter was somewhat nebulous in content, but it contained figures. That is, a code of some sort. It was not completely coded, but certain phrases and words were in code.

PROSECUTOR—What, approximately, was the text like?

LASHKOVA—It spoke of Nos. 101, 102, and 103, etc., and of the relations among them.

PROSECUTOR—No. 101 did not want to call on No. 103?

LASHKOVA—I said: the relations among the numbers.

PROSECUTOR—There was something that could not be done at No. 104's apartment—

LASHKOVA—That's the letter.

It was established in court that the voluntary lackeys of NTS received from abroad large sums of money in American dollars and Soviet rubles. This was the payment for their treason. Through intermediaries, Yu. Galanskov sold the dollars to foreign currency speculators for rubles. This did not come off without incident. After receiving some $50 bills from Galanskov on one occasion, the black marketeers contrived to palm off on him a packet of mustard plasters in exchange. All sorts of things happen among one's own kind.

As for the rest, matters seemed to be proceeding successfully and had manifestly gained in scope. One after another, NTS emissaries arrived from abroad under the guise of tourists. Brooke, an Englishman; Philippe, a Frenchman; Schaffhauser, a citizen of the F.R.G.; and Mikulinskaia, the daughter of a colonel in the Tsar's army—all of them hastened to look up Ginzburg, Galanskov, and Dobrovolsky. The three were given fat parcels of anti-Soviet literature and the latest instructions on obtaining, in return, information of interest to them. Special messengers were sent to them from Paris, Stockholm, Heidelberg. Their names figured in the foreground of the manuals compiled for NTS couriers. These zealous collectors of fraud were passed off as budding titans of the pen. Who would not go all out in such circumstances?

Ginzburg labored ceaselessly at compiling an entire anthology of slanderous materials. He had gotten hold of, among other works, "A

Letter to an Old Friend," a sample of the primitive anti-Soviet con-
coctions disseminated by our enemies. Under the guise of discussions of
events of the recent past, it trotted out ideas deeply hostile to socialism
and contained crude and slanderous fabrications that denigrated the
Soviet people and our country.

An NTS emissary, introduced as Heinrich, soon arrived from France.
With Ginzburg's consent and approval, Galanskov secretly handed over
to Heinrich the slander that had been collected. The NTS magazine
Grani published the material forthwith and exultantly told its readers
of its growing ties with the "Russian underground." The reactionary
newspapers and magazines also threw themselves greedily at this package of slander that had come their way and boldly proceeded to unwrap
it in issue after issue. The anthology compiled by Ginzburg was issued
in Russian and German by the NTS publishing house Posev. With a
haste that left no doubt as to the motives, it was promptly published
in France and Italy. And every copy bore the words: "Compiled by A.
Ginzburg."

Now the partners had new concerns. From the lies still left in reserve,
they compiled a new anthology with the pretentious title of *Phoenix*.
Again, the title page said: "Edited by Yu. Galanskov." Through a resourceful NTS emissary, this work was conveyed to Paris. And *Posev*
and *Grani* again went into ecstasies. They sent the newly received materials to the editors of bourgeois newspapers and magazines and to radio
stations; all these made wide use of them in the ideological sabotage
against the Soviet Union.

This was followed by promises to acquaint the public with the
"latest" as soon as it arrived. For reasons beyond the control of mes-
sieurs publishers and commentators, however, an urgent change had to
be made in the plans that had already been drawn up. In lieu of the
promised messages came an announcement that the enterprising seekers
of glory had been arrested.

However, the general dejection was short-lived. Such a turn of events
was a sensation too, after all. It presented a real opportunity to raise
another furor in defense of "writers fallen victim to arbitrary rule." And
the merry-go-round of slander and fantastic fabrications was sent spin-
ning in the opposite direction with renewed force.

Unfortunately, massive misinformation often accomplishes its purpose.
If such celebrities as the Nobel Prize winner François Mauriac, the
well-known actor Jean-Louis Barrault and Françoise Sagan could have
swallowed the bait, what about ordinary people, who are quite inexperienced in such matters? It was precisely such inexperience and dangerous lack of responsibility that played a filthy trick on the young
Venezuelan Nicholas Brocks-Sokolov, who arrived in the Soviet Union
from Grenoble in December of last year.

Before coming to our country this very young towheaded fellow had
attended a lecture by a certain Mikhail Slavinsky devoted entirely to
the "problems" of developing, in the U.S.S.R., underground and clan-

destinely exported literature. Nicholas, who had come to France from Venezuela only recently, could not know that before him was an experienced and cunning intriguer specializing in slander and sabotage against the Soviet land and its people. Slavinsky had once headed the anti-Soviet Young Russia Organization in France, had worked at the NTS center in Frankfurt-am-Main (F.R.G.), had headed a group of agents organizing provocations against Soviet citizens at the Brussels World Fair, and had engaged in preparing hostile actions on the eve of the World Youth and Student Festival in Vienna. He is now a member of the NTS leadership. It is extremely noteworthy that this specialist in provocations and sabotage has changed his specialty and is now engaged in so-called underground literature. Slavinsky spoke with inspiration and at length of Ginzburg, Galanskov, and Dobrovolsky, who have now come to grief. . . .

The masters of prevarication, together with those who have not taken the trouble to ponder what has happened, are making efforts to present Ginzburg, Galanskov, and Dobrovolsky as some sort of meek creatures who, at worst, did not realize what they were doing. This is followed by lengthy arguments on the necessity to make allowances for their youth, on the inevitable mistakes of young people. Enough of this, gentlemen! We are not dealing with childish pranks, nor with a mischievous pen wielded by youngsters who have just left their parents' care. The people on trial here are far from boyhood. One of them is 30, and the two others about the same. Galanskov has even been married twice. Dobrovolsky has a son who has long been playing soccer. It is time that those fond of attributing all sins and abominations to youth realized that their position is fallacious in principle and utterly unfounded in this case. These innocent lambs kept track of their "rewards" with the calculation of seasoned merchants and maintained utter silence with the cunning of hardened criminals. Strange reasoning, indeed.

Dobrovolsky and Lashkova admitted their guilt and told the court about everything, which, by the way, was taken into account in determining their punishments. Ginzburg and Galanskov, on the other hand, continued to wiggle, cringe, and play unexpected tricks to the very end, though pressed to the wall by the material evidence and the testimony of witnesses. For example, both suddenly declared that they did not consider what they had done in collaboration with the NTS organization, which is hostile to our people, as anti-Soviet activity.

But what, then, are we talking about? How else is one to term their stealthy abuse of our country and the dignity of Soviet man? How else is one to brand betrayal and base behavior?

There was something else one could not help reflecting on in the courtroom: the brazen, unpardonable speculation in people's interest in and natural respect for literature, in people's confidence in the writer's personality, which is of long standing in our country. After all, it was not for nothing that Ginzburg and Galanskov, pushing hard for fame, fervently craved to become known as writers. There was a careful calculation here. They knew full well that nothing but general approval would greet sentences, no matter how severe, handed down to, say, speculators in foreign merchandise, currency speculators, or spies. But the role of a writer persecuted for his convictions is an entirely different matter. So if plenty of noise could be made ahead of time ("Help! They are infringing on freedom of creativity!"), then, you see, not only would the ordinary man be shaken but even more important people would swallow the bait and express sympathy.

The defendants were called writers, but, when it was ascertained that this role was clearly inappropriate to them, they were reclassified as "Moscow intellectuals." A very "intellectual" shuffle and very bright scoundrels indeed!

The criminal activities of Ginzburg, Galanskov, Dobrovolsky, and Lashkova have been completely exposed. Their guilt has been incontrovertibly proved by the testimony of a large number of witnesses, by numerous documents, material evidence, and authoritative expert conclusions. Taking into account the defendants' personalities, the degree of their sincere repentance, and a number of other circumstances important in principle, the Moscow City Court sentenced Yu. Galanskov to seven years' deprivation of freedom and his accomplices in crime A. Ginzburg, A. Dobrovolsky, and V. Lashkova to five years', two years', and one year's deprivation of freedom, respectively. The Muscovites present in the room received the sentence with applause and exclamations of approval.

A. M. Gorky once made the following contemptuous remark concerning the intrigues of enemies of our state and their servile hangers-on: "What poverty of thought. What destitution of spirit. And what hypocrisy!" Almost forty years have passed since this was said, but our foes, both covert and overt, at critical moments, continue to turn up in the same old spiritual rags. There is the same depressing puniness of ideas. I daresay only their hypocrisy has increased. This is true of the slanderers themselves, as well as of those who are clumsily attempting to shield and protect them.

85. *"Sham Daring," by A. Chakovsky* (from **Sovetskaia Rossia**)

Moscow
January 28, 1968

. . . Our upbringing work is directed at the people of the 1960's. Their world outlooks, joys, and anxieties took shape under the influence of many factors characteristic of our times.

Yes, these people are dedicated to the great Communist idea, to their Communist Party, and have faith in it. But it should not be forgotten that many of them are young. They did not go through the school of political struggle, as their fathers and older brothers did. . . .

These people were formed in the 1950's and early 1960's, which, like all the past stages in the development of the Soviet state, will go down in our history as years of great creative accomplishments. But one should not lose sight of the fact that these years were complex and in many ways contradictory.

In solving concrete tasks of Communist upbringing, we have no right to forget that our enemies abroad are waging a struggle for the souls of people, especially of young people, and, with monstrous cunning and hypocrisy, are flooding us every day with their murky radio waves.

In recent years the enormous, purposeful work done by our Party has not only activized the creative thought of Soviet people but also made them more active socially. Such concepts as daring creative quests, further socialist democratization of our lives, and aspirations to civic activeness and high principles have become especially attractive to the broad masses.

But our enemies, in seeking to play on precisely these chords, exploit this circumstance, for contrabandists have always sought to export their wares in packaging that is attractive and arouses no suspicion.

We have many good books, plays, and motion pictures, but the Soviet public often criticizes certain writers, scenarists, and theater directors for losing their sense of the real proportions between the bright and shadowy aspects of our lives, for their despondency and the shallowness of their themes, for their unthinking modernization of the classics, wherein an actor, at the will of an "innovating" director, foists upon his contemporaries the philippics an author long dead had addressed to the decadent society of Tsarist bureaucracy.

We should be not disconcerted but, on the contrary, pleased when a Soviet artist armed with genuine knowledge of life fearlessly invades it by posing in his works urgent problems of our times. Failure to understand the logic of this aspiration means failure to understand the spirit of the times.

The chief line of development of literature and art in our period is marked by just such aspiration, and this cannot fail to gratify Soviet people. However, in recent years, certain different, collateral tendencies, so to speak, have become characteristic of the artistic creative process. Though opposed in content, these tendencies are similar in their fundamental inadmissability.

We have already spoken about one of them: Its meaning lies in an unqualifiedly negative approach to entire periods of Soviet history. This is unquestionably a harmful and unjustified tendency.

But there is another tendency that deserves condemnation—when the artist attempts to portray particular events of the past without regard for the critical-analytical work conducted by the Party, beginning with its Twentieth Congress. Both tendencies contradict the truth of life and are, hence, false.

It is paradoxical but true that the bearers of such tendencies usually appear under the flag of daring. "I dared!" a given literary figure says or thinks. "And, whereas everyone before me maintained that man the creator was the chief hero of Soviet life, my hero will be the contemplative milksop who reviles everyone and everything!"

"I dared!" another announces in portraying particular events in the history of Soviet society and its struggle for Communism as if he had drawn no conclusions from our Party's analysis of the complexity and contradictions of this struggle.

"I dared!" a director who shall remain nameless says in attempting to convince himself and others by drawing analogies between events of the last century or remote antiquity and the present day. And there are those who see daring in overtly or covertly flirting with our class enemies.

There is no denying that, today, in the West, it is easier than ever to win the title of Soviet writer. All you have to do is write some anti-Soviet slogans on a fence and you are a writer. Our class enemies announce that they too are writers who, on orders from the foreign White Guard riffraff, have composed anti-Soviet proclamations. The title of writer is also given to the person who bound these proclamations into a magazine of sorts. And the typist who made copies of NTS appeals is also a writer. Why not? Are not they all writers? Does not this word come from the word "to write"?

The ease with which one can acquire, in the bourgeois West, the title of "Soviet writer" or, better yet, of "well-known, outstanding, progressive writer" unfortunately tempts some, though happily very few, of the professional litterateurs among us.

Apparently, "glory" becomes especially enticing to them when it is achieved not through great labor for the good of the people but merely through a widely circulated copy of a declaration or through showily signing some sort of letter dear to the hearts of our ideological opponents. A Party official who spoke at a conference on the tasks of ideological work made a very apt and scathing remark about this. He said that, if it were too much to ask such litterateurs to display the "Soviet pride" celebrated by Maiakovsky, one might wish them at least to follow the example of Maupassant's Boule de Suif, who, as is known, refused to flirt with the enemy.

Of course, the absolute majority of Soviet writers are implacable toward our ideological opponents and contemptuously reject their advances, their slanderous attempts to exploit the title of Soviet writer for their own ends. *Literaturnaia gazeta* carried Galina Serebriakova's angry exposé of the Polish *émigré* publishing house Kultura. This foul-smelling Kultura published in Paris an incomplete, unfinished novel entitled *The Sandstorm*, which, in manuscript form, had surreptitiously landed in the publishing house's portfolio. In this case, it had violated not only the author's rights but also elementary moral norms. . . .

The writer Vladimir Tendriakov resolutely repudiated the provocational methods of an Associated Press correspondent who crudely distorted Tendriakov's ideas in an interview with scholars and students at Keele University in Britain. Valentin Kataev, the author of many favorite books of the people, publicly exposed the unworthy action of Alexander Werth, who had resorted to what he subsequently admitted was a "dubious journalistic trick" and attributed to the Soviet writer ideas he had never expressed.

All these cases exemplify the real civic daring of the Soviet writer. The concept of pseudo-daring must be discredited on a nationwide scale. For it is not daring but cowardly to replace the labors of real creativity by trickery, serious analysis by the pursuit of cheap and superficial analogies, criticism by veiled nose-thumbing, and only half-veiled at that.

No indeed. Poseurs and "glory seekers" have no right to appear under the banner of daring, for daring is inseparably linked with creative quests, with the struggle for genuine truth—*i.e.*, for the construction of communism—with joint struggle alongside the Party and the people.

86. *"Writers and Spies: Some Parallels," Letter from a Reader and Reply by A. Chakovsky* (*from* Literaturnaia gazeta)

Letter from G. Novikov:

Leningrad

To the editors of *Literaturnaia gazeta*:

Esteemed Comrade Editor Chakovsky!
For more than ten years, I have regularly read *Literaturnaia* with great satisfaction.

The controversies and discussions about major literary problems arouse my special interest. At the last Writers' Congress, Sholokhov's speech rightly expressed alarm at the fact that very few young writers were represented (13 per cent) and that their voices were not fully heard.

This is why I think that *Literaturnaia gazeta* is making a mistake in keeping silent now about the campaigns launched by the world press over the trial of the group of young writers. Most important, it is evading its readers' desire to know the true situation, at least within the bounds of counterpropaganda.

I expected *Literaturnaia gazeta* to carry comprehensive articles on this troubled situation in the literary world. For not only is this a matter of gross violations of the principles of legality at a trial; the problem of the treatment of the Soviet intelligentsia, its creative daring and freedom of opinion, is growing more pointed, and this is linked to the consequences of the cult of personality. It is unclear on the basis of what considerations (I would like to say—expediency) it is possible to hush up questions that are now so well known to the Soviet reader from radio broadcasts and the world press.

This is why I ask *Literaturnaia gazeta* to show its true worth and respond to the latest events in the literary world.

Chakovsky's reply:

Moscow
March 27, 1968

Esteemed Comrade Novikov!

It is possible that you are right in reproaching *Literaturnaia gazeta* for failing to carry "comprehensive articles" in connection with the campaign launched by the bourgeois press and radio after the trial of the anti-Sovieteers. I tell you frankly that the editors of our *writers'* newspaper simply did not deem it necessary to make a *special* reply to bourgeois propaganda, which has importunately passed off as Soviet *writers* people who *never* (at least in our country) published one line *anywhere*.

But, obviously, the propaganda has left its traces. Even you, Comrade Novikov, call this group of anti-Soviet undergrounders "a group of young writers." Why? *Only because* that is what they are called by Voice of America and BBC and the German Wave?

If Western radio were the only source of information about this trial, I would understand your delusion, although some essential doubt, based on many years of experience and natural to a Soviet person, as to the purity of bourgeois propaganda's intentions should, it seems to me, have put you on your guard here.

But other sources of news exist. Soviet ones. *Izvestia* wrote about the trial (January 16, 1968). *Komsomolskaia pravda* covered it in detail (January 18, 1968).

Perhaps these reports failed to satisfy you? Perhaps something in them seemed inaccurate to you or inadequately argued, or perhaps something aroused doubt?

I assume this to be the case. And had you sent a letter to the above-mentioned newspapers, a letter describing the specific points that puzzled you, and had you asked for exhaustive explanations, I have no doubt that you would have received them. However, there are no such specific questions in your letter as published here.

Nevertheless, we deem it necessary to answer it. And not within the bounds of "counterpropaganda," as you say, but in terms of the substance of the questions touched upon. That's how.

Press reports and eyewitness accounts by people who attended the court examination are the natural and customary sources of information for citizens about any trial.

Later, we shall return to the eyewitnesses. Now, we shall discuss the press.

We learned from its reports about four people who came in contact with a foreign counterrevolutionary organization—the NTS [The People's Labor Alliance]—that sets as its goal the overthrow of the socialist system in our country and that collaborated in the last war with the Hitlerites and is stained with the blood of Soviet citizens.

This foursome received anti-Soviet materials from the NTS for clandestine circulation in our country, participated in machinations with foreign currency supplied from abroad, and sent slanderous materials to the West.

From an article published in *Komsomolskaia pravda*, we know that, during a search, dozens of anti-Soviet publications received from abroad were confiscated from Ginzburg, Galanskov, and Dobrovolsky. Among them were the NTS program and charter, the White Russian newspaper *Posev*, issued in the form of eight leaflets, the confirmed anti-Soviet journals *Nashi dni* and *Grani*, and works by NTS ringleaders and ideologists. The materials Galanskov received from this organization and passed on to Dobrovolsky and Ginzburg contained recommendations and instructions on forms and methods of struggle against the Soviet system, including armed struggle, and appeals for terrorist acts and for the organization of NTS cells in the Soviet Union. These materials contained such statements as: "The destruction of the Communist dictatorship in Russia will serve as a beginning for the purification and renewal of the entire world"; their terminology included expressions like "Communist yoke," "liberation from Communism," etc.

These are the basic facts we know. From the dialogue between the prosecutor and the defendants, which was also cited in material that has been published, it is known that several of the accused confessed their crimnal ties with NTS. The others were convicted by objective evidence.

Now, I would like to say the following.

As a Soviet citizen, I feel repugnance for the sort of activities that the defendants engaged in. I have no grounds not to trust the court or the information in the Soviet press and, consequently, no grounds to doubt that these people were convicted in accordance with the laws of the Soviet Union.

I also want to say that, as a writer and publicist, I am aware of other forms of public protection against anti-Soviet propagandists. I favor, if you will, a more severe punishment from the moral standpoint. I think that, if these four were placed face to face with a broad audience consisting of workers and members of the intelligentsia—a meeting that, most likely, would tell them everything it thinks of them—and if, as a result, the anti-Sovieteers were subjected to public ostracism, the punishment would prove more severe and effective. I also want to add that it would be worthwhile to give the people who hate the Soviet system and are seduced by the fate of Tarsis, who vanished into a Western Lethe, the opportunity to share his fate. And, instead of giving such people food and drink in prison or corrective-labor colonies at the people's expense, it would be worthwhile to shift the responsibility for their maintenance to American, British, or West German taxpayers. Such, frankly, is my opinion.

But let us return to the trial. We are told by some people abroad that it was illegal. Why? Because it was "closed." What does that mean? Is it the rule in bourgeois judicial practice that trials of people who threaten the security of the capitalist system are held in New York's Lincoln Center or London's Trafalgar Square? Do American courts send invitations to Soviet correspondents with a most humble request to attend a trial of the latest "Red spy"? Has it never happened in American, British, or other bourgeois courts that a courthouse attendant has stood before the closed door of a courtroom where a case is being tried, shrugged, and said in dismay:

"I'm sorry, gentlemen, but there is no space, the courtroom is over-crowded."

And yet—oh, what magnificent propaganda casuistry! If foreign correspondents were not invited to the Moscow trial, it meant the trial was "closed" and "secret." If they had been invited, the testimony of "impartial eyewitnesses" would have been circulated to present the accused as innocent lambs whose guilt was absolutely unproved.

Some Soviet writers, who were not present at the trial, have attempted to discredit it in their letter broadcast by the Voice of America. But why must I believe them and not, say, Prof. V. Menshikov, Doctor of Medicine; Prof. A. Gromov, head of the Forensic Medicine department; and docents K. Tarasov and V. Tumasian, candidates of Philosophy and History, respectively? Why am I obliged to believe Litvinov and his proclamations and not the letter from the above-mentioned scientific workers? This letter, addressed to the U.S.S.R. Writers' Union, says, incidentally, the following:

We, a group of teachers at Moscow Medical Institute No. 1 who attended the trial, are deeply angered by the fabrications contained in the statement by a group of writers; we express our resolute protest against such manifestations, which are aimed at misinforming public opinion and discrediting Soviet legal bodies. We did not see in the courtroom the individuals who signed the statement, and we are baffled as to where they obtained their information.

All the defendants and witnesses, and about forty of them were called, enjoyed complete freedom of speech. The defendants' relatives and friends sat in the courtroom, and not one of them, throughout the entire trial, expressed doubt as to the objectivity and conclusiveness of the materials in the inquiry.

The trial proceeded in an atmosphere of calm, thorough, and serious examination of the case. The defendants' guilt was obvious even to inexperienced people. It was openly and sincerely confessed by Dobrovolsky and Lashkova and corroborated by the testimony of witnesses, in particular Brocks-Sokolov and others. Moreover, we were astonished by the patience of the Soviet state bodies, which repeatedly warned the accused but the latter drew no conclusions for themselves.

The bourgeois radio stations allege that the courtroom audience consisted of handpicked people—plainclothes "KGB men," "militiamen," etc.

In which category should the authors of the quoted letter be placed?

Do you want still another letter? Fine. It is also addressed to the Writers' Union and is also related to the bourgeois radio stations' "popularizations" of the declarations of some Soviet writers:

> We were present in the courtroom, together with many other citizens. We declare that the open trial of Ginzburg, Galanskov, Dobrovolsky, and Lashkova observed all established procedural guarantees of justice. . . .
>
> The actions of certain individuals who continue to sell abroad false information about the trial arouse profound indignation. Individuals who sign "protests" and speculate in freedom of convictions, as well as the members of the intelligentsia who secretly hope to gain fame in the West, must realize that they will have neither glory nor popularity—only a shameless flirtation with our ideological enemies.

This letter was signed by a number of teachers at the Moscow Highway Institute—Comrades V. T. Yefimov, G. F. Yudin, N. S. Kuznetsov, N. M. Vasilyev, V. A. Yelizarov, Ye. V. Starostin, and I. I. Kravtsov.

The Writers' Union and the U.S.S.R. Artists' Union also heard from a group of scientists from the All-Union Raw Materials Research Institute: Comrades G. S. Momdzhi, N. D. Sobolev, Ya. D. Gotman, L. M. Shamovsky, A. D. Yershov, V. M. Grigoryev and V. I. Kuzmin, all Doctors of Sciences and senior staff scientists. Their letter protests the attempt to discredit a Soviet court that was "immediately exploited by the hostile propaganda apparatus of a number of capitalist countries in order to reinforce the myth that political opposition to the policies of the CPSU and the Soviet government exists in the midst of the Soviet intelligentsia." A letter with similar contents was sent to the Writers' Union by a group of workers (thirty people) at State Bearing Plant No. 1.

We are assured from abroad that, because the courtroom audience was relatively small, the trial was "closed." A strange argument. The fact that a courtroom holds 100 people means that the audience is "handpicked." If it holds 500, the "argument" remains the same: After all, hundreds can also be "handpicked." Are not the Western champions of human rights urging us to hold trials in public squares? Are they not implying that only these conditions can ensure painstaking inquiry and a calm atmosphere remote from hysterical passions?

How is one to know? At any rate, I heard with my own ears an American radio broadcast in the Russian language that, immediately following the latest accusations of "secrecy" with respect to the trial of the four anti-Sovieteers, went on to report that China had held a trial of Mao Tse-tung's opponent in a stadium holding 20,000 people, after which the principal defendants had been executed.

Let us take another example—one our newspaper recently reported.

A case was fabricated against the American poet and playwright Le-Roi Jones, in "full conformity" with the laws of the state of New Jersey. He was accused of illegal possession of a weapon. Penalties in cases of this sort in this American state usually do not exceed six months' imprisonment. But Jones was sentenced to three years' imprisonment and was fined $1,000. The whole point is that LeRoi Jones is a fighter for the civil rights of the Negro population. A journal with his poems figured in court as "material evidence." Before the sentencing, the judge quoted Jones's verses. How many such trials are now taking place in the United States, where fighters for civil rights and fighters against the dirty war in Vietnam are being tried in the name of the law!

The Moscow trial had nothing in common with such excuses for trials. So, on what basis, by what right are those who organize and encourage legal reprisals in the capitalist countries attempting to teach us legal procedure and democracy!

Now we shall discuss "creative daring" and "freedom of opinion." It is essential for us, Comrade Novikov, to reach agreement on the most important thing: Do you feel that freedom of opinion in our country should include freedom to urge the overthrow of the Socialist system, freedom of contact with foreign counterrevolutionaries, and freedom to circulate their propaganda materials?

If so, then I resolutely differ with you. But if you favor freedom of criticism that presupposes, as an indispensable condition, the preservation and improvement of socialism, then I am completely with you. If you feel that criticism and self-criticism must be developed in our country even more actively (although, in order to estimate the level of their development, it suffices to direct one's gaze to the relatively recent past), then I also agree with you.

Bourgeois propaganda has also set in motion the following version: It alleges that the accused were not anti-Sovieteers but zealots for improving Soviet life.

In this connection, Comrade Novikov, let us ask whether history has known even one case when a man undertook hostile actions against his country under the flag of hatred for it. No, he has always shouted about his love for his people, trying, thereby, to provide moral justification for his act of betrayal.

Now, something else. A number of foreign writers, including several quite respected ones, came to the defense of the accused. Why? I think this can be explained by several factors. First, they are not immune to lies, especially when these lies are reproduced daily by all the propaganda media. Obviously, these writers believe they are defending a just cause.

There are also the Western writers who profess the principle of "fifty-

fifty," or "half-and-half." They fear being suspected of showing un-
qualified sympathy for Communism and believe that, if, yesterday, they
signed a protest against the war in Vietnam or against racial persecution in the U.S.A., today, they must "balance" this by joining in some
action against our country. Of course, there are other factors at work
here. There are writers who have failed to gain fame through their literary works, who crave easy popularity and are ready to link their names
to any sensationalism.

Well, what is the situation with Soviet people, including a few professional writers, whose letters addressed to Soviet organizations arrive
with astonishing synchronism, and sometimes even ahead of time, in
America, Britain, and West Germany? Incidentally, it was in connection with the bourgeois radio stations' broadcast of one such letter that
a number of Soviet citizens sent their protest to the Writers' Union.
Perhaps my opinion of the Soviet writers who authored the letter will
be of interest to you. Well, in this case, I do not want to "tar them all
with the same brush." Obviously, there are those among them who are
sure that they are fighting for the restoration of the truth, although the
astonishing readiness of the anti-Soviet radio stations to broadcast their
letters should have put these comrades on their guard. I think there are
also others among them who cannot resist the temptation to flirt with
the enemy, particularly if this flirtation gives them the fame that takes
many years to win through literary works.

And one last item. This is not the first year that all kinds of lying
"voices" have devoted broadcasts to Soviet writers. These broadcasts
long ago turned into a sort of radio comedy serial portraying Soviet
writers as people who dream, day and night, of a capitalist paradise. If
one believes the bourgeois "radio-illusion," our writers think of nothing
else than how to sell their socialist birthright—if not for a mess of
pottage, then for British porridge or American apple pie.

I want to say that this is an abominable, provocative lie. For many
years, I have known hundreds of writers—Moscow and Leningrad
writers, Russian, Ukrainian, Belorussian, Uzbek and other writers—who
live and work in our fraternal republics. As a writer and simply as a
Soviet citizen, I know that the overwhelming majority of those engaged
in the complicated, laborious writer's trade are genuine citizens of the
Soviet Union, convinced builders of a socialist culture and a Communist
society. And, on this point, I would also like to say something for everyone to hear in connection with the "radio broadcasts" and "world press"
reports that you mentioned, Comrade Novikov.

In the concluding lines of your letter, you call on *Literaturnaia gazeta*
to respond to "the latest events in the literary world." If you, as the
contents of the letter imply, mean that same trial and what is happening
around it, I would like once more to clarify something. This is not an
event "in the literary world." It is an episode in the ideological struggle
—the same struggle that never ceases for a minute, a struggle in which,
for our enemies, all means are fine and the end justifies the means.

87. *"Whose Side Are You on?"* by S. Mikhalkov
(*from* Literaturnaia gazeta)

April 3, 1968

. . . Our writers' Party *aktiv*, which met on the eve of the capital's Nineteenth Party conference, asked me to report to you, comrade delegates, that the capital's Party organization can count on the 1,500-strong detachment of Moscow writers, the largest writers' organization in the Soviet Union. (*Applause.*)

We consider literature a Party matter, and never will we betray this principle. (*Applause.*) . . .

International imperialism spares neither forces nor funds in its subversive work against the countries of the socialist camp. It resorts to all possible means: bribery, blackmail, slander, and ideological subversion. It lures, snares, and pushes into a web and labyrinth of lies, falsehood, and misinformation the weaker, less stable, shortsighted, politically immature, and hence unprincipled persons. As you know, this has been graphically demonstrated in Poland, where the Party Central Committee and the working class succeeded in disclosing in time the secret machinery of provocational antipopular subversive work aimed against all the gains of socialist people's Poland. Unfortunately, a segment among Polish writers played quite an ignoble role in reaction's political adventure.

Comrades! The Moscow writers' organization is boundlessly devoted to the Communist Party. It sees its chief task in serving the people. But we cannot and must not gloss over certain developments that have occurred in the past two years and are still occurring in our writers' life.

Yes, as they say, "there is no family without a black sheep." I have in mind those few writers who have forgotten that the citizen of a socialist society must answer to society for the political and moral consequences of his acts. . . .

A Soviet court condemned two political slanderers and double-dealers. Strange as it seems, among our writers, volunteer spokesmen appeared who took up the defense of the accomplices of the camp hostile to us. Seventeen Party members out of 700 Communist writers in Moscow followed the lead of those who concocted a written protest to superior Soviet and Party bodies. This message hardly had time to be delivered to its addressees in the capital before it was published, by some miraculous means, in the foreign press. . . .

In all fairness, it should be noted that, if one does not count three or four famous writers' names, most of the signers of these letters have not added luster to our literature, have not enriched it with anything substantial, and it is not they who determine the true image of the writers' community. But among them are Party members, and we have the right to ask them: Is this your political stand or political immaturity? Whom are you defending? In any event, the behavior of these Communists has nothing in common with the concept of the class consciousness of likeminded Party members, of responsibility to the Party and society. Especially since many have no idea of the essence of the case or the people on whose behalf they appealed.

"What impelled you to sign such dubious political documents?" they were asked. "Writers should be humanists," they replied. It is appropriate to remind these writers of Maxim Gorky's interpretation of humanism. The great son of a great people considered genuine humanism to be the militant humanism of uncompromising struggle against the hypocrisy and falsehood of those who are trying to save the old world.

"The heart that is tired of hating cannot learn to love," Nekrasov wrote. Yes, to hate enemies untiringly—this is humanism for the sake of friends, for the sake of one's people. (*Applause.*)

Comrades! I have spoken here of so-called collective letters. Bourgeois propaganda took these letters into its arsenal, hailed the writers of these documents for "progressive" views, for "boldness," and advertised their names. But it is not only letters that alarm us. The position of some writers, particularly Communists, who speak at some meetings and literary evenings alarms us no less.

Recently three Communists in our organization received strict Party reprimands for making profoundly mistaken public statements. Two of them were punished not by our [Writers' Union] Party committee but by the bureau of the Frunze Borough Party committee and the bureau of the city Party committee. Why were we ourselves incapable of strictly and promptly calling to order those who deserve our condemnation? Because attitudes of general forgiveness and tolerance have not been completely overcome in our Party organization; we must honestly admit this.

Some time ago, we adopted a decision by the secretariat of our Union's board, sharply condemning the writers who signed the above-mentioned letters. We talked with them in the Union's Party committee and hoped then that they would realize their mistakes. Of course, there are some who "bark first and scratch their heads afterward." But there are also those who, to this day, remain stubborn and fail to draw the appropriate conclusions for themselves. This is why we consider the criticism addressed to us to be timely and quite just. Our Union's Party committee and, together with it, the secretariat of the board should be more principled in future in the appraisal of such phenomena.

We cannot fail to be alarmed also by certain phenomena in related arts, in particular the theater. It is no secret that there are some directors who, in their productions, however interesting these may be, present arbitrary interpretations of classical works, thereby arousing unhealthy agitation among the audience—the audience, not the public. This agitation is aroused not by the originality of the play's staging but by the political coloration of modernized lines of the characters, addressed directly to the audience and aimed at politically immature bystanders. If this is done for the sake of cheap effect and not deliberately, it is, in any case, politically and socially irresponsible. Since the classic writers cannot, themselves, speak out about this or have it out with the directors, it is our duty to do this for them. (*Applause.*)

I do not conceal that, in our everyday literary work, there are still regrettable, painful questions and unresolved problems of a professional and organizational nature. We naturally devote great attention to these questions, but, in settling them, we shall manage somehow to do without the services of dubious defenders scribbling appeals to reactionary circles in the West. We shall manage! We know where to turn. We have the Central Committee of the Communist Party! (*Stormy applause.*)

Comrades! As is known, our writers' Party organization unfortunately does not represent all the Communist writers of Moscow. Of the 640 writer members of the Party, only about 350 are registered in our Union's Party committee. In addition, a large number of them are persons of pension age or well past pension age. (*Animation in the hall.*)

Many dropped active political and literary work long ago. What can you do? Age is age. At the same time, about 300 active writer-Communists are registered as members of other Party organizations in Moscow. We almost never hear their voices at meetings held by our Union's Party committee. They have, as it were, cut themselves off from Party life in the Moscow writers' organization. Is this normal? Not very normal, we think. We have a Party group that, in name, unites all Moscow Communist writers. But, as a rule, it meets no more than twice a year and never decides current, timely problems of literature. We ask the Moscow Party organization, in the person of its headquarters, the city committee, to help us to rally all the forces of Moscow Communist writers. . . .

88. *Official Censure (from* Literaturnaia Rossia)

Moscow
May 1, 1968

At a session held on April 17, 1968, the secretariat of the board of the Moscow Writers' Union discussed the question of the writers who signed a statement in defense of the convicted Ginzburg, Galanskov *et al.*

The course of the discussion disclosed the unsavory role of a number of Moscow writers, who displayed inadmissible political dereliction and lack of principle and lent their names to arm our ideological adversaries.

The antisocial actions of these writers were aggravated by the fact that their letters appeared in various bourgeois newspapers and foreign radio broadcasts to the U.S.S.R.

Such actions on the part of several members of the Moscow Writers' Union evoked the unanimous and severe condemnation of the members of the secretariat. They noted in their speeches that these actions do not represent the opinions of the Moscow literary public and, moreover, arouse legitimate protest and indignation not only among our writers but also among the Moscow workers and representatives of the scientific and technical intelligentsia, who sent letters of protest to the U.S.S.R. Writers' Union.

The secretariat noted that the voluntary defenders of the renegades fed the ideological propaganda launched by the most vicious enemies of the Soviet state, for these letters, after being clandestinely sent abroad through the traitorous actions of their direct organizers and printed there in various bourgeois publications, are being disseminated by foreign radio stations and special broadcasts to our country with the aim of discrediting the Soviet way of life and provoking certain unstable and politically immature representatives of the Soviet intelligentsia to some sort of anti-Soviet action.

The authors of the "declarations" proved to be a find for bourgeois propaganda. Use was made of them to misinform public opinion, since they had presented the political swindlers Ginzburg, Galanskov, and Dobrovolsky as Soviet writers and distorted the real situation with respect to our intelligentsia's work.

The secretariat went on to note that some of the statements openly slandered the nature of social processes in our country. For example, L. Kopelev's statement pointed out that "Lenin's principles are so often taken in vain that, for many, they have in fact become rhetorical abstractions." And this was said with such assurance as to suggest that it was not to the Party and its decisions that we are obligated for the successful struggle against the consequences of the personality cult but to the slanderers who take the liberty of lecturing our entire ideological front and leveling shameful accusations at the Soviet public. It is natural that such statements, political falsifications, and exaggerations aroused the just anger and protests expressed by the working people in their letters.

With deep regret, the secretariat deemed it necessary to note that the Moscow writers' organization contained a small group of members who systematically participated in so-called "collective" letters and statements, which, as a rule, came into the possession of hostile bourgeois press agencies and leaflets published abroad.

The fact that some members of the Writers' Union who signed these statements not only drew no conclusions whatever from the fact that their names were published in the foreign anti-Soviet press but also did not even deem it necessary to react in the proper manner to the substance of the comments accompanying the aforementioned publications has shown that the authors of the letters are unwilling to give serious consideration to how far such political lack of principle and responsibility can lead them.

The secretariat placed special emphasis on the fact that the organizers of the collection of signatures in defense of Ginzburg, Galanskov *et al.*, who had been convicted by a Soviet court, had used unworthy methods and approaches to obtain the signatures of the members of the Writers' Union; evidence of this was provided by Yu. Ye. Piliar's letter to the secretariat of the Moscow writers' organization. After officially withdrawing his signature from the collective "statement" and condemning his action, Yu. Piliar wrote: "Now that I have become acquainted with the full text of the document, I cannot refrain from expressing my condemnation of the organizers of this whole letter business who so abused the confidence of a number of writers. . . . I am outraged that this document, which was addressed to official Soviet bodies, was sent abroad by puny dishonest souls without the permission of the writers."

In this connection and also on the basis that the letters and statements under consideration attest to a violation by their authors of the regulation of the U.S.S.R. Writers' Union obligating its members to wage an ideological struggle against bourgeois and revisionist influences, the secretariat announced that it could no longer condone such instances of irresponsible behavior by members of the writers' organization who ignored a decision previously handed down by the secretariat with regard to a similar incident.

The decision of the secretariat states: "Anyone who does not fully understand his responsibility to the people in a period of uncompromising conflict between the two ideologies of socialism and capitalism cannot call himself a Soviet writer."

The secretariat resolved to demand explanations from the members of the Writers' Union who, by signing all sorts of statements, had become involved in the case of Ginzburg, Galansbov *et al.* The secretariat will again take up this question in the form of individual cases.

The decision was adopted unanimously by the secretariat. Those who took part in discussing it were: S. Mikhalkov, M. Alekseyev, V. Rosliakov, V. Telpugov, B. Galin, Ye. Knipovich, V. Rozov, S. Narovchatov, V. Ilyin, and Yu. Korolkov.

89. *"Bureaucrats Versus Writers," by Sergei Mikhalkov* (*from* **Pravda**)

Moscow
May 11, 1968

. . . The foreign press regularly publishes surveys of the state of Soviet literature, but written on a single assigned theme for a single purpose—to prove the "bankruptcy" of the basic principles of socialist realism. Here is the core of these surveys, which always crudely obtrudes through their florid, verbose wrappings: Service to the people, fidelity to their interests, and ideological content supposedly render Soviet literature lifeless, rob it of artistic value and originality, and condemn it to embellishment of reality. . . .

Like jugglers in circus shows, our ill-wishers manipulate the words "critical outlook." They would very much like to see our literature take a "critical outlook" by mocking everything for which our grandfathers, our fathers, and our contemporaries gave their lives and shed their blood. The "critical outlook," as we see it, is exposure of ideals alien to us and not betrayal of the achievements of the Soviet people. . . .

Only recently, noisy stage appearances of writers reciting their own poetry seemed to be becoming fashionable, and readings aimed at publicity seems to be displacing the reader's communion with the printed poem. But this impression proved deceptive. What, at first, had been striking became tiresome. What had been thought to be "the latest thing" is losing its impact. Fashion has given way to mature reflection, genuine civic spirit, and spirituality that is not counterfeit. The readers have chosen and properly appreciated collected poems of M. Svetlov, Ya. Smeliakov, L. Martinov, and B. Ruchiev, each different in style, artistic character, and vision of the world. . . .

Some of our ill-wishers abroad feign puzzlement at the fact that we recall the last war so often in our works. This was all consigned to oblivion long ago, and it is time to forget it, they say. No, we won't forget! We do not want to forget it and have no right to.

Despairing of frontal attacks on our country, our enemy has now decided to "take us from the rear." Hesitating at military aggression, which, obviously, could bring him only crushing defeat, he is concentrating his efforts on ideological aggression. But we know that when he realizes this kind of struggle against us is also hopeless, he may lose his sense of reality and turn once more to the idea of military ventures. . . .

Our opponents are not interested in Soviet literature as it really is. On the other hand, they shamelessly include among "Moscow writers" people who have no connection with any literary genre, neither the short story nor the novelette nor poetry, but only certain articles of the Criminal Code.

Moscow writer! This is a lofty literary title. Moscow literature! We have the right to think that the only synonyms of this definition—Moscow!—can be words such as talented, highly artistic, filled with ideas! Party literature!

Always—in this century and in the past—only literature of the most brilliant intellectual and artistic qualities was considered literature of the capital. In 1838, *Severnaia pchela* published a "Letter from Moscow." Addressing himself to St. Petersburg readers, the writer of the letter said: "By the way, concerning literature: Why have some people in your city taken it into their heads to call cheap novels, pulp books, and meaningless poems 'Moscow literature'?"

More than 100 years have passed; St. Petersburg has become Leningrad. Moscow too has changed. We have a true Moscow literature! But we do not want to apply the term "Moscow" to some works that, unfortunately, were written in Moscow but were published in Russian, against our interests, thousands of kilometers to the west of the Soviet capital.

This also applies to some notorious epistolary works that crudely flout the laws of the intimate genre of letter writing. After all, *co-authorship* is, in my view, abnormal in a letter, especially such a strange form of co-authorship as occurs when one person writes and others sign a letter, sometimes without even having read it.

This is exactly what happened. A few "initiators," desirous of compensating for their lack of artistic talent by creating a political scandal, organized letters in defense of common criminals, who were at once proclaimed "Soviet writers" abroad. The signature collectors, in one case, took advantage of the severe illness and softheartedness of some prominent writer, in other cases, took advantage of ignorance of the facts, in still other cases, of lack of political understanding or a vague concept of "humanism in general." How strange! Why, then, did we not hear them raise voices of alarm in defense of Dr. Spock and his friends, in defense of Glezos and Theodorakis, in defense of Martin Luther King and his companions-in-arms, who were and are continuously threatened by bullets from ambush?! . . .

The Party *aktiv* of Moscow writers and the secretariat of the Moscow Writers' Union have unanimously condemned the authors of these irresponsible documents, who, wittingly or unwittingly, provided ammunition for enemy propaganda. These authors cannot even be called an "overwhelming minority." You simply cannot see them in the mighty ocean that is called Soviet literature. As the saying goes, "only three or four can be sighted." . . .

90. *Attack on Solzhenitsyn* (*from* Literaturnaia gazeta)

Moscow
June 26, 1968

The Great October Revolution, which opened a new chapter in the history of mankind, also laid the foundation for a new art. Soviet literature, inspired by the ideas of Marxism-Leninism, has truthfully reflected the life of the people and the moral image of the new man, the active builder of Communism. In the works produced by Soviet writers, one can trace the whole glorious and difficult path our country has traversed during half a century. Major works of prose, poetry, and drama have been devoted to each stage in our history—the October Revolution and Civil War, the early five-year plans and the socialist transformation of the countryside, the heroic struggle against the fascist invasion, and communist construction in the postwar years.

The strength of Soviet writers lies in wholehearted dedication to the ideas of Communism and boundless loyalty to the cause of the Party. This is why the tie between Soviet literature and Communist Party politics evokes such fierce attacks by hostile propaganda. Our foes cannot understand the futility of their efforts to drive a wedge between the Party and Soviet writers.

The ideological centers of the Western world experienced a bitter disappointment last year: The fourth U.S.S.R. Writers' Congress, which reviewed major problems of the development of our literature, demonstrated the writers' firm solidarity with the Communist Party of the Soviet Union and its Leninist Central Committee. Representatives of thirty-three world literatures attended the Congress. In answer to the turbid wave of slander abroad, many statements were made that objectively appraised the work of the Congress and noted its businesslike, constructive nature, corresponding to the entire atmosphere of Soviet life.

Some 600 writers from fifty-five countries visited our land during the [50th] anniversary year, 1967. Upon returning to their own countries, they truthfully described to broad circles of readers how the Soviet people live and work and what a great role the creative work of writers plays in the life of our society.

The world significance of Soviet literature finds expression in the constant expansion of the international ties of the U.S.S.R. Writers' Union. Regular meetings among heads of the writers' organizations of the socialist countries, close ties among literary periodicals, international gatherings of writers, poets, and translators—all foster creative contact among men of letters and arts throughout the world.

Western propaganda does everything in its power to distort the statements made by Soviet writers at meetings and discussions with their foreign colleagues. The enemies' provocational activities are dealt a fitting rebuff. Our writers display political maturity, lofty humanism, and Communist conviction at international forums. Their speeches have won universal recognition for creative spirit, consistent defense of the fundamental principles of the art of socialist realism, and readiness to wage uncompromising struggle against the enemies of peace, democracy, and socialism.

This struggle requires class mobilization, ideological arming, and the ability to recognize the forms and methods to which bourgeois propaganda resorts. It is extremely tempting to our enemies, of course, to try to pit the Soviet people against the Party, to sow dissension among the intelligentsia, to divide it into "right" and "left," "progressives" and "dogmatists," to oppose some writers to others. They employ any means to present the wish for the reality.

Everything goes into the score. Some ne'er-do-well speculator is lured by nylon rags or is drawn into currency manipulations—and a legend is created of the moral instability of Soviet young people. Some circus acrobat fails to return to his motherland from a foreign tour, and the bells peal forth: he is allegedly seeking "political asylum" because Marxism deprived him of freedom of acrobatic creativity. Someone sends a letter of inordinate praise to a foreign radio station in enthusiasm for its concert programs—a perfect excuse to howl about the poverty of musical culture in the Soviet Union. But this is mostly for arithmetical score-keeping purposes and for expanding the "assortment" of cases in the record of incidents chalked up. See, they say, how dissent against socialist surroundings spreads to every aspect of these surroundings.

Western propaganda gloats most over any incidents that can be connected in one way or another with the names of writers, artists, and composers. Naturally! After all, they enjoy such popularity among the people. This is not just one more mark in the score; it is a jackpot. Here you can expound at length the idea that a "real" Soviet writer is not obliged to use his art to serve the people who are building Communism and believe in it, since, if you please, true art stands outside and even above politics. In saying this, the gentlemen of the Western world experience no embarrassment at ignoring one awkward detail; the fact that they proclaim as ideal models for a writer those who would attack Soviet policy—that is, those who by no means stand outside politics.

Such models are not so easy to find in our country! Well, then, one has to engage in cheap tricks, and, like the alchemists of old, raise homunculi—artificial dwarfs—in a flask and proclaim any mediocrity a talent. So the graphomaniac and schizophrenic V. Tarsis was promptly made a writer when he scribbled vast outpourings of untalented but openly anti-Soviet writings spiced with fierce anger and hatred for our social system. After "escaping" from socialism to capitalism or, more precisely, after being kicked out of the Soviet land, whose bread he had eaten and which he slandered, Tarsis thundered in radio broadcasts and sensational news sheets that he would appear before the world as a new Dostoevsky.

Although political publisher-merchants abroad managed to make something out of Tarsis's manuscripts, the interest in him was short-lived, and the businessmen did not get the profits they had expected. Tarsis himself lost the hopes of Judas millions. But the "trainers" of this kind of "talent" are unwilling to forgo methods that have been compromised. And so they raised another homunculus in the flask: They championed Svetlana Alliluyeva and her "memoirs." The outcome was the same—readers turned away disgustedly from her petty book.

Now, new supertalented "intellectuals" have been "discovered": Ginzburg, Galanskov, and their ilk. Never mind that none of them ever published a single line in the Soviet press or has the slightest connection with the Writers' Union. All the same, the underground lampooners who had swallowed the bait of the NTS and who linked their destinies to this bandit organization were immediately registered in the books, scores, and records kept by Western propaganda: See how many Soviet writers are actively fighting Soviet policy!

Our entire people and our entire creative intelligentsia regard renegades with scorn. Only individual writers who had failed to examine closely the spiritual make-up of these renegades gave bourgeois propaganda an excuse to list them among the "supporters" of Ginzburg, Galanskov, and their crew and appeared before public opinion in their own country as politically immature and irresponsible persons.

Unfortunately, letters defending such anti-Sovieteers as Ginzburg and Galanskov bore the signatures of several long-respected writers. And this was just what hostile propaganda desperately needed. It hastened to circulate along with the fabrications of inveterate slanderers and adventurers, documents signed by such "tender hearts."

The secretariat of the board of the U.S.S.R. Writers' Union and the secretariat of the Moscow writers' organization severely condemned the political irresponsibility of the writers who signed letters in defense of the anti-Sovieteers. Though very few did so, nevertheless, the writers' organization cannot tolerate such acts, for they represent a fundamental departure from the norms of public life customary among Soviet men of letters.

Writers who cherish their good name and the honor of their homeland, writers deeply convinced that their work cannot be divorced from the interests of the people and the Party and from the ideas of socialist society—when such writers become involuntary targets of hostile propaganda, they deal fitting rebuffs to their unbidden foreign champions. A whole series of examples can be cited. A few years ago, for instance, our ideological foes failed in an attempt to turn an Anatoli Kuznetsov novel against Soviet rule. This novel, *Continuation of a Legend*, recounted the story of a young man who, on finishing school, went to work at a construction project and developed spiritually on the job. Employees of a French publishing house took paste, scissors, and a dishonest editorial pen, changed the title, printed a spider's web of barbed wire on the cover, and tried to give readers the impression that the action of the book took place not at a construction project but in a concentration camp. Kuznetsov issued a press statement publicly slapping the swindlers' cheeks and instituted legal proceedings against them. The upshot of the trial was that even a bourgeois court was obliged to punish the falsifiers.[1]

In recent times, there have been more frequent instances of gross falsification of statements by Soviet writers. There has also been an increase in the frequency with which Soviet writers' manuscripts, not yet ready for publication, have been obtained in fraudulent ways and published for the purpose of presenting the authors in the role of political oppositionists. Naturally, all this arouses resolute protests from Soviet writers. This was how V. Tendriakov responded on one occasion. *Literaturnaia gazeta* published a letter from V. Kataev that categorically rejected the attempts of foreign propagandists to ascribe to him unfriendly statements about Soviet literature. G. Serebriakova protested in print against the unlawful publication in the West of a work stolen from her in unfinished form.

Today *Literaturnaia gazeta* publishes a statement by A. Solzhenitsyn.[2]

It must be said, however, that A. Solzhenitsyn was told many months ago, at a session of the secretariat of the board of the U.S.S.R. Writers' Union, that his name had been taken into the arsenal of reactionary Western propaganda and had been widely used for provocational anti-Soviet purposes. A. Solzhenitsyn remained deaf to such a warning at that time and was unwilling to express his attitude toward this unseemly publicity, whose "hero" he had become.

A. Solzhenitsyn is a man of wide experience who had a higher education in physics and mathematics and has worked as a teacher. Solzhenitsyn spent the last years of the Great Patriotic War at the front as commander of an anti-aircraft battery and won awards. Shortly before the war ended, he was convicted on a charge of anti-Soviet activity and served a sentence in the camps. In 1957, he was rehabilitated.

A. Solzhenitsyn has not taken part in the public life of the Writers' Union. He preferred to take another path—the path of attacking the fundamental principles that guide Soviet literature and are set forth in the statutes of the U.S.S.R. Writers' Union, which Solzhenitsyn had indeed pledged to observe on entering the Union.

Several days before the opening of the Fourth Writers' Congress, A. Solzhenitsyn sent the Congress a letter and simultaneously, in violation of generally accepted norms of behavior, circulated it to at least 250 of the most diverse recipients, apparently reckoning that, now beyond control, it would be further reproduced and passed from hand to hand and would become a literary sensation.

Naturally, Western propagandists easily obtained this letter and promptly raised an anti-Soviet hullabaloo over it, since the letter claimed that our literature is in the grip of oppression and completely ignored all the achievements of Soviet literature that have gained worldwide recognition.

Furthermore, A. Solzhenitsyn demanded that the constitution of the Writers' Union include a special clause providing "all the guarantees of protection that the Union affords to members who have been slandered and unjustly persecuted." Such a clause would place the Writers' Union constitution above statewide laws ensuring equal protection to all Soviet citizens against slander and unjust persecution. Western propaganda greeted this demand of Solzhenitsyn exultantly and interpreted it as "proof" of the complete defenselessness of Soviet writers in the face of the law.

Bourgeois propaganda found greatly to its liking A. Solzhenitsyn's claims that state security agencies had taken files and manuscripts from him. In answer to an inquiry from the Writers' Union, however, the U.S.S.R. Prosecutor's Office reported that no searches had ever been conducted in A. Solzhenitsyn's apartment in Riazan and no *manuscripts* or files had been taken from him. *Typewritten copies* of certain of Solzhenitsyn's manuscripts, *without his name*, were found in a search of [the apartment of] a certain Citizen Teush in Moscow and were seized along with other compromising materials; when a customs inspection of a foreign tourist brought to light slanderous manuscript fabrications about Soviet life, the course of the investigation instituted by the appropriate agencies led to Teush.

Among the manuscripts taken from Citizen Teush was, for example, the play *Feast of the Victors*, in which A. Solzhenitsyn presents the Soviet Army that had freed the world from the fascist plague as a horde of blockheads, rapists, marauders, and vandals, interested only in their own skins. He also comments quite sympathetically on the Vlasovites.[3] The play blasphemously ridicules the immortal exploits of Zoia Kosmodemianskaia and Aleksandr Matrosov. The author's sympathies are with a Captain Nerzhin, a "hero" who helps a woman traitor to the homeland make her way secretly across the front line to the Vlasovites.

In his letter to the Fourth Writers' Congress, A. Solzhenitsyn declared indignantly: "This play is now being described as my most recent work." And, at a session of the secretariat of the board of the U.S.S.R. Writers' Union on September 22, 1967, which was devoted to a consideration of his letter, he objected to any mention of *Feast of the Victors* on the ground that he had composed this play in his mind in the camp and had set it down on paper only after rehabilitation. In fact, *Feast of the Victors* is not A. Solzhenitsyn's "most recent work." But how can we pretend that such a play does not exist if A. Solzhenitsyn, having entrusted the safekeeping of his works to a supplier of anti-Sovietism to the foreign world, thereby lost all control over them and over the play in particular? How can he object to mention of *Feast of the Victors* without protesting publicly against the central fact that his name itself, all of his literary works in general, and the letter to the Fourth Writers' Congress are being exploited by Western propaganda in the ideological struggle against the Soviet Union?

Nevertheless, at the secretariat meeting, in which well-known Soviet writers took part, the discussion of A. Solzhenitsyn's letter and all his "complaints" was conducted in a businesslike tone, with sincere concern for the writer's creative destiny.

The participants in the discussion naturally expected A. Solzhenitsyn to heed their advice and express his attitude toward hostile Western propaganda's political provocations connected with his name. But Solzhenitsyn's entire behavior at the secretariat meeting bore an emphatically demagogic stamp. Citing "lack of time," Solzhenitsyn refused to acquaint himself with the statements of the foreign anti-Soviet press that had bestowed praise on his letter. Instead, he insisted, in the tone of an ultimatum, on immediate publication of his new novel *Cancer Ward*, which, as the secretariat noted, was in need of substantial ideological revision. He then tried to strike a kind of bargain with the secretariat regarding the "concessions" he was prepared to make if the secretariat would meet his demands.

On November 25, 1967, the secretariat of the board of the Writers' Union sent A. Solzhenitsyn a letter asking him to state whether he intended, after all, to express his attitude toward the unceasing anti-Soviet publicity surrounding his name. An answer followed, again reproduced in many copies, from which it appeared that Solzhenitsyn intended to continue using "public opinion" in the West as an instrument of pressure on the Writers' Union.

And A. Solzhenitsyn adhered to his stand at subsequent personal talks with him in the secretariat.

In April, 1968, A. Solzhenitsyn circulated two more communications, again in many copies, expressing feigned alarm over the forthcoming publication of *Cancer Ward* by extremely reactionary Western publishing houses and hypocritically placed moral responsibility for this on the secretariat of the board of the U.S.S.R. Writers' Union. This time, incidentally, the recipients of Solzhenitsyn's letter also received a supplement to it—a transcript of the secretariat meeting, which he had prepared himself and prepared tendentiously and extremely unobjectively, hoping to create an impression of the nature and tone of the discussion that would be favorable to him. This transcript, naturally, was promptly included in the register of anti-Soviet materials circulated by bourgeois propaganda.

Radio centers hostile to us, in building up a provocational ballyhoo over *Cancer Ward*, armed themselves with a further "document," which they called "An Open Letter from V. Kaverin." In giving a perverted interpretation of many events in our literary life in recent years, V. Kaverin distorted the attitude of some secretariat members toward publication of *Cancer Ward* in the same spirit as characterized the transcript by A. Solzhenitsyn distributed in the West.

There is no need to analyze this letter in detail. Suffice it to say that, although V. Kaverin heard it recited almost every day by foreign "voices," he did not deem it necessary to speak out against this hostile "chorus."

A. Solzhenitsyn wrote his letter this April, when, according to the words of the author himself, the publication of excerpts from *Cancer Ward* in various Western publications had *already begun*. It was clear —to Solzhenitsyn above all—that publication of the letter could not change anything, especially since, in essence, it expressed concern only lest, God forbid, the publishers distort the text of the novel in their haste. But A. Solzhenitsyn failed to protest against the exploitation of his name and his works for anti-Soviet purposes.

One hopes that A. Solzhenitsyn would finally recognize the need to speak out in sharp protest against the actions of foreign publishers, would disavow his unbidden "guardians," and would declare, for all to hear, his unwillingness to have anything to do with the enemy provocateurs of our country. But Solzhenitsyn did not do so.

Nor did he do so after a number of foreign publishing houses, continuing to inflame anti-Soviet passions, recently announced that they were preparing to publish another of A. Solzhenitsyn's works, *The First Circle*, containing malicious slander of our social system. It has become clear once and for all that the role assigned to A. Solzhenitsyn by our ideological foes is entirely satisfactory to him and that he is prepared to voice protests only of the kind printed here today.

The writer A. Solzhenitsyn could devote his literary abilities completely to his homeland and not to its ill-wishers. He could, but he does not want to. Such is the bitter truth. Whether A. Solzhenitsyn wishes to find a way out of this *cul-de-sac* depends primarily on himself.

History has charged Soviet writers with the great and noble responsibility of heralding the advanced ideas of our age, the ideas of Communism, and of fighting for the social and spiritual values achieved by the socialist system. This is a responsibility to history, to society, and to their own talents, which flourish only in serving great goals, in serving the people. This is the responsibility of a person who feels he is not a detached observer in today's world, or a grumbling nihilist, but a fighter for Communist ideals.

The decisions of the April plenary session of the CPSU Central Committee once again remind every worker on the ideological front that the spearhead of the enemy's main thrust is now aimed precisely against the spiritual values of socialism.

When we cast our mind's eye over all that our literature has accomplished in the years of Soviet rule and think of the new tasks confronting this literature, we perceive clearly that much has been accomplished —much that has been needed by and useful to the people and that the people have received gratefully and appreciated highly. A new, highly ideological and highly artistic literature of socialist realism has been established whose creative potentialities are inexhaustible. We do not delude ourselves that there have been no grievous failures along our literature's complicated, difficult path. But the writers of the land of the Soviets have always remained with the people and the Party, have undergone every trial together with them, and will march with them into new battles for the triumph of Communist ideas, for peaceful labor on the entire planet, for genuine freedom for all mankind.

NOTES

1. Anatoli Kuznetsov, who defected to England in August, 1969, has since repudiated and apologized for his action in this matter.—ED.

2. Document 58.—ED.

3. The Vlasovites were Russians who served, or were forced to serve, in Nazi units headed by General Vlasov, a Soviet officer who joined the Germans when his troops were surrounded.—ED.

PART THREE

Literature of the Underground

"Underground literature" occupies a unique position in the Soviet literary world. Unauthorized—indeed, sharply disapproved—by the regime, it is nevertheless not, strictly speaking, illegal. And, despite being deprived of any financial or organizational basis, it has proved to be amazingly durable. The various journals that have appeared over the past few years, such as Phoenix 1961 and 1966 and the two issues of Sintaksis, are scarce and technically inferior; yet they seem to reach an inordinate number of readers thirsty for the uncensored word. Their contributors include not only "legitimate" and even well-established writers (such as Bella Akhmadulina) but also unknowns, some of them gifted artists and others devoid of any discernible talent. Although the "literature of the underground" is circulated in defiance of the political authorities and literary officials, its themes are seldom overtly political, and its genres, even by prevailing Soviet criteria, are conventional. Indeed, as one noted student of Soviet literature has observed, the underground journals are "underground" simply because "the Soviet authorities choose to make them [so] . . . they lead a clandestine existence because their appearance is not legally sanctioned by the authorities and not because the bulk of their contents would . . . preclude their authorized publication."* Yet it is this very attitude of the regime that endows these journals with a singularly important function and renders at least some of the works they publish so significant from an artistic as well as a broader sociological point of view.

For reasons of space, the small sample of underground literature reprinted here is not truly representative. A more characteristic sample would probably have to include a good many poor and mediocre essays, short stories, and poems. The items that follow were chosen either for their relationship to Soviet dissent in general or for their special literary merit. A few items were included to illustrate the "graphomania" (to use Siniavsky's term) that can flourish in a country where censorship has taken the place of bona fide criticism and readers' demand. For a discussion of past and current trends in Soviet underground literature, see the article by Friedberg cited below.

* Maurice Friedberg, "What Price Censorship?," *Problems of Communism,* September–October, 1968.

I. Historical and Political Essays

Selections from **Russkoe slovo** *(July, 1966)*

Public Announcement

On July 13 of this year [1966], the 140th anniversary of the execution of those founders of Russian freedom—Ryleev,[1] Pestel,[2] Muravev,[3] Bestuzhev-Riumin,[4] and Kakhovsky[5]—a meeting of the Ryleev Club took place on the grounds of the former Andronikovsky monastery in Moscow at which the following decisions were made:

1. To adopt Ryleev's poem "The Citizen" and his article "Culture and Man" as the philosophical basis for our activity.

2. To elect an administrative board of the Ryleev Club.

3. To conduct our work under the slogan "Culture, Truth, Honor."

The Ryleev Club was established on June 6, 1964, as a humanitarian society of a socioliterary and cultural-historical nature and as a successor to the Decembrists' literary "Society of the Russian Word," of which Ryleev was the leader.

The Administrative Board of the Ryleev Club
July 13, 1966

This Issue of the Literary and Political Magazine *Russkoe Slovo* Is Published After an Interruption of One Century

The monthly magazine *Russkoe slovo* was published originally in St. Petersburg in 1859 by Count Kushelov-Bezborodko. After 1962, publication was under the direction of the radical journalist Grigori Yevlampievich Blagosvetlov, who was a *"Shestidesiatnik"* [man of the 1860's], a staunch democrat, but not a socialist. From that time on, young authors with radical tendencies, such as D. Pisarev,[6] V. Zaitsev, N. Shelgunov,[7] and A. Shchapov,[8] wrote for the magazine. *Russkoe slovo* became one of the legal journals of the Russian radical-democratic movement; it was a mouthpiece for the revolutionary Populists' philosophy of the intelligentsia-*raznochintsy*, the so-called nihilists. After Dimitri Karakozov's[9] attempt upon the life of Emperor Aleksandr II, the magazine, as well as *Sovremennik*, was closed in May, 1866, by order of Muravev[10] the Hangman.

In May of this year [1966], the Ryleev Club, organized on June 6, 1964, by Vladimir Voskresensky and Yevgeni Kushev, adopted a resolution to revive the magazine *Russkoe slovo* (this is the only action taken by the Ryleev Club during the two years of its existence). The magazine is devoted to literature, art, culture, history, and philosophy, as well as to discussions of various themes.

Thus, the present issue of *Russkoe slovo* is the first after more than a century-long interruption.

THE EDITORS
Moscow, July, 1966

CULTURE AND MAN

To Russia's youth—those who are fighting, winning, suffering defeats, searching, observing, approaching the truth, and again retreating from it—we send brotherly greetings.

To Russia's youth—in cities and villages, in colleges and schools—we send unalterable, friendly, and cordial greetings.

Greetings to you, young workers, boys and girls.

You are the successors of the noble tradition of the freedom-loving Russian proletarians who gave to the world many heroes, among them Piotr Moiseev and Stepan Khalturin, the workers Alekseev and Obnorsky, and the first Russian Social-Democrats, those heroes of the Obukhovskaia defense, as well as the pure people who fell on "Bloody Sunday" in 1905, those who established barricades at Presna, and those who overturned the autocracy in 1917.

Greetings to you, young farm boys and farm girls! You whose family trees originate with Razin, Bolotnikov, and Pugachev—you are the most cherished hope of our Russian land, you who live on the farms, mothers and breadwinners of Russia!

Greetings to you, young Russian intelligentsia—on you rests the splendid mission of the battle for truth and for light, the battle for the reorganization and revival of Russia, to make her educated, enlightened, happy, deserving to take first place in the future within the universal, free, socialist society.

This mission has been passed on to you by the great Russian celebrities such as Radishchev and the Decembrists, Belinsky, Chernyshevsky, Dobroliubov, Lavrov, Bakunin, Mikhailovsky, Plekhanov, and Lenin, by the great Russian writers such as Pushkin and Lermontov, Nekrasov and Turgenev, Dostoevsky and Tolstoy, Chekhov and Korolenko, Tiutchev and Biusov, Blok and Yesenin, Platonov and Pasternak.

To educate the Russian youth in the spirit of these noble, patriotic, and truth-seeking ideals of social thought is the sole task of our times.

This objective cannot be fulfilled by the efforts of individuals; the unified efforts of many thousands of people are required to meet this objective. We need a wide cultural movement, reaching into the very midst of the masses of the Russian people, who are burning with genuine enthusiasm and inspired by great traditions.

Let the sacred name of Kondrati Ryleev—a romantic, a martyr, a great and enthusiastic patriot, a teacher of national valor and democratic consciousness—be the star to guide us on this difficult path, just as the *North Star* guided the Decembrists and illuminated for them all that was best among the Russian people.

Who among the young people is not familiar with Lenin's words written in printer's ink on the covers of student textbooks: "The most important task for us today is learning, learning, learning!"

In Lenin's time, in a country of universal illiteracy, this was an appeal to master reading and writing. But, even after mastering these skills, the Russian intelligentsia, the Russian people—as well as many other people of the world—are still far from being genuinely cultured. For culture to become a possession of the people, to reach like "Lenin's lamp" into each remote village, an immense cultural revolution must take place.

The cultural revolution must begin first of all among the intelligentsia, because to whom, if not to them, are the following words best suited: "Physician, heal thyself!"

During the years of the Soviet regime, the structure of the intelligentsia was widened considerably, embracing representatives from many social spheres to which education had been denied. This new segment of the intelligentsia eventually came to constitute its largest component. However, this increase in the size of the intelligentsia was the result of a lowering of standards. Today, a young person, after graduating from college, is very often nothing more than a highly qualified specialist: he knows his profession and nothing else, and, therefore, he quite often displays gross ignorance of everything that is outside his own professional province. He displays a complete lack of social awareness or of independent thought, and, at the same time, he is a profligate, a drunkard, a user of profanity—in short, a boor.

Let it not be said that we are making groundless accusations against these people. Although they are ethically deficient, they can develop into highly valuable workers if they use their natural intellect, common sense, and kind hearts. But such intellectuals cannot be educators or teachers.

Therefore, when we call for a cultural revolution, what we mean is a rebirth of humanitarian education *everywhere*, because it is only this kind of education that can broaden the mental outlook, awaken aspirations toward truth, elevate spiritual qualities, and teach us to understand human beings and to become human beings. It is necessary to give young people a genuine knowledge of Russian and foreign classics rather than lifeless rhetoric and platitudes, which, as presented in our schools today, are more capable of inspiring aversion than love for literature. An interest in philosophical problems and historical questions should be awakened in the minds of young people, because, without this knowledge, they cannot understand themselves.

It is also imperative that a moral wave of purification flood away debauchery, excessive drinking, and hooliganism. Certain results could be achieved by fighting these social problems with laws, administrative methods, and newspaper articles; however, these methods will not eliminate "the root of the evil"—that is, the ignorance that debases human character and drives people to violate morality. For the complete elimination of these abnormal characteristics from our society, the heroic dedication of our youth is needed, as well as the development of a strong character that will value noble actions and such social virtues as sincerity, veracity, and fearlessness. In no case should one speak words in which he himself does not believe or associate with something in which he does not believe. One must be courageous and brave; it is a disgrace for a man to be a coward, a hypocrite, and a traitor! . . .

What we have just offered is a philosophy of life and a genuine culture. The dissemination, broadening, and preservation of this philosophy are what constitute a cultural revolution.

Attempts to prescribe formulas by which this revolution could be accomplished would appear inexcusably ridiculous and pedantic; a revolution is called a revolution precisely because it destroys all types of formulas, canons, and dogmas.

Free discussions, comradely conversations, deep and comprehensive studies of both Russian and foreign culture should at the present time be the concern of the Ryleev Club's socioliterary, cultural-historical, and humanitarian society.

Let the wonderful motto of this club serve the cause of the moral and cultural rebirth of man, citizen and patriot!

NOTES

1. Kondrati Fiodorovich Ryleev (1795–1826) was a poet and revolutionary who helped to organize the December 14, 1825, mutiny of military units in St. Petersburg, for which he was arrested, tried, and executed.—ED.

2. Pavel Ivanovich Pestel (1793–1826) was one of the founders of the revolutionary Southern Society, a branch of the Decembrist group. He was arrested on the eve of the Decembrist uprising in 1825 and hanged.—ED.

3. Nikita Mikhailovich Muravev (1786–1843) was a prominent ideologist of the Decembrist movement and author of a draft constitution for a reformed Russian state.—ED.

4. Mikhail Pavlovich Bestuzhev-Riumin (1803–26), a leader of the Southern Society and a convinced republican, was executed for participating in the uprising of 1825.—ED.

5. Piotr Grigorevich Kakhovsky (1797–1826) was one of the organizers of the Decembrist insurrection of 1825, during which he mortally wounded the Governor-General of St. Petersburg. He was hanged the following year.—ED.

6. Dmitri Ivanovich Pisarev (1840–68) was a literary critic and historian who was arrested in 1862 for writing an article critical of the government. He produced some of his most important works over the next four and a half years while in solitary confinement in Petropavloskaia Fortress.—ED.

7. Nikolai Vasilevich Shelgunov (1824–91), a frequent contributor to such leading publications of his time as *Sovremennik*, *Russkaia mysl*, and *Russkoe slovo*,

was an advocate of general education, emancipation of women, and Western culture.—Ed.

8. Afanasy Prokofevich Shchapov (1830–76), historian, was an advocate of a federal—as opposed to a centralistic—Russian state. A Populist, he was dismissed in 1861 from the faculty of Kazan University and banished to his native Irkutsk.—Ed.

9. Dmitri Vladimirovich Karakazov (1840–66), a member of a terrorist group, made an attempt on the life of Aleksandr II, for which he was tried and executed. —Ed.

10. Count Mikhail Nikolaevich Muravev (1796–1866), was a Tsarist statesman and stalwart defender of the institution of serfdom who has gone down in history as "Muravev the Hangman" for his bloody suppression of the Polish revolt of 1863.—Ed.

N. Eidelman:

Serno

We know very little about one of the most splendid persons in Russian history.

What legacy has he left us? A few poems that are noble but artistically weak, about ten draft projects, and some articles.

But there was something else. He was one of those who constituted the very soul of a movement.

About this, however, he remained silent. Indeed, there were not many, fortunately, who knew and talked about it.

The lot of the historian is strange. The more the regime learns and writes down, the larger the output of scholars. So it was with the Decembrists.

The *Shestidesiatniki*, however, said less, and we know less about them. Chernyshevsky kept silent, and, to this day, there are many things we do not know—we know only that many things did take place. Hertzen kept to himself the secrets of his correspondents and assistants.

Serno-Solovevich also kept silent. However, the records of his interrogations do remain. Also a few letters. These records and the letters are probably the most unusual of all his works.

In one of his photographs, he stands leaning on a chair—tall, calm, but somehow light and wiry. There is perhaps something of a Rakhmetov or a Bazarov about him—but only in the eyes and certainly in his gestures.

One is reminded of a letter once written to the Tsar by a revolutionary, saying: "Your Majesty, if you meet a person with an intelligent and honest face on the street, be assured that he is your enemy."

The record of the interrogations starts as it is supposed to start: "Serno-Solovevich, Nikolai Aleksandrovich, a nobleman by birth, twenty-seven years old. . . ."

Having earned a silver medal, he graduated from the Aleksandrov

Lyceum with a respectable rank. And at the age of twenty-three, he was already a counselor, only five or six ranks below Gorchakov and Korfa. Then things began to happen. On February 18, 1855, Nikolai I, unable to endure the Crimean defeat and the consequent weakening of the monarchy, died.

That day people gathered in the streets, glanced around, joyfully shook one another by the hand, and glanced around again. And then, after thirty years of Nikolai's "winter," Aleksandr's "thaw" began. The word "liberal" ceased to be a curse. The bulk of the population, who had not thought before, began to think. The few who had already been thinking now began preparing to act.

The young official, Serno-Solovevich, had an unusual nature. He could in no way understand two very simple things: first of all, how it is possible to say one thing and do another; secondly, why one should depend upon others to act if one is capable of acting oneself.

Added to this was his manner of speaking directly, bluntly. . . . His first real enemies began to appear. They were the first to express and to inscribe the word "revolutionary" in certain newspapers.

Serno-Solovevich wrote later: "This type of enemy is dangerous in a country that knows no civil rights and where public opinion is so underdeveloped. Such an enemy always manages to arouse prejudice against a person, and, then, that person's actions are judged by noted circles of society on the basis of this prejudice. I had an opportunity to experience this myself."

But a man like Serno was not frightened by his enemies. The opposite occurred. He soon noticed that it did not make sense to waste his efforts fighting his enemies. Serno understood that a good wheel not only is useless in a bad mechanism but is sometimes positively harmful—which means that it is better, under such circumstances, not to be a wheel at all. Rather, one should tear apart the mechanism or, to put it more cautiously, "become engaged in private activities." The question remains —how? One has to think, study, discuss, and experiment.

And so Serno went abroad. It was the year 1860. He was to be arrested in 1862. Such a person can do a great deal in two years. If all his conspiratorial letters, meetings, contacts, appearances, and conversations had been published or recorded, they would comprise many books. But we hardly know one-tenth of what actually transpired.

In February, 1860, he was a guest in London with the exiled Hertzen and Ogarev.

"Yes," writes Ogarev, "he is a public figure and perhaps also an organizer!" And, later, in Petersburg, Chernyshevsky wrote to Dobroliubov: "Be happy, Serno-Solovevich and I are the closest of friends. . . ."

Nikolai and his younger brother Aleksandr Serno-Solovevich were among those who maintained contact between the revolutionary center in London (where Hertzen was) and the underground in Russia.

On February 18, 1861, after thousands of secret deliberations, serfdom was abolished in Russia. Almost instantaneously, the incorrigible Serno-

Solovevich traveled from Petersburg to Berlin, where he published in Russian "The Final Solution to the Agricultural Question," after which he returned to Petersburg. He wrote as he thought—sharply, directly, plainly.

The fact that Serno-Solovevich signed his work with his real name made a great impression. "I am publishing this project under my name because I think that it is time to cease being afraid. If we wish not to be treated like children, we should stop acting like children, because he who seeks truth and justice must be able to stand up fearlessly for them." Government officials were so astonished that they decided not to arrest him immediately. However, they made note of the incident and began waiting for another to occur.

In the fall of 1861 and the spring of 1862, the matter of Nikolai's defiant behavior approached the moment of reckoning. We know or surmise that Nikolai and his brother Aleksandr participated in almost everything in which the underground was involved at that time. In London, the appeal "What the People Need" was being prepared for publication at Hertzen's printing house. Nikolai was one of the authors. The large revolutionary party "Land and Freedom" was organized, and the brothers were among the organizers. During the year 1862, the clouds thickened. The infuriated government gathered its strength. At the end of June, about twenty people met in Hertzen's London apartment—among them the owner of the apartment, Ogarev, and Bakunin. Another guest was Pavel Aleksandrovich Vetoshnikov, an employee of a steamship company. The next day he was to leave for Russia, and Hertzen, Bakunin, and Ogarev decided to have him carry an important letter for them. But also among the guests was an agent of the secret police, Perets. . . .

There are many kinds of joy in the world, and among them is the joy felt by a police agent: the joy of a hunter who, with cold detachment, sets out to destroy another person. No doubt the agent Colonel Rakeev experienced such feelings on July 7, 1862, when he went to arrest Chernyshevsky,[1] and so did the agent General Levental, who waited in Serno-Solovevich's apartment for the owner's return.

From July 7, 1862, Serno's path to freedom was closed forever—from that time on he was imprisoned in cell No. 18 of Alekseev's section of Petropavlovskaia Fortress. Chernyshevsky was in cell No. 14.

Before their interrogations began, prisoners were kept in solitary cells, in whose senseless silence horror would be born. Some of the prisoners would break down. Petropavlovskaia Fortress crushed and depressed them. And so it would often happen that words were uttered that should never have been uttered and that friends would thus be betrayed. Another might defend himself, then grow frightened, his courage subdued; a third might become mentally disturbed; others perhaps did not betray their friends but stated, instead, that they did not know Hertzen and the other troublemakers and that they disagreed with the sedition these persons advocated.

Nikolai was called for his first interrogation in the middle of October, after a hundred days in prison.

During the first interrogation, the commission was taken aback by his calmness, his incredibly firm self-confidence. "I did not communicate with the exiles and their accomplices in London; I did not spread any propaganda hostile to the government; I did not know and do not know any accomplices."

In the succeeding interrogations, the commission tried to "trip up" the prisoner, but, in doing so, it was obliged to employ information received from others.

In the end, the commission did not find out anything new, while the prisoner learned much from the questions he was asked. He answered them skillfully, carefully, and thoughtfully.

Meanwhile, 1863 arrived, and bad news reached Serno from the outside: the revolutionary movement had been suppressed, and the Polish rebels were being mowed down. To Serno, this information was ten times harder to take than the deprivations of prison life.

His main task was to be and to remain a man!

Finally, the interrogating commission wrote its report and passed it on to the Supreme Court for examination. Of the thirty-two prisoners, Serno alone knew his legal rights and requested a copy of the report. His request was met. The other prisoners were the kind of people who, from childhood, had believed that the government was free to do as it pleased, that the citizen had no recourse and could not even expect to understand the crimes with which he was charged.

Serno read the enormous volume and gradually grasped what the enemy knew and what he did not know. He compiled a long report of fifty-five paragraphs, the so-called Signed Testimony, which, according to custom, had to be addressed to the Tsar.

Serno admitted certain things—but somewhat vaguely so that no harm would come to any of his fellow conspirators. Then, he explained the reasons for his views and for his defense. His report was so skillfully written that it was difficult to recognize the point at which he went over to the attack. He wrote very simply and clearly. People, he said, have different opinions, and they must be allowed to argue and discuss their differences openly:

> People are suffering and dying for no reason, while, under different circumstances, these sufferings could be eliminated and the people, though remaining in different political camps, would work collectively for the good of the Fatherland. . . .
>
> Two paths are open to the Russian government. One is to lead a reasonable [social] movement. . . . A government that does not stand at the helm of such a rational movement has no other choice but to retreat. This results in vacillations and half-measures on the part of the government and in rapidly mounting irritations among the people. . . . The people appear to be ungrateful. During Nikolai's regime, which was considerably worse, they refused to work, sat and sprawled about lackadaisically.

The present government awakened society with its partial reform measures but did not give it an opportunity to express itself. And the need for expression is the same type of need for society as chatter is for a child; therefore, nothing remained for society but to express its opinion without waiting to obtain permission to do so.

Serno attempted to send a letter from prison to his brother Aleksandr abroad. The police intercepted the letter, which said: "I am completely satisfied that I was able not to involve anybody and to endure two years of prison, remaining the same person." As a result of the letter, he was asked again and again about past events and his secret relations with Hertzen and Ogarev.

To talk about Hertzen and Ogarev as Serno-Solovevich did meant at least the doubling of his sentence. But to talk in a different manner would have meant incurring a moral sentence upon himself for the rest of his life—to become, as Serno said, a coward like Judas, who hanged himself from an aspen tree. . . .

When the trial of the thirty-two prisoners, held behind closed doors in strictest secrecy, was nearing its end, Serno was asked why he had not informed the administration of a visit by Kelsiev (Hertzen's and Ogarev's agent). He answered: To inform on a guest would have been "a violation of social ethics" and, consequently, would have been contradictory to the interests of His Majesty the Tsar.

The Supreme Court judges' astonishment reached the limit when Serno-Solovevich delivered an informer's report . . . on himself. It turned out that he found out about the Tsar's order "to set free from prison those persons who cooperate in disclosing their accomplices." Serno asked that this order be applied to his case and that he be released immediately. By providing information about himself, the development of his views, the circumstances that led him into battle, he also provided information about the paths of thousands of people, without mentioning them by name. By so doing, he got to the root of the problem. Thus, he helped the government to understand these matters and—if it so wished—to correct them.

The way I understand honor, I would rather be executed than become a Judas; and, according to my understanding of the matter, I know that, to the government, my sincere repentance would just be utterly useless chatter. . . . What kind of situation would the government be placed in if I decided to deliver an endless list of those persons who I know or suspect have criticized the government's actions or were dissatisfied with the existing order! Propaganda does not cause irritation, but irritation causes propaganda.

The government could not forgive nor forget such a report. When the sentence was handed down, it called for the deprivation of all civil rights, twelve years' imprisonment at hard labor, and then exile to Siberia for life. Serno's mother asked the Tsar to mitigate the sentence.

Tsar Aleksandr II commuted the sentence from penal servitude to banishment for life.

Even before he reached Siberia, Serno, still calm and businesslike, was already thinking about the possibilities of escape. He began to act, apparently, on the very first day of his arrival. He made arrangements with some exiled Poles to organize a revolt, with the objective of reaching the border. Immediately, he again became an activist and organizer. "Try to be ready by the end of February," he said to Sulimsky, one of the exiles. The revolt was to break out at the beginning of February in 1866. But Sulimsky appears to have been a government spy. He informed the officials about the daring plan, and the government took countermeasures. Nikolai Aleksandrovich did not have time to find out about this. . . .

Within a few months, the sad news reached London.

Kolokol, No. 219, starts with Hertzen's article, "Irkutsk and Petersburg." He compared the unsuccessful attempt on the Tsar's life with the death of a political prisoner.

> These murderers do not miss a chance to murder the most noble, the purest, the most honest among us, such as Serno-Solovevich. . . . He was one of the best of the flowering of prose writers that heralded the new era in Russia. . . . And he is dead. . . .

NOTE

1. Nikolai Gavrilovich Chernyshevsky (1828–89) was a radical philosopher, journalist, and literary critic. In 1862, he was imprisoned for two years in Petropavlovskaia Fortress, where he wrote his famous didactic novel *What Is to Be Done?*—a title Lenin borrowed in 1902.

II. Literary Criticism

Andrei Siniavsky:

In Defense of Pyramids

In the fourth issue [1965] of *Yunost*, Yevgeni Yevtushenko published a long poem that simultaneously sums up and plots the future direction of his creative activity. The poem is intended to summarize the experience of the present, to relate it to the past, to Russia's history, and to unfold a panorama of human destinies, ordeals, labors, and struggles. The common link, the author's preface states, is the debate between two themes: the "theme of unbelief" contained in the monologues of the Egyptian pyramids and the "theme of belief" as expressed in the monologues of the hydroelectric station and by all the figures, episodes, and lyrical reflections involved in its construction. We see before us the contours of a gigantic, monumental project; indeed, Yevtushenko's poem is considerably broader in scope than most of the poetry of our day. It is as if the poem, even in its outward appearance, tries to resemble the construction project that gave it life and a name—"The Bratsk Hydroelectric Station."

True, as the preface says, "perhaps this is not a poem, but simply my meditations united by the debate between two themes." We will not cavil. After thirty or forty digressions in Andrei Voznesensky's "Three-Cornered Pear,"[1] we have become accustomed to the freest of compositions and will not demand thematic harmony or purity of genre. Digressions, monologues, meditations, discussions—even when they run from one end of the poem to another—can all be interesting and poetically justified. So we propose to take advantage of the offered appearance of this easy yet fundamental dialogue between Yevtushenko and his readers to throw ourselves into it and try—even if it becomes necessary to digress somewhat—not to limit our analysis to "Bratsk HES," but to tackle several general problems that Yevtushenko's work poses for contemporary poetry.

The first of these problems is Yevtushenko himself and the extraordinary success he has had with his wide and primarily youthful audience. Even those who are reserved or skeptical about his verse (and this, frankly, includes the author of this article) are forced to admit that the poet's renown, as it spreads across the country and beyond our borders—

perhaps the greatest poetic renown of recent times—has a real foundation and cannot be called just a passing fad. Nor can it be attributed to the undemanding standards of the audience or to ignorance of other and worthier subjects for love and reverence.

Yevtushenko owes his popularity to himself, to the very brilliant qualities that are basic to his poetic character and talent and that have enabled him, for better or for worse, to enthrall the minds of men of his time and, to a somewhat lesser extent, to fill the gap left in poetry by Maiakovsky's departure. After a long interlude, he has given back to us a feeling of lyrical biography that unwinds before our eyes in a chain of verses linked together by a single topic—the personality and life of the poet. In new and different circumstances, and in his own Yevtushenkoesque way, he has adopted—to use Pasternak's phrase—that "spectacular conception" of poetic biography demonstrated at the beginning of the century by Blok and then variously developed in the poetry of Maiakovsky,[2] Yesenin, and Tsvetaeva. Notwithstanding all the many differences in individual interpretation, the essence of this "spectacular conception" is that the poet not only writes his verses but somehow lives in them for all to see, generously and without embarrassment offering his life to his contemporaries and heirs for review, making it his literary subject, his fascinating novel in verse that revolves around a vividly drawn hero—the poet himself. The gesture of invitation to this festive, tragic spectacle ("I won't melt before your eyes, look at me. . ."—Blok; "People of the future! Who are you? Here I am, all pain and bruises. . . ." —Maiakovsky); his utter frankness in telling about himself; the effort to put himself into his verses so completely that we perceive the hero almost physically, that we admire him, suffer for him, and unconsciously identify him with the author (although, of course, they are not, in fact, completely the same)—all these things Yevtushenko has directly or indirectly adopted from his great predecessors.

Without comparing the relative degrees of talent, one can, however, discern elements of profound dissimilarity in the very understanding of the concepts of the individual, his destiny, and biography. For all his penchant for self-exposure, Yevtushenko is devoid of the stamp of personal exclusiveness, of the sense of being chosen for a great and awesome destiny, a destiny both providential and immutable and, at the same time, one that allows the poet to elevate his private life to the level of a unique "existence," half real, half imaginary, created from day to day before the eyes of an astonished public. Next to the Titans, Hyperbolists, and Maximalists,[3] as the poets of the above-mentioned circle were called, Yevtushenko's hero is an ordinary man; all his attractive characteristics and high ideals do not prevent him from being "like everybody else," appearing most often in the role of the "nice fellow," the "good guy"—interesting, good, and brave, but in no way one of the chosen few. But while he is far removed from the mythmaking about one's own personality that so attracted Yesenin and Maiakovsky, to say nothing of Blok and Tsvetaeva, and while he is also remote from their spiritual storms and messianic aspirations, Yevtushenko is nonetheless like them: he brings into his poetry faithful details about his life and environment; he tells where he was born, where he lives, whom he sees, whom he loves, what he is like in appearance and morals, thus maintaining the [reader's] illusion of knowing Yevgeni or, better yet, Zhenia Yevtushenko ("so that they will read [me] more and more and simply say to me: 'You know, Zhenia—that's good!' "). Thus, we know for certain that he is not just anybody but that he is Zhenia driving Galia to the beach in his Moskvich.

It is here, precisely here—in the revelation of the concrete facts of his personality and biography—that Yevtushenko's secret lies. Beyond everything else, he creates an atmosphere of personal charm by virtue of the very fact that he introduces himself and we make the acquaintance of the man himself and not just a "faceless hero." It is for this faith, this friendliness, and this sociability that people have come to love him. . . . In short, we think of Yevtushenko as an old friend whose character, mimicry, and intonations express the essential traits of a whole generation that has seen in its midst no other prophet, apart from this "one of their own," of whom it could immediately be said that he was real and not imaginary, sincere and not a liar, as proven *inter alia* by his wholly believable "Mama," "Galia," and "Winter Station."[4]

But just the same, in comparison with his more demanding and self-assured forebears ("Aleksandr Sergeevich, permit me to introduce myself. My name is Maiakovsky"; "Thus, according to the Bible, spake the prophet Yesenin, Sergei"), Yevtushenko represents an alteration if not a degeneration of the tradition. We accept without question Yesenin's confused, muddled, ecstatic prayers:

> Even after all my sins,
> After giving heaven the lie,
> They put me in a Russian shirt,
> And under an icon let me die . . .

Troubled as it is, this has weight and sounds magnificent. But Yevtushenko's incomparably more timid and simple request (in "Russian Nature," 1960)—though Yesenin-like in its incongruity and disorder—gives an impression of affectation and unfounded pretense:

> Russian nature,
>   before you, prophetic,
> How I feel pathetic
>   always in my little rush!
> You don't hurry,
>   fuss and scurry
> You just go
>   powerful, slow
> When my time comes,
>   don't you mourn;

Dispose of me simply,
             don't you weep.
I won't die!
             you, Russian nature,
Like Russian nature,
             take me to your keep.

. . . The situation is different with respect to the Maiakovsky tradition of civic poetry. This tradition Yevtushenko has inherited and is continuing as one of the keenest and most urgent poets of the new generation, now willingly playing the role of tribune. In large measure, it was civic sentiment that dictated "Bratsk HES," with its special chapter dedicated to Maiakovsky, who served the author as a model for imitation, an example of fortitude, nobility, and revolutionary purity.

But on Yevtushenko's lips, the inspired verse of Maiakovsky, unfortified from within by a personality of equal charge and caliber, not infrequently sounds naked, thin, declamatory, and publicity-seeking (as does the verse of many other poets who try to imitate Maiakovsky). And, in the role of champion, tribune, and agitator, Yevtushenko seems to represent a very different and weaker version of civic consciousness. Not commanding the powers of a Maiakovsky, who always marched straight ahead to the goal, permitting himself no twists or turns, Yevtushenko is forced to resort to maneuvers, ambushes, detours, camouflage ("We tried to take orders but do them backwards"), and even to devise his own special "battle strategy." In his poetry, the poet "retreats in order to advance," tacks, lays traps, plays tricks:

His mighty hand sets into motion
             arms,
             wagons,
             flags,
Let them think it's the right flank
Where he has concentrated his men,
But he knows,
             he knows
                          it's the left,
At dawn awaiting the drum,
Ready for battle, cavalry alert,
Nostrils quivering, all ahum.

Much has changed and grown more complex since the time when Yevtushenko made no secret of the flank on which he was concentrating ("Who's that marching with his right foot? Left, left, left!"), when he went into battle erect, facing forward, deploying his troops in "parade formation." It is hard to blame him for the change that has taken place; yet one is inevitably distressed to see his fighting spirit, bravery, and implacable rejection of the "scum" coexisting in an amazing manner with compliance and caginess. All the complicated maneuvering, the shifting of troops from left to right, the whole "battle strategy," suddenly turns out to be mere adaptation to circumstance. He manuevers artfully enough to make you admire his unexpected fencing techniques, but it is hard to count on him, you don't want to follow him—he is capable of leading you Heaven knows where and abandoning you half-way for the sake of the next maneuver.

Yevtushenko himself is well aware of his pliability, the indecisiveness of his civic muse, because those same "strategic" considerations by which he justifies himself turn at other times into quite another sort of confession: "It's no time to be a coward, but I'm not very brave"; "I was halfway between wax and metal. . . ." Feeling himself to be the poet of a transitional period, a poet not fully formed and not fully consistent, he hails the future artist who will carry out his noble intentions, carry off what he has not dared:

> And where I throw down my pen, saying
>   "It's not worth it . . ."
> He'll say
>   "It's worth it"
>   and take up his pen.

. . . At the same time, these reproaches against himself have a sounder basis than self-glorification. By not making a walking paragon of himself, by admitting his weaknesses and shortcomings, the poet strengthens our feeling of contact with a living human being who, for all his simplicity, is not so very simple and not at all naive. But what these confessions show most of all is that he is capable of a self-analysis and doubt that enable him to look soberly at reality in all its complexity and contradictions, to contemplate his precarious position in the world, and thus to step away from his yesterday's self, rise above himself, and reveal other potentialities within himself. . . .

We will not rebuke the poet for vaingloriousness. Who doesn't hold success dear? Who hasn't dreamt of fame? But there is something else that is frightening—the treatment of oneself like a lottery ticket that can win if the right number comes up but that is essentially unimportant; a disrespectful attitude toward one's own personality, which, with one gesture, can cancel out all the lofty monologues about belief in mankind as master of its fate.

Fortunately that mood, which makes all life seem an endless merry-go-round and the poet himself a squirrel circling in a cage impatiently waiting for "his chance," is offset in Yevtushenko's work by other motifs, motifs that have been gaining importance of late—dissatisfaction with himself, the desire to break out of the vicious circle, to catch his breath, to meditate. It is these motifs that stand out in the . . . poem cycle "Trip to the North," the most mature and meaningful work, it seems to us, that Yevtushenko has ever written. The experiences described in it are perhaps hard, saddening, and contradictory, but they could serve as the condition for a more profound world view; they testify to the poet's growing demands and leave the impression that the constant hustle and bustle of the past have left him for a time, making room for serious reflections about life and himself.

> Hey, you orator! Hey, you seer!
> You're lost, soaked, chilled through.
> Your ammo's gone, your voice worn out,
> The rain has quenched your fire for you.
> But don't fret that this brings tears,
> There's much that needs consideration
> There's lots of time . . . "Long cries,"
> That's what's called transportation.

The note of dissatisfaction with himself and his milieu, the effort to take a new look at the familiar, boring round of activities, habits, and practices, is also clearly heard in "Bratsk HES," most of which was written somewhat earlier. Its appearance was in significant measure dictated by these new impulses: the poet does not want to waste any more time on trivia, he doesn't want to skim the surface, and he renounces certain of the sins common to his own and others' pasts.

> O my rivals, let's stop all this,
> This nastiness and flattery.
> Let's think about our fate,
> About the disease that afflicts us all.
> Superficiality—worse than being blind,
> You can see but do not want to.
> Are you ignorant, you?
> Or maybe it's from fear of ripping up roots
> Of sheltering trees, leaving not a trace,
> Not so much as a stick planted in their place.
> Isn't the reason we hurry on,
> Taking off on the top, because
> Manhood forgotten, we are scared
> Of the very idea, getting to the bottom?
> We hurry along with half an answer,
> Bearing our shallowness like a treasure.
> No, no, not in cold calculation
> But in an instinct of self-preservation.
> Then comes the snuffing out,
> The inability to flee or fight,
> And the feathers of our tamed wings
> Become nasty pillows for the night.

This is stated somewhat diffusively, but essentially it is very true. With all our heart, we share the poet's anxiety over the dominance of superficial thinking, premature decisions, half-answers, and half-truths.

Yevtushenko's point of departure is so serious and so applicable to the contemporary world he writes about, as well as to his personal progress, that one would like to take his own words (in their positive sense, of course) as the criterion for judging his poem. But, first, we should also acknowledge that this is necessary not only for the sake of an accurate critical analysis, which must observe the "rules of the game" and respect the rules and principles adhered to by the artist; it is also necessary as a precautionary measure—to keep from falling into a trap.

Yevtushenko is easy for the reader and hard for the critic. He knows how to make himself likable, to win you over, to arouse your sympathy. He is the first to criticize himself so severely that he can give a 100-point handicap to any critic. After he is through doing that, it's even a bit awkward for someone else to come along and take up the job. After all, the author understands everything and knows all about himself already, so what is there left to do? But, while he is aware of everything and makes perfectly just demands, Yevtushenko is far from consistent in applying them himself. His poetic thought often wanders, curves, turns back halfway, jumps from subject to subject, and evades the question it puts to itself. And, though it is not hard to understand his verses, it is often hard to catch their inner essence, for that essence is inclined to change as things go along, so to speak. . . . In tracing the logic of his work, one marvels at the art with which he touches on the acute and painful questions of our time, but without depth; at his ability to meditate about everything on earth, but without saying anything meaningful; at his capacity to proclaim one thing candidly while simultaneously doing something completely different with equal candor. This is not always the case with him, but it does happen, and it *has* happened in "Bratsk HES."

After diagnosing our common ailment—superficiality—and proclaiming his firm intention to conquer it, Yevtushenko has written his most superficial work. *Most* superficial because, in conception, in scale and scope of reality, it aspires to be more than just another simple verse, or poem, or poem cycle, and this means that more is demanded of him. *Most* superficial because the author has broken his own newly uttered commandment, a commandment extremely important and precious to him and to us, and he evidently never even noticed what he had done. How did this happen?

Let us return to that splendid tirade against superficiality which we quoted earlier. Let's go on reading it carefully and attentively to see how Yevtushenko develops his theme and what cure he prescribes:

> Let everyone go into life with this vow,
> To help that which deserves to flower,
> Never forgetting to avenge
> That which deserves to be avenged,
> Not vengeance for vengeance's sake

But vengeance as a battle incarnate
In the name of justice and honor,
In the name of affirming the good.
We shall not avenge out of fear.
When the possibility of vengeance is lost,
The instinct of self-preservation
Kills, it does not preserve.
Superficiality is a murderer, not a friend,
An enemy pretending to be a friend,
Laying the nets of delusion,
Squandering the spirit on details,
Running away from conclusions.
The earth will lose its powers,
Leaving conclusions to a later date.
Or will perhaps the defenselessness
And the inconclusiveness of human fate
Some century become clear?

Comparing this fragment with the earlier one, we see the pulsating thought grow thin and faint, the moral go flat, the language become clumsy. The verse no longer flows but marks time, unable to master its flabby notions about the need to do what must be done and not to do what must not be done. "Vengeance as a battle incarnate," "we shall not avenge out of fear"—is this what we expected from a poet who has gone into battle against superficiality, only to turn back suddenly in midsentence? And what is the point of repeating those empty words— "vengeance," "honor," "justice," "goodness," "avenge"? Or is this just a word game to trick the understanding so that one problem can be substituted for another and the author can jump to a conclusion about general inconclusiveness, sliding along the surface of his utterances in a way that is perhaps . . . effective but bears no relation to what has gone before? . . .

In Yevtushenko's new poem, the treacherous phrase is one about the "inconclusiveness" of the world, from which, supposedly, flows the necessity for reaching artistic "conclusions" that promise us salvation from the superficial hustle and bustle (as if a harmony of words guaranteed a correspondence of phenomena). In fact, Yevtushenko's resounding initial promise to present an authentically profound interpretation of life is never fulfilled. It is smothered by the false profundity of the "grand genre," by the grandeur of the subject, and by the prospect of creating something epic, universal, something having worldwide historical meaning. "The poet, undaunted, sums up everything that has gone before," Yevtushenko asserts with extraordinary ease. But it is precisely this promise that contradicts, excludes, and ruins his other promise—"to get to the heart of the matter." Summing things up over thousands of kilometers, over decades and centuries, "Bratsk HES" becomes amorphous and wordy (reading it straight through is, quite frankly, exhausting). It sins in its high-speed attempts to "tell everything," "taking only half a meter off the top." Though interesting in its separate episodes and vignettes, it leaves the over-all impression that the author, in trying not to be shallow and not to waste himself on details, draws "conclusions" that are only outwardly significant but that actually are generally superficial. . . .

Taking the "Bratsk HES" as his ideal and model, Yevtushenko set speculatively to work, giving preference to the quantitative method; summarizing all his observations, memories, and associations connected with a trip to Siberia, he monotonously weaves them into the one central, pivotal idea of the work, the essence of which is the "need to believe" regardless of difficulties. Though essentially worthy, this idea is reiterated over and over until it produces what is called a "bad infinity" and imparts a stereotyped pattern to the enormous amount of material assembled in this work. This is particularly evident in the historical chapters, which are written like paragraphs in a schoolbook. The Decembrists, the Petrashevskyites,[5] Chernyshevsky, Khalturin,[6] all appear as martyrs to faith, all with the same face and all arranged "in order," in keeping with a school curriculum.

"Will I be able? Not enough culture . . . A smattering does not promise prophecies. . . ." Yevtushenko expresses serious misgiving at the beginning only to reject it immediately: "But the spirit of Russia soars above me and boldly bids [me] try." However, the main trouble, in our view, is not so much a.lack of culture as the excessive erudition displayed by the author whenever and wherever possible, as if he had tried to put into the poem everything he had ever heard, seen, read, or come upon in his country's history or in world culture. . . . The cultural-historical references flow so smoothly into the text and in so hackneyed a form, just as we memorized them in childhood, that, for all their variety, they take on the character of a requirement without which no ever-so-slightly educated man could get along but which the artist could probably avoid—all that "common baggage," since he has his own special interests and tastes. . . .

Wishing to demonstrate the high intellectual level of the people building the HES, Yevtushenko brings in, along with the popular names, some more unusual and refined ones: Scriabin, Fellini, St. Exupéry. The construction workers say:

> Here in the *taiga* I see Gauguin's gardens
> And Cézanne's blue-gray stacks.[7]
> Amid the sparks of acetylene torches,
> I see the blue girls of Dégas.
>
> Forgive me for my fantasy,
> But when the blizzards blow,
> Sitting on the edge of the dam
> Is Rodin's Thinker, all in snow.

Tolstoy came to share our ordeal
Through the storm so wild,
Dostoevsky suffered, and Gorky
Toiled along, carrying a child.

And so every comma, every stanza, line after line, sets the "task" required of today's young person, if he wishes to understand art. There is no question that a variety of aesthetic tastes and cultural needs among our youth is a true sign of the times. The trouble is that, in Yevtushenko's patter, variety lacks a solid foundation, and the things the heroes of the poem (not its author) are supposedly thinking and saying are no different from the stylistic conglomeration that so fully characterizes the author's tastes. "Amid the sparks of acetylene torches, I see the blue girls of Dégas"—it is with such a formula that Yevtushenko often builds his images and links his words and motifs. Outwardly pretty, fashionable, with a certain pretension to refinement, reasonably industrial and proletarian, the formula shouts the poetic eclecticism to which Yevtushenko has again paid tribute in his new poem.

In this regard, he is not alone. At times, we encounter more pronounced attempts to unite the un-unitable—to wed Andrei Rublev to a radar set, to put it crudely—in the art of Andrei Voznesensky than we do in that of Yevtushenko, who is just a beginner in formalistic innovation. In the fine arts, we find a similar trend in the works of Ilia Glazunov, which caused such a sensation not long ago among young art lovers. The latter failed to perceive the tastelessness of his showy counterfeits of ancient Russian icons executed in a method that crosses Käthe Kollwitz, Johanson, and the Kukryniksi.[8]

It is not impossible that this eclecticism is the result of too ardent an acceptance and adoption of two ideas, both good and fruitful in principle. First, we all know (too well perhaps) that art grows out of the classical tradition. On the other hand, in contemporary art, especially in the works of the young pleiad of artists, there is the natural effort to broaden and renew tradition. But, in hurried practice ("Isn't the reason why we hurry on. . ?"), this combination of tendencies can produce unthinkable hybrids, like a crossbreed of a dachshund and a sheepdog. Once, a poet was content with the tradition of Demian Bedny, for example; today, this is not enough. So, without losing his old orientation, he "enriches" Bedny with Briusov. While both writers deserve continuation and a following, the mixture of their styles results in something a bit monstrous.

At the beginning of "Bratsk HES," Yevtushenko, like his pious masters in the Middle Ages, pronounces "a prayer before the poem." In it, he turns for help to all the Russian poets—Pushkin, Lermontov, Nekrasov, Blok, Pasternak, Yesenin, and Maiakovsky—making a thumbnail sketch of each and paraphrasing their winged words in his own way, most often in a banal, cheap, and sometimes parodistic way. . . .

But, what is worse, in his desire to adopt all that is most valuable from his great teachers, the deferential student does not stop to consider how it is all going to fit together in his poem. Although "Bratsk HES" is big and, so to speak, has room for everything, it is difficult to imagine how, in this poetic fusion, Pushkin's "melodiousness" (all the characterizations are Yevtushenko's and represent the "gifts" he asks from the classical writers) is supposed to unite harmoniously with Nekrasov's "inelegance," Blok's "mistiness," Maiakovsky's "rough-hewnness," Yesenin's "tenderness," and Lermontov's "venom." One imagines that, if the aforementioned writers had actually bequeathed those mutually exclusive qualities to the author of "Bratsk HES," the poem would have been a catastrophe and the structure would have fallen apart instantly. There remains another approach, and this was the approach actually adopted by Yevtushenko—that of taking just a little from each classical writer, a little "mistiness," a little "rough-hewnness," a little "melodiousness," etc. So what one gets is a neutral stylistic mix that is unexplosive, spiritless, and devoid of all the brilliant features of the givers; it is eclectic to some degree, original to some extent. But was it worth praying for so fervently? . . .

The "prayer before the poem"—over which we have lingered because it is, unfortunately, so typical of a widespread notion today about how to create a masterpiece—makes us want to compare it to another "prayer" composed before creation by an exacting artist. It was written by Kipling, for us not too authoritative a figure but sensible on questions of the psychology of art and the creation of unique aesthetic values. Kipling's poem "Evarra and His Gods" tells of a certain Evarra, maker of gods in a land across the sea," who personifies the Artist, to whatever country or culture he may belong. Accordingly, in each of his reincarnations he solves his problems differently. Depending on the place or time in which he lived, Evarra made his god of gold and pearl, hewed it from crude stone, carved an idol of wood with moss hair and a crown of straw, or, finally, molded it from mud and horn. And each time he left the proud inscription: "Thus gods are made, and whoso makes them otherwise shall die," so that, in the next incarnation, the past forgotten, he would always follow his immutable law in creating a completely different form.

> Yet at last he came to Paradise
> And found his own four gods; and that he wrote
> And marvelled, being very near to God,
> What oaf on earth had made his toil God's law.
> Then God said, mocking: "Mock not. These be thine."
> Then cried Evarra: "I have sinned!" "Not so.
> If thou hadst written otherwise, thy gods
> Had rested in the mountain and the mine,
> And I were poorer by four wondrous gods
> And thy more wondrous laws, Evarra. Thine,
> Servant of shouting crowds and lowing kine!"

The moral of this parable is that, in the process of creation, the artist must not be omnivorous. He is better off being intolerant of another's interpretation, being convinced of the unquestionable rightness of his own way. It is not that, in principle, he should be incapable of appreciating others' work, incapable of broadening his point of view and tastes. Like any other man, he can appreciate very many and very different things. But, as for himself, he knows that he can work in one way and no other, according to his own unwavering vision, his chosen stylistic system, tradition, unique aesthetic truth. "Thus gods are made." We know of many cases of one genius being unfair to another: Tolstoy reviled Shakespeare; Gorky had no sympathy for Maiakovsky at one period; Maiakovsky attacked the Art Theater. But they are still dear to us, and we often wonder at the unexpected narrowness, prejudice, and partiality of such judgments of theirs, forgetting that the excellent, many-faceted works of art we love so much came to be as a result of the fact that they were not supposed to resemble one another, because their creators, in their stubborn originality, were deaf to any other artistic conception. Of course, such conflicts need not be created artificially, but, in an indirect fashion, they do testify to the fact that, in the field of art, the ones who usually triumph are the loners, the fanatics about their own ideas and style.

For a long time Yevtushenko's connection with contemporary reality has been direct and immediate; he has a clear eye for everyday details and an ear unspoiled by a lack of faith in familiar, homely speech. As a result, when he is not trying to draw any general literary conclusions and is simply writing about his milieu, so to speak, everything is just fine. . . .

The best parts and sections of the poem ("Niushka," "Bolshevik," "Dispatcher of Light," "Night of Poetry") are written as scenes taken from nature, and the characters are taken directly from reality. Here, the poet is not playing his usual role of leading actor; he is a spectator and listener, carrying out his intention, declared earlier in the poem, "to hear everything at once, to see everything at once." From lyric biography, he moves on to the metamorphoses—about which he has also written in one of his recent poems ("I am bound by duty and love to be trees, tramways, and people")—and they are employed extensively in "Bratsk HES."

At the same time, that broad sweep, that Yevtushenkoesque hunger to give life to "everything at once," leads to places where even the best bits read like something we already know, something we have read or seen at the movies. . . .

Despite their concreteness, their animation, their authenticity, his images at times seem secondhand, the reflections of images. . . . He abuses pathetic intonations and moving gestures, trying too hard to make an impression and touch the reader. Hence the excess of tears shed in the poem, the theatrical parting words of the old woman in the "*Taiga* Flowers" section:

And she blesses us forever,
The excavators of land,
With that thin, knotted
Peasant woman's hand.

The author probably needed that parting gesture to tie up loose ends
and to cross the logical bridge back to another section nearer the beginning ("Fair in Simbirsk"), where the young Lenin is depicted in a
similar situation. But such bridges (there are no small number of them)
are too contrived, too planned, to say nothing of the fact that the
episode in which Lenin symbolically lifts a drunken woman up out of
the mud—signifying the renaissance of Russia—also sounds excessively
saccharine and false:

He takes her gently by the elbow,
Unconcerned over who might see.
"Jesus bless you, dear,
I'll get along from here."
And he goes off
          beside the barges
Along the Volga in the spring.
The old woman watching, sad and mild,
Blesses him
As she would her own child.

There can be no doubt that, in "Bratsk HES," Yevtushenko attempted to solve very serious problems, past and present, and, on such a
field of action, he was naturally unable to solve them all. It is sometimes
said that a writer is not obliged to "solve" anything; it is enough for
him to pose the questions of the day and let his generation, society, and
history itself find the answers. This notion needs at least one correction:
to pose a question does not mean simply to hint at something serious
and move on calmly, as if a simple reminder were the last word on a
given subject. Perhaps it would be better for an author not to concern
himself at all with those aspects of life about which he is in no position
to say more than has been said by others. Isn't a thoughtful "narrowness" better than superficial "breadth"? Can't a conscious limitation of
theme facilitate a more concentrated approach to reality and be more
effective than an easy, universal view of things?

These melancholy thoughts come to mind when Yevtushenko concerns himself with what is probably the most painful, most "accursed"
question of our recent past—the concentration-camp theme. It would
have been better if he hadn't. Without attempting to say how such a
subject should be handled, one can say with certainty that it should not
have been handled as it was in the poem published in *Yunost*. The poet
probably wished to extol the unbending faith of the people who innocently suffered under Stalin; so he took the familiar and easy path of
praising their enthusiasm for labor as if it didn't matter where, why, or
how that enthusiasm was manifested. As a result, the author's wishes

notwithstanding, concentration camps are transformed into strongholds of our military and industrial power—almost a pledge of victory—and the people destroyed there into some sort of Communist labor brigade, which sounds altogether blasphemous.

> Around us the guards stood watching.
> Comrade Stalin, you didn't understand
> That we numbered prisoners
> Were far from your guards, from our land;
> We went over the river, over the sea, and
> On to Berlin, with the army! . . .
>
> An "enemy of the people"—yet
> I built a power station on the Volga
> Hidden from foreign sight.
> We beat all records. Who cared
> That they never photographed or praised
> Us—not a word did they write!

The solution of the problem of "fathers" and "children" is too facile and illusory, attractive as it may seem at first glance. The "children" dare not condemn the honest "fathers," the ones who had faith and worked heroically even in the camps.

> But remember the other fathers
> Too, the midnight knockers, informers,
> The odiously silent and blind.
> Remember and spit on them, mean or kind!
> Go ahead, my boy, clean as a commissar, set forth
> Thy father's truth, leave the odious behind.

It is put sharply and boldly, but not profoundly. Pose the question a bit more deeply and the proposed division of "fathers" into honest (believers) and odious (nonbelievers) becomes a fiction: excuse me, but do you mean that, among the "other fathers," the "midnight knockers, informers," there were no people of sincere faith? Does that really entirely explain the tragedy we endured?

In conclusion, it would not be inappropriate to take the idea of "faith," around which a great many of the episodes in "Bratsk HES" revolve, and add to it another idea expressed by Yevtushenko—his special invocation to the young: "Let us Think."

> Let us think. We are all guilty
> Of things not so small—
> Of empty verses, countless quotes,
> Of standard speeches in the hall.
> We do not want to live
> Like the wind. On the brink,
> Greatness calls. Let us be
> Equal to it. Let us think.

Along with his other attractive qualities, this invocation, which is so expressive of the spirit of the times and which could practically serve as a motto for contemporary literature, has frequently enabled Yevtu-shenko to play the role of the pioneer and leader in recent years. This did not happen in "Bratsk HES." There he lags behind his own demands, if one can put it that way. So preoccupied is he with developing his theme in breadth that he forgets his own demand for depth, for thinking things through to the end, for penetrating to the essence. "Yes, higher and more deeply—simultaneously!" he calls on us in the poem. As always, he has figured out what must be done, but, instead of accomplishing his acknowledged task, he avoids it. It remains for us to support the poet and take up his call: "Yes, higher and more deeply!" Yes, thus and only thus.

—From *Phoenix 1966*
(translated by Gabriella Azrael)

Notes

1. For an English translation, see *Selected Poems by Andrei Voznesensky*, trans. Anselm Hollo (New York: Grove Press, 1964).—Ed.

2. Vladimir Vladimirovich Maiakovsky (1893–1930) was a poet and playwright who popularized revolutionary ideals in such works as *Ode to the Revolution* (1918) and *The Left March* (1919). Later, however, he became disillusioned with many aspects of Soviet life. His plays reflected his growing bitterness and were suppressed by Stalin. Under growing attack by the official literary critics, Maiakovsky committed suicide in 1930. Nevertheless, he is now portrayed as the apotheosis of the "Bolshevik" poet.—Ed.

3. Various literary schools that flourished in the 1920's.—Ed.

4. For an English translation of "Stantsia zima," see *Selected Poems of Yevgeni Yevtushenko*, trans. Robin Milner-Gulland and Peter Levi (New York: E. P. Dutton, 1962).—Ed.

5. The Petrashevsky Circle was a group of radical writers who met in home of M. Butashevich Petrashevsky to discuss philosophical and political issues of the day (1845–48). Most of its members were arrested after the uprisings of 1848. The Petrashevsky Circle has become a symbol of liberal aspirations brutally crushed by police tyranny.—Ed.

6. Stepan Nikolayevich Khalturin (1856–82) was a revolutionary who organized the Workers' Union of North Russia in 1878. He was executed for participating in the assassination of Tsarist officials.—Ed.

7. The "blue-gray stacks" are probably not Cézanne but Claude Monet.—A. S.

8. Kukryniksi is the composite name for three Soviet artists—Mikhail Vasilevich Kuprianov, Porfiry Nikitch Krylov, and Nikolai Aleksandrovich Sokolev—who for many years have collaborated as political cartoonists.—Ed.

Lev Kopelev:

At Anna Akhmatova's Grave

Akhmatova's poetry, her destiny, her every aspect—so fine and majestic—personify Russia during the hardest, most tragic, and most glorious years of her thousand-year history.

Anna of all Russia, that was what another great daughter of Russia, Marina Tsvetaeva, called her.

Anna of all Russia! Here is pride, unbending in humiliation or mortal fear. Here is humility—humility, not meekness—and contemptuous composure even in moments of exalted inspiration. Majestic sorrow and an eternally young and mischievous smile. The tenderest feminity and the most courageous masculinity. The tough, elegant mind of a scholar; the clear vision of a stern prophet mixed with genuinely naive wonder at the beauty of the earth and the secrets of life; and the ancient thrall of the sorceress, herself bewitched by love, the breath of the earth, the magic harmonies of the mischievous word:

> Our sacred profession,
> A thousand years old,
> A light to the world.
> But of the poets, not one
> Has spoken of wisdom—there is none;
> Old age—none; even death,
> Perhaps—none.

Anna of all Russia, twice crowned—with a crown of thorns and with the star-studded crown of poetry.

Her poetry is integral and many-faceted, it grows out of lively contradictions, out of the unity between a flaming, troubled heart and a mind that glitters like the snow on the heights of a mountain. Her poetry is open, wide open, and as secret and secretive as life itself. Her life is filled with boundless suffering and unprecedented victories, hours of sorrow and moments of happiness—a life as contradictory and fine as her poetry.

The sounds of Russian songs—laments, quiet prayers, clever ditties—are alive in her verse. Inconsolable longing, bright joy always touched by a shade of sadness, the breath of Russian forests and rivers, white nights, the hard rhythms of Petersburg's granite and dark gardens, the rustle of palace groves, bursting shells on the streets of a besieged Leningrad: all, all are alive in Akhmatova's verses. They are profoundly original. In the most dissimilar verses—dissimilar in mood, theme, rhythm, vocabulary—that special Akhmatova style is always clearly felt; that unique, inimitable voice is always heard. But, at the same time, a flesh-and-blood relationship to Pushkin is always obvious—the relationship of a direct poetic lineage, a relationship of words and of an attitude profoundly nationalistic and thereby universal.

The poetry of Anna Akhmatova personifies Russia not only because it is stamped with nature, with Russia's past and present, her life and reality, her sorrows and her joys, but also because—in the true Russian manner—it also embraces the whole world, embraces Europe and the universe, with love and wisdom. In speaking of Pushkin, Dostoevsky said: "The Russian's mission is to be undeniably pan-European and universal. To be a real Russian, to become fully Russian, means, perhaps . . . to become the brother of all people, to become a universal man."

The "universal responsiveness" that Dostoevsky found in Pushkin lives on in Anna Akhmatova, as it does in Blok, Tsvetaeva, Mandelshtam, Maiakovsky, and Zabolotsky.

Alive in her verses—literally alive—are the images of ancient Greece and Rome, the Biblical East, past and contemporary Europe. Her muses are the muses of Dante and Shakespeare. The suffering of London ablaze under fascist bombs, the pain of Paris captured by Hitler's armies are her suffering and her pain. When she translated the poetry of the ancient and contemporary East, the poets of all the Slavic countries, and the poets of Estonia, Rumania, and Norway, it was with genuine love and wise insight into the spiritual life of other peoples and epochs.

And, in every line of her poetry, her prose, and her poetic translations, "Russian speech, the great Russian tongue," works its miracles.

Akhmatova's greatness is all the clearer and more distinct in that it emerges against a background that is hardly lacklustre. She is the heir, the contemporary, and the countrywoman of giants. In the heavens of Russian poetry, our century sparkles with incomparable constellations. Poets, like dying stars, go right on burning in space as beacons to new generations. New people find in them new shades of the spectrum, new particles of living energy. Blok, Gumilev, Khlebnikov, Yesenin, Maiakovsky, Mandelshtam, Tsvetaeva, Pasternak . . . Akhmatova forms a link in the chain, she completes an era of such greatness and richness in Russian poetic diction that probably only our grandsons and great-grandsons will be able truly to evaluate it. Akhmatova is as immortal as Russian speech. Her detractors are condemned to either total oblivion or eternal shame in the fine print of the comments accompanying the last volume of her *Complete Collected Works*.

For those of us who knew Anna Andreevna, who had the great happiness of seeing her and listening to her, for all of us, life from now on will be more pallid, muted, and insipid.

However, we are left with one proud, sad comfort. Today, believers and unbelievers alike are convinced of the immortality of her soul, because, now and in centuries to come, the greatness of her art and life will be confirmed ever more incontestably.

Eternal life. No, these are not just the words of prayer, of mournful entreaty or hope, but of certain knowledge. Understanding and sensing the age-old essence of each word, we know and believe in—eternal life.

—From *Phoenix 1966*
(*translated by Gabriella Azrael*)

III. Short Stories

N. Karaguzhin:

Stalin's Charm

This happened long ago, years before the war, when Stalin was in his glory. The words "Stalin" and "great" were inseparable. "Stalin" without "great"? It was the same as being without pants—just as indecent.

True, the intelligentsia floundered about, trying to save its intellectual reputation. Its historical reputation. Paid for by the blood of the Decembrists.

But why are we so unfortunate? Our fathers—heirs of Radishchev—somehow managed to uphold their honor. But we? Why must we be disgraced, why did this happen no sooner, no later, not to some other generation but to us? What are our heirs going to say?

For shame! Servility, obsequiousness, "giving in to the boss!" Disgusting! Is there any comparison to the present? Abominations, abominations, abominations, we always have been and always will be. How can we look our children in the eye? Oh, our shameless eyes! Oh, lackeys!

A vague presentiment of future conflict between fathers and sons.

The mud overflowed, the intelligentsia floundered, grumbled, and told anecdotes about the tyrant.

"Listen, Comrade Radek, they tell me you're making up stories about me. Stop it, please: you know I'm a great leader."

"I didn't make up any anecdotes."

The young woman was a typical hereditary intellectual. On the walls of her room, among the Leningrad watercolors by Ostroumova-Lebedeva, hung good photographs of two naval lieutenants: Schmidt and her papa.

The young woman was an artist—a ballerina.

Like her comrades in fate—humiliated by oppression, disgraced by intellectual prostitution—she too found comfort in making fists in her pocket.

Despise her?

There are days when shadows lie sharp against the earth—like the demarcation drawn by a tautly strung carpenter's line. Here is the region of light; there, darkness.

The artist was still on the side of light.

No need to despise her.

Stalin loved to arrange splendid receptions at the Kremlin. Sometimes pianists, sometimes Stakhanovites, sometimes master harvesters, sometimes artistic masters. The ballerina landed at one of those receptions.

She came back from Moscow transformed. You couldn't recognize her. Something had happened there, something serious. A new light shone in her soul. You couldn't tell whether it was the clear light of day or another, more sinister, light; but the reflection of a new light burned in her thin face, and her silent eyes had the glitter of steel.

No one dared say a bad word about Stalin. There was a sense of superiority in her. As if she had a new faith, dedication, a secret—unsuspected by the ignorant—that had been opened to her. Oh, how she despised the ignorant!

"Why do you talk so, when you've never seen him? I've seen him, as I'm seeing you."

"And what about it, dear Yekaterina Dmitrevna?"

"Here's what. If you knew him from up close . . . you don't know, but you talk!"

"What's to know, Katia? Isn't it the same—from a distance or up close? He's not a monument, you know, but a political figure."

"A lot you understand about politics! Have you ever talked with Stalin? I have!"

"You talked with Stalin?"

"Yes, I did, just as I'm talking with you now!" And the artist looked at her interlocutors with unspeakable scorn, seeming to measure the distance separating their worthless selves from the shining heights that she had been fortunate enough to behold.

"What did you talk with him about, Yekaterina Dmitrevna?"

"Ah, can it be conveyed in words? It was simply a miracle."

"But Katinka, why can't it be conveyed in words? That's incomprehensible."

"Some things *are* incomprehensible. You have to see, feel, hear the intonations of his voice. No, you can't imagine how intelligent a man he is! And how loving!"

"He's just a . . . father, for the whole people . . . a father!"

There were lots of ohs and ahs at that; the feelings of tenderness, gratitude, and love flooding the heart of the woman were obvious enough, but the sense and content of the conversation that had caused such upheaval in the ballerina's heart remained unknown.

And when the passion inflaming her somewhat subsided and the artist was again capable of articulate speech, there came an explanation.

In the middle of the banquet at the Kremlin, the leader began circulating among the tables. He stayed a minute with some guests; others he passed, smiling affably. The ballerina was lucky. He stopped by her chair. He might perhaps have gone on, but someone quickly and helpfully told him her name. Stalin held out his hand and said hello.

"Hello, Comrade Stalin!" said the woman in great confusion: there standing next to her was he who was making history, he who was legendary, he about whom they sang songs and wrote music, he who was unknown and famous, hidden and in full view, he who inspired fear and love, respect and hatred, he whom she had read about in books and whom she had daily heard on the radio, he about whom she had gossiped.

"Hello, Joseph Vissarionovich!" she said, not releasing his hand from her own.

Stalin had to make an effort. Freeing his hand, he glanced at the ballerina's figure, thought a while, and said, "Why are you so thin?"

"I don't know," the woman whispered, embarrassed, upset, and already in love.

"Aha, very bad!" Stalin wagged his head. "Ought to eat more," the great leader concluded and moved on toward the other guests.

That was all. The whole conversation. But it was enough for her; the man had crossed the carpenter's line, sharp against the earth.

Great is the charm of power.

Stalin's Smile

He joined the conversation abruptly, but it was as if they had been expecting him. He cut the others off short, and there was no stopping him. He spoke easily, smoothly, as if he were telling a story. Well, maybe it was a story. And maybe he was being sly, maybe simple.

"Nowadays, they say a lot of irrelevant things about Stalin, bad things. It's not fair. No one will dispute that he was cruel, like a beast sometimes, but, with our people, you've got to be or you're lost. Yet there was something warm and human in him. He wasn't loved for nothing. And that he was loved to the point of adoration is no secret.

"Poskrebyshev[1] was a man very close to him. His title, as kind of a chief secretary, was 'private secretary.' He had important privileges and could see Stalin any time without asking. The leader, who had a suspicious and frightened eye, had no doubts about Poskrebyshev and trusted him completely, without checking on him.

"Sometimes Stalin would give him a slip of paper, a crumpled slip from the bathroom maybe, and on the paper would be names. Sometimes scrawled in pencil, sometimes in ink; two, three names, perhaps a dozen. And Stalin would add the little words, 'to be taken care of.' Poskrebyshev knew that the list should be taken to Yezhov or, when Yezhov was taken care of, to Beria. The private secretary would have laughed if any of those poor creatures had remained among the living after having been 'taken care of.'

"This happened so often and Poskrebyshev got so used to it that he lost his curiosity as to which names he had been given. When occasionally he read the list—what difference did it make? He was doggedly attached to Stalin as to no one else on earth. All the rest were so much wild grass in a flower bed, to be tirelessly weeded out by the great gardener.

"Nevertheless, on one occasion, Poskrebyshev stumbled and nearly deviated from the general line he had so bitterly adhered to all his life —so selflessly, shall we say?

"One day he received a piece of paper, left the office, bowing as he went, and proceeded at a firm pace to Beria, or perhaps to Yezhov, I don't remember exactly. On the very threshold of the sinister door, he gazed blankly at the paper, then rocked back on his heels. He, Poskrebyshev, so privileged and well trusted, had balked at Beria's door and spun around.

"The list was not a long one, but on it was the name 'Poskrebysheva.'

"His wife!

"No, not his guiding light—Stalin! His wife was part of his cheerless soul, they couldn't take her away! Who knows, if it had not been for her, her boundless love, her abandon in his arms, soothing his pain, her maternal forgiveness, he might have hanged himself one dark night. . . .

"Poskrebyshev reeled in fear from the dead-silent door and returned to Stalin.

"In the doorway, he plumped down on his belly—down on the carpeted floor. He crawled, crawled, sobbing, to his leader. He crawled the many yards and, grasping Stalin's boot in his trembling hands, pressed it to his face. From the burning wetness, the brilliantly polished boot began to lose its shine.

" 'Have mercy!' Stalin heard between sobs, but was silent. Poskrebyshev kissed the boot as, in his youth, he had kissed his wife in frenzied passion. . . . At length, he wrenched his stomach from the carpet, and, without daring to raise his eyes to the master, he backed, head bowed, to the door.

"But Stalin remained silent.

"A folksaying nudged Poskrebyshev's desperate, frozen brain, offering the faint hope that silence was the same as consent. He erased his wife's name from the list. The others he left to Beria—to take care of.

"And, once again, he was ministering to Stalin, carrying out the complex affairs of state.

"Stalin remained silent.

"But, on the third day, having finished his report, Poskrebyshev was preparing to leave the office when Stalin stopped him and murmured with a tender, mysterious smile: 'But you know I told you it was to be taken care of.'

"And so Poskrebyshev had, with his own hand, to write the name of his wife on a piece of paper and send it off. And soon, on lawful business, they appeared—the faceless officers—and took her away.

"And life went on its way; it didn't stop. There was great work to be done for the great leader. Poskrebyshev liked his work, and not a word was said between them about the irreparable. The private secretary did not change in the slightest, as a good dog does not change just because his master beats him for something. They lived, one might say, in perfect harmony. The master knew best.

"The first to break the silence was Stalin.

" 'We've been checking on you a little, Comrade Poskrebyshev. Go home, your wife is waiting for you.'

"His heart jumping for joy, beside himself, Poskrebyshev dashed home.

"Even from the outer vestibule, he could hear the sounds of music, his favorite song being played on the piano. Did they cure her? wondered Poskrebyshev. (His wife had not played at all in the last year: her fingers had begun to cramp.) It means they've found a cure! he thought, and a warm wave of happiness swept over him. Oh, Stalin!

"In his room, his wife was sitting with her back to the door. In a new dress, a new hairdo. And her hair was black. Had those clever hairdressers taken out the gray?

"She turned and got up. Poskrebyshev froze. It wasn't his wife at all! She was young, with black, frightened eyes, a slender figure—a girl of un-Russian beauty, an alpine flower.

" 'How did you get here?' asked Poskrebyshev, dumbfounded. 'Where's my wife?'

" 'But I am your wife!' cried the girl, and threw her arms around him, trembling like a blade of grass and dissolving into tears.

"No," the storyteller concluded, "no matter what they say about Stalin, he was a deep man, a thoughtful man. He took us peasants in hand, who can deny it?"

—From *Phoenix 1961*
(*translated by Gabriella Azrael*)

Note

1. Aleksandr Nikolayevich Poskrebyshev (1891–?) was chief of the "Special Section" of the Party Secretariat and Stalin's personal secretary from 1931 until the Premier's death. He was reportedly responsible for supplying lists of victims to be executed. Poskrebyshev has not been heard of since Stalin's death. Solzhenitsyn paints a chilling portrait of him in *The First Circle.*—ED.

Vladimir Bukovsky:

Stars

When I was small, my grandmother and I always went for walks around the Kremlin. We walked along the river, across Red Square, and in the Aleksandrov Garden. Red Square was always full of cars. They were green and dusty. Grandma always said that the color was meant to disguise them.

Whenever I walked in Red Square, I used to stamp my feet. It was fun to stamp your feet in the Square. I loved to walk around the Kremlin. Grandma would tell me all kinds of stories about it—about the theater, about Ivan the Terrible, about the King of Bells, and about the King Cannon. It's the biggest cannon in the world. And the oldest. Grandma told me really interesting things about the Tsars, about the boyars, and about the Kremlin bells. They always rang in the morning. And everyone went into the Kremlin. Many, many people. There were always huge crowds at the Kremlin. Everyone was dressed up. And everyone was happy. I always begged Grandma to tell me her stories. She had a marvelous way of telling them. And whenever we passed the Spassky Tower, she would recite:

> Who can lift the King of Bells,
> Who can move the King Cannon?
> Haughty the fellow who does not doff his cap
> By the holy Kremlin gates!

I always tried to picture this haughty fellow. He would stand by the Spassky gates, hands on his hips, and look up. He would throw his head back so far that his cap almost fell off his head. Very dauntless he looked, too.

Grandma and I took long walks. From morning to evening. In the evening we always sat in the Aleksandrov Garden. And when darkness fell and the stars on the towers began to glow, I would exclaim: "Grandma, look, the stars have lit up!" And she would answer:

"They didn't light up just now. They are always on. But, during the day, you can't see them because they are rubies. Enormous ruby stars. They were brought all the way from the Blue Mountains and made into stars that would shine forever. Rubies glow in the dark, you know."

And, thus, I knew that, as soon as the sun set, the big ruby stars would start to shine. I liked the fact that these were real rubies and that they glowed so beautifully. When we came home and I was tucked into bed, I would close my eyes and see the ruby stars. Brightly, very brightly they shone, and I felt warm and serene.

I saw strong, kindly men coming from the Blue Mountains. They walked for a long time. It was terribly hard for them to carry the rubies. But they walked and walked, fighting off their weariness and helping one another. They swam across rivers and trudged over mountains. They walked and walked in spite of their tiredness, because they knew they had to bring the rubies and make the stars that would shine for people in the evening, after sundown. Finally, they arrived, deposited the rubies, and fashioned the stars. I was certain of this. And no one ever told me that this wasn't so. Many years passed. I no longer took walks around the Kremlin. I was going to school. I had no time for walks. But I knew that as soon as the sun set, the stars would start shining. I was absolutely certain of this. Many years went by, probably four years, perhaps even more. Then, one day my entire class went on an outing to the Kremlin. I went, too. No one took off his cap. Everyone stood there and looked, listening to the guide. I took a few steps away from them. I already knew about the Kremlin, about the theater, about Ivan the Terrible, and about the Tsars. I wasn't interested. I stood by the King Cannon. It was big, of course, but I couldn't believe that it was the biggest in the world. Well, maybe it *was* the biggest. I didn't know for sure. I stood there and thought about it.

> Who can lift the King of Bells,
> Who can move the King Cannon?
> Haughty the fellow who does not doff his cap
> By the holy Kremlin gates!

I kept standing there. Then someone behind me yelled: "Hey! Watch out!"

I looked around. A truck was standing behind me. It was dusty and green—the color used for camouflage. Inside the truck, there were soldiers, lifting an enormous ruby star. From close up, the star looked very big and not very pretty. I walked up to the truck and looked inside. The star was made of glass. It was made of red glass, and inside there were ordinary light bulbs.

"Hey, careful! Don't break it!" yelled the soldiers as they pulled the star off the truck.

"What!" I said. "It's not made of ruby? It's supposed to be ruby! Rubies shine in the dark, after sundown."

The soldiers started to laugh. One of the passersby said:

"No, it's not ruby, it's plain glass. And furthermore, rubies don't shine in the dark."

"You're lying," I said, "—you bastard!"

"I'm not lying," he said. "And you don't have to curse. There's nothing you can do about it—it's the truth."

I knew that he wasn't lying, but I wanted to swear at him. I went home. I didn't want to look at the King Cannon any more, nor at the King of Bells either.

Many more years went by. Perhaps six—I don't know. I hadn't visited the Kremlin for a long time. I didn't want to. Then, one day I was suddenly seized with a desire to see the Alexandrov Garden again. I wanted to sit on the little bench—so I went. I must have sat there for a very long time, because it began to get dark. I just kept sitting there, looking at the pathway. Grandma and I had always walked along that very path, and she had told me about the theater, about Ivan the Terrible, about the Tsars, and about the ringing of the bells.

> Who can lift the King of Bells,
> Who can move the King Cannon?
> Haughty the fellow who does not doff his cap
> By the holy Kremlin gates!

I smiled. That, after all, had been a long time ago. How strange.

"Look, Grandma! The stars have lit up!" cried a little boy.

I looked. It was just a little boy and his grandmother taking a walk. Around the Kremlin probably.

"They didn't light up," I said. "They're ruby stars. Rubies glow in the dark, you know."

"Uh-uh," said the boy. "They're not rubies. I know. They're just glass with light bulbs inside. They turn them on when it gets dark. I know."

—From *Phoenix 1961*
(*translated by Rosalind Avnet*)

IV. Poetry

Yevgeni Kushev:

Decembrists

Ryleev

The verses will be used to roll cigarettes . . .
And the poems will be blown about the streets . . .
It's not the first time that you have been wrong—
So why rebel, little boy?
Crush, crush your feelings!
Pour, pour more in your glass!
But all things in the world are already alien.
You rebel against all, little boy.
They will break you, and hang your body
Like a drawing exposed for public view.
Gallows-bird, do you see that monstrous exhibit?
There you and I will be neighbors.
Constellations of planets will laugh.
As our legs start to dangle,
Only God can give us salvation,
Mankind offers only damnation.
You and I will be dragged along,
And our friends will renounce us.
"These boys"—the raven will say—
Have gagged on the Revolution.
And the gendarmes will say nothing.
They will stamp us out like the plague . . .
But it's too early to repent, I say.
Perhaps we should give it another try.

Pestel

If I be judged
And my soul laid bare—

The drumbeat of fate
Will give me no peace.
There will be a murmur, barely heard,
There will be red leaves,
Green uniforms,
And troops,
And ugly mugs—
Faces of the high brass,
Oblivion, defeat,
Betrayal, victory, a dream,
Holy Transfiguration,
And shining purity.
Only spirit will not suffice,
Or paper, pen, and ink,
To list all the souls
Now dwelling in graves,
Accompanying
The flight of time and falsehood . . .
Betrayals,
      gods,
            victories . . .
But one can't write this down!

Bestuzhev

So you too have decided to visit!
Come in. Put your coat on my chair.
Here is my room, please come in!
You are irreproachable, totally polite.
You are relentless, totally intent
Whenever you study me.
My papers and table—here is my homeland.
You can run your fingers over the keyboard of my life.
But forgive me—I cannot recant,
And I cannot repent.
Although it's the first time my testimony
Is written in red ink—
It will stick on my grave,
Once the order comes from above.

Muravev

In our heads, churchbells ring.
But there is no square below us—
Only a cluster of old aspirations,
Wary, pleasing to the touch.
We'll be led into an office,

And buried alive with questions.
Guards are marching below the window,
And thaw will be long in coming.
The memory of expert fortunetelling
Will force me to loosen my tie.
For there's freedom for a free man
And a raven's knife
For his ribs.
A clear text is brought before me.
I ponder every word.
But already I'm full of mirth,
And my mind is filled with rebellion. . . .

Kakhovsky

December . . . And, in that December,
Our passions rolled up in a ball,
Our vision became tangled, like rigging ropes
Of caravels sunk in the sea.
But we cannot sink to the bottom!
We all must batten down the hatches,
We all envision battles,
Prophets, gods—
And that palpitating agitation
In which one drowns
Or floats to shore.
Although our ship is laden with lead,
And its course leads to the bottom . . .
December . . . Still the same ado!
But nothing has been done!
Let the ship sink to the bottom,
We didn't ask to leave the hold . . .
We are destined for defeat! . . .

Thirteenth of December

When scope for thought is narrow,
Then spirits are aflame . . .
But the knot will be severed
In the middle of December.
Their noble hearts will taste
The bitterness of defeat.
Love, fervor, wrath, and valor
Will remain to the end!
But only ten revelations,
Divided by two,
Will blaze like their dying words

With a crimson hue.
And, on the windswept parade ground,
That nighttime conversation will be recalled,
And linger through all the moods of summer
Soon to rush upon us . . .

Fourteenth of December

The biting wind would like to thrust
Shrapnel into the face.
The dictator Trubetskoy
Does not appear on the square.
Stillness. Silence.
The instigators,
Like janissaries,
Are armed with yataghans.
But the spark smolders from the risk.
Dusk is falling.
Anguish will be caused
By the felonious grapeshot.
The fatal fleeting moment
Drags out like a year.
The Rosinantes of the rebellious gentry
Stand ready to be ridden.
The vision of prison looms in the eyes
Like a bitter tear.
Perhaps there's another way?
Perhaps it's time to turn back?
But it's too late.
The city is full
Of gendarmes and police carts.
At midnight the carts will be filled
By those lined up in square formation,
Who will be hung on the crownwork . . .
And whose tracks cannot be covered up . . .
Bestuzhev and Ryleev . . .
One hangman for them all. . . .
But conspiracies are not commandments—
They can't be circumvented!
The merchants have no regrets,
One Koran exists for them:
Order,
      satiety,
            celebrations
To be upheld by Cossack formations.
Does idleness ask:
"Pray tell, my friend, for what?"

But, in a land of soldiers,
Amidst the refuse and the drills,
The heroes of the Senate Square
Are desperately needed still. . . .

Thirteenth of July

Early morning. The capital is sleeping.
But the guards have changed.
Evil faces freeze
In the lacerated wind.
"O God, may they not realize
That criminals are being executed!
The devil take this masquerading!
To hell . . . hell with this execution!"
Thus thinks Colonel Sukin,
As he counts to himself
The manacled hands.
"One . . .
    two . . .
        three . . .
            five!
I can't understand it!—Nobility all.
They have wives and careers,
But they stood up for the rabble,
The mob, the poor, and the scum.
What else, sinners, did they want?
And why? I'll never understand it!"
Men and rifles grow cold
In the lacerated wind.
A white handkerchief is clutched
By the supervisor Sukin—
"A poet—yet he took part,
The hood on his head seems like a halo!"
Six o'clock.
    Mist.
        Morning.
Townsfolk sleep sweetly.
The man in charge, Mister Sukin,
Leads the execution like a parade.

Convicts

Russia's honor, like a teardrop,
Dries up in the wind . . .
There blind men are walking,
They're not walking, but are led

By three gendarmes,
          six gendarmes,
Or by a whole squad.
Take them, Siberia—we don't care!
We give them all to you!
Wear them out and exhaust them—
Then for certain they shall die.
Pines are monsters,
The *taiga*—an inquisition.
Snow sparkles under stars
Like emeralds in the dust. . . .
Decembrists, Decembrists, you knew
The path that you were taking,
Without yielding or repenting!
Seditious verse,
Like chains, for insurrection,
We shall melt into bayonets!

The Gendarme's Monologue

Cornets and lieutenants
Well taught, well taught.
Manacles, manacles
Attesting to my words.

Only five were hung
In the song of the wind.
We are not obliged
To spare the others.

Let the funny little boys
Gaze at the Senate.
We are now attentive.
We are—a wall.

We have learned gendarme methods
And acquired experience.
Manacled, manacled
Are liberty and honor.

Let all the little poets
Sing on their Parnassus.
Now they are hanged,
They are already hanged.

I say in all sincerity
That might makes right.

The warrants for arrest are issued,
Already they are signed.

Everything is prepared ahead:
The hangman, cell, and prison.
All assignments are discharged
According to the schedule.

We are the sentinels of the state.
We are our country's silence.
We fear not the Pechorins—
And the Muravevs are no more.

The throne is surrounded
By a multitude of servants.
Who dares to disturb
The comfort of His Majesty?

In the meantime, we permeate
Everything here and there.
We are the investigators—
Ours is a necessary task.

We are loyal and assiduous
And sensitive, like Orpheus.
When there are no more critics—
The hangman will disappear.

But if this should not happen—
Manacles, manacles. . . .

From the Author

I am haunted by disquieting dreams . . .
Especially in December.
Then I walk to the Senate Square
And stand in square formation.

At that instant, I'm surrounded
In silence, without words,
By Ryleev, Pestel, Bestuzhev,
Kakhovsky, and Muravev.

In a childlike manner,
Later they will ask:
"Is it true that the noose
Is your sole inheritance?

Is it true that only Nekrasov
and our Bohemian bard
Have cleansed us of black colors
And brought us all to light?

That after a hundred years or so,
Years of flogging by the knout,
December's fire smolders
In every Russian lad?

Is it true, we've handed down
Hatred for the hangman?"
What can I answer? . . .
I weep—and stay silent.

—From *Russkoe slovo*, July, 1966
(*translated by Ludmilla Zemels*)

Yuri Galanskov:

Workers of the World, Unite!

Let Me Not Kill

Moscow!
New York!
Cairo!
All repudiate war
But, like a squirrel, the tortured world
Keeps turning on a cannon-wheel.
Birds of petitions.
And what of it?
Men spit in the faces of these questionnaires.
Men wish to wrap the bodies
Of rockets in human skin.
And as for people—
All-powerful people!
Staggering on a pair of bones,
They carry maternal breasts
To nourish children of bronze. . . .
Hold back, you cattle!
They'll drive you
Into a wooden pen,
Tether you with a rope.

The executioner, skilled in his craft,
Will fell you with a sure blow between the horns.
Then, gripping the steel in his hand,
Full of assurance and power,
With the blade of his knife, he'll tie
A red ribbon round your neck.
Let me not kill!
Bellow, deafen them,
Binding muscles in knots,
Tear off the leather reins,
Break the shafts,
A net of blood over your eyes.
The flame of rage kindling in your nostrils,
Dripping foam from your mouth,
Raise your head like a flag,
Your entrails winding round your neck!

Behind the Revolution—Another Revolution . . .

They seemed the same tired faces,
The same feelings,
And the same thoughts.
But I affirm that somewhere there lurks
A vast
Universal
Rebellion.
Over the bombs, a question arose,
And the world has grown expectantly still.
The poets muttered
Ancient verses under their noses,
Shouted hurrah,
Had hysterical fits,
Made a wreath of scarlet lips . . .
And suddenly—
In the enfeebled hands of America,
The sugar of Cuba was stained with blood.
In the chest of the pyramids, a bugle blew:
The Sphinx has awakened and emerged from the dusk.
And like a torch in the hands of a slave,
The oil of Iraq flared up.
Europe seemed to be crucified,
But little shoots began to grow.
The dictators and the diplomats
Shuddered upon the atomic barrel.
Famine,
Sickness,
Weariness

Hung like guilt over the world.
I felt that Mine
Was the ultimate word.

Down with the Pessimists!

Perhaps
I shall come, an unwanted doctor,
Into the cities of pestilence
And shall realize that the world
Is doomed forever to suffer and shoot.
But, in my opinion, that is not so, not so!
Just look, what a daybreak,
Just look, what a dawn
Awaits me—the Rebel.
I shall come,
Bringing the generals a dish
Of coarse Martian meat.
And I shall remake the bombs
Into juicy pineapples.
I'll pass through the tangle of the labyrinths
And tear down and cast off the prison bars.
And, from the hands of the laboratory assistants, the rats will rush
At the throats of the creators of the plague.
This is not evil, but a museum offering—
The superbombs,
The pestilential sores,
And tuberculosis—
These I shall bring with me and carelessly throw them
To the pessimists, drenched with tears.

—From *Phoenix 1961*
(*translated by George Reavey*)

Yu. Stefanov:

Song About Science

1.

O, from century to century,
It's been the same since time began:
Man,
His skin like snow and skin like coal,

Looks in the sky,
Looks in the sea,
Looks out for bread,
And pleads with God.
          Rain falls
          God rains
          The battle roars
          The leader reigns.

2.

Oh, just look round—the world is so plain
Without microscopes or binoculars:
For either the meadows float,
   drenched in rain,
Or death prophesies the dances of stars.

Either the puddles resound with sun drops,
Or else the whole sun hides itself in the dusk.
Because of the all-mighty croaking of frogs,
You cannot escape from the thunderstorm's bursts.

3.

What's there—like a beacon from some unknown land
Up in the sky—Vega or Sirius?
Oh, close the eyelids of your unbeliefs,
And let your hearts become your compasses!
Like bloodhounds on a reindeer's track,
Seek out the scents of secrets in the ground,
So that the vessels of your body will be wrecked
Against the rocks of all your doubts, and drown.

—From *Phoenix 1961*
(translated by Elisavietta Ritchie)

Vladimir Batshev:

This Old Dream Once More

For L. V.

This old dream once more
I dream,

I dream . . .
From lips to toes
With interflow,
I see you run,
    I hear you call to me,
"I'll do it now!"
What are you doing in my dream—
Sharing my hardships?
Do you hear? Guests ring at the door.
Treat
    them
        kindly.
This old dream once more
Persists,
As if the wheel had caught a stick.
The spokes have broken, flown.
I stole your old dream,
Let me dream it,
    let me dream.
Old dream, why have you come?
Please go away!
Well, old dream, why hang on?
Why do you stay?
A year will pass, and two, and five.
Faces will fade.
Only this old dream again
I dream,
    I dream . . .

May–June, 1966: Exile, Siberia

—From *Phoenix 1966*
(*translated by Elisavietta Ritchie*)

Bella Akhmadulina:

Fifteen Boys

Fifteen boys and maybe more,
or fewer than fifteen maybe,
said to me
in frightened voices:
"Let's go to a movie or the Museum of Fine Arts."
"I haven't time."

Fifteen boys presented me with snowdrops.
Fifteen boys, in broken voices,
said to me:
"I'll never stop loving you."
I answered them more or less like this:
"We'll see."

Fifteen boys are now living a quiet life.
They have done their heavy chores
of snowdrops, despair, and writing letters.
Girls love them—
some more beautiful than me,
others less beautiful.
Fifteen boys, with a show of freedom and, at times, spite,
salute me when we meet,
their liberation, normal sleep, and regular meals.

In vain you come to me, last boy.
I shall place your snowdrops in a glass of water,
and silver bubbles will cover
their stocky stems. . . .
But, you see, you too will cease to love me,
and, mastering yourself, you'll talk in a superior way,
as though you'd mastered me,
and I'll walk off down the street, down the street. . . .

Sarah Bernhardt

Nobody believed her tears,
And tears, indeed, she had not shed,
Upon an all-white ostrich fan,
In response, she laid her cheek.

All her admirers in the orchestra,
Squeezing their handkerchiefs, gazed on
As both her hands were outlined white
Against the raspberry portiere.

They knew full well what fire the stones
Of her costume rings contained
And the eternal chill of the camellias
That wintered in her hands.

The handkerchief slipped from her hands
With such mortal resignation,

Her heart beat on with even calm
Without noticing these torments.

Him they forgave for what had happened,
And distantly the curtain fell,
And to her dressing room they brought
Bouquets of pallid yellow roses.

She held these roses in her arms,
But she could barely see them
While tears were running down her cheeks,
The dry tears of her mastered craft.

—From *Sintaksis*, No. 2, February, 1960
(*translated by George Reavey; "Fifteen
Boys" is reprinted from* The New Russian
Poets: 1953 to 1968 [New York: October
House, 1968])

Bulat Okhudzhava:

A Paper Soldier

In our world, there lived a soldier.
He was extremely handsome, very brave,
but he happened to be a children's toy—
for he was merely a paper soldier.

He wished to refashion all the world,
to make each individual happy,
but he dangled over a child's cot,
for he was merely a paper soldier.

He would have dashed through smoke and fire
and given his life for you twice over,
but you only derided him and laughed—
for he was merely a paper soldier.

You were unwilling to trust
him with your most important secrets.
And why did you not trust him? Oh, just
because he was a paper soldier.

And kicking against his wretched lot,
he thirsted for a life less tranquil
and kept demanding: "Fire! Yes, Fire!"
forgetting he was a paper soldier.

Into fire? All right. Why not plunge in?
And bravely forward he marched off.
And there he perished, nothing won—
for he was merely a paper soldier.

Vanka Morozov

Why do you blame Vanka Morozov?
It really wasn't his fault at all.
She's the one who led him on.
And it wasn't his fault at all.

He visited the circus in the square,
And there he fell for a circus girl.
A simple girl would have been better,
But he had to fall for a circus girl.

She was a tightrope walker,
And she would wave her lily-white hand,
And passion grabbed Morozov
And held him in its calloused hand.

He threw money around in the "Pekin"
(It was all the same to him).
But Marusia is pining for him,
And it's not all the same to her.

To please his circus girl,
He dined on jellyfish.
And he tried to seduce her
To please her, obviously.

He didn't think she'd deceive him:
One doesn't expect trouble from love . . .
Oh Vania, Vania! What's with you, Vania!
It's you who's walking the tightrope.

(*translated by George Reavey;* "A Paper
Soldier" *reprinted from* The New Russian
Poets: 1953 to 1968 [*New York: October
House,* 1968])

Aleksandr Timofeevsky:

The Word

The word fell down like a coin worn through.
And I want to pick it up anew!
One life is not enough to show
The world its bright metallic glow!
As bare as truth, the word was born,
Quivered like doves in the sky at dawn.
Some followed it even to hunger and death.
It pounded in heartbeats, resounded in breath,
And suddenly fell in a murderer's hands.
By all the signs, the word was found
Where the thief was using his knuckles of brass.
It covered up his thieving snatch,
And covered itself with filth and blood.
The thief then launched a fraud on the world,
Sewed similar words to line his fraud.
The idea was snatched by hypocrites
To issue millions of copies of it.
Inside rich dachas they frayed the word,
And in cheap broadcasts where it was heard.
The word was repeated in unctuous speeches
With daily use and holiday features.
The word became swollen and fat,
People got fed up . . . and it fell flat.
The word fell down like a coin worn through.
Who but ourselves can lift it anew?

—From *Sintaksis*, No. 2 (February, 1960)
(*translated by Elisavietta Ritchie*)

Yosif Brodsky:

Verses About the Acceptance
of the World

All this has been, has been,
All this has burned us.
All this has poured down, battered us,

Jerked us, shaken us,
And robbed us of our strength,
And dragged us into the grave,
And pulled us on top of pedestals,
And then knocked us down,
And then forgot about us,
And then challenged us
To seek various truths,
So that we might lose our way again
In the sparse bushes of ambition,
In the wild grove of prostrations,
Associations, conceptions,
And—very simply—emotions.

But we learned to fight,
But we learned to warm ourselves
By the hidden sun
And to reach the shore
Without pilots and sailing directions;
But—most important of all—
We learned not to repeat ourselves.

We like constancy,
We like the folds of fat
Round our mother's neck,
And also our apartment,
Which is rather small
For an inhabitant of a temple.
We like to spread ourselves.
We like to sprout like wheat.
We like the rustling of satin
And the rumbling of a solar prominence;
And, in general, our planet
Resembles a recruit
Who sweats as he marches.

Past Hippodromes

Past hippodromes, pagan temples,
Past fashionable cemeteries,
Past churches and bars,
Past large hazards,
Past the world and its grief,
Past Mecca and Rome—
Scorched by the blue sun,
The pilgrims
Trudge over the earth.

Misshapen they are, humpbacked,
Hungry, and half-clothed.
Their eyes are brimming with sunset.
Their hearts are brimming with dawn.
Behind them deserts sing,
Heat lightnings flare,
Above them rise the stars,
And birds call hoarsely to them
That the world will remain the same.
Yes. Will remain the same,
Dazzling with snow
And doubtfully tender.
The world will remain a liar.
The world will remain eternal,

Attainable, perhaps,
Endless all the same.
And that means there's no sense
In believing in oneself and God.

And that means that only illusions
And the road remain.
There will still be sunsets on earth.
On earth there will be dawns . . .

Improve the earth with soldiers.
Approve the earth with poets.

A Jewish Cemetery

A Jewish cemetery on the outskirts of Leningrad,
A sagging fence of rotting plywood.
Beyond the sagging fence, next to each other, lie
Lawyers, tradesmen, musicians, revolutionaries.
They chanted for themselves.
They saved up money for themselves.
They died for others.
But, first, they paid taxes,
        respected the police,
And, in this inescapably material world,
Discussed the Talmud,
        remained idealists.

Perhaps they saw more.
Perhaps they were blind in their belief.
But they taught their children to be patient
        and become persistent.

They sowed no grain.
  They never sowed grain.
They simply lay down in the cold earth like seeds
And fell asleep forever.
And then they were covered with earth,
Candles were lit,
And, on the Day of Atonement,
The hungry old men in loud voices,
Choking with cold,
Wailed about eternal rest.
And they achieved it.
  In the form of disintegrated matter.

Remembering nothing.
Forgetting nothing.
Behind the sagging fence of damp plywood.
Four miles from the last trolley stop.

     —From *Sintaksis*, No. 3, April, 1966
      (*translated by George Reavey*)

Vadim Delone:

Evening

Dedicated to Aleksei Dobrovolsky
as a token of great friendship.

Evening—a frivolous cornet
All spruced up in a blue uniform,
Lies about his brilliant conquests,
Crushing autumn in a passionate embrace.

He begs for tender love
And toasts with sunset-flavored punch,
Spitting wind on debts,
He gives change in stars as payment.

Autumn will rebuff the shadow-hand,
Evening awaits refusal as an answer.
And the village cobblestone
Awaits the cornet in a coach. . . .

Autumn squints with a red eye,
Loosening its yellow hair,
Autumn asks for ten chapters
On awakening at dawn.

—From *Sintaksis,* No. 3, April, 1966
(*translated by Ludmilla Zemels*)

Dissent and Opposition: A New Phase?

This book by no means exhausts the supply of protest documents available at this writing; it is obviously impossible for a single volume to include all the expressions of the increasingly complex and dynamic phenomenon of Soviet dissent. Further, many more protest documents have come out of the Soviet Union since the manuscript of this book was sent to the printer, and no doubt still more will have become available by the time this volume is in the hands of readers. In a collection of current materials, some arbitrary cut-off date must be established. But there is one document that could not be excluded, even at the cost of delaying publication—the petition of fifty-two Soviet citizens, addressed and forwarded to the Commission on Human Rights of the United Nations in late May, 1969.

In some respects, the petition covers the same somber ground as many previous protest documents. Most of the factual data had already been disclosed elsewhere—although the emphasis on and implicit equation of "Crimean Tatars struggling for a return to their Crimean homeland" and "Soviet Jews demanding the right to depart for Israel" are surely novel and significant. The incidence of familiar names among its signatories is striking—yet so is the number of heretofore unknown protesters, among them seven workers and four who describe themselves as "employees."

What distinguishes this from previous protest documents, however, is, first of all, its purpose. No longer merely an impassioned appeal to Soviet authorities, or to Communists outside the Soviet Union, or to "world public opinion," it is, in a very real sense, a legal brief of Soviet citizens requesting an international body to exercise its legal prerogatives in their behalf. Thus, a regime that recently asserted its right to challenge the sovereignty of other countries now finds its own sovereignty challenged by its own citizens—and before an international tribunal at that.

Second, and perhaps more important, the petition offers both direct and indirect evidence that the struggle for civil liberties in the Soviet Union is taking on a more pronounced programmatic and organizational form. Earlier confirmation of this trend was furnished by the Chronicle of Current Events, *six issues of which have appeared thus far.[1] (For excerpts, see the sections "In Defense of Czechoslovakia" and "Reprisals.") The regular appearance of this underground journal, and the breadth of its coverage, are clear indications of coordinated and sustained activity by a number of people. Significantly, the letter to the United Nations is signed not by individuals but by a body that calls itself "The Initiative Group for Defense of Civil Rights in the U.S.S.R." Equally revealing is the reference to Major-General Grigorenko as "one of the most notable participants in the move-ment for civil rights in the U.S.S.R." (emphasis added)—a phrase, inci-dentally, that has also appeared with increased frequency in recent issues of the* Chronicle. *The journal is unattributed and distributed clandestinely; the letter is signed, and its origin is open and explicit. Together, they well may mark the beginning of a new phase in the development of Soviet dissent —the rise of an organized movement of political opposition.*

NOTE

1. Two more issues have appeared as of this writing, September, 1969.—ED.

To the Commission on Human Rights of the United Nations

We, the undersigned, deeply disturbed by the unending stream of politi-cal persecutions in the Soviet Union, which we see as a return to the Stalin era when our entire country was in the grip of terror, appeal to the United Nations Commission on Human Rights to come to the defense of human rights that are being trampled upon in our country.

We appeal to the United Nations because our protests and complaints, addressed for a number of years to the highest state and judicial authorities in the Soviet Union, have elicited no response of any kind. The hope that our voices might be heard, that the authorities would put an end to the lawless acts to which we have repeatedly called their attention—this hope has proved to be vain.

Therefore, we appeal to the United Nations, believing that the defense of human rights is the sacred duty of this organization.

In this document, we shall speak of the violation of one of the most fun-damental rights of man—the right to have independent convictions and to propagate them by all legal means.

At political trials in the Soviet Union, one often hears the phrase: "You are not being tried for your convictions."

This is profoundly untrue. We are being tried expressly for our convic-tions.

The words "You are not being tried for your convictions" mean simply this: "You are entitled to your convictions, but, if they contradict the offi-cial political doctrine, do not dare to disseminate them." And, indeed, the arrests and trials described below occur precisely when people of opposing viewpoints begin to voice them in the open.

But propagation of convictions is a natural outgrowth of the convictions themselves. This is why Article 19 of the Universal Declaration of Human

Rights states: "Each person has the right to freedom of convictions and freedom to express them; this right includes the freedom to uphold one's convictions without hindrance and to freely express, receive, and disseminate information and ideas by all means, regardless of state boundaries."

The formal reason, then, for persecution [in our country] is propagation of convictions; in reality, people are tried for the convictions themselves.

The defendants are accused of undermining the Soviet state and social system (Article 70, R.S.F.S.R. Criminal Code) or defaming the Soviet system (Article 190-1, R.S.F.S.R. Criminal Code). None of the people condemned at political trials we know about either intended to slander the Soviet system or, what is more, acted with the purpose of undermining it. Thus, at all these political trials, people were censured under fictitious accusations.

We offer several examples, which have become the objects of wide publicity both in the Soviet Union and abroad:

—The trial of Siniavsky and Daniel, who were condemned for publishing abroad artistic works critical of Soviet reality.

—The trial of Ginzburg and Galanskov, condemned for publishing the literary journal *Phoenix 67* and the *White Book* about the trial of Siniavsky and Daniel.

—The trial of Khaustov and Bukovsky, who organized a protest demonstration against the arrest of Ginzburg and Galanskov.

—The trial of Litvinov, Larisa Daniel, and others for demonstrating against the dispatch of Soviet troops into Czechoslovakia. An important point at these last two trials was that the charges against the participants were based on the content of their slogans.

—The trial of Marchenko, formally accused of passport violation—a charge, incidentally, that was not proved at the trial—but who was in fact tried for his book *My Testament*, which describes conditions of prisoners in the post-Stalin years.

—The trial of I. Belgorodskaia for the attempt to distribute letters defending Marchenko.

—The trial of [Yu.] Gendler, [Lev] Kravchevsky, and others in Leningrad, who were condemned for distributing foreign-published books.

—The trials of persons defending national equality and the preservation of national culture.

—In the Ukraine, the trial in Kiev in 1966, at which more than ten persons were condemned; the trial of Chornovil in Lvov, sentenced for his book about political trials; and many others.

—The trials of Crimean Tatars struggling for a return to their Crimean homeland. Over 100 of them have been sentenced in the more than twenty trials that have been held in recent years; as these lines are written, ten representatives of the Crimean Tartars are being tried in the latest and largest of all political trials, in Tashkent.

—The trials in the Baltic republics, in particular the trial of Kalhinsh and others.

—Trials of Soviet Jews demanding the right to depart for Israel; at the latest trial in Kiev, engineer B. Kochubievsky was condemned to three years.

—Trials of believers demanding the rights to religious freedom.

All these political trials, given their essentially illegal nature, were conducted with gross violations of procedural norms, above all openness, as well as the impartial nature of the judicial inquiry.

We also wish to call your attention to an especially inhuman form of persecution: the confinement of normal persons in psychiatric hospitals because of their political convictions.

Recently, there have been a number of new arrests. In late April, 1969, the artist V. Kuznetsov, of Pushkino, Moscow *oblast*, was arrested and charged with distributing *samizdat*, that is, literature not published by Soviet publishing houses.

At the same time I. Yakhimovich, former *kolkhoz* chairman in Latvia, was arrested in Riga and charged with writing letters protesting political persecutions in the Soviet Union.

In early May, former Major-General P. G. Grigorenko, one of the most notable participants in the movement for civil rights in the U.S.S.R., was arrested in Tashkent, where he was to appear, at the request of nearly 2000 Crimean Tatars, as public defender at the trial of the ten Crimean Tatars.

Finally, Ilya Gabai, teacher of Russian literature, was arrested on May 19 in Moscow, several days after a search during which documents containing protests of Soviet citizens against political repressions in the Soviet Union were seized. (In the spring of 1967, I. Gabai was confined for four months during an investigation into his participation in the protest demonstration organized by Khaustov and Bukovsky.)

These latest arrests lead us to believe that Soviet punitive organs have resolved once and for all to suppress the activity of persons protesting against arbitrariness in our country.

We believe that freedom to have convictions and to propagate them has been placed in the most serious jeopardy.

We hope that the information contained in our letter will provide the Commission on Human Rights with a basis for undertaking a review of the violation of fundamental civil rights in the Soviet Union.

THE INITIATIVE GROUP FOR DEFENSE OF CIVIL RIGHTS IN THE U.S.S.R.:

G. ALTUNIAN, engineer, Kharkov
V. BORISOV, worker, Leningrad
T. VELIKANOVA, mathematician
N. GORBANEVSKAIA, poetess
M. DKHEMILEV, worker, Tashkent
S. KOVALEV, biologist:
V. KRASIN, economist
A. LAVUT, biologist
A. LEVITIN-KRASNOV, church writer
YU. MALTSEV, translator
L. PLIUSHCH, mathematician, Kiev
G. PODIAPOLSKY, scientific associate
T. KHODOROVICH, linguist
P. YAKIR, historian
A. YAKOBSON, translator

Supporting the appeal are:
Z. ASANOVA, doctor, Begovat, Uzbek S.S.R.
T. BAIEVA, employee
S. BERNSHTEIN, literary worker

L. Vasilev, jurist
Yu. Vishnevsakia, poetess
A. Volpin, mathematician
O. Vorobev, worker, Perm
G. Gabai, educator
E. Egaidikov, mathematician
V. Gershuni, mason
Z. M. Grigorenko, pensioner
A. Grigorenko, technician
R. Dzhemilev, worker, Krasnoiarsk krai
N. Yemelkina, employee
L. Ziugikov, worker
A. Kalinovsky, engineer, Kharkov
L. Kats, employee
Yu. Kim, teacher
Yu. Kiselov, artist
V. Kozharivov, worker
L. Kornilov, engineer
V. Lapin, literary worker
A. Levin, engineer, Kharkov
T. Levina, engineer, Kharkov
D. Lifshits, engineer, Kharkov
S. Mauge, biologist
V. Nedobora, engineer, Kharkov
L. Petrovsky, historian
S. Podolsky, engineer, Kharkov
V. Ponomarev, engineer, Kharkov
V. Rokitiansky, physicist
I. Rudakov
L. Terpovskiy, doctor
Yu. Shtein, movie director
V. Chernovil, journalist, Lvov
I. Yakir, employee
S. Vintovsky, student.

Biographical Notes

The notes below synopsize the available information on many of the people referred to but not identified in the foregoing articles and documents, including defendants at recent trials, individuals who have publicly protested, in person or in writing, in behalf of defendants, and representatives of the regime.

BELLA AKHMADULINA (1936–   ); Poetess and former wife of Yevgeni Yevtushenko. For years, was denied admission to the Writers' Union and thus prevented from publishing her poems, but finally gained membership as a translator. Author of a book of verse entitled *A String;* her work also appeared in the underground journal *Sintaksis.* (Document 5)

ANNA ANDREEVNA AKHMATOVA (1888–1966): Poetess whose verses dealing with such proscribed topics as love, loneliness, alienation, and religious experiences led to her denunciation by Zhdanov in 1946 as "half-nun, half-whore" and her expulsion from the Writers' Union; was reinstated in 1954. In 1959, a month after Khrushchev had upbraided writers who had ventured beyond the confines of socialist realism, A. was nevertheless accorded high praise by *Literaturnaia gazeta* for "talented and noble" work. Many younger writers were deeply influenced by A.'s writings. For Kopelev's eulogy at her funeral, see pp. 426–28.

VASSILI AKSIONOV (1932–   ): Member of the editorial board of the monthly journal *Yunost* (Youth). Works include *Colleagues* (London: Putnam, 1962) and *Oranges from Morocco* (1963). *A Ticket to the Stars* (New York: Signet, 1963), about modern youth, provoked much criticism in the Soviet press. A. is the son of Yevgenia Ginzburg (below). (Document 5)

PAVEL GRIGOREVICH ANTOKOLSKY (1896–   ): Poet and stage producer; member, U.S.S.R. Writers' Union. Spent early years working for the National Arts Theater and various other playhouses. Recipient of two Orders of the Red Banner of Labor, the Badge of Honor, and a Stalin Prize. In the mid-1930's, abandoned theatrical career to devote himself to literature. In the 1940's, was censured for "aestheticism" and "formalism"; in the 1950's, for "eulogizing" Pasternak's work. In October, 1967, defended Solzhenitsyn in a letter to P. N. Demichev, CC Secretary responsible for ideological matters, and received a severe Party reprimand. (Documents 28 and 50)

463

ZAMIRA ASANOVA: Physician; a leader of the Crimean Tatars. (Document 32)

VLADIMIR BATSHEV (1947–): Poet, believed to be the son of a senior *Glavlit* censor. Member of SMOG underground writers' group (see p. 29). Was arrested during the December, 1965, demonstration demanding an open trial for Siniavsky and Daniel, released, then rearrested in April, 1966; sentenced a few months later to five years' hard labor in Siberia for "parasitism" (see p. 447).

LARISA BOGORAZ-DANIEL: Philologist; wife of imprisoned writer Yuli Daniel. On June 17, 1967, wrote to Soviet authorities protesting conditions of her husband's imprisonment, later described in an article published in *Die Zeit* (Hamburg) and reprinted in *Atlas* (New York), December, 1967. For her participation in the Red Square demonstration against Soviet intervention in Czechoslovakia, was exiled to the Irkutsk region for four years. (Documents 7, 32, 64, 65, and 69)

YOSIF BRODSKY (1940–): Poet and translator. In 1964, was sentenced to five years' hard labor as a "parasite." Such leading Soviet creative personalities as Shostakovich, Paustovsky, and Akhmatova protested his imprisonment, and he was reportedly released before serving his full term. Although little of his work has been published officially in the U.S.S.R., his poems have circulated from hand to hand.

VLADIMIR BUKOVSKY (1941–): Writer; son of a journalist associated with the conservative journal *Oktiabr*. In 1961, contributed to *Phoenix*, an underground literary magazine, took part in unauthorized poetry readings in Maiakovsky Square, and made critical speeches at Komsomol meetings at Moscow University. Expelled from the university and the Komsomol, then committed to a mental asylum from 1963 until spring, 1965. Participated in the December 5, 1965, public demonstration calling for an open trial for Siniavsky and Daniel, and, in 1966, was again detained in a mental asylum, this time for six months. In January, 1967, demonstrated in support of Galanskov and Dobrovolsky and subsequently received the maximum sentence of three years at hard labor.

A. CHAKOVSKY: Editor-in-chief of *Literaturnaia gazeta*, the organ of the U.S.S.R. Writers' Union. (Documents 85 and 86)

VYACHESLAV CHORNOVIL: Ukrainian television journalist. In November, 1967, was sentenced to eighteen months in a labor colony for distributing a document exposing the methods of the KGB. According to the *New York Times* (February 24, 1964), he was recently released after serving his full sentence. (Document 37)

LIDIA CHUKOVSKAIA: Writer, daughter of novelist Kornei Chukovsky. Best known for her novel *The Deserted House* (New York: Dutton, 1967), an account of the Stalinist terror. The manuscript, written in 1940, was rejected for publication by the Soviet authorities and was eventually published in the West "without the author's permission." (Documents 35 and 74)

YULI MARKOVICH DANIEL (1925–   ): Poet and translator. Some of his stories—"This Is Moscow Speaking," "Hands," "The Man from Minap," and "Atonement"—were published in the West. In September, 1965, was arrested, with Andrei Siniavsky, and accused of "slandering" the Soviet state (which both defendants unqualifiedly denied). In February, 1966, was convicted with Siniavsky. Sentenced to five years at hard labor.

GRIGORI ABRAMOVICH DEBORIN: Historian at the Institute of Marxism-Leninism, specializing in World War II. During the immediate postwar period, was attacked, with a number of other historians, for "cosmopolitanism"—*i.e.*, lack of patriotism—a charge made most frequently against Jews.

VADIM DELONE: Young poet, member of SMOG. Was arrested in January, 1967, with Bukovsky and Kushev, for participating in a demonstration in support of Galanskov; was tried in September, 1967, and given a one-year suspended sentence. (See p. 455.)

ALEKSEI DOBROVOLSKY (1939–   ): Typographer and poet. In 1964, after serving a three-year sentence for disseminating "anti-Soviet propaganda," was again arrested, imprisoned for six months, then confined in a Leningrad mental hospital—an experience to which he was subjected for another two months in 1966, after helping to organize a protest meeting. Published one of his works in *Phoenix 1966*. Rearrested in January, 1967, turned state's evidence against Ginzburg, Galanskov, and Lashkova in January 1968, and received a two-year sentence.

YEVGENI ARONOVICH DOLMATOVSKY (1915–   ): Poet, known for political as well as artistic orthodoxy. In a series of poems published in *Oktiabr* in November, 1962, expressed shock at the vehemence of the de-Stalinization process, reminding the younger generation that Stalin, despite his "excesses," had ushered in a quarter century of revolution and progress. Siniavsky, in his last "legally" published review (*Novyi mir*, March, 1965), took a volume of D.'s verse as point of departure for a disquisition on poetic mediocrity.

YEFIM YAKOVLEVICH DOROSH (1908–   ): Writer, member of the editorial board of *Novyi mir*; known especially for his honest and compassionate writing on Soviet rural life. (See Ronald Hingley, "Home Truths on the Farm: The Literary Mirror," *Problems of Communism*, May–June, 1965.)

IVAN DZYUBA (1931–   ): Ukrainian literary critic and writer, for years a member of the editorial board of *Vitchyzna*, official organ of the Ukrainian Writers' Union. In 1962, was threatened with expulsion from the UWU for advancing "politically false concepts." Has not been permitted to publish since 1965, when he wrote on "The Honesty of Creative

Research." His literary works have nevertheless circulated clandestinely, and some have been published in Czechoslovakia and the West, most recently *Internationalism or Russification?* (New York: Humanities Press, 1968). During the mass arrests of young Ukrainian intellectuals in 1965–66, was interrogated by Party and security organs but was released, apparently because of his incurable tuberculosis. (See Document 38)

ILIA GRIGOREVICH EHRENBURG (1891–1967): Writer, journalist, poet. At first, opposed the Revolution but "accepted" it in 1921. From 1923 to 1937, was European correspondent for *Izvestia* and had wide acquaintance among Western intellectuals; was war correspondent and propagandist during World War II and a member of the Jewish Anti-Fascist Committee. In 1954, published a novel whose title (*The Thaw*) has become synonymous with the changes in the Soviet Union since Stalin's death. In the last years of his life, was a steadfast supporter of the liberal cause and instrumental in rehabilitating a number of Soviet writers. His memoirs, *People, Years, Life*, were serialized in *Novyi mir* and published in many Western languages. (See Victor Erlich's essays on E. in the July–August, 1963, and September–October, 1965, issues of *Problems of Communism*.)

NATAN YAKOVLEVICH EIDELMAN (1928–   ): Candidate in Historical Sciences, writer, journalist, authority on nineteenth-century Russian literature. Until 1964, was director of a small municipal museum near Moscow and member of the editorial board of *Znanie sila*. In 1966, compiled a collection of excerpts from public speeches by M. A. Sholokhov, which were not allowed to be published. (See his "Serno," pp. 405–10.)

KONSTANTIN ALEKSANDROVICH FEDIN (1892–   ): Novelist; first secretary, U.S.S.R. Writers' Union. Interned in Germany during World War I, returned to Russia in 1918. His epic novel *Cities and Years* (New York: Dell, 1962; originally published in 1924) portrayed the difficulties of intellectuals who were reluctant to accept the new order. Between 1923 and 1928, published stories anticipating the clash between the peasants and the Party, and was accused of idealizing the *kulaks*. K. gradually adapted to Soviet life and the socialist-realist genre and—despite the narrow limitations of the approved literary model—produced some of his finest works after World War II; *e.g. Early Joys* (New York: Knopf, 1960). (Document 57)

ILYA YA. GABAI (1936–   ): Schoolteacher and editor at Institute of Asian Peoples. With Bukovsky, Delone, and Kushev, participated in the January, 1967, demonstration demanding repeal of Article 70 of the R.S.F.S.R. Penal Code and protesting the arrest of Galanskov *et al.* Was arrested and sentenced to four months in prison, but sentence was annulled for lack of evidence. In May, 1968, was dismissed from a geological team on direct orders from the KGB. (Documents 6, 27, 30, and 32)

YURI TIMOFEEVICH GALANSKOV (1939–   ): Writer. After finishing secondary school, worked as an electrician and administrator at the Evening Machine Tool Technical School of Moscow. Author of several books of verse, some of them printed abroad (*e.g.*, *The Human Manifesto*). In 1961, was arersted for distributing the journal *Phoenix* and confined for several months in a psychiatric hospital. In 1965, staged a solitary sitdown demonstration in front of the U.S. Embassy in Moscow to protest American intervention in the Dominican Republic. Arrested on January 19, 1967, for distributing *Phoenix 1966*, tried a year later with Ginzburg, Dobrovolsky, and Lashkova, and sentenced to seven years' hard labor under Article 70 of the R.S.F.S.R. Criminal Code.

ALEKSANDR ILICH GINZBURG (1936–   ): Editor, actor, journalist, and technician. After completing secondary school, worked as a lathe operator and subsequently as correspondent for *Moskovskii komsomolets*. In 1959–60, edited three numbers of *Sintaksis*, and was arrested in 1960 on charges of "distributing an anti-Soviet journal" (*i.e.*, under Article 70 of the R.S.F.S.R. Criminal Code). Charges were dropped for lack of evidence, whereupon G. was prosecuted under Article 196-1, concerning forgery of documents—alledgedly on the ground of having once taken an examination on behalf of a friend—and imprisoned for about a year. Arrested in May, 1964, again on charges of distributing anti-Soviet literature, but again the charges were withdrawn. In 1966, compiled the so-called *White Book* of documents on the trial of Daniel and Siniavsky, which he sent to the Supreme Soviet of the U.S.S.R. and the KGB with a demand that the case be reviewed. Again arrested in January, 1967, charged with violating Article 70; tried January 8–12, 1968, with Galanskov *et al.*, and sentenced to five years at hard labor. (Documents 4 and 10)

LUDMILA ILINICHNA GINZBURG: Pensioned economist, mother of Aleksandr Ginzburg. Her protests in defense of her son (Documents 19 and 20) drew a warning from the KGB that she could be charged with defaming the Soviet state if she continued her "antisocial activities." The charge carries a maximum penalty of three years' imprisonment.

YEVGENIIA SEMIONOVNA GINZBURG (1907–   ): Author of *Journey into the Whirlwind* (New York: Harcourt, Brace & World, 1967), a firsthand account of Stalin's purges and her own eighteen-year imprisonment, never published in the Soviet Union. Mother of writer Vassili Aksionov.

PIOTR GRIGOREVICH GRIGORENKO (1906–   ): Construction engineer, former Major-General and lecturer at the Frunze Military Academy in Moscow. Active in various protest movements since 1961, when he sent an "open letter" to Moscow voters protesting restraints on freedom in the U.S.S.R. and was consequently dismissed from Frunze Academy. Arrested in February, 1964, and sent to Serbsky Institute (a so-called special psychiatric prison). Released in April, 1965, and, after continuous pressure, obtained a certificate of sanity, but was discharged from the army and the Party, deprived of his war-invalid certificate, and forced to take job as a loader. Early in 1966, was again arrested, with several other dissenters, for preparing a public demonstration on the anniversary of Stalin's death (March 5). In May, wrote to Kosygin protesting mistreatment and then, receiving no reply, sent an open letter to *Pravda* and *Izvestia* charging Kosygin with "full responsibility" for the crimes of both the Stalin and the Khrushchev governments. Protested trials of writers in 1967 and 1968 (Documents 6, 24, and 32), the measures against Crimean Tatars (Document 40), the persecution of Marchenko (Documents 64 and 65), and Soviet intervention in Czechoslovakia (Document 66). At funeral of Aleksei Kosterin, delivered a devastating attack on "Soviet totalitarianism" (pp. 208–13). On December 4, 1968, wrote to Procurator General Rudenko (Document 83) detailing KGB harrassment. Arrested in May, 1969, in Tashkent, where he was to testify at trial of ten Crimean Tatars. (See Peter Reddaway, "Five Years in the Life of Piotr Grigovenko," *The Listener* [London], February 20, 1969.)

VASSILI SEMIONOVICH GROSSMAN (1905–   ): Novelist and playwright. Published freely in the 1930's, but came into conflict with the postwar censors. A play, *If We Were to Believe the Pythagoreans* (1946), was banned as "ideologically unacceptable"; a war novel, *For a Just Cause* (1962), was condemned for its "idealism," its failure to exalt the Party's role in winning World War II, and for dwelling on the hardships of the Soviet people. Nevertheless, in 1956, was elected—with other writers who had previously been reprimanded—to the executive board of the Writers' Union.

LEONID FIODOROVICH ILICHEV (1906–   ): Ideologist, journalist, and propagandist. Served as editor of both *Izvestia* (1944–48) and *Pravda* (1951–52); as head of Agitprop (1958–61); and as chairman of the CC's Ideological Commission during the 1962–63 campaign against unorthodox writers and artists. Also served as press chief for the Foreign Ministry, accompanying top Party leaders to important conferences around the world from 1954 until the end of the Khrushchev era. Awarded the Order of Lenin three times, Order of the Red Banner of Labor, Order of the Patriotic War, Badge of Honor, and Lenin Prize.

FAZIL ISKANDER: Author of poems and tales of his native Abkhazian Autonomous Republic as well as satires on the Soviet bureaucracy; works include *Green Rain* (1960), *Children of the Black Sea* (1961), and *Youth of the Sea* (1964). (Documents 5 and 28)

VALENTIN PETROVICH KATAEV (1897–   ): Prominent novelist and playwright, known for sympathetic but objective descriptions of developing Soviet society. An early novel, *The Father* (1925), deals with the conflict of generations in postrevolutionary Russia, a theme now officially frowned upon. *Squaring the Circle* (1928), a bedroom comedy, hinges on the relaxation of Soviet divorce laws. Despite his many awards, including the Order of Lenin, K. has not always managed to satisfy the censors: *For Soviet Power* (1949), a novel about the partisan movement in Odessa during World War II, was denounced for having "neglected" the role of the Party in the underground resistance. His more recent works include *A Winter's Evening* (1960) and *Time for Love* (1962).

VENIAMIN ALEKSANDROVICH KAVERIN (ZILBERG) (1902–   ): Novelist. Early works, such as *The End of a Gang* (1926), are concerned with fanciful subjects. In 1931, his *Unknown Artist* upheld personal ethical responsibility as an essential social value and expressed fear that it might vanish as Soviet collectivism developed. Subsequently conformed to the precepts of socialist realism in the novel *The Larger View* (1934–35). During World War II, was correspondent for *TASS* and *Izvestia*. Recent fiction includes the novel *Quests and Hopes* (1962). Protested the Galanskov-Ginzburg trial (Document 28) and the attacks on Solzhenitsyn (Document 57).

YURI KAZAKOV (1927–   ): Writer, associated, since 1963, with the Molodaia Gvardiia publishing house. *Going to Town*, a collection of short stories, has been translated into English by Gabriella Azrael (Boston: Houghton Mifflin, 1963); individual stories have appeared in *Encounter*, *Esquire*, and *Odyssey Review*. (Document 28)

IVAN KHARABAROV (1940–   ): Poet. Was "exposed" as a disciple of Pasternak at the 1958 Congress of the R.S.F.S.R. Writers' Union and expelled from both the Komsomol and the Gorky Literary Institute; was reinstated in 1959. His poems are represented in Patricia Blake and Max Hayward (eds.), *Dissonant Voices in Soviet Literature* (New York: Pantheon, 1962), and in George Reavey (ed.), *The New Russian Poets* (New York: October House, 1968).

YULI KIM (1936–   ): Secondary-school teacher of literature, poet, composer and performer of popular songs. Dismissed from job and all performances and a contract to star in a film were cancelled. (Documents 27, 30, and 32)

VSEVOLOD ANISIMOVICH KOCHETOV (1912–   ): Author and journalist. Chief editor of *Literaturnaia gazeta*, 1955–59, and of *Oktiabr* since 1961, when he published *Sekretar Obkoma*, a novel containing laudatory references to Stalin. *Bête noire* of the liberal writers, K. led attacks on Dudintsev in 1957, Solzhenitsyn in 1963, and Tvardovsky in 1966. There are contemptuous allusions to him in Siniavsky's *Makepeace Experiment* and Daniel's *This Is Moscow Speaking*.

LEV ZINOVEVICH KOPELEV (1912–   ): Writer and critic specializing in foreign literature. Served in the army as a political officer but was sentenced to ten years' imprisonment on "political charges" at the end of the war. In 1962, was attacked for defending the right of Soviet artists to develop abstract techniques. In 1966, wrote in behalf of Siniavsky and Daniel and signed a petition urging their release. As a result, was expelled from the Party and dismissed from the Institute of Historical Sciences. Also, some of his books previously approved for publication were removed from the publication list.

ALEKSANDR YEVDOKIMOVICH KORNEICHUK (1905–   ): Ukrainian playwright and critic. Chairman, Ukrainian Supreme Soviet; secretary, U.S.S.R. Writers' Union; member, U.S.S.R. Academy of Sciences. Author of numerous plays on Ukrainian themes, such as *On the Ukrainian Steppes* (1940), as well as essays on classic Ukrainian literature. During the "thaw," wrote

Wings (1954), an anti-Stalinist play. His awards include five Orders of Lenin and five Stalin Prizes.

VLADIMIR KORNILOV: Poet; author of a volume of poems, *The Wharf* (1964). (Document 28)

ALEKSEI YEVGRAFOVICH KOSTERIN (1896–1968): Writer, former editorialist for *Trud, Gudok,* and *Izvestia.* Spent seventeen years in Stalin's concentration camps. Signed appeal to the Presidium of the Consultative Conference of Communist Parties in Budapest (Document 32), protested arrest of writers (Document 18), and was active in behalf of Crimean Tatars (Document 40) and Czechoslovakia (Document 66).

YEVGENI IGOREVICH KUSHEV: Young poet, one of the organizers of the "Ryleev Circle."

VERA LASHKOVA: Student. Received a one-year suspended sentence for typing manuscripts of Ginzburg and Galanskov. Reported to have been one of the organizers of the March 5, 1966, demonstration against Stalin's partial rehabilitation.

MIKHAIL ALEKSANDROVICH LEONTOVICH (1903–   ): Nuclear physicist at Kurchatov Atomic Energy Institute in Moscow; full member, U.S.S.R. Academy of Sciences. Since 1959, has been associated with Sakharov in research on controlled thermonuclear fission. Twice awarded the Order of Lenin.

ANATOLI E. LEVITIN (KRASNOV) (1915–   ): Religious writer, former priest. Spent seven years in a concentration camp; released in 1956. Prolific author on religious freedom (Document 46) and civil liberties in general (Documents 25, 30, and 32). For more information, see the article by Peter Reddaway, pp. 62–78.

PAVEL MIKHAILOVICH LITVINOV (1937–   ): Grandson of the late Soviet foreign minister; dismissed from faculty of Moscow Institute of Precise Chemical Technology for participating in protests against trials of dissident intellectuals. For his protest against the Soviet invasion of Czechoslovakia, was exiled for five years to the remote region of Chita, near the Chinese border. (Documents 2, 3, 6, 7, 8, 32, and 70)

VICTOR LOUIS (1928–   ): Soviet citizen of French extraction, employed as a journalist, *inter alia,* by the *London Evening News.* In 1947, was arrested on political charges and was imprisoned for nine years. In 1959, engaged in translation and staging of *My Fair Lady* (without the authors' permission). Later arranged a television interview with Khrushchev, shown in the U.S. in 1967. In February, 1966, accompanied Valeri Tarsis to London as public-relations man and interpreter. In the summer of 1967, created a stir when he offered certain West European publishers an unauthorized version of Svetlana Allilueva's memoirs, together with photographs from the Stalin family album. This version, portions of which were published by *Der Stern* (Hamburg), seemed designed to undermine the credibility of the copyrighted text.

ANATOLI TIKHONOVICH MARCHENKO (1937–   ): Worker. Convicted for currency speculation in 1960, served six years in a labor camp. In 1967, wrote *My Testimony* about his camp experiences. Expressed approval and support of Czechoslovak liberalization program in July, 1968 (Document 63) and was thereupon arrested, charged with violating probation and passport regulations, and sentenced to forced labor in a Siberian lumber camp. Now suffers from near-total deafness as a result.

GEORGI MARKOV (1911–   ): Conservative writer; secretary, U.S.S.R. Writers' Union; frequent critic of liberal writers, especially Aksionov and Voznesensky. In 1963, became chairman of the Moscow Writers' Union. At the Fourth Congress, in May, 1967, voiced displeasure at the alienation apparent in the works of some younger writers but denied there was a conflict of generations in the Soviet Union. Ironically, M. is the author of a novel entitled *Fathers and Sons*.

NOVELLA NIKOLAEVNA MATVEEVA: Poetess; collections include *Lyrics* (1961), *The Little Ship* (1963), and *The Soul of Things* (1966); individual poems have appeared in *Izvestia, Novyi mir,* and *Yunost.* (Document 28)

SERGEI VLADIMIROVICH MIKHALKOV (1913–   ): Dramatist and poet; first secretary of the Moscow Writers' Union and secretary of the board of the U.S.S.R. Writers' Union. Co-authored lyrics of Soviet national anthem. Order of Lenin, Order of the Red Banner, Order of the Red Star, three Stalin Prizes. (Documents 87, 89)

VIKTOR PLATONOVICH NEKRASOV (1911–   ): Writer. With Ehrenburg, bore the brunt of Khrushchev's March, 1963, attack on outspoken Soviet writers. *Both Sides of The Ocean,* his memoir of visits to Italy, France, and the United States (New York: Holt, Rinehart and Winston, 1964), was found particularly objectionable because of its favorable comments on certain aspects of Western society and its criticisms of the Soviet way of life. (See Colette Shulman, "New Vistas for Soviet Readers," *Problems of Communism,* 1965, No. 6.) Was also reprimanded by Khrushchev for his praise of Khutsiev's film *Gates of Ilich,* which deals with the conflict of generations in the Soviet Union.

BULAT OKHUDZHAVA (1924–   ): Poet, short-story writer, and balladeer. Served in the Soviet army during World War II and worked as a village schoolteacher for a number of years thereafter. In the early 1960's, won wide acclaim for his guitar concerts and poetry readings, gaining rank with Yevtushenko as an idol of youth.

KONSTANTIN GRIGOREVICH PAUSTOVSKY (1892–1968): Elder statesman of Soviet letters. Early works, such as *Naval Sketches* (1927–30), *Ships*

That Were Met (1928), and *The Romanticists* (1929–30), were followed by more realistic portrayals of Soviet life, including *Karabugaz* (1932), *Kolkhida* (1934), and *The Black Sea* (1936). In 1956, made a strong defense, unpublished in the U.S.S.R. of Dudintsev's *Not by Bread Alone* at meeting of Moscow writers called to condemn it; also denounced anti-Semitism in the U.S.S.R. and several times attacked orthodox Soviet writings. Although he once withdrew a letter in behalf of Siniavsky and Daniel, he protested Brodsky's imprisonment and, shortly before the Ginzburg trial, publicly defended the Soviet Union's "brilliant" young writers, appealing to the older generation to "spare them from the hindrances that did not elude us" (*Novyi mir*, November, 1966). Despite such protests and appeals, was awarded the Order of Lenin in 1967. The first part of his autobiography, *Story of a Life* (New York: Pantheon, 1964), was widely acclaimed when it appeared in the West. (Document 28)

SERGEI PAVLOVICH PAVLOV (1929–   ): first secretary of the All-Union Komsomol since 1959. Has often attempted to intimidate outspoken young writers such as Yevtushenko, Aksionov, and Tendriakov. Decorated "For Valiant Labor" in 1960.

YURI YEVGENEVICH PILIAR: Writer, author of *All This Happened* (1956), a description of his internment in a Nazi concentration camp. (Documents 28 and 29)

G. S. PODIAPOLSKY: Geologist, author of an article published in *Physics of the Earth* (1966, No. 6) about seismic waves. (Documents 26, 28, and 30)

VLADIMIR POMERANTSEV: Soviet literary critic. Less than a year after Stalin's death, wrote an appeal for "sincerity in literature" calling upon writers to introduce "genuine conflict" into their work (*Novyi mir*, 1953). Shortly thereafter was expelled from the Writers' Union.

G. S. POMERANTZ: Writer and philosopher, employed at the Main Library of the Social Sciences; contributor to such journals as *Narody Azii i Afriki* and *Voprosy filosofii*. (Documents 30, 75)

ANDREI DMITREVICH SAKHAROV (1921–   ): Nuclear physicist; member, U.S.S.R. Academy of Sciences; Order of Lenin; Stalin Prize. Pioneer in the field of controlled thermonuclear fission. In 1964, was criticized for opposition to Lysenko's doctrine that hereditary characteristics of plants can be influenced by environmental factors. In 1966, joined other intellectuals in appealing to Brezhnev against the rehabilitation of Stalin. Later signed a petition objecting to a decree making unauthorized protest demonstrations punishable by law. (Document 76)

MIKHAIL ALEKSANDROVICH SHOLOKHOV (1905–   ): Writer, best known for *And Quiet Flows the Don*, an epic novel of Cossack life in the revolutionary era (New York: Knopf, 1941), for which he won the Nobel Prize in 1965. His public statements (notably his implication at the

Twenty-third Congress in 1966 that execution without trial would be an appropriate fate for Siniavsky and Daniel) have identified him with the ultraconservative wing of Soviet literature. Ironically, his latest novel, *They Fought for Their Country*, has now been banned in the Soviet Union, allegedly for its excessively critical view of Stalin's role during World War II (*New York Times*, February 8, 1969). (Document 62)

BORIS N. SHRAGIN: Philosopher specializing in aesthetics; film critic. Expelled from Party; discharged from position at Institute of Art History. (Documents 18 and 32)

KONSTANTIN MIKHAILOVICH SIMONOV (1915–   ): One of the most successful writers of the Stalinist era; awarded six Stalin Prizes for his poetry, plays, and novels. Under Khrushchev, however, joined other intellectuals in denouncing the Stalin cult. His war diaries, also critical of Stalin, have been suppressed by the present regime. Published works include *Days and Nights* (New York: Simon and Schuster, 1945) and *The Living and the Dead* (New York: Doubleday, 1962).

ANDREI DONATEVICH SINIAVSKY (1925–   ): Writer, candidate in Philological Sciences, former senior member of the Gorky Institute of World Literature, U.S.S.R. Academy of World Literature, U.S.S.R. Academy of Sciences. From 1959 to 1966, published various novels, short stories, and critical articles abroad under the pseudonym "Abram Tertz." His best-known novellas are *The Trial Begins* (New York: Pantheon, 1960) and *The Makepeace Experiment* (New York: Pantheon, 1965). *On Socialist Realism* (New York: Pantheon, 1960), his principal critical work, stresses the difficulties of dramatizing Communist ideals within the literary framework of realism, a form he considers more appropriate to the nineteenth century. Tried in February, 1966, with Yuli Daniel (*q.v.*) and sentenced to seven years' hard labor for "slandering" the Soviet Union in his foreign publications.

SERGEI VASILEVICH SMIRNOV (1913–   ): Poet, board member of the R.S.F.S.R. Writers' Union. Replaced the conservative Kochetov as editor of *Literaturnaia gazeta* in 1959 but was dismissed the following year for publishing the works of "formalists."

ALEKSANDR ISAEVICH SOLZHENITSYN (1918–   ): Novelist. Commissioned in the artillery in 1942, served continuously at the front until February, 1945, when he was arrested and sentenced to eight years' forced labor on what was later officially acknowledged as "an unfounded political charge." After completing his sentence, was exiled to the provinces until 1955. Since 1957, has taught school in Riazan. Author of *One Day in the Life of Ivan Denisovich* (New York: Praeger, 1963), a moving description of a Stalinist concentration camp, of numerous short stories (also translated into English), and of two monumental novels, *The First Circle* (New York: Harper & Row, 1968) and *The Cancer Ward* (New York: Farrar, Straus & Giroux, 1968), both of them suppressed in his own country. (See "Writers and Censors," pp. 245–72.)

ALEKSEI ALEKSANDROVICH SURKOV (1899–   ): Poet and editor. First secretary of the U.S.S.R. Writers' Union, 1954–59; chief editor of *Literaturnaia gazeta*, 1944–46, and of *Ogoniok*, 1949–53. As a writer, is best known for his war poetry, including the collection *Victory* (1943). Order of Lenin, Order of the Red Banner of Labor, two Orders of the Red Star, Badge of Honor, two Stalin Prizes.

GRIGORI TS. SVIRSKY: Novelist, short-story writer, and essayist. Expelled from the Party after a January 16, 1968, speech protesting censorship at a party *aktiv* of Moscow writers. (Document 61)

VASYL SYMONENKO (1935–63): Poet whose impassioned championship of Ukrainian national and cultural values has been compared to that of Taras Shevchenko in the nineteenth century. Also defended the rights of other Soviet minorities, notably the Kurds. His militant underground poetry, as well as excerpts from his diary, were published in the West after his death. *Bereh chekan* (New York: Prolog, 1965)

VALERI YAKOVLEVICH TARSIS (1906–   ): Writer. Joined the Party as a young man and worked as an editor in a state publishing house. In the early 1960's, had several novels published abroad, including *The Bluebottle* (London: Collins and Harvill, 1962) and *Red and Black* (New York: Knopf, 1963). Arrested in 1962 and kept in an insane asylum for seven months after writing a letter to Khrushchev calling the Soviet Union an unbearable place to live. After his release, wrote *Ward 7* (London: Collins and Harvill, 1965), a barely fictionalized account of his confinement in which he predicted the inevitable overthrow of Soviet totalitarianism. In 1966, was permitted to go to England, where he bitterly denounced the Soviet regime.

ALEKSANDR TRIFONOVITCH TVARDOVSKY (1910–   ): Poet; editor of *Novyi mir*, 1950–54, and again from 1958 to the present. Has sought to make the journal a platform for progressive writing of all kinds. In the late 1950's, published *Tiorkin in the Other World*, a devastating satire on Stalin's bureaucracy (for an English translation, see Priscilla Johnson, *Khrushchev and the Arts: The Politics of Soviet Culture, 1962–64* (Cambridge, Mass.: M.I.T. Press, 1965). In 1963, Khrushchev unexpectedly invited T. to read this work before prominent authors from both East and West. A known admirer of Solzhenitsyn, whose *Ivan Denisovich* was first published in *Novyi mir*, T. has reportedly tried hard—though unsuccessfully—to publish the latter's *Cancer Ward* and *The First Circle*.

BORIS BORISOVICH VAKHTIN: Member, U.S.S.R. Writers' Union; senior scientist on the staff of the Leningrad Division of the Institute of the Peoples of Asia, U.S.S.R. Academy of Sciences; candidate in Philology. (Document 14)

YURI BORISOVICH VAKHTIN: Senior scientist at the Institute of Cytology, U.S.S.R. Academy of Sciences; candidate in Biology. (Document 14)

KONSTANTIN VASILEVICH VORONKOV: Writer, secretary of the U.S.S.R. Writers' Union in charge of organizational questions.

ANDREI VOZNESENSKY (1933–): Leading contemporary poet, encouraged by Pasternak, whom he greatly admired. In 1963, forced to recant his "failings" (including giving foreign interviews, a practice he has not abandoned). See *Selected Poems of Andrei Voznesensky*, trans. Anselm Hollo (New York: Grove Press, 1964); and *Voznesensky: Selected Poems*, trans. Herbert Marshall (New York: Hill and Wang, 1966). (Document 7)

IVAN A. YAKHIMOVICH (1930–): Philologist, appointed chairman of a collective farm in Latvia in 1960. Lauded as a "model collective-farm chairman" in an article which appeared in *Komsomolskaia pravda* (October 30, 1964). In 1968, wrote appeal to Suslov on behalf of Ginzburg and Galanskov (Document 16), which cost him his job. In July, 1968, declared his support of the Dubcek regime in Czechoslovakia (Document 66), reaffirming it on two other occasions in 1969 (Documents 72, 81, and 82). After numerous reprisals (see Document 80), was arrested on March 25, 1969.

PIOTR IONAVICH YAKIR (1923–): Historian on staff of the Institute of Historical Studies, U.S.S.R. Academy of Sciences. His father, Major-General Iona E. Yakir, was executed in 1937 during the Stalinist purges of the Red Army. The same year, Y. was sentenced to seventeen years in a concentration camp; was rehabilitated in 1956. In February, 1968, was reportedly accused of being a principal instigator of "antisocial" activities, including protests against both the Galanskov-Ginzburg trial and the partial rehabilitation of Stalin. (Documents 27, 30, and 32)

ANATOLI ALEKSANDROVICH YAKOBSON: Poet and translator; member of the council of writers attached to the Sovietskii Pisatel publishing house. His "Brief Notes on Contemporary Poetry" appeared in *Phoenix*. (Documents 18, 23, and 30)

KAMIL YASHEN (1909–): First secretary, Uzbek Writers' Union, and secretary, U.S.S.R. Writers' Union. His *Selected Works* appeared in 1962, and his awards include the Order of Lenin (1959) and the Order of the Red Banner of Labor (1965).

ALEKSANDR SERGEEVICH YESENIN-VOLPIN (1924–): Mathematician and poet-philosopher. Twice imprisoned (in 1949 and 1959), the second time for smuggling an "anti-Soviet" philosophical treatise to the West. A collection of his poems, *A Leaf of Spring*, was published in 1961 (New York: Praeger). On December 5, 1965, led a rally in Moscow's Pushkin Square to protest the arrest of Siniavsky and Daniel. On February 19, 1966, challenged the legality of the Siniavsky-Daniel verdict in an interview with a *New York Times* correspondent. An active protester against the Galanskov-Ginzburg trial, was arrested at his home in February, 1968, and taken to a mental institution. In March, 1968, ninety-five mathematicians protested his forcible confinement in a letter to the Minister of Health, the Procurator General, and the Chief Psychiatrist of the City of Moscow; fifteen withdrew their signatures after the letter was made public by the *New York Times* (Documents 33 and 34)

YEVGENI YEVTUSHENKO (1933–   ): Poet whose outspokenness in the late 1950's and early 1960's made him an international celebrity and an embarrassment to the Soviet regime. Was twice expelled from the Komosomol, the second time, in 1963, after a visit to western Europe, where he permitted *L'Express* (Paris) to publish his *Precocious Biography* without Soviet sanction. The political candor that marked many of his earlier poems (such as "Babyi Yar," 1961) has been less evident (perhaps suppressed) in recent years. Has been permitted to travel on four continents as an official cultural envoy. See George Reavey's edition of *The Poetry of Yevgeny Yevtushenko* (New York: October House, 1965). (Document 71)

VITALI ALEKSANDR ZAKRUTKIN: Member of the U.S.S.R. Writers' Union and the editorial board of *Literaturnaia Rossiia;* known for his severe antipathy to liberal writers.

MIKHAIL VASILEVICH ZIMIANIN (1914–   ): Chief editor of *Pravda;* former diplomat. Served as Soviet Ambassador to Hanoi and Prague and rose to Deputy Minister of Foreign Affairs in 1965. Order of the Red Banner of Labor. (Document 53)

The Contributors

ABRAHAM BRUMBERG—Editor, *Problems of Communism*; Editor, *Russia under Khrushchev* (New York: Praeger, 1962); U.S. Editor, *The Soviet Union and Democratic Society—A Comparative Encyclopedia* (Freiburg, Germany: Herder Verlag); contributing Editor, *Atlas* magazine (New York); contributor to *The New Republic, The New Leader, Commentary, The Reporter, Interplay,* and other journals.

SIDNEY MONAS—Professor of History at the University of Rochester (New York); author of *Third Section: Police and Society in Russia under Nicholas I* (Cambridge, Mass.: Harvard University Press, 1961), as well as a number of translations from and studies of Russian literature.

STEPHEN M. WEINER—Associate with law firm of Goodwin, Procter, & Hoar; former Teaching Fellow at the Boston College Law School.

GEORGE LUCKYJ—Professor of Russian and Ukrainian Literature at the University of Toronto (Canada); author of *Literary Politics in the Soviet Ukraine: 1917–34* (New York: Columbia University Press, 1956); contributor to *Problems of Communism, Survey* (London), and other journals.

PETER REDDAWAY—Lecturer in Political Science at the London School of Economics and Political Science; coeditor (with Leonard Schapiro) of *Lenin: The Man, the Theorist, the Leader: A Reappraisal* (New York: Praeger, 1967); editor of an anthology of Russian "underground" literature to be published later this year by Longmans (London), and Praeger (New York); author of numerous monographs on religion and politics in the Soviet Union.